RESOLUTIONS

CONTEMPORARY
VIDEO
PRACTICES

Michael Renov & Erika Suderburg, editors

University of Minnesota Press
Minneapolis
London

A French-language version of chapter 6 appeared in *Passage de l'image* (Paris: Editions du Centre Pompidou, 1990), translated and reprinted by permission; chapter 9 first appeared in *Lynn Hershman: Chimera Monographie,* ed. Lynn Hershman (Montbéliard: Editions du Centre International de Création Vidéo, 1992), copyright David E. James; a French-language version of chapter 11 first appeared in *L'Entre—Images* (Paris: Editions de la Différence, 1990), translated and reprinted by permission; an earlier version of chapter 22 appeared in *Quarterly Review of Film and Video* 15, no. 1 (1993): 15–26, copyright Harwood Academic Publishers, by permission; "Slipping Between" copyright 1991 by Sandra P. Hahn, by permission.

Every effort has been made to obtain permission to reproduce copyright material in this book. The publishers ask copyright holders to contact them if permission has inadvertently not been sought or if proper acknowledgment has not been made.

Published by the University of Minnesota Press
111 Third Avenue South, Suite 290, Minneapolis, MN 55401-2520

Second printing, 1997

Printed in the United States of America on acid-free paper

Library of Congress Cataloging-in-Publication Data

Resolutions : contemporary video practices / Michael Renov and Erika Suderburg, editors.
　　p.　cm.
　Includes bibliographical references and index.
　ISBN 0-8166-2327-9 (alk. paper)
　ISBN 0-8166-2330-9 (pbk. : alk. paper)
　1. Video recordings.　I. Renov, Michael, 1950–　.　II. Suderburg, Erika.
PN1992.935.R47　1996
384.55'8--dc20   95-10972

The University of Minnesota is an equal-opportunity educator and employer.

This book is dedicated with great love, respect, and a

sense of immeasurable loss to the memory of *Marlon Riggs*,

who contributed such eloquence, rage, beauty,

and deep poetry to the world of the moving image.

Contents

ACKNOWLEDGMENTS   ix

INTRODUCTION: RESOLVING VIDEO > *Michael Renov and Erika Suderburg*   xi

1   **The Politics of Video Memory: Electronic Erasures and Inscriptions** > *Marita Sturken*   1

2   **Qualifying the Quotidian:**
Artist's Video and the Production of Social Space > *Christine Tamblyn*   13

3   **The Image of Art in Video** > *Maureen Turim*   29

4   **Video: The Access Medium** > *Tetsuo Kogawa*   51

5   **Looking through Video: The Psychology of Video and Film** > *John Belton*   61

6   **Videor** > *Jacques Derrida*   73

7   **Video Confessions** > *Michael Renov*   78

8   **The Electronic Corpse:**
Notes for an Alternative Language of History and Amnesia > *Erika Suderburg*   102

9   **Lynn Hershman: The Subject of Autobiography** > *David E. James*   124

10   **Longing for Real Life** > *Rosanna Albertini*   134

11   **The Images of the World** > *Raymond Bellour*   149

12   **Dweller on the Threshold** > *Bill Horrigan*   165

13   **Operative Assumptions** > *Gregg Bordowitz*   173

14 **Tongues *Re*-tied** > *Marlon Riggs*   185

15 **Sex Lies with Videotape:**
Abbreviated Histories of Canadian Video Sex > *Sara Diamond*   189

16 **Talking Heads, Body Politic:**
The Plural Self of Chicano Experimental Video > *Chon A. Noriega*   207

17 **New Visions/New Chinas:**
Video — Art, Documentation, and the Chinese Modernity
in Question > *Bérénice Reynaud*   229

18 **Taking Aim: The Video Technology of Cultural Resistance** > *Monica Frota*   258

19 **Video: The Politics of Culture and Community** > *Ron Burnett*   283

20 **Fetal Tissue: Reproductive Rights and**
Activist Amateur Video > *Patricia R. Zimmermann*   304

21 **Female Transgression** > *Laura Kipnis*   333

22 **Julie Zando's Primal Scenes and Lesbian Representation** > *Judith Mayne*   346

23 **Wedding Video and Its Generation** > *James M. Moran*   360

24 **Vision after Television:**
Technocultural Convergence, Hypermedia,
and the New Media Arts Field > *Michael Nash*   382

C ONTRIBUTORS   401

I NDEX   405

ACKNOWLEDGMENTS

This volume is a long-awaited follow-up to a previous collection of essays, *Resolution: A Critique of Video Art*, published by Los Angeles Contemporary Exhibitions (LACE) in 1986, edited by Patti Podesta in conjunction with an exhibition and symposium of the same name. That book engendered an ongoing series of discussions within LACE's video programming committee regarding the paucity of material addressing video as an art form, as well as the absence of collected material that charted the history, radical changes, and rapid growth of the medium since 1986.

Many people contributed their time and energy to this book; it is a volume that owes a great deal to the earlier *Resolution* project as well as to the current and past membership of the LACE board, staff, and VideoLACE committee, and to the National Endowment for the Arts. We would like to thank especially Gwen Darien, the executive director of LACE, under whose patient eye this project came into being, along with the many people connected with LACE who contributed to the book at many stages. In that number are included Peter Kirby, VideoLACE member and LACE board chair, as well as the following past and present members of the VideoLACE curatorial committee: Claire Aguilar, Nancy Buchanan, David Bunn, Wendy Clarke, Ed. De La Torre, Frances Salomé España, Steve Fagin, John C. Goss, JoAnn Hanley, Bill Horrigan, O. Funmilayo Makarah, Branda Miller, Patti Podesta, Adam Soch, Erika Suderburg, and Bruce Yonemoto. A debt of thanks is also due the previous executive directors of LACE, Joy Silverman and Roberto Bedoya, along with the former LACE video coordinators, Anne Bray, Adriene Jenik, and Tom Dennison.

Other individuals have offered invaluable assistance over the many months of this volume's preparation, among them Akiba Onada-Sikwoia and Kirsten Jones of Signifyin' Works, Lynne Kirby, Kathleen McHugh, Sylvere Lotringer, Marita Sturken, and Casandra Morgan. Finally, we wish to acknowledge the extraordinary level of support provided by Janaki Bakhle of the University of Minnesota Press. Hers was the task of steadying our course during what seemed an endless period of author solicitation, writing, editing, and manuscript preparation. We were the beneficiaries of that rare mixture of critical intelligence, professionalism, and forbearance that is hers.

RESOLVING VIDEO

Michael Renov and Erika Suderburg

In the introductory chapter to his *Techniques of the Observer: On Vision and Modernity in the Nineteenth Century,* Jonathan Crary suggests the necessity for tracing the "points of emergence" of a modern and heterogeneous regime of vision as it moves toward a "relentless abstraction" of the sort associated with digital technologies, computer-generated imagery, virtual environment helmets, texture mapping, and the like.[1] These are the techniques of an emergent visual culture in which "spaces" can be fabricated without recourse to preexistent referents. Crary argues that modernity is coincident with the collapse of classical models of vision and their stable space of representation, that there is a kind of "freeing up" of vision that contrasts with the rigidly linear perspective of the camera obscura invented some three centuries earlier:

> But almost simultaneous with this final dissolution of a transcendent foundation for vision emerges a plurality of means to recode the activity of the eye, to regiment it, to heighten its productivity and to prevent its distraction. Thus the imperatives of capitalist modernization, while demolishing the field of classical vision, generated techniques for imposing visual attentiveness, rationalizing sensation, and managing perception.[2]

Crary thus describes a kind of historical tension between freedom and restraint accompanying the nineteenth-century transition to a new cultural economy of value and exchange in which mass-produced photographic signs began to circulate like the money form itself. While representation and the vision it engendered were released from the mimetic restraints of earlier ages, formidable social forces were being mounted to control and capitalize upon these new possibilities.[3]

On June 21, 1993, an organization called HealthRIGHT launched its "Speak Out, America!" tour, a thirteen-thousand-mile odyssey that crisscrossed the United States with stops in sixty-eight cities and innumerable spots in between. Organized by the Foundation for Hospice and Homecare, sponsored by organizations ranging from the March of Dimes to the American Federation of State, County, and Municipal Employees and the National Council of Senior Citizens, the primary goal of the HealthRIGHT crusade was to give Americans the opportunity to speak out about the nation's health care system at a time when its future was being debated by legislator and pundit alike.[4] The key to the campaign was contained in the much-traveled HealthRIGHT van: a battery of video cameras and editing setups used to record and assemble the thoughts, experiences, and expressed needs of thousands of American citizens. Less than two months later, campaign organizers presented to the president and Congress the first ever video petition. Six hours in length, culled from seventy hours of raw tape, the HealthRIGHT petition delivered concretized audiovisual documentation of a collective need for health care reform, bringing to the floor of the Congress the words and images of hundreds of Americans, many of them facing severe illness, financial hardship, even death.

Carolyn Marvin, whose more culturalist approach to the social impact of new communications technologies in the late nineteenth century nevertheless corroborates Crary's at crucial points, notes that new media forms build upon but reconfigure existing patterns of social stratification and hierarchy. Rather than focusing on technology as instrumental knowledge unleashing an array of effects, Marvin attends in great detail to the manner in which emergent media forms confirm, contest, and rearticulate the field of social forces in which they arise. In her analysis, the *apparatus* as such is less at issue than the tracing of incipient *media practices*, the social applications of scientific devices:

> The model used here is different. Here, the focus of communication is shifted from the instrument to the drama in which existing groups perpetually negotiate power, authority, representation, and knowledge with whatever resources are available. New media intrude on these negotiations by providing new platforms on which old groups confront one another. . . . New practices do not so much flow directly from technologies that inspire them as they are improvised out of old practices that no longer work in new settings.[5]

The work of both Crary and Marvin suggests that new technologies are never as new as they appear to be; they are experienced in relation to older and more familiar media, which they challenge and destabilize. Efforts to maintain control of the expanded social opportunities afforded by emergent cultural forms are exerted within settings that range from the familial to those of professional or expert communities. According to Marvin, the impulse to check the expansive horizons of a new electrical culture in the late nineteenth century resulted in a fixing on one-way communication issuing from familiar cultural, political, and geographic sources rather than two-way exchange, "with its greater presumption of equality and risks of unpredictable confrontation."[6] The impact of this two-stroke action—the expansiveness of technological promise engendering its conservative reflex via regulatory contraction—can be felt throughout this volume of essays on the video practices of the late twentieth century.

In December 1993, astronauts Kathryn C. Thornton and Thomas D. Akers succeeded in making a spacewalk swap of a $101 million replacement camera for the damaged Wide Field and Planetary Camera. WFPC (pronounced "wiff-pick") was the main scientific instrument aboard the $1.5 billion Hubble Space Telescope, which had been orbiting the earth for some three and a half years.[7] Working in conjunction with corrections made to the telescope's 2.4-meter primary mirror, the 629-pound replacement camera contained eight CCD imaging detectors developed at the Jet Propulsion Laboratory; it was easily the most sophisticated electronic imaging device (or camera of any sort) ever engineered.[8] With the Hubble telescope functioning as a kind of supertelephoto lens, the camera could record and transmit images of a firefly 8,500 miles away; it could see "with clarity" objects twelve billion light-years from Earth.[9] WFPC 2 was a video camera whose depth of field could be measured in light years.

From the halls of Congress to the far reaches of outer space, video is indeed transforming our culture and our world. In the aftermath of a bomb blast that shook New York City, investigators of the 1993 terrorist attack on the World Trade Center directed a robotic probe equipped with sensing devices and a video camera to the depths of an unstable crater lying beneath the damaged towers, producing a close-up assessment of the damage in a manner unavailable to the human eye.[10] In Los Angeles, camcorder-wielding civilians have formed the Volunteer Surveillance Team as a way to bolster crime-stopping efforts in their neighborhoods. Called by one police official "the crime-fighting technique of the future," volunteer video surveillance resulted in more than forty (lower-cost) arrests in a one-year period while reinforcing a sense of citizen involvement in law enforcement. The L.A. program is being studied by police forces in Seattle, Tampa, Baltimore, Portland, and Norfolk.[11] In the aftermath of George Holliday's taping of the Rodney King beating, the Los Angeles Police Department has begun installing its own video cameras in selected squad cars, the cost of the pilot program diminished by camera donations from community groups such as DARE America.[12]

But the technology that enables police forces to surveil populations has the potential to be turned against its state-sanctioned purveyors. Indeed, many of the essays contained in this book draw our attention to the independent and resistant uses of the same video apparatus that patrols the often invisible borders of banks, convenience stores, and private estates. Foucault addressed the potential reversibility of surveillance in his discussion of the panopticon, a late-eighteenth-century design for a system of penal surveillance. The work of British philosopher Jeremy Bentham, the panopticon was a blueprint for a transparent society, visible and legible in all its parts, an Enlightenment dream of unobstructed knowledge and social exchange. In practice, however, the panopticon organized its absolute visibility around a dominating, overseeing gaze that issued from a central point. In contemporary cultural studies, the panopticon has frequently become a touchstone for dystopian views of surveillance technologies that assume them to be the jailor's unerring servant. But Foucault insisted that the panopticon was a machine that embroiled both the subject and the object of the surveilling gaze:

> This indeed is the diabolical aspect of the idea and all the applications of it. One doesn't have here a power which is wholly in the hands of one person who can exercise it alone and totally over the others. It's a machine in which everyone is caught, those who exercise power just as much as those over whom it is exercised. This seems to me to be the characteristic of the societies installed in the nineteenth century. Power is no longer substantially identified with an individual who possesses or exercises it by right of birth; it becomes a machinery that no one owns.[13]

From this point of view, surveillance is never a flawless, one-way exercise of power; the police are themselves caught in the same machine as the presumed perpetrator whom they so relentlessly track.

A recent pronouncement by Cmdr. David Gascon, a community affairs officer for the Los Angeles Police Department, displays an acute awareness that, in fact, the LAPD does not own exclusive rights to the machinery of surveillance it deploys: "We all have to realize that everything the Los Angeles police officer does in 1994 is under a microscope. . . . Whether it's for television news or documentaries, or other police departments, or John Q. Citizen, we have to perform as though we are clearly on center stage, and that there are cameras out there watching every move."[14]

While Gascon's remarks were in reference to Police Chief Willie Williams's decision to allow the taping of *Cops* episodes in the streets of Los Angeles, they may now best be understood in the context of the live TV coverage of the police pursuit of O. J. Simpson during the twilight hours of 17 June 1994. With the skies above teeming with a battalion of news choppers competing for the best camera angles, the white Ford Bronco led a bizarre caravan of police vehicles and well-wishers along freeways usually choked with rush-hour traffic; much of America stayed tuned as the melodrama unfolded. During a press conference held after Simpson's surrender to police, Gascon admitted that officers had watched the TV coverage right along with the rest of us; indeed the intelligence resources of law enforcement were mightily overmatched by those of the electronic newsgatherers. In the next morning's newspaper, TV critic Howard Rosenberg acidly noted the imbalance:

> Soon police arrived. In much greater numbers, so did the media. About 2:30 pm, Channel 2 and Channel 4 choppers were above the townhouse. Then Channel 2 was live on the ground. Then KTLA-TV Channel 5 was live in the air. Then KCAL-TV Channel 9 was live on the ground. Then Channel 11 and

KCOP-TV Channel 13 were live in the air. Although the Channel 7 Newsvan appeared stuck in traffic, even it would ultimately arrive at the townhouse, joining the gawkers and others who had turned out for the show. The place was surrounded.[15]

With NBC cutting away from its coverage of the National Basketball Association finals to join ABC and CBS in live coverage, the nation was treated to a spectacle of the real unrivaled in its dramatic potential. Of course, unfettered media access to the chase fueled widespread second-guessing of LAPD's handling of the case from the outset. Gascon's belief that the police were themselves the subjects of an unceasing public surveillance ("We have to perform as if we were on center stage") materialized on a scale no one could have predicted.

If we consider Foucault's description of the panopticon as "an apparatus of total and circulating mistrust,"[16] then we can begin to see the camcorder as one source of that capillary action through which the power exercised by the surveilling gaze circulates: the means of (surveillance) representation—an inexpensive video camera or a TV chopper prowling for the news—is so widely available, indeed pervasive, as to dissolve a meaningful state monopoly. Video has begun to play a significant role in the balance of power effected among state, corporation, and citizen even as a pure potentiality.

In all the aforementioned instances—video petition, interplanetary camera, robotic probe, surveillance eye—video technology has moved well beyond the function of artistic expression or exploration common to artists' video to encompass every discursive function of documentary media: recording, preserving, persuading, and analyzing events—public and private, local and global—at an astonishing rate.[17] It is a sense of this volatility, this expansiveness of video's social usages, that impels this book's efforts to describe, evaluate, and critique the range of video practices in evidence as we move toward the close of this century. With a mere three decades of public availability to serve as its history (the Sony portapak was introduced in 1965), video technology continues to confound its academic chroniclers, those who would award video its niche as artistic medium, marketing tool, newsgathering vehicle, or amateur recording device. In this volume, we hope to test some of the received boundaries of video culture. As the editors of this book, we have sought out contributions that provide support to our thesis of video's ubiquity and protean power without resorting to either a reification of the technology or a hagiography of its practitioners.

Despite the attention to a new horizon of electronic sound-image possibilities, this book privileges a notion of media *practice* rather than technical *device*. Attention to new communications forms all too frequently reinforces determinist historical readings, treating technologies as bundles of instruments or techniques abstracted from an active network of social relations, capable of producing radical transformations overnight. In a chapter of *Marxism and Literature* titled "From Medium to Social Practice," Raymond Williams argues that a "medium" is always a form of social organization, never an abstraction or autonomous force. Williams seeks to reestablish "the full sense of practice, which has always to be defined as work on a material for a specific purpose within certain necessary social conditions."[18] Williams's decades-long passion for a theory of culture that could productively link up with historical materialism (that is, "cultural materialism") offers one source of inspiration for the current project, an assessment of contemporary video practices viewed on a global stage.

Resolutions is a volume of original critical essays that seek to alter the terms of discussion and debate into which video, as a medium and as a practice, has been historically cast. The project's focus is not, therefore, on "video art," as that term is commonly understood, or on video as an autonomous medium possessing essential features,[19] but on video in relation to ongoing cultural, aesthetic, and political agendas and activities—video as a source and as a medium for contemporary expression that is allied with and paralleled by myriad cultural and critical discourses in specific and sometimes surprising ways. The book represents a cross section of possible approaches to the context and content of video production. It is informed by contributions from quite disparate sources and cultural arenas: from artists, independent television producers, media activists, alternative space and museum curators, programmers, and academics working at the borders of critical theory.

These essays seek to address video as a global medium: many of the chapters have been written within or about contexts far removed from the standard Euro-American art video histories. Whether it is Tetsuo Kogawa's theorization of video as a medium of performance rather than of taped preservation and display—an account rooted in Kogawa's decades-long relationship to performance and installation work in Japan—or Bérénice Reynaud's discussion of video's emergence in China as a more accessible, often entry-level alternative to film production, or Chon Noriega's analysis of Chicano experimental videomakers whose work has extended the tradition of the *testimonio* so central to the post-1960s narrative arts of Latin America, these essays are cognizant of the particularities of cultural context and historical imperative. They are also informed by the technological and conceptual shifts that have reconfigured media arts communities in the 1990s, in the United States, and worldwide.

The collapse of previously-adhered-to notions of media specificity mark the end of the eighties. Video and film are not so diametrically squared off in aesthetic opposition; cinema, once considered unshakable, has become enmeshed in diverse delivery systems no longer dependent on collected mass audiences. The advent of user-based editing systems and consumer video models of ever escalating sophistication bring home production capabilities incrementally closer to broadcast potential, while sublevel movements of creators connected via e-mail, satellite, tape swaps, 'zine exchanges, and QuickTime computer video notes force a reconfiguration of our definitions of time-based media. As the idea of a necessarily fixed site for making and receiving images has been erased, so too has the delineation of the "essential characteristics" of contemporary media forms been undermined as a useful enterprise. Technologically driven shifts in materials and environments have cast electronic media adrift on the infobahn where monolithic designations such as "video aesthetic" or "video culture" retain little signifying force.

It is time to revamp the media lexicon, to reshape and pluralize the words we use to describe our media culture. But the plurality that marks *Resolutions* is not the ideological residue of a liberalism that replicates the sheer profusion of new technologies so much as it is a testing of specific conceptual boundaries that confounds absolutism or orthodoxy. James Clifford has written that cultural identity is conjunctural rather than essential; we are the convergence of a vast network of diverse affiliations and determinations—genetic as well as social.[20] Video in the 1990s is an equally hybridized domain deserving of treatment that preserves its discontinuities and multivocality. The knowledge presented on these pages is therefore situated and particular; specific questions address dispersed cultural objects from diverse critical positions. But if we have abandoned the search for a globalizing knowledge of electronic media, we have not therefore resorted to a sheer relativism. There is a politics that suffuses these pages.

For indeed this collection grew out of a very real need to speak about marginalized work, videomaking that has been forced to build its audience in ever more diverse venues with little institutional support. To us these works and the cultural practices that subtend them are deserving of our collective investigation; the work needs to be looked at critically, given a space in which to serve as a catalyst for debate and as an alternative to the exclusionary canons of avant-garde film and video. *Resolutions* began as one response to the collective programming mandate of Los Angeles Contemporary Exhibitions (aka LACE) that developed a model of programming and advocacy much like that of other art and media arts centers of the early 1980s. This was a model defined against certain hegemonic cultural institutions—the museum, broadcast television, and the film festival circuit—but in continuity with other sites of cultural opposition (particularly the experimental or alternative film and video exhibition spaces of the 1960s). In the United States, this tradition of alternative sites encompassed the cinematic— Millenium Film Workshop, Filmmakers Cinematheque, Filmforum, and the Pacific Film Archive—as well as the electronic—Raindance Video Collective, VideoFreex, and Video Free America.

As the history of alternative media in the United States is reinvented in a cycle of historical unearthing, appropriation, exhaustion, and rebirth, it is useful to recall the originary function of LACE, particularly as a pretext to the present volume. If the preexisting cultural venues were hopelessly bureaucratized, politically conservative, or resistant to the new, alternative sites had to be fashioned at the border, margin, or subculture. VideoLACE began within this context as a group of artists curating contemporary media collectively, with the work to be shown in an alternative space administered by a director equally committed to challenging received notions of art-world propriety. The work curated in this way could only be eclectic, contentious, and ever mutating. *Resolutions* exists as a kind of critical supplement to the activities and aspirations of the VideoLACE committee.

The appearance of Doug Hall and Sally Jo Fifer's *Illuminating Video: An*

Investigation of Video Art during the planning stages of this volume also helped to sharpen our focus. *Illuminating Video* made available the most diverse and insightful critical writing on video within the art context to date. The direction of our collective project could now more sensibly expand to encompass new investigative sites well beyond the scope of broadcast television or the art world.

We also imagined a more expansive global reach for *Resolutions*. To that end, we enlisted the participation of some of the writers and producers who have offered material and conceptual support to independent video initiatives around the world: in the United States, Japan, France, Italy, Brazil, China, Canada, and Mexico. Given that the structures of current alternative media production and distribution are undergoing transformations of the sort that respect neither linguistic nor national boundaries, it seemed important to maintain a diversity of critical approaches and geopolitical objects for the essays making up this volume.

Our focus is on independent video production, whether it falls within the rubric traditionally defined as "art" or not. This continuum includes video installation, single-channel video, "experimental" video, broadcast intervention, cable, interactive video, computer-generated video , experimental documentary, home video, video documentation services, video collectives, and ethnographic applications and implications. The essays contained in this volume also begin to address the very real pedagogical problems inherent in such categorizations. There is also attention given to the direction and emerging structures of new media forms as they find and recreate their audiences.

But our sense of the new has been sharpened by an attentiveness to what has come before, particularly to the politicized appropriations of media forms. A number of the essays in this volume examine the ways in which thirty-year-old portable video technology continues to find new applications in response to particular social needs, many of them within the arena of sexuality. Williams's sense of a media practice as the fulfillment of "a specific purpose within certain necessary social conditions" is dramatically illustrated by the community-based video practices of AIDS activists discussed by Gregg Bordowitz or Patricia Zimmermann's examination of new media strategies within the prochoice movement. Indeed, the many-faceted politics of sexuality emerges as a key arena for the essays of this volume. Sara Diamond painstakingly charts a history of Canada's state censorship of sexual imagery and the attendant evolution of state-mandated content restrictions that inspired a rich body of oppositional video work and social activism. Laura Kipnis writes on a body of work produced by women artists that typifies the nineties "bad girls" trend: female transgression that confronts a litany of gender-based clichés while erasing any comfortable notion of fixed identity. Judith Mayne's essay explores the video work of Julie Zando as specifically lesbian representation for the ways in which its patternings of sound and image rearticulate received notions of romantic love, the mother-daughter dyad, even sisterhood. Marlon Riggs's "Tongues *Re-tied*" is a reply to the furor caused by his epochal video work, *Tongues Untied* (1989). A mixture of autobiography and polemical celebration of black gay male subjectivity, *Tongues* unleashed a torrent of invective from the Right whose ripple effects were felt during the 1992 presidential campaign.[21] Taking a different tack, Bill Horrigan writes about the infiltration of AIDS into the daytime soap opera world of network television, a medium that has failed miserably in its prime-time efforts to document or dramatize the epidemic. But, notes Horrigan, "Nobody does death better than the soap operas."

Many of the essays gathered together in *Resolutions* address video's interventions in the fabric of everyday life in the United States and around the world. Monica Frota's work on the uses of video by the Kayapo Indians of the Amazon basin shows that media practices are best understood in their effective plurality; the electronic applications of the Kayapo fulfill a range of social needs (the documentation of ritual, intervillage communication, the affirmation of social hierarchy) while creating others that arise in the aftermath of growing international media celebrity. Ron Burnett's essay is a call for a more intensive examination of the meaning and breadth of alternativity in the diffusion of community-based videomaking in the north or south. Burnett suggests that the rhetoric of "empowerment" that suffuses the important struggle for media access has been applied ahistorically and with too little regard for what we know about the variabilities of reception. James Moran's analysis of the wedding video as a new subfield within the commercial video marketplace attests to the speed with which technologies can be mobilized to serve perceived social needs, in this instance by supplying a personalized (although highly generic) documentation of a public ritual for an affordable price.

Other authors in this volume take up the analysis of the dynamic borderline between emergent and residual cultural forms, the ways in which video has developed from, interpreted, and freqently displaced its media predecessors. While these essays on video in relation to radio, photography, film, television, painting, performance art, and literature begin to trace an incipient media specificity for video, what emerges is far from the essentializing endeavor against which Williams warns us:

> It reaches its extreme in the assumption of the independent properties of the "medium," which, in one kind of theory, is seen as determining not only the "content" of what is communicated but also the social relationships within which the communication takes place. In this influential kind of technological determinism (for example, in McLuhan) the "medium" is (metaphysically) the master.[22]

What emerges is a very different (and historical) sense of how one medium—and the cultural criticism that supports it—can provide a platform for the development of new possibilities within another format. Jacques Derrida writes about the difficulty of specifying the features of a "new art" for which one lacks a ready discourse. In the end, Derrida abandons the search for the irreducible elements of video, arguing instead that its defining terms can only emerge historically, through "an active, vigilant, unpredictable proliferation."

Other contributors undertake the task of constructing historical linkages between video and its predecessor forms. John Belton suggests that the current historical sense of video's emergence has been hampered by a relative inattention to the importance of sound technologies in the formation of "video," a term whose very etymology discourages that historical awareness. Maureen Turim looks to a centuries-old tradition of easel art for the antecedents of an important current in contemporary video art. Turim shows how artists such as Mary Lucier, Thierry Kuntzel, and Doug Hall have produced work in an electronic medium that responds to and advances particular aesthetic inquiries recurrent within post-Renaissance painting. The historical linkage suggested by Raymond Bellour's essay is a critical one in that it extends his earlier and groundbreaking studies in the close textual analysis of film to the domain of video through his microanalysis of Woody Vasulka's *Art of Memory*.

A number of the volume's contributions share an interest in aesthetic questions, most often by way of investigating the theoretical implications of particular video art practices. Marita Sturken, Erika Suderburg, and Christine Tamblyn examine the works of artists mining the intricacies of memory, history, and electronic inscription. Sturken concentrates on the construction of memory engendered in the act of recording "screen memories," Tamblyn on video's occupation of social space and its connection to interior speech. Suderburg examines the representation of history, memory, and eulogy within the works of Jean-Luc Godard, Alexander Kluge, Marc Karlin, Michael Klier, Jan Peacock, and Janice Tanaka, situating these works as alternative recodings of given historical narratives. Rosanna Albertini examines the project of video time in relation to the reinvention and collapse of video grammars and their relation to the philosophical construct of the real. David E. James, who has previously written on the film diary in relation to its literary precursor, looks at the diaristic practices of Lynn Hershman in their electronic specificity. Michael Renov examines the emergence of the first-person video confession, with video understood as an apparatus that, owing to its potential for privatized production and consumption, is particularly well suited to the role of facilitator of self-interrogation. Moreover, Renov argues that video confessions produced and exchanged in nonhegemonic contexts can be powerful tools not only for self-understanding but also for two-way communication. Finally, Michael Nash writes about the prospects for ensuring the future vitality of independent videomaking and the media arts more generally in the aftermath of the censorship battles and diminished public funding. Nash describes a brief window of opportunity in the current technological transition (and the concomitant battles over corporate control) in which artists, critics, curators, and activists can forge necessary alliances and help create a community of readers in search of new ideas, capable of sustaining a viable alternative culture.

One approach to the writing of a developmental history of electronic imaging devices might well make reference to the expanding potential of the medium to store and display information. From the beginning, the resolution of the TV image—that is, picture definition, understood as the ability to distinguish clearly two small, closely adjacent objects—has been set against that of 16mm and 35mm film as well as the still photograph.[23] On this basis, TV has remained the poor relation, delivering less information per frame than its cinematic counterpart. The U.S. standard of 525 lines per frame (with only about 280 usable lines for the color image) compares very unfavorably to the 1,000-line equivalent for the 35mm film frame. Of course, high-definition television and the digitization of the video signal have all but closed the gap between the resolving power of photochemical as opposed to electronic imaging devices, but the entire mode of comparison is ill conceived from the outset. Emergent cultural forms tend to be evaluated in terms of their antecedents and are frequently found lacking; their perceived inadequacies may well serve to palliate the threat of the new. The novel mix of characteristics and capabilities attached to an emergent medium requires that the old standards and measurements be reassessed, the value-determining criteria reimagined. This is certainly the case with video in its aesthetic relation to film. As a number of video artists and critics noted throughout the 1970s and 1980s, video's palette, texture, sound capabilities, and pulse (the twice-scanned thirty fields per second for NTSC as opposed to cinema's twenty-four frames per second) distinguish it from other moving image forms. Subsequent variations in the world of electronic sound-image reproduction—laser disc, CD-ROM, and so on—offer their own range of characteristics.

In this book, we have approached the matter of video "resolution" in another way, not after the technologically based habit of providing hard edges that define the object, but by offering to view a range of critical perspectives—multiple, even disjunctive conceptual and ideological matrices through which to *know* video as a contemporary cultural phenomenon. As we have noted throughout this introduction, the plurality of this enterprise is necessitated by an explosion of forms, functions, uses, and effects of electronic media in the 1990s. Rather than serving to "resolve" the matter at hand, our hope for these essays is that they will engender argument, debate, contestation, and, in the end, new thinking on video in all its manifestations.

NOTES

1 Jonathan Crary, *Techniques of the Observer: On Vision and Modernity in the Nineteenth Century* (Cambridge, Mass.: MIT Press, 1990), 1-3. "Most of the historically important functions of the human eye are being supplanted by practices in which visual images no longer have any reference to the position of an observer in a 'real,' optically perceived world. If these images can be said to refer to anything, it is to millions of bits of electronic mathematical data. Increasingly, visuality will be situated on a cybernetic and electromagnetic terrain where abstract visual and linguistic elements coincide and are consumed, circulated, and exchanged globally" (2).

2 Ibid., 24.

3 A number of cultural critics have written about this epochal shift and from many perspectives, among them Walter Benjamin ("The Work of Art in the Age of Mechanical Reproduction," in *Illuminations,* ed. Hannah Arendt, trans. Harry Zohn [New York: Schocken Books, 1969]), Michel Foucault (*Discipline and Punish: The Birth of the Prison,* trans. Alan Sheridan [New York: Pantheon Books, 1979]), Jean Baudrillard (*Simulations,* trans. Paul Foss [New York, 1983]), and John Tagg (*The Burden of Representation* [Amherst: University of Massachusetts Press, 1988]).

4 "HealthRIGHT seeks to fill a void in the health care reform debate by giving the American people a voice in the political process. Physicians, drug companies and hospitals all have well-funded lobbies. HealthRIGHT is the people's lobby" ("Speak Out, America!," a press release issued by HealthRIGHT ["A

nonprofit coalitition for comprehensive, compassionate health reform"], 513 C Street, N.E., Washington, D.C. 20002-5809; 202/547-6586 [n.d., n.p.]). The full roster of sponsoring organizations that joined the Foundation for Hospice and Homecare to form the coalition includes the ALS Association, AFSCME, the Caring Institute, the Child Welfare League, the Hospice Association of America, the March of Dimes, the National Association for Home Care, the National Center for Health Care Law, the National Consumers' League, and the National Council of Senior Citizens.

5 Carolyn Marvin, *When Old Technologies Were New: Thinking about Electric Communication in the Late Nineteenth Century* (New York: Oxford University Press, 1988), 5.

6 Ibid.

7 Robert Lee Hotz, "Astronauts Swap Hubble Cameras in Swift Work," *Los Angeles Times*, 7 December 1993, A1, A28.

8 Richard Tresch Fienberg, "Hubble's Road to Recovery," *Sky and Telescope,* November 1993, 17.

9 Robert Lee Hotz, "Fixed Hubble's Sharp Photos Cause Elation," *Los Angeles Times*, 14 January 1994, A1, A25.

10 John J. Goldman and William C. Rempel, "Probe of N.Y. Blast Scene Uses Videotapes, Robotics," *Los Angeles Times*, 2 March 1993, A1, A10. This use of the video apparatus is altogether consistent with the theorizing of the early Soviet filmmaker Dziga Vertov, whose passionate writings on the "kino eye" stressed its unceasing perfectibility. The following lines excerpted from his 1923 manifesto, "Council of Three," may well strike the contemporary reader as both prescient and utopian for their anticipation of robotics, computer-generated imagery, and even smart bombs: "We cannot improve the making of our eyes, but we can endlessly perfect the camera. . . . I am kino-eye, I am a mechanical eye. I, a machine, show you the world as only I can see it. Now and forever, I free myself from human immobility, I am in constant motion, I draw near, then away from objects, I crawl under, I climb onto them. I move apace with the muzzle of a galloping horse, I plunge full speed into a crowd, I outstrip running soldiers, I fall on my back, I ascend with an airplane, I plunge and soar together with plunging and soaring bodies. . . . My path leads to the creation of a fresh perception of the world. I decipher in a new way a world unknown to you" (Dziga Vertov, *Kino-Eye: The Writings of Dziga Vertov,* Annette Michelson, ed. [Berkeley: University of California Press, 1984], 15-18).

11 Jim Herron Zamora, "Volunteers Give L.A. Police Extra Eyes in the Night," *Los Angeles Times,* 18 March 1993, A1, A3, A30. The matter of the accelerating arrival of a "surveillance society" and its political effects is a complex one indeed. There have been countless books and articles written on the topic, many of them sounding a decidedly dystopian alarm, ranging from the early sociological studies of Jacques Ellul (*The Technological Society* [New York: Vintage Books, 1964]) and James Rule (*Private Lives, Public Surveillance* [London: Allen-Lane, 1973]) to the highly influential writings of Michel Foucault (for example, *Discipline and Punish: The Birth of the Prison* [New York: Vintage, 1977]). The approach of sociologist David Lyon (*The Electronic Eye: The Rise of Surveillance Society* [Minneapolis: University of Minnesota Press, 1994]), is somewhat different. He begins by noting that surveillance exceeds its function as a means of social control and "is not unambiguously good or bad." He cites widespread public approval for the way in which electronic databases can disperse lifesaving information with unprecedented speed and efficiency (for example, consumer alerts regarding newly discovered health risks for pharmaceuticals, product recalls for unsafe items, international sharing of information on terrorism, and so on) (4-5). While acknowledging the complexity of the surveillance imperative, for us Mike Davis's corruscating vision of Los Angeles as a city whose divisions of race, class, and ethnicity are scrupulously enforced by high-tech law enforcement techniques remains unchallenged—"good citizens, off the streets, enclaved in their high-security private consumption spheres; bad citizens, on the streets (and therefore not engaged in legitimate business), caught in the terrible, Jehovan scrutiny of the LAPD's space program" (Mike Davis, *City of Quartz* [London: Verso, 1988], 253). The Volunteer Surveillance Team is only another proof of the ways in which the hegemonic exerts its power through the willing participation of those it holds in thrall. Contrarily, this book is dedicated to the ways in which individuals and social groups have invented alternatives for video technologies that countervail the top-down terror of surveillance society.

12 Marc Lacey, "Thirty-six Squad Cars to Be Outfitted with Cameras," *Los Angeles Times,* 7 October 1993, B1, B8.

13 Michel Foucault, "The Eye of Power," in *Power/Knowledge: Selected Interviews and Other Writings—1972-1977* (New York: Pantheon Books, 1980), 156.

14 Daniel Cerone, "'Cops' Hits Streets of L.A.," *Los Angeles Times,* 21 May 1994, F13.

15 Howard Rosenberg, "Chase Outran the Usual TV Theatrics," *Los Angeles Times,* 18 June 1994, A10.

16 Foucault, "The Eye of Power," 158.

17 For a discussion of the notion of "documentary function," see Michael Renov, "Toward a Poetics of Documentary," in *Theorizing Documentary,* ed. Michael Renov (New York: Routledge, 1993), 12-36. This argument for video's documentary status—despite the echoes of an outmoded bifurcation of video practitioners into "artists" and "documentarians"—responds to its increasingly significant role as an apparatus of information storage and retrieval.

18 Raymond Williams, *Marxism and Literature* (Oxford: Oxford University Press, 1977), 160.

19 We tend to agree with Sean Cubitt's position that "there is no essential form of video, nothing to which one can point as the primal source or goal of video activity. It isn't intrinsically good or bad" (*Videography: Video Media as Art and Culture* [New York: St. Martin's Press, 1993], xv). Cubitt employs the term *video media* to stress the plurality of relationships, sources, and discursive modalities that constitute the electronic sound/image. We have chosen the term *resolutions* for the title of this book as an indication of our own sense of the multiple and overdetermined character of video culture and of the impossibility (as well as undesirability) of producing anything like a "definitive" account of this cultural phenomenon.

20 James Clifford, *The Predicament of Culture: Twentieth-Century Ethnography, Literature, and Art* (Cambridge, Mass.: Harvard University Press, 1988), 11.

21 Dissident Republican presidential candidate Pat Buchanan assailed George Bush for presiding over a National Endowment for the Arts that could fund such "obscenity" as *Tongues Untied.* To this day, the tape serves as a catalyst for continuing public debate on state subsidy for the arts, as well as on the power of the religious Right's lobby in the halls of Congress.

22 Williams, *Marxism and Literature,* 159.

23 For a useful overview of broadcast technologies, see chapters 4 ("How Broadcasting and Cable Work") and 5 ("Relays, Recording, and the Digital Revolution") in Sydney W. Head, Christopher H. Sterling, and Lemuel B. Schofield's *Broadcasting in America: A Survey of Electronic Media,* 7th ed. (Boston: Houghton Mifflin, 1994), 111-81. For all its utility, this standard text's framing of the physical aspects of electronic media is markedly determinist and, thus, far from the view espoused in these pages: "Our theme is that technology largely determines both electronic media's potential and their limitations" (111).

CHAPTER 1

THE POLITICS OF VIDEO MEMORY:
ELECTRONIC ERASURES AND
INSCRIPTIONS

Marita Sturken

I remember that month of January in Tokyo, or rather I remember the images that I filmed of the month of January in Tokyo. They have substituted themselves for my memory. They are my memory. I wonder how people remember things who don't film, don't photograph, don't tape. How has mankind managed to remember? ~ CHRIS MARKER, *Sans Soleil*

Since its invention, the camera has figured centrally in the desire to remember, to recall the past, to make the absent present. Photographic, cinematic, and video images are the raw materials used to construct personal histories: events remembered because they were photographed, moments forgotten because no images were preserved, and unphotographed memories that work in tension with camera memories. The memories constructed from camera images are not only personal, but collective. History is represented by the black-and-white photographic or cinematic image, and increasingly by a faded color film image or low-resolution television image. The camera image produces memories, yet in offering itself as a material fragment of the past it can also produce a kind of forgetting.

Projected and transmitted on screens, these images can be seen as "screen memories." According to Freud, a "screen memory" functions to hide painful memories that are too difficult for a subject to confront; the screen memory offers itself as a substitute, while "screening out" the "real" memory. The camera image can often screen out other often unphotographed memories and offer itself as the "real" memory, "becoming" our memory.

Freud demonstrated that memory is essential to the notion of a self and described the complex ways that we disremember those memories that are too damaging or painful. Similarly, the construction of memory and history is essential to a specific culture or nation; we often "forget" as a nation. I am employing the term *cultural memory* to designate cultural processes that stand outside official history and mainstream culture yet have served as a catharsis for healing, the sharing of personal memory, and community building. History in the United States is constructed through a complex apparatus of media, written texts, and popular culture. Cultural memory is a kind of living memory that is produced at sites of disruption in history; it intervenes and tangles with history-making. For instance, both the Vietnam Veterans Memorial in Washington, D.C., and the AIDS Memorial Quilt are sites of an intense production of cultural memory, where people have actively shared memory, usually anonymously, in order to construct meaning out of the grief and loss of those events. The stories shared at these memorials are powerful testimonies that actively question aspects of their historical narratives.

Similarly, independent video constitutes a field of cultural memory, one that contests and intervenes with official history. This is not to say that all memories produced with a video camera constitute modes of resistance or political intervention—in the 1990s, videotapes as cultural forms shift meaning all the time. Yet many independent videotapes are deliberate interventions in history and conscious memory constructions. The politics and phenomenology of television and video converge to both produce and negate history and memory.

THE TELEVISION IMAGE MAKING HISTORY

In the late twentieth century the photograph, the documentary film image, and the docudrama are central elements in the construction of history. Yet electronic images have a constantly shifting relationship to history. The television image is an image of immediacy, transmission, and continuity. "Flow," as defined by Raymond Williams—the incorporation of interruption until it becomes naturalized in the stream of images—is a central aspect of television. Television is the image without an original, for which the status of the copy is ultimately irrelevant. Stanley Cavell has noted that the primary "fact" of television is its serial format; we do not distinguish the particular television episode so much as the ongoing series or event; hence, the series is what is memorable in television.[1]

In contrast, most videotapes that fall under the rubric of video art or independent video are meant to be seen not as interruptions in the flow but as unique events. Certain works are designed for the context of satellite transmission and other videotapes are identified as "art for television." However, most independent videotapes aspire to be seen in contexts that separate them from the ongoing information flow of TV.

Yet the video image is implicated in the relentless electronic flow of the television image. Television is coded, like all electronic technology, as live and immediate; it evokes the instant present, in which information is more valuable the faster and more immediate it is. Television technology has thus never been conceived in terms of preservation, and videotapes deteriorate rapidly. Videotapes that were made as recently as the 1970s look like distant antecedents to contemporary television, with their blurred

MARITA STURKEN

and worn images and muffled sound. Many videotapes and early television shows are in fact already irretrievable.

Despite this problematic relationship to preservation, television-video has inevitably become a medium in which memory and history are recorded. Since the early 1980s, an increasing number of "historical" incidents have been recorded on television (until the late 1970s, most television news footage was still shot on film). The Challenger space shuttle exploding, the lone Chinese student halting a tank in Tiananmen Square, the people clambering on top of the Berlin Wall, and the "targets" taken from cameras on bombs in the Persian Gulf War: these are distinctly television's images of history. Slightly blurred, often shot with the immediate feeling of a hand-held camera, these images seem to evoke not a fixed history but rather history as it unfolds— the making of history. While the feverish immediacy of these images connotes an instantaneity, their status as historical images is somewhat muddied. They will, in a sense, always be coded as live, immediate images—their blurriness or lack of image resolution is often read as evoking the speed of information rather than their electronic materiality. The electronic image thus presents a paradox for memory and history, connoting the immediate instead of the past. This has led certain cultural critics to declare television as the site of memory's demise. For instance, Fredric Jameson has written: "But memory seems to play no role in television, commercial or otherwise (or, I am tempted to say, in postmodernism generally): nothing haunts the mind or leaves its afterimages in the manner of the great moments of film (which do not necessarily happen, of course, in the 'great' films)."[2]

Yet, despite Jameson's pessimism, it is too easy to declare memory dead in a postmodern context. Jameson nostalgically mourns the passing of history in the postmodern "weakening of history, both in our relationship to public History and in the new forms of our private temporality."[3] But what is the history mourned here, a pretelevision history? I would argue that the stakes in memory and history are ever present in electronic media (and postmodernism)—that despite its paradoxical relationship to the preservation of memory, television-video is a primary site of history and cultural memory, where memories, both individual and collective, are produced and claimed.

VIDEO MEMORIES

In independent video, the preservation of images and recording of history has been an underlying desire in the accumulation of videotapes. Video collectives in the 1970s, such as the Videofreex and Raindance, were interested in compiling databanks of alternative images and in accruing an alternative visual history to the nationalist history produced by broadcast television. Concerns with preservation were deemed irrelevant; consequently most of the early videotapes by the collectives have not survived, and television stations routinely destroy master tapes of old programs. The maintenance of collective memory is a problem, it seems, in the case of bulky one-inch tapes or old heat-sensitive reel-to-reel videotapes. While the notion of a video databank utopically envisioned by these collectives conjured up alternative histories stored neatly in electronic space and accessible to everyone, in reality tapes are material objects that stick, erode, and warp.

Yet in this dual role of image retention and loss, video has increasingly become a medium in which issues of collective and individual memory are being examined. The politics of memory and identity, the elusiveness of personal memory, and the relationship of camera images to national and cultural memory have become topics explored by artists in video. I would like to examine several of these artists' works in order to explore how the phenomenology of video intersects with a contemporary politics of memory, and how video has been used to create counterimages to nationalistic histories: Woody Vasulka's *Art of Memory* (1987), Rea Tajiri's *History and Memory* (1991), Janice Tanaka's *Memories from the Department of Amnesia* (1990) and *Who's Going to Pay for These Donuts, Anyway?* (1992), and Jeanne Finley's *Nomads at the 25 Door* (1991). These tapes are concerned with the memory of political and historical events, how those memories are preserved and embodied, how they permeate the present, and the intersections of personal memory, cultural memory, and history. In all these works, the role of video as a technology of memory is ever present: remembering, forgetting, and containing memories.

Among these tapes, Woody Vasulka's *Art of Memory* is concerned most directly with the different phenomenological relationships of film and television-video to memory and history, and the fluctuating cultural meanings of images that are coded "history." *Art of Memory* takes as its material the black-and-white photographic and filmic images of the "historic events" of the twentieth century: the Spanish Civil War, the Russian Revolution, World War II, the atomic bomb. Vasulka mixes codes and tropes to make the signification of historicity his central topic. Cinematic tropes for the passage of time, such as images reeling past or flipping by, are contained within stylized, electronically created shapes that deny these cinematic codes their narrative potential. Vasulka's project is to use video to examine and ultimately consume cinema.

In *Art of Memory*, newsreel and documentary footage and still photographs are transformed into image objects that appear to sit on a southwestern desert landscape. These image objects are evocative, strange, and unpredictable. Sometimes they resemble large movie screens in the desert, at other times their shapes are awkward and bulky. They function to decontextualize the film images: one cannot read them as windows onto the world, but only as generic images of history. Some assert themselves to suggest narratives—Oppenheimer's famous postbomb speech, in which he quotes the Bhagavad Gita, for instance—but then are submerged again in the stream of images contained within the object forms that deconstruct narrative in the tape.

Yet within this dense layering of images, Vasulka does hint at a narrative of history and the image. In one of the few purely video images, a mythical figure with wings sits on a cliff. Seeing it from a distance, a man tries to capture its attention. He tosses a pebble at it, and then, when it turns toward him, he photographs it, causing it to rise up in apparent anger and swoop down upon him. The creature is ultimately unex-

MARITA STURKEN

plained in this tape, but it evokes many possible meanings—an unattainable, mythic man/beast that the nervous and distracted middle-aged man, haunted by images of history, tries to capture with his camera. It is as if he is trying to photograph the well-known "angel of history" described by Walter Benjamin:

> His face is turned toward the past. Where we perceive a chain of events, he sees one single catastrophe which keeps piling wreckage upon wreckage and hurls it in front of his feet. The angel would like to stay, awaken the dead, and make whole what has been smashed. But a storm is blowing from Paradise; it has got caught in his wings with such violence that the angel can no longer close them. This storm irresistibly propels him into the future to which his back is turned, while the pile of debris before him grows skyward.[4]

This sense of a propelling forward of history permeates *Art of Memory*. Vasulka's alter ego tries to create an image of the figure to hold it in place, to prevent it from hurtling toward the future, away from the photographic into the electronic grids created by Vasulka's machinery. The images of history lose their individual meaning and become a tangle of memories swallowed by the electronically rendered desert landscape. Voices echo and haunt these images; we cannot understand them, but we know, with their scratchy sound and intonation, that these are the voices of history. Still photographs, some of famous historical figures such as the anarchist Durruti and the revolutionary Rosa Luxemburg, scroll across the screen, processed until they become almost translucent and shredded by the passage of time. These images of history are set in the desert, a landscape coded as both timeless and postapocalyptic.

In its form and its contrast of the cinematic and the electronic, *Art of Memory* is an attempt to chart the death of cinema. Here, the cinematic is the past, the fading black-and-white images of history, swallowed up by the electronic. In the structure of the tape, Vasulka is attempting to configure an electronic language that defies the legacy of cinematic codes. He uses complex wipes and fades to avoid the "cut," which he considers to be a cinematic trope that is not inherently a part of the language of electronic imaging. In creating image "objects" on the screen, he is attempting to defy the fetishizing aspect of cinema, to render the cinematic images into a relentless flow in which any pretense of realism gives way to the simple code of cinema as history. *Art of Memory* is a meditation on the ways in which cinema defines and creates history, and on redefining its legacy in the realm of the electronic.

While the status of the cinematic image as history propels *Art of Memory*, the tape does not attempt to trace the meaning of its historical images or their consequences. In *Art of Memory*, the images of war meld together into a totalizing image of history, one that does not question the status of the image as history. In contrast, Rea Tajiri's *History and Memory* presents video as memory (as opposed to cinema as history) as a means to construct countermemories to history. For Tajiri, the critical issue is the construction of history and how the historical image screens out the images of personal memory. This is a dense work of found and reconstructed images, a cathartic reworking again and again of history.

History and Memory attempts to understand the intersections of personal memory and historical events, specifically the history and memories of the imprisonment of Japanese Americans in the United States during World War II. Tajiri is compelled by the gaps in her mother's memory and her own sense of incompleteness to counter the historical images of the internment of her mother and her father's family in California, specifically in U.S. propaganda films. The story of her family forms a microcosm of the consequences of racist American policy: her father served in the army while the government interned his family, all of them Americans, in concentration camps and took their possessions. Their house was not only confiscated by the government but literally moved away; they never found out where. Tajiri's task is a kind of retroactive witnessing; cameras were not allowed in the camps, so her raw materials are the images she has carried in her mind of this nonimaged past. From her mother's stories of the camps, recounted to her as a child, she creates an image of her mother filling a canteen at a faucet in the desert, an image for which she wants to find the story. When cameras are not there to witness, when memories fade and people forget, the sole witnesses are the spirits of the dead:

> There are things which have happened in the world while there were cameras watching, things we have images for. There are other things which have happened while there were no cameras watching, which we restage in front of cameras to have images of.
>
> There are things which have happened for which the only images that exist are in the minds of observers, present at the time, while there are things which have happened for which there have been no observers, except the spirits of the dead.

She imagines the spirit of her grandfather witnessing an argument between her parents about the "unexplained nightmares that their daughter has been having on the twentieth anniversary of the bombing of Pearl Harbor." Where are the memories of those events for which there were no witnesses? Where are those memories when the witnesses are gone? Where are the unphotographed images? The prohibition of cameras in the camps asserts itself often in the narrative weavings of this work. An unearthed home movie image of the camps, made with a smuggled camera, contrasts sharply with the evenly lit, steady, and clean images of government propaganda films in its jerky camera movement and, unexpectedly, its everydayness.

When we do not have access to images to construct memories and histories, Tajiri makes it clear, we make others. Her sister follows a young man with her camera, too shy to talk to him except to ask him to pose for her. His photo ends up in her box of movie stars that only years later Tajiri realizes is filled only with images of white people. Her own task is to create images to fill the void of those absent images of the camps, to make the absent Japanese American—absent from the box of movie stars and from history—present. The war in the Pacific produced a kind of hypervisibility of the Japanese Americans. Tajiri notes, "Whereas before we were mostly ignored and slightly out of focus, the war brought us clearly into view and made us sharply defined." The historical camera focused and saw not citizens but enemies of the state.

These are not just the memories of survivors, now fading, but the memories of their children as well. Tajiri has lived this memory:

> I began searching for a history, my own history, because I had known all along that the stories I had heard were not true and parts had been left out. I remember having this feeling growing up that I was haunted by something, that I was living within a family full of ghosts. There was this place that they knew about. I had never been there, yet I had a memory for it. I could remember a time of great sadness before I was born. We had been moved, uprooted. We had lived with a lot of pain. I had no idea where these memories came from yet I knew the place.

Her tape is in many ways an attempt to coexist with the ghosts of the past by creating images in which to place them.

History is constructed not only through documentary images and propaganda films, it is also constructed via popular culture. American cultural notions of World War II, for instance, are for the most part constructed through Hollywood films. These are screen memories that both substitute themselves for the personal memories of survivors and supersede documentary images in signifying history. These are, in Tajiri's words, the events that we restage in front of cameras. The history of this era in American history is signified for Tajiri by the jingoistic film *Yankee Doodle Dandy* (1942) and the absent presence evoked by *Bad Day at Black Rock* (1955), in which Spencer Tracy investigates the death of a Japanese American man in the United States after the invasion of Pearl Harbor. Kimoko, the murdered man, is never seen in the film; Tajiri notes that his murder was one the townspeople wanted to forget, just as the people who live near Poston, Arizona, where the internment camps were constructed on a Native American reservation, attempt to forget until an Asian face reminds them. The narrative film presents itself as both history and memory, filling and supplanting our memory gaps, offering images when there were none. Tajiri's nephew, in reviewing the Hollywood film *Come See the Paradise* (1990), a sentimental depiction of the camps seen through the eyes of an internee's white husband, actively resists the capacity of these film images to replace memories, although, he says, his grandparents didn't tell him any stories.

Tajiri's desire to fill in the memory gaps with new images and reworked images of the past allows her to re-remember for her mother. When her mother cannot remember how she got to the camp, Tajiri goes back to film the drive for her. Imagining her mother filling the canteen, she says, "For years, I have been living with this picture without the story. . . . Now I could forgive my mother for her loss of memory and could make this image for her." The camera image thus participates in a process of healing, allowing through recreating, reimaging, a kind of memory closure. Yet, Tajiri makes it clear that this is a partial memory and a partial healing, one remembered and constructed in opposition, one peopled with multiple subjectivities, racist images, counterimages, fragments of the past, absent presences.

Public commemoration, as a memorial or a videotape, is a form of bearing witness. Tajiri, in questioning historical narratives and creating countermemories, attempts to create memory out of forgetting. For Janice Tanaka the video form also becomes a means of bearing witness and reclaiming memories. Tanaka states that in her childhood home, "silence was the keeper of memories," and her videotapes are a means of speaking through that silence. *Memories from the Department of Amnesia* reflects on the death of her mother, and *Who's Going to Pay for These Donuts, Anyway?* chronicles her search for a father she hasn't seen since she was three, a father she continues to search for in the frail man with a confused memory whom she comes to know.

In both these tapes, Tanaka juxtaposes "official" historical accounts with personal memories and anecdotes. On paper, both her parents clearly suffered because of their internment as Japanese Americans during World War II, yet it is the different ways in which they responded to American racism that Tanaka investigates. In *Memories from the Department of Amnesia*, she opposes a chronology of her mother's life events with the seemingly "unimportant" quirks and anecdotes remembered by herself and her daughter. Tanaka uses cryptic and dreamlike images to suggest the elusive nature of memory: a figure rides a bicycle through a restaurant; a surgeon walks through deep snow; a white figure stands in a white space, perhaps a hospital waiting room; the bicyclist and surgeon pass each other in the snow—images of passage, remembering, and death.

The photograph as a marker of the past, as a totem of death, infuses this tape. A hand lays photographs on the screen, creating negative and positive layers of images, each shifting with movement, focusing and refocusing. The photograph is both stationary and moving, freezing the past yet moving within the present. As the hand lays these still images on the screen, they appear to briefly come alive and then resume their two-dimensional form, as if floating in and out of consciousness.

Tanaka and her daughter tell stories about her mother as the statistical events of her life are written on the screen: Born December 15, 1919, Los Angeles, California . . . Abandoned by mother, 1925 . . . Molested by father . . . Married, February 1940 . . . First child born, September 1940 . . . Government freezes bank account, 1941 . . . Interned Manzanar, 1942 . . . Spouse declared insane, 1942 . . . Nervous breakdown, 1963 . . . Finds mother, acknowledgment denied. . . . This visual litany of trauma, abuse, and hardship displaces the amused rememberings of Tanaka and her daughter. We see the layered existence of a woman whose life is unalterably changed by the actions of the government, the memory behind the history, the memories that emerged from the "department" of amnesia. The history of Tanaka's mother is told through a roll call of the traumatic events of her life, the institutionalization of her life's events. Yet her memory is evoked through video images, hands touching photographs, voices remembering her humor and her humanness.

In *Who's Going to Pay for These Donuts, Anyway?* this tension between history and memory emerges in the absence of memory of Tanaka's father. When she

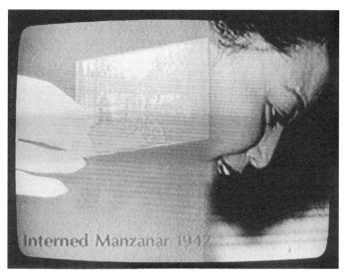

FIGURE 1
Janice Tanaka, *Memories from the Department of Amnesia* (1990)

discovers him after several years in a halfway house for the chronically mentally ill in Los Angeles, it is unclear whether he ever recognizes her to be his daughter, although he knows he has a daughter named Janice. Similarly, it remains unclear whether or not his mental instability was sadly coincidental with or actually the direct result of the Japanese internment. Tanaka remembers that her mother told her in anger not to make a hero of her absent father and, to prove his insanity to her daughter, said that he had written letters of protest to the president about the Japanese

internment, that he had been questioned by the FBI, that he was diagnosed as a schizophrenic with paranoid tendencies, and that he had outbursts of anger—all of them, on the face of it, potentially sane responses to being interned in one's native country. Tanaka says, "You hated being a Jap and you hated your wife and children for being Japs."

Tanaka juxtaposes this portrait of her father as a man destroyed by history with one of her uncle, whom she also rediscovers: a calm, reserved man who speaks of the events of the war and their effects with a sad irony. Just as her uncle has devised a personal philosophy to reconcile his memories of interrogation and internment, so clearly her father has lost his memory not only through shock treatment and drug therapy but also perhaps by a strategic forgetting of things too painful to remember. In this light, those things that he does remember seem remarkable—his understanding of redress, for instance, and why he was given money by the government to compensate for his internment.

Like Tajiri, Tanaka uses the video camera as a tool to mediate between herself and the past that is also part of her memory; she states, "Observing the effect of the past could only be dealt with from behind the distancing lens of the camera." Focusing the camera on her father, however lost, makes him finally tangible. Her videotaping is thus an attempt to counter the antimemory of her family, the lack of souvenirs and memorabilia, the lack of family cohesion. Memory, according to Tanaka, allows us to live more in the present: "When you have a past, it is easy to believe the present has a reason."

Tanaka's tape serves as a countermemory to history, providing, like Tajiri's work, memories that tangle with history and disrupt its narratives. American national identity is constructed through the remembrance of certain historical events, as well as through the forgetting and rescripting of certain events. The historical event of the internment of Japanese American citizens during the war is not easily rescripted from its historical narrative—as necessary though regrettable, as different somehow from what other countries did. It is survivors, in particular their physical presence, who prevent history from being written smoothly and without disruption. In these three tapes it is the children of survivors who are refusing to leave history alone and whose image interventions place the bodies of their parents in the cracks of history.

The displacement so powerfully evoked in Tajiri's story of the house moved from its foundations and in Tanaka's image of her father as a man destroyed by history is echoed in Jeanne Finley's *Nomads at the 25 Door*, in which the ruthlessness of history-making and issues of home are presented within a context of bearing witness and memorializing fleeting moments in history's rapid accrual. The tape examines two separate worlds that are infused by displacement: Yugoslavia in 1990 and a women's prison in Carson City, Nevada. Finley toys with notions of history by drawing analogies between the two situations: the upheaval of Yugoslavia and the burden of its rapidly changing history, and the ways in which the displaced women in the prison create a sense of home and bear witness for each other.

That history is a process of displacement is played out daily in the upheaval of Eastern Europe. Finley captures this painful process of history via videotape and the television screens on which it was played. Ironically, the historical upheaval she documents seems trivial when compared with the brutal destruction of Yugoslavia that has taken place since that time. While in Yugoslavia she watches the televised images of the Romanian revolution that are broadcast twenty-four hours a day for a week. Yet the television revolution is confusing and chaotic. We see scenes of people speaking, lined up before the camera, trying desperately to get into its view. Finley remarks that the coverage was "incredibly confusing," and even the Romanians she knew could not decipher the scenes. A British newscaster tells us that "residents have placed their televisions in the windows of their homes so those who are engaged in street fighting can watch their own revolution as it is taking place." History is presented in the relentless flow of television, although finally it elucidates nothing except that power has changed hands. Yet the political stakes in what gets designated history and imaged as history are high. A friend of Finley's writes her notes every morning about tricky phrases in the Serbo-Croatian language, a hybrid language created by historical whim, which are mini-commentaries on history and home:

> You might think you are in a vacation *paradise*, but you are not. You're in a complicated part of the world, used by a cruel and ongoing history.

The possibility of a home for me has always been based on the whims of history. And history never seems too indulgent. It is always displacing people.

The search for a history represents a search for stability, community, a home. In the tape we see Finley write on someone's hands, "If only I could find history simply by pressing the palms of your hands against my chest." Yet history is elusive, intangible, ever changing: it stands outside these bodies.

It is through the unusual juxtaposition of the two disparate worlds of Eastern Europe and the women's prison that Finley pushes at notions of personal history, national history, and the desires within both for community and home. Her interviews with the women in the Carson City prison are moving and compelling and ultimately overshadow the images of Yugoslavia because of their direct emotional intensity. These women speak of lives of abuse and fear and, strangely for those of us on the outside, the ways in which they finally found acceptance, love, families, and a sense of home in prison. The tape centers on Mickey Yates, a young woman who very slowly tells her story of receiving two life sentences for her complicity in the brutal killing of her mother. For Yates, the notion of a home is profoundly troubling; she went *home* to find her mother dead. At first, she is reluctant to tell her story, her history, but then its telling becomes cathartic and essential. She actively constructs her history. Ironically, she reveals the paradox of history in a simple idiomatic expression: when the judge asked her about the sexual abuse she was subjected to, she started to cry—"I was history after that."

In its elliptical style, Finley's tape is about inserting personal memories into the mass of history. She begins and ends the tape with an image taken by her own mother of herself and her brother waving while going off to school. These were images her mother took for family calendars showing the children dressed in different outfits for each month, standing and waving—a project that crudely evokes the passage of time. They were instructed, says Finley, to stand and wave, walk, wave again, and then walk away without looking back. Yet clearly her tape is asking, How can we not look back? Isn't it cruel to ask a child not to look back? History and memory in this work are intimately allied, each pushing the boundary of the other, each permeating our lives.

The relationship of history and home is clearly evoked in Finley's tape. The women in the prison find their voices after establishing a sense of home. "I never realized that I would have to come to prison to find acceptance," one says. The displacement of the Japanese Americans during the war was equally a negation of home, of the right to call any place home. It is from the place of home that a historical voice can speak, and it is home where memories reside.

All these tapes are infused with the desire to create countermemories to official historical narratives. While Vasulka wants to reorchestrate the images of history and to show the empty frame of the totalizing historical image, these other videomakers want to bear witness: the prisoners in Finley's tape bear witness for each other; the Romanians bear witness before the television cameras, watching themselves "make history"; Tanaka bears witness for her mother and father; and Tajiri bears witness for her family. Video thus acts as a form of cultural memory, providing a form through which personal memories are shared, historical narratives are questioned, and memory is claimed. Television will continue to play a central role in how Americans and other nations construct their national identities. Yet video's memories are tangling with its narratives, appropriating its images, and telling different stories.

In these tapes, memory is not seen as a depository of images to be excavated, but rather as an amorphous, ever-changing field of images. This memory is not about retrieval as much as it is about retelling and reconstruction. It is about acknowledging the impossibility of knowing what really happened, and a search for a means of telling. This is memory within a postmodern context, not destroyed but different, memory that is often disguised as forgetting.

NOTES

1 Stanley Cavell, "The Fact of Television," in *Video Culture: A Critical Investigation,* ed. John Hanhardt (Rochester, N.Y.: Visual Studies Workshop, 1986), 192–218.

2 Fredric Jameson, *Postmodernism; or, The Cultural Logic of Late Capitalism* (Durham, N.C.: Duke University Press, 1991), 70–71.

3 Ibid., 6.

4 Waler Benjamin, "Theses on the Philosophy of History," in *Illuminations,* ed. Hannah Arendt, trans. Harry Zohn (New York: Schocken Books, 1969), 257–58.

CHAPTER 2

QUALIFYING THE QUOTIDIAN:
ARTIST'S VIDEO AND THE PRODUCTION OF SOCIAL SPACE

Christine Tamblyn

In *The Practice of Everyday Life*, social historian Michel de Certeau sketches the rudiments of a discursive trajectory that he does not develop further: "The analysis of the images broadcast by television (representation) and of the time spent watching television (behavior) should be complemented by a study of what the cultural consumer 'makes' or 'does' during this time and with these images."[1]

Everyday life is a notoriously obscure object of academic scrutiny; its ubiquity (paradoxically) renders it invisible, protecting it from panoptic surveillance. Recent work in cultural studies tends to position consumers as active, critical users of mass culture, creators of a multiplicity of fragmented and contradictory discourses. I will attempt to decipher how the consumer operates when receiving television by examining some of the scattered video products she concocts as bricolage from televisual refuse. Because the elusive "consumer-sphinx" is a hybrid creature,[2] I found it necessary to search for her products in cultural arenas ranging from recordings of ACT-UP demonstrations to broadcasts of *America's Funniest Home Videos*.

While conducting these investigations, I discovered that the consumer-sphinx has already devised a multitude of enterprising applications for the disposable, quasi-obsolete technology of video. Capitalizing on its capacities for representing visceral sensations and interior speech, consumers have used video to create new spaces for cultural intervention. The presence of a camcorder does not merely function to passively witness and record events; it also facilitates intrapsychic communication, abrogating the monadic isolation of the postmodern subject.

Who uses consumer video technology? The major corporations that manufacture camcorders no longer aim their marketing campaigns solely at the bourgeois heterosexual family. Camcorders are used to document town council meetings, ballet classes, group therapy sessions, and sports events, as well as weddings and birthday parties. Does the proliferation of camcorders within new markets signify that the democratization of video so fervently advocated by independent producers and communication theorists in the late 1960s has finally been accomplished? I am skeptical about assertions that the nonprofessional use of small format video necessarily demystifies mass media or facilitates democratic participation in government. However, the multiple interfaces between video and daily life indicate that video is now a primary tool in the production of social space.

Social space emerges from representations of space and representational spaces. As sociologist Henri Lefebvre observes: "Spatial practice is neither determined by an existing system, be it urban or ecological, nor adapted to a system, be it economic or political. On the contrary, thanks to the potential energies of a variety of groups capable of diverting homogenized space to their own purposes, a theatricalized or dramatic space is liable to arise."[3]

Because video has the capability for registering and recording moving images and synchronous sound more cheaply, quickly, and efficiently than other mediums, it offers unique possibilities for responding to the demands of the body transported outside of itself in the virtual space of the society of the spectacle. On an institutional level, video technologies continue to abet the elision of the public and private realms through their multifarious applications in commerce, entertainment, education, the military, the legal system, and medicine. Nevertheless, deterministic views of technology that equate video with totalitarian mechanisms of surveillance and control must be refuted. As an aspect of systems of social relations and discourses, video may also help to create counterspaces through its "real time" potentials for immediacy and spontaneity.

Consumer video applications bridge high and low cultural spheres in their modes of distribution. Video artworks shot on VHS or Hi-8 may be shown in galleries and museums, rented from hip emporiums, or broadcast on TV. As a medium that is economically accessible and requires minimal technical skills to master, video is ideally suited as a vehicle for the close integration of art and life. Several recent examples of video art extend or parody consumer video's modes of interfacing with everyday life. Many genres of home video have already emerged: video diaries; video letters; commemorations of holidays and other special occasions; vacation tapes; video wills; documents of such phenomena as natural disasters, accidents, and police brutality; and home pornography.

Do any of these genres bear a reciprocal resemblance to small format video made by artists? The amateur porn video, for example, that has recently become available through video rental stores or swapping clubs libidinizes the human/technological interface. The authenticity of the performers and their willingness to do more than simulate the mechanisms of genital penetration make amateur productions more erotic than their professional analogues. The crude camera work, muddy sound, and harsh lighting serve as earmarks of an authenticity that titillate the postmodern voyeur's appetite for an always already absent referent. But the utopian potential of home pornography is counterbalanced by its makers' attempts to replicate many of the conventions of commercial pornography regardless of inherent technical limitations. Rather than aestheticizing these limitations as artists often do, makers of amateur porn tend to ignore or attempt to circumvent their low-budget production apparatuses.

CHRISTINE TAMBLYN

If homemade pornography must be discounted as a site for practices that resist dominant ideologies of representation, where may such resistances be located? As I followed the elusive chimera of home video, it initially seemed it would be efficacious to investigate two other cultural phenomenona. The first, *America's Funniest Home Videos*, is a broadcast television program that solicits consumer video from its audience. The best submissions are aired and awarded prizes in a game show format. Unfortunately, the clips selected by the show's producers usually focus on unwilled accidents, perturbations in a texture of banality that remains unchanged after its temporary disruption. Occasionally, viewers send in something more arcane and it slips by the censors. Instead of waiting for a propitious slip on a banana peel or a capsizing boat, they engineer a sight gag or pratfall. For example, in one show a woman hid inside a jack-o'-lantern, her head protruding through a hole cut in the table the pumpkin rested on, surprising her daughter when she lifted up the stem. The grisly implications of this scene were amplified in another narrative vignette that recast a typical Japanese monster movie within a domestic milieu. The monster in this elaborate parody was the couple's baby, whose scale was magnified by tricky camera angles. His beleagured parents just sat in their car and screamed.

However rife with psychoanalytic subtexts, *America's Funniest Home Videos* presents a very limited purview of home video's potential applications. My second lead, the annual *Visions of the U.S.* home video contest sponsored by Sony corporation and administered by the American Film Institute, did not furnish many new insights about the medium. Like the producers of *America's Funniest Home Videos*, Sony solicits open entries and awards prizes. There are five categories: fiction, nonfiction, music video, student, and experimental. But rather than utilizing consumer video in genuinely amateur or unorthodox ways that would convey the propinquities of the tape makers' daily lives, the 1990 and 1991 winning entries tended to emulate professional feature films or documentaries. Most of the entries in the experimental category were sent in by aspiring video artists. These outcomes can probably be attributed to the context of the contest itself; only individuals who have a certain level of ambition bother to submit their work in public competitions. Within this particular discursive domain, then, valid criteria for distinguishing between amateur and professional work cannot be established. Oddly enough, the appellation of "home video" does not seem to carry any sort of stigma for the video artists who chose to participate in the contest.

Abandoning further attempts to conduct an empirical survey of amateur video artifacts, I will now utilize a more theoretical framework. I will apply de Certeau's model for discovering how ordinary people use the culture imposed on them by the technocratic elite to an analysis of certain video art practices. According to de Certeau, the weak manifest ways of utilizing the strong through their tactics of consumption. Composing with the vocabularies and prescribed syntactical forms of established languages, ordinary people contrive to "trace out the ruses of other interests and desires that are neither determined nor captured by the systems in which they develop."[4] The everyday practices cited by de Certeau for their tactical character include talking, reading, walking, riding in trains, shopping, and cooking. Readers, for example, juxtapose fragments of texts to create something new in the space opened up by the capacity of all texts to permit multiple meanings. The arbitrarily constituted distinction between readers and writers must therefore be quafied; reading can be regarded as a form of creative bricolage. The reader poaches on the author's text by insinuating her countless differences into it.

The new stories that de Certeau envisions the reader composing from selected fragments of the dominant text have been given a material aspect in postmodern modes of appropriation. Rap music, voguing, and video collages all feature the recombination of preexisting elements by shifting them into new discursive registers. The subversive rhetorical movements characteristic of these heterogenous formats violate the legalities of syntax and "proper" significance, as well as copyright laws. Verbal economy and condensation, double meanings and misinterpretation, displacements, alliterations, and multiple use of the same quotations are among the procedures employed by consumers to recontextualize found texts. De Certeau observes that such devices are not merely ornamental; they are the verbal equivalents of the trickery and deception the weak must use to outwit the strong. Because consumers are not given a secure place to strategize from, they must instead be ready to seize opportunities for intervention as they arise. They "must vigilantly make use of the cracks that particular conjunctions open in the surveillance of the proprietary powers."[5] The surface of the constructed order can then be abruptly punctured by "ellipses, drifts and leaks of meaning."[6]

De Certeau's astute descriptions of the dispersed, tactical, and makeshift creativity of individuals or groups who superimpose different and interfering kinds of functioning on the disciplinary nets that attempt to contain them provide an interesting correlative to the historical avant-garde's endeavour to integrate art and life. From the posturing of dandyism in the nineteenth century through Dada, Russian constructivism, Marcel Duchamp's persona art, and French surrealism, the major avant-garde movements aimed at developing an innovative relationship between high art and mass culture.[7] After happenings and pop art made any category of recycled cultural debris available for artists' use and minimalism redefined the contributions the viewer was expected to make to complete the work of art, the stage was set for the emergence of video art in the late 1960s.

As Martha Rosler has noted, the ambitions of early video art were twofold: to provide an alternative to *both* broadcast television and the mainstream institutions of the art world.[8] Video art found its impetus in the utopian project of tranforming the sites of art production with their emphasis on passive reception. But perhaps it was the utopian aspect of this project that can be held accountable for its failure. If the dichotomization of active producer/passive consumer was inherently flawed to begin with, then the boundaries video artists intended to transgress were erroneously constructed. I do not mean to imply that a utopia had already been achieved without video artists realizing it, but rather that their project should have been conceived differently. Interventions rather than revolution seem more appropriate within the socioeco-

CHRISTINE TAMBLYN

nomic structure of late capitalism, "a skill of ceaselessly recreating opacities and ambiguities—spaces of darkness and trickery—in the universe of technocratic transparency, a skill that disappears into the network of already established forces and representations and reappears again, taking no responsibility for the administration of a totality."[9]

Risking the possibility that I may be doing a disservice to these protective opacities by situating certain daily practices within the rational confines that circumscribe the writing of this essay, I want to suggest some ways that video art and consumer video now overlap as vehicles for cultural intervention. Each of the home video genres I listed earlier seems to have analogues within the video art canon. I want to cite several artists' tapes that feature some of the rhetorical tropes associated with consumer video and then develop these examples in greater detail.

George Kuchar's *Weather Diary #3* (1988), Lynn Hershman's *Binge* (1987), and Sadie Benning's *It Wasn't Love* (1992) are video diaries.

Video figures as a therapeutic tool in Joe Gibbons and Tony Oursler's *Onourown* (1990).

Video records vacations or other journeys in Chip Lord's *Motorist* (1989) and Susan Mogul's *Prosaic Portraits, Ironies and Other Intimacies* (1991).

Video is used as a family album in Jeanine Mellinger's *In Those Days* (1988) and Janice Tanaka's *Memories from the Department of Amnesia* (1989).

Paralleling the consumer video documents of natural disasters, accidents, and police brutality that are aired regularly on network news shows, activist video that records demonstrations serves the dual functions of witnessing what occurs and bringing the message to a wider audience. Some Paper Tiger Television tapes may be included in this category.

Paper Tiger Television seems like an appropriate example with which to begin a survey of the eradication of the boundaries separating "high" and "low" video culture, because this public access show has always emphasized by necessity a handmade look. Foregrounding the specificities of the production process is an aspect of Paper Tiger TV's policy of demystifying media apparatuses. There are two reasons that Paper Tiger TV contrives to let its audience see what goes on behind the scenes. Besides wanting viewers to feel empowered enough to get involved in making TV, it also intends to demonstrate that television is always an artificial construction made by particular people to promote their own ideological purposes. Paper Tiger TV's updated repertoire of Brechtian alienation effects include the use of handwritten titles and crudely painted backdrops. When they are shooting in a studio, the videomakers often make their sound cues audible and turn a camera on the crew shooting the scene. The deliberate inclusion of such mistakes creates a stylistic texture that differs markedly from the seamless flow of normative broadcast television.

The content of Paper Tiger Television's shows dovetails with such self-reflexive gestures. Over one hundred artists, activists, and academics have worked on the series since its inception in 1981. These commentators have contributed to Paper Tiger TV's ongoing project of analyzing the corporate structures of the media and the commodity culture it services. The ad hoc character of Paper Tiger TV's approach is apparent in *Judith Williamson Consumes Passionately in Southern California*, a 1987 tape that deconstructs a magazine advertisement for Burlington Prima Sport athletic socks. Because Williamson, a British journalist, was teaching at California Institute of the Arts when the tape was made, the tape utilizes the school's pool as a site for a mock water ballet performed by students.

The humorous attitude evidenced by the inclusion of a scene like this in a tape that deals with the expansion of capitalist markets into the bodies of consumers typifies Paper Tiger TV's unpretentious aesthetic. Although the information the tapes offer about the corporate media industry is intellectually rigorous, the activists who volunteer their services to produce the shows want their work to be accessible to diverse audiences. Accordingly, the shows often include hyperbolic dramatic tableaux or silly sight gags that physicalize the abstract issues the commentators have addressed. Williamson's piece features images of her getting buried under an avalanche of socks as she shops at a Target discount store; these images effectively underscore the program's theme about the overabundance of choices consumers must make between competing brands when they purchase commodities.

Paper Tiger TV always concludes its shows by revealing its production budget. In *Judith Williamson Consumes Passionately in Southern California*, the prices of the tape stock, gas, and socks used to make the program are printed in ink on Williamson's heel, framed in a tight close-up through a hole in her sock. Low-cost visual heterogeneity is provided throughout the piece by the unauthorized appropriation of clips from Hollywood musicals. These brief quotations ironically counterpoint the main themes the show tackles by invoking a more naive bygone era of capitalist expansion.

The promiscuous admixture of appropriated feature films, hand-held camcorder footage, and set-up studio shots that constitutes the Williamson tape is characteristic of what Ernest Larsen has dubbed "impure cinevideo."[10] Larsen defines purity as the aesthetic alibi of authority. But an "impure" collison of image registers facilitates a collison of contradictory discourses attuned to the heterogeneity and lack of finality of the quotidian. Larsen states: "An impure art digs right into the dirt of the world. It revels in imperfection, in the mess, in the existing contradictions. This is how it stays close to its audiences and how it remains conscious of and responsive to their needs and desires. . . . The site of the struggle is the quotidian. There we find the jagged edges, the rough surfaces, the unclassifiable smells, the apparent babel of voices. Certainty and universality escape the everyday."[11]

In literature, the diary format most faithfully conveys the shifting nuances of daily life. The only structural consistencies in the diary genre are date headings to mark the passage of time and a concomitant chronological succession of entries. Diaries are inherently fragmented because they cannot begin at the birth of their authors; they always commence in medias res, with their narratives already in progress. And because diary writers are not capable of recording their own death, diaries must end abruptly, at a point that is more likely to be arbitrary then predetermined.

Whereas literary diaries are written and read by isolated subjects and thereby contribute to the construction of interiority, video technology provides more opportunities for social interaction. Other people besides the diarist often participate in the production of a video diary. The finished tape is usually viewed in a communal context, whether it is broadcast or shown in a gallery or museum. Because using video equipment is more cumbersome than writing, video diaries are less spontaneous than their literary equivalents. But camcorders, with their technical advantages of portableness, minimal lighting requirements, and efficient operation on battery power have made the production of video diaries more feasible.

George Kuchar's *Weather Diaries* have already attained definitive status in the emerging video diary genre. Kuchar's extensive experience as an independent filmmaker may have helped to prepare him to make maximal use of minimal means. He does all of his editing in the camcorder, thereby introducing aspects of randomness and improvisation into his pieces. First, he records a basic track. Then, like a jazz musician playing around with riffs, he punctuates this material by inserting new shots. This method makes it impossible for the tapes to be assembled in strict chronological order; Kuchar's compositional strategies thus differ markedly from those used in written diaries.

However, the *Weather Diaries* do resemble more traditional diaries in some respects. The tapes, which Kuchar began making in 1986, chronicle a habitual activity that the artist engages in. Each year Kuchar travels to Tornado Alley in Oklahoma to experience the storms that sweep through this region in the spring. Since Kuchar can't drive, he can't actually chase the storms. Instead he spends most of his time waiting in sleazy motel rooms, alternately watching the cloud formations in the sky and the weather reports on television.

Kuchar's obsession with his own bodily functions parallels his interest in the weather. Using dialectical montage, he juxtaposes images to draw explicit connections between the downpour outside his window and the excretion of his bodily fluids in *Weather Diary #3*. Bizarrely reviving the "pathetic fallacy" of nineteenth century Romantic poetry within a more mundane cultural context, Kuchar also dramatizes his sexual tension when the anticipated storms fail to materialize. Offscreen narration by a weather forecaster predicting scattered thunderstorms accompanies a shot of boys in swimming trunks roughhousing around the motel pool. This is followed by a close-up in which Kuchar turns the camera on himself as he licks his lips and says, "Hot." Next we see shots of water pouring out of a shower spigot and Kuchar masturbating in the spray. This sequence epitomizes the complex system of condensations and displacements Kuchar sets up throughout the piece. These metaphorical links are often based on the physical similarities of objects or on a chain of sound-image-text substitutions that operate as transitional devices. When Kuchar murmurs, "Hot," and licks his lips, his saliva connects the sound bite about thunderstorms with the ensuing torrent of water in the shower. The word "hot" also functions as a figure of speech connoting both sexual desire and water and weather temperature.

Kuchar's meticulous accumulation of the synedochal details of his daily life in the *Weather Diaries* conveys a sense of rural America in the 1980s that transcends the scope of the personal and opens out into social history. Like Judith Williamson, Kuchar is concerned about the commodification of the body under late capitalism.[12] In *Weather Diary #3*, Kuchar visits the junk food emporiums and discount stores in the strip malls that make up the shopping district of El Reno, Oklahoma. A shot of a sweatshirt bearing a University of Oklahoma logo is qualified by Kuchar's voice-over commenting, "I did buy a new shirt out here. This one is only 50 percent polyester." There doesn't seem to be much to do in El Reno besides eat pizza or watch baseball games on television. The sense of time passing with excruciating slowness figures palpably in the tape. A natural disaster such as a tornado begins to seem like it would break the monotony, serving as a welcome relief from the dreary vicissitudes of the ordinary.

In a perceptive essay on the significance of the coverage of catastrophes for television,[13] Mary Anne Doane posits that catastrophes serve as both the exception and the norm in television practice. Television has a great deal at stake in perpetuating the illusion of its liveness and relevance to the present moment. Even though almost nothing shown on television actually occurs in "real time," television hooks viewers by continually holding out the lure of referentiality. On-the-spot depictions of crises simultaneously generate and assuage anxiety, ensuring that viewers become addicts who can't stop watching. It is as though the audience is waiting for some magical apocalyptic moment when their visceral experience of a catastrophe and its television portrayal will coincide.

Kuchar's *Weather Diaries* offer a salubrious corrective to the habit-forming spectacle of disaster offered by the broadcast networks. In his work, the focus is on the absence of catastrophe. Kuchar presents an alternative to television's quantification of video as a disciplinary time machine. Freud defined anxiety as the reponse to a need that the analysand is incapable of fulfilling. But Kuchar sublimates his own anxiety about the metronomic passage of time by creatively employing the temporal medium of video. The meaning he imparts to the humble rituals of his daily life by closely observing and representing them on video redeems their existential vacuousness. The apocalyptic lure of gathering storms provides the excuse for Kuchar's storm-chasing, but as he remarks in *Weather Dairy #3*, he is really a "storm-squatter" rather than a "storm-chaser." The Proustian isolation of his motel room serves as a sanctuary where he can reflect on his life, while the electronic palimpsest of videotape serves as the vehicle for his reflections.

Binge, the second part of Lynn Hershman's three-part *Electronic Diary*, was also videotaped under circumstances that facilitated solitary reflection. The piece was recorded over a period of several months as Hershman tried to lose forty-five pounds. Each day she set up the camera in her studio, addressing its fixed lens as one might address a therapist. She free-associated about her feelings toward her changing body. The footage generated through this procedure was subsequently altered using special effects. Thus, Hershman's tape is more like a written essay than Kuchar's improvisational

CHRISTINE TAMBLYN

diaries. The postproduction process provided an opportunity for Hershman to review and revise the raw material she had accumulated.

Although the visual texture of *Binge* is more homogeneous than the rapid montage style Kuchar favors, the tape is equally redolent with precise details about Hershman's daily life. Her narration is the source of this anecdotal richness. Chronicling the circumstances surrounding her weight gain, Hershman describes how her husband went out to buy a newspaper and never returned. Her solace for losing him became cookie binges, "romances with caloric strangers." As the tape proceeds, Hershman reflects on her dieting regime from a variety of perspectives. Her mood swings are documented; rather than unfolding as a smooth continuum, her weight loss is erratic. She is not always faithful to her diet, and her body responds to her behavior in ways that are often unpredictable.

Hershman's philosophical meditations enlarge the tape's scope from its potentially trivial focus on one woman's eating obsessions. The process of videotaping her body as its size alters over time makes her more aware of the changes that are occurring. Viewers can also gauge their reactions to the transformations her corporal image undergoes. Hershman anticipates viewer responses, speaking eloquently about the prevalent alienation in social relationships and the undue emphasis our culture places on physical appearance. As she remarks, "We deal with things through reduplication, facsimiles," her visage multiplies into successively smaller replicas of itself, forming a disorienting electronic portrait of potential selves.

Throughout the tape Hershman employs special effects in an inventive manner to illustrate the ideas she broaches in her monologue. For example, as she talks about avoiding looking in mirrors, her image splits into two symmetrical halves. A verbal allusion to physical distortion is counterposed with a squeeze zoom that compresses her body into a thin column. When she states, "We're taught to filter out our originality," an electronic filter applied to the image removes its color. These postproduction devices are comparable to the figures of linguistic trickery that de Certeau has categorized as tactics of consumer poaching. According to de Certeau, "A tactic boldly juxtaposes diverse elements in order suddenly to produce a flash shedding a different light on the language of a place and to strike the hearer. Cross-cuts, fragments, cracks and lucky hits in the framework of a system, consumers' ways of operating are the practical equivalents of wit."[14]

Sadie Benning's *It Wasn't Love,* the third video diary I want to consider, is also characterized by verbal and visual ingenuity. Benning's tape certainly can be classified as consumer video; it was shot with a Fisher-Price camera, a toy sold for under two hundred dollars that uses audiotape cassettes as its recording format. Although Benning is only nineteen years old, she has produced an extensive body of work in the four years she has been making videotapes. For Benning, as for Hershman, identity is process. Whereas Hershman was attempting to transform herself by slimming down, Benning is rapidly growing up. *It Wasn't Love* focuses on her infatuation with a tough young dyke. Because the lesbian subjectivity she expresses has been insufficiently represented in public discourse, her revelations are fascinating indications of the vagaries of youth and same-sex desire.

The impressionistic collage of brief clips in *It Wasn't Love* is stitched together by Benning's husky voice-overs and appropriated bites of popular music that range from "Why Must I Be a Teenager in Love?" to "My Funny Valentine." Although it tells the story of an aborted trip to Hollywood, the purview of the piece is mostly limited to the four walls of Benning's bedroom. When Benning needs a shot of a car to advance her narrative, she moves a toy car across the floor. Rather than functioning as constraints, the technical limitations of the Fisher-Price camera inspire Benning to creative invention. Because the camera doesn't have a zoom lens, Benning pushes her face close to its aperture, achieving an eerie fish-eyed sense of presence. Lacking access to a titler, Benning makes hand-lettered signs and holds them in front of the lens. The length of the shots, a consequence of the camera's weak batteries, becomes

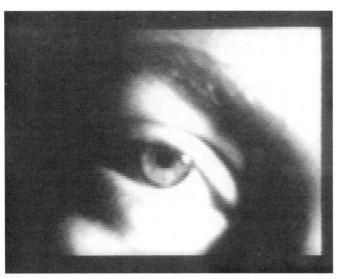

FIGURE 2
Sadie Benning, *It Wasn't Love* (1992)

a stylistic asset as the piece careens dizzily from one suggestive fragment to the next. Serving as a metamorphic mirror, the camera witnesses Benning's experimentation with myriad personae, many of which are based on pop cultural icons. At one point, Benning looks like James Dean; in another excerpt she resembles Jean Harlow.

Both Hershman and Benning use video as a catalyst for self-transformation in their tapes. Joe Gibbons and Tony Oursler satirize the deployment of the medium as a therapeutic tool in *Onourown*. Whereas the video diaries by Kuchar, Hershman, and Benning have a "factual" basis, *Onourown* is a fictionalized diary. However, the characters Gibbons and Oursler play seem related to their real-life roles as marginalized artists. The tape's premise is that the two protagonists have been discharged from a psy-

CHRISTINE TAMBLYN

chiatric hospital due to budget cutbacks. To aid in their rehabilitation and adaptation to independent living, their therapist suggests they keep a video diary. He also makes videotapes of mock counseling sessions that they are supposed to watch daily. These videotapes consist solely of the therapist's pat responses; Gibbons and Oursler are supposed to "fill in the blanks" by talking back to their TV set. In one of the tape's funniest scenes, Gibbons and Oursler follow these instructions, but the content of their dialogue makes the therapist's commentary grotesquely inappropriate; Gibbons asks if he should kill Oursler and the therapist in his soothing manner replies, "Yes."

Shot with consumer-grade equipment, *Onourown* delineates a preoccupation with the vicissitudes of daily life that is similar to the other tapes I have described. However, daily life in this case has a nightmarish intensity as Gibbons and Oursler perform such unpleasant tasks as grocery shopping and looking for a job. The multitudinous hypocrisies of sane society are astutely encapsulated as the tape's protagonists are rudely brushed off by employment counselors, feel traumatized by watching TV stars suffer in soap operas, and engage in paternalistic conversations about the inevitability of death with their dog. Video figures as a dystopian appliance: the video diary functions as a mode of surveillance, and Gibbon and Oursler's canned interactions with the tape of the therapist signify the medium's failure to promote communication. Yet even this critique of the gimmickry of prevalent "therapeutic" modes of electronic connectedness contributes by implication to the search for genuine ways of promoting dialogue via technological conduits.

Although video operates as a detriment to interpersonal contact in *Onourown,* it is represented differently in Susan Mogul's *Prosaic Portraits, Ironies and Other Intimacies.* Mogul uses the presence of her camcorder as an excuse to converse with people in her travel diary about Eastern Europe. During the fall of 1990, she visited Poland for five weeks. Mogul has worked extensively as a performance artist; the vivacious, extroverted persona she exhibits in her comic monologues also made it feasible for her to make contact with a wide variety of Polish people, even though she did not speak their language. *Prosaic Portraits, Ironies and Other Intimacies* revolves around Mogul's encounters with over thirty different individuals. Because her trip was not undertaken to accomplish any particular goal, the tape's structure differs markedly from conventional documentaries with their prescribed purposes. Astutely juxtaposing redolent slices of everyday Polish life, Mogul offers a perspective on Eastern Europe that seems alternatively intimate and foreign.

Certain themes do recur in the tape. When they discover that Mogul is Jewish, many of the people she meets offer to take her to Jewish synagogues and cemeteries. Also, since she is an artist, she is introduced to various sculptors, filmmakers, and photographers who discuss their work with her. Political issues are broached obliquely; for example, a Polish film critic discusses his trepidations about Lech Walesa's rise to power ("Walesa was an electrician; Hitler was a plumber"), and a newspaper layout director informs Mogul that he hasn't told his children they are Jewish. But Mogul's attention is equally drawn to the seemingly insignificant contingencies of daily life. She

23

shoots herself bathing (without hot water) and applying lipstick in preparation for a date with a dentist. Like Kuchar, Hershman, and Benning, she makes extensive use of voice-over narration, creating a portrait that reveals as much about herself as it does about the people she interacts with.

In his discussion of the figures associated with walking, de Certeau identifies the "ambiguous dispositions" that divert and displace meaning in the direction of equivocalness. Walking consists of tours and detours; "the crossing, drifting away, or improvisation of walking privilege, transform or abandon spatial elements."[15] *Prosaic Portraits, Ironies and Other Intimacies* positions Polish people and places within a fluctuating spatial-temporal matrix, because Mogul visited the country during a crucial turning point in its history. The rhetorical tropes de Certeau associates with walking are similar to the structural elements that organize Mogul's travel diary. *Synecdoche* is the device of substituting a part for the whole that contains it. *Asyndeton* entails a suppression of linking words like conjunctions or adverbs, either within a sentence or between sentences. When applied to spatial practices, synecdoche extends a spatial element, while asyndeton opens gaps in the spatial continuum. Mogul employed comparable strategies by excising electronic fragments that represented her trip and assembling them in an elliptical manner.

In contrast to Mogul's journey with its hyperactive focus on social space, the leisurely cross-country trip the protagonist takes in Chip Lord's *Motorist* seems lonely. Richard, the tape's fictional character, has been charged with delivering a 1962 Thunderbird to its new Japanese owner in Los Angeles. Richard's monologues, delivered from behind the wheel, enliven the monotony of the long trip. His favorite subject is cars; he delineates the interface between his personal history and the social history of the United States through his reveries about these fetishized objects. As he remembers the automobile design contests he entered as a child, images from 1960s commercials advertising new models appear onscreen.

FIGURE 3
Chip Lord, *Motorist* (1989)

Nostalgia for the United States' heyday as an industrial superpower is counterpointed in the tape by disquieting indications of its current decline. The sublime landscapes of Arizona are supplanted by California's smoggy sprawl as Richard hints at his disillusionment with the American dream.

CHRISTINE TAMBLYN

The production values employed in *Motorist* are much higher than those used in any of the other tapes I have mentioned. But like Mogul's tape, it utilizes a "How I Spent My Summer Vacation" format, its discursive demand an elaboration of the tourist's desire to make a record of his adventures. The unvarying motion the tape documents as the road unwinds outside the Thunderbird's windshield promotes the sense of distraction Margaret Morse has identified as endemic to the ontology of the freeway, the mall, and television.[16] Being situated within the iron bubble of the automobile fosters a partial loss of touch with the here and now. The driver can daydream, but he must also devote some of his attention to the task at hand to avoid accidents. Similarly, the typical TV viewer divides his attention between the media's simulated world and his immediate physical surroundings, often eating, carrying on a conversation, or performing some other task while he monitors what's happening onscreen.

Although the viewer of *Motorist* may be theorized as doubly distracted by watching a 2-D representation of a 3-D experience of distraction, a routine state of disorientation is essential to the contemporary individual's mobile subjectivity, in Morse's view. The no-space of the freeway, mall, and television that the mobile subject routinely inhabits is "disengaged from the paramount orientation to reality—the here and now of face-to-face contact. Such encounter with the other is prevented by walls of steel, concrete, and stucco in a life fragmented into enclosed, miniature worlds."[17] Yet *Motorist*'s existence as an artwork suggests possibilities for an ironic reversal of this situation. Because it astutely chronicles the vicissitudes of a distracted consciousness, this tape creates an empathetic link between the protagonist Lord has created and the viewer. The virtual journey the viewer makes across the vast geographical expanse of the western United States while watching *Motorist* mirrors the recorded video signal's capacity to bridge conventional spatial-temporal barriers to communication.

The last two art tapes that I want to discuss, Jeanine Mellinger's *In Those Days* and Janice Tanaka's *Memories from the Department of Amnesia*, resemble Susan Mogul's *Prosaic Portraits, Ironies and Other Intimacies* in their exploration of the ritualistic employment of video as a tool for promoting deeper intrapsychic rapport. The witnessing presence of the camcorder simulates a retreat to a ceremonial enclave within which the focused attention of the cameraperson and her subject can trigger revelations about past events and relationships. Both Mellinger's and Tanaka's tapes might be described as virtual family albums. Old family photographs form part of the visual texture of *In Those Days*. Structured like an oral history project, the tape is based on interviews with Mellinger's mother and maternal grandmother (Grandma Grace). Their descriptions construct a portrait of Grandma Ann, Mellinger's paternal grandmother, an ordinary Minnesota farm wife. Because Mellinger is taping them, the two women are prompted to make insightful revelations about both Grandma Ann's character and their own. Although Grandma Grace certainly would not consider herself a feminist, a feminist subtext emerges in her discussion of her own marriage, as well as in her admiration for Grandma Ann's independence.

During her interview, Grandma Grace keeps one eye on the soap operas she watches faithfully, mixing the recitation of her memories with responses to what she sees on TV. Her fluid monologue epitomizes the way consumers use broadcast television to enrich their own fantasies. Speaking of Grandma Ann, she states, "I don't think she could have been happy with any man. I heard her say a lot of times that she didn't think that husbands should treat their wives like they did." Without pausing or giving any indication of a change in discursive register, she switches at this point to a comment on the TV drama: "I wouldn't put up with that. She should divorce him. It never occurred to me to get a divorce."

With its focus on domestic concerns and the intertwined lives of family members, *In Those Days* neither glorifies nor denigrates the everyday. Mellinger avoids the clichéd methods used in many documentaries, with their celebrations of the heroism of subjects who have accomplished brave deeds or overcome devastating disabilities. Instead, she investigates the kind of compromises people commonly make to get through their lives, as when Grandma Grace confesses that she ignored her husband's infidelities to save her marriage.

The ordinary trials of living Tanaka alludes to as she outlines her mother's biography in *Memories from the Department of Amnesia* were exacerbated by extraordinary events. Tanaka's parents were sent to a relocation camp for Japanese-Americans during World War II. Tanaka discloses this in a matter-of-fact way that foregrounds its horrifying implications. As a series of family snapshots appear onscreen, Tanaka reminisces with her daughter Becky about their recently deceased relative. The presence of the video camera as a silent witness provides a suitable occasion for memorializing the dead. The women's warmly intimate conversation on the sound track is augmented by text describing milestones in Yuriko Yamate's life. Thus, the still photographs, audio recording, and written inscriptions convey three different aspects of a complex video portrait. Whereas the images depict an unremarkable middle-class woman, the text chronicles her physical and mental illnesses, as well the injustices done to her by her husband and the U. S. government. But the dialogue between Tanaka and her daughter ameliorates the bleakness of these misfortunes as the women fondly remember Grandma's reckless driving style and eccentric eating preferences.

The discrepancy between oral and written language in the tape parallels the distinction de Certeau makes between "the scriptural economy" of writing and oral culture. According to de Certeau, "Combining the power of *accumulating* the past and that of making the alterity of the universe *conform* to its models, the scriptural economy is capitalist and conquering."[18] The law is inscribed on the bodies of its subjects, whereas orality is an expression of the voice of the people. Because video is a hybrid medium that preserves traces of oral and written speech, its sociocultural role is still being defined. But the ways in which video is employed to facilitate new forms of intersubjectivity that link artists to their audiences or their subjects in the tapes I have examined suggest that video is not merely a technological conduit for narcissistic self-absorption. This thesis is corroborated by fictive explorations of how consumers might employ video, explorations that feature prominently in two recent mainstream films,

26

CHRISTINE TAMBLYN

Steven Soderbergh's *Sex, Lies and Videotape* (1990) and Atom Egoyan's *Speaking Parts* (1989). Innovative uses of video enable the characters in these films to overcome their passivity and inability to communicate effectively with others.

The plot of *Sex, Lies and Videotape* revolves around Graham, an impotent young man whose desires are sublimated into a video project. He persuades women to allow him to film them with his Sony camcorder as they discuss their sexual experiences. Later, he uses the tapes as a masturbatory aid. However, the film's happy ending occurs when Graham overcomes his narcissistic isolation. He permits his best friend's wife Anne to make love to him after she reverses their roles by turning the camera on him during her interview. Video becomes the vehicle for the characters to express their unspoken feelings.

Speaking Parts includes scenes of encounters between an actor and a feature film writer. They are romantically linked but geographically separated, so they decide to use the film company's two-way satellite link-up for a clandestine meeting. In an interaction that functions like a technological extension of phone sex, they watch one another masturbate as one sits at the end of a long table in a conference room facing a video projection system that displays the live image of the other. Appropriately enough, a video mausoleum also appears in the film. The mausoleum contains marble slabs that slide up to play a tape of the deceased. Sex and death are thus electronically mediated in a complementary manner, with the image substituting for the presence of the body. Interactive video seems to promote more intimacy than face-to-face contact, because face-to-face contact has become too threatening.

If the development of the novel contributed to the evolution of bourgeois interiority, as Fredric Jameson has posited in *The Political Unconscious*,[19] perhaps video now functions as a communication medium that fosters the "post-interiority" of the postmodern condition. Video may be instrumental in eradicating the boundaries modernist modes of interiority have erected between subjects. The world of video images and signs is situated between directly lived experiences and thought processes. Thus, video efficaciously chronicles the differences that emerge within the body from the repetition of rhythmns, gestures, and cycles. By making the medium accessible to larger numbers of people, the existence of consumer video tools facilitates its integration into everyday life. Consumer video modes also connect the formerly elite practice of video art with more pedestrian uses of home video. Validating poststructuralist theories that demystify art production and qualify modernist attributions of genius and originality to canonical artists, consumer video art occupies new cultural niches. By surveying works that utilize consumer video formats in novel ways or elaborate on home video genres, I have tried to indicate the scope of video's potential to reconcile mental space with the social sphere.

NOTES

1 Michel de Certeau, *The Practice of Everyday Life*, trans. Steven Rendall (Berkeley: University of California Press, 1988), xii.

2 Ibid., 31.

3 Henri Lefebvre, *The Production of Space*, trans. Donald Nicholson-Smith (Cambridge: Basil Blackwell, 1991), 391.

4 De Certeau, *Practice of Everyday Life,* xviii.

5 Ibid., 37.

6 Ibid., 107.

7 See Andreas Huyssen, *After the Great Divide* (Bloomington: Indiana University Press, 1986).

8 See Martha Rosler, "Video: Shedding the Utopian Moment," in *Illuminating Video: An Essential Guide to Video Art*, ed. Doug Hall and Sally Jo Fifer (New York: Aperture, 1990), 31-50.

9 De Certeau, *Practice of Everyday Life,* 18.

10 Ernest Larsen, "For an Impure Cinevideo," *Independent* 13, no. 4 (May 1990): 25.

11 Ibid., 25.

12 I am indebted to Margaret Morse for this insight. See Margaret Morse, "Cyclones from Oz: On George Kuchar's *Weather Diary I*," *Framework* 2, no. 3 (1989): 26.

13 Mary Ann Doane, "Information, Crisis, Catastrophe," in *Logics of Television: Essays in Cultural Criticism*, ed. Patricia Mellencamp (Bloomington: University of Indiana Press, 1990).

14 De Certeau, *Practice of Everyday Life,* 37.

15 Ibid., 98.

16 Margaret Morse, "An Ontology of Everyday Distraction: The Freeway, the Mall and Television," in *Logics of Television: Essays in Cultural Criticism,* ed. Patricia Mellencamp (Bloomington: University of Indiana Press, 1990), 193.

17 Ibid., 200.

18 De Certeau, *Practice of Everyday Life,* 135.

19 For an account of the sealing off of the psyche under emergent capitalism as manifested in realist novels, see Fredric Jameson, *The Political Unconscious: Narrative as a Socially Symbolic Act* (Ithaca, N.Y.: Cornell University Press, 1985).

CHRISTINE TAMBLYN

CHAPTER 3

THE IMAGE OF ART IN VIDEO

Maureen Turim

From Steina and Woody Vasulka's *Golden Voyage* (1973) to Juan Downey's *The Looking Glass* (1981) to Mary Lucier's *Ohio at Giverny* (1983) to more recent works, including those in which the reference to painting and photography is less direct and more implicit, video has taken diverse views of art. What constitutes the attraction of the already recognized structure (for example, a well-known painting) for those attempting to define video as itself an art or as a discursive practice? In this chapter I will look at several invocations of visual art in video to explore the theoretical implications of this reimaging. The artists seem to be exploring concepts parallel to recent theoretical art historical writing. Video works become a way of inscribing ideas about art, the image, and aesthetic perception.

Sometimes the reference in a video work is to an artist whose works seem to prefigure video. Steina and Woody Vasulka have looked to the work of René Magritte as a precursor of videography, seeing in his paintings the type of collage, juxtaposition, and image manipulation that current video techniques afford.

The Vasulka's homage to Magritte is most direct in their tape *Golden Voyage*. This work acts as a reimaging of past aesthetics, implicitly claiming that those principles can be found in a painting, *La Légende dorée* (*The Golden Legend*, sometimes translated as *The Gilt Legend*, 1958), that was already prevideographic in the same way certain devices and images have been called precinematic. The painting depicts loaves of French bread, in front of a landscape and evening sky, framed by a gray stone wall on the left and bottom edges of the canvas. Steina, explaining the video's genesis, has said, "We were looking at this picture and joking about how many cameras we would need *to reproduce* it. Of course three. One camera would be on the frame, one on the landscape, and one on the bread."[1]

One way to consider this project is, as this quote suggests, as reproduction. The impulse to reproduce a modern painting and its means of transforming spatial and temporal representation signals an attempt to define videography as prefigured in modern art. Mechanisms of multiple camera setups, horizontal drift, colorizing, and keying allow one to reproduce effects of modernist representation.

In an earlier article, "Video Art: a Theory for the Future," I suggested the limits of such aspirations, although as is clear from that article as it develops, I by no means wished to foreclose this area of video exploration, only to force what could be merely reproduction to be pursued as intertextuality, difference, and development:

> The artist must move beyond video versions of image redefinition that have already been accomplished by artists working with non-electronic craft. It is intriguing to know that multiple cameras put through a sequencer (a video device that arranges simultaneously transmitted images into patterns of superimposition and sequential order) can "simulate" cubism. But the added factor of temporality is not enough to justify the reworking of cubism per se, especially when the subject matter of the representational images used to create the video vision is still lives, portraits, landscapes. Painters have already done this. The same is true of Futurism, Impressionism, etc. The risk here is that video art will limit itself to kitsch citation, with no new imagination.[2]

I look back at this statement now with a great sense of irony. It was made before the tremendous attention garnered by the work of postmodernist artists such as Sherri Levine. Levine created a series of works devoted to reproduction. Her photos of artworks present themselves as new artworks, engaging critics in theorizations of an artwork's aura or reproducibility in the terms introduced by Walter Benjamin. They indicate an obsession with reproduction as the repetitive metacommentary on the loss of aura and authenticity in contemporary artistic practice. In contrast to Levine's framing of the photographic reproduction, the Vasulkas' *Golden Voyage* always looked less like an effort at reproduction or even citation and more like a drifting beyond the fixity of the Magritte image to an elaborately different project of temporal and spatial transformation.

The tape's duration, twenty-nine minutes, expands the purview of the original painting as the "loaves of French bread embark on a journey. They travel across various backgrounds—a mesa, a beach, a building, as well as a nude woman."[3] This voyage beyond the space of the original tableau through different scenes, engaging a symbolic, even a surrealist displacement, invites a look at this work as metadiscourse on painting and video, if one made playfully, visually. Although the Vasulka tape never insists upon its theoretical implications, it allows spectators to reconsider the complex intertextuality and reference already inscribed in the Magritte image. Magritte's title, *La Légende dorée*, is taken from a fifteenth-century lives of the saints. The floating loaves evoke the legend of Christ's miracle of the loaves and fish, in which he is said to have fed a multitude on five loaves of bread and two fishes, and its commemoration in the Catholic doctrine of transubstantiation. The painting also recalls earlier works by the artist. In *L'Ami intime* (1958), whose imagery refers to transubstantiation, loaves and wine float in front of a man, turned away, looking out at land and skyscape through a window framed by the same brick wall as later appears in *La Légende dorée*. In *Le Bouquet tout fait* (1956), the same male figure hosts an embedded citation of Botticelli's *Primavera* figure of Flora. These three paintings then become a group, reworking symbolism and celebrating intertextuality of representation. Magritte's reference to Botticelli prefigures the Vasulkas' reference to Magritte; in fact, Magritte is constantly rearranging references to his own paintings and to art history. *The Golden Legend* may be an oblique reference to religious icons of the fish and loaves imagery, including the Byzantine mosaic in the Basilica of San Apollinare Nuovo in Ravenna, A.D. 520.

Magritte continues to be a crucial intertextual reference for the Vasulkas' work. *Scapes* (1981) uses the same semicircular curved "screen" interior to its frame that we find in Magritte's *Les Mémoires d'un saint* (*Memoirs of a Saint*, 1960). In the painting, this screen appears as a freestanding cylinder with an open space in the center. The exterior is draped as a theater curtain, and the interior is an image of a sea and sky. In the Vasulka tape a similar geometric abstraction of theatricality contrasts with nature; the landscape curves before our gaze, elegantly inviting us into its realm while it remains a sculptural object of illusion.

Even the feedback-distorted raster lines that emerge from the representation in the Vasulkas' *Vocabulary* (1973) compare with Magritte's wood-grain inserts in his paintings *Découverte* (*Discovery*, 1927) and *La Passion des lumières* (*Passion for Light*, 1927). That Magritte's wood grain is itself an ironic transposition to oil painting of the mark of the woodcut indicates a migration of this pattern from the revealed trace of the image's production to artifice that comments on this, and back to becoming a sign of image production, now electronic. Finally, the back and front recombined bodies of *Violin Power* (1978) and *Somersault* (1982) recall Magritte's continual play with the recombined body in such works as *Les Liaisons dangereuses* (1936), where a nude woman facing front holds up a mirror that displays the reversed image of the section of her body that the mirror obscures.

While a recent Magritte exhibit includes a catalog essay that suggestively traces Magritte echoes and homages in any number of painters and sculptors, the Vasulkas are not mentioned, nor is there more general discussion of Magritte's prefiguration of video art technique.[4] So if we are struck that a work, *Le Blanc seeing* (1961), in which the image of a woman on horseback in a forest is interrupted by vertical bars of forest imagery alone, shows us the interlaced pattern of two images one gets using a wave form generator and switcher to thread together two separate video camera images as vertical bands, this has not entered into contemporary reassessments of Magritte.

However, the catalog cites a 1952 version of the CBS logo that borrows the transparent eye/cloud image of Magritte's *Le Faux Miroir* (1929).[5] The painting was undoubtedly well known to CBS, as it is displayed at the Museum of Modern Art in New York, around the corner from the network's studio, and certainly this logo predates the Vasulkas' own video references to Magritte. This early commercial borrowing, like numerous print ads that borrow Magritte's images, seems to have ignored willfully the painting's title and its irony. Its existence suggests, however, that Magritte's imagery becomes more relevant in the context of video technology, a point the Vasulkas make with more respect for Magritte's mode of naming and making meaning. As the homage to Magritte in the Vasulkas' *Spaces I* (1972) joins segments named as homages to Escher, Tanguy, and Dali, the precedence for video technique in painting and graphics certainly extends beyond Magritte's work. Yet it rests on a combination of drift, exchanges of multikeyed elements, and geometric reconfiguration of spatial planes. Timing and image recombination are what link this art to video fabrication.

We can look to the way the National Gallery in London uses computerized imagery to didactically introduce spectators to its collection in what it calls its "Micro Gallery" for further reflection on the interstices between video imaging and the history of painting. When a viewer looks up a painting, the program offers an analysis using a digitized display of elements of the composition. Articles and books on the paintings provide the basis of many of these analytical points, illustrating that digital display is not necessarily intrinsic to performing the analysis, but rather that it serves to inscribe a preexisting method of reading. Yet the illustration of a composition using a reproduction of a painting and a sketch of its elements differs perceptually from the Micro Gallery experience. The Micro Gallery then has the color and detail disappear, leaving only the outlines. Consider, also, how it examines the shape of the surviving rectangular panel of Paolo Uccello's *The Battle of San Romano* (1455). We see the panel as a fragment within the geometry of its original form, which included an arched over-piece, since lost. In these examples, art history conditions our visual perception of the surviving object, allowing us to animate a less object-centered vision of an artifact in favor of a multidimensional recontextualization. The computer animations that graphically enact the analysis of a painting do nothing that could not be done by other means, by illustrations, slides, diagrams, and lectures, or even by filmic animation such as those used in cinematic documentaries on the history and theory of art. However, in another sense, with the expansion of CD-ROM technology, such pedagogic use of video technology will transform art historical writing, turning this use of video and computer technology into the pedagogic form of the painting-video relation, in which reproduction is potentially a transformation, an analysis, a learning device.

The potential for artistic use of digital deconstruction and collage is displayed by Simon Biggs's *A New Life* (1989) and *The Temptation of Saint Anthony* (1990) and Luis F. Camino's *Velazquez Digital* (1989). Biggs uses digital manipulations to rearrange shapes in paintings and to exchange motifs between paintings, adding his own motifs to the ever changing collage. In *A New Life,* selected devotional works of Andrea Mantegna are the subject of this graphic play. The central figure and the column of Mantegna's two Saint Sebastian panels are presented on either side of the frame. The Saint Sebastian of about 1459 (now in the Kunsthistorisches Museum in Vienna) is on the left, while the Saint Sebastian of about 1480 (now in the Louvre) is on the right, although inverted left to right. This inversion causes the fragmented arches behind each figure and the three-quarter profile and directed eyeline in each depiction of the saint to appear to connect to each other across the center. Arrows like those that crisscross the saint's body in each panel are animated in video flight across the whole of the image. Although the background of both Saint Sebastian panels is eliminated in the video, those who know the original images are privy to an added humorous irony, as these Mantegna compositions depend on similar fragments, such as the broken Greek statues scattered about in what might appear to be a seemingly incongruous conjunction until it is read as symbolic construction.

Despite such humorous treatment of Renaissance space, each transformation of a composition hints at a knowledge, virtually lost except among art historians, of how to decipher and appreciate the complexities of this space and the shifting historical forms of representation.[6] The tape reshapes the use of architectural elements, for example as significant internal framing devices. It uses the motifs of the heart and a scientific beaker (introduced at the beginning, when a heart appears inside a beaker) to wrest its own alchemical mélange of Christian imagery and computer science. It ends by isolating the sky in a frame that recalls the symbolic weight given the sky in Renaissance painting.[7] There is much humor in the play between computer generation and Renaissance composition, so that, for example, figures of three top panels of the San Zeno altarpiece (1456-59) appear divorced from the panel's background and overlaid on a different one. The columns that demarcate the panels float into and out of the image, while the figures shuffle their positions several times. The Christ child is absent from the Madonna's hands, an absence repeated toward the end of the tape when the empty space is filled with the beaker motif. Similarly, the top half of the *Circumcision* panel (circa 1460) appears as only architectural elements, eliminating the figures entirely. This allows for the collaging of a distinctively Mantegna column into other contexts, as well as a focus on its own geometric form. *Lamentation over the Dead Christ* (circa 1466), Mantegna's famous foreshortened image, drifts back into the depth of an image. We see *Death of the Virgin* (circa 1460) with all the attending figures eliminated, their places covered by a simple seamless continuation of the elements of the picture plane behind them that their presence had obscured. The Virgin floats down to her bier and up again, while the river scene framed by columns behind her becomes a video window for the collage of other motifs. The play in all these instances is so comic and so reminiscent of filmic animation collage used primarily for humor that one has to underscore that such moves can also be seen as delineating the sharp planar representation of Mantegna and its connotations of insistence on and faith in presence within representation. The moves Biggs makes deconstruct that absolute, creating a more "virtual" space.

Similarly, Biggs's *The Temptation of Saint Anthony* plays with the reshaping of Marcel Duchamp's *The Bride Stripped Bare by Her Bachelors, Even (The Large Glass)* (1915-23), *The Chocolate Grinder, No. 2* (1914), and other elements as a meditation on the image and Duchamp's abandonment of the pictorial and painterly image for his virtual, imaginary machines.[8] The Duchamp images are not directly represented here, but mimicked with similarly shaped objects collaged into a construction with similar design. Throughout the tape, elements are surrealistically collaged together, as when a virtual desert folds into a cube to metamorphize into the diamond floor under an arcade, as found in Renaissance painting. Objects whose points and shapes, as well as their isolation tilted against a ground as they float through space, recall the readymades, especially the ones like *Trap* and *Hat Rack* (both originally made in 1917 but lost, then remade in 1964), which are, respectively, nailed to the floor and suspended from the ceiling at just such angles. This tape, with its emphasis on metamorphosis, is an homage to Duchamp's transformative project, in addition to being an extension (begged by its title) of the work on the meanings of techniques of representation begun in *A New Life*. If *A New Life* could be mistaken as merely a reinscription of religious spirituality rather than a more ironic commentary on an age that wrote and rewrote the spiritual, from the vantage point of an age that can't possibly simply rewrite that spirituality, *The Temptation of Saint Anthony* leaves us no doubt.

Camino performs a similar act of disassembly, which he combines with collage and montage. *Velazquez Digital*, too, has a light side, but it is also an attempt by the Latin American video artist to comment on his Hispanic heritage (he was born in Spain, lives in Mexico). The tape begins with Velázquez's *Las Meninas* (1651), with the progressive removal of each of the figures in the painting, beginning with the onlooker on the stairs and ending with the infanta. Each evacuation is punctuated by a single tone of music, and the spaces behind the missing figures are immediately filled in, as if they had left not a painting, but a space that remained behind them upon departure. Then figures from other Velázquez paintings fill the vacated space, first the workers from the genre pictures, then *Venus and Her Mirror*. After this game of substituting the commoners and the mythological for the court, the space of the room is rendered with increasing abstraction, minimizing its detail, retaining only the lines of its perspective and rear doorway. This is then collaged and transformed into modern painterly surfaces, yielding to abstract collages that interweave textures, broken letters, rope, and occasionally photographs, revisited by the figures from Velázquez's paintings. At the tape's end, there is a process of reassembling *Las Meninas*, starting with the introduction of the gilt frame into which the portrait of king and queen emerge in close-up. When this recedes to the back wall, the figures of *Las Meninas* reappear, one by one, until the image is complete, except that now one of the abstract paintings from the tape's midsection occupies one of the spaces on the back wall. The tape resonates with much of the theoretical speculation that *Las Meninas* and the whole oeuvre have inspired, particularly concerning the tension between court painting and genre aspirations, as the collected images trace the painter's own will and desire.[9]

In a different strategic move, the pedagogic view of video looking directly at art is taken to task by Juan Downey's videotape, *The Looking Glass*. A riff on the tradition of the art documentary, the tape looks at artworks that include Velázquez's *Las Meninas* and *Venus with Her Mirror*, Holbein's *The Ambassadors*, (1537), Picasso's *Woman in the Mirror* and Versailles, Fontainebleau, and the John Sloane house, linking these thematically with the mirror and the Narcissus myth. The tape collages fragments of interviews with three art historians, an erudite mirror salesman, and a tour guide, interspersed with theatrically performed scenes such as stealing the famous tableaux in question. Video reimaging techniques are used as supplements to create echoes and repetitions in the image.

Downey attempts humor alongside theory; although brushing with serious notions of subject positioning historically and covering a terrain mined by such theorists as Foucault and Lacan (although Downey's reference point from the French is to Roland Barthes), *The Looking Glass* insists on its playful speculation. If *The Looking Glass* uses discursive strategies and juxtaposition for analytical ends, if it calls into question the history of art and theories of visual representation, it refuses the seriousness that it frankly mocks in the scholars it sets up, who either appear to read images too reductively, without pleasure and multivalence, or as snake-oil salesmen for formal analyses presented as elaborate games. These caricatures are unfair to the contributions of Eunice Lipton and Leo Sternberg, respectively, whose writings on the paintings in question made suggestive contributions; however, Downey's interpretation of video as form or expression demands the foregrounding of video collage, which he does audaciously. Montage is not to be taken for granted when art history is in question or at any other time.

To construct the playful argument visibly is part of his effort at foregrounding video not as the invisible documentary tool of art, but as the artistic reinvention of discourse. Downey wrote of his addiction to "electrons shot to flash against the phosphorescent screen" as "his turpentine," in reference to a citation of Marcel Duchamp: "Some artists continue painting because they are addicted to the smell of turpentine."[10] Duchamp's sarcasm may be in line with Downey's own, but in this case Downey seems to be more willing to equate his own love of an alternative form of art-making with the painterly obsession than was Duchamp, who was, in such quotes, contrasting and justifying his own Dadaist moves away from oil painting. Coming after Duchamp, and addicted to machinery, Downey as video artist seems to seek his own sublime as he puzzles over the "code to an elevated landscape." This is the note upon which Downey ends his article, following a rumination on the exalted experience of listening to Bach.

Downey calls the question on the tendency of video art to lace its imagery with homages to the past of art. If Downey belongs among those video artists who "deconstruct . . . existing constructions of communication technologies and industries," this discursive gesture on his part seems to take place in awe and mourning of aesthetic experience in the past. *The Looking Glass* seems nostalgic, wistful, and therefore unable to align itself entirely with the art historical discourses of critical theory; Downey's own voice-over confession of his experience before *Las Meninas* in the Prado turns his aesthetic arousal into a self-consciously "dirty" joke, of the schoolyard variety. Yet if he is irreverent, it is as a measure of reverence, like his visit to the site where Roland Barthes was "crushed by a laundry truck." He doesn't know where to stand to look in this age of postmodern trafficking and the ambivalence of this uncertain desire, except, that is, from a vantage point of contradictory impulses.

In contrast, Thierry Kuntzel's *Eté—double vue* (1991) is an assured sculpting of a space of desire and aesthetic pleasure, using paradox. The reference to the painting of Poussin in the tape's title is reiterated in the illustration in the book on Poussin being looked at by a powerful, nude black male reclining on a divan. This figure is the link between the two images in the installation, the element who appears in both views, seen on opposite sides of the installation's room.[11] The views can be termed for reference the "close-up" and the "long-shot" view. In the "close-up," a digitized image produced by a camera programmed to slowly move through space explores this nude body in a large projected image. The result is the magnification of a sensual, microcosmic view of skin as surface, methodically covered by the fluid, exploratory, yet nonsubjective gaze. Produced by a motion-control camera usually used for animating objects, it is a view, not of the human eye, but of a perfectly measured seeing, a perusal of the body's space. Presented as a seven-minute loop, the close-up dissolves in on the subject's closed eyes, then travels over the body, traversing the corner of the Poussin book open to the page on which the photo of *Eté* appears. At this moment the fingers and corner of the book provide the image with a moment of concrete reference easily placed in the visual space of the larger image as spatial and temporal fragment. However, at most other instances, the dark skin forms its own abstract landscape of intense formal beauty, deep browns sidelit in graceful and powerful abstract curves sometimes contrasted against the white background.

The other image, presented on a monitor framed on the opposite wall, is a long shot of the room in which this figure reclines. The ratio of the image is an elongated rectangle, a ratio corresponding to wide-screen film projection. The divan is angled with its back to the viewer so that the image is dominated by three grand arches of windows and doors of the room's far wall. This archway frames a landscape beyond, in deep Renaissance perspective. A woman approaches this room from the distance of the shot, sits in the doorway, and finally departs across the foreground of the image.

The bifurcation of scale and placement between the two views creates oppositions between stasis and movement, near and far, still life and landscape, pivoting on the representation of sexual and racial difference, here treated not so much thematically as contrasting visually. That is, the tape uses figures less as actors than as models, with obvious reference to the history of art, but also to photography. The work of Ansel Adams, Paul Strand, and Robert Mapplethorpe figures intertextually (in fact, Ken Moody, the male model, is one of Mapplethorpe's most often photographed subjects). The parallel work on figures, landscapes, and extreme close-ups by these photographers is marked by framing the single, static image; Kuntzel uses video in reference to this photographic tradition, but as a reinscription that foregrounds movement, and thus the difference of his video images.

In an interview, Kuntzel speaks of Poussin's color as his impetus in choosing the artist as reference, saying, "In the long-shot you have the same colors as Poussin, though the work is not meant as imitation of Poussin. You have the same way to work the landscape, the yellow landscape and green trees."[12] This color reference is ironic, as the critical discourse originating in the seventeenth century places Poussin as the artist of drawing, contrasting him with Rubens as the master of color:

This controversy [the *colore-desegno* dispute] occupied the attention of critics, and especially of the Académie Royale, for about twenty years. . . . Briefly, Poussin here becomes, in the minds and writings of the critics who championed the cause of desegno or "le dessein," the ideal classic artist, embodying the virtues of correct drawing with its connotations of restraint and aesthetic, even moral, purity. The coloristes . . . demanded the recognition of those artists who did not conform to the orthodox canon of Raphaelesque standards—first, the Venetian and then the Flemish school, above all Rubens. The two sides were identified with the artists who were seen as their chief representatives: thus the dispute became known as one between "Poussinistes" and "Rubenistes."[13]

The terms of this controversy continue to influence art historians; for example, they are reproduced by H. W. Janson in his standard *History of Art* to devalue Poussin:

Poussin now strikes us as a man who knew his own mind only too well, an impression confirmed by numerous letters. . . . The highest aim of painting, he believed, is to represent noble and pious human actions. These must be shown in a logical and orderly way—not as they really happened, but as they would have happened if nature were perfect. To this end the artist must strive for the general and typical; appealing to the mind rather than the senses he should suppress such trivialities as glowing color, and stress form and composition. . . . His method accounts for the cold and over explicit rhetoric.[14]

This turns out to be not only a recapitulation of the Rubenistes' side of the historical argument, but also a very selective reading of Poussin's theoretical writing. In *Self Portrait I and II*, Poussin is posed with two fragments of canvases and a book in his hand titled *Lumine et colore* (Light and color). From our contemporary vantage point, we can appreciate how like conceptual art these self-portraits are. Oskar Bätschmann, in his *Nicholas Poussin*, argues that color was indeed extremely important to Poussin, although in the context of an exploration of light.[15] The entire debate brings into focus these issues underlying the referential play in Kuntzel's tape; the relationship of color to light and light to color, while significant to painting, is newly posed by artists using video with theoretical sensitivities to such questions of form. Yet much of the current treatment of video both by makers and critics centers not on such conceptualizations of the form of video representation, but on its usefulness as a tool of critical discourse more directly. Through reference to other artworks, Kuntzel signals his theoretical background and his conceptual framework, where the precision of form is the means of a statement. To put it directly, Kuntzel shares with Poussin an interest in pictorial discourse, in the relation of figuration to disposition.

  The statement made by this video work, though, will be oblique, the symbolism only suggestive rather than clear. The divan on which Moody reclines recalls a historical posing of desirable recumbent women—Titian's *The Venus of Urbino* (1538); Velázquez's *Venus with Mirror*; Goya's *Maja* images (1796-97), clothed and unclothed; David's *Madame Recamier* (1790); Ingres's *Venus* and *Odalisque* (1840); Manet's *Olympia* (1863); Rousseau's *The Dream* (1910)—each with her own challenging combination of display and self-containment. So, too, is this male figure absorbed; his male counterpart is to be found perhaps in another Poussin painting, the Narcissus of *Echo and Narcissus* (circa 1630). In this painting, Narcissus is depicted next to the water, at his moment of death, while Echo looks on at her unrequited love as she reclines against a rock, prior to her own transformation into stone. *Echo and Narcissus* has itself been analyzed by Bätschmann as immersed in intertextual references to de Cavalieri's engraving, *Dead Niobad* (1594) and Michelangelo's *The Punishment of Titus* (1532). Bätschmann suggests, "The loans and transformations have their literary counterpart in Ovid's *Metamorphosis....* Poussin's Narcissus differs from the existing pictorial schemata for the representation of Narcissus; he selects his sources with Ovid's legend in mind, and is aware of contemporary insight into mythology."[16] This not only illustrates Kuntzel's finding precedence in Poussin for intertextual processes of generating ideas in painting, but also suggests that pictorial art depends on a remapping of such intertextual reference to deepen its conceptual functioning, to move from visual emblem to narrative myth as a relay or layering of meaning.

On another level, we note that "sur le divan" is slang in French for being in psychoanalysis, a usage frequently employed by Jacques Lacan. So if the male figure studies art books languidly while reposed on a divan, the dream space evoked by this image is perhaps a fragment of the unconscious, manifest. The woman who arrives from the depth of the landscape to enter the doorway is disconnected and aloof, as well, as if she is the specter of a female character in a Marguerite Duras novel, walking and looking, detached.[17]

In Poussin's *Eté*, the foreground action depicts Boaz's encounter with Ruth; in contrast to the Adam and Eve image of spring, Boaz and Ruth represent a more mature love, later in the "history" of a people that the Old Testament represents and later in the lives of the characters in question. The juxtaposing of this meeting to the field labor in the middle ground of Poussin's image puts this love in the context of everyday life and fecundity. The relationship between male and female figures in Kuntzel's *Eté* is, in contrast, entirely ambiguous. It is restricted to the woman's movement from distance to foreground, where she looks at the man, preoccupied and oblivious to her presence, as if the two occupied different spaces (accentuated by the space of the man's body magnified, alone in the second, large image). The models, or characters, if you will, are mute in this interaction, as figures in painting must be. Their narrative is one of movement and contrast, whose minimal mode of exposition has only the suggestion of a private meaning, withheld from the viewer of the video installation. What we are allowed to witness is their visual impact; we can search perhaps for the traces of other figures in Poussin, his narratives of desire and death, such as *Echo and Narcissus* (circa 1630) or *Landscape with Pyramus and Thisbe* (1651) as somehow obliquely informing the space established between them.

The two sets of images can be seen as forming a highly displaced shot–reverse shot, (or, in French, the more poetic "champs-contre-champs"). The woman looks from a distance at the man's body. There is no cutting in, no "decoupage" of the scene that would give us a close-up of her looking. Instead, the close-up on the man's skin provides the insert of a reverse shot, not from her point of view, but from ours, the spectators on this scene. The play then of desire is through the spectator, reversing the order of things in the exchange of looks in filmic editing. Further, the spectator in the installation finds his or her body suspended between the space of these two images and must turn from one to another, canceling out the progression of one to follow the progression of the other. What is at issue here is the order of scenography itself. It was a similar issue of scenography that preoccupied Poussin, leading him to construct what was called a "grand machine," a miniature diorama in which wax figures, displayed in an oblong box, were seen through a small hole that provided a distant view of the model tableaux.[18] As for reversals, how intriguing that Bätschmann discusses Poussin's *Landscape with Pyramus and Thisbe* as the artist's attempt to reverse the "order of things" in *Marriage* (circa 1636-40), the last picture of the series *Sacraments*.[19] Here reversal means the systematic substitution of chaos for calm, asymmetry for symmetry, the confusion of signs for the "solemnization of the Sacraments." The video installation, in its reference to Poussin's tableau scenography, finds its energy through the restructuring of elements in a different order.

One is also reminded of Louis Marin's exploration of Poussin, *Détuire le peinture*.[20] Marin takes Poussin's remark that Caravaggio has come on earth to "destroy painting" as the title of his book comparing the approaches of the two painters. Marin looks at theoretical metalanguage in relationship to painterly representation to underscore the nuances of a double regime of reflexivity and pleasure. Similarly, Hubert Damisch, in his article "Eight Theses for (or against) the Semiology of Painting," explores how a semiotics of painting must move beyond the codification inherent in iconography to explore the discursive and contextual gestures of the visual in relationship to desire.[21] Kuntzel works in the context of the theorization of art in France, bringing to his video work the indirect echo of the principles otherwise presented as essays on the semiotics and discourse of painting.

Kuntzel's self-assured minimalism, reduction, and purity of expression let visual representation take a central place not often accorded it in video, in the manner painting has long pursued. To use terms reintroduced by Jacques Derrida in *The Truth in Painting*,[22] it is productive to see Kuntzel's installation as redefining relationships between "the ergon," the work, and "the parergon," the frame and framing of the image, its title, its reference to spaces outside itself. He means here more than the image-frame dialectic in its more literal sense, deployed as emblem of modernist self-consciousness or conceptual attacks on the art object.[23] Instead the parergon refers to extensive, metaphorical framing acts, operations producing truths that Derrida sets out to deconstruct, sometimes through juxtaposing and questioning interpretations, sometimes through citing contemporary works that use fragmentation and multiplication to deconstructive ends. Marin's observation that painting is marked by a centrality and closure of its discourse, as all referential elements are forcibly rendered meaningful only through their discursive disposition within a painting's schematic self-conscious representation and reflexivity, rests on a similar view of the discourse of painting.[24] These theoretical views of the operation of painting seem to be what Kuntzel is taking into account.

When the viewer stands before Kuntzel's video installation, between two video images, he or she confronts a work that takes its function as inheritor of the tradition of the tableau seriously. While willfully ambiguous at the level of narrative and symbolism, the work states its place as art, assured of its place in desire.

Similarly, Mary Lucier and Doug Hall have images express their concept of a video artist's relationship to painting. As Americans, they approach the art of continental Europe as a distant echo of its thunder, yet resonating nonetheless, brilliantly. A pursuit of autobiographical memory images spurs Mary Lucier to return to her birthplace in rural Ohio at the opening of *Ohio at Giverny* (1983). The views, although anecdotally subjective, are rendered as framed camera images whose mode ranges from the subjective to the objective to the ambiguous; rather than narrate this return directly, she does so obliquely, letting the image composition bear the weight of memory. The transition to France moves the image out the window of the two-story, wood-frame farmhouse with Victorian accents in rural southern Ohio as a white light overpowers the landscape beyond. This is joined by a fade-in to images taken from a train. This gives way to a montage of French landscapes, monuments, and streets. The exploration of Monet's Giverny house and garden then parallels the Ohio Victorian farmhouse.

Giverny was Monet's last dwelling. The garden he established there became an auxiliary work of art, which he subsequently painted as his only late subject. Some of it is a Japanese-style garden, but Giverny's garden bears traces of English gardening traditions, with lavish beds of flowers. The Japanese aspects of the garden find their echoes in Monet's large collection of ukiyo-e, Japanese wood-block prints. The flowers are likewise echoed in the remarkable color of the interior walls and woodwork in translucent shades of bright pastels. In effect, Monet styled the characteristic belle epoque French country home under the influence of Japanese aesthetics.

Lucier's installation alternates images that create temporal and spatial displacements. Tableaux are multiplied in a sculptural space. The preoccupation with light and its inscription of her earlier burn tapes becomes here a fixation of the light and space of Monet, as remembered from childhood, perhaps well before the reference to the Giverny paintings was known to her. The tape makes the connection as a journey across images, as one site bleeds over into images at the other. A dedication of the film to Lucier's uncle and his French wife is later echoed in the miniature ceramic memorial to "mon Oncle" shot in close-up at Pere LaChaise. Connections between Ohio and Giverny, given visually, are imbued with a floating personal memory that informs the work but retains only brief traces of reference of these personal associations. Lucier's eye for detail

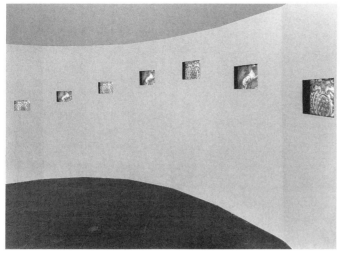

FIGURE 1

Mary Lucier, *Ohio at Giverny* video installation, Whitney Museum of Art
(1983). (Photo: David Allison.)

isolates elements in frames, similar to the way the rich sound track mixes distinct sounds of birds, train noises, and electronic music, composed by Earl Howard. These distinctly, precisely presented images repeat in patterns of symmetry and asymmetry from monitor to monitor and moment to moment. Slow motion or rapid motion, sometimes in conjunction with blurred focus, vary the textures of the imagery, creating a rhythm of enunciation that is thoughtful and exciting.

Lucier's installation acts as a reframing. She claims for video an impressionist palette, a subtlety of color, as well as the relationship between the pixels and the fragmentation of the colored brush stroke. The critical reception, mainly in response to the inclusion of the installation in the 1983 Whitney Biennial, marked this conjuncture. Grace Glueck in the *New York Times* called it "a stunning paean to Monet, . . . [which] orchestrates beautifully a brilliant melange of images in what is certainly the Biennial's most beautiful display," while Victor Ancona in *Videography* called it "a unified poetic narrative structure that rarely surfaces with such acumen in contemporary art," and Ann-Sargent Wooster in the *Village Voice* said, "Her studies of skies, reflections, and pure radiant light build on Monet's paintings and in certain instances surpasses them."[25] While critics recognized and praised the work's shared aesthetics with its Monet reference, most left aside the meaning and consequences of Lucier's strategic borrowing, or simply presented them as an aesthetic tautology, as in Paul Groot's praise of "the esthetically balanced work of a fine artist." Bruce Jenkins, in his notes to the Walker Art Center exhibit, posits the consequence of this work also as validating the "enduring terms of western art," although he sees it as part of a more recent subset of those values, based on a "phenomenology of artistic perception, the act of seeing that pictorializes the world and reworks it into art."[26] Wooster, in a separate piece in *Artnews* called "The Garden in the Machine: Video Goes to Giverny," however, contrasts Lucier's installation with Suzanne Giroux's *Giverny, le temps mauve*. She faults Giroux for seeing video as "ersatz painting" following the path of pictorialist photography. Wooster realizes that Monet's project is by no means unified and fixed for all time, as she gives a sketch of changing perceptions of Monet criticism:

> In 1939 Lionello Venturi called Monet "the victim and grave digger of Impressionism." By the fifties, Monet had come to be seen as a painter of pretty pictures, until Clement Greenberg became instrumental in transforming these

late paintings from the limbo they occupied after Monet's death into a precursor of Abstract Expressionism in his essay, "The Later Monet," by showing that his work was a path to Abstract art. The rebuilding of Monet's garden at Giverny, a project that opened to the public in the early '80s, gave Monet's reputation renewed vitality.[27]

This thumbnail sketch of Monet's fortune with art history, of course, selects only a few of the many vicissitudes to which his work has been subject, a flux that depends on shifting the focus on different periods or aspects of his work.

It is this historical flux in Monet and art reception that I feel makes the Lucier work most vital. Despite, or perhaps even because of, Monet's posthumous popularity as an artist, recent art historical work has relegated Monet's art to the "beautiful." This work does not ignore the fact that reception of Monet's work at first was not by any means uniformly favorable; in its own way the exploration of light, pigment, and brush stroke challenged the reigning aesthetic and was embraced only by those critics who were able to appreciate its difference. Yet the recent questioning of Monet's surface beauty might be seen as descended from Kant, as he positioned the beautiful as inferior to the sublime; it is more directly influenced by various forms of Marxist art criticism and various theories of modernism.[28] In such a move, the question of a bourgeois aesthetics resides, in which "bourgeois" is meant to indicate a pictorial art of complacency, a visual decoration given over to values that provoke no problematic visions.[29]

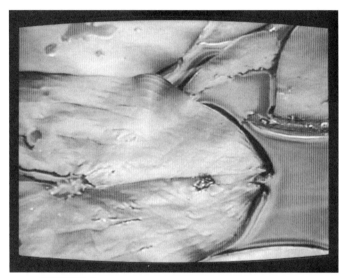

FIGURE 2
Mary Lucier, *Ohio at Giverny* video still (1983). (Photo: Mary Lucier.)

Seeing Monet's art as merely beautiful art is also, however, a symptom of a time when aesthetic appreciation is no longer central to art, even though, or perhaps because, it dominates everyday and commercial life. Our culture lives in ambivalence with beauty, seeking it endlessly in fashion, makeup, decor, the human body, but often either ignorant or disdainful of its appearance in art. If the critics in New York termed Lucier's work beautiful, they must have been aware that the adjective could be seen as a condemnation in many circles, at the very least connoting the trivial, at worst connoting the old-fashioned, the escapist, the reactionary. In a sense Lucier's montage means to take on just such connotations, reworking and commenting on them intelligently.

Lucier herself refers to the shape of the installation, the arched concave wall into which the seven monitors are set, as a "bower."[30] Often this shape is echoed internally in her video images. Wooster adds the association of the curving panoramic water lily paintings Monet made for the walls of the Orangerie.[31] The bower, a curved brace for flowering vines, is a construct for palace gardens and estates. It is adapted into a bourgeois vision, the luxury of ordered space. The bower gathers connotations of a sheltering property, a safe and glorious haven. In the United States bowers become tied to the image of the picket fence as the border of the proper middle-class household. The "Clos Normand" within Monet's gardens carries the bower to excess, with its central rows of flower beds striped by a main linear pathway, with bowers arching overhead.[32] Yet there is a cross-cultural investigation implicit in Monet's garden at Giverny that represents less the seeking of a personal ideal, less complacency than one finds in the social garden of bourgeois contentment. To arrive there, Monet left behind the established bourgeois society of Paris, as well as its route to escape in the Midi and the Côte d'Azur.[33] His Giverny was a cloistered world, intensely devoted to the production of a space and the production of the images of this space. There is much here to debate about visual aesthetics and social context, about the shifts of historical and political concern.

My personal associations with similar lace-curtained windows complementing antique decorated interiors from which you could look out at seemingly endless corn and soybean fields makes Lucier's point of departure particularly rich with association to another house, this one in Indiana, literally moved from a small town and transplanted to its rural setting in the thirties. Contradictions inhere in such Victorian farmhouses between culture and nature, the refined and the earthy, contradictions exaggerated in American film to yield the mise-en-scène of George Stevens's *Giant* (1956) or, more recently, Terrence Malick's *Days of Heaven* (1978). For the Victorian urban style, the house on the hill represents the triumph of the bourgeois in the small-town grandeur of American cities. Displaced onto the farm, it highlights even more the conflict in the United States between European culture and the wilderness. I think these are also associations churned by Lucier's *Ohio at Giverny*.

Mary Lucier, when asked in an interview by Peter Doroshenko whether her connection with landscape imagery was closer to the ideas of Caspar David Friedrich or Robert Smithson, took the opportunity to point out the dialectic between romantic and conceptual sensibilities that allows her an affinity to both.[34] For her the sublime reemerges in Smithson's and her own pragmatic, intellectual way of ordering things, their interest in process and materials, at the moment when the response is "visceral."

This is the tension that orders not only *Ohio at Giverny* but also her installation *Wilderness* (1986), where a variety of U.S. East Coast land and seascape images recall the Hudson Valley and Luminist schools of painting, with some images also reminiscent of Caspar David Friedrich, as well as the English and French romantics. The parergon here includes gray "mats" that enclose the borders of the video images as they are reduced in dimension, and then golden frames that outline the borders of the landscape images within the gray mats. Each of the seven monitors is set on symmetrically arranged pedestals designed as a series of columns and urns. As is the case with the bower shape, these formal white supports are echoed in the occasional ruin found in the imagery of the tapes, culminating in the snow-covered New York City Library, which offers itself as a metaphor of the historical and cultural archive. This time one tape is repeated three times, while two other tapes alternate with it in the asymmetrical pattern ABABCBC. It is even more obvious in this tape than in *Ohio* that Lucier is interested in her parergons, her acts of reframing, of the confrontation of modernism with the romantic ideal.

Caspar David Friedrich figures again in Doug Hall's work, *Storm and Stress* (1986), as does this same problematic. In his article "Thoughts on Landscapes in Nature and Industry," Hall speaks of the preromantic Sturm und Drang of nineteenth-century Germany, as well as with contemporary landscape painters who represent a new relationship drawn between landscape painting and abstract expression:

FIGURE 3
Mary Lucier, *Wilderness* video installation, Henry Gallery, Seattle, Washington (1986). (Photo: Richard Nicol.)

> As one part of me revels in the awe that one feels when in the presence of violent weather and technology—this is the Wagnerian side which I try to keep in abeyance since the dangerous romantic lurks there—the other is more distanced and is fascinated by the language of images, their sign system. I am attracted to the powerful image not just on the visceral level (the aesthetic experience transmitted through the bowels) but, more importantly, I am curious about the nature of these images; the means by which they're transmitted, and, once received, by their ability to affect (us).[35]

FIGURE 4
Mary Lucier, *Wilderness* (1986)

As Hall indicates, his tape is marked by a semiotic self-consciousness in the rigorous composition, in the obsession with scientific measurement and assessment of the storms in question, and in the purposeful juxtaposition of various types of images. Do the black-and-white images of wind crossing a road accompanied by a voice checking measurements signify a tornado, or does the classical (even sepia-toned) image of the long narrow funnel cloud to which we cut next? In the southwestern images of lightning storms where the bolts are visible in the far distance of a dramatically dark landscape dominated by low, dark clouds, an overwhelming visual beauty is wrested from space, in awe of the instant. Different instances of people isolated within the dwarfing, glistening machinery of power plants and other industrial assemblages explore conceptually the architectonic relation of humans in the spaces they have built. The positioning of these figures with their backs to the video camera echoes the dominant composition of figures in Friedrich's paintings. Humans are isolated, contemplating a distant horizon, forever in recession from the viewer, out beyond and unknown.

FIGURE 5
Doug Hall, *Storm and Stress* (1986).
(Photo: Kira Perov.)

FIGURE 6
Doug Hall, *Storm and Stress* (1986). Video-tape for the installation, *The Terrible Uncertainty of the Thing Described* (1987). (Photo: Kira Perov.)

There is a willful heterogeneity here, a collage of types of images, different sorts of signs. Never is this more pronounced than in the vignette that shows the inhabitants of a commercial strip in a small southwestern town emerging from their meager neon-signed frontier in fairy-tale formal wear looking out to the storm in a context that is quite clear from the image. Everyday life, captured, produces its own sort of narrative photography, in the tradition of Robert Frank; as in Frank, the real evokes the surreal.

Hurricanes, earthquakes, and floods have dominated parts of the American landscape throughout its history, but certainly the ravaging storms and stresses on our landscape over the past ten years make this tape a commentary on and prefiguration of the power of nature in our age of technology. The tension between postmodern aesthetics and the Romantic tradition that laces Hall's imagery complicates the direct awe of natural power, offering as counterpoint a technology neither uniformly heroic nor simply evil, transgressing, and futile. Instead, images explore this cultural struggle in artistic terms.

Another of Hall's tapes, *People in Buildings* (1990), takes up many of these same issues, particularly the relationship between the pictorial and the architectonic. Again images of various sorts are presented in a slow and elegant montage that compares the signs of computer technology to the occupation of public spaces. One set of images that bridges this relation is that of close-ups of workers at computers framed so that only their faces fill the screens. The evidence of their workstations is presented through the sound track, occasional reflections of their monitors on their glasses or pupils, and a preoccupied downward stare, sometimes seeming like an inner gaze or a hollow look. Like other images in the tape, these video portraits echo the painting style of the super realism (sometimes called hyper realism) of the seventies—certainly an ironic echo, as super realism itself borrowed its spatial and color representation from photography, using paint and canvas to underscore and overdetermine the transformation of reality inherent in photographs.[36] Hall's portrait segments are reminiscent of the portraits of Alfred Leslie and Chuck Close, but are less a meditation on the pose and the displaced ideal. They propose a fragmentary visual study of the ergonomic relations that define technoworkers, whose fixity in place makes them the epitome of "people in buildings." The portraits are surprisingly masklike, calm, in a space that seems to float even as it is anchored to the space of the offscreen monitor.

Similarly, some of the shots of corridors, escalators, and public spaces move the reflective surfaces and uncanny repetitions and symmetries of super realist street scenes, such as those by Richard Estes, into the buildings' interiors. Artificial lights and reflections are ominous in the decor of the Trump Tower shopping mall, but the plain corridors, whether transversed by a hand-held camera or seen in a static symmetrical framing, seem to provide the worst nightmare image of a purely visual prison. It is here that the architectonic image becomes the equivalent of the row of numbers of computer data or the lists of names produced by angry-sounding computer printers.

FIGURE 7
Doug Hall, *People in Buildings* (1990–1993). Two-channel video installation. Detail, channel two: Department of Motor Vehicles, Sacramento, California.

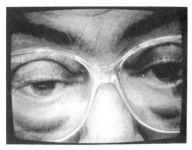

FIGURE 8
Doug Hall, *People in Buildings*. Detail, channel two (the interior): data processor.

A pornographic bookstore rack is juxtaposed with library stacks, a Greyhound bus station with a work station, and a professional photographic portrait studio with the informal portraits of those simply sitting. Often the oblique, fragmentary, and stationary angles on scenes mimic the view of surveillance cameras, forcing recognition of how often individuals in public buildings are the objects of the stare of power and control, subject to arrest or at least regulatory scrutiny at any time. The digitized insert that magnifies a portion of the scene as actions occur across both insert and the larger, framing image is reserved by Hall for those scenes in which little action by the individuals occurs. What ends up being magnified are the gestures of waiting, of passing time.

If this tape seems less involved in the reference to the history of art than Hall's earlier tape and the other tapes discussed in this chapter, the sequence of *People in Buildings* that unequivocally makes the connection is the one shot in the Shoshona Wayne Gallery, where viewers wander past an exhibit of paintings, some of texts, some of scenes. The works on the walls have some of the same visual concerns as the imagery of Hall's tape. It is a metatheoretical moment for the tape, positioning its video work in the history of contemporary painting. This same San Francisco gallery presented the tape in installation format as *People in Buildings II* (1991), combined with an exhibit of Hall's photos and a sculptural installation. The photos were of two groups, one consisting of large-scale views of empty institutional corridors and the other of portraits of people taken from enlarging portions of the video frames. This determined movement of imagery from format to format allows each to refer to and relay meanings via the others. This fluid intertextual-

MAUREEN TURIM

FIGURE 9
Doug Hall, *People in Buildings*. Emergency waiting room, San Francisco
General Hospital.

ity extends the specific references to the history of art to a contemporary practice in which imagery is continuously in citation.

In summary, what I have attempted to explore here are some of the specifics of a visual intertextuality between video and painting. If artworks are in some sense cited by such texts, they are also displaced. They are moved into the spatial and temporal parameters that define video and that video, in turn, helps reconceptualize. How does displacement operate in such texts? Between the immediacy of visual perception and the self-conscious inscription of art as signifier of a reified history, several tensions operate. Videos that reference artworks stress those tensions.

One implication of a video artist's citing a painting is a dissection of the compound phrase "video art" through an investigation of video's relationship to all the graphic arts that preceded it. Nam June Paik asserted early on, "As collage technique replaced oil paint, so the cathode-ray tube will replace canvas," and imagined shaping video "as precisely as Leonardo / as freely as Picasso / as colorfully as Renoir / as profoundly as Mondrian / as violently as Pollock and / as lyrically as Jasper Johns."[37]

Cinema previously opened this terrain of aesthetic retrospection in some recent works, such as Jean-Luc Godard's *Passion* (1982) and Jacques Aumont's book *L'Oeil interminable: Cinema et peinture*.[38] Avant-garde film, in particular, has not only referred to the history of art, but has also been a lively reinscription of nearly contemporaneous paintings, such as Stan Brakhage's mixed reworkings of expressionism and abstract expressionism. It is intriguing in this light to compare the use of the art historical book within the image in Kuntzel's tape with the use of a text on Cézanne in Larry Gottheim's film *Four Shadows*, Erie Loran's *Cezanne's Composition: Analysis of His Form with Diagrams and Photography of Motif*.[39] This parallel between images in Gottheim and Kuntzel is ironic considering the recent Edinburgh exhibition juxtaposing the two painters, the catalog of which is published as *Cezanne and Poussin: The Classical Vision of Landscape*.[40] Taken in its most extended sense of film or video citing modernist and especially postmodernist painting or sculpture, references and interactions between the avant-gardes and art movements are constant and ongoing. The sense in which Gary Hill's videos are conceptual or image-text art done in video form is the sense in which the boundaries of a medium might have long ago disappeared, but for our institutional need to categorize.

The history of one art form citing another is well established and is cer-

47

tainly charged with significance and burdened by detractors, those that find such citation tedious or beside the point. This is particularly true of "new" art form, as can be seen by the way photography and lithography in their own manner and historical perspective found themselves indebted to and obsessed with earlier pictorial art. The recent work of video that looks at or refers to the history of the graphic arts is particularly contentious in that video is unsure of its proper place and purpose. While often displayed in museums, it is after all linked to the communications apparatuses and functioning of television and film. In the museum context of the works it cites, these citations must still be seen as more than just a desire to be considered beautiful, important, or culturally valuable. If the reference to art is to be meaningful, it is its function as part of a larger project of visual signifier of video that will make it so. Ultimately it is the import of one art inscribing *our looking* at the other arts, by which emphasis I mean that the process asks for new attention to the spectator and to the techniques that inscribe our observation.[41] The artists I have looked at in this chapter do more than bring to their video imagery a simple debt to that history; rather, they engage that history.

NOTES

[1] Lucinda Furlong, "Notes toward a History of Image Processed Video: Steina and Woody Vasulka," *Afterimage*, December 1983, 15 (my emphasis).

[2] Maureen Turim, "Video Art: A Theory for the Future," in *Regarding Television: Critical Approaches—An Anthology*, vol. 11, American Film Institute Monograph Series (Los Angeles: University Publications of America, 1983), 132-41; reprinted in *Esthetics Contemporary,* ed. Richard Kostelanetz (Buffalo: Prometheus, 1989), 398-404.

[3] Furlong, "Notes," 15.

[4] Sarah Whitfield, *Magritte* (London: South Bank Centre, 1992).

[5] Ibid., 10-11. It is interesting to note that William Paley, founder of CBS, was an initial donor to the Museum of Modern Art.

[6] Pierre Francastel, *Le Figure et le lieu: L'ordre visuel du Quatrocento* (Paris: Editions Gallimard, 1967).

[7] Hubert Damisch, *Theorie du nuage: Pour une histoire de la peinture* (Paris: Editions du Seuil, 1972).

[8] See Thierry de Duve, *Pictorial Nominalism: On Marcel Duchamp's Passage from Painting to the Readymade,* trans. Dana Polan (Minneapolis: University of Minnesota Press, 1991).

[9] One famous instance of this discussion is Michel Foucault's opening chapter of *Les Mots et les choses* (1966), translated as *The Order of Things: An Archaeology of the Human Sciences* (New York: Vintage, 1973).

[10] Juan Downey, "The Smell of Turpentine," in *Illuminating Video: An Essential Guide to Video Art*, ed. Doug Hall and Sally Jo Fifer (New York: Aperture/BAVC, 1990), 343-48.

[11] See the discussion of ideological meanings of this figure and the installation in Timothy Murray, *Like a Film: Ideological Fantasy on Screen, Camera, and Canvas* (London and New York: Routledge, 1993), 11-14.

[12] Thierry Kuntzel in a videotaped interview with Anne Morgan and Randy Miller, 1989. Parts of the interview appear in two videotapes made by Morgan and Miller, *Directions in Contemporary French Art* (1991) and *Video Art to Virtual Reality* (1992), Museum of Modern Art, New York.

[13] *Felibien's Life of Poussin*, ed. Clare Pace (London: Zwemmer, 1981), 39–40.

[14] H. W. Janson, *History of Art* (New York: Abrams and Englewood Cliffs, N. J.: Prentice-Hall, 1965), 441.

MAUREEN TURIM

15 Oskar Bätschmann, *Nicholas Poussin: Dialectics of Painting* (London: Reaktion Books, 1990).

16 Ibid., 23-24.

17 Consider the similarity between the woman in Kuntzel's tape to the walks of Lol V. Stein that eventually take her to a field where she watches a window in l'Hôtel de forêt in *Le Ravissement de Lol V. Stein,* the look of the woman at the adolescent on the beach in *Les Yeux vert,* or the opening passages of *Les Yeux bleu, cheveux noirs,* where gender is reversed and a man on a road outside l' Hôtel des roches looks at a woman within, whose eyes are hidden in shadow.

18 Bätschmann, *Poussin,* 27-29.

19 Ibid., 93.

20 Louis Marin, *Détuire le peinture* (Paris: Editions Galilée, 1977).

21 Hubert Damisch, "Huit theses pour (ou contre?) la sémiologie de la peinture," *Macula,* no. 2 (1977): 17-23; trans. Larry Crawford as "Eight Theses for (or against?) the Semiology of Painting," *Enclitic* 3, no. 1 (Spring 1977): 1-15.

22 Jacques Derrida, *La Vérité en peinture* (Paris: Flammarion, 1978), trans. Geoff Bennington and Ian McLeod as *The Truth in Painting* (Chicago: Chicago University Press, 1987).

23 It would be intriguing to trace the use of this opposition as a theoretical principle in critical discussion of cubist collage, photography and the photographic series, conceptual art, and the like. To begin, consider the way artist Nancy Wilson Kitchel presents the opposition in her series of landscape photographs: "Better perhaps for me to circle it, draw a line around it with what I do know, find its boundaries. . . . The implication of something beyond . . . that which is unspoken, that which cannot be seen . . . some sense of an unknown . . . an invisible presence. Locating, then crossing boundaries. Stepping across boundaries" (Nancy Wilson Kitchel, in *Individuals: Post-Movement Art in America,* ed. Alan Sondheim [New York, Dutton, 1977], 149 [ellipses in original]. See allusions to the question of the frame in Lucy Lippard, *Six Years of the Dematerialisation of Art* (London: Studio Vista, 1973), such as in Marjorie Strider's notes on her *Street Work* of 1969, in which frames were deployed in streets as environmental, spectator-performance pieces (Lippard, 91).

24 Marin, *Détruire,* 29.

25 Grace Glueck, "Video Comes into Its Own at the Whitney Biennial," *New York Times,* 24 April 1983, 33, 36; Victor Ancona, "Video Fuses with Traditional Media at the Whitney Biennial," *Videography,* May 1983, 72–77; Ann-Sargent Wooster, "Mary Lucier," *Village Voice,* 24 May 1983, 89.

26 Bruce Jenkins, notes to the Walker Art Center exhibit, *Viewpoints: Paul Kos, Mary Lucier*, Minneapolis, Minn., 1987.

27 Ann-Sargent Wooster, "The Garden in the Machine: Video Goes to Giverny," *Artnews,* April 1992, 50.

28 Immanuel Kant, "Analytic of the Beautiful" and "Analytic of the Sublime," in *The Critique of Judgment,* trans. James Creed Meredith (Indianapolis, Ind.: Hackett, 1987), 43–232.

29 Consider this passage from T. J. Clark, *The Painting of Modern Life: Paris in the Art of Manet and His Followers* (Princeton, N.J.: Princeton University Press, 1984), 72: "It should go without saying that this situation—Haussmann's work and its aftermath—presented painting with as many problems as opportunities. Naturally, it offered occasions for a meretricious delight in the modern, or proposals in paint that the street henceforward would be a fine and dandy place. (I cannot see, for example, that Monet's two pictures of *Le Boulevard des Capucines* in 1873 do more than provide that kind of touristic entertainment, fleshed out with some low-level demonstrations of painterliness. Where Monet went, Renoir inevitably followed: his image of the grands boulevards in 1875 is untroubled by its subject's meanings, and not helped by this innocence.)" Clark then goes on to discuss painting of "a more serious cast—the kind that took Manet's example to heart," meaning, I take it, a more problematic and less bourgeois vision.

30 Mary Lucier, notes on *Ohio at Giverny* sent to exhibitors. Lucier is particularly detailed and eloquent in explaining her project, so that many of the journalists reviewing her work use her own enunciations in their remarks.

31 Wooster, "Garden in the Machine," 50–53.

32 Based on my own visit to Giverny. See also *Monet's Years at Giverny: Beyond Impressionism* (New York: Metropolitan Museum of Art, 1978); Stephen Shore, *The Gardens at Giverny* (New York: Aperture, 1983), and Charles Weckler, *Impressions of Giverney: Monet's World* (New York: Abrams, 1990).

33 John House, *Monet: Nature into Art* (New Haven, Conn., and London: Yale University Press, 1986).

34 Mary Lucier, interview with Peter Doroshenko, *Journal of Contemporary Art* 3, no. 2 (1990): 85–86.

35 Doug Hall, "Thoughts on Landscapes in Nature and Industry," *Resolution: A Critique of Video Art*, ed. Patti Podesta (Los Angeles: LACE, 1986), 38-39.

36 See Edward Lucie-Smith, *Super Realism* (Oxford: Phaidon, 1979), for an assessment of this movement at the end of the decade of its emergence.

37 Nam June Paik, *Video 'n' Technology*, ed. Judson Rosebush (Syracuse: Everson Museum, 1974), as cited in Ann-Sargent Wooster, "Why Don't They Shoot Stories Like They Used To?" *Art Journal* 45, no. 3 (Fall 1985): 204.

38 Jacques Aumont, *L' Oeil interminable: Cinema et peinture* (Paris: Librairie Séguer, 1989). Consider also the work done on the fluidity of theoretical principles between different forms of imaging in *Passage de l'image*, an exhibition at the Centre Georges Pompidou in Paris curated by Raymond Bellour, Catherine David, and Christine Van Asche, an exhibit that yielded a remarkable catalog (Paris: Editions du Centre Pompidou, 1990).

39 Erie Loran, *Cézanne's Composition: Analysis of His Form with Diagrams and Photography of Motif* (Berkeley and Los Angeles: University of California Press, 1943).

40 Richard Verdi, *Cézanne and Poussin: The Classical Vision of Landscape* (London: Lund Humphries, 1990).

41 Jonathan Crary, *Techniques of the Observer: On Vision and Modernity in the Nineteeth Century* (Cambridge, Mass.: MIT Press, 1990).

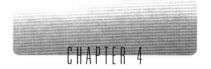
VIDEO:

THE ACCESS MEDIUM

⏚

Tetsuo Kogawa

FILM AND VIDEO

Video has not yet achieved independence from the cinema. Aware of its indebtedness, video has remained eager to receive its inheritance. But it is necessary to understand video's difference, to theorize the conditions of its specificity. Now that today's video technology achieves as high a definition as film, the video theater will gradually take over the movie theater. This does not, however, mean that the cinema will cease to exist.

Video can be a new type of movie. But the material differences of video and film are not the most crucial points for differentiation. After all, cinema itself has undergone many technological changes. The arc lamp is no longer the source of light; film is no longer simply celluloid; recent films rely more and more on computer-generated images. At the same time, nothing has changed for the audience of the video theater. The audience faces a screen in a dark space, watching it until the end of the show. No one "fast-forwards" or "rewinds" the sequences, nor do they "pause" motion. This renunciation of access to the control of the image on the part of the audience guarantees video's status as identical to the cinema. As long as this renunciation remains in place, the cinema is what it has been.

However, this renunciation of access is not inherent but historical. In transition, every medium is used and understood through the extended (time-tested) conventional standards, but sometimes new possibilities are revealed. The early stage of video art revealed its radical possibilities most explicitly: it was inseparably accompanied by bodily performance actions. In 1963 when Nam June Paik showed his "Exposition of Music—Electronic Television," the earliest video art work at Galerie Parnass in Wuppertal, he created artistic video images through improvisation, manipulating, as he did so, the electronic conditions of used television sets. It was a one-time event that could not be recycled in the future.

Starting in the late sixties, public broadcasting stations in the United

States such as WGBH (Boston), KQED (San Francisco), and WNET (New York) began programming artists' video.[1] These circumstances should have encouraged the interactive and performative aspects of video. The problem is that video art has not always developed its full potentialities. Ironically, the retreat from video's radical possibilities began with the advance of electronic technology. The recorded package took the shape of the videocassette, powerfully boosting video art into a new self-understanding. This was the inception of video art as a "work of art," a commodity to be bought and sold with the "live" process of creation separated from the video itself. Video has increasingly become an object of representation to be enjoyed without direct reference to the "nascent" process. The industrial pursuit of ever higher image definition—as well as ever greater compactness of the package—steadily compounds this separation.

Despite these circumstances, performance actions cannot be dispensed with entirely: viewers handle the television set when they change the channel or volume; they operate the VCR by fast-forwarding, pausing, and even recording. Furthermore, they watch not only the screen but also the environment surrounding it. The interactive aspect of performance actions cannot be ignored in an analysis of video. Indeed, video's performative dimension constitutes its defining difference from cinema.

Video holds the technological potential to realize direct sensory systems beyond the flat screen (for example, the hologram). However, when video images are packaged, a "screen" is structurally introduced. The packaged video *screens* out the very chain of events that initiates the entire process of showing and watching. Given its hermetic nature, the packaged video offers a mere window onto performative events, one that is technologically reified as monitor and projector. Thus, video becomes cinema.

SEMIOTICS AND VIDEO ART

Film theory has been applied to video art, but this is possible only as long as the aspect of performance in video is ignored. In fact, the semiotics of Christian Metz and others was fairly successful in articulating film and video images. However, it had to enter a cul-de-sac.[2] To the extent that semiotics considers video a capsule of image-signs, it must restrict its work to the signification system. To deal with the "outside" or to look beyond the image-sign system is illegitimate. Consequently, semiotics was unable to carry out any social critique, such as that of Siegfried Kracauer's *From Caligari to Hitler*, which succeeds in providing both formal analysis and social criticism of the filmic images of Germany's Weimar cinema.[3]

Semiotics had to tacitly assume that, when it gave up the "outside," it would be attended to by sociology or anthropology or psychology. The "slick" analysis by semiotics and the "vulgar" approaches of the human sciences (which deal with images as a social, cultural, or mental index) are complementary. It is not accidental that in spite of Ferdinand de Saussure's proposition that semiotics is "a science that studies the life of signs within society" while "linguistics is only a part of the general science of semiology," his followers never succeeded in overcoming the "either/or" of linguistics/sociology as separate disciplines with distinct fields of analysis.[4]

The difficulty of Saussurian semiotics has something to do with the fact that its basic model of language comes from the printed word, which is considered a capsule of "living" language. To the extent that the world is closed off, linguists and then semioticians must limit their working field to the bounds of the signifier and must maintain an indeterminate attitude toward the signified (with the referent existing entirely outside the domain of semiotic interest). In fact, Saussurian semiotics assumes that "the bond between the signifier and signified is arbitrary."[5] Consequently, this idealist theory comes into its own through analyzing abstract rather than socially oriented images.[6]

This may explain why semiotics and video art have found themselves in close association. Video art shies away from messages. The more "artistic" it tends to be, the less message-oriented it becomes. This implies that conventional communication theory has inflated the centrality of the message; it considers the media as nothing more than a vehicle for messages. However, the message is not a mere bullet shot from the media machine. As Félix Guattari wrote, the nature of media is "transversal." So radical media must belong to the "schizo-analyze" of the schizophrenic who is "floundering in a world in which relationships of signs, or productions of signification, far outstrip our individual madnesses and neuroses."[7] To the degree that semiotics cannot operate at this transversal level, it *screens* out the image's performative side.

However, every image—packaged or not—transcends itself and forms various horizons of the "signified," "content," the "social," the "transcendental," and so on. It is quite natural that when Gilles Deleuze wrote *Cinema 1* he had to deconstruct the sign itself, starting not from Saussure but from Charles S. Peirce, who established a systematic classification of images and signs without using the linguistic model.[8]

FROM PERCEPTION TO RESONANCE

Perhaps virtual reality's most instructive contribution is that it suggests possibilities beyond the standard, screen-style video monitor. The liquid crystal is already changing the conditions of watching that have been dominated by the cathode ray tube. However, even though it can extend the screen to an unlimited size and can easily support 3-D effects, liquid crystal is still screen-bound and is not free from a modernist perspective. Virtual reality (VR) is still problematic,[9] but it is a move toward new technologies of perception. Ultimately, it promises an interactive technology to directly link the video image with the brain/body organ.

The present head-mounted display is too awkward, but it already describes what the future imaginary system should be. Virtual reality could give not only images to our eyes, but also to our more organic senses. Thus, it pushes beyond a passive spectator position to the very threshold of action. Virtual reality lets us resonate rather than simply see and hear. It terminates the modernist perspective that integrates everything toward a center.

Maurice Merleau-Ponty never experienced virtual reality technology, but he provided a brilliant description for the perception that outstrips modern perspectivism, one that should provide a most viable hint for how to radicalize virtual reality. According to the modernist paradigm, the other person's sensuous experience is theoretically inaccessible to others. However, it is true that we often have an immanent experience by just talking with another person. "Through the concordant operation of his body and my own, " wrote Merleau-Ponty," what I see passes into him, this individual green of the meadow under my eyes invades his vision without quitting my own, I recognize in my green his green. . . . There is here no problem of the *alter ego* because it is not *I* who sees, not *he* who sees, because an anonymous visibility inhabits both of us, a vision in general, in virtue of that primordial property that belongs to the flesh, being here and now, of radiating everywhere and forever, being an individual, of being also a dimension and a universal."[10]

This account, however, already reveals the difficulty of applying Merleau-Ponty's description of the human body and perception from *The Visible and the Invisible* to a technological apparatus such as VR. The crux of this difficulty occurs in his use of the French word *"chair,"* which is translated as "flesh." David Cronenberg introduced "new flesh" produced through video in his *Videodrome*. This flesh presumes the idea of representation to the extent that it is merely an electronic reconstruction of the human body. Merleau-Ponty's *"chair"* is somewhat different from such a flesh. He even uses it uniquely in French. "What we are calling flesh, this interiorly worked-over mass, has no name in any philosophy."[11] "The flesh is not matter, in the sense of corpuscles of being which would add up or continue on one another to form beings. . . . Nor is it a representation for a mind: a mind could not be captured by its own representations; it would rebel against this insertion into the visible which is essential to the seer."[12] In this sense, Merleau-Ponty's account of the *"chair"* should prescribe the horizon and direction of electronic visual interfaces and the absolute uniqueness of body element.

MEMORY AND ELECTRONIC AMNESIA

Whenever a new type of media permeates the popular scene, the problem of memory arises. Printed media spoiled the popular customs of recitation and memorization, the typewriter weakened our handwriting ability, and video arouses a fear that it may dissolve not only literacy but also the liveliness of personal intercourse and encounter on which all face-to-face communication is based. However, our memory cannot work without transcending itself and referring to the "outside." Every memory demands its appropriate media. As Frances A. Yates pointed out, even a mnemotechnics, the ancient art of memory, "uses contemporary architecture for its memory places and contemporary imagery for its images."[13]

TETSUO KOGAWA

Memory has always been inseparable from media. Even oral memory demands its human organ as a medium. Oral culture is not immediate but is experienced through various media: rhythm, metrics, and punctuation of voices and gestures. As Walter J. Ong makes clear in *Orality and Literacy*, oral poets never sing the same way twice. Their memory does not repeat. "Basically, the same formulas and themes recurred, but they were stitched together or 'rhapsodized' differently in each rendition even by the same poet, depending on audience reaction, the mood of the poet or of the occasion, and other social and psychological factors." This is why "an oral poet is not working with texts or in a textual framework."[14]

The history of technology is a history of amnesia, but the technology has been extending memory outside our bodies. Thus, the outside field has been filled with numerous technological artifacts: cities, modes of transportation, and electronic media. The most radical thing about virtual reality is its appearance as the ultimate and most comprehensive expression of these artifacts and simulacra. Computer-generated images have no need for physical objects, which used to be indispensable for photography and cinema. The object of VR has no memory. It is not a wordplay to say that the object-oriented programming has nothing to do with objects.

As Martin Heidegger pointed out, the historical process of media technology is the acceleration of forgetting the origin of our existence and the hypertrophy of the technological apparatus. The history of technology is "the history of the forgetting of Being" (*Seinsvergessenheit*).[15] Although electronic media such as video or VR involve us in the strongest amnesia of the origin, it is specific to the age of reproduction, the age of the nonoriginal where every idea hides itself. Using Heideggerian and Deleuzian discourse, the idea becomes *virtual*. The idea is virtual: thus virtual reality appears.[16]

In "the history of the forgetting of Being," every epoch-making philosophical term such as Plato's "Idea," Descartes' "Cogito," Hegel's "Absolute Geist," and Nietzsche's "Nothing" expresses the extent and process of this forgetting. When Heidegger thinks this forgetting in relation to science and technology, the forgetting reaches its first peak in Hegel's "Absolute Geist." Interestingly enough, electricity had just begun to attract public attention in Hegel's period; his notion of "Absolute Geist" could be read as an idealist model of today's artificial intelligence.[17]

This transfer from human memory to media technology does not imply a necessary absentmindedness on the part of human beings who rely too heavily on modern conveniences. Heidegger writes of "a thinking outside of the distinction of rational and irrational still more sober than scientific technology," but one does not have to relegate this line of thought to esoteric naturalism or Zen.[18] Rather, I would like to take Marshall McLuhan's often ignored comment on Heidegger seriously. In *The Gutenberg Galaxy*, McLuhan wrote that "Heidegger surf-boards along on the electronic wave as triumphantly as Descartes rode the mechanical wave."[19] No one except McLuhan had related Heidegger to that very contemporary theme: electronic media.

Heidegger explained the decline of memory as "the fate of Being's

VIDEO: THE ACCESS MEDIUM

essence," adding that it had nothing to do with any pessimistic interpretation of world history but rather with the role and function of technology. Although he was a severe critic of modern technology, this argument is quite understandable when one thinks of the basic function of video and electronic media. Video actually functions to the extent that it brings the origin to nothing. Without forgetting the origin, the video image cannot be what virtual reality is.

VIDEO AS TRANSMITTER

Every medium transmits something. What is transmitted? If we are to undertake a fundamental reconceptualization of video, let us for the moment leave this question unanswered, rather than relying on terms such as *message, signified,* and so on. Video is not a capsule of images; rather, it is a transmitter. Yet we must be careful when using this term. Radio transmits sounds; television transmits images. A "transmitter" is usually thought of as a kind of "catapult" of information-objects. It makes an object move through the air from one place to another. This set of places is called "sender/receiver."

These categories of "sender" and "receiver" are, however, nowhere near as simple as conventional communication theories would lead us to believe. The "sender" sometimes sends nothing, while the "receiver" may receive much more than the "sender" sends. As Humberto Maturana and Francisco Varela already clearly explained, the "tube metaphor" in which a parcel of information passes from a "sender" to a "receiver" is obsolete. Communication is no relationship between isolated enclaves; on the contrary, communication always occurs, or mutates, as a holistic event. Maturana and Varela use the term "structural coupling" for what is happening at the transmitting and transmitted sides. In their definition, there is a structural coupling "whenever there is a history of recurrent interactions leading to the structural congruence between two (or more) systems."[20] They wrote:

> Communication takes place each time there is behavioral coordination in a realm of structural coupling. . . . According to this metaphor of the tube, communication is something generated at a certain point. It is carried by a conduit (or tube) and is delivered to the receiver at the other end. Hence, there is a *something* that is communicated, and what is communicated is an integral part of that which travels in the tube. Thus, we usually speak of the "information" contained in a picture, an object, or, more evidently, the printed word.[21]

Based on their analysis of the life of metacellulars, they argue that the metaphor of the tube for communication "is basically false. It presupposes a unity that is not determined structurally, where interactions are instructive, as though what happens to a system in an interaction is determined by the perturbing agent and not by its structural dynamics."[22]

The transmitter does not bring anything, but it does *relay* something. It literally *re-lays* something in a different context. Even in the transmission of a very simple image, innumerable information units are relayed, producing meanings that are both different from and similar to the source material. There is no original for the resulting similar (transmitted) images because the transmitter does not carry away anything intact. Instead, the transmitter does erase the origin. It substitutes an eternal circulation for origin.

When a video camera and microphone create a closed circuit (the camera points at the monitor screen to which it is connected and the microphone is brought close to the speaker), the monitor displays no image and the speaker amplifies nothing. However, the monitor begins to show Escherian images of the labyrinth as soon as some object is laid between the camera and the monitor; the speaker begins to "howl" (self-oscillate) as soon as the microphone catches even a faint sound. The transmitter makes a resonance rather than opening up a path or circuit.

Quite different from mechanical reproduction, the transmitter cannot reproduce the very same objects we handle, touch, smell, see, hear, and feel in our everyday lives. While the automated assembly line is designed to reproduce the same products, such as canned foods, this is beyond the transmitter's capability. Thus, radio or television alone will never succeed in homogenizing the consciousness of the listening or viewing audience. Even those transmitting fascist propaganda had to simultaneously organize oral rumor networks and violent enforcement to achieve their goals of persuasion. Printing was invented as a means of mechanical reproduction, but it produced too many interpretations.

Although Walter Benjamin wrote only about the still and motion picture cameras, his account of reproduction technology must be understood in relation to transmission. The camera reproduces not only the physically identical images, but also the qualitatively different meanings in the physically identical image. If television had been popular when he wrote "The Work of Art in the Age of Mechanical Reproduction," he might have more clearly argued his point. The examples he offered on the relationship of photographed actions to their textualized meanings, produced through editing after the fact, are altogether pertinent to video editing.[23] The notion of ontological relativity that he introduces finds far greater expression in digital video and computer graphics than it does in film, given the relative ease of manipulation of the digitized "original" in the creation of meanings and effects for the audience.

While Benjamin used the expression "the age of mechanical reproduction," his point of view exceeded the boundary of "mechanism" and moved toward "information." His article on mechanical reproduction is complemented by his essay on storytelling in which he compares recycling in the "new form of communication," "information," to the storytelling.[24] Benjamin is interested in Franz Kafka and Nikolai Lesskow because they were nourished by the tradition of storytelling, which does not intend to copy objects automatically but rather links them dialectically. In the media, any kind of "mechanical reproduction" must become *informational reproduction*.

Even a mass-produced canned beer can engender different drinking styles. This is a point overlooked in accounts of mass reproduction. That mechanically reproduced photographs can create totally different perceptions and interpretations is more obvious. These differences are compounded and intensified in electronic transmission. When an airwave is transmitted, its electronic field is not homogeneous. Every radio and television set catches the wave in different conditions. As a matter of fact, this polymorphism is usually undercut by seeking the "stable" and "clear" condition of transmitted images and sounds. Only artists are interested in exploiting this property of transmission.

In his large-scale media experiment *Bye Bye Kipling* (1986), Nam June Paik showed how these conditions create artistic images with his "Video Ball." The system was very simple: Paik and Ryuichi Sakamoto play catch with a ball containing a video camera and transmitter. The transmitted images are shown on a massive screen on the wall. The conditions of the transmitter's physical movements, the intensity of the airwave, and various unknown electronic conditions create what the audience considers an artwork in this event. This could be a critical metaphor of the "tube" theory of communication. The ball is posed as a message that is tossed between a sender and a receiver. However, the sent and received messages are never accordant but instead sporadic. In fact, neither Paik nor Sakamoto intended to send or receive any message. Only the audience could find its own *arbitrary* message on the screen, a message that is now created not by a person ("sender/receiver") but by the collective, physical, environmental, and structural context.

FROM PROCESSES TO ACCESS

Unlike the film screen, the video monitor cannot be seen as a window through which stored information comes to viewers. The video monitor is merely an access point from which unlimited relayed connections or, more precisely, resonances, will be created. The monitor should be considered a node of video resonances. It does not show the tableau of a closed accumulation of information, rather it provides an index to something. So television is an indexing device. However, television didn't develop this function further, despite its technological progress. On the contrary, it concealed the aspect of access, a necessary function for any index.

Today most television sets build in a computer. Viewers, in one sense, also use a "keyboard" when they operate their remote-controlling channel selector. The operation of advanced VCRs and television sets is as complicated as a simple personal computer. Nevertheless, the VCR and television continue to be considered as an information container.

Like the VCR and television, the computer has not made use of its interactive access function until recently. The computer is one of the most advanced access devices in electronic technology, but it is popularly understood as a process device. It is usually assumed that the computer acts for the brain. Actually, in Chinese the computer is represented by two characters literally meaning "electronic brain." However, the way computers function is more like a kind of tissue than like the brain, as the latter is considered the central locus of the body. Actually, today's studies of the cerebrum indicate that the brain itself turns out to be less central than a polymorphous "module" in which every unit is autonomous and at the same time interactive.[25] Both brain and computer can centralize the thinking processes to the extent that they deal with relatively primitive processes such as arithmetic, but they can also link, overlap, shift, stagger, and sample various processes. The computer is an endless interface to the more holistic processes of social life.

Television and the computer have been taking different courses of development: the former turned into a sending and receiving device while the latter became a processing and storing apparatus. It is perhaps the residue of several centuries of print culture that has retarded both the television and the computer from achieving their radical potentials. Thus, the television and the computer divided their work in contradistinction to one another. But while television belongs to the transmitting-receiving system, it performs at its best when processing and storing images. The single popular exception to this polarization of television/computer functions is the video game, which links a television set to a computer. Meanwhile, the computer, bogged down in the text intrinsic to print culture, has only begun to move beyond its conventional processing mode with the emergence of telenetworking and virtual reality.

To think radically, video is the technology that owes its virtuality and its polymorphism to "the complete forgetting of Being," the absolutism of copies or, put simply, virtual reality. Thus video is no longer a tool to represent, recollect the origin; it is a transmitter to terminate the origin completely. And the truth of the image consists not in the represented image itself—real or unreal—but in the relationship of access that obtains between the audience and the image source or environment. Therefore the audience as such has to become an activist of access.

NOTES

[1] On the historical relationship between video art and broadcasting, see Kathy Rae Huffman, "Video Art: What's TV Got to Do with It?" in *Illuminating Video*, ed. Doug Hall and Sally Jo Fifer (Seattle: Bay Press, 1990), 81-90.

[2] In order to evade this, Christian Metz reinforces his semiotics by phenomenology, writing, on one occasion, that every semiotics is an extension of phenomenology ("Semiotics and Phenomenology," in *Esse Semiotikku (Essais Sémiotiques)*, trans. Kieko Higuchi [Tokyo: Keiso-shobo, 1977], 184–87.

[3] Siegfried Kracauer, *From Caligari to Hitler: A Psychological History of the German Film* (Princeton, N.J.: Princeton University Press, 1947).

[4] Ferdinand de Saussure, *Course in General Linguistics*, trans. Wade Baskin (New York: McGraw-Hill, 1959), 16.

[5] Ibid., 67.

[6] Mikhail Bakhtin already revealed the limitations of semiotics within the literary field: "Semiotics deals primarily with the transmission of ready-made communication using a ready-made code. But in live

speech, strictly speaking, communication is first created in the process of transmission, and there is, in essence, no code" (Bakhtin, "From Notes Made in 1970-71," in *Speech Genres and Other Late Essays,* ed. Caryl Emerson and Michael Holquist, trans. Vern W. McGee [Austin: University of Texas Press, 1986], 147).

7 Félix Guattari, *Molecular Revolution: Psychiatry and Politics,* trans. Rosemary Sheed (New York: Penguin, 1984), 172.

8 Gilles Deleuze, *Cinema 1: The Movement-Image,* trans. Hugh Tomlinson and Barbara Habberjam (Minneapolis: University of Minnesota Press, 1986), 69.

9 Tom Piantanida, Duane K. Boman, and Jenniffer Gille explore the basic technological problems of VR in detail in "Human Perceptual Issues and Virtual Reality," in *Virtual Reality Systems,* vol. 1 (New York: SIG-Advanced Applications, 1993), 43-52.

10 Maurice Merleau-Ponty, *The Visible and the Invisible,* trans. Alphonso Lingis (Evanston, Ill.: Northwestern University Press, 1968), 142.

11 Ibid., 147.

12 Ibid., 139.

13 Frances A. Yates, *The Art of Memory* (London: Ark Paperbacks, 1966), xi.

14 Walter J. Ong, *Orality and Literacy: The Technologizing of the Word* (London: Methuen), 60-61.

15 Martin Heidegger, "Modern Science, Metaphysics, and Mathematics," in *Martin Heidegger: Basic Writings,* ed. David Farrell Krell (San Francisco: HarperCollins, 1993), 271-305.

16 Gilles Deleuze would never have thought that his brilliant description of "virtuality" and "the virtual" in *Difference and Repetition* (trans. Paul Patton [New York: Columbia University Press, 1994]) could be extended to such an extreme as it has with virtual reality: "The virtual is opposed not to the real but to the actual. The virtual is fully real in so far as it is virtual. . . . The virtual must be defined as strictly a part of the real object" (208-9).

17 In "Überwindung der Metaphysik," Heidegger wrote: "The consummation of metaphysics begins with Hegel's metaphysics of absolute knowledge as the will of Spirit" ("Die Vollendung der Metaphysik beginnt mit Hegel's Metaphysik des absoluten Wissens als des Willens des Geistes"; in *Vorträge und Aufsätze* [Lectures and essays] [Pfullingen: Neske, 1954], 76). It should be noted that, for Heidegger, "metaphysics" means "meta-physics" (all that is beyond the physical). So in one sense the historical process of metaphysics refers to the movement from physical object to information-object with the corresponding epistemic movement from modern physics to infomatics.

18 Martin Heidegger, "The End of Philosophy and the Task of Thinking," in *On Time and Being*, trans. Joan Stambaugh (New York: Harper and Row, 1972), 72.

19 Marshall McLuhan, *The Gutenberg Galaxy* (London: Routledge and Kegan Paul, 1962), 248.

20 Humberto Maturana and Francisco Varela, *The Tree of Knowledge: The Biological Roots of Human Understanding*, trans. Robert Paolucci (Boston: Shambhala, 1992), 75.

21 Ibid., 196.

22 Ibid.

23 Benjamin wrote that "a jump from the window can be shot in the studio as a jump from a scaffold, and the ensuing flight, if need be, can be shot weeks later when outdoor scenes are taken" (Walter Benjamin, "The Work of Art in the Age of Mechanical Reproduction," in *Illuminations*, ed. Hannah Arendt, trans. Harry Zohn [New York: Schocken Books, 1968], 230).

24 Walter Benjamin, "The Storyteller," in *Illuminations,* 88.

25 For a brilliant account of the brain as module, see Michael S. Gazzaniga, *The Social Brain: Discovering the Network of the Mind* (New York: Basic Books, 1985).

CHAPTER 5

LOOKING THROUGH VIDEO:
THE PSYCHOLOGY OF VIDEO AND FILM

John Belton

Video exists in a field of other representational forms, and our understanding of it necessarily derives, in part, from its relationship to these other modes of representation.[1] No technology develops autonomously. It is always a direct or indirect product (or by-product) of other technologies, which leave their imprint upon it. Video is no exception. Any definition of it needs to situate it within a horizon of related technologies and of cultural uses of those technologies.[2] This chapter seeks to do two things. It attempts to define video as a sound technology rather than as an image technology and to explore the psychology of video in terms of its differences from film.

FIGURE 1
The team of engineers that pioneered the development of the videotape recorder by Ampex in 1956. From left to right: Fred Pfost, Shelby Henderson, Ray Dolby, Alex Maxey, Charles Ginsburg, and Charles Anderson. (Photo courtesy of Ampex Systems.)

In part, the advent of video has changed the way we look at earlier forms of representation, such as the cinema. Today, we tend to look at the cinema *through* video. Indeed, video technology has radically altered our understanding of what Andre Bazin once referred to as "the ontology of the photographic (and cinematographic) image."[3] The plot of *Rising Sun* (1993), for instance, hinges on the ability of computer technicians to manipulate videotaped images. It even provides a brief demonstration in which Sean Connery and Wesley Snipes exchange heads by means of a computer that digitalizes and plays with their videotaped images. The video image thus has no inherently indexical relationship to a profilmic event.

In this and other respects, the existence of video forces us to reperceive the cinema, which is, as a result, forever transformed. At the same time, the existence of the cinema forces us to rethink our notions of video. Moreover, this mutual co-definition is a continuous process; it takes place over time, and, as a result, our understanding of film and video is constantly changing. What they mean to us at any given point in time is the product of the unique relationship of each technology not only to the other but to a field of different representation formats that is itself constantly changing.

In an attempt to focus this comparison of film and video, I will try to concentrate on issues of *technology* rather than on the many other bases for comparison that exist between the two.

Before starting, I need to explain and, to some extent, qualify the title of this chapter. "Looking through Video" poses a number of problems. The term *looking* would seem to give precedence to video as a visual medium and to ignore sound completely. But, as I hope to show, the process of "looking through video" begins with sound—with seeing video as a sound technology. Indeed, it is this feature that emerges as one of the chief characteristics distinguishing it from film.

The term *video* emerges, in more ways than one, as the most problematical feature of this essay (see note 1). The first stage of my argument attempts to defamiliarize popular notions of the term *video*. The very name *video* (literally "I see") suggests, especially in its contrast to *audio* ("I hear") and *radio* ("I emit beams"), its status as an image technology that exists in a linearly evolving chain of other image technologies. At the same time, video's invention, innovation, and diffusion occur *after* that of the cinema, implicitly suggesting a technological progression of sorts.

Yet television and video have traditionally been misperceived—by the average viewer, at least—as outgrowths of film. First came the movies, and then came television. This may be historically accurate, but it is not technologically correct. The two technologies evolved separately, not successively.[4]

Historians trace the genealogy of the cinema back to photography, photochemistry, and the so-called phenomenon of persistence of vision. Video, however, looks back to the telegraph and the telephone—to the transmission of coded, electric signals across a wire. Although video can't be traced back to the cinema, the cinema can be traced back, in part, to certain features of the phonograph, telegraph, and telephone—that is, to technologies that were crucial to the development of video. Certain mechanical, as opposed to electrical, features of sound technology did play a part in the development of the motion picture.

Using the phonograph as a model, Edison developed the motion picture camera in an attempt to "do for the eye what the phonograph has done for the ear."[5] He at first tried to pattern his kinetoscope after the cylinder phonograph, arranging tiny images successively around the circumference of a cylinder. Later, after having abandoned this approach, Edison drew upon his earlier experiments with notched strips of paper that he used to record telegraph messages (and that could then be played back) in his attempts to mechanize the movement of sequential images on motion picture film past a stationary viewing head.[6] This technology worked and is still with us in the cinema today in the form of sprocket holes.

Although the cinema and video may look back to similar nineteenth-century sound technologies, video is not cinema; it only looks like cinema. Its technology is essentially the technology of sound transmission, recording, and reproduction.[7] It's an extension of the telegraph, the phonograph, Marconi's wireless telegraph, and the radio, not of photography or the illusion of movement. The cinema was photochemical and mechanical, but in video there is no photochemistry and there are no moving parts.[8] *Technologically speaking,* video is entirely different from the cinema—except for their shared reliance upon a similar sound recording technology.

If the most problematic word in the title of this essay is *video,* then what exactly does the term *video* mean? Until the 1950s, it simply meant the visual (rather than the audio) component of a televised signal. But the term gradually came to stand for the entire apparatus of television itself—for the broadcast of electronic television signals through the air or through cable from a central source. With the development of the videotape recorder (VTR) in the mid-1950s, the original notion of video found itself fused with another; this "video" was a shortened form of a different technological apparatus—the VTR, which consisted of both the recording machine and the plastic tape on which a video signal was recorded.

The VTR and videotape, successfully demonstrated by Ampex in 1956, were the direct descendants of magnetic recording technology developed by the Germans during World War II for radio broadcasts.[9] After the war, several German Magnetophons were appropriated by the Signal Corps (by an electronics engineer assigned to the Signal Corps) and shipped back to the United States.[10] These spoils of war found commercial exploitation in American radio and motion picture production in 1947, when Bing Crosby used it to record his weekly radio show[11] and when Hollywood studios began to use modified versions of it in 1949 for recording dialogue, certain sound effects, and music and for mixing sound tracks.[12]

The connection between audio and video is driven home by the crossover between these two fields. One of the engineers who worked for Ampex on the innovation of the VTR was none other than Ray Dolby.[13] And one of the major breakthroughs in the development of the Ampex VTR involved the conversion of video signals to a sound format—to FM signals—before recording them.[14] At the same time, the tape used to record these signals was similar to that used in audio recording.[15]

It is no accident that film sound expert Ray Dolby was, as an undergraduate at Stanford, a central figure in the development of the Ampex videotape recorder in 1956. The technology for videotape recording and recording film sound was essentially the same. Later, Dolby, an American physics student at Cambridge, founded Dolby Laboratories in London in 1965. There, Dolby developed a crucial noise reduction system for sound recording (circa 1966) that enabled audiocassettes to match the quality of reel-to-reel audiotapes and thus opened up a new market in the recording industry. Later, at Dolby Labs in San Francisco, he perfected the first commercially viable optical stereo motion-picture sound system, introducing a four-track, optical stereo sound-on-film system (Dolby SVA, 1975). Dolby subsequently developed a six-track, 70mm magnetic format; a spectral recording system (Dolby SR, 1986); and a digital sound technology in 1991. As a pioneer in electronic signal recording and playback, Dolby serves as yet another example of the interconnection between video and sound.[16]

After the introduction of the VTR, video recording machinery slowly developed, becoming smaller and more portable; by 1974, "video" also meant the ENG (electronic news gathering) video portapak employed by TV news units, which was used extensively to cover the Vietnam War. In April 1975, Sony introduced the Betamax, a videocassette recorder (VCR) for use in the home, which could record television programs off the air.[17] About a year later, Matsushita began selling a home recording machine that used a noncompatible VHS (video home system) format. By the mid-1980s, over 30 million American households had VCRs, and *video* became a household word.

As a result of the VTR-VCR revolution, *video* came to mean not just the live broadcast video signal of television but also the audiovisual signal of broadcast TV on videotape. With the proliferation of VCRs in the 1980s and the exploitation of the home video market by producers of prerecorded videotapes, *video* has expanded its meaning to include prerecorded material as well as programming taped off the air.

Since the mid-1960s, when Nam June Paik began working with the medium, video artists, scholars, and critics have begun to distinguish between the terms *television* and *video* in an attempt to recognize the way in which video art refuses the identity of television. *Video* has, as a result, also come to be used as a term to describe video art. Indeed, the existence of video art actually predates the home video revolution and coincides with the shift to video for TV news. Video artists appropriated the portapak and other video recording technology several years before it became widely available for home use, moving beyond experimentation with live signals to include, during the late 1960s and early 1970s, that with prerecorded signals.[18]

Loosely defined, video art consists of works produced by the manipulation of video as a medium—either through special video installation pieces, through the experimental play with prerecorded material or with synthesized images, through film-like documentaries, through an artist's own performances recorded on video, or through the production of original works on video that explore the nature of the medium. This third notion of video can be seen, in part, as a mediation of the other two; it involves video both as broadcast signal and as a recording format. But for video art, routine transmission and recording give way to a play with transmission and recording functions.

As a technological format, video—either as television or as videotape—differs from film in fairly obvious ways. Television, like radio, is largely a medium of transmission. Indeed, the technology of transmission emerged independently of concerns for the content of what was transmitted. As Raymond Williams notes, "Unlike all previous communications technologies, radio and television were *systems primarily devised for transmission and reception as abstract processes, with little or no definition of preceding content."*[19]

Television technology takes preconstructed material and relays it to a receiver somewhere else. The form and content of this material preexists its transmission and is not significantly altered in its transmission. The signal that leaves the studio is more or less the same signal that is picked up by the home TV set. To some extent, the material that is transmitted is determined and given shape by the techniques and technology of television—televisual recording and editing practices influence the way(s) in which the medium uses TV cameras, lighting, editing, and sound. But the *technology* of television remains a transmission technology.

The most obvious example of television as transmission would be a live broadcast, such as the coverage of a news story or a sporting event. Of course, the broadcast of sporting events does include certain special effects—the superimposition of statistics, instant replays, and so forth. But this is all done to the original material prior to its transmission. If television is defined more broadly to include the equipment employed to produce the signal, this, of course, opens up a space for a certain amount of transformation and mediation of events. However, many of these transformations are not specific to the medium of video but have been borrowed from other forms of visual presentation, including the cinema. They certainly belong to any definition of television and/or video, but they need to be seen as add-ons to the original technological base and kept distinct from it.

This notion of television as transmission becomes clearer if we compare broadcast television to film.[20] Television transmits programming and it does this more or less instantaneously. Film deliberates. There is always a necessary delay between filming and the presentation of what has been filmed. At the same time, the film differs from the profilmic event—that is, from the event staged before the camera. The camera and microphone read the profilmic event. Framing, camera angle, distance, and/or movement present a specific view of the event. Editing and postproduction sound mixing constitute yet another reading of the original event, which has typically been broken down and reassembled in a specific way to express specific ideas. In other words, film transforms what it records.

Broadcast television, on the other hand, merely transmits programming. When a TV editor cuts from one shot to another or a camera operator reads the original action in one way or another, the original material is subjected to essentially filmic codes and conventions. The instant replay represents a transposition of filmic techniques, developed by Dziga Vertov and others, onto the procedures of television coverage. In other words, the technology of television has been geared to transmission, not to transformation; when it does transform, it is not television, but a copy of the cinema. Video art emerges as the exception that proves the rule. Video art transforms, but its transformative features and the unique formal language it has developed over the years derive from the techniques and practices of the avant-garde; that is, video art stems, in large part, from the appropriation of video technology by artists who worked in other media.

A similar argument might be made about the second notion of video—video recording via magnetic tape. All videotape does is to record. In recording off the air, it produces a simulacrum of the original broadcast. Indeed, for the average viewer, it is impossible to distinguish between a "live" broadcast and a videotaped recording of it. Indeed, this confusion is compounded when the word "live" is superimposed over the original telecast and recorded on the copy, which is then played back.[21] In this respect, the copy of a broadcast is the "same" as the broadcast; the original and the copy are identical. (Something a bit different happens, however, when prerecorded videotapes are made of motion picture films, as we will see later; in these instances, the "original" video signal differs from the original motion picture.) In other words, television technology—whether in the form of broadcast TV or videotape recording—possesses a certain invisibility. Transmission technology is designed to eliminate any signs of transmission or noise, and original video signals remain virtually indistinguishable from copies of them.

Another way of describing the difference between film and video as "transmission" and "recording" technologies is to point out that the cinema, for one reason or another, was forced to develop a formal language in order to facilitate its expressiveness. This formal language constituted a mediating consciousness of sorts, which stood between the profilmic event and the finished film—a consciousness that, in narrative cinema at least, we have come to identify as the narrating agency or narrator. With TV and videotape, what intervenes is largely mechanical—the narrating consciousness has not been constructed into a humanized presence but remains on the level of the machine. The epitome of television consciousness, I would argue, is the surveillance camera, whose machine eye and mechanical movements circumscribe the expressive range of broadcast television and videotape recording.

In other words, television and videotape are purely mechanical forms of reproduction. Their value lies primarily in the value of the things they reproduce and only secondarily in the mode of their reproduction, that in many instances is identical to the mode of production that they reproduce. Video art, however, problematizes video as a means of reproduction by calling attention to the medium of video as a medium. Video art makes visible that which is generally kept transparent. In this way it explores the nature of the medium and offers the possibility of a revolutionary way of seeing through it.

There is a problem, however, with the above notion of TV and videotape as purely mechanical modes of reproduction. The technology of these forms of video constitutes a way of seeing; although this way of seeing might be characterized as mechanical or—more accurately—as electronic, it is not entirely transparent. The medium of transmission is visible there. And it is the *visibility* of the medium that I would like to examine in the latter portion of this chapter, doing so through yet another comparison of film and video.

The cinema is based on movement that, as noted above, is produced

66

mechanically; video transmits and records movement electronically. The movement of film through a motion picture camera or projector is intermittent or noncontinuous. Contrary to popular opinion, the cinema's illusion of movement is not the product of persistence of vision. As described by Belgian physicist Joseph Plateau, persistence of vision is a physiological phenomenon in which discrete images supposedly dissolve into one another on the surface of the retina.[22] Plateau, however, was wrong. As Hugo Munsterberg insisted, the illusion of motion is the product of the phi phenomenon, a psychological phenomenon discovered in 1912 by Gestalt psychologist Max Wertheimer.[23] The phi phenomenon involves the fusion, through a kind of mental short circuit, of successive still elements, "giving rise to a single, continuous total event."[24] Munsterberg argued that, in the cinema, "apparent movement is in no way the mere result of an afterimage . . . but is superadded, by the action of the mind, to motionless pictures."[25] Thus, the illusion of movement was produced in the brain, which constructs it out of discrete but *whole* still images received in the retina.

Movement in video, on the other hand, is not intermittent but continuous. Video technology derives from sound technology, which can only transmit and record sound by duplicating its uninterrupted flow with a technology that is itself continuous rather than intermittent. Thus, video produces images through an endless scansion process. Broadcast signals are similarly continuous, as is the movement of tape in a VCR (except of course in the freeze-frame mode, when there is a limited, repetitious movement of the tape and the tape heads).

When we look at film and video, the difference we perceive between the kind of image produced by each is, in part, the product of the different technologies each uses to produce an illusion of movement. We see video movement directly—it is not mediated for us by the brain; it is immediate and uninterrupted. At the same time, with video and unlike film, there is never a whole image either on the TV screen or on our retina; what we have, instead, is always a partial image—a single pixel or dot of visual information is conveyed every four-hundred-thousandths of a second—in a continuous chain of electronic scanning.[26] Video images are always in the process of their own realization. Their association with immediacy and presentness is partly because they are always in the process of coming into being.

The different "looks" of film and video have, over the years, resulted in a kind of codification through which each "look" has come to have a different value. This value is, in part, a consequence not only of the different ways in which each medium produces the illusion of movement but also of the different ways each has been used. The video "look" has come to signify greater realism, immediacy, and presence. But it does so largely within a system of signification that includes the comparative "looks" of photography and the cinema as well.

Roland Barthes argued that the still photograph signified pastness; its reality consisted of conveying a presence—that of the camera—that was there, that is, that was once in the presence of the object in the photograph.[27] Building on this, Christian Metz argued that the cinema, which recreates in the present a past movement, achieved an impression of reality that had even more presence and immediacy than the photograph. For Metz, the cinema's illusion of movement undermined the actual pastness of its images to give it a "present tense."[28] Thus even film flashbacks seemed to be taking place in the present because they take place in both our presence and our present.

The advent of video and its use in films has added a new twist to the impression of reality, providing an even greater sense of presence and immediacy to the image than the cinema. It can do this because its "look" possesses a "psychology of the image" that is rooted in both its technological and cultural bases—in its electronic continuousness and its association with live broadcasting. (Television relied on film until recently to shoot prerecorded material, and everything else was live; thus the video look is associated with live TV.) In the age of video, cinema has been subtly redefined as a temporally deliberated present and as a mediated reality, while video comes to signify immediacy.

Ironically, the greater the presence of the video image, the greater the absence of that to which it refers. Television literally means "seeing from afar." It spans distances. Movies have a limited transmission range, circumscribed by the room, auditorium, or theater in which they are projected. When we watch a movie, we can sense its spatial properties. It is there with us in a sense, recreated for us by the actions of the projector, sound head, amplifier, and speakers. It does not (at least not at first) refer to another space—an elsewhere—from which it comes. Television does. Although television plays on a screen situated in our space, its ultimate source is elsewhere.

NASA, for example, outfits its space probes with special cameras, which electronically transmit pictures of outer space back to us on earth. This photographic technology creates a dramatically new sense of space, which can be crossed virtually instantaneously. Traditional limitations of space, which were indirectly communicated to us in the past in terms of the time it took for the photographer, newsreel cameraperson, or filmmaker to send footage back to be developed, assembled, and then presented to the public, no longer exist in the age of video.

The presence of a VCR next to the TV set may seem to locate the source of the transmission within our space. The tape, like the print of the movie, has been brought to a space where it can be played for a discrete audience of a roomful of people (rather than millions at once). Yet in a strange way, the tape is at one remove. I would argue that, although it is decidedly there, it just as decidedly refers to something that is not there—to the original cable or TV broadcast of which it is a record or to the original filmed (or taped) material of which it is the electronic transcription.

This latter point is fairly obscure but crucial to our understanding of the video medium. Most of us tend to view a videotape of a motion picture as merely another copy of the film. As Walter Benjamin argued, in the traditional arts there was an original work that existed at a unique place in time or space (or both) and that could be experienced only by those in its physical presence.[29] With photography and the motion picture, the notion of an original became moot. There were no originals, except of course for the original camera negative, which was never meant to be seen by viewers; there were only copies, and any one copy was just as original as any other copy.

Of course, this argument requires some qualification. Subtle differences do exist from print to print of photographs or of motion pictures, depending upon the type of film stock used and the quality of the lab work. More significant differences exist in the area of film gauges. Most spectators sense a difference between 70mm and 35mm versions of the same film, preferring the former. Since most 70mm films are blowups of films originally shot in 35mm, the difference that audiences sense probably has more to do with image size, sharpness, and brightness (which can be increased more readily with 70mm prints) and with sound, which is six-track stereo for 70mm and four-track stereo for 35mm. (Recent technology, in the form of Digital Theater Sound, which was used for *Jurassic Park* [1993], has expanded the number of tracks that can accompany 35mm films from four to six.)

As for 16mm, which is used in most college classrooms, there are obviously a number of compromises that are made in terms of the amount of audio and visual information that projection prints can contain; sound is monaural, not stereo; and the contrast ratio (ratio of light to dark) is not quite as extensive as with 35mm, so that its ability to convey the same detail in the darkest and brightest areas of the image is reduced. But given that 16mm is usually projected in classrooms on relatively small screens, its visual limitations are rarely apparent, and it serves as a close equivalent to the film that most spectators saw in the theater.

But with video, the shared nature of the identity of videotape and film is less easily maintained. The structure of the exhibition marketplace has tended to obscure these crucial differences. Over the last few years, video versions of films have played a more and more important role in the distribution and economic life of a motion picture. After a film has played in a theater, it moves to its next most profitable venue, pay-per-view, premium cable, and subscription television. After that, the film will go to home video, where it is available for purchase or rental on videotape or videodisc. Several months later it might appear on network television, then perhaps after that make its way to syndication. Three-quarters of its total audience is likely to see the film on some sort of TV screen.

The motion picture industry continues to make a lion's share of its profits on a particular film in the theaters, but the revenues from subsequent video marketing remain substantial. Given the video version's place in the economic chain, it is no wonder that the industry treats it as if it were identical to the film itself. But I want to suggest that it is not—that a videotape of a film is not a copy whose identity is the same as all other copies. Nor are the differences between it and other copies comparable to those outlined above in the comparison of film gauges. The difference between a videotape of a film and the film itself are significant enough to re-endow the motion picture with a kind of Benjaminian aura and originality and mark the video copy not as a copy but as a referent that is once removed from the actual film.

Television is not entirely transparent; it does transform. Motion pictures are significantly altered when they are broadcast on television or transferred to video. I want to concentrate on three particular practices that have recently been singled out for the ways in which they "materially alter" original motion picture films. These are panning and scanning, colorization, and lexiconning or time compression.

Since 1953, every American motion picture has been filmed and exhibited in one widescreen ratio or another. When these films are shown on narrow television screens, they are routinely cropped, losing in some cases as much as 50 percent of the original image. The process by which these films are adapted for television is called panning and scanning and involves (1) isolating one segment of the larger picture, (2) introducing pans across the original images, and (3) introducing cuts from one part of the image to another. All three pan and scan practices leave their marks upon the original film.

Colorization involves the use of computer technology to color films originally shot in black and white. The ways in which this process rewrites the cinematographic qualities of the original film are quite obvious and have become the subject of public debate.[30] Unlike panning and scanning, colorization can only be achieved electronically; a colorizer must work with a computer and a video copy of the original film. The black-and-white video signal on the videotape is digitized and entered into a computer where individual pixels are colored to produce a new version of the film in color. The transformation of the original is so total that the Copyright Office recognizes the colorization as a form of new authorship that can be copyrighted independently of the original black-and-white film.

Similarly, lexiconning or time compression takes advantage of video, using telecine equipment to accelerate (or slow down) the speed at which a frame of film goes past the telecine's raster. The lexicon telecine thus shortens or expands a film's running time in order to fill specific time slots and/or permit more commercials to be aired. In the cases of panning and scanning, colorization, and time compression, video technology is directly at odds with film technology. Video is clearly unable to transmit or record the original film. Instead, it writes its own technology over that of the original; what we see is a kind of modern-day palimpsest containing two texts—a video reading of the original through which we can still see fragments of the original film.

Panning and scanning is perhaps one of the grossest examples of how video technology has developed to answer the needs of a marketplace dominated by commercial television and of the way in which we see films differently through video. But video also possesses the technology to transmit widescreen films more or less correctly. Thus letterboxing preserves the full width of widescreen films by reducing the height of the widescreen image and leaving the screen area above and below the image blank. No matter how much video technology develops to find solutions to the problems it has in presenting films, inherent differences between film and video technologies will remain, forcing us to see film on TV through a technology that severely circumscribes it.

High-definition television, with its 1100 scan lines and 532,836 pixels, is barely the equivalent of 16mm film. Not only can it not deliver the amount of visual information available in conventional 16mm classroom screenings, but it is still years away and remains a potential standard upon which only the United States and Japan have agreed.

The contrast ratio, or ratio of light to dark areas of the image, of 35mm and 16mm motion picture films is roughly 300:1, which matches that of human vision. That of conventional (standard-definition) video is only 30:1, which means that it provides less detail in the image. Nor can video, which relies on an additive color process, reproduce the full color spectrum of motion picture film, which uses a subtractive color process. As a result, video will always have trouble with reds and will necessarily distort the hue and saturation of other colors.

Paradoxically, the emergence of video has resulted in the reinvestment of aura in motion pictures. Going to the movies has increasingly become a special event—a unique encounter with mechanically reproduced images that differ markedly from the more commonplace electronically reproduced images that we see more habitually on television screens when viewing films on cable or on prerecorded videocassettes. Videotape and cable have given theatrical movies a new lease on life, relegating them to a status of experience that has become increasingly rare in contemporary culture. Video has transformed the way we see movies in a positive as well as a negative way. For years we have taken films for granted. Video has given us a new technology that we can but do not always use to renew our perception of film as a medium. If we look through video in a certain way, we can rediscover what is unique not only about the cinema but about video, as well. If we look at video in terms of its differences from other representational forms, we can recover its unique identity as a medium. In order to look *at* video, we must also look *through* it.

NOTES

1 The term *video* has a variety of meanings ranging from broadcast television to video art. These different notions of video are discussed within the body of this chapter. For the most part, when I use the term *video* I am referring to television and videotape, not to video art. Video art constitutes a unique appropriation of video technology and regularly explores, manipulates, and/or violates its normal usage in these other forms of video. I try to distinguish between these different usages by employing *video* to refer to the video signal, broadcast and cable television, videotape recorders, and videotapes (and videodiscs) and using the term *video art* to refer to video art.

2 My methodology here is indebted to the writings of Walter Benjamin and André Bazin. In "The Work of Art in the Age of Mechanical Reproduction," Benjamin viewed the advent of photography and film in terms of traditional art forms and saw them as introducing new categories of image production that altered our perception of these more traditional forms. In "The Ontology of the Photographic Image," Bazin defined the photographic image in terms of its "psychology": that is, he defined it in terms of our understanding of its relationship to (and difference from) other modes of representation. See Benjamin, *Illuminations*, ed. Hannah Arendt, trans. Harry Zohn (New York: Schocken Books, 1968), 220, 234, and Bazin, *What Is Cinema?* trans. Hugh Gray (Berkeley: University of California Press, 1967), 10, 12, 13.

3 Bazin, "Ontology of the Photographic Image," 9-16.

4 See, for example, Raymond Williams's discussion of the parallel development of movies and television in *Television: Technology and Cultural Form* (New York: Schocken Books, 1975), 14-19.

5 Gordon Hendricks, *The Edison Motion Picture Myth* (Berkeley: University of California Press, 1961), 14.

6 W. K. Laurie Dickson, "A Brief History of the Kinetograph, the Kinetoscope, and the Kineto-phono-graph," in *A Technological History of Motion Pictures and Television,* ed. Raymond Fielding (Berkeley: University of California Press, 1967), 9-14.

7 Roy Armes, *On Video* (New York: Routledge, 1989).

8 This is something of an exaggeration; television technology does rely on scanning—on the motion of an electron beam in a cathode ray tube and/or picture tube and on that of videotape and rotating heads in a VCR.

9 John T. Mullin, "Creating the Craft of Tape Recording," *High Fidelity Magazine,* April 1976, 62.

10 Ibid., 62-63.

11 Ibid., 65-66.

12 William Lafferty, "The Early Development of Magnetic Sound Recording in Broadcasting and Motion Pictures, 1928-1950" (Ph.D. diss., Northwestern University, 1981), 191-206.

13 See, for example, Ray Dolby, "Rotary-Head Switching in the Ampex Video Tape Recorder," *Journal of the SMPTE* 66, no. 4 (April 1957): 184-88.

14 Yuma Shiraishi, "History of Home Videotape Recorder Development," *SMPTE Journal* 94, no. 12 (December 1985): 1257–58.

15 Ibid., 1260.

16 See Larry Blake, "Mixing Dolby Stereo Film Sound," *Recording Engineer/Producer* 12, no. 1 (February 1981), and Ioan Allen, "Fifty Years of Stereo Optical: From Blumlein to Dolby SR," paper presented at the Society of Motion Picture and Television Engineers (SMPTE) conference, 26 October 1987.

17 James Lardner, *Fast Forward: Hollywood, the Japanese, and the VCR Wars* (New York: Norton, 1987), 95.

18 Peter Frank, "Video Art Installations in the Telenvironment," in *Video Art: An Anthology,* ed. Ira Schneider and Beryl Korot (New York: Harcourt Brace Jovanovich, 1976), 204-5.

19 Williams, *Television,* 25; emphasis in the original.

20 Video art needs to be distinguished here from broadcast television in that the former uses the technology for purposes other than pure transmission (although the works of video artists are occasionally broadcast or transmitted as program material).

21 See Edward Stasheff and Rudy Bretz, *The Television Program: Its Writing, Direction, and Production* (New York: Wyn, 1951), 6, as quoted in David Antin's "Video: The Distinctive Features of the Medium," in *Video Art,* ed. Schneider and Korot, 177. The advent of videotape and the practice of time-shifting have, however, led to the qualification of television's identification with "live" broadcast. Nonetheless, even in the case of time-shifting, the signal playback and the on-screen programming are simultaneous, constituting a "recreation" of the "live."

22 Joseph Anderson and Barbara Anderson, "Motion Perception in Motion Pictures," in *The Cinematic Apparatus*, ed. Teresa de Lauretis and Stephen Heath (New York: St. Martin's Press, 1980), 78-79.

23 Hugo Munsterberg, *The Film: A Psychological Study, the Silent Photoplay in 1916* (1916; reprint, New York: Dover, 1970), 26-30. See also Anderson and Anderson, "Motion Perception," 81-82.

24 Anderson and Anderson, "Motion Perception," 81-82.

25 Munsterberg, *Film,* 29.

26 Dimitri Balachoff, "The Psychophysiology of Film and Video," *Perfect Vision* 2, no. 5 (Fall 1989): 54.

27 Roland Barthes, "Rhetoric of the Image," in *Image-Music-Text,* trans. Stephen Heath (New York: Hill and Wang, 1977), 45-46.

28 Christian Metz, "On the Impression of Reality in the Cinema," in *Film Language: A Semiotics of the Cinema,* trans. Michael Taylor (New York: Oxford, 1974), 5-6, 8.

29 Walter Benjamin, "The Work of Art," 222–25.

30 See, for example, *Technological Alterations to Motion Pictures: A Report of the Register of Copyrights* (Washington, D.C.: United States Copyright Office, March 1989).

CHAPTER 6

VIDEOR

Jacques Derrida

—[. . .]So one would say. It seems to me, at least, that this is the case: quite singular
operations, more and more numerous, put to "work" the new "video" power, the possibility that, in an apparently empirical fashion, is called "video." But I say "it seems to
me that . . . " since I am not sure I have at my disposal an adequate concept for what
today goes by the name video and especially video *art*. It seems to me that we will have
to choose from among three rigorously incompatible "specificities." To go quickly by
using common names, let us say that these are (1) the specificity of video *in general*; (2)
that of video *art*; (3) that of *such works*, or the putting-to-work of a general technique
that is called "video." Whether it is shared by these three possibilities, or whether it is
proper to each of them, the aforesaid specificity would suppose the determination of an
internal and essential trait. Now, despite the upheavals in progress, the use of a different technique or of new supports . . .

—But which ones exactly? What is a support for video?

—I am still wondering what these things have in common: for example,
video grafted onto the ordinary use of television, surveillance video, and the most daring
research, called "video art," which still remains confined in rather narrow circuits,
either public or private, and whose "pragmatic" conditions have nothing in common
with the other finalizations of video. The possibility of multiple monitors and of a freer
play with this multiplicity, the restructuration of the space of production and performance, the new status of what is called an actor, a character, the displacement of the
limit between the private and the public, a growing independence with regard to public
or political monopolies on the image, a new economy of relations between the direct
and the nondirect, between what is carelessly said to be "real" time and "deferred"
time, all this constitutes a bundle of considerable transformations and stakes. If, however, video can play such a visible role here, at a new rhythm, it is neither the sole nor the
first technique to do so, and this, at least for video art, constitutes an *external* determination. Once again, it seems to me therefore (*mihi videor*) that there is no essential

unity among these things that seem to resemble each other or that are assembled together under the name of video.

　　—But perhaps the video event, among others, reveals precisely the problematic fragility of this distinction between an internal determination and an external determination. That would already be rather disturbing . . .

　　—So why then do you say, quite rightly, "among others"? In any case, we would agree, I think, that giving up specific identity doesn't hurt anyone, and perhaps it's better that way.

　　—On the contrary, it always hurts a lot, that's the whole problem . . .

　　—Why should it still be necessary to try to identify? Especially in this case, why should one have to zero in on the irreducible property of an "art"? Why try to classify, hierarchize, even situate what one still likes to call the "arts"? Neither opposition (major/minor, for example) nor a genealogy ordered with reference to the history of supports or techniques seems pertinent any longer in this regard, supposing that they ever were. And if the very concept of the "beaux arts" were thereby to find itself affected in the dark core of its long life or its nine lives, would that be such a serious loss?

　　—One could say that my uncertainty in this regard—it has a long history but it keeps growing, it is both uneasy and joyful—has been encouraged by the experience of the "video" simulacrum into which I have seen myself, modestly, swept along for a little while now, ever since I was given the chance to participate, or rather to figure, in *Disturbance* by Gary Hill. Better still, ever since I seemed to see (*videre videor*, as Descartes would say)[1] my simulacrum do no more than *pass by* there, risk a few passing steps that would be led elsewhere by someone else, I didn't know where. Narcissism set adrift. I owe this chance not only the way one owes a chance but the way one is obliged by another to be involved in an experience, without knowing it, without foreseeing it—an experience that combines in such an inventive fashion luck with calculation and *tuchē* (chance) with *ananke* (necessity). But, for that very reason, I was in no position to talk and, finally, I had no desire to do so. The blind *passerby* was hardly even an extra; as to what may be said about that, others have done so with better results than I might even attempt, in particular Jean-Paul Fargier in "Magie blanche."[2] On the other hand, concerning that which cannot be said about it and which remains encrypted in the bodily contact with another simulacrum, with a text that, as I was told and as I believed up until the last minute, was "apocryphal" (the more or less improvised choices that I dictated to myself, almost without seeing—only once—in truth, let be dictated to me like the truth of oracular symptoms in the space of my own familial, tattered gnostic, these raveled fragments of the Gospel according to Thomas that Gary Hill put into my hands, the interrupted premeditations and the sheer chance of improvisation, the hasty crossing of repetitions or rehearsals in the course of an irreversible scene, which is to say unrehearsed, live, direct but without direction, in a direct that was to get carried away with itself, from itself in the course of a simulacrum of performance or presentation that would reveal that there is not and never has been a direct, live presentation, not even, as Virilio ventures to put it in a very fine text, a "presentation [of an] electro-optical milieu"),[3] concerning that which, therefore, cannot be said about it and that regards only me and mine, I will say nothing. And for lack of time, I will also reduce to silence a whole possible rhetoric on the subject of, precisely, "video silence," of video "mystique," in the sense that Wittgenstein speaks of "mystique" when he says that concerning that about which one cannot speak, one must remain silent. Here, what one cannot "say" other than by showing it, or rather by putting on a quasi presentation in video on the subject of video, must be silenced. One must put up or shut up, that is, do it or be quiet, take into account, as Gary Hill *does*, what happens to language through the "video" event (parti . . .)

—Ah well, but a moment ago you were saying that you did not see yourself as capable of speaking of an identity—already identifiable, already assured—of the "video" event . . .

—Not yet, one must take into account what happens to language (partitioned or distributed, cut, strung or tacked together, delinearized, palindromanagrammatized in more than one language and passing like a serpent across seven monitors at the same time) through the "video" event . . .

—But you are sure there is only one monitor, right here, and one line? What do you think you see?

— . . . Anything but mutism, a certain "being silent" of this writing—new but very impure and all the newer for that—which stages discourses or texts that are thought to be of the most "interior" sort. Is it just by chance that Gary Hill solicits, among others, gnostic texts or the writings of Blanchot? One never sees a new art, one thinks one sees it; but a "new art," as people say a little loosely, may be recognized by the fact that it is not recognized; one would say that it cannot be seen because one lacks not only a ready discourse with which to talk about it, but also that implicit discourse that organizes the experience of this art itself and is working even on our optical apparatus, our most elementary vision. And yet, if this "new art" arises, it is because within the vague terrain of the implicit, something is already enveloped—and developing.

—But someone who was neither an actor, nor an extra, just barely a passerby mobilized by a new interplay of the aleatory and the program, couldn't he say something about the way in which "video art" affects the essential status of its interpreters (I do not say its actors, even less its characters; one would say they are just barely its human subjects)? Whoever appears or sees himself appear in a video work of art is neither a "real person" nor a movie or stage actor nor a character in a novel.

—Are you talking about video art or about the art of Gary Hill?

—As this was my first video passion (passion in the sense that, seeing myself passing by reading in front of a camera against an absolutely white studio background that made me think, I don't know why, of the cemetery in Jerusalem seen from the Mount of Olives, I was all the more gravely passive in that I did not know what Gary Hill would do with what I saw myself doing without seeing myself, with me and mine, with my words, the words that I borrowed, selected, recomposed, repeated, nor what he would do with my passing steps whose rhythm was all I could calculate, not the trajectory, and in fact this image was swept along by a well-understood path of necessity, from one aleatory moment to the next, there where I could in no way have foretold or foreseen it would go, but passion also in the sense that right away I *loved* it, that is to say, as always when one loves, I right away wondered *why* I loved *that,* what or whom I loved exactly), I will say only a few words very quickly on the question that, like everyone, I have asked myself and am still asking: if it is an "art," that, and an absolutely new one, especially with regard to the analogues that are painting, photography, cinema, and television, and even the digital image, what would compose this irreducible difference, that very thing? What is going on there? What went on with me? What happened to the passerby that I was, using my body, my passing steps, my voice as no art, no other art, so one would say, would have done? It seems to me. Difficult. I tried out all the possible analyses—forgive me if I do not repeat them here—but nothing worked; I could always reduce the set of components of this "art" to some combination of givens older than *that,* video "properly speaking" as art "properly speaking." So one could say that the question is badly put.

      —Let us suppose Gary Hill to be exemplary here . . .

      —No, not exemplary, otherwise you are going to end up with the same classical problematic that you want to avoid; no, not exemplary, but singular, idiomatic, his work, each of his works is found to be singular and sweeps the general technique called video along in an adventure that renders it irreplaceable, but irreplaceable among other irreplaceables, other unique effects of signature, even if it puts to work many other things, many other "arts" that have nothing to do with video . . .

      —All right, but you are still insisting on the "work," on the shape of its unity, on the idiomatic singularity of the signature, as if it were self-protecting and self-legitimating, in an internal fashion, whereas today events called "video" *can* lay bare symptoms that are far more disturbing and provocative: for example, those that lead us to think the singularity of "works" and "signatures" beginning with the very thing that institutes them and threatens them at the same time. Supposing that there is in effect, so it seems, as an effect and as the simulacrum on the basis of which we are speaking, *some* work and *some* signature, let us then start out from this reminder: Gary Hill was to begin with a sculptor, and a sculptor who was first of all tuned into sonority, indeed to the singing of his sculptures, in other words to that unheard-of technical prosthesis that, at the birth of an art, grafts an ear onto an eye or a hand, right away making us doubt the identity, the name, or the classification of the arts. But he is also one of the few, I do not say the only, "video artists" who is now working, even if he has not always done so, with discourses, many discourses (this is a "new" visual art that—and it is our first enigma—appears to be one of the most discursive), and not only with discourses but also with textual forms that are heterogeneous among themselves, whether literary or not (Blanchot, the Gospels, for example), that seem to be altogether at odds with such a working, with what one thought "video" art had to be, especially if, as seems to be the case, they are anything but the simple pretext assumed by the videogram.

      —This obvious fact perhaps calls for the following hypothesis—I indeed say hypothesis, maybe even fiction: The specificity of a "new art"—or, in general, of a new writing—is not in a relation of irreducible dependence (by that I mean without pos-

JACQUES DERRIDA

sible substitution or prosthesis) and especially of synchrony with the emergence of a technical generality or a new "support." One would say that the novelty remains to come, still to come with regard to a technical mutation that, by itself, could give rise to the most mechanical repetition of genres or stereotypes, for example narrative, novelistic, theatrical, cinematographic, or televisual . . .

—So it would take time, a kind of latency period, to render the new support, the new technique indispensable, irreducible . . .

—No, not a homogenous period of latency, but the history of an active, vigilant, unpredictable proliferation that will have displaced even the future anterior in its grammar and permitted in return a new experience of the already identifiable "arts," and not only the "arts," another mode of reading the writings one finds in books, for example, but of so many other things as well; this without destroying the aura of new works whose contours are so difficult to delimit and that are delivered over to other social spaces, other modes of production, of "representation," archiving, reproducibility, while giving to a technique of writing in all its several states (shooting, editing, "incrustation," projection, storage, reproduction, archiving, and so on) the chance for a new aura . . .

—But there would have to be another name for that, other names for all these things, it seems to me . . .

—I wouldn't say that that is indispensable; one would have to see. It seems to me that an old name can always name anew: see how Gary Hill makes secret names and dead tongues resonate on his seven monitors . . .

Translated by Peggy Kamuf

NOTES

A French-language version of this essay appeared in the catalog for the *Passage de l'image* exhibition at the Centre Georges Pompidou in Paris, curated by Raymond Bellour, Catherine David and Christine van Asche. See *Passage de l'image* (Paris: Editions du Centre Pompidou, 1990), 158–61. The piece was written after Derrida had participated as one of the "readers" in Gary Hill's video installation *Disturbance (among the Jars)* which was featured in the *Passage de l'image* exhibition. EDS.

1 René Descartes, second *Méditation*, quoted by Jean-Luc Nancy, who writes in the course of his analysis: "The *videor* is the illusion that, through an extraordinary torsion or perversion, anchors certainty fully in the abyss of illusion. The place of the *videor* is indeed painting, the portrait, at once the most artificial and the most faithful of faces, the most unseeing and the most clairvoyant eye" (Nancy, *Ego Sum* [Paris: Flammarion, 1979], 71-72).

2 Jean-Paul Fargier, "Magie blanche," in *Gary Hill, Disturbance (among the Jars)* (Villeneuve d'Ascq: Musée d'art moderne, n.d.).

3 Paul Virilio, "La Lumière indirecte," *Communications* 48, "Vidéo" (1988): 45ff. The point would be to engage a close discussion around the very interesting but very problematic notions of "telepresence," of "present telereality in 'real time' that supplants the reality of the presence of real space." Already problematic with regard to video *in general* (the principal, even unique object of Virilio's analysis), these concepts would be even more so, it seems, with regard to the putting to work of "art" video, as well as the type of simulacrum that structures it.

CHAPTER 7

VIDEO CONFESSIONS

—|(—

Michael Renov

Every fidelis of either sex shall after the attainment of years of discretion separately confess his sins with all fidelity to his priest at least once in the year. . . . Let the priest be discreet and cautious, and let him after the manner of skilled physicians pour wine and oil upon the wounds of the injured man, diligently inquiring the circumstances alike of the sinner and of the sin, by which he may judiciously understand what counsel he ought to give him, and what sort of remedy to apply, making use of various means for the healing of the sick man.

~ CANON 21, Fourth Lateran Council of 1215[1]

Confession increasingly takes the place of penance. This development can best be recognized by considering the fact that, in its early period, the Church ordered the sinner to make a public confession as an exercise of penance. Modern Protestantism actually puts coming to terms with one's own conscience in the place of the external confession, thus unconsciously preparing for the future development that will go beyond confession and perhaps replace religion by other social institutions.

~ THEODOR REIK, *The Compulsion to Confess* (1925)[2]

Dear Lord, I'm sorry I fight with my mother, but my underwear is my own business and the business of my audience. It ain't that yellow.

~ GEORGE KUCHAR, *Cult of the Cubicles* (1987)

In an interview shortly after the publication of his groundbreaking first volume of *The History of Sexuality*, Michel Foucault suggested a trajectory of continuity that linked his latest work with such earlier projects as *Madness and Civilization*. In both cases, the problem was to find out how certain questions—of madness or sexuality—"could have been made to operate in terms of discourses of truth, that is to say, discourses having the status and function of *true* discourses."[3] For in his work on sexuality, Foucault had discovered "this formidable mechanism . . . the machinery of the confession," by which he meant "all those procedures by which the subject is incited to produce a discourse of truth about his sexuality which is capable of having effects on the subject himself."[4] Like autobiography, with which it can be aligned,[5] confession was, for Foucault, a discourse "in which the speaking subject is also the subject of the statement," but unlike other autobiographical forms (for example, the diary, journal, or Montaignian essay), confession was, by definition, "a ritual that unfolds within a power relationship, for one does not confess without the presence (or virtual presence) of a partner who is not simply the interlocutor but the authority who requires the confession, prescribes and appreciates it, and intervenes in order to judge, punish, forgive, console, and reconcile." And, finally, confession was a ritual "in which the expression alone, independently of its external consequences, produces intrinsic modifications in the person who articulates it: it exonerates, redeems, and purifies him; it unburdens him of his wrongs, liberates him, and promises him salvation."[6]

According to Foucault's formulation, psychoanalysis figured as simply the most recent and most scientifically explicit development of a confessional apparatus that could be traced back to Tertullian and to Augustine. For in all cases, confession was understood to be a restorative vehicle, of mind or spirit, yet one in which power was necessarily implicated. In the manner of the Augustinian model (Augustine's *Confessions*, a thirteen-volume work of the late fourth century, is universally cited as originary), confession could provide "a way to escape madness, to reveal secret, hidden places, and to face the world with a new and 'easeful' liberty."[7] But, according to confessional logic, the cure could be bestowed only through the guarantee of God or psychoanalyst; confession required submission to authority, divine or secular. Significantly, in neither case was the confessor the bona fide recipient of the confessant's unburdening. The priest was only a go-between in the dialogue between God and supplicant, while the analyst was the site of a transference, the object of "certain intense feelings of affection which the patient has transferred on to the physician, not accounted for by the latter's behaviour nor by the relationship involved by the treatment."[8] The implications of this dependency—confession as a play of authority, a regulation of desire—were the provocation for Foucault's critique of confessional "truth-telling."

A very great deal is at stake in this critique, far more than simply a revisionist view of religious ritual or psychoanalytic practice. As so many critics have noted, Western epistemology presumes a subject who must submit to the Truth, one whose substance and identity are constructed in relation to an authoritative Other (the truth as divine, God as the "transcendental signified," the final guarantor of meaning).[9] One could then say that the Western subject finds his sweetest repose in confessional discourse. Moreover, it was not just the individual-as-subject who had been conditioned by confession, as sacrament or compulsion; social effects followed. In *The History of Sexuality*, Foucault traced the influence of the confessional mode at the level of the organization of social life in the West:

> We have . . . become a singularly confessing society. The confession has spread its effects far and wide. It plays a part in justice, medicine, education, family relationships, and love relations, in the most ordinary affairs of everyday life, and in the most solemn rites; one confesses one's crimes, one's sins, one's thoughts and desires, one's illnesses and troubles; one goes about telling, with the greatest precision, whatever is most difficult to tell. . . . Western man has become a confessing animal.[10]

Risking a fall into absolutism, such a notion of confession is nonetheless compelling for the way in which it organizes an extraordinarily dense discursive domain (theological, juridical, psychoanalytic) articulated around the confessional act into an epistemological praxis, thoroughly imbued with relations of power.

THE THERAPY OF SELF-EXAMINATION

But few commentators, Foucault chief among them, construct confession solely in terms of submission to an authorizing and exteriorized source of power; confession has customarily been assigned a complex therapeutic value.[11] Peter Brown, author of the definitive English-language biography of Augustine, judged the Augustinian model of confession to be a precursor for the modern obsession for self-scrutiny: "It is this therapy of self-examination which has, perhaps, brought Augustine closest to some of the best traditions of our own age. Like a planet in opposition, he has come as near to us, in Book Ten of the *Confessions*, as the vast gulf that separates a modern man from the culture and religion of the Later Empire can allow."[12]

In the mid-1920s, psychoanalyst Theodor Reik pronounced Augustine "one of the greatest psychologists of Christianity."[13] For Reik, confession was a fundamental trope of psychic life, one response to repression: "The general urge of unconscious material to express itself sometimes assumes the character of a tendency to confess."[14] Functioning at the join of public and private domains, confession as public discourse (confessional literature or performative display) can be understood either as a kind of self-interrogation that produces spiritual reconciliation while implicitly challenging others to ethical action (a theological reading)[15] or as an acting out of repressed material that, when subjected to analysis, can facilitate the transfer of unconscious psychic material to the preconscious (a psychoanalytic reading)—therapeutic ends, both of them. And, of course, therapy has emerged as one of the growth industries of our age. Given an understanding of the multiform historical role confession has played in the development of Western thought, how can we now begin to talk about the transformations of confessional culture in the late twentieth century? And what place should we give to video in this account? Foucault's theorization remains pertinent.

Despite the historical sweep of Foucault's formulations, which take as their point of departure the advent of the "age of repression" in the seventeenth century, *The History of Sexuality* draws our attention to the dynamic and protean character of confessional utterance, particularly in this century. Far from censoring speech, repression has produced "a regulated and polymorphous incitement to discourse,"[16] which, as Reik notes in the opening epigraph, can find expression outside religion or the therapist's couch. Many commentators have remarked upon the decline of confession in its most parochial or doctrinal sense: William James, writing at the turn of the century, refers to "the complete decay of the practice of confession in Anglo-Saxon communities";[17] Norberto Valentini and Clara di Meglio, citing a dramatic statistical decline in the level and frequency of confessional participation in the Italian Church in the 1970s, deem confession to be "in crisis."[18]

And yet, in the 1990s, confessional discourse proliferates. In what follows I will look beyond both church and couch to the aesthetic or cultural domain and indeed to a very particular corner of that domain—toward independently produced, low-end video, which I shall position against capital-intensive, industrially organized, mass market cultural commodities, on film or tape. In doing so, I take as my focus selected work by independent videomakers working consciously (sometimes parodically) within the context of confessional and therapeutic discourses. What I will say about video confessions is not, therefore, ontologically grounded. I don't wish to make claims for something like a confessional potentiality intrinsic to the electronic medium; what I say will be limited and contingent. And yet I shall argue for a uniquely charged linkage between "video" and "confession" in the current cultural environment for reasons that I shall return to later in the chapter.

Regarding the aesthetic domain, it should be said that there are substantial grounds for a turn of the confessional impulse toward specifically artistic ends (never, of course, to the exclusion of coexistent theological, psychoanalytic, or criminological contexts). At least since the Greeks, art has been judged capable of yielding "cathartic" effects for artist and audience alike through the public disclosure of concealed impulses and secret wishes, secondarily revised. Indeed, a large number of books have been written on the topic of confessional literature (among the chief objects of inquiry, Augustine, Chaucer, Shakespeare, Rousseau, De Quincey, Dostoyevsky). But in the latter half of the twentieth century, the vehicles of cultural hegemony have been transformed dramatically, along the lines of what Raymond Williams has identified as a kind of ongoing but interstitial struggle of dominant, emergent, and residual cultural forces.[19] For while it can be said that there has been an explosion of confessional and therapeutic discourses within the public sphere of American culture, that efflorescence has been less "literary" than popular cultural—in the form of tabloid journalism, talk radio, and commercial television.

Mimi White's insightful book on American television's place within this emerging landscape of public confession, *Tele-Advising: Therapeutic Discourse in American Television*, examines a range of TV formats (daytime soaps, religious broadcasting, game shows, prime time series, advice shows, shop-at-home television), all of which decisively if unpredictably generate narrative and narrational positions for their audience.[20] White ingeniously shows how television programs not only borrow from the world of psychological theory and clinical practice, but also "construct new therapeutic relations."[21] Following closely on Foucault's premise that the production of confessional knowledge is equally an exercise of power and regulation, *Tele-Advising* nonetheless points to the multiplicity of subject effects created by these TV therapies, outlining as well the possibilities of resistant positions.

But I want to distinguish between White's field of inquiry and my own, between the worlds of broadcast television and independent video, and thus to begin to account for the very different confessional manifestations produced in each domain. Throughout White's discussion, it is clear that confession is not only narrativized but commodified. (One could say, as Nick Browne has argued, that the master narrative of television, in line with its "supertextual" function, *is* commodification.)[22] Given the profit orientation of broadcast television, all confessional transactions—from Dr. Ruth to *The Love Connection*—are also commercial ones. If successful, the show's presentation of embarrassing disclosures of newlywed couples entices a generous share of the viewing audience and thus higher advertising rates from sponsors. The lifeblood of such commercial ventures must be mass appeal, a requirement to which confession responds if we may judge by the number and variation of talk therapy vehicles. These therapeutic discourses offer illustration of Reik's characterization of confession as a kind of repetition compulsion[23] ("everyone confesses over and over again to everybody else" says White of TV talk formats),[24] only these secrets are made available to home audiences rather than to professional auditor-confessors. As participatory as televisual therapy may appear to be ("telling one's story *on television* is part of the process of recovery"),[25] there can never be a thoroughgoing disengagement from the consumer culture of which the confessional scene is a support. As we shall see, there is a rather different dynamic to be discerned in the realm of video confession.

CAMERA: INSTRUMENT OF CONFESSION

We have learned from Freud that verbal presentations are necessary to make consciousness possible. It is only the confession that enables us to recognize preconsciously what the repressed feelings and ideas once meant and what they still mean for us, thanks to the indestructibility and timelessness peculiar to the unconscious processes. By the confession we become acquainted

MICHAEL RENOV

with ourselves. It offers the best possibility for self-understanding and self-acceptance. ~ THEODOR REIK, *The Compulsion to Confess* (205)

Yes, the camera deforms, but not from the moment that it becomes an accomplice. At that point it has the possibility of doing something I couldn't do if the camera wasn't there: it becomes a kind of psychoanalytic stimulant which lets people do things they wouldn't otherwise do. ~ JEAN ROUCH[26]

Chronique d'un été (1961), Jean Rouch and Edgar Morin's monumental experiment in direct cinema, can also be seen as a milestone in the development of "camera confessions" in the documentary mode, an embryonic instance of what I have elsewhere called "techno-analysis."[27] There are two key confessional scenes enacted in the film: Marilou's face-to-face encounters with Morin, in which corruscating self-inquisition brings her to the edge of emotional collapse, and Holocaust survivor Marceline's soliloquy of wrenching wartime memory delivered to a Nagra she carries in her handbag as she strolls through Les Halles. During *Chronique*'s famous penultimate sequence, these are two of the most criticized moments of the film, as the subjects themselves argue over the sincerity of the personal testimony and the film's overall merits. The filmmakers, although far from sanguine about the prospects of success for their experiment, are convinced that they are onto something. In Rouch's words:

> Very quickly I discovered the camera was something else; it was not a brake but let's say, to use an automobile term, an accelerator. You push these people to confess themselves and it seemed to us without any limit. Some of the public who saw the film [*Chronique*] said the film was a film of exhibitionists. I don't think so. It's not exactly exhibitionism: it's a very strange kind of confession in front of the camera, where the camera is, let's say, a mirror, and also a window open to the outside.[28]

The camera is for Rouch a kind of two-way glass that retains a double function: it is a window that delivers the profilmic to an absent gaze and, at the same moment, a reflective surface that reintroduces us to ourselves. Rouch's insight brilliantly anticipates what the video apparatus (with the playback monitor mounted alongside the camera) realizes.

As founding a moment as Rouch's experiments may be in the history of filmic confession, a crucial break occurs when the camera as confessional instrument is taken up by the confessant herself. In this configuration, the camera becomes the "camera-stylo" first described by Alexandre Astruc, a moving-image equivalent to the pen, which has so assiduously transcribed two millenia of confessional discourses. There are indeed exemplary instances in which filmmakers have committed to film the ebb and flow of conscience and moral evaluation: Jonas Mekas, for one, whose ongoing project, the "Diaries, Notes, and Sketches," reinscribes and puts to the test the artist's life since his emigration to the United States in 1949. In a film such as *Lost, Lost, Lost* (1975), Mekas lays his narration, steeped in the memory of the people and places we are shown, over footage excerpted from fourteen years of filming (1949–63). The "present-tense" voice interrogates "past" images through a temporally disjunctive diaristic method that produces the confession of his own cinematic practice as a compulsion to remember: "It's my nature now to record, to try to keep everything I am passing through . . . to keep at least bits of it. . . . I've lost too much. . . . So now I have these bits that I've passed through."[29]

But the first-person, artisanal style that has been refined through five decades of the New American Cinema (Maya Deren, Mekas, Stan Brakhage, Bruce Baillie, and so on) has always strained against an industrial bias as economically grounded as it is ideological.[30] The legendary spring-wound Bolex—so light, so durable—and even Brakhage's hand-wrought signatures, etched into the emulsion itself, could not free the cineaste from a dependence on large-scale manufacturers who could discontinue stocks (even whole formats) if profit margins sagged. Then, too, there were the vagaries of the local labs to contend with.

The development of the Sony portapak in the mid-1960s provided visual artists with a greater possibility for relative autonomy. Not that the portapak, designed and manufactured as it was by a major Japanese conglomerate, and its descendants can be deemed a more artisanal format than 16mm film. Indeed, the potential for the hand-crafting so beloved by 16mm and 8mm enthusiasts has been lost in the transition to electronic pixels.[31] In exchange, the independent videomaker or home consumer has been relieved of certain mediating contingencies—material and temporal—that separate shooting from viewing, production from exhibition. It is the systematic solipsism and "immediacy" of video (the latter, in particular, a notion to be approached with much caution for its implicit metaphysical implications) that suit it so well to the confessional impulse. No technician need see or hear the secrets confided to tape. None but the invited enter the loop of the video confession.

THE ELECTRONIC CONFESSIONAL[32]

In its nearly thirty years of existence, the mass-marketed video apparatus has succeeded in colonizing the business of the preservation of family ritual (home video, wedding video), of information exchange (dating services, instructional media—from closed-circuit patient education in hospitals and clinics to aerobics tapes), and, in a less systematic fashion, of do-it-yourself or "techno-therapy." All of these are nonfiction applications consistent with that most elemental of documentary functions, the preservational.[33] Certain of the above-named instances combine preservation with persuasion or instruction (for example, health education or exercise tapes), while others (such as the home video) provide a moving-image catalog of domestic life to be stored and perused at will. But, compared with generic "home video," video confessions are deictic. (Most of the confessional video with which I am familiar is also artfully crafted. The distinctions I am delimiting here are based primarily on discursive function rather than aesthetic value.) Confessions of the sort that I am examining can also be functionally opposed to other preservational formats, such as the wedding video, in that they are autobiographical and counterindustrial.[34]

It is necessary to resolve the precise object of the present inquiry with even a finer grain. There have, for example, been some important confessional works in video made outside the autobiographical ambit, such as Maxie Cohen's *Intimate Interviews: Sex in Less than Two Minutes* (1984) and *Anger* (1986). In these pieces, Cohen expertly (and from off-camera) elicits the disclosure of intense emotion from a series of interview subjects. In *Anger*, for example, a man calling himself "Master James," a black hood masking his features, confesses to the pleasures he experiences through the whipping of compliant females; he traces his sexual preference to a mother who, although they shared a single room, punished him as a boy for looking at her unclothed body. Another man admits on-camera to four murders. While he displays no remorse for the crimes, only one of which he claims to have committed in anger, he does evidence an ironic self-knowledge. He describes the irreparable atrophy of his liver tissue caused by years of alcoholism and notes that Eastern medicine aligns that organ with one emotion—anger. In each of *Anger*'s seven sequences, people (as individuals, couples, or gangs) speak about an emotion that is very near the surface; anger is the lever whose expression frees discourse from repression. The confessing subjects have been raped, slashed with knives, betrayed, abused, and abandoned and have responded with tears, embitterment, or violence. The unresolved emotion they have lived with has in some cases driven them to unspeakable acts, which they nonetheless offer freely to the camera with only the occasional encouragement from Cohen offscreen. Clearly, as Riek predicted, confession has taken the place of penance. The subjects seek not forgiveness but expressive release in the form of dialogues—between imaged subject and a present but unimaged interlocutor—from which only monologues survive. I am suggesting that first-person video confessions, addressed to an absent confessor-Other, mediated through an ever-present apparatus, constitute a discursive formation significantly different from the truncated dialogue, one that offers particular insight into the specificities and potentialities of the medium itself.[35]

First-person video confessions satisfy Foucault's formulation of confession as "a discourse in which the speaking subject is also the subject of the statement," with the "speaking subject" understood as necessarily and simultaneously the "enunciating subject." (Here, enunciation entails the repertoire of tasks required to conceive, shoot, and edit a confessional tape.) The subjects of Cohen's works are thus "speaking" but not "enunciating" subjects. Indeed, it might be argued that *Anger*'s subjects, like those of other documentaries of the interactive mode in which the interview format prevails,[36] are more spoken than speaking. The distinction is pertinent to my earlier claim that confessional discourse is particularly well suited to the solipsistic potentiality of video.

With regard to the therapeutic value of diaristic video confessions, I do not wish to suggest that these practices provide actual substitutes for professional therapies. For its part, traditional psychoanalytic theory is fairly categorical with regard to the distinction between analysis and catharsis or "acting-out," which Reik, for one, never accepts as a therapeutic end in itself:

> Acting-out, if elevated to be the dominating element of psychoanalysis, ruptures the frame of the treatment and transforms the provisional device of analytical experience into a final phase which is nowhere essentially different from the experiences "outside." That technique gives the suppressed impulses and wishes, as well as the need for punishment, full gratification, while we wish to avoid just that in psychoanalysis, which should, according to Freud, be accomplished in abstinence.
>
> We said earlier that acting-out is not an emotional end in itself. . . . [T]he analyst reopens to him [the confessant] the way from acting-out to remembering which we expect. In this sense, acting-out, too, is an unconscious confession in the form of representation or display; its interpretation is an essential part of analysis.[37]

Of course, the reference to "abstinence" in the above quotation is indicative of the distance that separates a monastic Freudianism from the free-for-all that is artistic expression. It is worth noting that autobiographical forms, particularly in the public realm in which film and video reception gets defined, are frequently labeled "self-indulgent." The asceticism that effectuates analysis (and the narrative economy of popular cinema is, in its own way, ascetic) is anathema to the self-immersion of first-person video confessions, which obsessively track personal truths. It could hardly be otherwise. According to the Freudian orthodoxy, then, "acting out" (first-person confession) demands its analytical Other (the analyst-confessor). Could it be, however, that, in the stages of secondary revision we call editing, the videomaker-confessant has the potential, in working through the material, to produce, if only implicitly, something like an analysis, to move from acting out to remembering, from the unconscious to the preconscious or even to consciousness?

FIRST-PERSON VIDEO CONFESSIONS

A particularly telling instance of the transition from Rouch's incitational camera to first-person video confession occurs in Arthur Ginsberg's notorious documentary soap opera *The Continuing Story of Carel and Ferd* (1970–71), in which the San Francisco–based videographer set out to chronicle the vicissitudes of a former porn queen turned independent filmmaker and a one-eyed, bisexual junkie who choose to marry and live their lives before the camera in a Videofreex version of *An American Family*.[38] When, months down the line, celebrity and the connubial luster begin to wane, Carel and Ferd wrest the camera from "Awful Arthur," the better to probe the depths of their unhappiness through a one-on-one confrontation. (It seems that the couple had been "seeing a shrink"—Ferd's description—in the period just previous.)

Toward the end of an hour-long précis of the *Continuing Story* produced by WNET's Television Laboratory (1975), in which a reunited Carel and Ferd provide in-studio commentary for the edited compilation, the latter-day Carel describes this appropriation of the apparatus: "It was important for us to use the camera therapeutically. . . . So we took the cameras alone and used them." "And Arthur had nothing to do with it?" asks their on-camera interviewer. "He couldn't use this stuff," replies Carel, "It was too real."

But the footage *is* used in the hour-long version (now distributed by Electronic Arts Intermix). Ferd and Carel in turn focus in unflinching close-up on the fine gestures and bodily details of the other (Carel's fingers nervously flicking ashes from her cigarette, Ferd's unsmiling lips as he smokes, eats, and talks). The one interrogates the other, posing difficult questions from behind the lens, the camera straining to catch out truths betrayed or, better yet, to get under the skin. It is a kino-eye usage, an attempt to extend the perfectibility of the human eye to intrapsychic ends. While the ploy inevitably fails (at least their union—as well as the melodrama—dissolves), *The Continuing Story of Carel and Ferd* establishes the paradigm of interpersonal video therapy with an intensity appropriate to the genre.

In the twenty years since the completion of *Carel and Ferd*, there have been a great number of first-person video confessions produced by independent artists. And while I think it important to draw attention to the range and particularities of this work, I will only be able to discuss a few tapes in any detail. The criterion for selection is primarily a heuristic one (those pieces that most vividly illustrate a particular discursive strategy or conceptual affiliation). Artists who have produced video confessions of the sort I have described include Ilene Segalove (*The Mom Tapes*, 1974–78; *The Riot Tapes*, 1983), Skip Sweeney (*My Father Sold Studebakers*, 1983), George Kuchar (the *Weather Diary* series, 1986–; *Cult of the Cubicles*, 1987), Lynn Hershman (*Confessions of a Chameleon*, 1986; *Binge*, 1987), Vanalyne Green (*Trick or Drink*, 1984; *A Spy in the House That Ruth Built*, 1989), Sadie Benning (virtually all of her work to date, including *If Every Girl Had a Diary*, 1989; *Me and Rubyfruit*, 1989; *Jollies*, 1990; *It Wasn't Love*, 1992), Susan Mogul (*Everyday Echo Street: A Summer Diary*, 1993), and Wendy Clarke (*The Love Tapes* project, 1978–94; the "One on One" series, 1990–91).

Right now I'm sitting here with no cameraman in the room. I'm totally alone. I would never, ever talk this way if somebody were here. It's almost as if, if somebody were in the room, it would insure lying . . . just like eating alone. I think that we've become kind of a society of screens, of different layers that keep us from knowing the truth, as if the truth is almost unbearable and too much for us to deal with, just like our feelings. So we deal with things through replications, and through copies, through screens, through simulations, through facsmiles, and through fiction . . . and through faction.

~ LYNN HERSHMAN, *Binge*

Lynn Hershman's on-camera monologues in the various entries of her *Electronic Diary* (1985–89) tend toward the overtly confessional. Her pronouncements in *Binge*, as quoted above, certainly lay out some of the issues to be confronted in the analysis of first-person video confessions. It is a central premise of my argument that taped self-interrogation can achieve a depth and a nakedness of expression that is difficult to duplicate with a crew or even a camera operator present. At first glance, the physical isolation of the confessant appears to be at odds with the dynamic of religious and psychoanalytic confession, each of which requires a confessor. To return to Foucault's characterization, "One does not confess without the presence (or virtual presence) of a partner who is not simply the interlocutor but the authority who requires the confession, prescribes and appreciates it, and intervenes in order to judge, punish, forgive, console, and reconcile."[39]

This model would seem, however, to apply to work, like Maxie Cohen's, that depends upon the artist's solicitation and preselection, varying degrees of intimacy or distance toward the subjects during production, and the introduction of gestural or verbal cues to induce expansiveness, closure, and the like. But this method entails, precisely, "direction" of the more traditional sort; confession is coaxed and elicited rather than simply given the opportunity to issue forth as occurs in the first-person mode. In contrast, the work of the priest or analyst is typically undirected; it is the ear of the other as an organ of passive listening, mirroring rather than choosing, that facilitates confession. With the interactive or directed variant, confession is tendered (not always consciously) to the videomaker herself; confessional discourse of the diaristic sort addresses itself to an absent, imaginary other. Consider, for example, Cohen's *Intimate Interviews: Sex in Less than Two Minutes,* in which four men and women speak directly to the camera about the personal idiosyncracies of their sexual lives. It is a compressed, parodic play of souped-up self-disclosure, confession reduced to the very edge of legibility (TV-fashion), much in contrast to the extended, purgative narration—glorying in every pause, every parapraxis—in which Hershman engages in *Binge*. The latter approach, through its willingness to give center stage to unexpurgated self-disclosure as *the* enunciative act, tells us more about the specific character and potentiality of video as a medium suited to confession. From this point of view, video can be seen as a format historically joined to the private and the domestic, a medium capable of supplying inexpensive, synch-sound images, a vehicle of autobiography in which the reflex gaze of the electronic eye can engender an extended, even obsessive, discourse of the self.

From a crudely developmental perspective, one could say that first-person video confession has simply built on an evolutionary dynamic in which the public confession initially ordained by medieval church doctrine gave way to a private, one-on-one ritual. Then, in the sixteenth century, Protestantism eliminated the externalization of confession as a face-to-face ritual of reconciliation, fostering a kind of spiritual entrepreneurship. Video preserves and deepens that dynamic of privatization and entrepreneurship. Now, with the help of their cameras, videomakers can exhume their deepest fears and indiscretions all on their own, and then put their neuroses on display. In a

MICHAEL RENOV

sense, first-person video confession is uniquely suited to its moment. Born of late-stage capitalism, it endows therapeutic practice with exchange value.

There are other ways to understand the advantage of the first-person format. As Rouch demonstrated with Marceline's soliloquy in *Chronique d'un été,* the presence of the camera or recorder is sufficient to spur self-revelation. In the case of video confessions, the virtual presence of a partner—the imagined other effectuated by the technology—turns out to be a more powerful facilitator of emotion than flesh-and-blood interlocutors. Camera operators, sound booms, cables, and clapper boards are hardly a boon to soul confession. Hershman's statement, cited at the beginning of this section—the claim that she would "never, ever talk this way" if there were another person in the room—returns us to the heart of the matter.[40]

Given that Hershman's telling describes the travails of an eating disorder in which she ravishes a host of "caloric strangers," frequently in the privacy of her boudoir, we can assume that the artist knows something about the solitary character of compulsive behavior. But is the tape simply another repetition of binge behavior or does it enact a level of analysis sufficient to move it beyond the realm of catharsis or "acting out" against which Reik warns us? I would argue that the control Hershman exerts over the structure and design of her tape, signs of secondary revision, suggests that once-repressed unconscious material has been, at least temporarily, rendered conscious and malleable. There is also a way in which Hershman refuses to let herself off the hook in what she shows us of herself. She warns that we are a society that functions most comfortably by means of simulation rather than authentic action or emotion. As she intones her critique of the growing inauthenticity of everyday life ("so we deal with things through replications, and through copies"), her imaged self begins to reduplicate itself in an infinite regress of video boxes. Hershman's self-indictment might also be seen as a further indication of the analytical insight foreign to brute cathartic displays. Her sense of the limits of her "cure"—her confession as itself a kind of artful, socially acceptable repetition of her condition—speaks to the internally contradictory character of confessional discourse, which contains the symptom within the cure.[41]

While there are many more video confessions deserving of discussion, I would like to turn to the work of Wendy Clarke, whose twin vocations—as performance artist–videomaker and as psychotherapist—make her the ideal subject for this inquiry. Specifically, I want to focus on two of her projects, each of which explores video's confessional and therapeutic potentialities in new and surprising ways. The place to start is with Clarke's "Love Tapes" project, which, since 1978, has afforded thousands of individuals a chance to voice deep emotion through a process of mediated self-interrogation. The minimalism of the concept is compelling: individuals of every age and background are given three minutes of tape time in which to speak about what love means to them. Clarke facilitates rather than directs the process; she supplies her subjects with the opportunity to make tapes and the requisite tools to accomplish the task. A small boothlike structure is erected, usually at a public site (for example, a mall, a bus station, or a prison), containing a chair, a video camera mounted for a frontal medium close-up,

and a monitor.[42] Each participant chooses a backdrop and musical accompaniment as mood dictates before activating the camera. The subject is necessarily the first audience of the piece for it is only upon the granting of permission that the tape becomes a part of the installation—instantly available for public viewing—and of the larger project.

Clarke's only other role is as the bestower of a single animating word: *love*. As "anger" was the incitation for Cohen, so is "love" the emotional levering point that explains the power of "The Love Tapes." It is the mana-word that spurs confession.[43] The performance produced is undirected but not, I think, unprompted. I would argue that it is the video apparatus as "pure potentiality"—its capabilities for preservation, instantaneous replay, repeated consumption, mass duplication, and public broadcast (all of which have been realized by "The Love Tapes" project)—that effectuates response. Admittedly, the myriad soliloquys collected by Clarke are not so pointedly therapeutic as those contained in *Chronique d'un été* or *Carel and Ferd*. They may not, in fact, conform so closely to what Lacan has termed "full speech"—the talking cure that works through past trauma as an effect of language. The tapes do, however, tap remarkable, and unpredictable, affective wellsprings in troubled youths, guilt-stricken fathers, adoring dog-owners, those who have lost or never known love, others whose capacity for love has been revived. The monologues, which frequently pivot on the confessant's (in)ability to experience physical or emotional intimacy, repeatedly speak the unspoken. Why, we might ask, do these individuals, many of whom claim to be incapable of expressing their innermost feelings to those closest to them, choose to eviscerate themselves so profoundly for the camera?

It is as if, in an age in which the information superhighway breeds a kind of "knowledge dependency" via antenna, cable, and optical fibers, "The Love Tapes" effect a temporary inversion of technopolarities. Instead of spewing a one-way stream of words and images (which, at another level, only soften up the consumer for the kill), Clarke's installed monitor shows the subject only herself as she (re)produces herself. The screen-mirror also becomes a blank surface upon which an active projection of the self rather than a strictly receptive introjection reigns triumphant. At last, in a reversal of broadcast fortunes close to Brecht's dream, the television stops talking and just listens.[44] Video becomes the eye that sees and the ear that listens, powerfully but without judgment or reprisal. As for the potential critique of the tapes—that they simply commodify emotion or gratify narcissism—the truth is that only a tiny fraction of these pieces have ever been publicly viewed, and fewer still have been broadcast. The charge of media celebrity is unconvincing for work whose cumulative impact begins to feel more and more species specific, less and less individuated.

I remain convinced that it is video-as-potentiality that fuels the emotional impact of the "The Love Tapes." What makes the experience of the tapes so powerful for subjects and audiences alike can never be duplicated on the couch. Clarke's success taps into the staggeringly hegemonic media current and temporarily redirects the flow. The very force that, while informing and entertaining us, delivers us to the advertisers now becomes a vehicle for performing ourselves for ourselves. The professional analyst can elicit, mirror, and interpret the subject's desire but lacks the levering capacity that the media apparatus inchoately mobilizes.

"ONE ON ONE"

The main object that I really want is to see how open I can get to be and I think this is a unique opportunity for myself because I don't know you, you don't know me. We don't have to ever know each other besides these tapes.

~ KEN from *Ken and Louise*

It's possible I could say things to you that I couldn't say to anybody else. . . . Maybe, we'll see.

~ LOUISE from *Ken and Louise*

I find that it's that vulnerable place that I have to address. And you have let me touch yours in a short time. Sometimes people can be married even for years and years and never have allowed their partner to touch that place. And for that I'm very grateful. I'm very grateful. It was a type of a freedom because I knew I was like you. . . . When you said it, I felt what you were saying.

~ KEN from *Ken and Louise*

While "The Love Tapes" may be the most streamlined and populist of first-person video confessions, Wendy Clarke's "One on One" series may be the most complex, bearing as it does the traces of confessional discourse's triple legacy—the theological, psychoanalytic, and criminological. For four years, Clarke was an artist-in-residence at the California Institution for Men at Chino. During that time she led workshops in poetry writing, painting, photography, and videomaking. Late in 1990, Clarke proposed a new project to her video workshop: a series of video letters to be exchanged between the class members and people on the outside. Like "The Love Tapes," these video letters would be intimate and self-regulated but, unlike them, would be addressed, directly and exclusively, to an individual who would respond in kind.[45]

Clarke's concept included another key proviso: the relationship between subjects was to remain a video exchange only. "I wanted them to have a very pure video experience," Clarke has said. "And I felt that the relationships would be changed if they met in any other way outside of this video space."[46] To that end, Clarke functioned as a go-between, minimally facilitating the tapings (usually made in solitude, "Love Tapes" fashion), allowing participants to play back the entry and reshoot if they so chose, then shuttling the tapes to their proper recipients. And, indeed, the connections made between these individuals are remarkable, crossing as they do barriers of race, class, gender, age, and sexual orientation. Those incarcerated are mostly young men of color (black, brown, and red), while the "outsiders" are typically older, both black and white, and frequently female. (Members of the latter group were drawn either from the membership of a progressive church in Santa Monica or from a community of successful African American businesspeople in the Crenshaw district of Los Angeles.) Beyond this sketchy description, few generalizations can be made that apply equally to all fifteen of the tapes in the series except to note that the linkages among participants are in every instance effected entirely through a media apparatus. In this regard, the "One on One" series is a remarkable case study, one in which, in the words of one critic, "the camera, instead of blocking communication, seems to be a two-way umbilical cord that nourishes the candor of both parties."[47]

In an age in which face-to-face encounters have tended to be displaced by mediated ones (for example, American political campaigns) and in which that development is inevitably figured as a loss, "One on One" demonstrates that the contrary can also be true. "I can express all of my emotions and everything to you," says Raul, a twenty-three-year-old Latino, father of two, who struggles with alcoholism and is estranged from his wife. As the exchange progresses, Raul digs deeper: "To tell the truth, I'm happy without drinking, real happy without having the bottle and getting drunk, all of that. Because all of that time, I might have been with a smile but I was crying inside." How is it that Raul is capable of revealing himself in this way to the video camera? Is the answer to be found in the particular wisdom of his interlocutor, Jeanene, a Caucasian woman in her late thirties who teaches high school in a Latino section of Los Angeles? Or can it be that the "One on One" concept engendered a therapeutic experience for its participants and that, in certain cases, we witness something akin to a positive transference, as described by Freud, in which the removal of repression is aided by the formation of an attachment to the analyst, an attachment properly belonging to earlier (often parental) relationships?

If the latter is so (transference mingling with incipient bonds of kinship or affection), the wonder of the "One on One" tapes is that the transference tends to be both mutual and reciprocal. In almost every instance, vulnerabilities are shared, positions of confessor and confessant exchanged. In fact, the psychodynamic is such that the openness of the one induces greater openness in the other in a kind of therapeutic spiral. In *Ken and Louise,* a black man—married, restrained but confident, a talented songwriter and vocalist—exchanges tapes with an upbeat but somewhat distant white woman of similar age and interests. He suggests that she is putting on an "air." She replies that she is "afraid I'm going to say something wrong to you"; her distance is the result of an

Michael Renov

excessive sensitivity to racial politics ingrained from childhood. (Her father, once a member of the Communist Party, had been jailed for his political affiliations in the early 1950s.) With each tape exchanged, the emotional intimacy gathers a greater force. Ken writes and sings a song to Louise about the colors not of the skin but of the heart. He is a startlingly gifted singer whose lyrics reveal a delicacy and depth of feeling. In reply, Louise shares with him a small stuffed animal, a monkey named Lucky, whom she cuddles and kisses, giggling with nervous excitement. "Every day I hug her and squeeze her and you're just about the only person who knows about this." His gift to her has inspired an even riskier display of her secret self. ("It's possible I could say things to you that I couldn't say to anybody else. . . . Maybe, we'll see.") And it is through the incitation of the video medium that so powerfully fuses distance and intimacy that this cathartic pas de deux is effected.

As the exchange progresses and Ken nears his date of release, many of the viewer's expectations are overturned. Ken is increasingly buoyant of spirit, self-assured,

FIGURE 2
Ken from Wendy Clarke's *Ken and Louise* (1991)

FIGURE 3
Louise from Wendy Clarke's *Ken and Louise* (1991)

offering more than receiving emotional support. Louise strips herself bare, revealing layer after layer of emotion testifying to the loneliness of her life, her inability to find a man to love. Her mood darkens. Given the audio/visibility of the process, we are able to judge these interior changes through outward signs—gesture, facial expression, posture, and choice of attire, as well as vocal tonalities. Our initial assumptions about these tapes are likely to include an implicit belief in the position of the "outsider" as the more powerful and empowering one (with the attention paid to the inmates restoring their damaged self-esteem). And while the assumption may hold initially and even throughout many of the fifteen "One on One" dialogues, it proves to be far from universal. By her fifth tape, Louise is slumped deep into her chair. Her unmade-up face a mask of despair, she announces that she is in a "state of grief." In Ken's reply, he assures her that her "dark, over-clouded look upon things" will pass. He speaks of wanting to reach out to her "in a real way," adding "I don't necessarily mean the man-lady type of thing."

Both Ken and Louise struggle to define the growing connection between them. There is the flicker of sexual attraction, particularly in Louise's flirtatious beginnings. That edge never entirely disappears, evidenced by Louise's embarrassment well into the tape when she realizes that she has casually addressed Ken as "hon." And, indeed, what names do we have for such a hybridized relationship—intimate yet remote, equal parts human and electronic? The distance is the result of the bar to bodily contact, nearness the result of an intensity of discourse, a zeroing in on the other's affective domain. After Louise shares her Lucky with Ken, he shows her the guitar that he has played in previous tapes. He has christened it "Louise" in her honor, adding: "It's like a lady—curves and stuff like that. It happens to be brown, but that's no reflection on you." Exchanged confidences are gifts bestowed, producing and eliciting confession. As per the psychoanalytic literature, unconscious material is transferred into verbal presentations and perceptions, repressed material is unleashed, preparing the way for "the possibility for a better kind of adjustment to reality."[48]

But there are more directly political considerations to be encountered alongside the therapeutic ones. In the context of Brecht's critique of radio (see note 44), video exchanges such as those of the "One on One" series constitute a kind of resistance to the commercial broadcast model, which offers a "mere sharing out" of entertainment. Brecht imagined the potential of radio as "the finest possible communication apparatus in public life," as "a vast network of pipes" if only it "knew how to receive as well as to transmit, how to let the listener speak as well as hear, how to bring him into a relationship instead of isolating him."[49] If it can be said of the series that transferential relations between insiders and outsiders are mutual and reciprocal, it can also be said that the clear-cut distinction between producer and consumer is obviated. While a claim of media empowerment can be made for other public art projects, such as "The Love Tapes," in which thousands of individuals from all walks of life have made tapes by themselves about themselves, here the gains are even greater. Here, in a precise miming of the Brechtian prescription, "the listener speak[s] as well as hear[s]," indeed, speaks only after listening, perhaps speaks even while hearing. This delicacy of listening is in fact enhanced by the mediated circumstances; there are no auxiliary sources of information for these interlocutors. The subjects of the video letter exchanges learn to listen with a special intensity, frequently replaying the tape just received several times before beginning their own reply. Theirs is a very special kind of speech, one that teaches listening.

These exchanges are also profoundly communitarian in their power to overcome the isolation of those incarcerated. How rarely do contemporary media forms work to build bridges across human differences rather than simply make spectacles of those differences? In this instance, the bridges built transcend their apparent limits in demonstrable ways. People who have never and will never meet enter into relations in which trust grows incrementally, in which vulnerabilities are increasingly shared, in which emotions attached to long-buried experiences are allowed to surface. In *Ricky and Cecilia*, a young Latino man serving a sixteen-month jail sentence on drug charges develops a video relationship with Cecilia, a fifty-one-year-old white woman. In his very first tape, Rickey speaks about the mix of feelings he has for his younger brother who is also serving time. He is sorry to have failed as a role model, regretful that their relationship has soured. In her next tape, Cecilia replies in kind:

> I was very close to my younger sister and we were very good friends when I was in my twenties and she was in her teens. Then she became mentally ill and later, when she was in her twenties—and it was related to the mental ill-

ness—she died. I lost her completely except in my memories and feelings. So maybe you have a fear that you'll lose your brother. But maybe you won't, maybe there's still hope for you two and you'll be able to connect up when you're both out of prison.

The young man is clearly moved by this disclosure; he returns to the topic of his estranged brother several times more during the remainder of their exchanges. Cecilia has struck a nerve. In "One on One," relationships of trust are built upon a foundation of reciprocal confession, freely given and exchanged. Confidences, painful memories, the willingness to allow the other to touch one's own place of vulnerability and vice versa become the basis for a connection between people who will never meet except on videotape.

The "One on One" dialogues are remarkable from another perspective as well. For if, as I have claimed, the confessions exchanged are freely given, they can be contrasted to another kind of self-disclosure well known to the incarcerated subjects. Confession plays an important role in criminology and the practice of law, as evidenced in such prime-time cop shows as *NYPD Blue*. Detective John Kelly's most outstanding police skill is his ability to induce confessions through recourse to an emotional reper- toire ranging from the quiescence of feigned sympathy to the near edge of violence. If Kelly can move from tough guy to father confessor so adroitly, it is because, in ushering the accused into those airless rooms, he shares with them a zone of liminality. In crimi- nological terms, confession is a threshold moment, marking the possibility of the crimi- nal's first step on his way back to society. "By confessing, he finds the first possibility of a return to the community after he had put himself, through his deed, outside its lim- its."[50] In that liminal zone, no emotion, no promise, no sign of remorse remains unthinkable. Kelly's weekly performances are staged both for the perpetrators and for an audience of millions. But there is a particular legacy—visual representation as an appara- tus of social control—that haunts this spectacle.

Photographically based representation has played a substantial historical role in the recent history of state power. As John Tagg writes in *The Burden of Representation*, photography began to function as a regulatory and disciplinary appara- tus in the aftermath of the failed rebellions of the late 1840s, just at the moment of the consolidation of power of the modern state.[51] Tagg traces a rendezvous between a "novel form of the state and a new and a developing technology of knowledge" in which pho- tography could contribute to the control of a large and dangerously diversified workforce newly arrived to the urban centers.

> Like the state, the camera is never neutral. The representations it produces are highly coded, and the power it wields is never its own. As a means of record, it arrives on the scene vested with a particular authority to arrest, picture and transform daily life, a power to see and record. . . . If, in the last decades of the nineteenth century, the squalid slum displaces the country seat and the

"abnormal" physiognomies of patient and prisoner displace the pedigreed features of the aristocracy, then their presence in representation is no longer a mark of celebration but a burden of subjection. A vast and repetitive archive of images is accumulated in which the smallest deviations may be noted, classified and filed. The format varies hardly at all. There are bodies and spaces. The bodies—workers, vagrants, criminals, patients, the insane, the poor, the colonized races—are taken one by one: isolated in a shallow, contained space; turned full face and subjected to an unreturnable gaze; illuminated, focused, measured, numbered and named; forced to yield to the minutest scrutiny of gestures and features. Each device is the trace of a wordless power, replicated in countless images, whenever the photographer prepares an exposure, in police cell, prison, mission house, hospital, asylum, or school.[52]

Like the confession, the mug shot plays a recurrent role in *NYPD Blue*. Eyewitnesses whose testimony will be needed to convict are frequently given pages of images—head shots that have been illuminated, focused, measured, numbered, and named—from which they are asked to choose and thus provide the crucial i.d. In "One on One," the incarcerated, while also "isolated in a shallow, contained space; turned full face," are not subjected to an unreturnable gaze. These prisoners, after all, have already been "subjected" in countless ways: removed from social contact and from their families and given clothing, living space, and food meant to reinforce a regimen of mind-numbing uniformity. Indeed, the experience of incarceration is calculated to strip the inmate of all the trappings of individuation through which subjecthood is achieved. But, in seizing the opportunity to return the media gaze, to speak as well as listen, these men are endowed with a measure of subjectivity denied the most privileged TV viewer tuned to the broadcast signal.

The "One on One" project attests to a power latent in the video medium, a power that has seldom been explored. It is a power that is political, psychological, and spiritual: a power to facilitate the reversal of repression at the level of (confessional) speech and of experience and in so doing forge bonds that are wholly media specific. Contrary to expectation, these media-specific relationships appear to engender effects (the visible signs of bolstered spirits, as well as audible testimony) that are bidirectional, experienced by both video partners. It is my contention that this new kind of relationship is a fundamentally therapeutic one rooted in confession, freely and mutually exchanged. In "One on One," the inmates' confessions—the uncoerced expressions of unspoken pain or pleasure—elude authority rather than wholly submit to it, as Foucault would have it. These unsanctioned utterances serve no institutional master.[53] While indeed judgment, consolation, even reconciliation may be sought from the interlocutor "outside," the dynamic of dominance and submission is everywhere reversible. If the ear of the other indeed contributes to the (re)construction of the speaking self, it is only on condition that the positions of self and other, confessor and confessant, remain fluid and reciprocal.

As I stated near the beginning of this essay, I have little interest in the ontological purity of my claims for video confessions. I have, following Foucault, been interested in tracing a skeletal history of confession and of the forces of repression that have produced in the Western subject a "regulated and polymorphous incitement to discourse." I have claimed that a new and particular variant of ritualized self-examination has arisen over the past two decades in the form of the first-person video confession, with video understood as a format uniquely suited to that purpose owing to its potential for privatized production and consumption. While pointing to a considerable body of recent work made by video artists that I have characterized as confessional, I have given special attention to two projects undertaken by Wendy Clarke, "The Love Tapes" and "One on One." In the tapes of these series, people of disparate background and life experience are given the opportunity to reveal hidden parts of themselves through direct address to a camera that they control. Video, as apparatus and potentiality, becomes in these works a facilitator to self-examination.

But this is confessional discourse produced neither for profit nor for temporary celebrity in the manner of commercial talk formats on radio or TV. Rather I have argued, most pointedly in reference to the "One on One" tapes, that video confessions produced and exchanged in nonhegemonic contexts can be powerful tools for self-understanding, as well as for two-way communication, for the forging of human bonds, and for emotional recovery. In contrast to the legacy of photographic representation as a regulatory and disciplinary apparatus, first-person video confessions of this sort afford a glimpse of a more utopian trajectory in which cultural production and consumption mingle and interact, and in which the media facilitate understanding across the gaps of human difference, rather than simply capitalize on those differences in a rush to spectacle.

NOTES

1 Cited in Jeremy Tambling, *Confession: Sexuality, Sin, the Subject* (Manchester: Manchester University Press, 1990), 37. Canon 21, "Omnis utriusque sexus," mandated annual confession for the faithful, to be fulfilled before the Easter communion. The place of private confession within church doctrine was the subject of much debate and revision throughout the medieval period.

2 Theodor Reik, *The Compulsion to Confess: On the Psychoanalysis of Crime and Punishment* (New York: Farrar, Straus, and Cudahy, 1945), 302. The book is composed of a series of lectures delivered at the Teaching Institute of the Vienna Psychoanalytic Association in 1924; its exhaustive treatment of the

subject received the endorsement of Freud himself. (In a letter to Reik, Freud termed the treatise "thoughtful and extremely important.") In Reik's analysis of it, confession emerges as a functionally complex psychoanalytic term. The inclination to confess is "a modified urge for the expression of the drives" that "are felt or recognized as forbidden" (194–95). Confession produces a "partial gratification" of the repressed thought or act, a kind of emotional relief. While Reik posits a masochistic component to confession (a "need for punishment"), he claims for it another seemingly contradictory function, "the unconscious urge to achieve the loss of love" (208). Reik goes on to analyze the compulsion to confess in its several manifestations: in the fields of criminology and criminal law, religion, myth, art and language, child psychology, and pedagogy.

3 Michel Foucault, "The Confession of the Flesh," in *Power/Knowledge: Selected Interviews and Other Writings, 1972–1977* (New York: Pantheon Books, 1980), 210.

4 Ibid., 211, 215–16.

5 Jeremy Tambling makes the case for a distinction between autobiography, which he takes to be a "self-fashioning," and confession, which, of necessity, submits itself to the judgment of a higher authority. Despite these differences, however, "the intertwining of the two forms seems important, ultimately, rather than the possibility of attempting to see them as opposites" (Tambling, *Confession*, 9).

6 Michel Foucault, *The History of Sexuality: Volume 1, An Introduction,* trans. Robert Hurley (New York: Vintage Books, 1978), 61-62.

7 Peter Dennis Bathory, *Political Theory as Public Confession: The Social and Political Thought of St. Augustine of Hippo* (New Brunswick, N.J.: Transaction Books, 1981), 21.

8 Sigmund Freud, "Transference," in *A General Introduction to Psychoanalysis*, trans. Joan Riviere (New York: Washington Square Press, 1966), 448. Freud notes that the transference can be either affectionate or hostile, can evince faith in the treatment or deep-seated resistance. This is because the analyst becomes an object invested with libido, a process that stands as an absolute requirement for successful treatment.

9 "Even we seekers after knowledge today, we godless anti-metaphysicians still take our fire, too, from the flame lit by a faith that is thousands of years old, that Christian faith which was also the faith of Plato, that God is the truth, that truth is divine.—But what if this should become more and more incredible, if nothing should prove to be divine any more unless it were error, blindness, the lie—if God himself should prove to be our most enduring lie?" (Friedrich Nietzsche, *The Gay Science,* trans. Walter Kaufman [New York: Vintage Books, 1974], 283). Lacanian subject construction positions the Other as the source of desire and of meaning. "What I seek in speech is the response of the other. What constitutes me as subject is my question. In order to be recognized by the other, I utter what was only in view of what will be. In order to find him, I call him by a name that he must assume or refuse in order to reply to me" (Jacques Lacan, *Ecrits: A Selection,* trans. Alan Sheridan [New York: Norton, 1977], 86). In Lacanian terms, confessional discourse is always addressed to the Other; it is the desiring letter that always arrives at its destination.

10 Foucault, *History of Sexuality,* 59.

11 Any analysis that constructs the subject's dependency on an external, all-knowing source as separable from the therapeutic effects that accrue from confession clearly misrecognizes the functional dynamic of the confessional act. A sense of unburdening can only occur if one endows the auditor with the power to grant absolution.

12 Peter Brown, *Augustine of Hippo* (Berkeley: University of California Press, 1967), 181.

13 Reik, *Compulsion to Confess,* 250. Philip Woollcett, writing in the *Journal for the Scientific Study of Religion*, concurred with Reik's assessment: "Augustine was the greatest psychologist of his time and probably for many centuries to come" (cited in Bathory, *Political Theory,* 55).

14 Reik, *Compulsion to Confess,* 192.

15 Bathory claims that Augustine developed "a mode of instruction through public confession" (17). He examines Augustine's "therapeutic method," in particular his use of anxiety as a positive rather than negative force. "Anxiety was a necessary part of people's lives, and he offers them the means to face it. In the process, anxiety took on a creative potential in that it could—if properly perceived—challenge people and lead not to paralysis but to an active search for self-realization" (38).

16 Foucault, *History of Sexuality,* 34.

17 William James, *The Varieties of Religious Experience: A Study in Human Nature* (New York: Collier Books, 1961), 360.

18 Norberto Valentini and Clara di Meglio, *Sex and the Confessional*, trans. Melton S. Davis (New York: Stein and Day, 1974), 12, 211.

19 Raymond Williams, *Marxism and Literature* (Oxford: Oxford University Press, 1977), 121–27.

20 Mimi White, *Tele-Advising: Therapeutic Discourse in American Television* (Chapel Hill, N.C.: University of North Carolina Press, 1992), 81, 178.

21 Ibid., 19.

22 "The actual commodity, then, is the ultimate referent of the television discourse" (Nick Browne, "The Political Economy of the Television (Super)Text," *Quarterly Review of Film Studies* 9, no. 3 [Summer 1984]: 181).

23 "The compulsive factor eventually found its representation and objectification in the obligation to confess," says Reik in *The Compulsion to Confess* (300). Mandatory monthly confession after the Council of Trent finds its therapeutic counterpart in the obligatory scheduling of analytic sessions.

24 White, *Tele-Advising,* 179. The confessional display can also become the basis for the viewer's own repetition compulsion, as a number of television audience studies have shown.

25 Ibid., 182.

26 Quoted in G. Roy Levin, *Documentary Explorations: Fifteen Interviews with Film-makers* (Garden City, N.Y.: Doubleday, 1971), 137.

27 Michael Renov, "The Distrust of the Visible: Documentary's Psychoanalytic Encounter," paper presented at "Visible Evidence: Strategies and Practices in Documentary Film and Video," Duke University, September 1993. Technoanalysis refers to the displacement of the analyst by the apparatus itself, resulting in a kind of do-it-yourself psychotherapy. The technology becomes both a site of and a relay point for transference.

28 Jean Rouch, quoted in Mick Eaton, "The Production of Cinematic Reality," in *Anthropology—Reality—Cinema: The Films of Jean Rouch,* ed. Mick Eaton (London: BFI, 1979), 51.

29 Spoken by Mekas as narration over images in *Lost, Lost, Lost.* For further discussion of this remarkable film, see my "*Lost, Lost, Lost:* Mekas as Essayist," in *To Free the Cinema: Jonas Mekas and the New York Underground*, ed. David E. James (Princeton, N.J.: Princeton University Press, 1992), 215–39.

30 David E. James has written with great insight on the alternative cinemas that emerged in the United States during the 1960s in opposition to the hegemonic or industrial cinema. At issue is a notion of the "mode of cultural production" inspired by Max Horkheimer and Theodor Adorno but considerably qualified by, among other factors, the many "renegade uses" at the point of consumption (David E. James, *Allegories of Cinema: American Film in the Sixties* [Princeton, N.J.: Princeton University Press, 1989], 3–28).

31 Perhaps, rather than pointing to the limits of electronic "handcrafting," it would be more accurate to suggest that the artisanal potential for video culture is simply unlike the cinema's, which is organized around tactility (the "feel" of celluloid). The first and legendary video art events of the early 1960s, Nam June Paik's and Wolf Vostell's, were installations in which the televisual hardware was stripped of its techno-use value, then reworked "by hand" to suit the artist's vision. Banks of TV sets became the plastic medium. Video art thus began as a kind of artisanal reflex to the very technology that rendered it possible.

32 Long after I had begun to research this essay, which I planned to call "The Electronic Confessional," I chanced upon a book of the same name authored by a husband and wife team of writers specializing in sexology (Howard R. and Martha E. Lewis, *The Electronic Confessional: A Sex Book of the 80's* [New York: Evans, 1986]). The Lewises had, it seems, developed a computer service called Human Sexuality (HSX for short), a "videotex" service offering "discussion, information and advice on a wide variety of issues related to sex." The book offers an introduction to the system and its uses for the uninitiated while devoting itself primarily to the reproduction of a selection of HSX queries, entries, and exchanges. One example may serve to illustrate the tone of the book: a married man confesses to a predilection for masturbating while wearing diapers into which he has previously urinated. "My wife and I have 'normal' sex, but I need more sexual release than she does. So I turn to the diaper"(88). Through the services of HSX, the man is informed of a group called the Diaper Pail Fraternity out of Sausalito, California (with a membership of fifteen hundred), with whom he may presumably choose to find fellowship. The book certainly suggested whole new frontiers of confessional discourse for the 1990s. It also convinced me to find another title for this chapter.

33 "The emphasis here is on the replication of the historical real, the creation of a second-order reality cut to the measure of our desire—to cheat death, stop time, restore loss" (Michael Renov, "Toward a Poetics of Documentary," in *Theorizing Documentary,* ed. Michael Renov [New York: Routledge, 1993], 25).

34 Indeed the wedding video must delegate the first-person function to the roving or multiple eye of the professional. For a thorough treatment of this video phenomenon, see James Moran's chapter 23 essay, in this book.

35 Of course, all confession is spoken in the "first person." The distinction I wish to make is between confession that is produced through the intervention of another party who controls enunciation and that discourse that is self-activated, subject only to one's own editorial agency.

36 *The interactive mode* is the useful term adopted by Bill Nichols to describe the third of four documentary modes of representation in his *Representing Reality* (Bloomington: Indiana University Press, 1991), 32-75. In comparison with the expository mode, in which arguments are rhetorically developed, frequently via voice-over narration, or the observational mode, which opts for the noninterventionism of American direct cinema, films of the interactive type "stress images of testimony or verbal exchange and images of demonstration. . . . Textual authority shifts toward the social actors recruited. . . . The shift of emphasis [is] from an author-centered voice of authority to a witness-centered voice of testimony" (44, 48).

37 Reik, *Compulsion to Confess,* 210–11.

38 Over a period of many months in the early 1970s, *Carel and Ferd* remained a staple feature at the Video Free America exhibition site in the warehouse district of San Francisco. Local audiences were able to develop a long-term relationship with the unfolding melodrama in the manner of mainstream soaps.

39 Foucault, *History of Sexuality,* 61-62.

40 Hershman's statement is deliciously paradoxical, since she knows her discourse to be a public one, albeit an excruciatingly *private* public discourse.

41 Here I refer to Reik's analysis of the confessional impulse in which he notes that confession "grants a partial gratification to the repressed wishes and impulses" while also fulfilling the need for punishment. "Actually, we often see symptoms disappear in analysis when needs of this kind, at odds with each other, have found a completely adequate expression in confession" (204).

42 Is it only coincidental that the edifice in which "Love Tapes" are made is architecturally congruent with the increasingly obsolescent church confessional? The design of each, suited to the containment of a single confessing body, nevertheless provides windowed access to another space that underwrites and authorizes it.

43 I borrow the notion of the mana-word from Roland Barthes: "In an author's lexicon, will there not always be a word-as-mana, a word whose ardent, complex, ineffable, and somehow sacred signification gives the illusion that by this word one might answer for everything? Such a word is neither eccentric nor central; it is motionless and carried, floating, never *pigeonholed*, always atopic (escaping any topic), at once remainder and supplement, a signifier taking up the place of every signified." For Barthes, that word is *body* (Roland Barthes, *Roland Barthes by Roland Barthes,* trans. Richard Howard [New York: Hill and Wang, 1977], 129).

44 In "The Radio as an Apparatus of Communication," written in 1932, Bertolt Brecht critiqued radio for the singularity of its purpose: as a profit-motivated vehicle for delivering entertainment rather than as a medium of two-way exchange. "But quite apart from the dubiousness of its functions, radio is one-sided when it should be two-. It is purely an apparatus for distribution, for mere sharing out. So here is a positive suggestion: change this apparatus over from distribution to communication. . . . The slightest advance in this direction is bound to succeed far more spectacularly than any performance of a culinary kind. As for the technique that needs to be developed for all such operations, it must follow the prime objective of turning the audience not only into pupils but into teachers" (Bertolt Brecht, "The Radio as an Apparatus of Communication," in *Video Culture*, ed. John Hanhardt [Rochester, N.Y.: Visual Studies Workshop Press, 1986], 53-54).

45 Questions of various sorts arise when the tapes of the "One on One" series are exhibited or broadcast. Is there a pact of sorts between the two interlocutors, which the introduction of an audience external to the exchange necessarily breaches? Only recently, three years after the project's completion, as the tapes have begun to be shown in classrooms, at public screenings, and soon on the Los Angeles PBS affiliate, KCET, has public exhibition become an issue. In my own experience of talking about this work and screening it in classes and public venues, I have found that audiences tend to be uneasy with their perceived positioning as voyeurs of exchanged confidences. The fact that the very concept of the "One on One" series was conceived in collaboration with the video workshop participants, all of whom signed releases authorizing future screenings of the work, seems not to dispel the uneasiness. This response is likely connected to a historical tendency in the West in which public forms of confession have been displaced by forms of self-disclosure that are private and protected (such as the "privileged communications" between

MICHAEL RENOV

ourselves and our doctors, lawyers, and priests). The public display of exchanged confessions—when received as "real" rather than fictional and predicated on a one-to-one, reciprocal exchange—strikes some audiences as a violation of principle. It seems to me, however, that the project's fundamental value has always been as a kind of heuristic device, a model for interpersonal communication in a media age. From one point of view, the particulars of any confession are less meaningful than the potentiality of the project as a whole for the creation of human dialogue across a whole series of spatial and cultural disjunctures.

46 Wendy Clarke, cited in Howard Rosenberg, "'One on One' Is the Best TV Talk You Can't See," *Los Angeles Times,* 8 December 1993, F8.

47 Ibid.

48 Reik, *Compulsion to Confess,* 205.

49 Brecht, "Radio," 53.

50 Reik, *Compulsion to Confess,* 79.

51 John Tagg, *The Burden of Representation* (Amherst: University of Massachusetts Press, 1988), 60-61.

52 Ibid., 63-64.

53 In fact, while the "One on One" tapes were made in conjunction with Clarke's video workshop at Chino and were thus institutionally "legitimate," prison officials had no idea about the particulars of the project. Proposals for future projects of this sort would, in Clarke's opinion, face little chance of acceptance. Personal communication with Wendy Clarke, 19 January 1994.

CHAPTER 8

THE ELECTRONIC CORPSE:
NOTES FOR AN ALTERNATIVE LANGUAGE OF HISTORY AND AMNESIA

Erika Suderburg

A traveler once wrote, in our dreams of future cities, what frightens us is what we most desire, namely to be free from the tyranny of memory . . . to be sufficient without a sense of past or future. . . .

Imagine a city where the past is past and the time is always now. The very thought of memory being lost is as much a cause for alarm, as a memory being allowed to disrupt the city's daily life. In our city, in which dreams are living in a permanent present but dare not let go of its past, freedom is advertised as freedom from history, its promises, its temptations and its demands.

~ MARC KARLIN *For Memory*

She made him feel that history was not progressive but circular, a pocket flashlight examining relentlessly the same three feet of ground.

~ BLANCHE MCCRARY BOYD, *Mourning the Death of Magic*

THE RUMOR OF HISTORY'S DEATH IS GREATLY EXAGGERATED

Video, both the material hardware and its distribution network outside broadcast television, had an odd birth. Its awkward arrival continues to haunt its identity as a media arts practice. The aura of liberatory promise still clings to video art's historical trajectory. Video, the legend goes, promised grassroots television networks, a wired global village, Marshall McLuhan as pop star, the eventual co-opting of the networks by fringe elements, the education of all television's children, and the means of production delivered to the hands of the disenfranchised. Portions of the fable were implemented and over the next twenty years mutated, died, or were reborn in newly minted form. Within the myopic art world, video's "promise" was partially realized in the 1970s as conceptual artists, sculptors, and performance poets committed to a devaluation of the commodity side of the art object. They embraced video as a medium that could surely be neither bought nor sold. The circumnavigation of the gallery system was seen as a necessary step away from the production of redundant art baubles and into the realm of art about ideas.

Today video art is comfortably marginalized: within the international art museum, as pricey installation works, or in a dwindling number of crippled (read "reeling" after the NEA wars) alternative spaces. It also makes brief appearances on MTV and U.S. public television and is bounced around on grassroots satellite (Deep Dish TV Satellite Network). It is passed from one private VCR to another or gets folded back into and co-opted by a hungry film industry. Video art is produced cheaply with camcorders, but it is also manufactured lavishly in Hollywood production houses. It appropriates and is appropriated. It lives in the margins and simultaneously occupies the center. It has been codified as a component of image-making, integral as computer input device, absolutely necessary to visual literacy for the new generation of positivist cyborgs. However, it remains linked to its initial material form to such an extent that in most theoretical discussions of video as an entity, conceptual concerns are conveniently overlooked. It appears more seductive to speak of video as a stream of patterned electrons than to move beyond that limited discussion of medium specificity.

The vortex of clichés orbiting the word *video* is myriad. It is ugly, it is cheap (a type of degraded film for ingrates impatient with the craft of filmmaking). The tracing of the raster scan will hypnotize you. It is the medium of the thirty-second spot. Its only righteous subject matter is Television, its practitioners devout children of the box. The flip side of this litany clings to identifications of video's permanent malleability, what Sean Cubitt calls "timeshifting," which makes video a revolutionary tool, as we throw off our couch potato passivity and reorganize received information ad infinitum to create our own programming.[1] This fascination with video's "difference" contributes to its categorization as either fundamentally blank or so compactly layered that it can serve to illustrate everything. The reorganization of received televisual flow into new works of "appropriation" accepts all electronic material. The digital sample running through myriad art computers can potentially access any image by creating a layering or core sample derived from sources that could never be traced to a specific origin. Video work, the legend continues, becomes the ultimate postmodern demonstration model, bounding off into the ahistorical free flow without a past.

Fredric Jameson busily charts the disappearance of the autonomous original work of art, along with its supervising ego and subject, ascribing to video a singular and damning burden. He casts it as "the only art or medium in which the ultimate seam between space and time is the very locus of the form. . . . [I]ts machinery uniquely dominates and depersonalizes subject and object alike, transforming the former into a quasi-material registering apparatus for the machine time of the latter and of the video image or 'total flow.'"[2] Prior to this intriguing compartmentalization, video is posited by Jameson to be incapable of haunting, or evoking memory:

THE ELECTRONIC CORPSE

Indeed, if anything like critical distance is still possible in film, it is surely bound up with memory itself. But memory seems to play no role in television, commercial or otherwise (or, I am tempted to say, in postmodernism generally): nothing here haunts the mind or leaves its afterimages in the manner of the great moments of film (which do not necessarily happen, of course, in the "great" films). A description of the structural exclusion of memory, then, and of critical distance, might well lead on into the impossible, namely a theory of video itself—how the thing blocks its own theorization, becoming a theory in its own right.[3]

Is video's terrible burden then to have been born without the subject and after history? Immune to memory, dispensing floating signifiers to the terminally absented? Is it only allegedly chained to the content of television, while secretly lusting after the seductive power of film's modernist scale and its immersion in the classical master narrative?

Sean Cubitt dismisses Jameson's deadly video stigmata by taking an earlier version of his argument, "La Lecture sans l'interpretation," to task. He summarizes the argument by saying, "Jameson, patronizingly, comments that 'the most profound content (of experimental video) can be described as being that of Ennui: the culture of boredom, which is almost unavoidable as the conclusion of the hyperreal, is ascribed to all video art. It is not the least original aspect of video to have abolished the most traditional and oldest category of the "work."'" Cubitt counters that "had he investigated the lines back from video into performance art, this wild over-generalization might have been avoided."[4]

Jameson writes: "One would like to defend the proposition that the most profound 'subject' of all video art, and even of all postmodernism, is very precisely the reproductive technology itself." Cubitt counters by saying, "This last statement, itself remarkably close to Greenbergian modernism, is mercifully covered by the realization that 'if all video texts designated simply the process of production/ reproduction, then they would all have to own up to being "the same" in a particularly sterile manner,' yet there it is, the unmistakable finale of his own object."[5]

One ends with yet another realization of the paucity of material that addresses the content of video work rather than "mediumistic essences" or technological determinants. Is film doomed to speak only about the Industrial Revolution, video about the electronic one? Silent film is not spoken about solely in terms of the apparatus used to construct it and the floated silver particles used to fix its image. Why then, for the sake of argument, is video wedded to its charged electrons? What happens during all this uninterrupted "flow?" How does the artist choose to insert his or her own meager history into this purported void of electronic "ennui"? The employment of the term *video* seems to incessantly hinge, as Cubitt states, on "what video is, far more than on what it does." [6] If works were made beyond the catchy postmodernist proscription, what form might the subject of history take? Would the recall involve the image of recounted history, or an amnesiac's painful and inventive reconstruction of that image and its rep-

ERIKA SUDERBURG

resentation? Perhaps the declared demise of haunting within this electronic freeflow is premature?

The language used to castigate video as a convenient measure of cultural fracturing, as the ultimate postmodern referent, or as antiliterary bastard is no doubt similar to warnings of the dangers of the steam engine, the model T, rock and roll, virtual reality, a national health plan, the video phone, irradiated food, and satellite uplinks. The cycle of fear interwoven with acceptance of projected futurist impulses is a modality that is a cultural given, which we pass through with increasing swiftness before careening on. Sitting in our electronic city, we will plug ourselves in, in ever more convoluted and technologically remote ways. Whether we want to or not, we will embrace the cyborg as part of our existence, a necessity of survival. We will trust, fear, and lust after various microchip configurations and devise strategies to keep our historical inscriptions alive in the fiber-optic matrix. What might these traces look like?

Situated topographically as I am, in Hollywood, surrounded by people who buoyantly narrate the next technological revolution (D1, D2, morphing suites, and nonlinear editing), the fixity of the term *video* seems wildly illusionary. The once blasphemous suggestion that film and video technologies are merging, to the extent that they will be virtually indecipherable, leaves the examination of medium specificity behind. Delivery systems that accommodate each new mutation of the market collapse as quickly as Hollywood studio CEOs. It may come down to the difference between a small human head in a one-to-one ratio with a self-regulated screen, or several hundred heads dwarfed by a bigger screen. Video is after all just a bit of magnetic tape, a floppy disc, or an encoded CD-ROM. The question at hand is how specific works of video interrogate, cajole, and illuminate the representation of history, despite predictions otherwise, choosing to address the representation of memory and eulogy, history and forgetting, within these boundaried electronic fields. The methodology employed to foreground these choices and the representational choices themselves present an intriguing inquiry.

BUYING A SATELLITE

Contemporary artists working in video continue to fabricate evolving image "grammars." These grammars are located at the intersection of the poetic and the documentary: dialectical inferences, built upon the visual "retelling" or recalling of the historical moment, divorced from the traditional modes of documentary and narrative. A hybrid has developed that works the shifting borders between documentary, first-person "diary films"; traditional narrative; home video; and television reportage, and that specifically seeks to inform the questioning of historical representation. Video in this milieu has often been construed as an "intimate" vehicle whose delivery system is conducive to processing or "learning" history, "on site," within the home, through constant reprogramming and appropriation of received television input. The logical next step is to treat the broadcast apparatus as infinitely mutable, a platform for the reconstitution of alternative histories.

Alexander Kluge, filmmaker, lawyer, producer, and writer, presents a model of interventionist media designed to suggest the viability and necessity of philosophically alternative histories, tied neither to rhetoric-filled calls to arms nor to wispy meditations on society. Kluge speaks to the migration of cinema into television, working within that transfer by forming a consortium to buy satellite time for his *Hour of the Filmmakers*, or *Ten To Eleven*, a weekly time slot on private TV. Intimately involved with earlier reforms of state television and committed to the Oberhausen Manifesto's insistence on German State Television's responsibility to support and broadcast new German film, Kluge's commitment to independent coproduction specifically locates the "public sphere" as an identified point of friction between intimate and public language.[7] This "public sphere" is constituted in several different ways: as a topographical social site where meaning is located and exchanged, as the specific conceptual projects of media makers within this site, and more broadly as the "general horizon of social experience."[8] Kluge's project involves the search for a site where art can be interjected into the public sphere and for a redefinition of art's existence within society as a whole: "Against such a power to convince millions through television, all conventional means are powerless. That means that I also have to produce for this window. I can only influence a mass medium through a counter-mass medium. An entire public sphere through a counter-public sphere. I cannot counter a society through a counter-society. That is war. One has, therefore, to seek a way out."[9] Kluge's escape hatch is a collection of video sketches designed for *Ten To Eleven*.

Kluge manufactures this "new media" with specific modalities that remain the cornerstone of all his video production: constant recycling of historical referents cut loose from their traditional moorings and outfitted with new contexts designed to examine the previous one. "The challenges of the New Media, the ecological threat to the structures of consciousness, require nothing less than a return to the origins of all the products of the public sphere. The components of this capital, dating back to 1802 (and for the most part, earlier), must be updated, revitalized. As for the moving images of the cinema, the journey only goes back to Lumière and Melies, once again to the origins. In each of these origins, 'cousins' and other relatives of what actually developed can be found, and these can be adapted for the New Media in very interesting ways."[10] In *Why Are You Crying, Antonio?* (1988) Kluge constructs a sort of madman's TV program. A genteel, bland female talking head pleasantly counts off "Film 1, 2 3, . . . " while Kluge turns the video screen into a type of shadow-puppet theater, whose locus is a recurring still of a mammoth unpopulated movie palace. Its screen is animated with flickering images that range from silent features to *Heimatfilme*, from natural disaster footage to newsreels of Chamberlain and Mussolini.[11] Woven throughout is a narrative revolving around a crucial 1938 meeting between Lord Chamberlain, Hitler, and Mussolini at Dreesen. They are poised to begin diplomatic cohabitation while attending a performance of Verdi's *MacBeth*. Opera becomes the common ground for diplomacy, a site of spectacle not unlike Kluge's chosen transformation of the TV box into silent movie palace. Chamberlain and Mussolini are likened to opera characters involved in

ERIKA SUDERBURG

fatal intrigues. This particular intrigue, however, results in the invasion of Czechoslovakia. Intercut into this diplomatic attempt is the love story of a Nazi officer and his wife, their first visit to Rome in 1939, and his subsequent posting to the front. The story is played out in one room, mutely, in perfect television docudrama style, in sharp contrast to the cut-and-paste video effects grafted onto the historical footage of the Dreesen meeting. The linkages between these unnamed characters and their historical compatriots are forged in Kluge's underscoring of the minutiae of daily life.

In still photographs frozen on the screen, the negotiation room is marked with arrows indicating where each man sat. Pictures of Chamberlain and Mussolini are annotated by colorized spotlighting of their hats and umbrellas. Linkages happen because of the absurdity of their shared objects, not their invasion plans. The site, Dreesen, becomes the historical marker. The players are mute and frozen: Chamberlain and Hitler by means of still photography, the young couple through the excising of spoken language. The intertitle, "A Love Story's Relationship to Hitler," which introduces the segment on the officer and his wife, suggests the personal minutiae under the elaborate obsessiveness of historical documentation. The ironic gesture for Kluge is the denial of the "real" story, the historical narrative devoid of interpretation. Elements, divorced from a coherent recap of historical "fact," coexist, frame by frame, and are linked through sleights of hand, coincidence, and the sheer pleasurable violence resulting from montage. The live action ruins of a tearoom, contemporaneously situated on the site of the negotiation hotel, are intercut with a man attempting to tune in a live broadcast of Verdi's *MacBeth* on a period radio.

Kluge then segues into a child's cautionary tale about Isabella and the umbrella performed in paper cutouts. In the narrative Isabella is saved from falling into trouble because her mother saw it coming. Isabella is linked to Chamberlain through the graphic notations pointing to Chamberlain's umbrella, Hitler's armchair, Mussolini's dagger. The connective tissue of the work is spun of the utilitarian objects, the artifacts of history, not the narrative itself. We assume knowledge of how the negotiations turned out with England's entry into World War II. Kluge, however, negates this summary information and chooses to end the tape with fanciful paper cutouts of horse-drawn carts and soldiers from around 1918, traversing the landscape, inside the magic TV box, celebrating the end of World War I. History's closure is denied, and what remains are its odd objects held in common, moving in cycles of perceived repetition. Margaret Morse, writing about Kluge's process, states that "Kluge shows us myths half-emptied, almost in graphic outline, so that we can fill them with our own reflections. The connections we make between segments and programs mirror our compulsion to manufacture and endlessly repeat 'archaic hopes of a happy end, the end of the war and/or unrequited love. . . . [I]s the end rather the repetition of a voyage to another world, from which the white sailor imagines arriving safely home, unscathed but with a story to tell?'" [12] Is it more important to sink into this story, to map the voyage, or to visualize the engine below deck and analyze its source of power?

In *Why Are You Crying Antonio?*, Kluge interrogates the residue of history, the jerky newsreels and still documentary photographs, and expects that a certain familiarity with their components will lead to a secondary insertion of the audience inside the previously alien and blind historical continuum. He brings Mussolini's image up on screen. It is graphically annotated by an explanation of the Italian Fascist dagger salute. The arrow pointing at the photograph is labeled "Murder Weapons of the Renaissance," adding otherwise secondary information to a photograph of Mussolini inspecting a rack of spears. The act of recollection, minutes after the piece is finished, is difficult, almost absent. But the structure of being in the work itself seems to be about the act of visual recollection, requiring the audience to float within a field of historical signifiers that are not necessarily meant to add up in terms of narrative lessons.

Kluge's gesture of collected remnants points instead to the machinations of interpretation and the privileging of moments, dates, monuments, and figureheads that level the mundane with the historically privileged; hence Kluge's interpolation of the "Love Story" segment with the ongoing fragmented views of the Chamberlain-Mussolini talks. Video in Kluge's hands serves as a type of electronic recorder dream machine. He uses the video screen as an animated coloring book; dirigibles float above London, the lights below magically extinguish themselves for an air raid. Trenches are manned as World War II is fought on the tiny screen of a monstrous movie palace in lurid hand-tinted color. We can see Kluge's hand at play in the video switcher and synthesizer, adding a color here, a label there. Video literally becomes a writing pad, a place in which to scribble over historical representation.

All these "effects" are primitive, slapdash, and vastly overshadowed by contemporary standards of computer imaging and animation techniques. It is as if Kluge relished the idea of reinventing a medium from the ground up, searching for the video equivalent to the nascent aesthetic of silent film by utilizing the immediate in-studio gratification of the effects switcher. The minimal level of in-studio video effects employed by Kluge is comparable to the hand-tinting of photographs before the advent of color film. Kluge revels in the base technology, painting onto the video through electronic manipulation. For Kluge, silent film engenders silent video, as textual information is delivered solely through inner titles or an ambient sound track that suggests that the audience is actually in a room with the radio on circa 1935. He refuses our historical seduction by organizing samples of the master narrative we have grown accustomed to but are too intimidated to challenge or speculate about. Kluge acts as assistant interrogator, chiding us into confrontation with these familiar images while providing an entrée into memory itself. Miriam Hanson, writing in depth about Kluge's employment of early cinema, suggests that the range of temporality available to early cinema simply cannot be extracted from television. She posits that television is limited by the uninterrupted electronic signal and the economics of programming. However, she identifies Kluge's recycling of film history within his video work as "an attempt to endow that medium [television] with a different temporal dimension through a strategic overlapping of institutions."[13] Kluge's insertion of historical referent scraps becomes a thorny interruption in television's "flow"—a breaking into and reformulation of this public sphere.

If we subscribe to this notion of early cinema "lending" video a memory (therefore supplanting its supposed innate amnesia) and add, or counter with, a sample of video's early "pioneers," say Wolf Vostell and Nam June Paik, it will be clear that video's lineage speaks more to music concrete, Fluxus, Happenings, the Sony corporation, and Karl Heinz Stockhausen's multimedia performative event spectacles than to film history.[14] Video's past is a complicated one, not only linked to a "TV generation," but also to a European film avant-garde in uneasy concord with two 1960s performance modes—one located in electronic music and the other in the visual arts. In contrast, it is interesting to note the institutional framework of alternative television production that Kluge and Jean-Luc Godard both choose to explore, aided of course by their cachet as European celebrity filmmakers. Godard experimented in 1977-78 with an early version of Sonimage—a project designed to train videomakers in Mozambique through the establishment of village TV production centers, a strategy pioneered by many U.S. grassroots video collectives in the 1960s and 1970s.[15]

HARD HOME MOVIES

We were still looking for the path to our language. It was still the time of daily massacres in Beirut. It was already the time of glorious space flights to Mars and Venus. It was the time of private television's triumph and of the dollar's incredible rise. The time when trees were buried in the Black Forest and McEnroe was first defeated. The time of the fifth generation computer and the famine in Africa. More than ever it was the time when all the waters of the sea could not wash away the stain of intellectual blood. It was also the time of the penultimate analysis session. And of the last picture show. In fact we weren't really looking any more for the path to our own language because we were talking less and more softly. We weren't short of subjects for conversation. Or rather yes we were. What we weren't short of were objects. Masses of objects, each with its own name. Masses and masses of names. But the subjects real or false had disagreed. ~ INTRODUCTION TO JEAN-LUC GODARD AND ANNE-MARIE MIEVILLE'S *Soft and Hard*

Godard's choice of video serves several functions for him. *Scenario du film passion* (1982) is a deliberate postproduction video analytic sketch pad for the film *Passion* (1981). *France/tour/detour/deux enfants* (1978) is an extraordinary portrait of the society of the child in the realm of the "monsters" (adults). *Sur et sous la communication (Six fois deux)* (1976) is a prototype of what Godardian TV might look like as a type of media deconstruction hour. *Allemagne neuf zero* (1990), which revives Lemmy Caution, the noirish detective character from the film *Alphaville* (1965), sends Caution on a journey from fallen East Germany into recovering West Germany. His mission: no longer to uncover the evil overlords of a modernist sci-fi future, but to pick up the stray signals of German history and piece them together. These video forays share a reliance on the macro-investigation, performed either by Godard's stand-ins, the newscasters of *France/tour/detour*, or detective Lemmy Caution, or by an onscreen Godardian persona. This presence is epitomized by Godard's off-camera query to Camille in *France/tour/ detour/deux enfants* when he asks her why she doesn't pay her mother for taking care of her, or by the interjection of handwritten notes inscribed directly on the screen in *Six fois deux*.

Colin McCabe locates Jean-Luc Godard and Anne-Marie Mieville's *France/tour/detour/deux enfants* in this space between the image and the self: "To participate in the established forms, be they political or televisual, is to lose what is specific to your experience and situation, to communicate easily at the cost of communicating nothing."[16] Video in Godard's universe affords a stretching out of that space between self and representation of self, film and its extended notepad—video. It is the site for Godard where conversation is revived and language is given breathing space. During this extrapolated video focus, the Godardian eye is split between video monitor or trace signal and witness-interpreter. The screen in *Six fois deux* is constantly inscribed with handwritten script. In *Soft and Hard*, the onscreen Godard slips away from conversation with the house's other occupant, Anne Marie Mieville, to his workroom to scan the channels, while she slips away to her editing table. The cottage industry of image processing that marks their relationship to one another affords them the home laboratory in which to reveal and examine their collected representations.

On live local minicam during the Los Angeles rebellion of 1992, an African American women is stopped at an intersection. A microphone is shoved in her face through the open car window. She is asked, in the feeding frenzy of news gathering, simply "Why?," becoming for an instant a representative of the media's desire to provide instant bite summary. She answers, "We got your attention now, didn't we?" She has briefly located herself within the broadcast flow, as it momentarily collapses, attempting to contain the uncontainable and parcel it out in consumable news bites. Her image ran only once, live, never to appear as taped minicam humanism. But the apocalyptically "sexier" images of burning palm trees and K-Mart looting would be replayed over and over on the local hourly recap and in national broadcasts for the next four days. Perhaps it was too clear a message. In a sense, her brief moment of historical imprint exists solely now in memory, becoming a representation that is normally excised and only admitted in times of chaos.

In Mieville and Godard's *Soft and Hard (Soft Talk on a Hard Subject between Two Friends)* (1985) the question is also one of interrupting the flow, in this case with an eye to how one's personal image history is formed in the crosstalk between film history, the domestic refuge, televisual flow, the charting of a current historical news story, or the breakdown of these units in recollection. Mieville and Godard have the enormous advantage of a controlled authorship that the anonymous Los Angeles car woman does not. But, in a sense, they both move outside the control of their image: one through analysis and investigation, the other through on-the-spot indictment. *Soft and Hard* examines the collecting and categorization of these moments. Essentially a home

ERIKA SUDERBURG

movie of Godard and Mieville ensconced in the domestic, *Soft and Hard* persists in interrupting its own conversation, its "hard talk between two friends," with landscape, TV news, classic film stills, walks, and ironing— the topography of the modern home. This "hard talk" asks the question "Where has it all gone?"—or, where are these "masses of objects" laid to rest in a continuum that can include African famine *and* Lillian Gish? These two friends settle down to decipher the question by examining their own desire to make images. They do this by investigating the details of their formation via previous filmmakers' images, which are present as stills throughout the tape. It is a meditation that resonates through the piece as a kind of nostalgic chamber music, evocative of time lost, but occupied with the need to continue.

The tape begins with Mieville arranging flowers, then writing at a desk, Godard on the phone needling a producer about money for *King Lear*, Mieville at a film editing table, Godard's voice offscreen asking her questions, and then Godard at his VCR, popping in tapes of a soccer match. This is the home routine of normally shielded, moderately famous people. Godard cast himself as a tennis player bouncing around and batting toward an imaginary opponent. As Mieville enters the screen carrying clean linen, they run into each other and shake hands as if ending the game. The domestic order of performance and routine is perpetually infiltrated by the history of cinema. Film stills stand in for family snapshots. They are the only insertion that interrupts the domestic document, penetrating the dialogue between the two that forms the major portion of the tape. The markers of time for the two, in fact how they relate to one another, are signaled by and channeled through these film remnants. With Godard seated on a couch facing the camera, his back toward the viewer, the central dialogue unfolds. Mieville explains her entry into image fabrication by telling a story about projecting family negatives, with the help of a shoe box, onto the wall. Godard is interested by her early entrée into this world and contrasts this to his relatively late cinephile baptism at age twenty at the hands of Henri Langlois. These tales are recounted as the beginnings of consciousness, the definition of self, the start of a shared history, the attraction of two people for one another. The frozen film frames, which occasionally fade into the video image, obliterate the two sitting on their respective couches. Moving in and out of the domestic space, the film stills pierce this bubble of conversation that literally takes place on twin couches where the roles of analyst and analysand merge. The stills serve to ground the intimate regard that both Mieville and Godard invest in these histories of images. The selected frames are images of dramatic engagement and martyrdom: Lillian Gish stranded, take after take, on the ice floe for D. W. Griffith, Ingrid Bergman as Joan of Arc during her ostracism from Hollywood, and Jimmy Stewart worriedly hoisting a ridiculously long lens in *Rear Window*.

Godard likens their conversation to a "last analysis session." This particular appointment between the two asks fundamental questions about their choice to continue to produce images and their "respect" for the cinema. In a sense the tape is about that respect and the cultivation of history through cinema. Godard is interested in video because he can control all the technical aspects of it simultaneously: shooting, lab work, and playback exist in one unit. The whole production unit can inhabit his living room permanently, a studio in a box. Their discussion then circles around the erasure of memory via television. Ironically television in this environment serves as one of the last remaining historical containers, as it runs docudrama purportedly based on historical fact while simultaneously editing which current events will filter through to a captive receivership and which will fall into the margins. Godard says he likes TV because "it doesn't show things." He can become lost in its free-flow fall and interrupt the flow with a battery of his own images. Mieville's slightly addled retort is that "television makes you think that it never shows things, but it never stops showing things and that is what showing things is." Their contribution to the flow is under scrutiny as they feed their living-room intimacy back into video. It is indeed a "Hard Talk between Friends" who are speaking of a loss of virginity, their version of a private history reconstituted from their first memories of moving images. It is a tape that asks, "What makes up the past?" *Soft and Hard* ends with the shadows of Godard's and Mieville's hands covering a white living-room wall, which cuts to the segment from *Le Mepris* (Contempt; 1963) where the camera stalks Brigitte Bardot in an extended dolly shot and then abruptly swings toward the spectator, crane and camera encroaching on our dark safety. *Soft and Hard* further punctures that third wall by pulling back to reveal the TV box tuned to electronic snow, a new facsimile of Freud's mystic writing tablet waiting for its next inscription.

THE PLACE OF EULOGY

Kluge and Godard are as far removed from the art world locus of "video art" as they could possibly be; video for both of them is an intriguing, occasional, and new media alternative to film production. It is entered into as a way to occupy another site of delivery, entrenched broadcast television. Another, smaller, center of video activity resides in art practice, however that may be constituted. The linkage between video, writing, and audiotape recording had suggested to some artists a strategy of employing video for intimately elegiac purposes, conflating the private and public markers of mourning and witnessing. These gestures share a questioning of chronology and the impulse to mark histories passing, inscriptions made for memory, and memory's decline. It is a realm clinging cautiously to the aura of the photograph and early cinema, and only recently inscribed, however tenuously, in reference to cybernetic entities, a link made explicit in science fiction as the cyborg searches for its originator, its manufacturer, or its programmer. Witness "Data's" ongoing quest for tracings of his maker's intentions in *Star Trek: The Next Generation*. He is the cyborg Tin Man looking for a heart. Video may seem the coldest of tools with which to uncover memory, but its position, hovering between magnetic tape and photography, suggests it as a medium conducive to the writing of memory and origin. Jan Peacock's *Wallace + Theresa* (1985) and Janice Tanaka's *Memories from the Department of Amnesia* (1990) are short works that suggest a way of working through the notating of loss with a newly cleansed mystic writing pad.

Wallace + Theresa merges the word images of the poet Wallace Stevens and the artist-writer Theresa Hak Kyung Cha, both of whom dealt with the entropy of words, their disintegration and mutation. Cha's best-known text, *Dictée* (1982), was invested in the melding of feminism and psychoanalysis through graphic semiotic turns, heavily manipulating the revelation of words on a page as if the graphic placements were performative elements.[17] Peacock uses a video equivalent of Cha's texts to evoke Cha's history and violent death via the animation, graphic inscription, and disappearance of words. A softly spoken audio track furnishes a steady background murmur of commingled Korean, English, and French. A white, parchmentlike screen fills the frame (another glowing blank slate) until fragments of Cha's *Dictée*, an autobiographical poem, are laboriously inscribed alongside selections from Stevens's "The Pure Good of Theory," "Peter Quince at the Clavier," and "The Creation of Sound." The video writing of these texts is actually taking place on the other side of the screen—a literal third wall. A hidden hand is writing text backward, seen correctly only by the witness-viewer. The blurred edges of the laboriously etched written words and the semi-translucence of the paper suggest ghost writing or a ritual that must be performed by an obscured and protected hand, continuing without explanation, but producing audible signals in the forms of scratched-out words. There is a temptation to look at the screen itself as a surface on which the viewer could have an impact, perhaps rubbing away the translucence to quicken the process of the writing's fabrication and unveil the proper sentence form. In this same screen space, a sign language writer carefully begins tracing in the air, making the accompanying alternative language gestures.

The audio track employs Cha's definition of identity found in a fragment of *Dictée:* "She says to herself if she were able to write, she could continue to live. Says to herself if she could write without ceasing. To herself. If by writing she could abolish real time. She would live."[18] The tape's writer-performer, by inscribing the paper with Cha's words, memorializes her but also questions this particular death. The transfixing nature of the hand

FIGURES 1 AND 2
Jan Peacock's *Wallace + Theresa* (1985)

gesture, which is the predominant image of the tape, suggests the tying together of loose ends, the rubbing away of veneer, the scraping of patina to get at the core material (in this case a narrative closure), an answer to death. Ultimately this gesture neither supplies biography nor narrative tissue, but suggests that the witness inhabits this particular poem and this particular writer fleetingly, as long as it takes to remember the dead. It is as if Peacock gives illustration to Foucault's call to "reexamine the empty space left by the author's disappearance," a space as worthy of investigation for its nothingness as for its complexity.[19] "What I have done with *Wallace + Theresa* is to take (the) propensity to read and interpret as a given condition, and constructed a layering of images, sounds, printed and written words and voice—all and each of which reciprocally narrate one another, where narration is, substantially, the event."[20] Cha's face materializes briefly at the end of the work, with the word "absent" superimposed over it. The eulogy's purpose here is to narrate not circumstances but the history of the literal paper trace, a being inside the creation of the poem itself. The eulogy is merged with the artist Peacock's desire to mark both her entry into the life of Cha and the entry into the larger visceral memory of Cha. If we tell ourselves histories in order to live, we also may fabricate images indicative of where we would like to have been, or at least how we would like to be remembered.

Janice Tanaka's *Memories from the Department of Amnesia* is explicitly about this inscription of memory. Structured into three movements, it opens with a slow-motion bicycle ride through a fifties-style coffee shop. The rider, ignored by the patrons and always teetering on the brink of crashing, obsessively circles the populated interior space. His slow-motion circuit is accompanied by a howling slowed down audio track derived from the sound of pedaling. Brief flashes of a surgeon in green hospital garb, lost in a blinding snow storm, periodically slice into the biker's circuit. His image fragment can be alternately a vision, a trace memory, or an apparition. The surgeon beckons the rider from within his frame until the frustrated rider enters his snowy landscape, laboriously biking from one end of the screen to the other.

FIGURE 3
Janice Tanaka's *Memories from the Department of Amnesia* (1990)

Both apparitions occupy each other's vision, initially through inference, as the sense of place merges and the dream characters ultimately collide in the drifting snow, forcing a confrontation of two ephemeral states.

At this collision, the tape switches abruptly to a series of snapshots in negative, illuminated by a light table being methodically slid into view. The negatives reveal the photographic chronology of the life of Tanaka's mother, Yuriko Yamate. As the negatives slip in and out of frame, a clinical listing begins: abandoned by mother, molested by father, bank account frozen in 1942, interned in Manzanar from 1942-43, uses Chinese surname to get a job in 1945, hysterectomy in 1958, looks for mother in

ERIKA SUDERBURG

Japan in 1979 (finds her and is refused acknowledgment), becomes more reclusive, and dies in 1988. This register slowly fades in and out at the bottom of the screen as the negatives are cross-faded into positives. This accumulation vividly brings forth the grim realization of being able to so easily historically syncopate and notate a single life—and the dual realization that this recording will in all probability be the sole manifestation of one's own life. At the point when this factual litany becomes overwhelming, Tanaka begins to insert the voices of her children telling stories: Grandma's hot rodding, her joy in discussing men, and her outrageous sense of humor. The sequence of tragedy is fleshed out, the newly unearthed chronological trail mercifully augmented by the present tense of recollection from a third generation of storytellers.

Tanaka places her own image at the center of the third movement of the work. She appears in an extreme overhead shot, dressed entirely in white, circling a small patch of floor in a glaring overlit void. The work moves from mother, to children, back to mother/daughter. The recording is complete, but the absence still resonates as the image of Tanaka obsessively paces this void, suggesting the impossibility of forming any more images outside this self-representation. She arrives at both the end and the beginning of genealogy. It becomes an intimate moment of stock-taking, allowing the viewer to recall these tertiary and parallel stories; her children's story, the reality of California internment camps, the search by daughter for mother and mother for mother, and the recording of these traces. Tanaka demands retribution of history and memory, an explosion in the middle of the proffered time line: "Memories are not always an understood compilation of linear ideas. They seem instead to be fragments of stored, synthesized, edited sensory stimuli; bits of personalized perceptions. Film and television oftentimes play a major role in the process of subliminal inculcation by creating a criteria for self-evaluation. Consequently, our self image, our role models, what we know and expect of our society and the world, are greatly influenced by the media. Somewhere caught between the crevices of concept and production [lie] the elements or perhaps the reflective shadows of who and what we are. This exquisitely complex structure of electrons prophetically examines nature"[21]—In Tanaka's case a "nature" that demands a space for mourning inclusive of confusion and disorientation, the careening biker and the lost daughter.

FOR MEMORY

If Tanaka searches biographic family history for definition and a harnessing of amnesiac's time, Marc Karlin widens the scope considerably by collecting and examining primary historical texts of the documentarist: a series of interviews about the past. The aim is not, however, to represent a specific story or group politic, but rather to use these first-person primary accounts to ask how recorded history is structured and inherited and how the human interloper skews his or her participation within this sculpted narrative. Karlin begins *For Memory* (1983) with a cameraman's account of entering Bergen Belsen, the ultimate depth charge for amnesiacs. The photographer explains his preparation for Karlin's interview by saying that he had written everything down, finding the site of the concentration camp unfilmable. He relates how his shock suspended image-making. He could not look into his viewfinder. The apparatus breaks down when confronted by the unseeable. This declaration of horror segues into the fundamental trope of *For Memory*, a long tracking shot of what appears at first to be an actual nighttime city that slowly reveals itself to be an elaborate mock-up. Miniature lit skyscrapers line endless downtown streets. The viewer experiences this fabricated city as if encased in a hovercraft twenty-five stories above the street, drifting and scraping past the metropolis, buffered from the stories inside the model windows. The urban somnambulist is construed as a kind of giant Macy's Day parade float. Karlin uses this image to introduce each segment: "Fragile Stories," "A Memory's Invitation," "A Walk through the Strange Museum,"[22] "The Memory Keepers," "Tracing a Line Backwards into the Future," "A Historian's Remembrance Speech," and "Myths, Legends and Lesson." An omnipotent voice-over explains that *For Memory* was made in response to Hollywood's 1978 TV docudrama *Holocaust*. Karlin points to this fabricated trace that stands in for historical knowledge as both a trigger of personal memory and a panacea for cataclysmic historical accounts. This voice frames the complex levels of interrogation that constitute the rest of the tape and underscores the necessity to reform and recall what is designated "history." Karlin is embarking on a project that is designed to make manifest the danger of knowledge delivered in the form of melodramatic docudrama—a thousand times removed from the historical complexity of the first-person account—which is a model that Karlin returns to and revivifies.

Karlin's offscreen narrator (whose words often dominate the city tracking shots) voices the sentiment that memory is surrounded by guardians. Karlin's representative guardians include patients of a senile dementia ward, children playacting (with the National Trust Theatre Company) a voyage of Sir Francis Drake, two women recounting their work as nurses at the front during World War I, a labor historian's curation of a coal-mining town's photograph artifacts, the inhabitants of the town who visit that exhibit, the recollections of a socialist mural painter recalling 1930s labor battles, and an impassioned historian, Edward Thompson, in the process of delivering a rather lengthy commemorative speech on soldiers who refused to fight in Ireland. Karlin relies on the exchange between interviewer and subject to sample history's residue. What is unusual here is that the space created for recall appears immense in relation to established documentary form. All of the holes, lapses, and awkwardness of memory are retained. At times, the flow of the work seems to wait patiently for the memory to be verbalized. The cameraman of Bergen Belsen is allowed an eternity to search his notes, as later in another scene the faces of children lined up as naval hands in the Drake expedition are searched for reaction, and in another the silence and unintelligible murmurings of the senile

FIGURE 4
Marc Karlin's *For Memory* (the city model)
(1983)

116

dementia ward occupants are never cut short. Karlin allows us the time to scrutinize the daily act of forgetting and recall. He tempers this structure by inserting between these first-person accounts those of sanctioned "historians." A Marxist labor historian who has organized an archival photo exhibit is articulate about his position as catalyst for the unwritten village history.[23] His words are underscored by images of the public deep in examination, faces and hands pressed into the airspace between photograph and eye. This section is introduced by a segment focusing on a senile patient at Saint Clement's Hospital who explores a photograph and is asked about his duty as a sentry during World War I. He stares at the photograph as if waiting for it to answer. Photographs are given the same memory-inducing powers that Tanaka ascribes to them in *Memories from the Department of Amnesia*. They are the single source for both memory and memory's erasure. Karlin asks that this process be honored while investigating the collapse of its keepers. He leaves the afterimages of memory open-ended.

The voice-over carries on a dialogue with itself about the meaning of remembrance, broadcasting a faint signal through the canyons of a fabricated city. *For Memory* is adamant about its fascination with oral tradition, the mutation of narrative via public speech. As *Wallace + Theresa* depends on conjuring words out of paper, Karlin depends on an image of the muralist's sketches appearing on the other side of a piece of paper, as his hidden hand etches a visual shorthand while he answers the question, "Are you tired of being asked about the labor battles of the thirties?" The muralist answers that there are some things you can't live past, that you must recount; that the battles of the thirties are now battles for Asian rights in Britain; that in the future that battle will pass into another battle. He relates this litany as the sketches he is working on bleed into the frame, his hand obscured but the traces filling the frame. The voice-over, a master mediator, speaks of a fear of things forgotten, memory disappearing as easily as a breath.

In the section titled "The Memory Keepers—Tracing a Line Backwards into the Future," which examines the representation of the old mining town Clay Cross, this voice-over articulates the malleability of history in the hands of its creators and fabricators:

> The city, often described as a city without signposts, whose roads never lead out and whose citizens live only to the rhythm of the cities' headlines, seems to those outside as if it had all the makings of a paradise for amnesiacs. It is the way the city acts on its memories which enables it to forget. Memories no longer have to be held onto, protected and tended. They can be stored, replaced, rejuvenated and if need be made to appear and be driven out again without trace, leaving habit as their sole protector. Wisdom, goes the city proverb, does not only rest in graves. If there have to be remembrances let them be melted into marble, by the city walls where there are still sites of ancient wars and where things forgotten still depend on the living for their

survival. Memories lie waiting, listening for the sounds of the day, for their recall to the city.

For Memory works alongside the great "city" films of the twenties and thirties—Walter Ruttman's *Berlin, Symphony of a Great City* (1927) and Dziga Vertov's *Man with a Movie Camera* (1929). However, there is no specific city as subject here, rather it is the city as container, as corpus. Karlin's city is a beautifully realized cardboard canyon of skyscrapers that the viewer moves through in search of the next storyteller. The labor historian articulates his history by uncovering what the bourgeoisie excise: "making the past so that the future is possible." The kids miming the loading of cannons aimed at an imaginary Spanish fleet are impersonating history, immersed in standard-issue English myth. The woman standing next to a burning bonfire, an actress portraying the recently widowed Isabelle, wife of explorer Richard Burton, is burning all his papers and manuscripts. She is terrified lest his taste in erotica be found out. She creates and erases history simultaneously. Karlin's tape is a compendium of possible guardians circling the notion of historical veracity and articulating the fear of forgetting. It is no accident that these guardians are older people being asked, for the last time, to tell the story once more. The viewer-witness and the children learning Drake's story are the only future inheritors within the tape, except for the glowing miniature TV sets that shine through the windows of the cardboard city— little machines waiting to receive a broadcast of *For Memory*.

AN ABSENT RECOLLECTION

Michael Klier's *Der Riese* (The huge one; 1983) fulfills Jameson's notion of video's predilection to evoke ennui. It is not the ennui of boredom but the ennui of obfuscation—evoked by the realization of the body surveyed, its trace histories interchangeable and ultimately vanishing. *Der Riese* charts mechanical and human movement through the wiring of sites formalized as discrete blocks of video time, extracted from the millions of surveillance stations in various German cities. Klier termed these surveillance stations "the secret observatory of an art of light and visibility that shuns the light."[24] This is a history driven by compulsive documentation in the name of control and safety. It speaks to the erasure of the individual body's participation in the city and the dominance of the autonomous video eye. Civil control becomes the new repository of historical marking and, for Klier, marks a return to origin similar to Kluge's identification with silent cinema: "Apart from questions of control I was interested in the video images from surveillance cameras because of their obstinate power of expression, which has a resemblance to the visions of science fiction, as well as to the images of early cinema, that is the Lumière cinema."[25] *Der Riese* was fabricated from the extracted debris of the perpetually humming surveillance machine, the images of the automaton eye oversampled by the human eye hoping to glimpse a transgression or a fissure in the city's smoothly functioning fabric of airports, parks, city squares, psychiatric clinics, and traffic control. Klier tapped into these video signals, occasionally choosing to honor the intent of surveillance, choosing to include the moment of the shoplifters' decision in dinnerware, or the purse snatcher in a shopping mall, or a psychiatric patient's obsessive hand rubbing. However, these moments of narrative action are defused by Klier's method of leaving long unadulterated stretches that chart the mundane: a woman eating lunch next to a German shepherd, small children jostling each other on a train platform, and the endless stream of incoming city traffic exiting grey tunnels. These sections are unrelentingly banal and somehow pathetic, witnessed only by an apparatus that often broadcasts its culled images out to an empty security chair—a modular panopticon present on every street corner.

Klier provides the human witness to this undirected output. The surface of the tape is etched with the automated jerk of the surveillance camera. A huge wall map of Berlin blinks incessantly as men in white shirts glance at their traffic corners, punch buttons, and receive the news of each new traffic snarl with calm efficiency. This benevolent casting of the video eye is carefully counteracted by the insertion of a police surveillance setup on the roof of a high-rise building, the freshly installed cameras trained on a crowd of demonstrators far below. These frames of the installation of the apparatus are always shot in color, in contrast to the machines' own black-and-white low-resolution output. Hans Magnus Enzensberger, writing in 1979 on Dr. Herold's (West German) federal bureau of investigation computer network, INPOL, termed the West German state the author of the most sophisticated surveillance network in the world. Library checkouts, hotel bookings, demonstration attendance, car registration, and flights in and out of Berlin (whether you are the target of an investigation or not) feed automatically into a central data base. This repository compiles data for a projected potential audience. It constructs a specific unsolicited history out of allegedly mundane, private, and sometimes public gestures. Enzensberger terms these your "permanent traces," unerasable and collected from all citizens. [26]

The rumored introduction into U.S. Senate conference hearings of Supreme Court nominee Clarence Thomas's video porn rental lists inserted the video diet of the judge into the contents of his state profile.[27] Klier evades this specificity, but finds the remnants of a more public gesture—the body's insertion into the apparatus of the city. It is the individual's arbitrary trace image that Klier is working with. The surveillance camera renders all subjects anonymous, patterns performing without awareness of being monitored. We might be oblivious to the glass-eyed box in the corner of the local 7-Eleven, but Klier banks on our curiosity about its images. Speaking once more of Dr. Herold's special machine, Enzensberger states that "his ultimate ambition aims beyond repression, at prevention: planning a cybernetically directed, disturbance proof society. He has indicated more than once that he would like to convert the police into a research and planning apparatus able to function as an early warning system, spotting malfunctions and areas of risk, devising foresighted political strategies. The police as an instrument of applied social science generating mathematical models of social processes."[28]

Klier employs a surveillance image taken from a sleep disorder clinic. A woman is hooked up to a tangle of wires. When she finally falls asleep, a split screen appears that contains a readout of her vital signs and the pulses emanating from each wire. When she jerks or even shifts slightly, it records her personal earthquake. When she lies still, dreamless, it renders a steady line. Our intimacy with this stranger is frightening. One wants to cover up her exposed thigh, straighten and smooth the covers over her, and leave the room. We should not be here. She should not be there. We should not be with her in this moment. But her image now occupies a small sliver of public domain, anonymous, a history made up of the slight gesture and the "private" video record. She is literally Karlin's amnesiac, except that the patterns of her memory are inscribed by the machine and made manifest by the witnesses of the surveillance machine. Klier's version of the urban topography is a history of the remainder. The surveillance machine is just as interested in the movement of a pigeon as it is in the flight of a purse snatcher. He presents us with the fiction of the document. By removing any identifiable author of these images, the subjects are recorded and pass on, vaguely aware of being scanned or simply desensitized to being scanned. Klier focuses on the haunting of these moments as a type of new automaton-created history, a negative inference of nightmarish proportions and banal disregard:

> In the video images we have shots of streets, border areas, architectural monsters, sometimes with a remnant of nature, which as an electronic image have the effect of a quotation from afar. But the watching, the seeing without being seen, is no longer confined to the outside world. It is penetrating inwards. People's inner lives must be domesticated too. This starts with the numerous cameras that keep an eye on people while they are at work and runs through behavioral research. . . . It is this all-embracingness—outside and inside—that constitutes the tension and threat of these materials: the world becomes a labyrinth. Here appear aspects of life which, as electronic, immaterial sequences of images, warn us that in many places life already no longer exists.[29]

The strategies for the informing and creating of historical containers in this body of work from the eighties vary greatly. Karlin interrogates the realm of forgetting; Klier, the anonymous collection of traces left by the passing subject. Tanaka depends on resuscitated biography; Peacock, on the elegiac. Kluge works on the repatching of historical appropriations; Godard and Mieville, on the public history of cinema to decipher their own identity as image makers. Ultimately these gestures of inscription from a specific time period in video broaden the grammars and methodologies available to the writing or imaging of the historical body. These are the stories otherwise degraded by unbalanced chronological importance, selection, and archiving. This body of work suggests an alternative series of subjects and images counteractive to that which we have become acclimatized to. These works operate as challenges to Jameson's identification of a medium-specific ennui, the perimeters of video's historical address/redress. They serve

ERIKA SUDERBURG

as remunerations for the unquestioned time line that memorializes and erases simultaneously with little regard for the awkward spaces between occurences.

> It might be thought that because the city's inhabitants had resigned themselves to living in a permanent present, and yet are unable to overcome their fear of forgetting, that they would have to live with a constant sense of loss. But this strange museum, open all night, beams its maps so perfectly that the citizens can dream, away from their predicaments, knowing that nothing has been lost. ~ MARC KARLIN, *For Memory*

NOTES

The author would like to thank Kathleen McHugh, Judith Spiegel, and Micki Trager for reading many drafts. Special thanks also go to Marc Karlin, Kathleen McHugh, and Jan Peacock for their kind help, attention, and patience.

1 See Sean Cubitt, *Timeshift: On Video Culture* (London and New York: Routledge,1991).

2 Fredric Jameson, "Video," *Postmodernism, or, The Cultural Logic of Late Capitalism* (Raleigh: University of North Carolina Press, 1991), 76.

3 Ibid.,71. For a further discussion of this quote, see Marita Sturken's "The Politics of Video Memory: Electronic Erasures and Inscriptions," chapter 1 in this volume.

4 Cubitt, *Timeshift,* 123.

5 Ibid., 122–23.

6 Ibid., 122.

7 The Oberhausen manifesto was written in 1962 by a group of West German filmmakers (of whom Kluge was a signatory). It called for a "New German Cinema" to be created outside of traditional commercial systems and supportive of new experimental works oppositional to the imported Hollywood fantasy model. For a contextualization of this manifesto, see Eric Rentschler's introduction to the manifesto in *West German Filmmakers on Film* (New York: Holms and Meier, 1988), as well as Alexander Kluge's "What Do the Oberhauseners Want?" in the same volume. Kluge identifies three main demands: extracting film from its "intellectual isolation in the Federal Republic," working against solely commercial orientation for film, and making film and its audience aware of its public, political, and social responsibility.

8 See Oskar Negt and Alexander Kluge, "The Public Sphere and Experience: Selections," *October*, no. 46 (Fall 1988): 61, n. 1. Complete text can be found in Oskar Negt and Alexander Kluge, *The Public Sphere and Experience* (Minneapolis: University of Minnesota Press, forthcoming).

9 Stuart Liebman, "On New German Cinema, Art, Enlightenment, and the Public Sphere: An Interview with Alexander Kluge," *October,* no. 46 (Fall 1988): 30, 40.

10 Alexander Kluge, "Why Should Film and Television Cooperate?" *October,* no. 46 (Fall 1988): 99.

11 *Heimatfilme* (homeland films) were a postwar (now kitsch) genre of German film in the 1950s that stressed the mythologically noble German people and the power of the homeland soil to nostalgically restore and inspire a collective postwar identity. It was a genre deeply despised by the Oberhausen manifesto signatories. For a history of this genre, see Anton Kaes, *From Hitler to Heimat: The Return of History as Film* (Cambridge, Mass.: Harvard University Press, 1989).

12 Margaret Morse, in the Los Angeles Contemporary Exhibitions' program notes for a 1989 retrospective showing of Alexander Kluge's "Ten To Eleven" television programs.

13 Miriam Hansen, "Reinventing the Nickelodeon: Notes

on Kluge and Early Cinema," *October,* no.46 (Fall 1988):186.

14 I am referring here to nascent video art's intersection with performed audiotape works in the mid-1960s, and particularly its early connection with composers like Nam June Paik, who transferred his compositional methodology wholeheartedly into video production based on a chance model (derived from John Cage and Marcel Duchamp, and also in reference to "music concrete"—music made up of "found sounds"). This transference was fueled by the newly introduced Sony portapak and was inclusive of happenings or of Fluxus performers like Wolf Vostell, who utilized video as a performative element. For an overview of this aspect of early video art, see Rob Perree, *Into Video Art: The Characteristics of a Medium* (Amsterdam: Idea Books, 1988), and Marita Sturken, "Paradox in the Evolution of an Art Form: Great Expectations and the Making of a History," in *Illuminating Video: An Essential Guide to Video Art*, ed. Doug Hall and Sally Jo Fifer (New York: Aperture, 1990).

15 *Cahiers du cinéma,* no. 300 (May 1979), special issue devoted to Jean-Luc Godard's "Sonimage" project in Mozambique. See especially Godard, "Le Dernier Rêve d'un producteur: Nord contre sud ou naissance (de l'image) d'une nation," 70-129.

16 Colin MacCabe, *Godard: Images, Sounds, Politics* (Bloomington: Indiana University Press, 1980), 154.

17 See Theresa Hak Kyung Cha, *Dictée* (New York: Tanam Press, 1982), and Theresa Hak Kyung Cha, "Commentaire," in *Cinematographic Apparatus: Selected Writings,* ed. Theresa Hak Kyung Cha (New York: Tanam Press, 1980).

18 Cha, *Dictée,* 141.

19 Michel Foucault, "What Is an Author?" in *Language, Counter-Memory, Practice: Selected Essays and Interviews* (Ithaca, N. Y.: 1980), Cornell University Press, 121.

20 Jan Peacock, Art Metropole Video distribution catalog, Toronto, Canada, 1990.

21 Janice Tanaka, "Electrons and Reflective Shadows," in *Moving the Image: Independent Asian Pacific American Media Arts,* ed. Russell Leong (Los Angeles: UCLA Asian American Studies Center and Visual Communication, Southern California Asian American Studies Central, 1991), 206. For a further discussion of this tape, see Marita Sturken's "The Politics of Video Memory: Electronic Erasures and Inscriptions" and Christine Tamblyn's "Qualifying the Quotidian: Artist's Video and the Production of Social Space," chapters 1 and 2 in this volume.

22 Marc Karlin notes, "All the excerpts shown in the section called 'Strange Museum' came from tv programmes already made—part of the city's way of having memory at its disposal at a moment's notice. As such the two nurses in World War I are not guardians . . . but are more representative of the way that a city's amnesia can be tempered at any given moment, or 'at a moment of danger'" (letter to author, June 1994).

23 The man who organized the exhibition at Clay Cross is actually a former miner turned historian. In a note to the author Karlin states, "I say this only to emphasise his journey as a memory man of the industrial age." This redefinition of the movable historian helps to nicely underscore Karlin's entire project in *For Memory.*

24 Michael Klier and Brigitte Kramer, "Der Riese," *The Luminous Image* catalog, ed. Dorine Mignot (Amsterdam: Stedelijk Museum, 1984), 124.

25 From an interview with Michael Klier in the videotape documenting the *Luminious Image* exhibition at the Stedelijk Museum, 1984.

26 Hans Magnus Enzensberger, "Civil Liberties and Repression in Germany Today," *October,* no. 9 (Summer 1979): 114.

27 These records of video rentals were kept confidential and released only to the committee itself. They were never entered into public record, allegedly as part of a plea bargain with Anita Hill and the withholding of private information about her.

28 Enzensberger, "Civil Liberties and Repression," 114.

29 Klier and Kramer, "Der Riese," 124.

DISTRIBUTION INFORMATION

Soft and Hard is available from Electronic Arts Intermix, 536 Broadway, New York, NY 10012.

Wallace + Theresa is available from Art Metropole, 788 King Street West, Toronto, Ontario, Canada M5V 1N6.

Memories from the Department of Amnesia is available from Electronic Arts Intermix, 526 Broadway, New York, NY 10012.

For Memory is available from the British Film Institute, 29 Rathbone Street, London WIP 1AG, England.

CHAPTER 9

LYNN HERSHMAN:
THE SUBJECT OF AUTOBIOGRAPHY

David E. James

I should live no more than I can record. ~ JAMES BOSWELL

Lynn Hershman's *Electronic Diary* (1988) was a crucial breakthrough for her own career as an artist and indeed for artists' video generally. A summary restatement of many of the concerns of feminist video of the previous decade and a half, it turned out to be an immensely fertile matrix that quickly generated a series of tapes—*Longshot* (1989), *Desire Incorporated* (1990), *Seeing Is Believing* (1991), *Shadow's Song* (1991), and *Conspiracy of Silence* (1991-92)—further elaborating the themes it had developed. This chapter sketches what I take to be the major achievements of the *Diary* and places it and the tapes it engendered within the theoretical parameters of autobiography. My primary concern will be with themes of love and death, with the mutual imbrication of erotic and thanatotic impulses as they pass from the psychology of the autobiographical subject to the nature of video itself, which, as both text and social exchange, is the medium of that subject's realization. Hershman's work does indeed affirm video's ability to represent—to construct and deconstruct—a self; but that ability is at the same time challenged as the medium asserts its own specificity, its own authority, its own desire.

In its self-obsession, Hershman's work finds itself in the historical field of what, in a seminal article, Rosalind Krauss termed the "aesthetics of narcissism."[1] But in this field, her particular contribution is to have shown how that splitting of the subject and its imaginary reformulation in the electronic mirror that was so important in early video may and should be negotiated not only in the immediate apparatus—the camera and the monitor—but also in the total televisual environment—broadcast, interactive, cable, surveillance, medical, and so on—with which it is integrated. Only in the multiple, dispersed yet interconnected practices that constitute television as a whole can an adequately extensive, flexible, and nuanced metaphor for the self now be found. And television as a whole is the site of the self's own discovery and transformation, but also its imperilment. Given the chronology of recent art history, this reflexive concern

124

with the medium appears as a return to earlier problematics, and indeed, as often as not, correlatives for Hershman's innovations lie in avant-garde film of the late sixties and early seventies as much as in video. But it is also progressive—at least potentially so—in that rather than repressing the social economies among which artists' video lives, it opens out to these and so toward an understanding of the self as a social process constantly mediated by public institutions.

The parameters of such an autobiographical project were described some fifteen years ago (when the production of film autobiographies was at its apogee) in P. Adams Sitney's "Autobiography in Avant-Garde Film."[2] Tracing the film autobiographies of Stan Brakhage and others to the tradition of Saint Augustine, Rousseau, and Wordsworth, Sitney showed how the conditions of literary autobiography were renegotiated in the new medium. Much of his analysis is film specific—for example, the way the habit of collecting still photographs to accumulate a personal chronology inhabits and supplies a fundamental trope to autobiographical film, whose materiality consists precisely of a chronology of still photographs. But his formulation of the axioms of literary and film autobiography can readily be made over to video; they include the privileged status of "the moment at which the author realized his vocation as a writer"; the ubiquity of the search for cinematic strategies that can relate "the moments of shooting and editing to the diachronic continuity of the film-maker's life"; the frequent contingency of the tropes of film autobiography on the material nature of the medium;[3] and the observation that "the very making of an autobiography constitutes a reflection on the nature of cinema, and often on its ambiguous association with language." These issues, reconstituted in terms of video, are precisely Hershman's concerns, but the last—the reflection on video and its relation to language—is summary. As Hershman employs video to "write" her autobiography, she is drawn to investigate both its nature as language and the role of verbal language within it. For while video provides the arena in which an autobiographical self can be talked into being, that talking is realized only via video; the verbal is always mediated through its specific electronic visualization. Investigating this mediation in successive tapes, Hershman discovers that the social relations that constitute her life are themselves similarly mediated through video as text and video as social process, video as audiovisual electronic information and video as a network of social institutions and apparatuses in which this information comes into being.

The *Diary* is almost entirely composed of Hershman's own direct address to the video camera, a confrontation that recurs as her direct address to and positioning of the spectator. As in other notable video works—Vito Acconci's *Recording Studio from Air Time* or Lynda Benglis's *Now*, for example—the ostensible privacy of the artist's conversation with the camera mimics the scene of psychotherapy, securing a place where the self may be encountered, a self-image constructed. And, as is axiomatic in this tradition, the monitor supplies both a mirror in which the subject may perceive an objectified form of herself, partially reified but still in flux, and also a stage upon which she may set herself

125

to play in assumed personae. But unlike the received video tradition, which was typically premised on immediate image feedback as the vehicle of a drive toward personal authenticity, Hershman foregrounds artifice. As the effects of the work of image manipulation in editing make plain and the credits make explicit, her self-images have been worked on by many people, in the initial recording and since. While she does not, at least not explicitly, go so far as to admit that the claims for veracity and sincerity that have subtended the autobiographical tradition since Rousseau are not so much impossible as irrelevant,[4] Hershman constantly toys with her own credibility. She drops us in an abyss between belief and denial, between video and life. Her autobiographical confessions all deal in seduction.

The fundamental condition of her *Diary* is, then, the instability of herself as its subject. Initially set in play in her negotiations with the changes in her own video image, with its attraction and sometimes with its repulsiveness, this instability recurs in the spectator's parallel negotiations with the more elaborated forms of the same images as they appear on the finished tape. Inhabited by narcissism and exhibitionism, its overriding need is to make the artist-model perform a self sufficiently interesting and desirable to hold our attention—no mean task, given the competition. Linking these two points—that of Hershman's own approach to her video image in the one case and our consumption of it in the other—is the process of composition, of manufacture.[5] Here, two formal strategies are especially important in the mediation of the autobiographical discourse as video: first, an ongoing interfolding of the tropes of documentary with those of fiction; second, Hershman's distinctive montage style, which consists of very brief shots with the replacement (or displacement or consumption) of one by the next, commonly involving some kind of image manipulation—a wipe, for example, or a dissolve created by an initially inset second screen taking over the whole. The former, which becomes especially prevalent in the later tapes that contain other characters besides Hershman herself, prevents any secure differentiation of biographical truth from authorial fabrication for thematic or narrative effect. The latter—and it epitomizes the tapes' reflexive affirmation of the centrality of video in Hershman's construction of herself and others—vividly figures the impossibility of an autonomous, uninterrupted self; there can only be a succession of provisional, video-dependent images of it, as flux, the quality that since Raymond Williams's early writings has been taken as characteristic of television, is similarly the condition of the subject.

In each of the *Electronic Diary*'s three parts, Hershman investigates an aspect of the traumas that have shaped her and that have therefore become the recurrent themes of her autobiography. In the first part, subtitled *Confessions of a Chameleon*, she describes how she was abused as a child and in defense constructed imaginary personae for herself. She then immediately launches into a spectacular narrative of her teenage years. Finishing college at twelve, she married at fifteen and, when her husband disappeared, worked as a call girl to support herself and daughter. After some years spent in hospital, on the verge of death but nevertheless experiencing sundry adventures, an epiphanic experience of the overwhelming sensual immediacy of the material world, sparked by her own sexuality, compelled her to become an artist. This amazing account is capped by the flat claim, "I always tell the truth."

Binge (figure 1), the second part of the *Diary*, documents a period of several months when she tries to lose weight, the forty-five extra pounds that she first put

FIGURE 1
Lynn Hershman, *Electronic Diary: Binge* (1988)

on after her husband disappeared and that now, she claims, "separate me from my image of myself." Since the diet is in process all through the period the tape documents, the account of its erratic successes is demonstrated, sometimes very graphically, in the changes we observe in her body shape. Accounts of her other attempts to improve her appearance are interspersed with speculations about why modern society prizes slender women and the psychic pressures this value system exerts on her and on her daughter. In the end she appears to have failed, having regained the weight she had at one point lost.

First Person Plural (figure 2), the last part of the *Diary*, returns to her childhood abuse, but uses a public vocabulary to elaborate the masochistic fantasies and identity crises this caused. Her recollection of her childhood obsession with Dracula movies (fragments of which are interpolated) is negotiated into images of the Holocaust via a psychobiography of Hitler, himself a battered child born from two generations of teenage mothers. The pathology of cycles of abuse, passed down from generation to generation, is presented as a public event; the trauma of Hershman as a girl becomes the trauma of all women, of the Jewish people, of history. Again Hershman claims veracity, but this time it is qualified: "I always told

FIGURE 2
Lynn Hershman, *Electronic Diary: First Person Plural* (1988)

the truth . . . for the person that I was. But the personas kept fluctuating and they would see things from all sides and I would be afraid from all sides."

The greatest of these fears—the fear of talking about the abuse—is paradoxically the only way its wounds can be healed. Here Hershman's own autobiographical situation becomes a summary metaphor for the condition of all women; her triumph over her father, family, and subsequent lovers, all of whom threatened to destroy her if she talked about their depredations, reflects patriarchy's exclusion of women from art and discourse generally. The "talking cure" that helps Hershman find herself—however fragmented and provisional the self she finds may be—and then her making a video diary of the process paradigmatically reenact the historical intervention of a generation of feminists who refused to be silent, of women artists who found a voice and found themselves as artists, especially in autobiographical performance and video.[6] Hershman's act of making a video of herself talking about her abuse and the consequent problems of identity and sexuality is what makes her an artist, both in the sense of releasing her

127

own creativity and in the sense of acquiring a public identity as such. But as she goes public with her story, its conditions are transformed: the experience of abuse in life becomes useful in art. And even though art-making can never entirely heal the trauma, it may supply the self-awareness that will enable her to break the chains of pathological recurrence by not abusing her own daughter.

The identity as a video artist that Hershman makes for herself in *Electronic Diary* may be fabricated from the impossibly disjunctive fragments of her private selves, but it is eventually also a public role, a profession that becomes real as the tape finds its place in the social world of public art institutions and economies. As such an artist, she subsequently made tapes about people other than herself. But while the autobiographical component ostensibly diminishes, in fact it massively proliferates via a public extension similar to that begun in *First Person Plural*. Her autobiography is discovered to have been already a social story, for other people's lives are found to reenact her own and also to be subtended by the same two mutually contradictory axioms that framed the personal exposition of the *Diary:* on the one hand, the claim for a coherent, self-identified subject implicit in her initial protestation that she is speaking the truth; on the other, the refutation of such a possibility as the tapes reveal that this truth was always subjective and that the subject herself was multiple, schizophrenic, a repertoire of fantasy roles created in defense against the threat of annihilation, and extant only in art. As all women (and some men) are discovered to be her personae, in their differences they figure her various selves, as conversely her own plurality figures the multiplicity of women's selves. But since all are artists, the original disjuncture between the autobiographical subject and the subject of the autobiography (the speaking subject who makes the videos and the subject of speech presented in them), the multiple forms of their contingency on video become correspondingly more complex.

In the *Diary* the specificity of video irrupted into the autobiographical discourse in two main forms. The first is the foregrounded exploitation of video-specific image manipulation: in *Chameleon,* for example, the instability of Hershman's identity is figured in the fragmentation and multiplication of her image, and in *Binge*, she electronically flattens herself to represent a weight loss. The second is the metaphorical reenactment of real-life events in the social praxis of videomaking: a crisis in *Binge,* for example, occurs when technical malfunctions in the rented studio during taping persistently interrupt the depressed Hershman's confession of her own malfunction in losing only two pounds in six months. Proposing analogies between events in the medium and events in the reality the medium portrays, these two devices are the main tropes of the works subsequent to the *Diary*.

The major thematic cluster revolves around relations among women, particularly between mothers and daughters. Appearing as a brief aside in the *Diary*, in Hershman's self-prostitution to support her daughter and in her mother's abuse of her, these relations are the main subject of *Seeing Is Believing* (figure 3), whose central

DAVID E. JAMES

figures are Dawn, a teenager, and her mother, Coyote, who had her as a teenager by a Latino who deserted her when the child was born. The rudimentary narrative revolves around Dawn's attempt to make sense of her life and to control her mother's promiscuity and general dysfunctionality; she regularly resorts for comfort and assistance to Coyote's not-quite-so-irresponsible mother (played by Rachel Rosenthal) and to a father surrogate (played by Guillermo Gómez-Peña). Otherwise men are absent, precipitating the mother's loss of esteem, her sexual hunger and low-life lovers, and her inability to care for her daughter.

This schematic replay of *Confessions of a Chameleon* is itself elaborated by means of a loose allegory about video, a "family romance" of its relations to performance and film. The actors who play Coyote's mother and Dawn's "father" are both celebrated performance artists; the tape as a whole is presented as a video narrative made by Hershman herself, who introduces it as such and who often comments on the psychological motivation of her characters. And she insists that the critical event that enabled her to make it was her own shift from film to video as the medium of her art, which happened when she turned forty and her daughter left for college. The narrative is set in motion when, standing outside the shop where she has unsuccessfully tried to pawn her 8mm camera and projector, she encounters Dawn. She gives the film equipment to her, agreeing to teach her to use it in return for permission to tape her life. Thus both Dawn within the text and Hershman outside it as its overall maker are instances where the making of film in the one case and video in the other is the agency of self-understanding; indeed for Dawn, her camera very quickly becomes her only connection with reality. The exchange between the two mediums (in fact both 16mm and 8mm film, as well as several video formats, are combined in the film) figures not just the binary of Dawn's composite ethnicity, but also the plurality of her personality. Like her, the final tape is a composite of many formats, each of which has its particular texture, visual range, and so on. The use of these media as the vehicle for Dawn's attempt to understand herself and her mother, and for Hershman's attempt to understand herself through this narrative, is summarily figured in scenes where Hershman videotapes Dawn while the latter screens the Super-8 footage she has taken of her mother; the subjectivity—the projection—inevitable in both processes is underlined by the fact that, in her search for a satisfactory image of her mother, Dawn screens the footage she has taken of her on a variety of shifting surfaces—on a glass of water, on her clothes, even on her own body.

A parallel mediation of erotic desire informs *Desire Incorporated*, but here the apparatuses employed are extended to include broadcast television. For this,

FIGURE 4
Lynn Hershman, *Desire Incorporated* (1990)

Hershman paid to have broadcast over cable television, as if they were commercials, a series of thirty-second tapes she had made (figure 4). This kind of intervention in the public airwaves is not unprecedented in video art: Chris Burden and Joan Logue, for example, have both made their own forms of commercial, and of course in Reagan-era art the television commercial became a privileged, not to say exemplary, medium of artmaking. But Hershman's are innovative in the audience interaction they encourage.[7] The broadcasted tapes feature a provocatively dressed woman

addressing the viewer directly and inviting him or her to phone her. The number given was Hershman's own, and the final tape consists of the original ads, together with Hershman's interviews with the actress and with some of the respondents, men and women, who discuss their sexual desires.

Presented as an investigation of what Hershman believes to be a loneliness pandemic in our society, *Desire Incorporated* is sustained by a double parody; the original ads mimic the 900-number phone-sex solicitations,[8] while the tape itself mimics academic investigation of the possibility of subcultural practices mobilized around the edges of industrial culture—the currently fashionable instance of fanzines taking off from *Star Trek* would be a case in point. But, to continue with this example, the most fundamental parallel with *Desire Incorporated* is not the scholarly essay about the fanzine production so much as the fanzines themselves, for while the tape appears to investigate a social loneliness, Hershman admits that her main motivation was her own loneliness. The sexy woman who advertised on television and the respondents to the ad were all her surrogates. The erotics of television, fundamental in the original seduction of all these people into the orbit of her own power, are similarly instrumental in her future use of the tape to seduce its audience—and not only the limited audience for artists' video. For, just as the original ads ran on commercial television, so *Desire Incorporated* ran on PBS.

The violence that is never far below the surface of the erotic scenarios these works explore is brought into the foreground in *Longshot* (figure 5). Ostensibly a documentary about a young woman (Lian Amber), it juggles the mercurial shifts of her all-but-pathological identity crises through multiple representations of her, nested

Chinese-box-fashion in several different video and film narratives. On the one hand, despite her promiscuity and drug use, Lian appears to be a relatively stable, functional person; her delight in the sensual world and her own engagement of it is reflected in her spontaneous singing. On the other hand, specifically in the opinion of a social worker whose assessments of her are regularly interpolated, she is dysfunctional and fundamentally self-destructive. The latter's opinion is given credence early in the tape when Lian remarks that one of her previous lover's stories of killing people in the desert feeds her obsessional fear of being made into a snuff film—a fate that the tape finally enacts. For her then—and this is a trope that inhabits the entire autobiographical tradition—representation and death are inextricably combined. The interwoven scenarios for such a paradox set under way by the tape are again all centered around different forms of video.

The dominant one, the major frame of the tape, is narrated for Hershman's camera by a young man (Dennis Matthews) who works in a computer-operated video-editing facility. Obsessed by Lian, he wants to possess and control not her body but her video image, so he follows her around, taping her and then manipulating her image on his computer console. Competing with Dennis for Lian's image, yet another woman—yet another moving-image artist—intervenes. She (Zsuzsa Koszegi) also wants to possess Lian and to direct her life, but as a movie rather than as a videotape. The competition between lovers, modes of sexuality, and media comes to a climax in a final sequence in which Zsuzsa takes over Dennis's video camera and has him play the role of Lian's murderer in her movie. With a gun now rather than a camera, Dennis shoots Lian in a park in San Francisco, and as her bloody body lies in the street, tourists shoot the whole scene with their video and still cameras.

Like one of the most sophisticated metacinematic meditations ever made, Dennis Hopper's *The Last Movie* (the crucial scene of which it, in fact, quotes in a shot in which Lian gets back on her feet after having been "killed"), *Longshot* shuffles diegetic levels so completely that the possibility of an exterior, normative ontology is

131

entirely lost. The subject is dispersed across an abyss of mediations in which life and television fold endlessly into each other. Only death can halt this deferral and stabilize an identity. But death is also the only event that is inaccessible to the autobiographical subject.

While Hershman cannot represent her own death, she can represent her fear of it and the displacement of her fear onto the deaths of others, and she has done so in two other works. *Conspiracy of Silence* (1991-92) is a dramatic reenactment of some of the events surrounding the death of the artist Ana Mendieta; in this work she again treats the possibility of a woman artist being killed by a man. And in *Shadow's Song*, she confronts her own death.

Shadow's Song is part of the *Electronic Diary* series, but it is separated from the three others, not bound with them, and quite properly so since it is irreducibly exergual. The terminal contradictions that follow from the autobiographical subject's approach to her death are mobilized in a diary of the events that follow Hershman's discovery that she has a tumor on the base of her brain. Again, the significant contexts of this event are elaborated through allegories about media. Hershman's tumor can only be proven to exist by means of yet another form of photography, X rays, and while it turns out to be benign and operable, she is able to avoid surgery by her recourse to alternative medical procedures, which enable her to shrink the tumor by a technique of mental visualization. She triumphs over at least this first presentiment of death, but the inevitability of death's victory is admitted in a second story interwoven with and serving as a surrogate for her own.

Her meditations on her own death and dealings with doctors are intercut with scenes, also in direct address, of Henry Wilhite, a black man who talks about his knowledge of impending death from a tumor similar to Hershman's own and his plans for his remaining time. Previously a dog trainer, Wilhite is also an artist—he sings, and as always in Hershman's world, singing is a mark of self-actualization in art. Although the tape ends with Wilhite's death, in some sense he too still lives on in the tape, which, at his request, Hershman made of him, braiding his death to her temporary victory over death. Sustaining the life of his singing, the singing of his life, *Shadow's Song* allows him the vitality that video has allowed Hershman's own voice. But, like the Holocaust victims in *First Person Plural*, like Lian in *Longshot*, and like Hershman's Ana Mendieta—like all subjects who construct themselves in video—outside it, he too is invisible and silent.

NOTES

1 "Video: The Aesthetics of Narcissism," *October* 1, no. 1 (Spring 1976); reprinted in *New Artists Video: A Critical Anthology,* ed. Gregory Battcock (New York; Dutton, 1978), 43-64. In this essay, Krauss distinguishes between modernist reflexivity (as instanced by Jasper Johns's *American Flag*) and the autoreflexiveness of early video (as instanced by Vito Acconci's *Centers*). The argument I developed later is that Hershman negotiates each of these into and through the other.

2 P. Adams Sitney, "Autobiography in Avant-Garde Film," *Millennium Film Journal* 1, no. 1 (Winter 1977), 60-106; quotations are from 60–63.

3 Thus, of Jerome Hill's *Film Portrait,* which he proposes as a seminal and exemplary film autobiography, Sitney notes, "A chronology is constructed in a context in which the authority of chronology and the truth of imagery is denied; consequently the categories of memory and causal sequence cease to be the founding forces of the film and enter an indeterminate arena where they might well be seen as illusions derived from, or at least reinforced by, the very conditions of film production and its apparatuses" (67).

4 The distinction of the ontology of autobiography from that of biography—and the recognition of the intrinsic rather than incidental nature of the former's subjectivity— were first made in 1956 by Georges Gusdorf in what has become the seminal essay for modern studies of the genre, "Conditions et limites de l'auto-biographie," translated as "Conditions and Limits of Autobiography," in *Autobiography: Essays Theoretical and Critical,* ed. James Olney (Princeton, N.J.: Princeton University Press, 1980), 28-48.

5 I have considered the theoretical issues at stake in the manufacture of a publicly distributed diary from a private practice of diary making in "Film Diary/Diary Film: Jonas Mekas's *Walden,*" in *To Free the Cinema: Jonas Mekas and the New York Underground,* ed. David E. James (Princeton, N.J.: Princeton University Press, 1992).

6 During the 1980s much theoretical work on the diary and other autobiographical forms was done by feminists. For an overview—and an argument for the intrinsic femininity of the diary—see Rebecca Hogan, "Engendered Autobiographies: The Diary as a Feminine Form," *Prose Studies* 14, no. 2 (September 1991): 95–107.

7 In fact, in various performance pieces of the mid-1970s, Hershman herself made and broadcast commercials for her own hotel room.

8 One, for example, currently running in Los Angeles, features a provocatively dressed "model" who addresses the camera and, detailing the tedium of the model's life, solicits phone calls from men at $4.75 per minute.

CHAPTER 10

LONGING FOR REAL LIFE

Rosanna Albertini

The Infinite asked God, How can I appear to humans without petrifying them with fear? God disguised the Infinite as the blue of the sky.

What about me? Eternity asked. How can I reveal myself to men and women and not annihilate them with fear?

Then God said, I want to give them an instant in which they will understand you. And he created Love. ~ ARTHUR SCHNITZLER, *Beziehungen und Einsamkeiten*

Video time is neither a mirror nor a description. It is a great many times, which attempt to approach (an impossible project) the thin and changeable human reality. Human time seems to have been formed as an invisible thread between beginning and ending; artists walk this vibrant line, as if they were acrobats, or musicians playing the mind's cords without using a score. Every artist seems allowed to create his own combination of time and space, his own grammar and syntax.

In order to have something that really belonged to her, Gertrude Stein dismantled the syntax of English. At the present time artists, if they want to express themselves, might dismantle the world. In a sense, they do. Think about realism in video art during the last fifteen years. Diseases abound, injustice is everywhere, war, loneliness, technological splendor, human misery. It's life that rushes art; it is reality, quite frankly, that has become radical. The artist, as everyone, is bound to the world by a double chain: if he wants to know the world, he must hold it in himself; if he wants to know himself, he must be in the world. Many different answers to many unacceptable conflicts; one by one, scattered, without a common order of language. But a poetry of life is still kept, inside and outside the monitor, recycling our contemporary ruin. Even the poor, worn-out, communication material—the Word—is recycled.

As it is cut off from speech it becomes gigantic, a voiceless scream. For

Nancy Dwyer (1992) the word is a large block on wheels, like a grocery cart, "CARE" on one side, "LESS" on the other. We can push or drive our very heavy CARE/LESS letters. The certainty that life is lacking something important becomes a moving monument; the way to emphasize emptiness is to make it solid. A market image is made of something that can't be bought or sold. The artist creates an impersonal object, a standard model, a volume that needs human arms and legs to be moved (*Less*, installation, 1992). Words are heavier than ever; lazy, very slow. An old doubt: would LESS objects open new organs in our bodies, or make our organs function better?

Today artists know that it is not a new computer that will improve the quality of their language. Not even intelligence is able to solve conflicts, at least not alone. Video art collects what remains of a language, making a weightless text of light. I wonder if video art is going through a period of "realism" that could be compared to realism in literature, but only as Roland Barthes meant it.

This is my unfaithful transcription of a piece from Barthes (*Leçon*, 1977):

Freedom's strength in videography doesn't depend on an artist's public image, on his political involvement, nor on doctrines inspiring him, rather, it only depends on how he pushes the limits of language.

Videography includes more than one kind of knowledge. Videography is definitely realistic, or more precisely, it is a dazzling light from reality. Ideas come around, neither fixed nor made a fetish. Videography gives them an indirect place, which is as good as gold. It stores and then releases a flash of light, as a stone heated by the sun. Science is rough, whereas life is thin; in order to heal the gap, we take video to our heart.

Art in video doesn't say it knows something, but about something. Better: it knows what's what about human beings.

Knowledge is a statement in videography: it illuminates where the subject is and how strong. . . . It aims precisely at the reality of language: language an immense nebula of implications, effects, echoes, meanders, ravines, addictions. . . . Videography is wherever words and images are tasty, colored, sounding, luminous.

If things must taste as they are, the artist has to accept the evidence: reality and language are never parallel, that is why video art is realistic, it longs for reality. It is also stubbornly unrealistic, because it believes it is sensible to wish that which is impossible.

If we need more and more to write, with video, texts soaked in real bits of our actual history, this does not mean that art's territory has been invaded by the need for documentation. Otherwise, what about *War and Peace*, or the combines by Robert Rauschenberg? The fact is that an artist cannot be aware of himself if he doesn't connect his inner anxiety with the common life of everyone, if he doesn't find again a relationship between his own existence and that of the larger human society.

Technology has made his tongue sharper, perhaps richer. We are under the strong illusion that a more fluid writing, discontinuous, unpredictable, having more than one dimension, is closer to life. But the main problem is not canceled: languages of art still long for real life, believing it is sensible to imitate its manner of operation, or to copy the glimmer of reality we are able to perceive. Specific times and processes take the place of accomplished shapes. More and more artists are able to leave the closed room of their body, to break the very closed circuit between their body and its image, captured by the camera. The limit of experience, in art, has moved from the personal body of the artist to his personal vocabulary, to his dialogue with his instruments. The passage through many kinds of technology (the most primitive are still included), exploring the large landscape of physical and spiritual dynamics, has created a particular way of understanding life, life as made by humans in time, which becomes history, when someone writes it.

This is not far from the experience of Woody and Steina Vasulka; they have been engaged for over twenty years in the attempt to correct the linear geometry of Descartes. Between the two coordinates that define the space for visual elements they put image's intensity and sound's waves, so that time takes the place of space and images become pure moving energy. Nevertheless, this visual invention, and the technological ambiance that produced it, are nothing but a desert if human practice hasn't the power to inscribe new tracks of ideas, or at least a new *Art of Memory* (Woody Vasulka, videotape, 1989). In a strange way, Woody Vasulka has become a worth fellow of Cicero, even if Cicero's house of memory is not, for him, a mere method of remembering. The classic idea of mind needing, literally, an architecture containing and supporting its activity becomes an artificial video space where the power of memory can be seen, struggling against a human nature compelled to forget. What happens to human beings when their refusal of memory is nearly a removal? Woody digs into the continuity of a desert landscape, incredibly beautiful and colorful, the gray caves of history. A long history of wars. The places of memory are computer sculptures of events that only have a visual reality in films and pictures, sound volumes in which colors are forgotten. For men and women of our time, who could go toward their last days without any awareness, memory can be a nightmare. An angel with gold wings, perched on a mountain, looks from afar at our ugly story. He is perfect, not contaminated. So is the landscape. Man is an isolated presence, a simple intensity of one existence that is not able to find a common place, neither in a natural, forgotten history, nor in History. He would like to be blind. The angel is his impossible perfection already thrown far away, now ready to become a bullet hurting and punishing him.

Images of threatening hostility. The man, torn by conflicts coming from inside and outside, shut in a cage. While he dances his despair, his laugh turns into a grimace, his weeping into a savage pain. Years of intelligent investigation into the language of sounds and images have finally generated such a limpid idea, a true story that brings video art back into our unbalanced world. Human beings coming out from memory's caves rediscover themselves primitive.

To be in with memory is even more difficult. It means to stay inside time—that is, the measure of life. It means that human time is not only subjective. The seventies are not to be forgotten—so close, real-time performances, fixed on videotape, interesting as much as impossible to watch. Certainly, they are not objects to use up. Maybe they are prisoners of their excessive nearness to life as it is, not yet written. Books as well as ideas have become deadened, or they remain unheard. Too much noise and confusion and fear of the unfamiliar things. I still admire the artists of the seventies, so desperately idealistic: wanting to be separated from conventional ideas, they preferred to have their heads cut off. It happened both in Europe and in the United States.

Nil Yalter was living in Paris. She had just arrived from Turkey as a painter. The first videotape she made is still a milestone in French video art's history. Nil Yalter aimed the camera at her navel. Between the navel and the machine, a closed path in the room. For almost an hour she wrote a widening spiral of words on her belly, around the small mark left by the lost umbilical cord, how women had been lost. The written belly starts dancing and only the central part of the body appears on the screen, the center point of her balance. The unexpressed argument at the origin of this work belongs to a story that made any woman, for centuries, *La Femme sans tête* (The headless woman; videotape, 1976).

The headless man was living in New York. He used to spend his time stretched out measuring the floor, trying to walk with his feet on the wall and, without stopping, moving his back and arms like a large worm on the ground. Bruce Nauman. He will recover the head much later, and this time the head without the body, for a video installation revealing that Nauman's fondness for the closed room hasn't come to an end (*Spinninghead*, 1990). I saw the installation at the Musée Cantonale in Lausanne in November 1991: one monitor on top of another, one head on the top, and the same head, turned over, on the bottom. Both of them go round the neck as if they were screwed on. Because they are not light bulbs, they cannot be turned on. Green and blue, the colors of asphyxia. It was time for somebody to kill Narcissus.

Belgium, 1976: Jacques-Louis Nyst used to make his head empty. Often absentminded, he sometimes neglected to choose *his* medium. He shot, drew, wrote (in which order isn't important) the story of *The Object:* a tiny blue coffeepot. Nyst lifts the lid: he wonders if it is by chance the top half of a skull. Inside, it is empty. What civilization does it come from? One hypothesis: from a civilization whose ideas rest on emptiness, which is the essential spring of life. The object sleeps. Its body is full. Blue domes, at night, emerge from the sleeping earth.

In New York, William Wegman was thinking of his dog as if she had a human head and human reactions. Even now, his videotapes are the only ones that crack us up. Really, Wegman was truly serious. With the greatest seriousness he tells us how desperate the artist is in his attempt to resist the dog as a dog, her settled "is-ness," a conceptual artist resisting the concept. Sometimes he didn't expect the dog to think and feel as a human being, and he attempted to feel as a dog.

John Baldessari, more gently and less successfully, taught a plant the alphabet. Bill Viola put a microscopic camera between his teeth. Rebecca Horn wore long nails touching the floor, as if her fingers couldn't move away from their own shadow.

If reality was trying to balance the mind and feelings of people trapped in technological conformity, artists reacted by transforming machines into something that they made their own, and by making clear the absolute, impersonal value of the human body as a filter for our mental experience.

At the same time he was painting the boundless workroom of the mind, Jean Dubuffet hurled his *"batons rompus"* against the unfaithful culture of the word. Everything happened at the same time, in the midseventies. Some artists working with videotape, and also with paint, began to clarify their ideas. "I use video as a knife to cut to the heart of the matter and the matter is me," wrote Willoughby Sharp (Schneider and Korot 1976).

It was a special moment in which art thinking was going beyond McLuhan's understanding of media and beyond the natural habit of separating the person who knows, the object known, natural and artificial tools, natural history, and the histories of culture. The effect this had (and it is difficult to say if this was positive or not) was the failure to keep a clear line between life and art. The authors and theirs works were temporary and unsteady. In many cases they still are. Questions opened by artists at the beginning of this century were reconsidered. How to create an imaginary reality connected with our preconscious sensory perceptions? How to think a dynamic syntax joining sounds and images, although not following established cultural codes? Near the beginning of the century Russian artists who invented a poetry and aesthetic for a new language, named ZAUM, had taken to composing sounds slipping through and beyond the limits of words and of their automatic repetition. The subject of a work of art was a perceptive and associative process. A response from the spectator was required.

The problem was not, then and now, merely an aesthetic problem. Art was supposed to be the filter, changing the automatic perception of life, increasing our ability to pay attention.

Once more, in the seventies, video cameras and audio synthesizers confirmed that an age of technology had the power to transform consciousness and ideas—for instance, the idea of the point of view, as if the mind was pointed out toward a lifeless, indiscreet collection of matter. It makes a big difference, when thinking of the connection between subject and object, that we realize that video images are a kind of energy spreading from a source of light, creating in us colors, forms, density that can seem to be totally unnatural. But even in out natural life we are not entirely independent from light's neurochemical stimulus on our cells. It is our body, in a sense, that creates the millions of possible colors covering the natural world. How precisely it happens in each of us, and for other animals, is something we don't understand, but certainly nothing is geometrical, foreseeable, or inevitable.

Long before video art was born, artists felt that traditional media, blocking in one way or another what can be expressed by human activity, were not enough. In 1932 Edward Weston complained about how difficult it was to watch in a personal way through the camera lens, which is absolutely impersonal. Alberto Giacometti used to destroy his portraits several times, remaking them by scraping out and erasing colors and signs, in an endless competition with time.

How to face nature without taking any advantage? Letting things reveal themselves. Even cutting them from the world, wanting to create abstract bodies, we open holes in the landscape. Ellsworth Kelly, while driving a truck for the U.S. Army in France, tried for the first time to separate a church from the panorama, lost his bearings, and drove into a ditch.

How to not break the unceasing stream of life, how to listen to the way things happen, how to recreate the unexpected without any . . . remembering John Cage.

How to go on using words, knowing their limits too well.

"Tout ce qui précède oublier. Je ne peux pas beaucoup à la fois. Ça laisse à la plume le temps de noter. Je ne la vois pas mais je l'entend là-bas derrière. C'est dire le silence. Quand elle s'arrête je continue. Trop de silence je ne peux pas. Ou c'est ma voix trop faible par moments. Celle qui sort de moi. Voilà pour l'art et la manière" (*assez*, Samuel Beckett, 1965–66).

How to not renounce using the voice, that which comes from me. A pause of silence had to be taken before artists could begin talking again, finding a new vocabulary in a dictionary not yet written.

Jean Dubuffet's last paintings, from 1974 until the end of his life, can be regarded as a stony ground on which you see the relationship between stone and stone. *Crayonnages, Parachiffes, Récits, Théatres de la mémoire, Psycho-sites, Sites aléatoires, Non-lieux* are a kind of writing, more and more a repetitive handwriting. In video, Ed Emshwiller, in the same period, multiplied the human figure, also as a figure of speech, whose outline was sometimes filled with bricks (the bricks of a built reality), sometimes empty, or walking out from itself, coming back, going out again: autistic writing in a fixed, motionless landscape (*Crossing and Meetings*, videotape, 1975). Here the continuity between the living, thinking being and the world surrounding him has broken down. Dubuffet used to point out the same failure as a betrayal: as if culture's function had been to fragment the thousand things contained by nouns, nailing them to the dictionary in a list of words. Verbal cords would have tied our thoughts up (*Bâtons rompus*, 1983–84). Might they fly through new trajectories? If the transmitter doesn't change, this is impossible. Mankind can only endure its own wasteland. That is why each character painted by Dubuffet is a tiny man, as a child would draw. Legs and arms almost nothing, the head is big, features cannot be found. Every tiny man is different only by accident. Not far from automatic writing, with one more paradox. It is the writing that writes the man, not the other way around. Man is its own writing; once written it takes to splitting and multiplying in space, as if space was time, until the hand is tired, and falls silent.

A linear connection in space can be different from Euclid's rigid geometry. Wolf Vostell tried to reverse the relationship between a body and a stone. The body is heavy and the stone is light. Is the stone still thoughtless? The video screen says "yes." The stone is transparent and the body impenetrable. Breathing is the only sound coming from the monitor, and it is a most difficult voice to classify. We don't know who it belongs to (*TV Cubism*, videotape, 1985). An unknown connection is sculpted in light, but Vostell's videography lies on the woman's skin as simple handwriting on paper. Who blesses the surface's funeral? What is beyond? A depth, or nothing? I always thought of a well, the so-called well of the mind. Can we really watch our thoughts down there? Why not, instead, fly with Edmond Jabès, the poet who has released every weight from thinking? "The real link is to go from sight to sight, from word to word. Aerial. The wave's memory is a bird."

Jacques-Louis Nyst is also a poet. He makes books, photographs, paintings, videotapes. Moving continuously from one medium to another, attempting to escape the danger that every kind of writing traps and imprisons stories and images. Always the same obsession. Dubuffet's obsession that writing writes man, and the written (drawn) character kills the unlimited variation of vision.

     "Then, let's imagine we are able to go under the tale, to sneak in the writing's gate, like when we were children, looking for that point from which we can see again, as the first time . . . " (from *Hyaloïde*, videotape, 1985).

     Let's imagine that we go beyond the wall behind which images become "transparent, translucent, hyaloïde," opening the door to the light of a legendary universe. Here the images spark and multiply without order or categories.

     "Once upon a time . . . and, if it was always the first time, . . . which side of the wall would we be on?" (from *Hyaloïde*, videotape, 1985). It is not thought, but thought's geometry, that has broken down, its fragments littering the ground. Sense and nonsense are aroused by Nyst's video poems, fluid images, and precise shapes. Images, words, stories, all have a sexual life. Words, just over the border of the Nomala Desert (deserted by names), change into images. The pencil's tip becomes a round, soft nipple. The story has lost its feet, but history has lost its footing. The poet walks in the emptiness and silence of written history; living in this imaginary history, he shifts the wall of thought and discovers what the desert is: a junkyard of words, broken stories, stones. Were we seeing them for the first time? Many triangular sails outline the desert's surface (*Comme s'il y avait des pyramides* [As if there were pyramids], videotape, 1990). The videotape began with a transparent pyramid, the twin of a straw hut. Reason lives in both of them. Perhaps the opaque wall of reason is an obstacle that we need, separating us from visible things, making them imaginable. Maybe we are learning to know our human nature again. We are rediscovering the changeable life of our soul, and looking for a similar kind of extension of our tools, either natural or artificial.

> I assume that everything we accept as reality is merely private, a limited construction that is infinitely more alterable than we imagine. At the same time, I live in a culture that has no space for what is not rationally knowable. I find that the only way out of this unrealistic and untenable situation is to change the way to see and hear what I see and hear. When they come, these changes are always sudden, disorienting, almost incommunicable, often elusive, priceless. They leave the world itself surreal, somehow more transparent, full of immanence. *Videotape is the means I have of making changes that leave a trace.* (Ingrid Wiegand, in Schneider and Korot 1976)

The main trace was in the artist's personal experience, the rest, as much as possible, on the tape. Eighteen years later, our world being what it is, without any confidence in exchangeable, universal values, people making videotapes are often far from a critical vision of our culture. If visual perception itself becomes a value, what isn't visible can be forgotten, once again. And artists often suffer what is normally accepted today as a natural judgment: no harmony or connection between feelings, ideas, imagery, wishes. No hope.

Irit Batsry, for instance, tries to focus *A Simple Case of Vision* (videotape, 1991) as a process of animal life. It could be a metaphor on the page, but not in video: a human neck raises a head up and brings it back slowly, then raises it again. Silent profile of a man, an adult. Words in white characters arrive after: "I was born . . . My vision . . . Cross eyed . . . Two dark areas on a human face." It is a mute vision, without any human voice. The hand's cavity recovers the face, the white light of silent words fades, bends, becomes a swarm of flies burning the screen with a cold flame. We read in the final titles that the text was a piece by Buckminster Fuller about his childhood, but this doesn't explain the tape, which is essentially the declension of a perceptive experience, possible for everybody.

To remember the page is to be walking on the ruins. Let's change the tape: *Leaving the Old Ruin* (Irit Batsry, videotape, 1989). A tiny man crosses a bridge, lifting a leg, disappearing in midstride, appearing again. He can only repeat and repeat. Where does he come from? War and urban violence. Where will he arrive? For the moment he moves, every time leaving himself, maybe forgetting himself.

We do not know what it is we are like. One of the experimental sciences, neuropsychobiology, says that our body is a system of actions and reactions to the molecules moving around us in electromagnetic waves. Our nerves don't receive their stimulus in a codified way. Our nerve cells and neuron tree of knowledge is blind to the source of the stimulus, because they can only respond to the strength and length of the impulses. The brain, in the end, having received the incredible variety of recovered impulses, works out a nearly steady reality in thought. Heinz von Foerster spent most of his life doing experiments about knowledge as a work in progress. Making a hypothetical calculation, he found that our body might have 100 million sensors and about 10 billion synapses in the nervous system. Synapses are nodes, not so different from a plant's nodes, in which an arriving impulse combines with a chemical substance that activates the neuron. Therefore, we are supposed to respond one hundred thousand times more to our inner changes than to the stimulus coming from outside. "One hundred thousand," in this case, isn't a turn of phrase, but a scientific calculation as correct as it is hypothetical in its possible consequences.

Let's imagine each of us as a container and source of a chain reaction. Of course a container having only one mold. René Descartes can rest in peace: there is no mechanical connection between the thorn in our finger and our ability to tell the name of our pain: synapses are silent. The passing of quantity into quality is still a secret. As long as life lasts, we bring off an unsuspected number of energetic exchanges, of which we are only vaguely aware. Maybe we realize how important they are if we pay attention to our unconscious or follow the imagination, rather than walking on reason's thread.

I have read more than once the romantic idea that science and art have something in common, artist and scientist both being suspected of a mental disorder, or at least of being acrobats of the mind, forming theories, feeling the beauty of the theoretical, the unseen. Statements emphasizing the gap between mental and physical reality. I have never seen such a clear similarity as that between von Foerster's numbers and the art of Bill Viola. Spiritual and chemical energies are impossible to split. Bill Viola is the only artist that I know who has the courage to show his feeling life as a real life. The meter of his art is the intensity of feelings, which is the inner breathing of the mind. Literally, taking air into the lungs and sending it out again; you have to hold your breath when you suffer, when you are at your mother's death, and when you are under water. *The Passage* (videotape, 1991) talks a language that comes before the brain's order: breathing images and sounds of breathing. The normal effects of love. But no one is allowed to be sentimental. Not even the table, flying in an empty room, losing the napkin, the vase with flowers . . . losing its balance on the ground. The metaphor is dead, the metaphor as idea was too stringent, nothing but an image moving from one room to another. No, Bill Viola isn't fixing feelings in a shape. He enables us to perceive what belongs to our feelings, when they are still like a kind of sensitive thinking, not yet settled in our mind. There is the *Sleep of Reason* (installation, 1988) in Bill Viola's mind: just the opposite of Hegel's and Goya's idea that monsters and imaginary creatures emerge when our reason sleeps. Good-bye surrealism. Henry Miller says, "When do we begin to know that we know? When we have ceased to believe that we can ever know. Truth comes with surrender. And it's wordless. The brain is not the mind; it is a tyrant which seeks to dominate the mind" (*Big Sur and the Oranges of Hieronymous Bosch*, 1956).

We are terribly disturbed by the evidence that emerges every time we face the mirror of our physical fate, carrying our death since our first day. So we look for illusions that seem to defy time and last forever. But we do know, as science and art tell us without any sorrow, that we are time beings. Two spoons turn around a pivot (Rebecca Horn, *To Sleep as Little Spoons,* sculpture, 1989). Turning as a clock's hands. They are perfect twins, identical. They are short dancing figures in a short time, one after the other. Where is the real time? For whom? Of what? Video art's culture couldn't have found a more ill-timed expression. What Rebecca Horn is saying is clear: time in art is an artifact, not simply because you can alter the clock's click, but because it belongs to a machine just conceived as a source wasting the small energy that makes the movement, wasting in space the tracks of its mechanical life. Sometimes the tracks are impossible to perceive, as is the mood: another machine (*La machine de la mariée bleue de Prusse,* installation, 1992), the three legged bride drips the Prussian blue on the shoes hanging from a nail over dirt on the floor. The lady cries blue. It was a hectic exhibition in Paris at the Galerie de France. Even the moon was rebelling.

La Lune rebelle (The rebel moon; installation, 1991), a horizontal line of typewriters, neither electric nor electronic, looks like a big black insect hung from an iron beam, near the ceiling. The carriages slip down, the black ribbons fall. As the machines write, they loose their tongues. Nobody is writing. But something is typed, characters produced by a small motor. Impossible to read. If we forget the mechanism, we could imagine a spiteful ghost. But it is Rebecca's red head sprinkling writing's decline with magic, and the black ribbons in mourning, sucking the characters in, erasing them each time they return.

She is leaving her first experiences in performance and videotape and becoming a sculptor and a painter, even when she makes installations. Just like Peter Greenaway, whose paintings need to become installations, or sets for his films, in order to find their final shape. Rebecca's hopeless machines are tools creating a noncodified writing, without characters, alphabet, or grammar. They produce a visual and audio texture that affects our mind directly, as any physical sensation. The texture itself becomes something living that you can't interpret. Maybe our mind could stop being flat on the page, exhausted from interpreting and following abstract threads. We could discover the mind's colors and sounds . . . Enough.

Michel Chion, a French composer who wrote a manifesto of concrete music, discovers in recorded sound a creative resource. Tape can capture the most inner and elusive vibrations of a particular sound (or image), an unsteady reality that we perceive. The artist and the material of his art are not opposed as a living being and inert material; on the contrary, they are both dynamic, difficult to train, changing each other:

> To compose is for me to work with a soft, escaping matter which slowly hardens, takes shape. I must certainly recover the same accuracy of the written note, therefore I need my hearing which is my own . . . I have to go with and

against the sound, from time to time contrasting with its natural movement or creating a new conflict between sounds. The finished work is not fluid, or a continuity starting from the original curve of the sound. I cannot follow that curve without resistance, nor can I ignore it. To question and cut the sound is very interesting, paying attention to what it is saying, what it is saying to me. . . . I have to watch myself. The shape of sound makes many proposals, often awakening my memory of music as a fixed object (on paper). The shape of sound is never an already existing object, my ear is my living instrument. I discover again and again the real sound of my music, changing it until the end. (Michel Chion, *L'Art des sons fixés*, 1991)

Finally, what results is a work of art that cannot be separated from the author's senses, or from a spectator's sensitivity. We can watch and listen endlessly and every time the work is, for the spectator, an experience in real time; every time we are losing or grasping something, every time we perceive something different because we are aware of ourselves in a different way. I doubt that looking at a painting is any different. The real difference is that this kind of contemporary art gave up imitating the surface appearance of nature, and makes the attempt to imitate nature in her manner of operation. This was John Cage's idea about Jasper John's paintings: structures, not subjects, signatures of anonymity—even if sometimes Johns introduces "signs of humanity" to intimate that we, not birds for instance, are part of the dialogue. A dialogue between art and nature from which John Cage, obstinately, erases every individual point of view, every possible clue.

It remains true, nevertheless, that each manner needs its own time, and the way indelible marks have been engraved by time in human history is something impossible to imitate. The human experience of time is only lived experience.

Marina Abramovic creates, in her videotape *Terra degli dei madre* (1987), an experienced time that she shares with the viewer: a shape in time floating between the monitor and the viewer, a flowing connection of camera/eye and microphone/ear. To perceive this time is to feel how passively we endure it. We see on the screen a circle of women sitting around a table. They barely move their eyelids, like statues plunged into a density of sound, a strange language that blends many languages, some dead, some not, a language that doesn't belong to anyone, not even the artist. The voice doesn't reflect any thoughts we can recognize. The images and the voice sound out of history. Never disturbed, neither happy nor unhappy. Human history and time, far from the natural order of things, lie in the peace of art. A spiral of concentration brings everybody to the threshold of hypnosis. Opening the door to the feeling of our physical existence, moving from an anxious consciousness toward the fluctuating quiet that precedes sleep, the frontier between life and death is lost.

"But once you are in videotape, in a sense, you are not allowed to die," wrote Nam June Paik (Schneider and Korot, 1976) about the videotapes of Shigeko

Rosanna Albertini

Kubota, Paul Ryan, and Maxi Cohen dealing with their fathers' deaths. To die, actually, is a long process not separate from life. Video, in its own way, doesn't die. It can be repeated, repeated, repeated. . . . The tape, for people watching and listening, is never the same. "Video art imitates nature not in its appearance or mass, but in its intimate structure . . . which is the process of AGING (a certain kind of irreversibility)"—Nam June Paik again.

Only words in video seem ready to disappear, or simply to exist as just another thing in the world of things. White on black, they look like writing itself wishing to forget they had been Utopia's vehicle, or the well-organized substitute for a historical situation that has never been really perfect. How to make art after the Holocaust and Hiroshima? Jochen Gerz says that a cemetery will never be used as a readymade (1993).

The "how " is interesting. Shalom Gorewitz makes an attempt in video. *Ten Thousand Things* (videotape, 1992) is to say: everything in the world. Everything is, apparently, difficult to move. Shalom Gorewitz writes on the screen their fragility and his own. The light dissolves, cancels the borders, decreases the image's definition, whitens the colors, empties and dismisses the symbols of a multitude without civilization. The images of the crowd are borrowed from Japan, a country with an old civilization, about to lose it imitating ours. The man of the book, creating in one image a column of soldiers and columns of text telling their story, is finally realizing that the mind's power will destroy the world. Oriental culture comes to his aid, our enlightenment is overturned: "To study the self is to forget the self. To forget the self is to be enlightened by ten thousand things" (Dogen, Japanese Zen master, quoted from the tape). A couple of centuries ago Robinson Crusoe turned to nature, or to a hypothetical state of nature, hoping to find the single man's place in an already senseless history. But our Robinson, of this time, is so contaminated that he can't help coming back to history, listening to his heart. In a fragment of the tape, lifted from *Hiroshima Mon Amour*, she is leaving; he opens his eyes to the city's emptiness and ruin. "Emptiness is not different than form." It is not strange that Shalom Gorewitz needs to empty himself and his images. This has been practiced by artists for a long time. What is new is that, renouncing himself, overloaded by judgment, he writes a story in light, as if light had feelings.

"Form is not different than emptiness." This is the silence of Samuel Beckett and John Cage, and it is also the reversed perspective of recent video art: recycling cold pieces of reality in a new written body that is filled with feelings, even the desperate feeling of a lost paradise of form. Human reality is the subject, calling for somebody who could understand and listen.

Let's visit its visible surface: a sock with a hole in it sticks out from a bench. The sock, the foot, the leg, and the body lie down. We are watching *Homeless* (1989–90), a video installation by Joan Logue. Pieces of life are held within four tiny monitors that pierce the backside of a small, old wooden cupboard, hung on the wall. A

LONGING FOR REAL LIFE

series of precious video miniatures in a frame protected by a house that is also a tabernacle. This house is hung on the wall, with no address, no specific site. Without a name. The homeless haven't. On one of the monitors is a burning candle.

Three portraits in the other monitors take the same, very long, time of the candle. The homeless outside in the street, inserted one after the other in one of the tapes, as a stream of bullets. Repetition. Nine times out of ten they are lying down. Their life is parallel to the ground. They don't look upset or anxious. The cardboard houses lie on the steps, on the threshold of other people's existence. It's an unopened book of sleeping people. Sometimes food is given, to the homeless and the birds in the park. A terse slogan cut into a stone in the park:

You are free to question authority.
You are free to believe what you wish.
Your right to privacy has been guaranteed.

There is someone scratching himself. In the second monitor, no homeless, only a home: a dog tied in the yard, smoke from the chimney in a white landscape. The most frequent sound is that of Joan blowing her nose. Nothing happens. Life is hidden and protected, a no-ness that evaporates into smoke. In the third monitor we are again in the street, in Brazil. Reality? Once upon a time there was a pedestrian island, in the middle of the street between stands of yellow and red buses, going in opposite directions. On the island is a person, very busy with a pile of garbage. The movements are as accurate and as uninterrupted as those of a bird making its nest with recycled material. The black bird is an old woman. When she has finished her work, she sits down on the pile, arranged as an armchair, and watches the world. Waiting. She scratches her back, she stops and waits again. Her face is solemn, her hands in her lap. She picks a louse from her hair and crushes it between her nails. She must have been beautiful. We have no news about her. She is a woman, she is there. The most we can say is: she is a woman who loves to be precise. The artist keeps these three images of life delicately, without disturbing them. She doesn't want to explain. Nothing but love can understand what is always the same in our life, and repeated forever.

ROSANNA ALBERTINI

BIBLIOGRAPHY

Albertini, Rosanna, and Sandra Lischi, eds. *Metamorfosi della visione: Saggi di pensiero elettronico*. Pisa: ETS, 1988.

Barthes, Roland. *Leçon: Leçon inaugurale de la Chaire de Sémiologie Littéraire du Collège de France*. 7 January 1977. Paris: Seuil, 1978.

Beckett, Samuel. *L'Image*. Paris: Minuit, 1988.

———. *Sans et le dépeupleur*. Paris: Minuit, 1970.

Cage, John. *A Year from Monday*. Middletown, Conn.: Wesleyan University Press, 1985.

Chion, Michel. *L'Art des sons fixés*. Paris: Editions Metamkine/Nota Bene/Sono Concept, 1991.

———. *L'Audio-vision*. Paris: Editions Nathan, 1990.

Dubuffet, Jean. *Asphyxiante Culture*. Paris: Minuit, 1986.

———. *Bâtons rompus*. Paris: Minuit, 1986.

———. *Les Dernières Années*. Catalog of the exhibition at the Galérie nationale du Jeu de Paume, Paris, 20 June to 22 September 1991.

———. *L'Homme du commun à l'ouvrage*. Paris: Gallimard, 1973.

Gerz, Jochen. "Invisible Monument." Interview by Jacqueline Lichtenstein and Gerard Wajeman. *Art Press* 179 (1993).

Jabès, Edmond. *Le Livre des questions*. Paris: Gallimard, 1963.

———. *Le Livre de Yukel*. Paris: Gallimard, 1964.

Kaprow, Allan. "Introduction to a Theory." *bull shit 01*, October-November, 1991.

Kelly, Ellsworth. *Les années françaises*, 1948–1954. Catalog of the exhibition at the Galérie nationale du Jeu de Paume, Paris, 17 March to 24 May 1992 and the National Gallery of Art, Washington, D.C., 1 November 1992 to 24 January 1993.

Minkowski, Eugene. *Le Temps vécu*. Paris: Delachaux and Niestlé, 1936.

Nauman, Bruce. *Sculptures et installations*, 1985–1990. Catalog of the exhibition at the Musée Cantonal des Beaux Arts, Lausanne, 5 October to 5 January 1992.

Nyst, Jacques-Louis. *Hyaloïde*. Brussels: Yellow Now, 1986.

———. *L'Objet*. Brussels: Yellow Now, 1976.

———. *L'Ombrelle en papier*. Brussels: Yellow Now, 1977.

Nyst, Jacques-Louis, and Daniele Nyst. *Le Sourire de la phrase*. Editions du Centre International de Creation Video Montbeliard Belfort, 1992.

Rebecca Horn. Catalog of the exhibition at the Galérie de France, Paris, 24 November 1988 to 7 January 1989.

Schneider, Ira, and Beryl Korot, eds. *Video Art: An Anthology*. New York: Harcourt Brace Jovanovich, 1976.

Schnitzler, Arthur. *Beziehungen und Einsamkeiten*. Frankfurt: Estate Vienna and S. Fischer, 1967. Translated by Pierre Deshusses as *Relations et solitudes*. Paris: Rivage poche Petite Bibliotheque, 1988.

Stein, Gertrude. *The Geographical History of America*. New York: Random House, 1936.

———. *Look at Me Now and Here I Am* (writings and lectures, 1909-45). London: Penguin Books, 1967.

Tapies, Antoni. *La Réalité comme art*. Paris: Daniel Lelong, 1989.

Valéry, Paul. *Cahiers*. Paris: Gallimard, 1973.

Watzlawick, Paul, ed. *La realtà inventata*. Contributi al costruttivismo. Milano: Feltrinelli, 1988. See particularly the essay by Heinz von Foerster, "On Constructing a Reality," published initially in *Environmental Design Research,* ed. W. F. E. Preiser et al. Stroudsbourg, 1973.

VIDEOTAPES

Abramovic, Marina. *Terra degli dei madre*. 1987.
Baldessari, John. *Teaching a Plant the Alphabet*. 1972.
Batsry, Irit. *Leaving the Old Ruin*. 1989.
————. *A Simple Case of Vision*. 1991.
Emshwiller, Ed. *Crossing and Meetings*. 1975.
Gorewitz, Shalom. *Ten Thousand Things*. 1992.
Nauman, Bruce. *Bouncing in the Corner 1 and 2*. 1968-69.
————. *Flesh to White to Black to Flesh*. 1968.
————. *Stepping in the Studio*. 1968.
Nyst, Jacques-Louis. *L'Objet*. 1974.

Nyst, Jacques-Louis, and Daniele Nyst. *Hyaloïde*. 1985.
————. *Comme s'il y avait des pyramides*. 1990.
Vasulka, Woody. *Art of Memory*. 1989.
Viola, Bill. *The Space between the Teeth*. 1976.
————. *I Do Not Know What It Is I Am Like*. 1986.
————. *The Passage*. 1991.
Vostell, Wolf. *TV Cubism*. 1985.
Wegman, William. *Selected Works, Reel 1 to 7*. 1970–77.
Yalter, Nil. *La Femme sans tête*. 1976.

Rosanna Albertini

CHAPTER 11

THE IMAGES OF THE WORLD

Raymond Bellour

The images of the world have returned, every one of them. Those of History and of legend. Like those of the machine-body that receives and emits them. They arrive with a violence that heightens our sense of urgency. We need to know what these images have become, and how they come back to us—today when the world has disappeared, vanished, has been swallowed inside itself and devoured by its own expansion. Today when, as Gilles Deleuze says, we no longer believe in this world because the bond with man has been broken, how can we believe, in spite of everything, in a world in which we find ourselves "as though in a pure visual and aural situation"?[1]

In Woody Vasulka's videotape, *Art of Memory* (1987), at least four levels of memory are presented. Let us examine each level of memory separately.

First is the memory of the artist as a child returning insistently through a memory: it is the end of the war, he's ten years old, he lives near a military airport that has become a cemetery of planes; in the German fighters, he finds ultraperfected war machines in pieces, which he takes apart and reassembles, subjecting them to an endless autopsy. "Europe was a huge junkyard after the war. You could find everything from weapons to human fingers in the dump."[2]

The next memory level is that of the grown-up Vasulka, who remembers the power these war machines had on him as a child. He has since become an amazing creator of vision-producing machines, in his search for new images. For years, with Steina, he has gathered, constructed, and deconstructed the basic elements of a language that he sometimes envisions as a new "natural language": a "vocabulary" capable of establishing, then developing, the immaterial physicality of images created in real time both from simple reality and from the video signal, through the machines' half-blind, half-visionary power.[3] Jean-Paul Fargier has demonstrated how this basic research grew into an oeuvre, for Woody, through the "selection of a subject matter" that accorded the "story" a particular "destiny" entirely contained within its mode of processing (for example, the decline and death of a virtuoso musician in *The Commission* [1983]); for

Steina, the subject matter is the "West," understood as a vanishing of limits.[4] Paganini's life, decline, and death in *The Commission* is depicted by his body being subjected to a perpetual motion, undergoing a figuration-disfigurement (like that of Berlioz, who also plays a part in the violinist's fall). "There are always two images on the screen: a virtually complete image, and one of the partial and transitory states presented by its constant mobility."[5] This is *The Commission*'s great novelty: it creates new states of the images for a fictionalization that both employs and reinterprets the high-contrast lighting of German Expressionist cinema (in its lines and image fields), as well as the diffused lighting of Impressionist or Fauvist painting (in its strokes and pointillist touches). *The Commission*, which displays a filmic aspiration to opera, thus lends unsuspected vitality to the narrative archetypes of Romantic subjectivity (death, the contract, guilt, castration, and so on) that, to my knowledge, video has never before attempted to return to so directly.

Art of Memory departs from the concerns of *The Commission* toward another subject matter, which itself has a dual aspect: its own particular mode of processing and experience of the world. The world proceeds by incorporating the medium that historically has been entrusted with conveying and instilling memory in the child and the teenager born out of war: cinema, as witness to all wars of this century, whose memory video seeks to extend and renew here. A twofold memory, that of the war and that of cinema as a place of passage between an old and a new way of waging war—projecting images as well as missiles, projecting missile images—war and cinema both being on the point of vanishing, as Paul Virilio has shown.

The third memory in *Art of Memory*, which plunges us deeper into the work, is that of the performer/character that Vasulka has assigned to be his alter ego. He is the man with deeply etched features who appears at the beginning of the second section to challenge the enigmatic creature—angel, devil, sphinx, Spirit of History, Icarus, or Superman—standing in the landscape (figure 14); the man whose wrinkled face bears the mark of experience that in itself is the subject of the tape. Later, in a powerful image at the start of the third section, the man is faced with his doppelgänger, all wrinkles, who speaks to him from behind with Oppenheimer's voice, as if from the inside of a materialized brain/consciousness: he is made of pure webbing, through which electronic memory is suddenly, exemplarily, blended with the web of history (figure 19). It is between these two extreme points of representation (photographic and processed imagery) that the actor's body oscillates—in a more direct way than in *The Commission*. Here, the man is either one *or* the other in order to be one *and* the other for the spectator. Similarly, the tape as a whole is determined by the double, vertiginous use of cinema *and* video.

At the start of the second section, in the foreground, the protagonist faces the mythical creature; suddenly, the sky in the background changes, turning into an abstract grayness split into particles, while a kind of metallic rain comes down like a heavy curtain (figures 14, 15). The following shot—a wholly unique shot— is edited with a very rapid matching cut: the protagonist, up to this point seen from behind in three-quarter profile, is reframed in a side close-up, hurling himself onto the ground to escape the threat of an unidentified flying object that darts across the screen (figure 16). Here is a truly *filmic* shot, without any video processing—a shot one might imagine coming straight out of Steven Spielberg's *Close Encounters of the Third Kind*. This is followed by the effect Vasulka uses again and again in the tape—splitting each of the shots in the middle—which governs the transition from one shot to the next. The character of the fiction/opera is thus distinguished from the start; the strategy that makes him the conscience of the drama is made clear from the onset in terms of both shot construction and the substance of the image; thus conflicts and changes that affect the shot construction also become elements at stake in the narrative and in what it suggests.

Finally, there are the spectators, whose memories are being put to the test because, as moral subjects, they must mentally go back over the terrifying space opened up by the metaphysical upheaval of modern war from World War I to the end of World War II, reabsorbed in the images of nuclear apocalypse. This is true particularly because, as psychophysical subjects, they have to try to memorize what is presented to them as a particular *reading* of the event. In Vasulka's work, the ungraspable or just graspable aspect of what is shown becomes very acute. The vertigo thus created is less subtle than in *The Commission*; but it becomes more interesting conceptually (albeit at the cost, sometimes, of a certain heavy-handed didacticism) because the spectators are led to a more active consciousness in order to maintain the visible coherence of everything they see. Echoing the tension that occurs between "real" bodies and bodies made of webbing, we attempt to grasp the two levels of the circular dialogue that is set up between cinema and video, as well as between analog and digital representation. The first level denotes a trend toward the shot (and the filmic segment, as well); the shot, while imploding and redefining itself in the act, still forms narrative and dramatic units whose perceptible divisions give expression to the ungraspable character of the event. The second level—internal to the first, yet quite specific in itself—seems to be the one that gives this tape particular import: it lays out a "theory" of the single-frame image and the photographic image as the most intimate part of the relationship between video and cinema.

Art of Memory is divided into seven clearly defined acts or sections. Sections three to six each correspond to a particular theme: nuclear holocaust, the Spanish Civil War, the Russian Revolution, the war in the Pacific. An overture of sorts, the second introduces the performer/character (who returns in sections three and four); the last section reintroduces him, changing his status as part of an epilogue.[6]

The effect used to pass from one shot to the next (for all but one shot) is a sort of sinusoidally shaped "wipe" that opens up (and closes) from the center of the frame (figures 8, 10, 11, 17), lending new versatility to the ancient "wipes" of silent cinema (the same "wipe," without motifs and in a solid gray, marks off the different sections). From the fifth section on, this transition process is doubly complicated: either only the top part of the image seems to change, because the bottom part of the two images is identical, or, most frequently, the top part of the image, when pushed away, instead of

151

moving off the top of the frame, narrows and becomes a sort of scarf that seems to wave within the frame before moving off (or reentering: special effects always work both ways) on the left. This second variation is very disturbing for the eye of memory because it adds to the confusion between the two separated shots, thus increasing the time the image lasts even as it is already being "drained away." This, however, is nothing as compared with the process that permeates the sixth section: an image strip, frayed at the edges, enters sideways, passes through, breaks up the shot (figure 36), and then expands, imposing the new image in combination with the dividing "wipe"—so that we witness a sort of dilation of the time-space the two shots share, like the very long dissolves that stunned the spectator's gaze in the early cinema. Thus this kind of effect somehow recreates the shot and redefines editing, as it has always done in cinema—marking the limits of the shot at the same time that it challenges them: "video" is one of the names for the passage that leads from the marking out of the shot to the vanishing of its limits. As one might guess, however, the strongest challenge created by the effect arises from *within* the shot, destroying its unity by multiplying it—thus opening the perspective to two connected levels: the single-frame image and the apparatus.[7]

Nearly all of the shots are divided between two motifs. The New Mexico landscape—mountains and desert—makes up the background: this image is wholly photographic, even if its color is often a processed one; inscribed against this are large digitally created gray shapes whose complexity comes from their relationship with analog representation—they either redouble it by mimicking its motifs or they capture and redistribute it. In the first instance, the first shot (over which the opening credits are shown—figure 1) simultaneously shows a background of red mountain and yellow sky, and in the foreground a series of gray waves are propelled with a slight rotating motion that evokes the mountain shapes. The simultaneous appearance of these motifs sets up a reversibility between nature and artifice, form/figure and background, while the contrast between them remains highly conspicuous. In the second instance, which comes up as early as the second shot, a gray, geometric shape, like a double folded screen, stands out against a background of rocky desert (figure 3); on one of its sides, one can make out an obscure, fascist-revolutionary sign,[8] on the other, a spinning globe of the earth on which the shadow of the sign is projected (to the accompaniment of sounds of wars, of the language and words that punctuate them: "Stalingrad . . . Africa . . . ").[9]

The primary interest of the tape comes from the activity of the large gray shapes. Their role is either to represent something—animate or inanimate—or to serve as a kind of image support. In the first instance, they create a certain confusion, allowing for alloys, ensuring transitions between various levels (of ideas, of categories, or matter). In the second and more profound instance, these shapes involve the functioning of memory, of the memory-image, at the core of the experience comprised both by the vision of the tape and the double history displayed in it (figures 5, 7, 9, 12, 13, 28): the history of this century and the history of the medium—the transition from cinema to video and the computerized image—and the photographic images that hover between

RAYMOND BELLOUR

them. As an example, I will analyze one shot, in which, at the very beginning of the second section, the protagonist faces the devil-angel, casts a stone at him, and then photographs him five times (figures 14, 15). At this point, the sky, which forms the background, changes into a gray shape (the only case in this tape, I believe, of a clear transformation of the analog into the digital, of the figurative into the abstract). The sky becomes a screen of metallic rain whose imaginary drops, propelled by a constant motion (upward, then downward), are actually many solid microfragments, juxtaposed and welded together. It is as if each fragment of this part of the artificial image, born out of the act of taking a still photograph, is reduced to the equivalent of a single-frame image—and that whole is a simultaneous image of the shot itself (or, by analogy, of the tape insofar as it is the sum of all the shots). The single-frame images, rendered two-dimensional although in motion, both construct and represent the screen that contains them. Thus, we can then pass on to the only shot of the tape that is purely filmic—the gray shape—because it penetrates the film from within it, jogging and reviving its memory, and is charged with representing film mutation.

With the third gray shape of the first section, the die is cast: the elbow-like "bachelor machine" that straddles the landscape is composed of unequal parts that appear to be welded together (figure 9); onto this entire surface, however, film is projected, modulated by the cuts, recomposing so many shots and/or single-frame images, both real and virtual. Eight (out of thirteen) shapes of this sort can be counted in the first section (figures 5, 7, 9, 12, 13). The images that throng and follow on each other constantly reach the limit of visibility and legibility, mostly because they match up with the most unexpected compositions of the gray shapes: thus they become moments of a sort of global phenomenal body, mutating, external/internal—as well as fragments of perception, originating from an autonomous vision. They are at once propelled by a constant motion and ceaselessly interrupted, one might say, by moments or points of fixity that imply barriers from one scene to the other and images "lifted" within the same scene. Finally, one does not know if the scene (minimally) changes or is (merely) reproduced from one shot, from one single-frame image, to the other, if it is sheer repetition or constant difference. (Rather, one has the feeling of going *beyond*, as if toward a possible image, a visible beyond the divisible yet made of it, close to repetition, as Deleuze defines it, as difference within concept.)[10] Nothing is really decipherable, not even for the analyst-spectator who struggles against this decomposition of memory in order to see how it is composed. Everything happens too rapidly, or too obscurely, or too undefinably, even if one guesses or "sees" the totality of what escapes vision: army movements, cities on fire, aircraft carriers, charges, assaults, rocket launches, flights, takeoffs, silhouettes, frightened faces.

Thus, the gray shape seems to harbor the body of film, its purely material substance, and make the film unravel beneath "the other film";[11] however, the variations of figures, rhythms, and frequencies are also in themselves possible echoes of the content of the scenes. The gray shape materializes the thousand and one shapes of this body—the film—only to the extent that it functions at the same time as a screen (figure 15). This takes place in the third section, just after a section that engenders the most beautiful of imaginable shapes: a machine worthy of Kafka's *The Penal Colony* crosses the desert like a rake or a mad insect (figure 18), while scenes of extreme violence seem to vanish and rebound against the edge of the receptor panels, where they may be halted yet may also pass through. The effect is enhanced by a movement sweeping the landscape that serves as a background to the machine, which appears to be followed by a tracking shot (this is an extremely rare occurrence in the tape, where movement almost invariably arises from within the image). This shows the extent to which this quite short third section, involving three singular shots (the conflict between the protagonist and the mythical figure, with the steel rain coming down; the "filmic" shot of the protagonist; and this gray shape), underlines points of tension between video and cinema.

The screen is first placed behind the actor, as a memory toward which he turns back: a huge concave screen, a cinemascope spread over the landscape, like a Richard Serra sculpture that's finally found its natural surroundings (figure 21). The solid gray is gradually disturbed; clouds float by; the light rises, gathers, and vanishes. The atom bomb explodes. All the world's memory. All the energy of a single movement in a huge, still, single-frame image.

The screen thus returns as a leitmotiv for the entire third section, with or without the protagonist or the spectator interposed (figure 23). The interest of that section, however, lies mostly in the other gray shapes, which appear in ambiguous yet powerful alternation. Nearly all these shapes are spinning, spiraling, and most are prismatic, composed of microelements arranged in curves and shattered with intense vibrations that recall the steel curtain-screen originating in the sky (figure 22). The atomic explosion, commented upon by Oppenheimer's voice and processed face (figure 20), is represented both on the screen and by the infinite division of abstract cells conveying pure energy on shapes that function as screens. These all function together as a revival, an amplification of the gray shapes, a background for the projections dispersed in the first section.

Up until this point (roughly in the middle of the tape) one can find three main kinds of gray shapes:

the undivided screen, with the single event that seems to be reabsorbed in the shot/ single-frame image (figure 23);

the myriad form, whose own "empty" event is the processing of the screen, fluctuating from the pure pulsing and twisting of light to a nearly infinite division of cells (figure 22) (these cells, produced along a model of geometric progression, are nevertheless largely unequal because of the form of the gray shapes, but they, too, come close to achieving singularity);

the gray form with a divisible screen (an average of ten unequal screens, themselves dependent on the variations of each form) onto which historical scenes are projected, in an extremely broad range of speeds stilled by brief motionless moments (figures 5, 7, 9, 12, 13, 28).

Thus, the attentive viewer will appreciate what is being carried out around the single-frame image/screen: a single-frame image per twenty-fourth or thirtieth of a second, one screen per single-frame image. This is what should be visible. For example, in the Spanish sequence (IV) the photograph (or the single-frame image?) of a man's face glides upward and downward (figure 26): the chain is interrupted by dark spaces (like black leader on the filmstrip) that run so fast that a single-frame image seems to occupy the whole screen, even though its connection with the other images is perceptible (every occurence of the image is, in addition, underlined, mechanically punctuated by a voice that repeats, like a broken record, "Por la Revolucion, Durruti!"). The same thing happens in the Soviet sequence (V). Here, the gray shape first consists of two identical images (of Lenin, Trotsky, and so on) turning on themselves (figures 29, 30). These fragments of filmstrip coiling and uncoiling, which look like the beginning of a series that stops at the moment an image is split in two, are situated precisely in the interspace between (unique) still photography and (individual or multiple) single-frame image. This feeling grows even stronger when the Spanish sequence starts to glide again, in a more significant way: moving horizontally now, the images take up nearly the whole screen (one only catches a glimpse of the colored desert landscape) and assume the shape of the screen. Two women's faces glide by, from right to left—both single-frame images and still photographs (figures 31, 32); by themselves they nearly fill the shot, which they set in undulating motion. This "parade"[12] ends with the image of a book, which has become emblematic of the psychic leafing through produced by the filmic apparatus; this image, long inscribed by cinema, has been recognized in film theory (by Thierry Kuntzel) and reworked by video as an after-product of cinema (by Vito Acconci, Kuntzel, and others).

Earlier, by way of introducing the transformation affecting the gray shapes, I used the phrase "from a single-frame image to the apparatus." The single-frame image is at the heart of this transformation, but only because the screen is in itself reworked as a variable of the photo-cinema-video apparatus. Recall, if you will, the two-sided screen on which, at the very beginning of the tape, the fascist-revolutionary sign and globe of the earth were inscribed (figure 3). This effect is not connected with the gliding and stratification of the images, but with their spatialization within the apparatus, that is, the virtual position of the spectator's eye. When the screen is only (and variously) double—instead of becoming polymorphic (as in the gray shapes with multiple images, where the gaze confronts a sort of tactile multiplicity)—it is the apparatus's mirror structure that is the direct subject of vision. What, then, happens to my mirror/body (facing the screen), which continues to function, even if my eye has already become a polymorphic body? The sixth section (war in the Pacific) tackles this problem by setting up *two* double screens *twice* and, what is more, *together* (to multiply the effect). On the left side, there is the two-sided screen, very close to the first one (although with multiple size variations between its two parts) and, in the middle, an even stranger double screen (figure 35). The part of the image this latter screen covers is split in two and folded vertically at a right angle: its top portion appears in frontal view like a normal movie screen, while its bottom part, much larger, stretches down slant-wise to the bottom of the image. Thus the action—here, mainly bombers taking off—occurs twice: the second time partly as a mirror and partly as a ghostly, excessive pro-longation of the first one. Meanwhile, on the other pair of double screens, the action embodies other motifs (the soldier's dirty work). Thus, the gaze is constantly relayed from a crossing or breaking of the mirror it continues to face. Each section, in effect, advances one step further in the systematic exploration of a virtuality of images as an extension of the theater of war.

The seventh and last section takes a decisive leap: it draws the charac-ter/actor back within the field of memory and casts him, as a being made of pure web-bing, within the gray shapes. He is enclosed in a split screen, with one of the two images lagging behind the other (figure 37). He suffers within this frame and, as his younger, former self, turns back into his own spectacle, a bygone image. This double, strained face is subjected to two other unfoldings—all I was able to project in this borderline, ungraspable, and enigmatic section, where the unfolded screens are vibrating over them-selves, multiplied, and substituted for one another, and are inhabited by exchangeable figures with exchangeable features. The first unfolding shows the protagonist, half recog-nizable, half made of fiber and folds, abandoning himself to a performance/dance that leads the images of the world back to video art and its origins, to the exertion of one's body, triumphant inside its screen-cage (figure 39). The second unfolding turns this standing body into a sitting body, making it a spectator, *its own* spectator (figure 38). One cannot say that these three figures of the same— metamorphosing and gliding under one another—are tied in a loop, for no image has the power to prescribe an overall meaning, but one has the feeling, nonetheless, that the images of the world are hostage to a memory designated within the very art that calls them forth.

To further convey the complexity of the work and conclude this analysis, which is part-ly a description, I offer a few additional remarks, if only to convey how hard it is for mere words to render some of the new *states* of the image, given the extent to which, in this work, a truly "unattainable" text[13] is composed. The word *text* no longer makes any sense, except as a reminder that language's sole prerogative is still its ability to try to say something, to remonstrate against anything. The first striking fact is the interde-pendence created, with the gray shapes, between figure and background; what exists as figure, or moves toward the figure, may also be background. Some of the most disturb-ing moments of the tape are caused by the way the screens/backgrounds become in themselves objects that seize *some* meaning, some *possible* meanings, such as the sever-al gray shapes that are loaded with films and single-frame images. In the Spanish sec-tion, for a huge stratified mass on which a still projection that could be mistaken for a fresco is inscribed, like an immense mausoleum (figure 24), a comparable mass appears at the end, as a false background for the credits: it is hollow this time, however, as though frayed from within and laden, so to speak, with all the undone memory that has accumulated throughout the tape—for the spectator as well as for the protagonist and the author he represents: this mass might be (and this is where its power lies) tomb, monument, brain, rock, face, a mass of undifferentiated memory (figure 40).

Next comes the very substance of the shapes—particularly of the shapes that are also backgrounds for a projection. I depicted them as being both full and flat (in spite of the strange profiles that can be seen in the illustrations). Yet, part of their power comes from their malleability, their transformability. A gray shape can become thick like a wall (figure 24), the screen a mass that accumulates memory and part of the real things of the world, even if it is a mere mirror for its images. A gray shape can be translucent, like a silhouette cutout. Curiously then, the shape is no longer really gray but gradually takes on color, having a less clear-cut relationship with the natural background than the other gray shapes in the tape. Finally, the gray shapes can be frayed, cloudy, hollow. In the Spanish sequence (where the backgrounds for multiscreen projection powerfully reappear), these different occurrences of the gray shapes are combined in the most extraordinary way: images are projected onto false dissolved screens where representation seems to collapse within the very time-space in which it is presented. This process grows more vertiginous when the actions of the bodies contradict the nature of the background that holds them: soldiers charging with guns and bayonets, or digging up the moving ground of this screen (figure 25), which is always on the verge of splitting open under the weight of its own lightness. There is as well an extraordinary moment in the Soviet sequence: shots or photographs of women glide by, from right to left, nearly filling up the entire screen; they are followed by the image of a man that moves past in a similar fashion (figure 33), except that the gray shape has now become both thicker (like a wall or screen) and hollow, distended, with its lines of memory left agape. In this image, volume and surface compete and verge on disappearance; in turn the image spawns a series of screens-words-images-books: the very image of the stratified and layered[14] cultural memory that could be emblematic of the entire "art of memory."

One may imagine how the transformations I just described are combined with those I mentioned earlier, and especially how this continuous mutation of the gray shapes within their own space, as within the entire screen, is ceaselessly combined with the constant yet variable special effects that establish transitions between shots or moments (figures 8, 10, 11, 17). A continuous mobility results, one of unceasing intersections and crossings and one that would seem to defy any drawing of distinctions. Nonetheless—and such is the power of the tape—the idea of the shot, the feeling of the shot, although split, fractured and, as it were, vaporized, still endures. The shot remains the *découpage* and memory device, for the contemporary spectator as well as for the spectator whose mind scans the history of wars captured by cinema in this century, which has become a history of cinema itself. The effort to maintain the shot as a unit of comprehension, destroyed then renewed, is quite close (yet with extremely different applications) to Marcel Odenbach's work on the strip-form:[15] there is the same repossession, the same distance-taking from the world, proceeding from video's formal rearticulation of major works from the past—Hitchcock for Odenbach, Eisenstein and Vertov for Vasulka. Destroying, then reconstructing the shot, then making this work visible: this, too, is the art of recognizing the memory of and within cinema.

There is, however, within this very movement, a more profound way to reach cinema while being *beyond* it. I have spoken of the structure of the cinematic apparatus—as screen, scenic place, solid memory—as constantly renewed with the aim of materializing the filmic apparatus and thereby capturing the single-frame image, both actually and virtually. More precisely, the single-frame image is shown in its infinitude, multiplicity, and singularity, but primarily in both its immobility *and* movement—one overlapping the other without completely encompassing it. One comes to realize, as in Vertov's work, how this immobility itself creates movement, and also how, at the very moment this movement (here infinitely accelerated) speeds up, motionlessness *might* at any point fall back on itself. The photographic function emerges as an element both visible and invisible, but always di-visible, of the transformation process that carries it to infinity. *This* is fundamental. The whole of Woody Vasulka's art is directed toward a processing of the image that aims at determining its substance and modes at every point, beyond the natural dictates of photography and its corollary, analogy. It is directed, in effect, toward a cameraless art. The power of this work lies in its ability to restore to us, *in real time,* the conditions of memory, at the very moment when we can glimpse an abstract time devoid of all connection to a preexisting visible world. One might say, as long as lines and points bear the mark of a preexisting photography, memory is still matter for history, and cinema is still captured in the course of its own development.

Translated by David Jacobson and Bérénice Reynaud

RAYMOND BELLOUR

1 Gilles Deleuze, *L'Image-temps* (Paris: Minuit, 1985), 223.

2 Woody Vasulka, quoted in Ken Ausubel, "Woody Vasulka: Experimenting with Visual Narrative," *News and Review,* 11 May 1983, 8.

3 Untranslatable pun: Bellour uses *extra-lucide* (visionary), an allusion to *voyante extra-lucide,* the French version of "readers and advisers." TRANS.

4 Jean-Paul Fargier, "Steina et Woody Vasulka: Zero un," in *Où va la video?* (Paris: Cahiers du Cinéma/Editions de l'Etoile, 1986), 76–82.

5 Ibid., 79.

6 I have deliberately "cheated" on the *découpage.* Syntagmatically, there are, strictly speaking, eight sections, if one follows the logic of segmentation demonstrated in the demarcation device—the gray "wipe" that closes shut (with a clapping noise that heightens the image-effect). From the point of view of the theme, however, section 3 and what would hypothetically be section 3a or 4 are homogeneous, since both deal with nuclear holocaust and are based on comparable elements. We find here, in an amusing but significant way, the basic problems of segmentation of classical cinema.

7 The word *apparatus* is used in English to translate two different French concepts, *appareil de base* and *dispositif. Appareil de base* denotes the situation of the subject in relation to the mirror stage and Renaissance perspective. *Dispositif* denotes the whole filmic situation, including the spectator's unconscious. In film theory, both meanings are used, but in this text, the second meaning is most often what is referred to. TRANS.

8 In fact, the sign bears the letters "UFA"—the initials of the biggest producer of German movies, which later became the producer of propaganda films for the Nazis.

9 There are exceptions to this omnipresence of the gray shape: the single "filmic" shot; several shots with the devil-angel in the landscape (for example, six in the first section), two shots of Oppenheimer in the third section (a third shot turns Oppenheimer into the gray shape), and a few colored solarizations behind the protagonist in the same third section.

10 This is the emblematic formula used by Gilles Deleuze in *Difference et repetition* (Paris: PUF, 1968).

11 By "filmic apparatus" Thierry Kuntzel designates a space both material and mental, between the "projected film" and the "film stock." See Kuntzel, "A Note upon the Filmic Apparatus," *Quarterly Review of Film Studies* 1, no. 3 (1976): 266–71.

12 Untranslatable pun. Bellour uses the verb *défiler* (to glide, to glide by) for the images; the beginning of this sentence reads *cet album-défile:* in this sense, *défile* means fashion parade (hence the connection with religious procession and, more significantly, military *march*). TRANS.

13 See Raymond Bellour, "The Unattainable Text," *Screen* 16, no. 3 (1975): 19–27.

14 Untranslatable pun: *feuilleter* means both *to layer apart* and to leaf through, so the past participle *feuilleté* connotes both books and "stratification." TRANS.

15 See Raymond Bellour, "The Form My Gaze Goes Through," *Afterimage* 16, no. 4 (November 1988): 4–6.

FIGURE 1

FIGURE 2

FIGURE 3

Figures 1–40: Woody Vasulka, *Art of Memory* (1987). (Photos: Marita Sturken.)

FIGURE 4

FIGURE 5

FIGURE 6

FIGURE 7

FIGURE 8

FIGURE 9

160

FIGURE 10

FIGURE 11

FIGURE 12

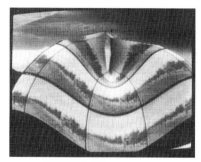

FIGURE 13

FIGURE 14

FIGURE 15

FIGURE 16

FIGURE 17

FIGURE 18

FIGURE 19

FIGURE 20

FIGURE 21

FIGURE 22

FIGURE 23

FIGURE 24

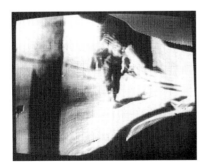

FIGURE 25

FIGURE 26

FIGURE 27

FIGURE 28

FIGURE 29

FIGURE 30

FIGURE 31

FIGURE 32

FIGURE 33

FIGURE 34

FIGURE 35

FIGURE 36

FIGURE 37

FIGURE 38

FIGURE 39

FIGURE 40

DWELLER ON THE THRESHOLD

Bill Horrigan

The things that you lost by the way were guiding you. And you tried to replace them. Which do you think you will see again, them or their replacements? Unless you lost the replacements as well, which sometimes happens. And sometimes you had grown to like the replacements better. . . .

So you went on losing and losing, as the rain loses, the mountain loses, the sun loses, as everything under heaven loses. You came along together and here you are.

~ W. S. MERWIN, "Speech of a Guide"

[For Gregory Patton, 1960-1993: friend of fox's friend]

The story thus far:

The force of the pull of the backward glance. You think you never want to suffer to hear another word on the "issue" of AIDS and television, and yet, just as you think you've safely pitched your tent in the western lands, you pivot (thoughtlessly, sentimentally, trigger finger itching) to hear the keening voices from the plain.

AIDS and television.

Yes, I know.

Repent from a wild place.

If you really want to understand about AIDS and television (*do* you? I ask because I don't know), read Paula Treichler's "AIDS Narratives on Television,"[1] which has the forbearance to trace in microscopic detail how and why television is the way it is in relation to a profoundly traumatic social and sexual crisis such as the AIDS pandemics embody.

AIDS didn't make television the way it is. Television has always been the way it is. AIDS just came along to present itself as one more thing for television to miscomprehend or deny (and don't fall for television's hurt feelings when it cries that it's doing the best it can—that's what television, lower lip aquiver, *always* tells you). Treichler's analyses of the made-for-television movies *An Early Frost* (NBC, 1985) and *Our Sons* (ABC, 1991) concludes with the comment that "AIDS narratives on television tell the story of network television, still on its fearful, cautious, deadly path to self-destruction"—that is, AIDS (even *that*) is incapable of shattering the mirrored surface of corporately engineered communication vehicles and hence, in that failing, is compelling us, as sadistic observers, to conclusively visualize that industry's pending demise in vignette format, a snapshot's negative of the agonized perfect moment in which the network's clueless masterminds would be caught tanning in the ghoulish light of corporate obsolescence while AIDS, whistling ("Lost in the Stars" or "Wooden Ships" or, I'm wondering, *what?*), strolls up and down Wilshire Boulevard.

It's a climax shot through like any other with. . . .

It is, if nothing else, the favored face to the mirror of television, and why is this so? According to one key futurist, circling the quarry from another direction, the imminent death of television must be a cause for great joy throughout the republic, because it's been, after all, only a matter of time, and we've waited too long, and now we, on the plain, are all just sick past death with having to put up with television's unhappy faults: television's self-loathing submission to Western dicta of pictorial perspective, its exhausted replication of photographic legibility orthodoxies, its terrified adherence to theatrical and novelistic notions of dramaturgy, its profiteering enchantment with a one-way system of communication, and so on and on.

The list does go on. You want to expire.
You do.
I'm here.

The time now is wired to say good-bye to all that, and sweep clear the stage for the next big thing, which (it sez here) looks and feels to be a post-virtual-reality-type theatrical *drench*, experienced uniquely in the home according to need and want, yet paradoxically contrived to reground those fantasies of community or commonality (or, uh, *consensus*) that "television" as heretofore practiced has, in simply heeding its parasitic when not craven nature, connived to undermine or thwart, withering all dreams of a happy *heimat*.

This evolutionary ascension will carry television as a phenomenon light years beyond its present fallen state and light years beyond its presently emerging interim paradigm of "interactivity," as exercised most rivetingly in home shopping expeditions, which as now practiced represent a merely incremental slither for television, taking it from the murky sea to the slimy shore.

A merely pathetic failure up until now (since, like, *forever*), television (or "so-called television") is poised on the brink of its epistemological transubstantiation, which hinges, futurists agree, on the (guaranteed) success of technology (so-called) in abetting its break—please, please, please let me get what I want—from "viewpoint dependency."

Mourning is a bequest from time. Time puts its head on your shoulder and lends itself to you, to be fashioned, for the mourning work to be completed.

I (and, of course, you) have never witnessed television as an expressive vehicle for the representation of mourning practices, *except on daytime soap operas*. (In the spirit of life-is-too-short, those readers for whom it still must be proven or hammered in that the daytime soap opera is a cultural practice capable of repaying a dependent viewer's commitment should probably spare themselves the heartache and stop reading here.)

Soap operas are exempted from those rules of television governing the lame failures described by Treichler because soap operas famously lack—actively fore-stall—closure. In Scheherazade fashion, stories are recounted in order to prevent the story, any story, from ever really ending. (Modern parent of soap opera: Isak Dinesen, who told stories to thwart the departure of her lover, and whose *Out of Africa* resorts to a pastoral masquerade to recount the desperation of a lover uncertain about the certainty of the beloved object returning.) The stories are, of course, just the demented days of our lives, lives timid and mundane, middle-aged and complacent, trapped in no other world but this one, which, furthermore, seldom turns. These stories routinely, if wearingly righteously, "tackle" social issues, by which I mean such issues as drug dependency, spousal abuse, racism, and so on, and to that anecdotal extent they do on occasion glance outward to the presumed stale hell of the viewers' worlds, if never, however, being able to provide a recondite analytical understanding of these issues as they would appear if unattached to the plot contingencies they flesh out. Soap operas are not materialism's handmaiden. Nowhere is this more evident than in soap opera's discovery of AIDS.

AIDS has infiltrated the soap opera world, and much has been made of this in the self-regulating industry journals (*Soap Opera Weekly, Soap Opera Digest, Soap Opera Update,* in descending order of credibility) directed at the soap opera viewer. Various shows have introduced, for very limited durations, gay characters (who aren't asked and don't tell), invariably as adjunct mouthpieces for, or as saintly exemplars within, AIDS-related plotting involving the main characters.[2] Various shows have, under the same circumstances, introduced minor characters who were HIV positive (always infected by rape or an offscreen junkie ex-spouse). One show even presented a prolonged story involving the AIDS quilt being brought to the fictional town, which spectacle (in addition to providing a platform for the good characters to demonstrate tolerance and the bad characters to dig deeper their own graves) reconciled a homophobic father to his surviving straight son, the dead gay son having never been seen on the show, although his surviving companion did briefly materialize, memorial quilt panel in hand.[3]

What to say about this? First, that these efforts, such as they are, far outpace any dramatic attempts made by evening television to address AIDS; and that this has everything to do with time. On soap operas, nothing ever *needs* to be conclusively wrapped up. Issues, conflicts, relationships—all of these can be dramatically and discursively extended for years. And, characteristically, *years* provide the measure of the viewer's allegiance. Which makes all the difference, in terms of the extraordinary empathetic bond typically in place between viewer and character; this is a phenomenon altogether different from the one put in place between the viewer and the characters in a two-hour movie or in a once-every-seven-days prime-time drama.[4]

Nobody does death better than the soap operas. Soap opera viewers know this, and the soap opera industry does, too; one of the industry's journals has a regular column assessing how recent deaths have been handled (for example, praising or damning as inappropriate the funeral hymns, criticizing what certain characters were wearing graveside, noticing conspicuous absences from the funeral service, and so on). More to the point, though, is this kind of commentary's sensitivity to how the removal of a character—and to the form of that removal, and to that removal's arbitrary or plot-dictated nature—affects the viewer, because to the extent that the deceased character has been on for many years or has become a lead player, the withdrawal comes closer to simulating the distended trajectory of genuine loss than any prime-time television fictional death could ever hope to achieve. Contrary to the high-minded notion that the typical soap opera viewer is a half-educated agoraphobe incapable of distinguishing serial drama from life, viewers are perfectly capable of containing fiction. It's simply that the particular structures of identification between viewer and character—which are shaped, dramatically, by a "redundant" verbalizing of emotional nuance and by an implicit worldview privileging, mainly, groups of two or three people trapped in an interior (Benjamin's "the horror of apartments") and resolving or, thrillingly, reliving conflict and difference through (what else?) *words*—produce this "excessive" response as the normal, desired one. Which is why reading letters from viewers in response to a popular character's death is the serenest eavesdropping agony. On every level save one, viewers *do* know the difference, but they feel and cultivate it *anyway*. Yes, yes . . . *mais quand même . . .*

Still, because the presence of AIDS on soap operas has yet to be more than an ancillary elaboration of the moment's dominant plots, no AIDS-related death has produced this level of intensely sustained identification. In order for that to happen, a major, sympathetic character on a soap opera (for example, a character who had been married to other major characters, which is a common destiny in this antiquely dynastic world) would have to be revealed to be bisexual or gay; would have to be allowed to have a romantic life or entanglement; would have to be allowed, say, to also be HIV positive; and would have to be further allowed, say, to die. This would be epochal, because it would in that event represent the weaving of AIDS, recognized as a common curse, into the very fabric of the contemporary disorder, rather than as a sideline plague visiting a community, doing its damage, but leaving the community and family essentially intact.

BILL HORRIGAN

In the story thus far, AIDS has not been allowed to make such visitation in the soap opera world. Which is not to say that people don't die for no reason.

Not long ago, I read that an extremely popular character on an eternally running soap opera I'd never watched was about to die. The article fretted over this death's arbitrary nature: the character wasn't sick, the character was actively involved in key storylines (she was a wholesome wife, mother, and, to the entire town, nonjudgmental confidante), and the actress had been involved in the show for years and was not having contract disputes.

And yet the character, a doctor's wife, was going to die.

I tuned in to watch.

So did you.

The character did die, in a car accident, in the mountains, following a domestic argument concerning adultery. The entire town was bereft.

This was many months ago. The town still talks about it.

They can't get over it.

Even the villainous characters can't believe it. "What did she ever mean to *you*?," hissed one virtuous citizen to a villain's profession of grief. "She was *different*," he whimpered, and we all understood what he meant: the only person in town—hence the only person in the world, hence the only person ever born—who would ever not want to see this villain dead on sight.

No other popular dramatic form is able and willing to simulate the grieving and loss in the wake of a loved one's death with the emotional accuracy it's given on soap operas, which trajectory clarifies, among other forms, into a mortifyingly incredulous repetition, a compulsive retelling or referencing, of the fatality. Coming as a shock to the entire narrative and domestic system, loss produces a situation in which nothing can ever be forgotten and pain can never leave. It will appear to be forgotten, in the higher or highest expedient interest of the narrative juggernaut and because life has to go on and new couplings are required, but the dead are always among the living, perpetually maintained there both in the spoken memories of the surviving characters and in the memory indexes of the faithful viewers—faith, indeed, or fidelity, being the patron virtue of the entire soap opera addiction. (Sometimes sacrificed characters literally return from the dead, as conniving twins, baffled changelings, or with altogether reassigned identities, but that's another story having more to do with actors' contracts than with anything else; viewers, in any case, placidly accept the conceit.)

However fundamentally deviant soap operas may be from the dramatic paradigms of prime-time corporate television, they are every bit as implicated in that model of obsolescent television whose imminent demise we're being bullied into embracing. If anything, they would be first sacrificed as being even more deeply implicated in the fallen state of television than whatever is grudgingly granted the cachet of "quality" television, given that they lack even more profoundly, along with other "female" cultural forms, most vestiges of critical credibility or any sufficiently warrior-like partisans.

What they share with all television, of course, is its "viewpoint dependency," its monocularity, its corporately engineered birthright. Within that totalized identity, soap opera also falls under the subset of "fiction," further tainting and making suspect its authorial origins.

These notes would be neither a premature lament for the disappearance of the form in the *tsunami*-like wake of The Television To Come (that is, The Television We Deserve) nor an argument (in the event, undeliverable) in favor of a minor cultural phenomenon heretofore providing peculiar solace to legions of individuals.

These notes, instead, would—and, like, *do:* they just *do*—labor around all sides of an idea without, however, wanting to halt to speak this idea (and not wanting to, even now, even now), which in rough terms would ascend to embrace two lonely facts adjacent for this moment alone: one would reference AIDS, and suffering and death from AIDS, and AIDS as an agent of suffering doing its job in bringing on grief to people; and one would recognize television, and the distractions and uses of television, and television in one of its minor practices, as formally and discursively embodying an unending compulsion to understand a community's daily lives and losses, in a way otherwise unavailable, unpracticed, within the dramatized purgatory (the shadowed fallen world, the half-world) television delivers into the home.

These two facts would converge and cohabit, not cozily, on a terrain overlooked by and indeed virtually wholly unassessed within commentaries on the degenerate nature of present television and, especially, in the forecasts of what kinds of empathetic relationships are likely to be provided by the impending transfigured television of the future.

These notes would just notice that . . . just *notice*.

Done.

Since you left, the neighbors have taken to clustering on the front porch to glimpse what I'm inside watching (sometimes wearing clothes, sometimes wearing thin) on television. Of course, as you know, I seldom ever *watch*, really. But these neighbors . . . they tolerate the window (curtained, semidrawn) as the framing condition of their viewing pleasures, the habit's cost, the price of the ticket. You know I could invite them inside, but I don't, ever (would you? did you? no), not for sweeps week, not for play-offs, not for music video or for mourning events. Once in a while, if I remember, I'll turn up the volume, but since I don't have exterior stereo speakers, I guess that courtesy is lost on them.

They miss you, of course, but mostly they're content, and they appear— I'm just guessing—to get by on very little. They're so dependent on me, but you're the one they dream about. They need me but they want you. Despite my not knowing how they're going to cope without you being here to guide them, sooner or later I'm going to have to let them know about all of this . . . and I'm dreading this, you know, just dreading the day when they'll have to find out, if they haven't half figured it out already . . . (they don't always tend to the speech of the guide; sometimes they end up leading the guide; sometimes they're the ones, not the guides, who implore all listeners to repent) . . . yeh, you know, I do think they've figured this out . . . they have mouth and all eyes open . . . so it's kind of crazy, this business about my not telling them *anything*, but about them *knowing*, all the same . . . so I could tell them . . . *whatever*, you know, but by this point, don't you think they'd know *everything*? on some level? and so why bother having to say it? I could say this and I could say that, and then I could say all the rest, but by day's end (the word you have *said* is your master) I'd have said everything wanting to be said, or heard . . . and then what would remain, still, would be the facts, all this house's bleak facts (fuck facts) . . . and I'd still be talking and they'd still be wondering, or wanting, and you'd still—well, you know, there it *is*, isn't it? (I'm sorry, you know, because *I did not want this to happen*)—be dead.

NOTES

[1] Paula Treichler, "AIDS Narratives on Television," in *Writing AIDS: Gay Literature, Language, and Analysis,* ed. Timothy F. Murphy and Suzanne Poirier (Columbia University Press, 1993), 161–99.

[2] *Soap Opera Weekly*'s article, "The Daytime Closet: How Homophobic Is the Soap Opera Industry?" (by Joanne Douglas Lampe, 3 August 1993, 12–14) surveys the way things are now, asking, "Why aren't soaps, which pride themselves on being topical, featuring more gay-rights stories and teaching tolerance by using homosexuality as regular parts of their storylines?" The piece's conclusion provides a weird absolution: "While gay men and women are making some strides toward gaining equal rights in the real world, progress has been painstakingly slow. In that sense, the soap opera business is truly a mirror of real life."

[3] The career of the annoying red ribbon AIDS awareness lapel symbol within the soap opera universe is peculiar from a number of angles. On a day in June 1993, soap operas were beseeched to have actors wear the red ribbon as one effort within a national "Day of Compassion" campaign. On the one ABC soap opera I saw that day, the full cast (even the children) sported the symbol for an entire episode, during which, however, not a single character or incident made mention of it; and the next day, during which a number of scenes were continued from the previous day, no one who had been wearing it the day before was sporting it. More than an error in "continuity," the gesture seemed to perfectly epitomize the well-intended but ultimately narcissistic implications that the AIDS red ribbon bears within show business

circles. On the other hand, the entire debate about the red ribbon—for instance, the argument among some activists that those who sport the red ribbon do so not as a sign of actual involvement but as a hollow, self-congratulating fashion accessory that in fact relieves them of any further commitment—has been thrashed out in the popular press, most acutely within soap opera publications. In *Soap Opera Digest,* 3 August 1993, 52–57, an article is devoted to one popular actress's refusal to wear the red ribbon when she appears on awards shows or attends benefits because, in her words, "it misguidedly politicizes human tragedy. These red ribbons provide a means by which public figures can appear to make a 'politically correct' statement in favor of a cause they do not support," to which position the article then offers a rejoinder from fellow soap actors as to why they support it: "I have found the red ribbon to be a valuable prompter of questions, leading to responses that have educated the questioner," and so on.

[4] ABC's Sunday night family drama, *Life Goes On,* received extensive publicity for its 1992-93 story focusing on the boyfriend of one of the main characters, a teenage girl. This boy arrived on the show after having already found out that straight "unsafe sex" had led him to be HIV positive. In six noncontinuous episodes (the final installment in May 1993 coming some weeks after the penultimate one), this story was in some ways extraordinarily enlightened vis-à-vis its companion evening programs, going so far as to explain and illustrate, if quite obliquely, how these two characters were still able to have sex with each other. Still, part of the feeling of irresolve produced by this story and its telling was due directly to the con-

straints of the form, which led each of the individual episodes into some manner of more or less forced closure, and led the entire story into a wholly unsatisfying resolution not purporting to be, but only tolerable if considered as, wishful fantasy: it is "years later," and the girl, now a mother, is telling her young son about his brave father, who lived considerably beyond the common term of the illness, married, produced a healthy child, and so on. While not diminishing the accomplishments of this series, it does seem striking in comparison with soap opera's understanding of AIDS, which, albeit greatly limited, folds it into other narratives and deploys it generally, and in my view more productively, as *one more blight* to the body/family politic.

BILL HORRIGAN

CHAPTER 13

OPERATIVE ASSUMPTIONS

Gregg Bordowitz

You are living mockery of your own ideals. If not, you have set your ideals too low.

~ CHARLES LUDLAM[1]

For the past five years I have worked as a videomaker for the Gay Men's Health Crisis (GMHC)[2] where I have been the coproducer, with Jean Carlomusto, of the "Living with AIDS" cable show,[3] as well as the producer of many videotapes addressing the concerns of people living with AIDS or HIV and members of groups hardest hit by AIDS—lesbians and gay men, drug users, poor people, people of color, women.

In 1985, I started making video as a young artist searching for ways to represent the manifold processes through which people come into being as subjects. I realized that by making video I could introduce the element of time into my work in ways I couldn't possibly achieve by making static images or installations. I wanted to represent the formation of subjectivities by creating conflicts between sound and image over time. Video seemed to be the most effective medium to picture the ways representations assign us places from which to identify. I was excited by its counterhegemonic potential. Additionally, video was relatively cheap and I had access to equipment. It was easy to learn how to use.

As a student I began to question the ways video art had been canonized within art world institutions. In general, video made for galleries and museums pursued two tendencies. One tended to be preoccupied with the formal limits of the medium and the other used the medium as a means to further the concerns of performance art. There were exceptions. Dara Birnbaum's work addressed issues of representation in video by appropriating and questioning network television. I have in mind Birnbaum's video *Wonder Woman,* which repeated an image appropriated from a popular weekly television show of the superheroine transforming from a mild-mannered woman into Wonder Woman, spinning in circles and exploding. Viewing this video rendered open the possibilities of a critical video practice.

Around the same time I was introduced to the works and writings of Martha Rosler and Dan Graham—two distinctly different artists, yet both used video to interrogate mass culture. Rosler's *Global Taste: A Meal in Three Courses,* a video installation at the New Museum in New York in 1985, was a fragmented collage of material presented on three monitors housed within a structure that did not permit the viewer to see all three monitors at the same time from any one vantage. The "interlocking motifs in its videotapes are children, food, commercials and learning." The theme of the installation was "colonization of the self and of other countries, by media and advertising."[4] As a student, I was overwhelmed by the complexity of the work and its ambition to map complex social forces. Rosler's printed works, specifically, *The Bowery in Two Inadequate Descriptive Systems,*[5] introduced me to criticism of left-identified documentary practices.

Dan Graham's video *Rock My Religion* (1984–85) introduced me to the idea of the video artist as cultural critic. *Rock My Religion* legitimated the idea that an artist could and should take popular culture seriously.

The idea that video did not have to be relegated to monitors in separate, well-defined spaces in galleries and museums came to me through watching Paper Tiger Television as it waged its own weekly cable struggle against dominant media. Paper Tiger comes out of a recent but not well documented history of alternative media, including but not limited to Third World Newsreel, Videofreex, and other groups of alternative makers grounded in movements for social change. An article by Dee Dee Halleck, founder of Paper Tiger, "Some Arguments for the Appropriation of Television,"[6] inspired me at the same time I began to think of myself as an "activist videomaker."

I was very much influenced by all this work for many reasons, but the one attribute all these makers shared was an interest in using video, both inside and, more important, outside the context of galleries and museums. All the work I mentioned fostered the idea that video could be used as a means to organize audiences around critical activities—questioning the culture industry. These makers considered viewers as participants in a process of making meaning. In making my own work I began to think of critical pedagogy as an ideal practice.

I think many video artists were and continue to be daunted by the monolithic enterprise of broadcast television. Artists feel that they can't possibly compete with it because of lack of resources and lack of access to broadcast venues. Video can be, and often is, employed in installation work to address conditions of spectatorship in the gallery or the museum. I can't limit myself to using video in this way. The broadcast dimension of television is the fundamental component of the medium. I have been much more interested in television's broadcast capacity than in its multichannel capacity employed in constructing installations and shows because I am interested in exploiting television's capacity as an organizing tool. Further, I view broadcast television as a field within which to intervene and bring about meaningful change.

Commercial television is produced with an agenda: to dominate the leisure time of its audience in order to sell products, to engender a public of consumers. Fundamentally opposed to this, I have attempted to travel the way of Bertolt Brecht: to employ forms of entertainment that engage the critical skills of an audience, galvanizing the potential for collective action. I approach television production as an activist, employing video as a means of organizing. My work is a hybrid of concerns derived from critical theory and concerns affecting my own conditions of existence. I place my own subjectivity at risk within my work, drawing on my own daily experiences, using my own identity and the various subject positions comprising it. My interest in videomaking developed at the same time I was coming out as a gay man and coming to consciousness about the AIDS epidemic. My first video, " . . . some aspect of a shared lifestyle . . . " (1986), considered the topic of the emerging AIDS epidemic in view of my concerns about the formation of subjectivity. It's a raw tape, juxtaposing first-person narration with varying medical opinions and differing representations culled from the dominant media—news reports, television specials, magazine and newspaper articles. While making this tape, I realized that I was part of an emerging identity. The AIDS crisis precipitated the formation of a new subjectivity— the person living with AIDS— a subject with a disease asserting his or her right to determine the conditions of his or her own health care. The formation of this identity was significant. People with a disease organized as a constituency, a political identity, questioning the ways they are positioned by authority and subjugated within the dominant culture. After the first tape, I became involved with the emerging AIDS activist movement, participating in several AIDS activist video collectives— Testing the Limits and DIVA (Damn Interfering Video Activists)— and producing television for GMHC. I tested positive for HIV antibodies in 1988. This informed my decision to make tapes by and for people living with HIV.

Over the past six years of AIDS activist television production I have come up with a set of fundamental organizing principles underlying my efforts. The following is a manifesto to which I have added explanatory notes to clarify specific concerns. I hesitate to use the word *manifesto*. This text lacks the force of certainty that often justifies the use of the term. It's riddled with ambivalences and ambiguities. In spite of these, I use the term. The following principles are intended to foster the spread of participatory democratic forms of media production and reception.

OPERATIVE ASSUMPTIONS CONCERNING THE COMMUNITY-BASED PRODUCTION OF TELEVISION

DEFINITIONS

Two concepts shape my understanding of what I will repeatedly refer to as "dominant culture." The first is "hegemony," which Raymond Williams defined as "a more or less adequate organization and interconnectedness of otherwise separated and even disparate meanings, values, and practices, which it specifically incorporates in a significant culture and an effective social order."[7]

The second concept is "tradition," defined by Williams as follows: "For tradition is in practice the most evident expression of the dominant and hegemonic pressures and limits. It is always more than an inert historicized segment; indeed it is the most powerful practical means of incorporation. What we have to see is not 'a tradition' but a *selective tradition:* an intentionally selective version of a shaping past and a pre-shaped present, which is then powerfully operative in the process of social and cultural definition and identification."[8]

Dominant culture is culture produced in the interests of the current hegemony. Its material means of support come from sources with an interest in maintaining the status quo. These are the corporations, the big businesses, and the government interests that determine the content and form of newpapers, magazines, television, films, and so on. "Tradition" is the principle that upholds the sanctity of the forms and the values determining representations. Dominant culture borrows and steals from alternative cultures that are produced on the margins of societies by communities whose lives and experiences aren't accounted for within the current hegemony. Dominant culture changes and grows constantly to account for historical change. Disenfranchised communities must act on and intervene within dominant culture to get the recognition and resources necessary to their survival.

There is a distinct difference between the production of commercial television and the community-based production of television. The latter is produced by disenfranchised groups who are not recognized, or are recognized in limited ways, on dominant television. Community television is no less deserving of the label "television" than what is considered appropriate for broadcast. The fight is to expand the notion of television to include the kinds of production now assigned only a place at the margins of broadcast and production.

In this context, community must be understood as a shifting, horizontally expanding entity open to change and growth. Communities of the disenfranchised are formed through negation. Forces within the dominant culture construct differences among subjects and establish exclusive principles that govern group formation. Subjects excluded by these criteria identify with each other along the lines of differences that have been established within the dominant field. Identity formations arise among the disenfranchised as a means to speak in a society that has refused them the opportunities to represent themselves. Alliances among different disenfranchised groups create the possibilities of new communities that transgress constructed boundaries. New alliances and coalitions give rise to communities that promote social equity, dismantling the structures of power that have shaped dominant culture.

Two Challenges

1. *Ask yourself, "What images would I like to see more of in the world?" Make them.*

2. *Face the representational problems of the day in ways that affect your daily life.*

The most widely recognized problem among community producers is lack of access to the means of television production. Disenfranchised groups affected by AIDS have had limited access to the equipment necessary to produce programs addressing the concerns of their communities. Access to broadcast standard equipment is limited, but the increased availability of small-format consumer production equipment has enabled television production by disenfranchised groups. Additionally, programs that are produced have little access to broadcast venues. Video activists have been gaining access to this kind of equipment by organizing resource pools and collectives.

Alternative distribution networks have been established to get these works shown—cable broadcasts, organizational newsletters, and relations among AIDS service organizations are just some of the means used to distribute activist video. Many of the videos produced at GMHC, including videos produced for the "Living with AIDS" cable show, are available through the GMHC catalog of AIDS educational material distributed nationally to health care institutions and service providers. An excellent example of community education efforts that employ video is the "Seeing Through AIDS" program in New York—an innovative mobile teaching event that uses alternative and activist video as a stimulus for training and discussions about AIDS in many different workplaces.[9]

The kinds of representations, or the lack of representations, addressing disenfranchised subjects within the field of dominant media can be a primary motivation for making video work. Television legitimates the experience of some subjects, and it provides a witness to the current times for anyone willing, or able, to identify as a member of the "general public." The "general public" is a fiction established to organize consumers around purchasing products. Anyone who may not fit the image of what advertisers want television viewers to imagine as the kind of people who want a particular product is excluded from the field of representation. For example, people with AIDS and HIV infection are often invited to speak about some of their experiences on television, but they are never pictured speaking to members of the audience who may also be people with AIDS and HIV. It may be a long time (perhaps never) before we see public service announcements directly addressing people with AIDS in the audience of television. No one wishes to be the subject of that address. The repressed fact is that the many people living with HIV and AIDS don't have a choice. The production, distribution, and broadcasting of video work intended for an audience of people with AIDS and HIV, representing some the complexities of living with HIV, creates opportunities toward the inclusion of groups affected by AIDS into the audiences of television.

NINE OPERATIVE ASSUMPTIONS

1. *Video is a medium, but television is a situation.* Video describes a means of production, a specific technology. Television production engenders a set of relations among workers: producers, writers, camera operators, lighting designers, sound engineers, and so forth. It also engenders relations between makers and viewers.

2. *Don't trust technology.* Did you have a hand in its development? Is it developed in

your interests? Take what you can use and use what you can take. Technology is designed within the context of social relations. Thus, relations of power and dominance inform all decisions concerning its design, use and implementation:

> We have now become used to a situation in which broadcasting is a major social institution, in which there is always a controversy but which, in its familiar form, seems to have been predestined by the technology. This pre-destination, however, when closely examined, proves to be no more than a set of particular decisions, in particular circumstances, which were then so wide-ly if imperfectly ratified that it is now difficult to see them as decisions rather than as (retrospectively) inevitable results.
>
> Thus, if seen only in hindsight, broadcasting can be diagnosed as a new and powerful form of social integration and control. Many of its main uses can be seen as socially, commercially and at times politically manipula-tive.[10]

3. *Television can be used in directed pragmatic ways as a means of defensive action.* Television is a form of intervention—interfering with the current social order. Television can be a crudely fashioned weapon, like a handful of nails bound by electrical tape thrown at a group of armed soldiers. It can be a form of sabotage, like a wrench thrown into the works of an engine, or like a virus introduced into the hardware of a computer system.

4. *Television should not be limited to a means of defense. It can be proactive.* Make television in the interests of community. This is the spiritual dimension of production. It requires faith. Have faith in the power of collective action and document the efforts of many different people working together toward common goals. Enfranchisement is the primary goal. The most significant feature of television production is its capacity to create opportunities for the formation of new audiences and communities.

I have seen groups of people accomplish great tasks through collective efforts—for example, the ACT-UP, ACT NOW nonviolent takeover of the Food and Drug Administration in October 1988, and subsequent New York ACT-UP actions at New York City Hall, the New York State Capitol, Saint Patrick's Cathedral, and so on. I have witnessed and documented all these actions.

5. *On dominant television, images, words, and ideas have no causal relation to each other, and there are no beginnings or ends.* Dominant television is an immanent domain. There is no outside to dominant television. Television necessarily refers to itself to establish its own veracity. Exclusions and marginalizations figure within the field of the dominant as signifying absences that play a determining role regarding the choice of subject matter on television.

6. *In community television production the ends are the means because new possibilities emerge when the means of production are in the hands of a self-determining group of*

people representing themselves. A community creates itself as it represents itself. Video-making can foster a process of consensus building and can provide the arena in which goals are identified by a group.

7. *Ontology and tactics merge on the television screen. The subjective conditions of the makers must be acknowledged as a fundamental factor informing all productions, broadcasts, and screenings.* Static, the hissing, grainy emission of light and sound present on the screen of an operating television, is the presence of nothing—the positive, substantive form of nothingness. That we produce television at all is an attempt to cope with the existence of this static state. I realize that this may sound pretentious, but I think it's necessary to recognize the existential dimension of production, to state what is fundamentally at stake for the individual maker.

Two fundamental dialectical formulations structure my understanding of the contradictions inherent in making television. (1) I accept as a given fact that the dialectic between eros and thanatos is a determining factor affecting our actions. A dynamic tension exists between desire and death—the strong impulse toward the experiences of pleasure that disclose one's being to oneself exist alongside strong impulses toward the self-negation of one's being. The knowledge that one may die gives life its value. (2) I accept as a given fact the existentialist dialectic between being and nothingness. The agency of the subject is opposed by the abitrary nature of the sign— when I speak I risk being understood in very different ways than I intended; perhaps I will not be understood at all. Meaning is always threatened by non-sense. Reason is always humbled by contingency. There are forces at work beyond one's control that can thwart one's best devised plans.

To avoid facile, vulgar, deterministic accounts of events one must admit that there are limits to what one can know. All accounts must allow for unknown factors. No single cause can explain a situation. No explanation can sum up the totality of a situation. Truth, like tradition, is an absolute category established in the interests of an established order. Work that questions the status of truth in representation runs a great risk of exclusion within dominant media, but it serves the interests of those whose history has been done great violence by the official record.

8. *Television cannot instrumentally affect the actions of viewers.* Television presents options and possibilities for action. Community producers can picture forgotten options and ignored possibilities.

9. *Television doesn't belong to the producer.* The producer is its reason for being, but this is a legitimate claim any spectator can and should make.

NAGGING AFTERTHOUGHTS

1. *The issue of whether to make video or film is not only an issue of medium. It can be framed as an issue of idiom.* Choosing between video production and film production is often framed as an economic decision by many producers. Video is cheaper to produce,

but film has greater avenues for distribution. In general, the distinctions between the two media are breaking down. Most broadcast television is filmed in production and many films are now edited on videotape.

Neither television nor cinema are pure categories anymore. Accepting that as a given, I am committed to making television. I produce video work that draws upon, refers to, and comments on the history of television. The decision to make television is a choice to produce within and improve on a set of idioms within a specific history of production. I like television because it is cheap, fast, superficial, and disposable—like a daily newspaper. To make film is to work within the idioms of cinema. A decision to work within either category is founded on the belief that there are still tendencies within each worthy of pursuit.

2. *The category of experimental work in video has been challenged and broadened over the past decade.* It now includes work concerned with the relation between the speaking subject and the subject of address. The structure and formation of identity is being questioned with new rigor. Addressing new audiences, communities, and constituencies is the goal of much new work. Even more ambitious is new video work that attempts to form new audiences by picturing alliances among disenfranchised groups.

There has been a shift away from previous areas of experimentation. The limits of the video medium and the science behind television have been explored by artists like Nam June Paik who strongly identify with the notion of the avant-garde and whose concerns were formed out of formalist problems rooted in the history of painting and sculpture. Video has been used effectively to make viewers question their presumptions about time and space within the context of galleries and museums by Dan Graham, Vito Acconci, Bruce Nauman, and many others. The status of truth in documentation has been questioned and dealt serious blows by artists mentioned before—Rosler and Paper Tiger. Godard and others associated with cinema have made their contributions by posing tough philosophical questions about television.

Many contemporary videomakers start from a critical interrogation of dominant television, developing complex, rich, and affirming representations of disenfranchised subjects and communities —*Tongues Untied* by Marlon Riggs or *L Is for the Way You Look* by Jean Carlomusto.

In general, significant shifts have occurred in theoretical conceptions of audience. The notion of an audience composed of artists and videomakers has been under assault for the past two decades. In the eighties, under the Reagan presidency, decreases in arts funding and conservative attempts at censorship have limited the resources of arts institutions and strained and severed the ties of arts communities. They have also politically charged the atmosphere, resulting in a resurgence of identity politics. My work is the product of these times. The AIDS crisis created a situation in which my identity as an artist became subordinate to my identity as an activist, although making video has remained my primary activity.

GREGG BORDOWITZ

CRITIQUE OF PREVIOUS WORK IN VIEW OF MY
EXPERIENCES AND THOUGHTS ON THE FUTURE

In the spring of 1988, within two months, I tested HIV-antibody positive, came out to my parents as gay, and decided to seek help concerning my alcohol and drug use. This was the densest moment of my life. Since then I have come to realize that there is no reason why I'm HIV positive, why some people get sick and why some people die. Although there are historical conditions that explain the crisis, there is no reason behind AIDS. But there is meaning. My experiences are rich with meaning. They're full of pain, irony, and hope.

The work I've done in the past few years was predicated upon the conviction that action must be taken toward ending government inaction on the AIDS epidemic. This conviction led me to a representational practice with a set of pragmatic goals. This work was often limited to performing a specific function: the documentation of the 1988 nonviolent takeover of the Food and Drug Administration, the provision of vital information concerning alternative medical treatments for HIV-antibody positive people, safer-sex educational videos for bars and theaters. There is some amount of certainty behind the production of this work. Positions must be stated clearly and asserted authoritatively, leaving little room for speculation. Fear of death often goes unacknowledged in much AIDS activist videos. Sexual identities are often presented unproblematically. Safer-sex educational materials often don't consider the complexities of desire.

I still hold the same convictions that motivated me to do this work, but now there is also a need for video work, that explores the subjectivity of a person living with HIV infection. Much of the work done about AIDS and HIV has been documentary work. I've contributed to the development of this body of work. Now I think it is important to produce work that grapples with the subjective conditions of living with HIV in ways that challenge conventional means of representation. We must consider the uncertainties inherent in the experience of being a person with HIV, uncertainties regarding sexuality, agency, and death.

The AIDS epidemic calls all previous notions of sexual identity into question because the epidemic necessitates talking about sexual behavior rather than identity. For example, new categories such as "men who have sex with other men" were developed in the field of sex education to account for the many men who do not identify themselves as "gay." Now, as the lesbian and gay liberation movement enters a new decade, new ideas about identities and alliances are being considered among lesbians and gay men. Established identities are being questioned. Media artists doing work about AIDS now have to recognize the fragility and historical specificity of identities. The shifting forces that shape identity during the AIDS crisis must be named and studied.

Also, new work about AIDS must question agency, the role of the individual in social change. The AIDS activist movement has posed a significant threat to the dominant order. It has been a catalyst for a growing health care movement in the United States. People with AIDS and HIV have been cast as agents of change in a number of intersecting fields, such as medicine, law, government, and business. Our struggle raises fundamental issues concerning people's rights of choice to control their own bodies. We have called into question long-held assumptions about government's sovereignty over matters of life and death.

People with AIDS and HIV must conduct their lives in the face of death because no person with HIV knows if or when she or he may get sick or die. Activists rarely see concrete results from their efforts, yet they continue to struggle. Identity is a fragile construct shaped by historical conditions. Work that addresses these issues will radically change current thinking about representation and AIDS.

Personal records and testimonies are valuable additions to the growing body of work that is shaping the ways the AIDS epidemic affects our lives. They are part of efforts to legitimate the concerns of people hardest hit by the AIDS epidemic and to pressure established institutions to take responsibility for some of the work that needs to be done in facing the continuing crisis. New video work that explores the psychic complexities of living with HIV can bring an acute awareness of mortality into debate with the ordinary tasks of daily existence. I have started a new series of portraits in video of people living with HIV. They are going to be a regular feature on the Living with AIDS cable program. I've completed six so far and would like to make as many as fifty. The first five portraits are two to five minutes in length. Each features a subject who looks directly into the camera and identifies as a person living with HIV. Then the subject is pictured in a variety of settings—the home, the office, a restaurant—talking about a variety of topics, not necessarily about HIV. However, once the subject discloses his HIV status, whatever follows in the video—a walk down the street, a game of pool, a discussion about pets—becomes a metaphor for living with AIDS or HIV. I am interested in exploring this. Perhaps, new ways of discussing mortality can develop out of this effort. In the portraits, I'm trying to reconcile an acute awareness of mortality with the monotony of daily life.

There has been a shift in the focus of this text that exemplifies a shift in my thinking about video work concerning AIDS. The first part of this text is an attempt to sum up aspects of community television paying special attention to pragmatic concerns. These ideas were formulated at a time when AIDS activist video was not yet an identifiable body of work, as it is today. When they were developed, I was motivated by the need for progressive cultural work about AIDS and I gave much thought and energy to fostering its existence. With the establishment of this small but visible category of video, new questions arise concerning the representation of AIDS, so I have recently become preoccupied with more subtle and complex questions about illness and death, issues that preoccupy my mind for the obvious reason—my own HIV infection. Sometimes I question whether or not I should continue making work about AIDS. I feel trapped by my infection, reduced and diminished. Yet, I can't exclude AIDS and HIV from the frame of my thinking. It has become a prism through which I view the world, and I expect that it will unfortunately take up more space on the horizon of my future.

Currently, I'm at work on an hour-long video concerning the problem of remaining hopeful in the face of increasing loss and despair. It attempts to picture the rage and sense of futility many people with AIDS or HIV experience. I feel a great sense of urgency motivating me to make the tape. Much is at stake.

Sometimes the forces motivating one to make work are not easily located in an identification with a cause external to and greater than the subject making the work—a movement, a group, an audience. Sometimes one has no conscious understanding of why one is making the work. Am I regressing into some kind of expressionist position mystifying the creative process? As a student, I made a commitment against any mystifying practices assigning privilege to an author, a figure, a signature, a gesture. I resisted the notion of the artist as a lonely alienated soul who is the bearer of a unique mark, the product of his individuality, a testament to the universal and transcendent nature of the human spirit. I formed some early assumptions behind my work arguing against neoexpressionism and the "return" to "traditional values" that was taking over the art world during the first years of the Reagan revolution. My peers and I vigorously opposed this tendency. These were the formative circumstances of my education as an artist. They continue to inform the decisions I make today.

Has my opposition to some formulations of expressionism enabled me to ignore the presence of my own unconscious? Has it limited my ability to understand the role of my unconconsious? There have been times in the recent past when I repressed my own ambivalences in order to convey a sense of certainty in my activist work. When I was most intensely involved in AIDS activist politics, I was unable to admit any sense of doubt in my work. Doubt, uncertainty, and contingency were temporarily removed from my vocabulary. This was not a crime. I feel more curious than guilty about this. Circumstances seemed to demand it, and now I understand why. It was necessary for me to focus on the problems of representation concerning people with AIDS in general rather than become mired in the circumstances of my own infection—the arena in which I experience fear about the future. This was a good but inefficient means of coping. It left much unattended. Now, I must pose new questions and maybe formulate some answers.

The more rules I try to establish, the more questions arise. Every time I formulate a principle, I feel burdened by the demand to locate its origin of thought. Every assumption is founded on a previously established received idea. My thinking is a rickety structure that can barely support the weight of surrounding circumstances. I call it home.

NOTES

1 Charles Ludlam, "Manifesto: Ridiculous Theater, Scourge of Human Folly," in *The Complete Plays of Charles Ludlam* (New York: Harper and Row, 1989), vii.

2 The Gay Men's Health Crisis is the nation's oldest and largest AIDS service organization, providing services and advocacy to people with AIDS.

3 "Living with AIDS" is a weekly cable program produced by GMHC addressing concerns of people with AIDS and those who care for them.

4 Martha Rosler, gallery statement, "Global Taste: A Meal in Three Courses," in *The Art of Memory: The Loss of History* (New York: New Museum of Contemporary Art, 1985).

5 Martha Rosler, "The Bowery in Two Inadequate Descriptive Systems," in *Martha Rosler III Works*, Nova Scotia Pamphlets, no. 1 (Halifax: Press of the Nova Scotia School of Art and Design, 1981), 11–57.

6 Dee Dee Halleck, "A Few Arguments for the Appropriation of Television," *High Performance,* no. 37 (1987): 38-44.

7 Raymond Williams, *Marxism and Literature* (Oxford and New York: Oxford University Press, 1977), 115.

8 Ibid.

9 Seeing through AIDS is organized through Media Network, which publishes a catalog of the videotapes used in the program.

10 Raymond Williams, *Television: Technology and Cultural Form* (New York: Schocken Books, 1975), 23.

CHAPTER 14

TONGUES *RE*-TIED

Marlon Riggs

The vice squad of American culture is once again on the attack. After being rebuffed in their attempts to ban the homoerotic images of Robert Mapplethorpe and, more recently, the Todd Haynes film *Poison*, after suffering embarrassing defeat in the "antiobscenity" court case against the black rap group 2 Live Crew, the nation's self-appointed media watchdogs have regrouped and found another, seemingly perfect target: my experimental documentary, *Tongues Untied*, which unabashedly celebrates the struggles, lives, and loves of black gay men.

Tongues Untied was motivated by a singular imperative: to shatter this nation's brutalizing silence on matters of sexual and racial difference. Yet despite a concerted smear and censorship campaign, perhaps even because of it, this work is achieving its aim. The fifty-five-minute video documents a nationwide community of voices—some quietly poetic, some undeniably raw and angry—that together challenge our society's most deeply entrenched myths about what it means to be black, to be gay, to be a man, and above all, to be human.

Tongues Untied has achieved a host of international awards. The Berlin, London, and New York documentary film festivals, the National Black Programming Consortium, and the Black Filmmakers Hall of Fame, as well as the Whitney Museum and the Los Angeles Film Critics Association—to name a select few—have accorded this work top honors.

Ironically, just as the Reverend Don Wildmon of the American Family Association was first citing *Tongues Untied* as an offensive misuse of "American tax-payers' dollars" (it never seems to occur to his ilk that gay, lesbian, and bisexual Americans are taxpayers, too), the documentary was screening at this year's International Public Television Festival in Dublin. Selected by an international jury of public broadcasters, my work was offered as exemplary, innovative programming in U.S. public television. Since then, England, Spain, Australia, and Sweden have commissioned *Tongues Untied* for their own public television broadcasts.

FIGURE 1
Marlon Riggs, *Tongues Untied* (1989). (Photo: Ron Simmons, Frameline.)

This, of course, has not meant a hill of beans to white archconservatives and religious fundamentalists, who pointedly minimize or ignore altogether the abundant evidence affirming *Tongues Untied*'s artistic and social merit. Among these would-be guardians of American culture, sexuality as such remains taboo: shrouded by even deeper layers of silence, stigma, and aversion is black heterosexuality. Black homosexuality, the triple taboo, equates in their minds with an unspeakable obscenity.

Predictably, the moral censors have pounced on both PBS and the National Endowment for the Arts in an ongoing effort to force American Culture into line with their rigid, narrow notions of morally correct art. Any public institution caught deviating from their puritanical morality is inexorably blasted as contributing to the nation's social decay.

In a rhetorical equivalent to hate-filled fag bashing, the morality watchdogs have smeared and disfigured *Tongues Untied* beyond recognition. A recent editorial in the *Washington Times* suggested in all seriousness that the PBS broadcast of my work was tantamount to disseminating raw homosexual "pornography" across the public airwaves, transforming the households of America into a "gay striptease joint"!

Equally predictable in the current "obscenity" controversy (and also more dis-

MARLON RIGGS

heartening) is the collusion—through silence—of mainstream black America in this nakedly homophobic and covertly racial assault. The legacy of Harriet Tubman, Sojourner Truth, James Baldwin, Bayard Rustin, and Martin Luther King Jr., and the many thousands more who lived and died to free us all from prescribed social roles defined by a dominant majority, that legacy has come to this: black straight Americans (many of whom consider themselves "progressive," even "Afrocentric revolutionaries") passively, silently, acquiescing as political bedmates to the likes of the Reverend Wildmon, James Kilpatrick, and Jesse Helms.

Suddenly, traditional conceptions of America's Left, Right, and Center prove bankrupt. The general desire to suppress any realistic acknowledgment, let alone exploration, of homosexuality in the United States has engendered the ultimate postmodern coalition!

Sandwiched uncomfortably amidst this improbable collection of censorship coconspirators are a significant number of public television executives and newspaper critics. Generally more politic than the Wildmons of America, the broadcasters and the critics nonetheless cite the "offensive language" of *Tongues Untied* and its affront to "community standards" as justification for banning the work or scheduling it in the wee hours of the night.

The question such critics never ask, because the answers are profoundly revealing, is, *Whose* community and *whose* standards?

Implicit in the much overworked rhetoric about "community standards" is the assumption of only one central community (patriarchal, heterosexual, and *usually* white) and one overarching cultural standard (ditto) to which public television programming must necessarily appeal. By this reasoning, any work seriously affronting majority biases and beliefs guarantees a highly marginal place, if any at all, on public television.

Defining imagery and language as either "acceptable" or "impermissible" then becomes a critical tool of cultural domination: the charge of "obscenity" or of being "grossly offensive" offers the perfect pretext for silencing a minority's attempt at ending its subjugation and challenging the majority's social control. Tongues untied are thereby *retied*. The suppression of the culturally (and politically) disfranchised thus continues without compunction. How convenient.

That this dynamic has shaped the cultural distortion and outright erasure of many groups throughout American history—African, Native, Asian, and Latin Americans, working-class communities, women as well as homosexuals—wholly escapes most who object to the "language" and homoerotic imagery of *Tongues Untied.*

"We are uninvited guests in people's homes," one station executive in Detroit explained. "We have to be careful about what we put on the air so as not to alienate and offend our community." Public television, on this basis, offers little if any distinction from its commercial counterpart.

Like most of mainstream American media, public television serves merely to consolidate the myths, power, and authority of the majority: minorities might be granted the right to speak and be heard, but only if we abide by the "master codes" of courteous speech, proper subject matter, conventional aesthetics, and "mainstream" appeal. Disobey this often unwritten rule and you risk banishment into cultural oblivion.

The present censorship hysteria has paradoxically rekindled an essential public debate: Who is to have access to so-called public media, and on what terms? Who should represent and define "minority" perspectives? Above all, whose authority draws the thin line between "diversity" and unacceptable "deviance"?

James Baldwin, renowned black homosexual novelist and essayist, once wrote that the general aim of white Americans was to refashion the Negro face after their own, and failing that, to make the black face "blank." Straight America, black as well as white, now demands much the same of homosexual men and women: to win majority acceptance, we are asked to represent ourselves in ways that, in effect, reaffirm the majority's self-image of privilege. The alternative is erasure.

But there is another alternative, and this for many is the real outrage of *Tongues Untied,* and for many, many more, its principal virtue: its refusal to present a historically disparaged community begging on bended knee for tidbits of mainstream tolerance. What *Tongues* instead affirms and demands is a frank, uncensored, uncompromising articulation of an autonomously defined self and social identity. (SNAP!)

FIGURE 2
Marlon Riggs and Essex Hemphill (right) in *Tongues Untied* (1989). (Photo: Ron Simmons, Frameline.)

CHAPTER 15

SEX LIES WITH VIDEOTAPE:
ABBREVIATED HISTORIES OF CANADIAN VIDEO SEX

Sara Diamond

In l992, the Supreme Court of Canada, after viewing what included several selections of gay male video pornography, passed the *Butler* decision, taking the significant Canadian anticensorship movement by surprise and initiating another battle against sexual images in film, video, and print.

     Butler crept into the prairie winter of Winnipeg stealthily, pursued by the antipornography committee of the Legal Education and Action Fund (LEAF).[1] The *Butler* brief was written with the aid of Catherine MacKinnon, who, in what could be read as a colonial gesture, used Canada as a test bed for the legislation she and Andrea Dworkin have fought so unsuccessfully for in the United States. The *Butler* decision claims to "protect" women and others from "degrading" and "dehumanizing" sexual images. In a major leap of legal faith, it blames pornography for social dysfunction. The concepts of degradation and dehumanization are as always ambiguous; the interpreters are police, customs agents, and judges.

     This decision came at a time when many feminist activists had finally realized that legislative remedies to pornography only result in the seizure of sex and AIDS education information and trigger wholesale crusades against feminist, gay, and lesbian books, films, and tapes. Add to this the confusing mobility of the commercial porn market. There is a growing availability of "couple-oriented" or "female" porn that centers on women's fantasies, does away with the money shot, and makes use of melodrama and romantic narrative as plot forms. Many women had shifted into media literacy and sex education campaigns, organizing for social services for victims of violence and tougher laws against child abuse.

     Anticensorship activists wept for good reason. In the year since *Butler*, many books, publications, videotapes, and exhibitions have been seized or busted. Some recognizable titles include Jean Genet's *Querelle, Body Art* magazine, *The Advocate*, Suzie Bright's *Sexual Reality*, and, ironically, Andrea Dworkin's *Women Hating* and *Pornography: Men Possessing Women*.[2] Panic-ridden commercial porn distributors have divested their shelves of a variety of videos, and a number of alternate cinema spaces are facing court cases for exhibiting *In the Realm of the Senses* by Nasia Oshima and other media works. This renewed policing vigor intervenes into a rich subculture of independent video that negotiates sexuality and sex. It will form another yet-unwritten chapter of a medium in which Canadian artistic and curatorial practice has been shaped as much by resistance to the boundaries of state repression as to any other structuring of desire and thus must provide an introduction to this essay.

Before, during, and after Canada's intensified censorship of the 1980s, Canadian video artists made work about sex and sexuality, but production intensified in angry response to censorship, and defiant audiences grew. With eager and sophisticated viewers in place, practice soon eclipsed the narrow boundaries of censorship issues or transgression, and complex video discourses about sex and sexuality continued in Canada, flowing into new territories and involving emerging artists. Actual explicit sex tapes form a tiny portion of a practice that spans the counterculture era of the 1970s until the present. Sex operates within larger social and psychic structures. I have chosen to include videotapes that construct and react around discourses of sexuality in critical ways and thus frame sex, as well as videos that include the apparatus of seduction, romance, desire, and loss.

While black-and-white video was barely pubescent there was a first date between tape and desire. This was no surprise; independent video's inheritance of body art, modernist voyeurism, and popular and community documentary made sex and sexuality surefire concerns. In the early 1970s, at least for the alternately cultured video man, sex was the ultimate truth, melding with utopian globalism and technoliberation. Video made its first foray into the bedrooms of the counterculture, documenting masturbation, fucking, and baby's first breath through a blur of pixels. Tapes about sexuality were not always predictable: for example, *Orgasm* by Michael Goldberg (1975) is inadvertently humorous as an interview between a man and two women becomes a debate about orgasm. John Mitchell's *The Agony and the Ecstasy*, made in the early 1970s, is an illustrated pun. Mitchell attempts to "penetrate" good literature, Joyce's *Ulysses*, by boring through it with a giant screw. The book is the object of obscurity and pursuit, but gives way to "woman," who becomes the butt of the joke, an Oedipal analogy.[3]

In early feminist work the body became a discursive site, constructed by difference, operating in ideological as well as linguistic terms:

> The body is the physical agent of the structures of everyday experience. It is the producer of dreams, the transmitter and receiver of cultural messages, a creature of habits, a repository of memories, an actor in the theatre of power, a tissue of affects and feelings. Because the body is a boundary between biology and society, between drives and discourse, between the sexual and the categorization of power, biography and history, it is the site par excellence for transgressing the constraints of meaning or what social discursivity prescribes as normality.[4]

SARA DIAMOND

Lisa Steele's *Birthday Suit—with Scars and Defects* (1974) adds new meanings to nudity, pain, and memory. Steele tours the viewer through a gentle chronology of her body scars, carefully placing each in extreme close-up view of the camera, pausing, stroking, speaking its genesis, until the scars culminate in an adult female body, but one reinvented through memory. At the end, she walks naked into a long shot, singing, "Happy birthday to me," dresses, and leaves the room.

In marked contrast, Rodney Werden documented perceived marginal sexualities with the scrutinizing camera gaze of a Diane Arbus, mostly fascinated, occasionally identified. This direct use of video foreshadowed its current use as a tool of sexual documentation.[5] In *Pauli Schell* (1975), a young working-class woman talks about her experiences of sexual abuse as a child and her continued interest in sadomasochism. Werden later produced *"I'll Bet You Ain't Never Seen Noth'n Like This Before"* (1980), a tape with the woman's father, a man who artfully penetrates himself with his own penis. He speaks openly of his abusive relationship with Pauli, his daughter. The status of this work as video art screened in the gallery context can enhance the sadistic pleasure of the viewer. Polli Schell's need to disclose seems desperate and naive, intensifying the spectacle for the media literate. Other of Werden's tapes use less transparent approaches, signaling their construction. The young man in *Baby Dolls* (1978) divulges plans for a sex change, while the camera intimately documents sexual intercourse, and an audio confession of the artist-voyeur is heard on the audio track in *A.M. Radio Was His Only Friend* (1979).

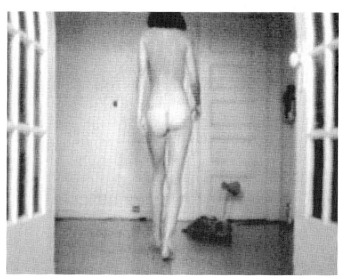

FIGURE 1
Lisa Steele, *Birthday Suit—with Scars and Defects* (1974)

Even if a gap exists between sexual object choice and other aspects of subjectivity, tapes about sex might still empower without enforcing the state's rigorous codes of morality by considering both the relationship between the artist and the subject(s) depicted and the positions made available to us as viewers. *Money Talks, Bullshit Walks* (1986) came on the scene during intensified police harassment of prostitutes but never once refers to this context. Prostitutes enter the frame and seat themselves before a map of the world. Werden buys their time for a small fee and hears their confessions; he is not seen, only his omnipotent voice is heard. He questions them about their reasons for working the streets, the kind of the sex they practice, and their price. Wanting more for his money, Werden continually challenges them for more disclosure, asks them to strip or, in the instance of a young male prostitute, masturbate for the camera. Does visibility make them vulnerable? The work echoes the classical cinema in which aberrant women humiliate themselves through disclosure, the spectacle of the female body overrides any plot development, and the modernist flaneur is celebrated.

This documentary sits uncomfortably next to Werden's more compelling narrative works, which also examine sex at point of sale, but allow us some distance. Werden's sexual fictions are perennial, almost literal, reminders of castration anxiety: money is exchanged between john and prostitute for an illusive reassurance in which men become powerless after the act of exchange. There are never pimps in Werden's scripts; the bargain is struck directly. Each encounter leads to loss: in *The Story of Red* (1984), the prostitute berates Red. In *Blue Moon* (1983), the protagonist dies, perhaps because of his implied homoerotic yearnings. There the prostitute is also a fecund mother, as womb envy meets the vagina dentura.

In other artists' work, "self" ricochets endlessly off the body. In *Janus* (1973), Colin Campbell presents himself, naked, statuesque, available to our gaze. This piece provides contiguity with other early works by the artist, *I'm a Voyeur* (1974), *True/False* (1972), and *Love Life* (1974), all of which explore the impossibility of self-knowledge and truth. In *True/False* Campbell makes a series of confessions to the camera and includes his sexual practices on the list. It is up to the viewer to choose which stories they will credit. While Campbell began with the culture of narcissism's multiple mirrors, so typical of early video, he quickly moves on to provide "a pseudonym, presenting himself as a false identity to begin with." Bruce Ferguson argues that this is a very Canadian act, for while Canada is part of commercial North American culture, we are always positioned as "other" within that culture: "It is inevitable that a Canadian artist would choose the evacuation of self rather than narcissism in the first place."[6] Stuart Marshall elucidates narcissism, suggesting that video functions as a "nonreversed mirror" that can allow the subject to search for his or her appearance in the world. Video is a metaphor for the duality of the self; the new self, through ritual and repetition, forms an "identity," but a fragile one indeed. The technology turns the sadomasochistic relationship; activity and passivity interplay in voyeuristic, exhibitionist pleasures. The artist engages in fantasy with an absent spectator, or with an other, imagined self.[7] This activity is most important when communal identities are brought into being, cutting across narcissism.

As a viewer we act upon the artist or we identify with him or her, and Campbell plays self-reflexively with these relationships. At times the imagined "I" is differently gendered. In *Conundrum Clinique* (1981), Colin Campbell addresses a feminine "self" in the mirror, providing a commentary on the assumed masculinity of the "other" viewing subject. Over years of videomaking Campbell has consistently produced a decentered subject; his works consist of complex narrative explorations of cross-gendered identities or scathing farces about cultural politics. Campbell uses gender as a soluble substance, a set of positions that can be assumed, biology aside, a means with which to explore identification. *No Voice Over* (1986) is a leap of imagination free of envy. He explores the allegiances and eroticism of feminine friendship. *Skin* (1990) challenges racism and class bias in a visually lush docufiction about women and AIDS. Crossing over a biological boundary, Campbell makes it possible for at least some men to speak for some women.

This sense of looking in upon a culture of narcissism formed an important component in the early works of Paul Wong, such as *Prime Cuts* (1981). Here, an insipid group of models loll on beaches, pose, flirt, party, flirt again, to no specific end; the technology of sexual artifice is laid bare. The tape's meaning amplifies through authorship since the artist, a Chinese Canadian, would have been excluded from full entry into Canada's racist glamour culture.

In Quebec, the 1970s were a self-conscious time with deep attention to language and narrative form. *Delirium*, a terrifying and hallucinatory tale, was made by Le Videographe collective. A woman turns on a man who is obsessively tracking her in the hilly countryside, somehow enters his cabin, and castrates him. Robert Morin and Lorraine Dufour's *Ma vie c'est pour le restant de mes jours* (1980) spends "a day in the life" with male go-go dancers, strippers, and the clientele in a rural Quebec bar. A mini-orgy swings into action, triggering a domestic dispute. We're never quite certain if we are watching vérité or fiction, as certain characters disrupt our sense of the spectacular by pointing out the cinematic nature of the "real."[8]

Many a commentary on the sex of the nation had screened on Canadian public television since the late 1950s. The National Film Board, Canada's postwar propaganda entity, worked with its fledgling flatbedmate, the Canadian Broadcasting Corporation, to warn against rising promiscuity, juvenile delinquency, "deviance," and family crisis. It's no surprise that when cable casting became available in the early 1970s, communities subject to public television rose to the televisual occasion.

Video is a truth guarantor in *Transsexual Lifestyle* (1973), as street kids who had been harassing and beating transsexual prostitutes are brought together with their victims. The mediator is a gay liberation activist. The threat of violence zings through the conversation as one disenfranchised group tries to talk to another. *Music for Stocking-Top, Staircase and Swing* (1975) by Cosey Fanni is a drag document in which two queens masturbate and play with phallic-shaped objects. *Suzanne et Lucie: Danseuses à Go-Go* (1973) by Richard Boutet steps through the routines of two exotic dancers and their heroin habit.

The strongest documentary impulse came from the early Canadian feminist movement. Tapes taught breast and cervical health, demonstrated birth control, held debates about abortion and prostitution, explored lesbian lifestyles. In *Women's Breast Self-Examination* (1973) a confident counselor encourages women to take pleasure in touching their own breasts. Early Quebec efforts combined fictional and documentary strategies. In the midseventies, *Les Seins de Louise* (Louise's breasts) speaks up for "eros" and stages hilarious candid camera perspectives that expose our culture's obsessive and fetishistic relationship to the breast. It's an everything-bared, shoot-from-the-hip treatment which insists that it's context, not image, that's the problem.

The initial curve of women's sexual imagery, tied to ideals of "control of our bodies," subsided by the later 1970s, increasingly replaced by a feminine sexuality characterized by victimization and pain. *We Will Not Be Beaten, A Rule of Thumb, A Common Assault, A Sign of Affection*, by Peg Campbell (1979-81); *Great Expectations* (1981), by Gay Hawley of Amelia Productions; *Chaperons rouges* (1979), by Groupe Intervention de Video and La Femme et le Film; *Fashion as a Social Control, Rape Is a Social Disease, Reclaiming Ourselves: A Feminist Perspective on Pornography* (slide show), *A Respectable Lie, That's Not Me They're Talking About*, by Women in Focus (1975-80); and *Fight Back: Transition House* (1984), by Speak Out Productions, all examine women's vulnerability to sexual abuse and violence. The impact of these tapes was contradictory. By speaking of sexual abuse, even within relationships where erotic love was acknowledged, feminist media created a needed public space for Canadian women to resist extreme forms of stereotyping, to fight for legislative initiatives against rape and domestic violence and services. While testimonial tapes did not always provide solutions, the solidarity they induced shifted attitudes toward violence. Unfortunately, feminist discussions of sexual imagery increasingly conflated with concerns about sexual violence. It was hard to speak of pleasure.

Of these tapes, *Chaperons rouges,* by Montreal-based Groupe Intervention de Video, exudes the inventiveness of the highly politicized Quebec documentary milieu of the 1970s. The video parallels Bruno Bettelheim's analysis of fairy tales as cautionary socializing tales of terror. It deconstructs Little Red Riding Hood as a metaphor of sexual assault, in which the wolf alludes to the myths that surround male sexuality. In a compelling scene a woman dancer reenacts a rape experience. Unlike this tape's sophisticated analysis of the unconscious reading of imagery, many other videos simplistically linked violence with sexual imagery, usually by showing "degrading" and "inciting" pornography. Documentaries that sidestepped this tendency deserve an honorable mention. *It's Not My Head, It's My Body* (1978), by Riseau Video des Femmes, is about stripping; it argues that the job is an economic choice. Victoria's Women against Pornography shifted their focus to organize with sex trade workers instead of against them. Their video, *She Works Hard for the Money* (1980), indicts the inequity of power between prostitutes, police, and johns. The first volleys in what came to be known as "the porn wars" were fired in the United States. Willing to play the comprador, the Canadian women's movement jumped to the fray, as did conservative women. Respected Canadian feminists such as Frances Wasserlein supported Andrea Dworkin and Catherine MacKinnon, arguing for provincial governments to intensify the monitoring of sexual imagery and allow those "harmed" by pornography to lay charges. Theorists such as Geraldine Finn believed that sexuality was a masculine construct, arguing that visual activity is inherently a masculine pleasure. Women should have sex but not sexuality; sexual imagery, "alternative or otherwise," authored by women or not, was reprehensible. Entire women's centers devoted themselves to fighting pornography.

The hostility toward sexual imagery brought on by the antiporn women's movement ironically gave rise to more sexual images than most Canadian women had

SARA DIAMOND

ever seen. For many, feminist media practice centered on denunciation, in turn predicated on show-and-tell. Karen Knights describes the problem with much of the analysis:

> The literalness which arose from the definitions debate hampered a creative approach to sexual imagery. Several slide shows were produced. All were didactic and flaunted the most clichéd of erotic conventions: soft focus, tasteful nudes, sunsets. Worse yet, some insisted on pronouncing, "This image is erotic, this one is not." This approach meant that some of the audience were first aroused by a picture and then punished by it. . . . Predictably, there were no discussions amongst men about abandoning explicit representations of sex. . . . [W]e are left with a visual wasteland. . . . [N]o matter how marginal gay and lesbian porn may be, heterosexual alternatives are even more scarce.[9]

Another Canadian voice quickly emerged, arguing not for free speech but rather for the transformation of social and psychic structures. Drawing from psychoanalysis and socialist-feminist critiques of the state, some women suggested that censorship only worked to strengthen patriarchy and thus, inevitably, a regime of antiwoman images, whether commercial or underground. Repression intervened between fantasy and activity; women, as well as men, desired media fantasy. These feminists sought thorough social change, alternative erotic production, and the opening up of a public discourse about sexuality led by women.

They argued that the obsession with explicit sexual imagery, with the evidence of male sexism and violence, was part of a withdrawal of the women's movement from the struggle for larger social transformation in the face of a growing right-wing backlash. They pointed out that, ironically, the organic link between sexual freedom, access to birth control and abortion, and lesbian rights was less often spoken, and that alliances with the Canadian right-wing women's movement against offensive imagery were more frequent and dangerous. Women's sexual identities were spaced on a continuum, not fixed by biology or in any essential difference. Although much pornography functioned as reassurance for men, it also offered ground for discourse and intervention, so rather than suppress the evidence, use the evidence to solve the problem! To criticize women for taking pleasure in viewing like a man would only intensify that pleasure in a culture in which sexual pleasure, particularly feminine sexual pleasure, was illicit. Certainly, serious reconsideration of the images with which women wished to be represented was needed, but why would pleasure diminish women's desire to resist? Did women want to embrace traditional nurturing and humanist values, more prevalent in melodrama and realism than in experimental and hard-core forms? Why couldn't one both be a feminist and enjoy fantasies about unequal sexual power? Women artists set about addressing these questions.[10]

Not everyone wanted to approach sexual imagery through documentary practice. Documentary makes us think we know a topic. Realism reinforces the idea that the image stands in for the real, a double problem when encouraging media literacy.

Like conventional narrative, documentary creates an identity between the camera and the subject position of the maker, reducing the object of the work to visual spectacle, reproducing relations of control whether structures of class, race, or gender. The viewer, working through the narrative, moves between identification and distance. Documentaries that focus on victimization often revictimize the object of their narrative, especially if the subject is isolated from a social context and critique.

Most nondocumentary work by women excluded itself from a direct critique of pornography, concentrating rather on creating an erotic language. A number of men found fertile ground to express guilt, confusion, and pain in relation to explicit sexual imagery; their work is an antidote not only to commercial sexual images but to the current of video art by men in which misogynist sexual narratives had played a significant part.

Accessory Transit Company (1980), by Jorge Lozano, imagines the loss of voice that Susan Griffin describes in *Pornography and Silence*.[11] A male actor is tied into a chair; helpless, he screams silently. Might men identify with women and operate within "loss," not in fear of it? The actor meets an actress; neither can communicate. A voice-over reads excerpts from the Griffin text, and clips of heterosexual pornography flash on the screen, intentionally or not, overwhelming the silence.

In *A Demonstration of the Fear of Pain* (1980), Kim Tomczak posits masculinity as an authoritarian regime. Porn images are projected onto a man's face and body while an interview subject rants. The image is kept at an uncomfortable distance from the viewer; pictures fall, fragmenting, distorting, and disintegrating the male viewing subject. A later Tomczak tape, *Paradise Lost* (1981), proffers this thought, "The problem with men are men's problems," in a searing critique of masculine narcissism. Tomczak also warns against a bourgeois feminism that looks only within the individual. A male New Left activist and a newly realized feminist squabble over their domestic future. She has shifted her focus from caretaking both her mate and the revolutionary project; he refuses any responsibility for their problems and devalues women's oppression and personal change. The worse the quarrel becomes, the more he finds solace in drugs. The drama is shot in relentless single takes and enacted with wry humor; it hurts to watch as politics kills desire.

From the 1970s, the Canadian video environment was prolific, literate, and versed in international practice, working with hybrid forms before these were popular elsewhere and with inflections of regional expression. Toronto favored narrative experiments and documentary deconstruction; both the West Coast and Quebec played with faux realism; the Prairies bred highly personal and alienated narratives. Classic narrative was pulled apart, as seduction, genre and identity fixer, or spectacle. Canadian video art had borrowed genre only to shatter it, written marginalia into the grand scene, broken expectations of form altogether. Many had anticipated or echoed Teresa de Lauretis's prompt to women film- and videomakers to push the Oedipal crisis of narrative to excess, her homeopathic suggestion that exaggeration begins the cure.[12]

Elizabeth Chitty becomes the feminine pornographer, writing an erotic

SARA DIAMOND

text that she never claims as "hers," masturbating while confronting the camera in *Desire Control* (1981). Ardele Lister assumes the role of her father's mistress, wearing leopard spots and speaking in the voice of the father's desired in *Sugardaddy* (1980). Like the artist, we quietly worry about the implied betrayal of the invisible mother. Marshalore relives her past as a goofy and rejected child in *You Must Remember This* (1979), then plays the vamp, singing siren songs to heal her wounds. Seduction, she suggests, is a compensation effect, and the need to forgive lies hand in hand with the need to punish. Kate Craig produced *Delicate Issue* in 1979. An extreme close-up camera perspective scans her body; like Steele in *Birthday Suit—with Scars and Defects*, she ejects the erotic altogether as body parts become impossible to recognize and the viewer is continually asked how close is too close for comfort.

Lisa Steele's *Gloria* tapes (1980) follow a composite character, a welfare mother.[13] Sexuality is part of the character's tribulations and pleasures. She suffers from an ectopic pregnancy; after the operation she tries to educate her boyfriend about the female body using pornography as her reference material. She asks her father for advice: can she have sexual intercourse in her condition? The discussion turns to her boyfriend's need for money: in humiliation she borrows it for him from her father. Social and economic systems, with women caught in the middle, mediate sexuality: every action has consequences.

Anne Ramsden's three-part *Manufactured Romance: Chance for Love; Beauty, Passion and Power;* and *Emotional Ground* (1983–85) stars Candie Cane, a romance writer trying to produce a more "realistic" form of fiction through the twists and turns of her own life. Soap opera is appropriated for its lack of narrative resolution and reference to daily life.

All five of the artists above act in their tapes. The performative presence in the work of this group of women is summarized well below:

> A conceptual space was created where the limits of narrative could be challenged or dominant genres such as soap opera revisited. Autobiography blurred the boundaries between fiction and documentary. Addressing the audience directly, or utilizing voice-overs, women were able to articulate the context and critique of their representational strategies. The mechanisms of voyeurism were called into question.[14]

Canadian media artists had created important explorations of sexuality from the 1970s through the early 1980s. It is in this charged period that censorship expands in a virulent attack against visual art, independent films, video, and books. Many works, even the National Film Board's notorious indictment of pornography, *Not a Love Story*, were banned or limited in their circulation. As censorship grew so did sexual resistance work, as "power operated as a mechanism of attraction; it drew out those peculiarities over which it kept watch. Pleasure spread to the power that carried it; power anchored the pleasure it uncovered."[15]

Censorship was not new to Canada, either federally or within the provinces. Like other bourgeois legal systems, Canadian law has always regulated sexual behaviors; practices such as birth control (until recently), abortion, male homosexuality, and presentation of sexual images have all been subject to repression. In the 1980s arrests, interventions, and seizures of tapes and technology would interlace with artists' protests, campaigns in the courts, and extensive public exhibition of work about sex and sexuality. Artists, particularly in the video community, refused to comply with the spread of regulation to video. Censorship became the core of video politics, especially tied to issues of identity, as feminists, gays, lesbians, and people of color experienced the suppression of their images. The state perceived these as marginal, offensive, or vulnerable—indicators, in fact, of the fundamental crises of patriarchy.[16]

The campaign against censorship had two centers—Ontario, where the notorious Ontario Board of Censors banned, cut, and seized films and tapes, and British Columbia, where the powers of the censor board were extended to include video in 1985. Women artists and cultural activists led groups such as the Coalition for the Right to View (CRTV, an acronym joke on the CRTC, Canada's federal telecommunications regulatory body, the Canadian Radio and Television Commission), Women against Censorship, and the Ontario Film and Video Appreciation Society (OFAVAS), which took up the fight to defend censored materials and build public awareness. Artists' and feminist groups joined ranks with the gay and lesbian community, whose literature and media were consistently seized by Canada Customs. When the federal government made two attempts to introduce sweeping procensorship amendments to the Criminal Code, prohibiting images of lactation, menstruation, and teens under age eighteen kissing, the coalition broadened to include civil libertarians, major museums, book publishers, and progressive clergy, librarians, sex educators, and teachers. The use of public exhibition as defiance, coupled with strong advertising campaigns, brought new communities into art spaces. Energetic outreach propelled anticensorship lobbyists onto country-and-western talk shows and pop radio; into public debates with right-wing clergy and procensorship women on television; into forums with policymakers, political parties, the substantial Canadian labor movement, and lawyers. Victory was declared, the legislation was jettisoned, and provincial regulation was liberalized, both marks of public opinion.[17]

Curatorial activism and intensified video production made these campaigns possible. Censorship intensified tolerance and opened readings of works: "yes, that is an anus being penetrated, now what's the big deal?" Video sex allowed a rare moment of sexual consensus in viewing, but unlike the porn theatre of old, audiences tended to cross boundaries of gender, age, and race and to articulate differing responses to the image. Screenings were a scale model of the anticensorship movement's larger program for change: they allowed audience members to satisfy sexual curiosity, discuss, and eventually question each others' experiences and pleasures. Some women, for example, were surprised at their pleasure in watching gay male erotic tapes, realizing that they identified without implicating their bodies. On the other hand, an image may elicit narcissistic and fetishistic pleasure that no one else finds sexy. Familiarity or memory

SARA DIAMOND

seems to work within sexual subcultures as well. Some lesbian sex might elicit delight-ful identification from some in the lesbian community at the same moment that a sigh of "ho hum" might arise from other viewers. Responses to alternate heterosexual erotica varied from "That's exactly how I feel about my sexuality, finally someone's showing it," to the comment, "That's gross." What excites the audience in the first place is the idea that they are there to see sex, then the possibility that a video might be made for them, and finally a belief that their proximity is enabled: "Desire requires a sense of attraction, a change in the interview or the relations of nearness or distance from sub-ject to object."[18]

Writers and viewers initially linked these exhibitions primarily to politi-cal strategy, although others pushed for more critical thinking in curatorial practice and the reception of imagery, warning against libertarianism. Perhaps initially, misogyny, archaic modernist pieces, essentialist ritual, and deconstruction sat benignly side by side as markers of resistance. As organizing continued, issues of form, and problems of repre-sentation, appropriation, and the need for cross-cultural presence emerged. The tradition of critical sex exhibition continues in Canada, with recent exhibitions such as *The Priapic Black Stud*, curated by David Odhiambo to explore images of masculinity from the African diaspora; *Out on Video* by Kellie Marlowe, Karen Knights, and Joe Sarahan, a show concerned with the role flip between lesbian and gay male experience of the 1970s and 1990s.[19]

Large institutions either rallied to the anti-censorship call or used the opportunity to embed a more conservative mandate. Paul Wong was asked to participate in the opening show of the new Vancouver Art Gallery in 1984, and *Confused*, his most comprehensive project, which included a drama and an installation made up of talking head interviews in which individuals told coming-of-age stories and chatted about their favorite pleasures, was commissioned. At the eleventh hour the gallery can-celed the exhibition, deeming it too controversial. This decision resulted in a protracted law suit against the gallery; ten years and several directors later, the gallery still lacks the respect of the local art community.

The need for a counterdiscourse spurred video production. *Snip, Snip*, a cross-dressed send-up of the Ontario Censor Board, was made by Colin Campbell and Rodney Werden. In *In the Dark* (1983), by Lisa Steele and Kim Tomczak, the artists have sex while commenting in voice-over on the complexity of gendered sexual identi-ty. The sound track blasts away all of our expectations of an easy erotic sight. In another tape, *See Evil* (1985), they chronicle the police attacks in Ontario, with poignant

FIGURE 2
Kim Tomczak and Lisa Steele answer questions at "The Heat Is On: Women on Art and Sex" conference, Vancouver, 1984. (Photo: Paula Levine.)

FIGURE 3
"The Heat Is On: Women on Art and Sex" conference, Vancouver, 1984. (Photo: Paula Levine.)

testimony from victims of legal cases. Other videos, such as Gary Kibbins's *Henry Kissinger Won the Nobel Peace Prize* (1986), explored the limits of representation and community "tolerance," scattering scatological connections in among politics, power, and actual fecal matter.

Not surprisingly, surveillance became both subject and means for many video works. Through the interventions of the church and certainly since the development of the panopticon, the internalized gaze of the patriarchal state as censor has been a part of the social construction of sexuality and the nuances of desire. Video technology was used early on in Canadian policing of public sex, particularly of gay male behavior and prostitution. The categorizing gaze of the surveillance apparatus discriminates among practices. Surveillance articulates the ways that sex—"a narrow but varied" set of activities—and sexuality—the construction of desire(s)—are linked, for the social and now literal surveillance of sexual practices, the insistence on proper forms and sites of expression, and the use of monitoring technologies to infer social disapproval as well as to collect evidence add to a culture where sight is given primacy in the definition of desire. As many have pointed out, surveillance folds into actual practices, so that the eroticism of the glory hole combines anonymity and danger. Form follows function.[20]

Just as the viewer, official and otherwise, is a central trope in pornography, the power of the technological gaze is present within many critical tapes. John Greyson, Margaret Moores, Rodney Werden, and Paul Wong all eroticize and underline the danger of surveillance. Gay and lesbian artists played a key role in developing alternate sexual materials, with lesbian tapes taking up a public space for lesbian desire and gay works providing complexity in relation to the existing substantial and increasingly regulated gay porn market. In Moores's *Frankly Shirley* (1987), the lesbian lovers make love in a variety of barren sites around the city, claiming their right to public space and its implied surveillance through the long shot. In this instance, the lack of surveillance of lesbian sexuality testifies to the invisibility of lesbian desire.

John Greyson's humorous video hybrids combine musical sequence, dance, comedy, films within films, and drama, sparing few agencies of regulation, including history and colonialism. *Breathing through Opposing Nostrils* (1982) indicts RCMP surveillance of the gay community; *The Jungle Boy* (1985), one-third of the Kipling trilogy, manages to divulge Rudyard Kipling's colonialism and homoeroticism, while linking the former to other forms of control, in this instance the arrest of a gay man for tearoom sex and his subsequent suicide within a culture of media hype. Clips of pornography interrupt the video narrative in many of Greyson's works, providing both pleasure and timely reminders of censorship. Greyson's later work, *Moscow Does Not Believe in Queers* (1986) and two films, *Urinal* and *The Making of Monsters*, explore the repression of gay identities within radical as well as bourgeois cultural traditions, reworking both identities and narratives to quite different historical outcomes.

In 1987, *Visual Evidence*, an eleven-event marathon series about sex and representation, hosted a gay and lesbian pornography production workshop, led by John Greyson and Blush Productions. Three men joined the men's workshop and sixteen

SARA DIAMOND

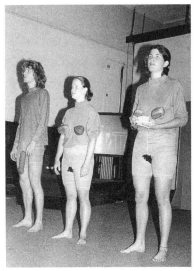

FIGURE 4
Visual Evidence conference, "In Formation: Youth on Sex" panel, Vancouver, 1987. (Photo: Meaghan Baxter.)

women participated in the lesbian group. Women divided into groups based on shared erotic fantasies and struggled to find metaphors, fetishes, words, images, sounds, and short narratives to depict what turned them on. These were then shot and within a weekend three short erotic tapes were made. Lesbians had desire and they certainly had sex, but they didn't yet have an auditory and visual language.[21]

Lesbian artists in Canada worked less for a commercial market than with the feminist tradition of narrative and humor. Margaret Moores works closely with Almerinda Travessos, making lighthearted tapes with winding, absurd plots. In *Frankly Shirley*, a voice-over traces the waxing and waning of an affair; in *Surely to God* (1989), two lovers lose a lottery ticket in the midst of having sex, then attempt to redeem it once it's discovered affixed to their frozen chicken. Lorna Boschman has made numerous explicit tapes, including *Drawing the Line* (1992), *True Inversions* (1992), and *Butch/Femme in Paradise* (1988), as well as two groundbreaking experimental documentaries that look at the complexity of sexual and physical abuse in women's lives, *Scars* (1984) and *Our Normal Childhood* (1988). *True Inversions* investigates censorship and the gap between real and represented sex. Marusia Bociukiw's *Playing with Fire* (1986) and *Night Visions* (1989) are narratives that challenge the radical feminist community with representations of sexuality within a discourse that they had prescribed: egalitarian, politicized, yet erotic. *Bodies in Trouble* (1990) is a short collage about antilesbian repression.

These videos suggest the need for a wide-ranging definition of objects, rather than a set of appropriated stereotypes. Bociukiw's, Boschman's, and Moores's women are attractive to the other women in the video, and it's that dynamic that signifies desire. The quotation of realism in the work engages an audience raised on documentary and narrative conventions. While this wave of lesbian works may have been in part given a supportive context by the anticensorship movement, lesbian sex video continues in Canada, spurred on by a dearth of mass media imagery. Susan Harman in Vancouver and Charlene Boudreau in Montreal have recently begun to create lesbian erotic tapes.

Other women artists play with quest myths and identity. Elizabeth Schroder's *The Bisexual Kingdom* (1987) and *I Can't Believe What I Saw* (1985) send up the sexual pretensions of the art world; in the latter a woman artist asks the question: "How many male artists do you have to fuck before you become one?" In the former an independent woman artist loops through complicated liaisons while trying to explain her sexuality to family and friends, the operative metaphor being *Wild Kingdom. The Lady Killer* (1986), *A Place with No Name* (1989), and *Where Does the Mess Come From?* (1992) attempt to speak to desires that are hard to represent, across the complex boundaries of gender or race.

201

Tanya Mars buffoons sexual stereotypes, first the virgin, Elizabeth the First in *Pure Virtue* (1985), then the whore, Mae West, in *Pure Sin* (1990). Each of these characters represents the price of power for women: the denial of sexuality or the masquerade, yet Mars's Elizabeth is desiring and her Mae West threatening to men in her hyperphallic state. Mars's construction of feminine subjectivity is cumulative; the series also includes the performance *Pure Nonsense*, a send-up of Alice in Wonderland. The videos quote cultural forms aligned with a history of feminine sexual representation. In Elizabethan drama young boys played women. The endless sexual banter read as double entendre; nineteenth-century burlesque was a woman's genre.

Cornelia Wyngaarden bends gender. In *Starling Man* (1983), a man weeps at his incapacity to control nature; In *As a Wife Has a Cow* (1985), the traditional tough-talking cowboy is replaced by Keelie, an androgynous and witty "Marlboro woman" who defies "Nature" while living in harmony with nature. *The Dead Man Was a Woman* (1993) is a noir "true" flirtation, leading to death and intrigue in Vancouver's now historic lesbian bar, the Van Port.

The project of subverting narrative is not owned by women alone. Three gay artists explore the construction of class, race, and language in their work. Joe Sarahan embraces yet critiques the class-bound images of homoerotic beef cake. *Holy Joe* (1987) is a rollicking if macabre romp through phallic icons of religion, fundamentalism, architecture, and heroism. In a barrage of images the tape underlines the role that religion plays in suppressing and creating a rhetoric of sexuality, while the music blasts us forward in ecstasy. An S-M ritual stops the diegesis in its tracks, but the tape moves on posthaste. In *111* (1989), three male subjects, a boxer, a race car driver, and a fencer push against the hard edges of masculinity. His recent multimedia works explore the eroticism of danger, reframing Anger and Genet.

FIGURE 5
Richard Fung, *Chinese Characters* (1986)

Richard Fung's work includes safe sex tapes and documentaries about racism and gay Asian identity and HIV—*Orientations: Gay and Lesbian Asians* (1985), *Fighting Chance* (1990), and *Out of the Blue* (1991)—and fragmented historical explorations of the artist's family. *Chinese Characters* (1986) looks at the ways that Chinese gay men in the West are forced to articulate their desire through images of white men, while struggling with stereotypes of Asian sexuality. Rather than a didactic strategy, Fung uses staged interviews, reenactments of porn, and fantasy voices.

Battling institutional discomfort and outright censorship, Quebecois artist Marc Paradis has created a series of visually piercing and strongly atmospheric video letters and later fantasy narratives. *Le Voyage de l'ogre* (1981); *La Cage* (1983); *L'Incident Jones* (1986), a collaboration with Simon Robert; *Délivre-nous du mal* (1987); *Lettre à un amant* (1988); *Reminiscences Carnivores* (1989); and *Harems* (1991) are narrative poems, painterly or sculptural meditations on alienation, prostitution, violence, sensory perception, thwarted love, the intensity of sexual encounters, and dreams placed against the iconography of gay male sexual culture. The tapes are dense sexual imagery: blow jobs, masturbation, ejaculation, poses, with ambient sound. For example, *Reminiscences Carnivores* is a requiem to "hope, memory and the end of life." The tape overflows with lyrical gestures: a man presses himself against the wall, his hand touches it; two lovers argue without content in a garden, their postures and movement suggesting conflict; a man looks out the window, washes sensuously in a shower in a sunny place; a man stands in a barred window yearning; two men sit below a tree; a man masturbates; the men undress and have oral sex; the men in the garden touch their fingers together. The text refers to time, the brief but interminable space of an affair, of "living without food or drink, on desire and cigarettes."

AIDS educational material seemed particularly subject to censorship, whether seizure by Canada Customs, who blacked out key information about anal sex, or the suppression of safe sex educational information by provincial governments. As in the United States, an activist documentary tradition emerged as various communities used media for internal education, agitation, and outreach. Some producers chose to focus specifically on sexuality and sex in their work about AIDS. In *Steam Clean,* a safe sex tape addressed to Asian men by Richard Fung, a surveillance camera happens to discover two men having sex in a steam bath. The surreptitious camera style naturalizes the activity shown, but also reminds us that marginal sexualities are always monitored. Growing numbers of artists used experimental strategies to address the subjective and social experience of HIV. John Greyson's *The ADS Epidemic* (1987) is a snappy commercial for safe pleasure. *Survival of the Delirious* (1988), by Michael Balser and Andy Fabo, compares the windigo and HIV. In

FIGURE 6
Richard Fung, *Steam Clean* (1987)

Blood Risk (1989), two gay lovers traverse a dangerous landscape. *Beyond the Helms of the Sensors* (1992) is a suite of pornographic vignettes, constructed with historical footage of masculine space and a commitment to safe sex. Art McP's *Fascist in Love, A Good Boy, Statues in Love,* and *Seize in Love* (1989) all confront loss, death, or desire. *AnOther Love Story: Women and AIDS,* by Debbie Douglas and Gabrielle Micallef, is a docufiction addressing culpability and transmission, particularly in the lesbian and black women's communities. In *Bolo, Bolo,* by Ian Rashid and Gita Saxena, images of two South Asian men kissing and of bodies moving together in slow motion are intercut with interviews about AIDS prevention, gay identity in South Asian communities, and invisibility; intertitles that remind the viewer that we are "Talking Silence"; and a discussion of racism and sexuality with Toronto writer Himani Banerjee. The tape skips through conventions of narrative, documentary, and experimentation. A recent series of AIDS PSAs titled *Second Decade* was produced by the Banff Centre for the Arts in collaboration with Michael Balser and a group of directors and composers. The PSAs were destined for broadcast and community use; all speak enthusiastically about safe sex to a wide range of audiences, from aboriginal viewers to heterosexual teenagers to lesbians.

FIGURE 7
David MacLean's Public Service Announcement "Marilyn," from the *Second Decade* series. (Photo: Don Lee, The Banff Centre.)

With important exceptions many of the first wave of sex works in Canada were by white artists. Relationships among race, gender, and sexual difference constitute key areas of current investigation. Some artists concentrate on self-censorship and community regulation. David Odhiambo and Jennifer Abbott's layered video *Skinned* (1993) exposes the emotional erotic of their relationship while the sound track peels away the hostility they feel from both white and black contexts. Shani Mooto's humorous *Wild Women of the Woods* (1992) tramps through stereotypes of South Asian women as her heroine is seduced and athleticized by a dancing goddess of the woodlands and mountains. Zackery Longboy's meditative urban performance document *From Another Time Comes One* (1990) examines fantasies of aboriginal masculinity. *Fresh Talk: Youth and Sexuality* (1991), by Craig Condy-Berggold and Teresa Marshall, is a 1990s version of *Confused,* in which young people from a range of cultures hold forth on Image, Responsibility, Power, and Pleasure. Through lyrical and layered montages, artist David Findlay rewrites received fantasies in *Gender, Lace, and Glass* (1992).

As new readings enter the cumulative knowledge of the video community, meanings of older works shift. For example, *Mirror, Mirror,* by Paula Levine, is a playful gambol with the mirror phase, but one that sounds discomforting chords in relation to race. The video is shot in the muscle section of Venice Beach. Levine takes up the problem of who is supposed to look at whom, fixing her camera on an unsuspect-

204

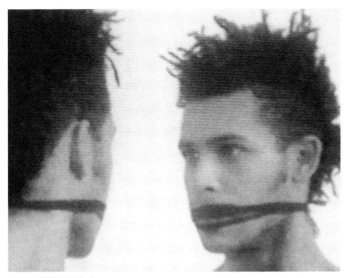

FIGURE 8
David Findlay, *Gender, Lace, and Glass* (1992)

ing young man. The latter, positioned at the center of a gaggle of girls, preens. In a sudden double take, he notices the camera, realizing that he is the object of its attention. Anger turns to playfulness as he converts the camera to a mirror, meeting its steady look with his own. Movement in the tape articulates at a very slow speed, providing the effect of analysis. That the young man is not white adds an additional layer to the gaze, perhaps especially for the white viewer. The look is no longer a simple reversal, gaze for gaze, but a look at the Other's other, an already sexualized subject within the discourse of white racism.

Video sex may seem to fit snugly into voyeurism, but its deconstructive nature, whether through an emphasis on sound over vision, extreme close-up angles, or its play on narrative and codes, has allowed the emergence of critical fantasy. Video plays with the linear, with repetition and fuzziness, allowing an articulation of difference as well as triggering memory. Placed in the political and social context of surveillance, censorship, and repression, video has provided a central tool for Canadian artists and activists to construct a kaleidoscope of resilient and resistant gazes, views, and desires, which nuance and shift continually. Video sex functions within a culture that still holds the discourse of sexuality as fundamental to notions of subjectivity. Difference articulates fundamental rifts in possible positions or sight lines, and one remains challenged to define a place to speak, to not say that desire cannot be represented, while surreptitiously stealing glances at the theoretical monitor. Alternate sex and sexuality tapes operate to build ego identification for collectivities, deploying relationships between signifiers that are only tied down by meanings constructed by communities, at least this side of the Nielsen ratings.[22] As Luce Irigaray suggests, "Desire occupies or designates the space of the interval. A permanent definition of desire would put an end to desire."[23] That's why, no matter how tired anticensorship activists may be in Canada, we can't allow censorship to fill or still the interval.[24]

1 There was no publicity surrounding this case until the courts declared for LEAF, as there would have been massive opposition had the anticensorship movement been alerted.

2 Lucinda Johnston, "Censorship and Receiving," *FUSE* 16, no. 4 (1993): 10–14, provides information about recent book seizures. See also Kika Thorne, "Refusing Censorship," *FUSE* 16, no. 3 (1993): 7–8, for information about resistance.

3 There are many tapes made between 1970 and 1980 with an uncritical misogynist vocabulary. *Steel and Flesh* by Dana Atchley and Eric Metcalfe, for example, uses noir style and story line in a genre-driven sex and violence narrative.

4 Nelly Richards, "The Rhetoric of the Body," *Art and Text* 21 (1985): 65.

5 Paul Wong, "True Enough," *Video Guide* 39 (1986): 12.

6 Bruce Ferguson,"Colin Campbell: Otherwise Worldly," in *Colin Campbell: Media Works* (Winnipeg: Winnipeg Art Gallery, 1990), 20.

7 Stuart Marshall, "Strategies of Dissemblance," in *Colin Campbell: Media Works,* 26. This brief text builds on several groundbreaking articles that Marshall wrote about video in the 1970s.

8 Dan Walworth,"Cascadage," in *Robert Morin, Lorraine Dufour* (Toronto: A Space, 1991), 64.

9 Karen Knights, "Explicit but Equal, Towards a New Pornography," *Video Guide* 39 (December 1986): 6.

10 See Varda Burstyn, ed., *Women against Censorship* (Toronto: Douglas and MacIntyre, 1985). The book collects a series of arguments for a social and cultural program.

11 Susan Griffin, *Pornography and Silence: Culture's Revenge against Nature* (New York: Harper Colophon Books, 1981).

12 Teresa de Lauretis, *Technologies of Gender: Essays on Theory, Film, and Fiction* (Bloomington and Indianapolis: Indiana University Press, 1987).

13 Other Steele videos, including *Waiting for Lancelot, Part 1 to 7,* deal more directly with sex. In *Lancelot* Steele chronicles a woman caught between marriage and an affair, "both male defined confines."

14 Dot Tuer, "From the Father's House: Women's Videos and Feminism's Struggle with Difference," *FUSE,* Winter 1987–88, 22.

15 Michel Foucault, *The History of Sexuality: Volume 1, An Introduction* (New York: Random House, 1976), 45.

16 Peter Stallybrass and Allon White, *The Politics and Poetics of Transgression* (Ithaca, N.Y.: Cornell University Press, 1986).

17 See A Space Exhibition Committee, ed., *Issues of Censorship* (Toronto: Our Times, 1985), for a chronicle of Ontario anticensorship organizing and for valuable arguments.

18 Luce Irigaray, "The Politics of Difference," trans. Sean Hand, in *Sexual Difference,* ed. Milan Women's Collective (Bloomington: Indiana University Press, 1990), 120.

19 Both of these occurred at the Video in Vancouver, the former in 1993, the latter in 1991.

20 Michel Foucault, *History of Sexuality,* 45.

21 *Visual Evidence* included many video screenings of historic and current work, including a retrospective of Colin Campbell; a performance and video evening "In Formation" by and about youth sexuality; a conference on sex education; a workshop on race, sex, and representation; discussions with Paul Wong and Candida Royalle; and the workshop described.

22 Brian Rusted, *Site Unseen* (1990), a video and talk presented at the Video in Vancouver, in which Rusted suggests that video creates temporary and strategic alignments of meaning and groups.

23 Irigaray, "The Politics of Difference," 120.

24 For distribution information about the videotapes mentioned in this article, please contact V/TAPE, Toronto, at 416/863-9897. They can facilitate access to tapes from across Canada and Quebec.

CHAPTER 16

TALKING HEADS, BODY POLITIC:
THE PLURAL SELF OF CHICANO
EXPERIMENTAL VIDEO

Chon A. Noriega

Always remember yourself, even if you remember nothing. ~ JAMES BROUGHTON[1]

Forget what I just wrote. It is a lie. I remember everything. ~ HARRY GAMBOA JR.[2]

Is there a "history" between these two ironic gestures about history? Broughton: beat poet and pioneer of the U.S. "underground" cinema of the 1940s and 1950s, mediated by the movement's heir unapparent, Guillermo "Willie" Varela, an artist who happened to be Chicano, mistaken for a Chicano who happened to be an artist. Gamboa: cofounder of the art collective Asco (Nausea), which was rejected by both the nationalist Chicano Art Movement and the alternative performance and conceptual art of the 1970s and 1980s.[3] Both artists must be seen as "postmodern" by default, insofar as neither fits easily within modernism or modernist categories, while both remain insistent on the truth claims of memory for media. In their art and artist personae, Broughton and Gamboa trade in the Brechtian "social gest," "the mimetic and gestural expression of the social relationships prevailing between people of a given period."[4] But, if the periods are a given, the social groups constituted by these gests remain unnamed, somewhere between hypothetical and emergent.

But is there a "history" between these two figures? And, if so, what is at stake in how it is told? Despite the similarities between Gamboa (and Asco) and the "established" avant-garde of the 1970s—with its historical antecedents—it is not a matter of the center's unacknowledged influences on the margins. There were none.[5] In fact, Varela is perhaps the only Chicano media artist to situate his work within the aesthetic trajectory of New American Cinema: Maya Deren, James Broughton, Stan Brakhage, and so on.[6] But I am not sure that the answer lies in an all-too-easy call for multiple or simultaneous histories, without a corresponding account of the spaces occupied by each. As Lawrence Grossberg points out, "History—or rather, different histories—are always placed somewhere. . . . It is not so much a question of when the other speaks, but

207

where."[7] The history of Chicano producers—whether commercial, independent, or experimental—has been one of expression outside or at the margins of the institutional and discursive domains for film and video. What this means in a practical sense is limited access to or exclusion from film schools, funding sources, production facilities, national programming, and the media curriculum.[8]

If I have focused on the individual media artist it is because the film and video histories that have been written thus far tend to limit themselves to certain bodies and—by extension—to certain bodies of work. And, if critical discourse rarely engages in the heroic modernism of auteur-driven histories, it nonetheless works with the primary sources of those same histories. As a consequence, one can easily detect the political project inherent in "la politique des auteurs" beneath the theoretical project of postmodernism. Fredric Jameson touches upon this contradiction with respect to video when he acknowledges that "the discussion . . . of a single 'text' then automatically transforms it back into a 'work,' turns the anonymous videomaker back into a named artist or auteur, and opens the way for the return of all those features of an older modernist aesthetic which it was in the revolutionary nature of the newer medium to have precisely effaced and dispelled."[9] But, in characterizing video according to its supposed "twin manifestations as commercial television and experimental video," Jameson never considers why it is that video functions as a postmodern *medium* with modern *features*. In other words, rather than examine the contradiction as a functional one, perhaps a necessary one, he suggests that certain discourses somehow thwart the revolutionary potential of the medium.

Part of the problem is that Jameson treats these "twin manifestations" in terms of formal strategies without considering their institutional structures: the television network and the art museum/gallery/school. In both contexts, it is precisely the slippage between the anonymous and the autonomous—or total flow and discrete works—that serves to obscure the question of access to the technology for production and distribution.[10] Thus, if video is the postmodern medium par excellence for the "pure and random play of signifiers," access to both television and the museum continues to be guarded by a modernist gatekeeper, according to whom access is a simple matter of "freedom of expression" within the economic-minded parameters of "popularity" (television) and "quality" (museum).[11] In other words, access is refigured as an individual question, rather than one of communities, cultures, and languages.[12]

Jameson's contrast between commercial television and experimental video is perhaps not as sharp as he would require. Experimental video enters quickly into the commodity system of the art market, so that museums and art collectors can purchase a one-of-a-kind video by Bill Viola or Nam June Paik under pretty much the same conditions as that of any other art object. As a consequence, there is a useful distinction to be made within the category of experimental video between those works circulated within art institutions and those distributed by the "independent" or "alternative" media sector. In the past decade, both grassroots organization (including lobbying for legislation) and advances in video technology have opened up an "alternative" to

CHON A. NORIEGA

the dichotomy Jameson describes. In public television, the minority consortia and the Independent Television Service have struggled against the privatization of CPB and PBS. Video technology itself has become a democratic commodity, another affordable consumer good, as cable access (and related efforts to open up new technologies) has provided opportunities for alternative broadcast and narrowcast, however limited: Paper Tiger Television, Deep Dish Satellite Network, DIVA-TV, and Hermandad National Media Center are examples.

But the question of the "I" of experimental video remains one in which the medium is defined by the relationship of aesthetic production to a specific technology. Scant attention is given to the third "signal"—as Jameson calls it—for the term *media:* social institution. The "I" of experimental video is seen at one extreme as a "narcissistic" subjectivity cut off from social context by means of the medium itself; hence, the argument that video is *the* postmodern medium.[13] The "other" of experimental video, the marginal, the minority, is recast in realist and modernist terms, not as a "politics of aesthetics," but rather as determined by social position, little more than historical "raw material."

TESTIMONIO NARRATION AND THE PLURAL SELF

Having raised questions of both historiography and subjectivity, I hope to avoid the deceptive debate over the precise relationship of the minority or postcolonial subject to the "social" and the "real."[14] In other words, I do not want to claim that the Chicano subject is different *from* the Euro-American subject, existing on an "other" axiological dimension; rather, I want to propose that Chicano video discourse registers differences *within* the national culture, approaching "American" from a metonymic perspective, and not a metaphoric one. That is, rather than focus on a particular identity, I want to draw attention to the national context within which identities (including the "normative" one) are articulated.

Given that the relationship of Chicanos to video-as-medium occurs, for the most part, outside either of Jameson's "twin manifestations," there is a need to look beyond the corresponding frames of reference and concepts for video.[15] In particular, I want to introduce different textual structures and concepts into the discussion of video, keeping in mind always how these are positioned within discourse and institutional practices. The Latin American *testimonio* (testimonial narrative) offers one such vantage point from which to discuss issues of form (in particular, genre), subject-camera relations, and reception. Of immediate interest is the tendency of recent scholarship to characterize the *testimonio* through the calculated use of the word *self:* "plural self," "self in a collective mode," or the "unquiet self."[16]

The *testimonio* emerges as a new narrative genre in the 1960s, in particular in postrevolution Cuba, where Casa de las Américas has recognized the genre in its annual international literary contest since 1970.[17] John Beverley defines the *testimonio* as "a novel or novella-length narrative in book or pamphlet (that is, printed as opposed to

209

acoustic) form, told in the first person by a narrator who is also the real protagonist or witness of the events he or she recounts, and whose unit of narration is usually a 'life' or a significant life experience."[18] In its development, the *testimonio* draws upon "roots" in diverse Latin American nonfiction narratives and oral histories since the colonial *crónicas*. But although Beverley cites Ché Guevara's direct-participant account, *Reminiscences of the Cuban Revolutionary War* (1959), as the most immediate model for the Cuban and, later, Nicaraguan *testimonio*, the testimonial workshops, handbook, and literature of Margaret Randall provide the best single case with which to define the genre's essential features.[19] In either case, the *testimonio* is intimately tied to the need to legitimize the postrevolutionary nation or struggles against state terror through the production of counterdocuments. In its production, the *testimonio* is often the result of a collaboration between an "illiterate" narrator—who seeks to inform the world at large about the conditions of his or her people and of the urgent need for social change—and an "intellectual" interlocutor who tapes, transcribes, and edits the narrator's testimony.[20]

There has been considerable debate over the precise generic features of the *testimonio* and of its relationship to autobiography. Nonetheless, as a general rule, one can situate the *testimonio* somewhere in the space between first- and third-person accounts of historical events: between autobiography, chronicle, and film or video diary, on the one hand, and biography, history, and social documentary, on the other. In blurring genres, while also insisting on its own truth claims, the *testimonio* places the speaking subject outside the theoretical binarism of the autonomous individual versus the decentered subject. Rather, the speaking subject initiates an "ethics of identity" that places him or her into direct relation with other people, albeit mediated through language.[21]

Doris Sommer provides perhaps the clearest delineation of the processes for such an "ethics of identity" in the *testimonio*, distinguishing between the metaphor of autobiography and the metonymy of the *testimonio*. She concludes: "The testimonial 'I' does not invite us to identify with it. We are too different, and there is no pretense here of universal or essential human experience."[22] The reader or spectator does, however, become "complicit," not through a one-to-one identification with the narrator, but through an identification with the narrator's project. This "lateral identification" encourages the reader to assume a role as an extension of the narrator's community.[23] The *testimonio*, however, must sustain several inherent contradictions: "The narrator often strains between affirming her singularity and denying it in favor of the first-person plural."[24] But even more, the narrator must be mediated through an interlocutor. The "I" of the *testimonio*, therefore, is marked with tension, not between stable categories (self, community, interlocutor, others), but in an ironic stance toward both "preestablished coherence" (of form) and the status quo (of social relations).[25]

In a suggestive aside, Beverley likens the interlocutor to a film producer. It is not print per se that distinguishes a *testimonio* from oral histories, but rather the fact of (and tension between) the interlocutor's editing and the narrator's intention.[26] But despite Beverley's allusion to cinematic practices, literary scholars have yet to acknowledge a crucial fact about the *testimonio:* it emerges in the 1960s as both a literary and a

CHON A. NORIEGA

film genre. The concept of "cine testimonio" has been outlined in a number of manifestos and genre analyses[27] and has served as the name and socio-aesthetic principle for at least two collectives, in Mexico (1969) and in Argentina (1982).[28] The publications tend to be self-conscious about the genre's literary genealogy as well as its social function, and an argument could be made that the increased use of the term in the 1980s is related to the concurrent proliferation of the print *testimonio*. But in addition to the self-proclaimed *testimonios,* there are signs that a testimonial mode operates in the social documentaries of radical film and video collectives in Latin America, including the "photodocumentaries" and *Tire Dié* (1960) of Fernando Birri and the on-site, participant reenactments of Jorge Sanjinés and the Ukamau Group since 1971. Overall, the goal is to give "voice" to communities or a national identity, not in a passive sense, but rather through "constant, ongoing discussion" between filmmakers and film subjects.[29]

Both the film and print *testimonio* can be described as a "blurred genre" that ranges from the expression of a single narrator to a composite of several "talking heads" within a social group.[30] In either case, however, the ambiguity and tension in the narrative between first- and third-person address (and corresponding nonfiction genres) originate in the relationship of the speaking subject(s) to the interlocutor. It is this relationship—whether masked in the service of a "reality effect" or made self-reflexive—that enables the genre's "ethics of identity" or "lateral identification" between the speaking subject(s), the community-of-origin, and an "external" audience.

There is a danger in equating the representational strategies of the *testimonio* with geopolitical, cultural, and racial formations, thereby producing a rigid taxonomy in which form determines ideology. This can be seen in Tom Waugh's distinction between "talking head" and "talking group" documentaries, in which the "talking head" shot becomes "symptomatic of a social ideology of the individual."[31] I am not questioning Waugh's distinction per se, which seems quite valid, but rather the assumptions and implications that derive from it within his overall argument. The problem, as I see it, is that Waugh takes the ideology of the individual at face value, a move that, oddly enough, aligns him with the "jaded postmodernist and orientalist tastes" that stand in contrast to his critique. That is, in marking out a third space for the collective subject in third-world documentary (including U.S. racial and sexual minorities), Waugh does not so much reject as qualify the theoretical binarism of the autonomous individual versus the decentered subject, delimiting its application to Euro-American culture. In this manner, the Euro-American subject lacks both group identity and individual agency. But is this *really* the case? In fact, Waugh's attention to the social dynamics within the mise-en-scène has wider implications, suggesting a third axis (of social formation) within film and video theories *and* practices that foreground discrete subject-camera relations. Thus, even if the subject is isolated within the frame, the mise-en-scène nonetheless remains a site in which we can read social relations; for example, in the subject's speech, address, gesture, and dress. In other words, the "talking head" must always belong—at some level—to a body politic.

In the 1970s, Chicano filmmakers turned to the films and manfestos of New Latin American Cinema in order to develop an alternative model to Hollywood. This project emerged as the most recent in a series of "plans" within the Chicano Civil Rights Movement (1965–75) that rearticulated identity around Chicano cultural practices (language, visual arts, literature) asserted within and against the public sphere (education, politics, labor).[32] The "plans" and other pivotal texts drew upon the Mexican and Cuban revolutions, as well as the Declaration of Independence, in a complex mediation between a public call for "revolution" and a behind-the-scenes negotiation for "reform."

For Chicano filmmakers, the efforts to develop a "Chicano film language"—expressed as an extension of New Latin American Cinema—often took place within commercial television stations, since Chicanos were able to protest for public affairs shows aired during prime-time access.[33] Chicano producers were able to introduce a number of cultural narratives as a way to supercede or transform the budget-imposed "talking head" format: *teatro, corrido, telenovela, floricanto,* and *testimonio*.[34] In the 1970s, television documentaries were shot and edited on film, which allowed some Chicano producers to make "films" out of these documentary segments. In this manner, the *testimonio* could continue to circulate after broadcast, reaching the classroom (mostly Chicano studies courses), film festivals (Chicano, independent, and international), and community *centros*.

Each of the above forms became a way of naming an emergent community within a number of contexts: mythopoetics, historical revisionism, cultural affirmation, and social melodrama. In addressing a diverse television audience, filmmakers drew upon cultural references and language (Spanish and caló) in order to foreground a "Chicano" interpretive community. In doing so, the filmmakers used audience stratification as a means to achieve "lateral identification" with the Chicano community and its struggles.

Many of the first Chicano filmmakers had been involved in the Chicano student movement and antiwar protests, an involvement that brought them into direct contact with biased news coverage. It also made them the subject of police and federal surveillance. This experience motivated a generation of Chicano student activists to become filmmakers, while it also called into question the visual media as an inherently objective discourse. As Harry Gamboa recalls:

> As a result of my activities I was listed in the Senate subcommittee report on un-American activities. And that was based on information provided by the high school and by the L.A.P.D. But of all the things I had seen, I was always constantly amazed at how people could manipulate material—your story—and change it. I guess it was right after high school that it kind of clicked that they had pictures, and I didn't have pictures to prove my point.[35]

Like the other cultural narratives, the Chicano *testimonio* was a form of counterdocumentation against the "horizon of expectations" established by the news and entertainment media. In particular, the *testimonio* sought *concientización* through the personal recollection of a communal experience, offering subjective histories as an alternative to these official accounts. In the Chicano *testimonio*, the narration is that of an individual who somehow represents the community and can therefore speak on its behalf in telling his or her own story as a part of that community: *pintos* (prison inmates) in *Carnalitos* (1973), an elder *curandera* (folk healer) in *Agueda Martínez: Our People, Our Country* (1976), and *santeros* (saint makers) in *Santeros* (1986). The *curandera* and *santeros* represent traditional social hierarchies (seniority, rural context, folk or religious belief systems), while the *pinto* represents the urban male youth in conflict with dominant societal institutions.[36] In these films, there is no external narrator, so that the subject's recollections appear to direct or motivate the visual sequence. The films break from the strident or militant style of the protest films and express resistance in unexpected ways: the gentle understatement of the gang members in *Carnalitos*; the folk lyricism of *Agueda Martínez*; and the numerous voice-overs of exterior shots in *Santeros*, set in northern New Mexico. These films emphasize quotidian resistance, conveying an urgent need for cultural maintenance (*Agueda Martínez*) and community-based institutions (*Carnalitos*).[37]

In the 1980s, changes in the mass media infrastructure provided the material base for a shift in the predominant form of the *testimonio*, from social documentaries to experimental videos. Deregulation of commercial television left Chicano documentary filmmakers with one, limited option: public television. The cancellation of Chicano public affairs shows meant that social documentaries lost the immediacy necessary for the *testimonio* to function as a means of communication. Documentaries took years to produce once they were no longer tied to a regular broadcast series. Because of these changes, the social documentary became more historical and ethnographic.

At the same time, however, cable access and advances in video technology attracted Chicano artists with backgrounds in Super-8 film, poetry, and performance art. In the experimental video produced since the late 1980s, self-reflexivity replaced the "reality effect" of earlier Chicano *testimonios*, and the artist often became both the interlocutor and the (surrogate) speaking subject of the *testimonio*. The sociopolitical content of the *testimonio* becomes increasingly fragmented, from the multiple selves of Guillermo Gómez-Peña in *Border Brujo* (1990), to Frances Salomé España's surreal narrative in *El espejo/The Mirror* (1991), to Sandra P. Hahn's elliptical poetic "autobiography" in *Slipping Between* (1991), to the performed subjects of Harry Gamboa's series, *El mundo L.A.* (1992–).

The remainder of this chapter will look at three experimental video artists whose work exemplifies the recent transformation of the *testimonio* in its aesthetics, production, and distribution. By and large, these artists are self-taught and independent, receiving little to no outside support for their projects. These artists belong to a loose community of Chicano artists, writers, and musicians in Los Angeles.

I grew up in East L.A., and the environment there was so violent that it was almost like absurdist theater. I went to Garfield High School at the time that it had the highest dropout rate in the country, and the whole school was oriented to prepare you to work in a factory or to join the military. By the time I arrived on the campus I was already a decidedly angry youth, and was involved with the organization of the walkouts that took place in 1968. In the early part of the twelveth grade, I was still organizing students, and I was cornered by the vice-principals and they struck a deal with me that if I stopped organizing and if I joined marching band—if they saw me in a uniform—that they would give me enough units so that I could graduate. I mean, that was like the deal under the table, right? And so, I graduated with a 1.1 GPA from high school, and that was like cause for big celebration. But during the years I was in junior high and in high school I had seen a lot of physical abuse of students. I had seen instances where the police came on campus and beat the shit out of kids.[39]

It is because of these experiences and the subsequent realization that "they had pictures, and I didn't have pictures to prove my point" that Gamboa turned to performance, writing, and photography. Between 1972 and 1987, Gamboa served as the polemicist and documentarist (in photography, film, and video) for the Chicano art collective Asco.[40] In street performance and conceptual art, Asco provided a "postmodern" voice within the Chicano Art Movement, one that questioned both the essential identity of cultural nationalism and societal and institutional racism in Los Angeles. Throughout, Gamboa rejected the movement's impulse to counter mass media stereotypes with alternative historical or political documentaries. For one, he argued, these cost too much, took too long, and reached too few people. Instead, Gamboa applied a snapshot aesthetic (in photography) or cinema verité (in film and video) in order to document "events" staged by Asco members. These images were then packaged and offered to the world press and cable access channels, reaching a potential audience in the millions.[41] Thus, these efforts insinuated themselves into the mass media, operating like a computer virus, the glitch in the system that, however briefly, reveals the system-as-system. In this manner, Gamboa made the processes of mass media (rather than its content) the real issue, exploring a postmodern condition in which Chicano identity and history are increasingly mediated through electronic culture. As such, sociopolitical content became a structured absence, often hidden behind a deceptive nihilism.

In the 1970s, Gamboa and other Asco members—Gronk, Patssi Valdez, and Willie Herron—produced a series of "no-movies" that satirized, among other targets, Chicano cinema and those filmmakers associated with KCET-TV and the Chicano Cinema Coalition.[42] The no-movies included media hoaxes (such as press kits for non-existent films) and performance pieces. In one performance, Gamboa portrayed a gunshot victim (perhaps a revolutionary?) whose last gesture had been to scrawl "Chicano

Cinema" on the nearby wall. While the gesture links Chicano cinema with street expressions (murals and graffiti), it adds an insightful ephemeral dimension: "Chicano Cinema" is written on a paper roll taped to the wall, with small portions of the first and last letters spilling over onto the wall itself. The paper roll, like the silver screen, lacks the material "fact" of graffiti, but is nonetheless portable, leaving behind some traces of its impact.

The no-movies share affinities with Sheldon Renan's notion of "expanded cinema," wherein "the effect of film may be produced without the use of film at all," an idea developed further by Gene Youngblood.[43] But Gamboa and Asco were not after the "effect" or experience of cinema, per se, but rather performance as critique of cinema: "It was sort of like a political protest based on the economics of financing films, and also based on the reality that maybe I only did have five dollars." Thus the no-movie comments on the film medium as a tool for social protest and parodies the concurrent debate over a "liberal" versus "radical" ideological function for Chicano cinema, pointing out that both camps sought the same goal: access to and success within the American film and television industry.[44] Still, the no-movies also exemplified—in an absurd context—the ideals of Chicano cinema, in that they reached international audiences and had a disruptive impact on the status quo.[45]

In the mid-1980s, Gamboa turned from the no-movies and Super-8 films to video, working through Falcon Cable Television (in Alhambra, California) to produce a series of "conceptual dramas" or experimental *telenovelas* that deconstructed both stereotypical and traditional notions about the Latino family. These videos also provide an extended metaphor for Asco itself, which was then in the process of dissolution.[46] When Falcon Cable changed ownership, the equipment was allowed to fall apart, and Gamboa did not make videos again until he acquired his own equipment in 1990. Since then, he has produced a number of innovative shorts that situate the *testimonio* within nonfiction television formats: on-location news coverage (*L.A. Merge*, 1991), news magazines (*Vis-a-Vid*, 1991), and educational documentaries (*Fire Medicine*, 1992). Gamboa's use of these documentary forms combines an unusual mix of parody and appropriation, wherein the viewer must confront both ironic distantiation and an ambivalent desire to emulate and subvert television.

Since 1992, Gamboa has been working on a series of *testimonios* related to his recent photographic series on the media representation of Chicano men: *Chicano Male: Unbonded* (1991–). The photographic series plays with viewer expectations that Chicano men be bonded to group structures—family, gangs—and presents Chicano friends and associates in isolation, often in dark clothes at night. The subjects look at the photographer (and, hence, the camera), creating a displacement that often leads viewers to feel that they were being confronted. This effect is increased by the use of a wide-angle lens that mimics the ubiquitous surveillance cameras in the Los Angeles area. But in contrast to these overhead "panoptic" views, Gamboa documents Chicano men from a slight low-angle shot, a move that places the viewer in a position of inferiority to the subject.[47]

In the video series *El mundo L.A.*, Gamboa acts as the interlocutor for a performed subject. Gamboa invites many of the same men to present themselves before the camera in an unrehearsed performance in which the subject is "in character" as himself, a self identified by profession: artist, actor, writer, poet, curator, professor.[48] That Gamboa names his subjects by profession comments on patriarchal conventions for the "professional" of late capitalism. But, at the same time, Gamboa draws attention to the unexpected fact of a profession for his subjects, especially professions within the cultural or "intellectual" arena.

In *El mundo L.A.: Humberto Sandoval, Actor* (1992), Sandoval performs in character as an ex-con become "street preacher"—an urban wise fool whose social critique is a pastiche of Chicano political discourses. The video is divided into three segments in which Sandoval appears in different locations—a street corner, a parking lot, and a graveyard—with ambient sound of the ubiquitous Los Angeles traffic. In almost all his recent videos, Gamboa uses traffic as an aural and visual backdrop to the *testimonio* or *telenovela* narration. It is an intrusive backdrop that must be read on both realist and allegorical levels as the condition for Chicano narrative.

FIGURE 1
Harry Gamboa Jr., *El mundo L.A.: Humberto Sandoval, Actor* (1992). (Copyright 1992, Harry Gamboa Jr. By permission.)

The video is presented as a compendium of Sandoval's thoughts on the state of postriot Los Angeles, with the refrain, "I've been thinking, I've just been thinking," opening and closing the narration. In the first segment, Sandoval zeros in on self-interest as the reason "the city looks like trash," and associates this with the "system" and politicians. He concludes, "Fuck, for all I know everybody is a politician: 'What are you going to give me, so I can give you a piece of the pie?'" The phrase "a piece of the pie" becomes the major trope for the failure of race relations in Los Angeles. Sandoval's goal is to get a piece of the pie for Chicanos, which places him in the position of asking blacks and Anglos to invite him to the table to share the pie.

In the second segment, Sandoval presents his rationale, which links the major tenets of Chicano cultural nationalism to the reformist goal of being *given* "a piece of the pie." In a stunning pastiche of Chicano political discourses, Sandoval argues that "we forgot to put pyramids in Aztlán . . . so the Chicanos and la raza that live here can never quite get their bearings, although I think we are making some progress." Aztlán, the mythical homeland of the Aztecs, grounded the cultural nationalism of the Chicano Movement in the notion of the Southwest as a Chicano Ur-nation. Sandoval, however, links Aztlán to the reformist notion of incremental progress, and makes the reification of "a great culture" (in Aztec pyramids and names) the prerequisite for a respect of origins and, subsequently, a piece of the pie. It is at this point that Sandoval announces himself as someone who represents the interests and needs of the Chicano

CHON A. NORIEGA

community. But he does so in a way that reveals the slice of pie as itself the precondition for something else: "So I can feel that I've been done right, me and my people, that's what I'd like." The "I" in this statement is both self and community ("me and my people"), but it is tied to self-esteem within a paternal social structure. The Chicano community, then, must reach a state of meriting recognition from the system.

In *El mundo L.A.*, Gamboa uses the technique of freeze frame with continuous sound in order to create a photographic effect that recalls both his photographic series and his earlier foto-novelas. The foto-novelas were a transitional format between the no-movies and video that simulated film narrative through the use of slide projection, recorded music, and lecture. The foto-novela and photograph series fall somewhere in between the still and moving image and newspaper and television news. Likewise, *El mundo L.A.* occupies the same indeterminant space in its attempt to give voice to the invisible majority of Los Angeles.[49] But rather than do so in the manner of the earlier social documentaries, Gamboa draws attention to how Chicano political discourse locates authority outside the community, splitting itself between mythical past and hypothetical future.[50] This is further implied in the third segment, which takes place in a graveyard, where Sandoval calls out to his father, mother, and other relatives, as well as the "politicians, the abusers, the people who don't want to share the power, the money." Death, or Dia de los Muertos, becomes the great equalizer, "el emparejador de la vida." But it is uncertain how such an appeal translates into social change, leaving Sandoval to retreat into rumination: "I've just been thinking, that's all." For the first time, the camera pulls back, no longer allowing Sandoval to situate and define himself within the social environment.

SANDRA P. HAHN: HIGH-TECH *RASQUACHE*

Sandra P. Hahn, who works with computer animation, produces videos that can be described as high-tech *rasquache*, that space where the remnants of "new technologies" are mixed into the "slapdash vitality" and "make-do" inventiveness of Chicano working-class culture. Tomás Ybarra-Frausto defines *rasquachismo* as a Chicano sensibility, "an underdog perspective . . . rooted in resourcefulness and adaptability, yet mindful of stance and style."[51] Hahn works with basic consumer electronic equipment available in the mid to late 1980s: a home video camera, a Macintosh computer, and a cassette recorder. "I'm limited with the equipment I have," she explains, "so you just do what you can." This results in a "one-time shot" to synch and record the images and sound. Working at home late at night—after her husband and daughter have fallen asleep, and mindful of the phone and nearby train tracks—Hahn videotapes directly from the computer monitor, covering the camera lens with nylon in order to flatten out the image and to add a grainy look similar to an old photograph. For *Replies of the Night* (1989), Hahn recorded the sound and music on eight different tapes, and used twelve borrowed cassette recorders in order to "mix" the sound as the home video camera recorded the computer animation.[52]

217

Hahn's background is indicative of the close relationship of art to every-day life outside an institutional framework. The child of Mexican immigrants, Hahn grew up in an extended household in Whittier, then East Los Angeles, where she was able to communicate (in her native Spanish) and learn English. In the seventh grade, Hahn became involved with gangs and disaffected with school. In response, her family moved back to Whittier, where Hahn enrolled in a beauty college. Upon graduating at age seventeen, Hahn had saved ten thousand dollars, which she invested in a twelve-chair hair salon. Hahn sold the business four years later and enrolled in college courses, joined a local band, Los Illegals, and married and had a daughter: "I had my little girl and that's when I started to focus into one direction. Children do that to you. They do." Hahn purchased an early home computer, the Commodore 64, and became fascinated with its graphics capability. She enrolled in a new computer school in Orange County, purchased a Macintosh computer, and started to freelance, eventually working as art director for a manufacturing company. It is through her freelance work in computer graphics that Hahn became involved in Chicano art exhibition, producing flyers for Marisela Norte, then video installations and window displays.

The above trajectory from working class to artist, however, is deceptive. Throughout her life, Hahn organized what she calls "productions": murals in schools, fashion shows to promote her hair salon, trade shows, installations. Until the late 1980s, these productions took place outside "art spaces" and, in fact, often oscillated between commercial function and personal expression. While Hahn knew many of the Chicano artists of her generation, including Gamboa and other Asco members, it was on personal and not artistic terms: "I just knew them." Instead, in an unrelated, parallel context, Hahn and several friends performed private "exhibitions" in the early 1980s, unaware of the performance art movement: "We were just doing a show."

While Hahn has become more involved with gallery exhibition, she maintains independence through her professional career, preferring to locate her "influences" in people and personal relationships rather than aesthetic discourse. In contrast to the cultural reclamation project of the Chicano Art Movement, Hahn describes her work as concerned with the future, both in terms of form and content. Part of this derives from a certain cultural and generational distance from the movement: "No. I can't relate to that. No. I was twelve years old on top of an avocado tree when the East L.A. thing was going on . . . the riots. It was down the street from my house. All I knew was, 'Chicano Power,' 'La Raza.' We just knew that it was a riot and we would give the cops coffee. See, that's how ironic it was. We weren't informed and so we didn't know what was going on."[53]

Nonetheless, Hahn sees her expertise in computer technology (including the professional end) as part of an effort "to give back to the community someday." In terms of the thematic content of her work, Hahn has tried to piece together her family history and cultural practices. *Replies of the Night* was commissioned for a Day of the Dead exhibition. Hahn, who had to learn about the practice, also discovered that her grandfather had died in a duel with one of her uncles on the Day of the Dead. The video resists an explicit and objective account, because of the incomplete and partial memories about his life, as well as Hahn's ambivalence about the presentation of personal memories within a "public" context of film festivals and gallery exhibitions.

Slipping Between (1991) is another video poem that attempts to come to grips with the death of a relative, Hahn's aunt, who had recently died of cancer. Hahn attempts to reconcile the aunt's painful and protracted death with the fact that the aunt was a mean-spirited person. Both *Replies of the Night* and *Slipping Between* can be described as what Nancy Miller calls "memoirs of a dying other," or autobiographies in which the author recounts the death of a loved one. Miller argues that these texts exceed the self-referential, turning back to "the world of facts," and offers a neomaterialist reformulation of Paul de Man's "linguistic predicament": "the world as language lived in experience."[54] Looked at from one perspective, Miller provides an instance in which the autobiographical narrator is most similar to the *testimonio* narrator. Here, both narrators speak in the first person singular about a metonymic or lateral identification (with a friend, relative, or community), although for quite different ends.

But in the case of *Slipping Between*, Hahn goes one step further, "slipping between" the interlocutor and narrator of a *testimonio*, so that she occupies both positions. In effect, the interlocutor stands in for the other. Hahn uses a poem in the first-person voice of the aunt in which she recalls her life and describes her death (see the appendix to this chapter). But it is Hahn's own "talking head" that is presented as that of the aunt. In the poem, the refrain—"Slipping between life with death, / is there a reason for trust?"—becomes an ambiguously rhetorical question, especially insofar as Hahn finds in the aunt's difficult life a mirror to her own.

In the elision of the interlocutor and narrator, *Slipping Between* turns the *testimonio* inward toward the extended Chicano family and away from its social function as a communication act between a community in need and the outside world. But while the aunt's plaint is highly personal, the fact that it gets read through Hahn as a public statement suggests the familial and social reproduction of the aunt's condition. Thus, *Slipping Between* is an urgent call to reconstruct an "ethics of identity" *within* the Chicano family and community. But the video poem itself must be reconstructed before something as clear as a "message" comes through the foreboding images and sounds. The "talking head" consists of a scanned photograph that is manipulated and distorted against a backdrop of patterns, shapes, and lines. At one point, the phrase "Love U" appears across the "talking head," followed by the entrance of a ghost image of Hahn's face that settles on the "talking head," then moves off screen. The video ends with the "talking head" in the center of a nestlike vortex. The *testimonio* narration itself consists of a digital reworking (and layering) of the poem beneath an eerie instrumentation. As a result, the viewer strains to make out fragments—a word, phrase, line—but is able to detect a continuous narration.

In its displacement, *Slipping Between* recalls Simone de Beauvoir's own astonishment in *A Very Easy Death:* "Someone other than myself was weeping inside me. I had put Maman's mouth on my own face and in spite of myself, I copied its movements. Her whole person, her whole being was concentrated there, and compassion wrung my heart."[55] But Hahn's own acknowledgment belongs to a larger narrative structure that is revealed only at the end in the credit sequence, which includes the first stanza and the refrain of the poem. Hahn credits six "characters" drawn from the six stanzas of the poem: "The Fields," "Young and Busy," "So Proud," "A Daughter Then Two," "Why Listen," "A Sickness." Given the memory demands of computer animation, Hahn must divide her pieces into segments that can be run from floppy disks. She gives these segments character names and identifies them by the amount of memory they use. In *Slipping Between*, each segment (with its images and effects) corresponds to a stanza of the poem.

As a *testimonio*, rather than, say, a modernist video poem, the video requires a direct relationship with the artist, in the same way that New Latin American Cinema often used the screening as a means toward dialogue (either among the viewers or with the filmmaker), rather than an end in itself. For Hahn, the text belongs to a body, her body, with the videos originally intended for local exhibition.

FRANCES SALOMÉ ESPAÑA: UNCOMPROMISED VISIONS

Frances Salomé España has a similar background in poetry, visual arts, and performance. Unlike Gamboa and Hahn, España attended film school in the late 1970s, although she quit the program because of its emphasis on "industry standards" rather than on aesthetics and experimentation. Since then, she has worked in small formats—Super-8 film, 8mm video, and half-inch video—and has financed postproduction in public access stations with her own money. España has also been involved as a curator for "L.A. Freewaves," a multisite exhibition of independent media in Los Angeles.

España, like Gamboa, belongs to the generation that took part in the high-school "blowouts" of the late 1960s. In describing the Chicano Moratorium and subsequent police riot, España likens its effect to the Aztecs' prophetic accounts of the conquest:

> So for me, when the city blew up, that was like some kind of an omen. It was something that was really positive that prophesied that I can do whatever I want, you know. It wasn't until after I got out of high school and went through all this meaningless stuff that it just hit me. It didn't come from the schools. It came from the community. For all of us [media artists] it manifests itself in different ways, but we all have very deep roots to the community.[56]

The slippage in the referent for the word "it" is indicative of the conflation of community, public struggle, and personal expression. In her images and music, España extends this mixture (or *mestizaje*) across pre- and postcolonial timeframes, blending together ancient indigenous and contemporary Chicano sources. *Anima* (1990), for example, blends indigenous wind instruments with contemporary jazz guitar, playing off the visual contrasts set up between the tradition of "Day of the Dead" and its contemporary inflections by Chicano cultural nationalism and Chicana feminist rearticulations.

In *El espejo/The Mirror* (1991), España becomes the speaking subject for her parent's generation as well as for the entire barrio, using metaphor and indirection to relate the broader historical forces of immigration, deportation, and internal colonialism.[57] While the camera is set up before España, she does not look into the lens, as is often the case in autobiographical video. Instead, España looks to the side of the camera at an implied interlocutor, turning to speak into the lens at key points in her narration. It is in that mediated distance that España fragments the autobiographical voice, so that it does not become equated with the camera. Likewise, España fragments the autobiographical body through crosscut images of her face and feet.

The video sets up the narrative as an alternation of a three-shot sequence: España's "talking head" (close-up), her dangling feet (close-up), and her parents' backyard (medium to long shot). Like Harry Gamboa's recent videos, *El espejo* relates the Chicano experience marked by the sights and sounds of transportation "progress" in Los Angeles: in this case, the ever-present trains that impose a border around her parents' huge backyard, where the video was shot.[58] The trains establish a physical border that contains the barrio home and an aural one that penetrates the "edenic" spaces of the backyard with its apple trees and chickens.

In the "talking head" shots in the first part of the video, España strains against first-person narration as she assesses her situation: "Things weren't so bad. Things were actually quite clear then—heaven was the sky and hell was somewhere under the dirt, you know. It was pretty clear but I was . . . it couldn't have been that bad . . . people survived, you know." In not allowing herself to speak from the position of an "I" or "we," España's description seems to come from outside the community, internalized like the sounds of the trains. When the location shots shift to night, however, España's narration offers two sentence fragments that resemble "self-evident" declarations about the community: "that this place had a *corazón* unto itself, something very special that we had to learn to . . . embrace"; and "that we drew our breath from an urban area, something removed and yet so close to the homeland." These declarations initiate a shift in the meaning of the "edenic" images of the backyard, from the religious (as repressed past) to the nationalist (as romanticized past).

It is in the final third of the video, however, that España finally attains the position of the *testimonio* narrator, speaking in the first person singular as a member of the community. But what makes *El espejo* remarkable is that the *testimonio* occurs at the level of the surreal as a dream. In the dream, España describes giant bees that build an invisible wall around East L.A. that the *gente* cannot see, but also cannot see beyond. The bees refuse to let her return from the dream until she shows them her papers. Here, the notion of an edenic space slips outside a hegemonic/counterhegemonic framework and becomes ironic, with the bees insistent that the narrator shouldn't leave East L.A.: "Girl, don't you know, you're already in Wonderland." The narrator plays out the irony with a translation into the Spanish-language place name: "Even the county signs confirmed it. Man, I lived in Maravilla."

The shift from day to night, and the alternation between "talking head" (speaking subject), feet (sexual fetish), and landscape (social environment), collapses the psychological and sociological registers around the narrated dream. In fact, the video interrupts the three-shot sequence at this point, dropping out the expected landscape shot. In this manner, the "talking head" narration of the dream is framed by the shots of España's feet.

In effect, España remaps the unconscious along social lines, so that the fetish and castration threat become both racial and sexual mechanisms. Here, in contrast to Laura Mulvey's distinction, the woman-as-spectacle provides the way into the repressed narrative of Chicano history. The video ends with the line, "You got to show them something all the fucking time . . . disgusting," and returns to a shot of España's dangling feet. Although her disgust (and return to a wakeful state) suggests a will to change, it must be read through the last shot (of her dangling feet), which suggests both the absence of a material base for collective action and the corresponding displacement within U.S. discourse on Chicanos from a social to a psychological (pathological) register. Thus, in the telling of her absurd dream, España holds up a mirror that offers a surreal reflection that insinuates (through metaphor and visual images) the psychological, cultural, and economic violence inflicted upon the Mexican American Generation of her parents: repatriation, Zoot Suit Riots, Bracero Program, Operation Wetback, and the vivisection of communities (railways, highways).[59] It is a mirror, like that of *Entelequía* (1978), that fragments, decenters, and questions the Chicano subject, rather than provides for his or her (imaginary) completion. This is most apparent in her non- or mistranslation of the bilingual dialogue, which opens up a space between the languages. For example, in Spanish, España refers to the bees as *moscas*, which means flies and is slang for the helicopters that search for undocumented workers. As with the mention of Wonderland, English functions as the language of metaphor, while Spanish becomes either opaque (for those who do not understand) or the site of historical displacement.

In order to reach that site, *El espejo* invokes the unconscious. But it is crucial to understand that it does not remain there, cut off from social context. In other words, the video is about the Chicano community in a historical sense, not a psychological one. But this is easily misread, as in a review in *Artweek:* "The fragmented body paralleled a fragmented narrative, an autobiographical account that mixed memory and desire, reflection and projection, past and present, reality and nightmarish dreams to reveal the psychological trauma of cultural displacement."[60] Given the sharp social humor that underlies España's narration, which relies upon a "situated knowledge" based in the languages of cultural conflict, it is perhaps more apt to speak of the "trauma of cultural displacement" as historical rather than psychological.[61]

In proposing that Gamboa, Hahn, and España perform variations on the *testimonio* tradition, I am caught with an obvious contradiction: these artists produce texts that are obscure rather than direct in their attempts to speak for the community. But this is more than a matter of a simple "genre shift" from documentary to the experimental, since that shift becomes possible only as a consequence of the reconfiguration of video

CHON A. NORIEGA

in the late 1980s. That Gamboa, Hahn, and España could make videos, then, was at once a democratic extension of their artistic expression within a consumer society and a sign that the Chicano community had been exiled from an "active citizenship" within the public domain of broadcast television and the art museum.

It is in that condition—whether it is called postmodern, postcolonial, or some older name—that Chicano experimental video rearticulates a plural self outside social institutions. If the earlier *testimonios* "must assume that language always relates to the world, even when it does so imperfectly," theirs is an assumption central to the print and electronic media within which the *testimonio* acted as a counterdiscourse. In the 1970s, at least, Chicano filmmakers had some level of access to local broadcast stations and programming and could, therefore, act as interlocutor between a community in need and the outside world. In the 1980s and 1990s, the experimental *testimonio* cannot make the same assumption, nor can it assume the privilege necessary to stand in ironic distantiation, where the "pure and random play of signifiers" acquires the discursive trappings of the lost referent. To follow either path—of either counterdiscourse or postmodern discourse—requires a social institution with a modernist gatekeeper. It is that predicament, and not the linguistic one per se, that becomes the focus of Chicano experimental video.

España's own words shift the discussion from the usual questions of video and postmodernism, suggesting access as a central axis upon which to discuss the content of form:

> Colonization permeates every level. It's not just taking land. It's robbing a culture of its spirit. So for those of us who have managed to *sobrevivir* somehow, you know, I think that the gift is to give back to our community an uncompromised vision, because they have had to deal with compromises historically. In that sense our work is very, very explicitly connected, but it's in a new way. I think that for myself and for most of my peers, our interest with an art form, whichever one we're using, is to address a whole world with our perception of things. The work may be culturally specific or it may not be, but, for myself, I am definitely working for a specific community, for a specific culture that exists, but the work is for everybody. An uncompromised vision sets the record straight.[62]

These remarks are neither the expression of a naive faith in the communications model nor a retreat into self-referential abstraction. Rather, they are part of a complex mediation of an ineffable memory and silenced presence. Or, as Sandoval's street preacher explains in *El mundo L.A.*, these may look like "just small little relics of the past, but they're not, because we're going to come back, because we're la raza . . . and I'm not going to forget about it."

Slipping Between. . . .
Sandra P. Hahn

The fields are painted red,
a past that has left decay,
a future unwillingly surrenders into the final day.

Slipping between life with death,
is there a reason for trust?

Young and so busy, hard work and reality left dizzy,
filled with love struck between jealous sentimental
    hate,
broken blood with mended fate.

Slipping between life with death,
is there a reason for trust?

So proud yet so blind to see,
I'll put on the pants and carry the keys,
paying the bill, ironing the sheets, cook for the family,
misunderstand all their needs,
clean the house, wash the car,
importance so bright, vengeance is light,
I'll do it all.

Slipping between life with death,
is there a reason for trust?

A daughter then two,
with false cares and an other that is fair,
my life will mend if I can just pretend,
but my meddling gives reason for being pushed away,
alone I'll protect them anyway.

Slipping between life with death,
is there a reason for trust?

Why listen instead I talk,
open minded and repetitiously lost,
the family needs me,
afraid of the truth,
goodness lost between verbal abuse,
believing I am needed reliving a lie,
the tearing inside holding in a surrender's cry.

Slipping between life with death,
is there a reason for trust?

A sickness devouring from inside then out,
no more words but mere mumbling,
with visitors so few,
so tired yet distant denial,
the room grows foggy,
am I slipping. . . . I pray in cool water. . . .

3-12-91

VIDEOTAPE DISTRIBUTION INFORMATION

Carnalitos, Agueda Martínez, and *Entelequía* are available from the UCLA Instructional Media Library, 405 Hilgard Avenue, Los Angeles, CA 90024.

ART COM distributes a compilation on Chicano Experimental Video, which includes Gamboa's *L.A. Merge,* España's *Anima* and *El espejo/The Mirror,* and Hahn's *Replies of the Night* and *Slipping Between.* The video

also includes work by Isaac Artenstein, Sandra Peña, and Luis Valdovino. The address is 70 12th Street, 3rd Floor, San Francisco, CA 94103. Telephone 415/431-7524.

Gamboa's videos are also available from the artist: P.O. Box 862015, Los Angeles, CA 90086-2015. Telephone 213/269-0560.

NOTES

1 From *James Broughton* (1985), a Super-8 portrait by Willie Varela; available from Canyon Cinema in San Francisco.

2 Harry Gamboa Jr., "Past Imperfecto: Essay and Photographs," *Jump Cut,* no. 39 (June 1994): 93–95, 107–11.

3 On the Chicano Art Movement, see Shifra M. Goldman and Tomás Ybarra-Frausto, *Arte Chicano: A Comprehensive Annotated Bibliography of Chicano Art, 1965-1981* (Berkeley: Chicano Studies Publication Unit/University of California, 1985).

4 Bertolt Brecht, *Brecht on Theatre: The Development of an Aesthetic,* ed. and trans. John Willet (New York: Hill and Wang, 1964), 136.

5 See, for example, the discussion of Asco in Ramón Favela, *"Entrance Is Not Acceptance:* A Conceptual Installation by Richard Lou and Robert Sanchez," in *Third Newport Biennial: Mapping Histories* (Newport Beach, Calif.: Harbor Art Museum, 1991), 51.

6 Interestingly, Varela's first video and narrative, *A Lost Man* (1992), can be read in autobiographical terms as an account of how he has been "lost" in the spaces between the acknowledged experimental movements (lyrical, structuralist, feminist, and new narrative), as well as the nationalist "ethnic" cinemas. A similar process happens to Raphael Montañez Ortiz, a now forgotten veteran of the film avant-garde in New York of the 1950s.

7 Lawrence Grossberg, *We Gotta Get Out of This Place: Popular Conservatism and Postmodern Culture* (New York: Routledge, 1992), 26-27.

8 In 1993, employment reports by the guilds revealed a nearly constant rate of underrepresentation for Hispanic actors (0.8 percent of continuing television roles), writers (0.7 percent of Writers Guild of America membership), and directors (1.3 percent of available television and film work) since the 1970s, when the U.S. Commission on Civil Rights released *Window Dressing on the Set* (1977). Since the Hispanic population doubled to about 10 percent of the national population in this period, these figures represent an actual decline in employment opportunity. See Chon Noriega, "The Numbers Game," *Jump Cut,* no. 39 (forthcoming).

9 Fredric Jameson, "Video: Surrealism without the Unconscious," in *Postmodernism; or, the Cultural Logic of Late Capitalism* (Durham, N.C.: Duke University Press, 1991), 78-79.

10 Interestingly, Jameson examines a video produced at the School of the Art Institute of Chicago.

11 Both television and museums use this argument in response to demands for cultural diversity and equal employment opportunity.

12 In chapter 20 of this volume, Patricia Zimmermann also identifies access as the "fulcrum upon which 'rights' can be imagined" within both discourse and practice.

13 Rosalind Krauss, "Video: The Aesthetic of Narcissism" (1978); reprinted in *Video Culture: A Critical Investigation,* ed. John Hanhardt (New York: Visual Studies Workshop Press, 1986), 179–91. On the problematic conflation of poststructuralism and postmodernism, see Andreas Huyssen, *After the Great Divide: Modernism, Mass Culture, Postmodernism* (Bloomington: Indiana University Press, 1986), 206–16.

14 As I discuss later, there seems to be tacit agreement that such a relationship is more direct, less mediated than that of the "Western" subject. In its most reductive sense, this is often expressed as a position about postmodernism; that is, it may explain whites, but not people of color.

15 For an overview of Latino media artists, see Coco Fusco, "Ethnicity, Politics, and Poetics: Latinos and Media Art," in *Illuminating Video: An Essential Guide to Video Art,* ed. Doug Hall and Sally Jo Fifer (New York: Aperture/BAVC, 1990), 304–16.

16 These phrases are from, respectively, Doris Sommer (see n. 21), John Beverley (see n. 17), and Sylvia Molloy, (see n. 24).

17 John Beverley, "The Margin at the Center: On *Testimonio* (Testimonial Narrative)," *Modern Fiction Studies* 35, no. 1 (Spring 1989): 13. On the impact of Casa de las Américas on minority literature in the United States, see José David Saldívar, *The Dialectics of Our America: Genealogy, Cultural Critique, and Literary History* (Durham, N.C.: Duke University Press, 1991).

18 Beverley, "The Margin at the Center," 12.

19 Beverley acknowledges Randall's central role in the development of the *testimonio* in a footnote (Beverley, "The Margin at the Center," 15). See Margaret Randall, "¿Que es, y como se hace un testimonio?" *Revista de Crítica Literaria Latinoamericana,* no. 36 (1992): 21-45; based on a manual prepared for an oral history workshop for the Sandinista Ministry of Culture in 1979 and published as *Testimonios* (San José, Nicaragua: Centro de Estudios Alforja, 1983) and *Testimonios: A Guide to Oral History* (Toronto: Participatory Research Group, 1985).

20 The most renowned example of such a *testimonio* is Rigoberta Menchú's *I, Rigoberta Menchú,* written in collaboration with Elizabeth Burgos-Debray. As Beverley concludes, "*Testimonio* above all must be a story that *needs* to be told, that involves some pressing and immediate problem of communication" (John Beverley, "'Through All Things Modern': Second Thoughts on Testimonio," *Boundary 2* 18, no.2 [1991]: 21).

21 Nancy K. Miller, "Facts, Pacts, Acts," *Profession* 92 (1992): 13. While Miller does not write about the *testimonio,* her phrase is an apt one. Her essay is significant for its attempt to locate a plural self outside a first- and third-world binarism. Doris Sommer makes the same case for the *testimonio:* "The narrator and her public must assume that language always relates to the world, even when it does so imperfectly" (Sommer, "'Not Just a Personal Story': Women's *Testimonios* and the Plural Self," in *Life/Lines: Theorizing Women's Autobiography,* ed. Bella Brodzki and Celeste Schenck [Ithaca, N.Y.: Cornell University Press, 1988], 130).

22 Sommer, "'Not Just a Personal Story,'" 108.

23 Ibid., 118.

24 Ibid., 123. See also Sylvia Molloy, "The Unquiet Self: Spanish American Autobiography and the Quest of National Identity," in *Comparative American Identities: Race, Sex, and Nationality in the Modern Text,* ed. Hortense J. Spillers (New York: Routledge, 1991), 29.

25 Sommer, "'Not Just a Personal Story,'" 122.

26 Beverley, "The Margin at the Center," 18.

27 The most extensive article is written by Cuban filmmaker Victor Casaus, "El género testimonio en el cine cubano," *Cine cubano,* no. 101 (1982): 116–25. Michael Chanan provides an overview of the *testimonio* and of Casaus and Eduardo Maldonado, founder of Grupo Cine Testimonio in Mexico, in "Rediscovering Documentary: Cultural Context and Intentionality," in *The Social Documentary in Latin America,* ed. Julianne Burton (Pittsburgh: University of Pittsburgh Press, 1990), 40-42. For an earlier version, see Michael Chanan, *The Cuban Image: Cinema and Cultural Politics in Cuba* (London: BFI, 1985), 168–71.

28 Cine Testimonio formed in Argentina in 1982 and received international recognition for three *testimonios* on the country's "marginal cultures": *Martin Choque, un telar en San Isidro, Causachum Cusco,* and *Los Totos* (all 1982) ("Exito en Montevideo de tres cortos argentinos," *La voz,* 17 February 1984, 27; and Jorge Abel Martin, "Cine Testimonio," *Tiempo Argentino,* 27 June 1983). On the Grupo Cine Testimonio in Mexico, see Chanan, "Rediscovering Documentary."

29 Fernando Birri, "The Roots of Documentary Realism," *Cinema and Social Change in Latin America: Conversations with Filmmakers,* ed. Julianne Burton (Austin: University of Texas Press, 1986), 6. See also Julia Lesage, "Women Make Media: Three Modes of Production," in *The Social Documentary in Latin America,* ed. Burton. 315–47.

30 In print, the latter is something more akin to New Journalism or the *novela testimonio* of Elena Poniatowski and other Latin American journalist-writers.

31 Tom Waugh, "Words of Command: Notes on Cultural and Political Inflections of Direct Cinema in Indian Independent Documentary," *CineAction,* no. 23 (Winter 1990-1991): 36.

32 For an overview of the Chicano Movement, see Carlos Muñoz Jr., *Youth, Identity, Power: The Chicano Movement* (London: Verso, 1989), which also reprints the "Plan of Santa Barbara." Armando B. Rendon's *Chicano Manifesto* (New York: Macmillan, 1971) ends with a "personal manifesto" or *testimonio,* and reprints "El Plan de Delano," "Plan de la Raza Unida," "The Del Rio Mexican American Manifesto to the Nation," and a portion of the "Spiritual Plan of Aztlán"—all under the appendix heading, "Four Declarations of Independence." The entire "Spiritual Plan of Aztlán" is reprinted in *Aztlán: Essays on the Chicano Homeland,* ed. Rudolfo A. Anaya and Francisco Lomelí (Albuquerque, N.M.: Academia/El Norte Publications, 1989), 1–6.

33 Prime-time access aired between the news and prime time (7:00 to 8:00 P.M.). While the minority public

CHON A. NORIEGA

affairs shows often generated high local ratings, they were not looked upon as profit generating, but rather as a service to the public interest, as was the news. With deregulation, these shows were replaced by syndicated game shows and reruns.

34 I provide an overview of these cultural narratives in my article, "Between a Weapon and a Formula: Chicano Cinema and Its Contexts," in *Chicanos and Film: Representation and Resistance,* ed. Noriega (Minneapolis: University of Minnesota Press, 1992), 156–64.

35 Personal interview with Harry Gamboa Jr., Los Angeles, 27 May 1991.

36 The *pinto* was an important part of the Chicano Movement, with numerous *pinto* newspapers, literature, and visual arts produced.

37 See also Sylvia Morales's *Vayan con Dios* (1985) and *Faith Even to the Fire* (1991).

38 Harry Gamboa Jr., "Urban Exile," *Artweek,* no. 35 (1984): 3.

39 Gamboa interview.

40 See Harry Gamboa's own account of Asco: "In the City of Angels, Chameleons, and Phantoms: *Asco,* a Case Study of Chicano Art in Urban Tones (or *Asco* Was a Four-Member Word)," in *Chicano Art: Resistance and Affirmation, 1965-1985,* ed. Richard Griswold del Castillo, Teresa McKenna, and Yvonne Yarbo-Bejarano (Los Angeles: Wight Art Gallery/UCLA, 1991), 121–30.

41 As Gamboa explains, "One might as well just forgo that format and try to reach as broad an audience as you can, and maybe do it for five dollars" (Gamboa interview).

42 Ibid. The Chicano Cinema Coalition was a major force in the efforts to situate Chicano cinema within the institutional contexts (funding, training, and exhibition) of New Latin American Cinema and U.S. Independent Cinema.

43 Sheldon Renan, *An Introduction to the American Underground Film* (New York: Dutton, 1967), 227–53.

44 See the manifestos reprinted in Noriega, ed., *Chicanos and Film,* 275–307.

45 Harry Gamboa Jr., "Harry Gamboa, Jr.: No Movie Maker," interview by Marisela Norte, *El Tecolote* (San Francisco Mission District), n.d. (ca. 1983), 3ff.

46 These videos are *Imperfecto* (1983), *Insultan* (1983), *Blanx* (1984), *Agent Ex* (1984), *Vaporz* (1984), *Baby Kake* (1984), and *No Supper* (1987).

47 In many respects, the project finds its counterpart in recent efforts within cultural studies to develop a "poetic" self-examination of Chicano masculine expressive culture. See, for example, Renato Rosaldo, "Politics, Patriarchs, and Laughter," *Cultural Critique* 6 (1987): 65-86, and José E. Limón, *Mexican Ballads, Chicano Poems: History and Influence in Mexican-American Social Poetry* (Berkeley: University of California Press, 1992).

48 To date, these include Raul Villa, professor; Rene Yañez, artist-curator; Max Benavidez, poet-writer; David Avalos, artist; Humberto Sandoval, actor; and John Valadez, artist.

49 Latinos make up about 42 percent of the population; whites, 37 percent; and blacks and Asians, 10 percent each.

50 I discuss this general process in "El hilo latino: Representation, Identity, and National Culture," *Jump Cut,* no. 38 (June 1993): 45-50. Gamboa has returned to the theme of the Chicano nuclear family in *L.A. Familia* (1993), a thirty-seven-minute narrative that combines both self-reflexive and "direct" aspects of the *testimonio* with an unscripted ensemble performance.

51 This makes it different from the middle-class orientation of kitsch. For an overview of *rasquachismo* as an aesthetic concept, see the exhibition catalog *Chicano Aesthetics: Rasquachismo,* which contains essays by Tomás Ybarra-Frausto, Shifra Goldman, and John L. Aguilar (Phoenix, Ariz.: MARS [Movimiento Artistico del Rio Salado], 1989). An expanded version of the essay by Ybarra-Frausto is published in *Chicano Art: Resistance and Affirmation, 1965–1985* (Los Angeles: Wight Art Gallery/UCLA, 1991), 155–62. Nicolás Kanellos discusses the development of a *rasquache* aesthetic in *teatro* in "Folklore in Chicano Theater and Chicano Theater in Folklore," in *The Chicano Experience,* ed. Stanley A. West and June Macklin (Boulder, Colo.: Westview Press, 1979), 165–89.

52 Personal interview with Sandra P. Hahn, Los Angeles, 27 May 1991.

53 Ibid.

54 Miller, "Facts, Pacts, Acts," 12–13. For an expanded treatment of "memoirs of a dying other," see Nancy K. Miller, "Autobiographical Deaths," *Massachusetts Review* 33, no. 1 (Spring 1992): 19–47.

55 Simone de Beauvoir, *A Very Easy Death,* trans. Patrick O'Brian (New York: Pantheon, 1985), 31; quoted in Miller, "Facts, Pacts, Acts," 13.

56 Personal interview with Frances Salomé España, Los Angeles, 27 May 1991.

57 Internal colonialism arose as one of the first concepts within the Chicano Movement. By the mid-1970s, Chicano scholars reevaluated and critiqued the internal colony model and its role within the university and the community. See Mario Barrera, Carlos Muñoz Jr., and Charles Ornelas, "The Barrio as Internal Colony," *Urban Affairs Annual Reviews* 6 (1972): 465–98. For a more recent critique of the legal basis of the internal colony model, see Tomás Almaguer, "Ideological Distortions in Recent Chicano Historiography: The Internal Model and Chicano Historical Interpretation," *Aztlán: A Journal of Chicano Studies* 18, no. 1 (Spring 1987): 7-28.

58 The year that España was born, her parents acquired a "ranch" in East Los Angeles, complete with horses and tractors, and built two houses for the extended family. España's father, a Yáqui immigrant from Sonora, worked in the foundries.

59 On the Mexican American Generation, see Mario T. García, *Mexican Americans: Leadership, Ideology, and Identity, 1930–1960* (New Haven, Conn.: Yale University Press, 1989).

60 Connie Fitzsimons, "L.A. Freewaves: Celebrating the Existence of Independent Video," *Artweek,* 7 December 1989, 20. *El espejo* was a work in progress at the time.

61 As Donna Haraway explains, "Situated knowledges are always about communities, not about isolated individuals" ("Situated Knowledges: The Science Question in Feminism and the Privilege of Partial Perspective," *Feminist Studies* 14, no. 3 [Fall 1988]: 575–99, at 590).

62 España interview.

CHON A. NORIEGA

New Visions/New Chinas:
Video—Art, Documentation, and the Chinese Modernity in Question

Bérénice Reynaud

Typically, as the history of the non-West is divided into the classical/primitive and the "modern" stages, modern non-Western subjects can be said to be constituted primarily through a sense of loss—the loss of an attributed "ancient" history with which one "identifies" but to which one can never return except in the form of fetishism. The "object" with which Chinese people are obsessed— "China" or "Chineseness"—cannot therefore be seen as an emotional simplism, but must rather be seen as the sign of belated consciousness. ~ REY CHOW, *Woman and Chinese Modernity*

THE YELLOW RIVER AND FRACTURED MODERNITY

In June 1988, CCTV (Central Chinese Television) broadcast a six-episode television program throughout Mainland China. Directed by Xia Jun and narrated by Su Xiaokang and Wang Luxiang,[1] the series, entitled *River Elegy,* took the meanders of the Yellow River as a metaphor for China's political fate in order to analyze why the "people's spirit [was] hurting" and why Chinese civilization was "in decline." Broadcast twice, *River Elegy* generated such controversy that it was subsequently banned, and it is said to have somehow fueled the Democracy Movement in the spring of 1989. Su Xiaokang became one of the most wanted intellectuals in the aftermath of the June 4 massacre. The series engages in a soul-searching attempt to analyze a long succession of "Chinese failures" as responsible for the suffering paid by the country upon entering modernity. Among these failures, *River Elegy* lists the Confucian organizing of intellectuals as a class separated from the rest of the people, but also what it deems cultural narcissism and blindness, which made China not only incapable of taking advantage of its own inventions on the international market, but also of resisting foreign imperialism. The Great Wall ("the only piece of human architecture that is visible from the Moon," as the Chinese say) symbolized this attitude, since it had been designed to prevent inland invasions—while

Western powers entered China through its harbors and waterfront. For the makers of *River Elegy*, the solution lies in an opening toward the sea, toward the West.

It is difficult to judge the entire scope of the message carried by *River Elegy* and its real subversive value, for, subsequent to its banning, the series is only available in a fifty-seven-minute compilation curated by Mi Ling Tsui and distributed in the United States by film- and videomaker Shu Lea Cheang. What can be said is that *River Elegy* is one of the many video documents recently produced by Chinese artists— living either in Mainland China, Taiwan, Hong Kong, or the various communities of the Chinese diaspora—that strive to articulate the dilemma of Chinese identity facing modernity. For such a "modernity" is the result of a violent cultural shock that started in the nineteenth century with the systematization (and militarization) of the contacts between China and the West. Previous contacts, such as Marco Polo's visit (1275) or Matteo Ricci's trip (1601) were not designed for colonialist purposes. In 1533, Macao was seized by the Portuguese, and around 1650, Taiwan was occupied by the Dutch, and then the Russians invaded the area around the Heilong River, but these imperialistic incursions did not shatter the identity of the Chinese people. A radical change occurred when King George III of England tried to impose on the Chinese emperor Qian Long (1736–95) commercial treaties based on the principles of free trade—a formidable tool for the expansion of British capitalism. Qian Long's response was haughty and clear: "The Heavenly Empire has everything in plenty and lacks nothing within its boundaries. Consequently we do not need to import the products manufactured by the Barbarians from the outside and exchange them against our own products."[2] The judiciousness of such a response has been questioned by Chinese themselves—in particular by the makers of *River Elegy*. Indeed Qian Long's response threw China into a disaster such as it had never known: it gave George III and his successors an argument to start the Opium War against China, to force the emperor to go back on his 1800 decision to forbid the sale of opium to his subjects. Although the decision of a sovereign state, it had been deemed by George III an attack on the principles of free trade, which gave him a reason, in 1840, to send his gunboats to "open up" the doors of the Chinese Empire.[3]

Consequently, France, Germany, Russia, England, and the United States imposed "unequal treaties" to open up "concessions" in the empire, lend money to the emperor at high interest rates, force unilateral most-favored-nation treatment to their advantage, and encroach upon national sovereignty (ensuring that their nationals were not accountable to Chinese authorities). *River Elegy* also makes it clear that the price paid was not only a loss of political and economic power, but also a long-lasting feeling of inferiority that is still affecting Chinese in their ideological and cultural life and that lies at the core of the many issues affecting Chinese identity. This kind of alienation can easily be analyzed and discussed within the parameters of postcolonial discourse, since it was caused by the uneven encounter between two forms of imperial power: a millennial empire ready to collapse, subjected to internal forces of decay (as exemplified, on the political-melodramatic level, by the numerous intrigues woven by Empress Dowager Ci Xi to keep power, or the "unhappy" fate of Pu Yi, the "Last Emperor," and the imperialistic designs of Western powers. Technically, China remained a "sovereign state" and was never colonized, but the "concessions" were treated as no different from colonies, that is, as pieces of property belonging to the Western powers, designed to be exploited and exchanged at leisure, as proven by China's setbacks during World War I. In 1917, the newly proclaimed Republic of China (established in 1911) had taken the side of the Allies, thus hoping to recover the concessions attributed to Germany and to be on equal footing with the Western powers. Yet, at the signing of the Versailles Treaty, the German concessions were treated as if they were mere colonies, confiscated from Germany and handed over to Japan, which had its own imperialistic designs on China.

The "unfair" decisions of the Versailles Treaty had another result: they triggered, in 1919, the May Fourth Movement—a movement of students and intellectuals that was both a protest against the interference of foreign powers in China and a call for modernity. This "call for modernity" was itself two-sided. What the May Fourth intellectuals had in mind was the destruction of an authoritarian literary tradition, perceived as "life-crushing," as well as of the principles of Confucianism. Westernization represented another "pole of modernity," one that didn't always coincide with the nationalistic aspirations of the movement. This is why, in her wonderful book *Woman and Chinese Modernity*, through an argument too complex to reproduce here, Rey Chow can define the paradox of Chinese modernity as being "as intent on self-destruction as it is on self-strengthening."[4]

James Joyce once said of the modern man that he is a displaced individual, who lives and works in a culture that is not his and who often speaks a language that is not his native tongue. The complex dialectic between Chinese culture and modernity is a striking figure of this condition—as demonstrated, for example, by the plight of Hong Kong residents. After the 1842 Treaty of Nanking, which turned their city into a colony of the British Crown, they were constituted as a population "marked" (in the linguistic sense of the term) by colonialism: they are indeed Chinese and speak Cantonese, but are subject to the British rule that imposes the use of English in all official circumstances, but are deprived of the right to have a British passport. Hence the forced modernization undergone by Hong Kong residents alienates them from their fellow Chinese living in the Mainland or in Taiwan after 1949 without turning them into British citizens.

It was while studying medicine in a Japanese hospital in 1902 that Lu Xun, considered "the father of contemporary Chinese literature," realized the intellectual and moral confusion of his fellow citizens and decided to devote himself to literature as "the best means to raise [their] spirits."[5] The main political events marking China's entry into contemporary history (the 1911 democratic revolution, the triumph of the Communist Party in 1949) are the results of a constant interaction between the East and the West, between the imperialistic strategies of the Western powers and China's efforts toward modernization, self-government, and self-definition. Sun Yat-sen's democratic principles (enunciated in 1904-5) may not have been formulated the same way if the Boxer Rebellion—triggered by a populist resistance against foreign inference—had not taken place (and hadn't been harshly repressed by the Western powers) in 1900. Sun Yat-sen himself had studied in Honolulu. And the founding of a Communist Party in China (1921) wouldn't have been possible without the existence of an international labor movement at the turn of the century in both Western Europe and Russia. It is also interesting to note that the first major strike organized by Chinese workers in 1922 was to protest against the treatment of Chinese sailors under British authority in Hong Kong.

The product of an intimate interaction between the effects of Western and Japanese imperialism and the development of internal forces and contradictions, contemporary Chinese history can be seen as a series of ruptures—ruptures of the Chinese sovereignty symbolized by the colonization of Hong Kong and the opening up of free ports to European powers; loss of Taiwan after the first Sino-Japanese war (1894–95; the islanders underwent Japanese occupation and were forced to speak Japanese till the end of World War II); and rupture between the Communist Party and the Kuomintang, generating a bloody civil war and ending up in the retreat of Chiang Kai-shek's army and government to Taiwan, where they established a "provisional government" in Taipei, intending to use it as a base to reconquer Mainland China (the "Republic of China" in Taiwan and the "People's Republic of China" on the Mainland are still technically at war). Western powers have played with the rivalry between the two governments, siding with Taiwan as a rampart against Communism, then opening up diplomatic relationships with Beijing, and so on. (Taiwan's exclusion from the United Nations in 1971 and the diplomatic rupture between Taipei and Washington in 1972 caused a serious ideological crisis among Taiwanese.)

Another violent rupture, this time internal to Mainland China, was caused by the Cultural Revolution (1966–76), whose far-reaching effects are still affecting Chinese contemporary art, literature, and cinema. "Our millennial system of belief was broken at the time," explains "Fifth Generation" film director Chen Kaige.[6] "Traditional art and culture were totally destroyed. Currently, our major problems are *not* political or economic, but lie in the fact that we don't know how to deal with the incredible *loss* we experienced during the Cultural Revolution. And there is no way to set another kind of culture or tradition in a short time."[7]

The development of a huge, and permanently growing, Chinese diaspora represents another form of fracture. Here again, one should be careful about *not* viewing Chinese emigration as a "natural" phenomenon, but rather analyzing it as an element of a postcolonial situation. After winning the second Opium War in 1860 and entering Beijing, the Western powers imposed the right to "import" Chinese workers abroad—to Malaysia, Australia, Latin America, and the West Indies, as well as to the United States, where manpower was needed to build the railways; this was the beginning of a lucrative "coolie trade."

CHINA AND THE WESTERN GAZE

If it is to colonialism that China owes its first real contacts with the Western world, it is also to the invasion of foreign capitalism that it owes the import of cinema (Shanghai,

BÉRÉNICE REYNAUD

1913), then television (Hong Kong, 1957). For Chinese, as for people formerly submitted to colonialism, cinema and television are technologies that are imported, alien, foreign. Here we are faced, once again, with the polemics generated by the former colonized using the tool of the colonizer. For example, West Indian poet Aimé Césaire was fond of saying that the French language, as a tool of the colonizer to brainwash black populations, could be reclaimed by black writers who'd turn it into their own tool and transform it for their own use (as exemplified by the large body of African and West Indian literature written in French). For Chinese, the problem does not lie in the loss of the mother tongue[8] but in issues relating to the mastery of audiovisual language. Cinema was delivered to them, all constructed, with an "apparatus" (as described by Jean-Louis Baudry) reflecting the ideology of the capitalistic bourgeoisie, the space of Renaissance painting, and an epistemology representing nineteenth-century Europe and America. In 1913, the first Chinese film production company, Asia Motion Pictures, was created in Shanghai by two Americans, Isher and Suffer. They controlled all aspects of the financing and distribution of their products, but hired a twenty-one-year-old Chinese man with a good knowledge of English, Zhang Shichuan, to direct the films.[9] Zhang eventually opened his own production company and became one of the pioneers of Chinese cinema, which developed very quickly in prewar Shanghai, generating films that successfully merged the narrative conventions received from Hollywood and Chinese visual and literary traditions.

Until recently, though, Chinese cinema was virtually ignored in the West, except by a handful of "specialists." And eyebrows are still raised in surprise when one talks about "Chinese video." In the field of representation, the game is uneven. The images that the West has "of China" are either the documents shot by its own cameramen and constructing more or less exotic figures of "the Other"; or television programs under government control that, whether they are produced in Mainland China or in Taiwan, are heavy propaganda tools; or Chinese feature films, which must resort to allusion or metaphor to circumvent censorship (in Mainland China, the film studios are state controlled; in Taiwan, numerous subjects were still taboo until quite recently; in Hong Kong, the British government imposes a very strict political censorship). And Chinese communities established in industrialized countries (the United States, Canada, Australia, England, France) are still "minorities" usually less organized and less visible than, say, African Americans,[10] still struggling for their "right to representation." Here again the "real" is difficult to grasp, to construct, to recognize.

This chapter, which itself should be read as a series of fragments and ruptures, has no claim to "objectivity." At best, it represents the efforts of a Western woman—albeit "displaced" within American culture and the English language—to articulate her own seduction by contemporary Chinese media. There is a risk: that the "displacement" I perceive in Chinese culture might become a metaphor for my own displacement—the way, in Derrida's work as analyzed by Gayatry Chakravorty Spivak, the displacement of "woman" is treated as a convenient metaphor for the displacement of the male subject.[11] However, this text is far from being "closed," and I hope to avoid falling in the trap laid under my feet by initiating a dialogue in two directions: first with other Western critics and scholars interested in seeing in multiculturalism something other than a glorification of the U.S. melting pot, that is, an authentic reflection on the interactions between Western and non-Western cultures in our present context (hence the didactic aspects of the first part of this text, which succinctly describes basic aspects of contemporary Chinese history for the use of non-Chinese and nonspecialists); and second with my Chinese friends and colleagues, whose help and support have been invaluable throughout the years in which I have been involved with Chinese culture. The viewing of Chinese media constructs two kinds of spectators: it empowers Chinese audiences (but we should beware of an essentialist vision of "Chineseness" and carefully examine *which* Chinese audience we are talking about) and, on the contrary, *displaces* the non-Chinese spectators who have to face their lack of knowledge and understanding of the images represented, the language spoken, the social rituals explored, the history alluded to, *without constructing an exotic Other as a convenient substitute for the specific forms of alienation they are undergoing.* Another issue is raised when dealing with Chinese *video,* since this is a still-marginal form of artistic expression among the various Chinese communities. What position can we adopt in front of this marginalization? My goal is not to fully answer this question, but to generate among readers the desire to see, and show, the works examined in this piece.

For this is not a theoretical essay, but a text that developed as the result of my own activity as a curator. In 1993, the Galerie Nationale du Jeu de Paume in Paris gave me the opportunity to present works that I felt addressed the question of "fractured Chinese identity." The present chapter is an expanded version of the catalog essay written for the Jeu de Paume and a lecture-presentation given in February 1993 at the same museum—which means that it was originally intended as an introduction to the works in the exhibition and a guide for the potential viewer. Hence its limitations.

I also want to insist on the collaborative aspect of my research, that is, its specific positioning in an "in-between" space in world cultural politics. My interest in Chinese video was triggered at two levels: first, by my involvement in the Chinese American community in New York, where my mentors and guides were Taiwanese-born video artist Shu Lea Cheang, publicist and spokesman Norman Wang, and the staff of Asian Cine Vision; second, by the screening at the 1991 Vancouver Film Festival of an extraordinary work from Mainland China, *Bumming in Beijing: The Last Dreamers* (1990), directed by then thirty-four-year-old Wu Wenguang, presented as part of the Asian program curated by British critic Tony Rayns. Again, Rayns's own investigation of Chinese culture couldn't have happened without the help and collaboration of Chinese scholars, producers, and distributors; in this case, the tape was made available to him by Hong Kong distributor-critic-filmmaker Shu Kei. Later, when I developed the program, a few people were my key "informants": Hong Kong video artist Ellen Pau, who put me in touch with video artists from Hong Kong and Taiwan; Wong Ain-ling, Asian programmer of the Hong Kong Film Festival; film critic Peggy Chiao (Chiao Hsiung-ping) in Taiwan; critic and producer Roger Garcia in Hong Kong and New York; and French specialist of Chinese cinema, Sophie Laurent.[12]

While screening the 150 minutes of Wu's *Bumming in Beijing: The Last Dreamers*, I had the feeling that a new chapter of the history of representation was being written in front of my eyes. For the real subject of the tape was the struggle of an artist with the documentary form, his (re)discovery of cinema verité and "camera-stylo." The only kind of documentary that officially exists in China is the traditional form (images plus voice-over commentary) produced at the Beijing Documentary Studio and for television. The only foreign films that are imported are feature films, so Chinese artists have had no exposure to different forms of documentary and have had to "reinvent everything themselves" (Sophie Laurent), hence their trial-and-error approach. In a potentially subversive gesture, Wu took his camera into Beijing's back alleys and run-down apartments, where his best friends, nonconformists in their twenties—painters, writers, photographers, theater artists—were trying to survive "in the margins," outside the "system." From a Western point of view, the tape is "too long," and it includes many moments in which "nothing happens," nothing is said, and the only sound is that of a brush or pencil on a piece of paper.[13] Like a classical Chinese painting, *The Last Dreamers* is organized as much around its blanks and its silences as around what it shows and says, but this aesthetics has a new resonance in the contemporary context. Historical "slips" overlap with the outward "awkwardnesses" of the structure. The student movement of spring 1989 and the June 4 massacre are totally elided. Wu resumes filming his buddies as if "nothing had happened," but the young artists are less cocky, more sullen, more depressed. All of them but one (the theater director) manage to find a foreign spouse and leave the country. One extraordinary sequence, which gives the feeling of having been shot "in real time," with a minimal amount of editing (hence the repetitive, tedious, but also poignant aspect of that moment), is when a young female painter, Zhang Xia Ping (born in 1961), suffers a violent mental breakdown the day of the opening of her show in a public gallery. She rolls on the floor, uttering broken words (which, significantly, have to do with questions of sexual difference: who is man, who is woman),[14] screaming, laughing, crying, in short making a spectacle of herself. The strength of such an image has to be understood in context: in Chinese culture *women do not freak out in public.* (In traditional fiction they cry, or hang themselves in a hidden corner when their "honor" is sullied, and if they become mad with sorrow they remain silent.) In the tape, Zhang Xia Ping's delirium functions as a metaphor for the violence done to the Chinese youth at Tiananmen Square; it also points out tears in the social fabric, particularly in the discourse of Confucianism still prevalent (although repressed) on issues of propriety and the education of women. Yet, the real "event" in Zhang Xia Ping's breakdown is that a camera was there to record it, unflinchingly. It is a sign that young Chinese are picking up video cameras to bear witness to *their realities* and to the changes their society is currently undergoing. This in itself constitutes a break with official art, where the mission of "representing the masses as they are" conceals the desire of representing them as they "should" be. Wu is part of a new generation of film and video artists whose work tends to communicate what I would call "the grain of existence," struggling to achieve another form of realism. So, far from being the mere portrait of a "lost generation" of young Chinese artists, *The Last Dreamers* reveals the existence, within the Chinese social structure, of "pockets of difference" that could potentially become "pockets of subversion."

Another major work in this respect is *Mama* (1990) by Zhang Yuan (born in 1963), hailed as "the first Chinese independent film since 1949." It is the story of a poignant, impossible tenderness between a young single mother, Liang Dan, and her little boy, Dongdong, who is mentally handicapped. Written by the actress Qin Yang, who also plays the main part, the fictional part of the film is shot in black and white with a subtle, sensuous touch, calling to mind the intimist masterpieces of the "Golden Age" of Chinese cinema in the thirties and forties. Then the film turns to color video transfer, and a frontal shot displays the medium close-up of an ordinary woman talking about her own experience as the mother of a handicapped child.

The film skillfully interweaves fiction and documentary. After a sequence in which Liang Dan is embarrassed when a neighbor curiously and none too subtly gazes at her child, we see a real mother discussing situations of similar embarrassment in the bus or in the street. The next sequence, returning to fiction, continues to develop the theme of the gaze, but this time it is the little boy, Dongdong, who is its bearer. While Liang Dan is applying makeup, her son, until now the *object* of inquisitive and pitiful gazes, looks at her with a poignant mixture of tenderness, love, longing, and desire. I see in this "return of the gaze" a metaphor for the empowerment that the mastery of video documentary represents for young Chinese filmmakers, now ready to become the *subjects* of their own audiovisual discourse.

"Talking heads" might be a cliché in Western media, but in China, apparently, nobody had ever thought of asking the mothers of handicapped children their point of view about their plight and the situation of health care in China. Their emotion when asked to talk in front of the camera, to state their feelings and opinions, is almost tangible. Here again, one has the distinct feeling that filmic history is being written. Furthermore, the decision to shoot the "documentary" parts of *Mama* in video, to contrast them with the luscious fictional parts (shot in 35mm), not only is bold in artistic terms; it also demonstrates that young Chinese artists are determined to use video as a means in a search for objectivity. "To go into the streets with a camera, directly ask somebody a question and listen to his or her answer—this had never been seen in China," says Laurent.[15] And, defining himself against the filmmakers of the "Fifth Generation," Zhang states: "Our thinking is completely different. . . . They are intellectual youths who've spent time in the country, while we're urbanites. . . . They all went through the Cultural Revolution and they remained kind of romantic. We don't. . . . I make films because I am concerned about social issues and social realities. . . . I don't like being subjective, and I want my films to be objective. It's objectivity that'll empower me."[16]

Partaking of this idea are Shi Jian (born in 1963) and Chen Jue (born in

BÉRÉNICE REYNAUD

1961), the founders of the Structure, Wave, Youth, Cinema Experimental Group, who state their intentions as follows: "By means of observing and recording reality on a massive scale, and through the authors' detached contemplation on reality, we want to present a more truthful and more expansive document on the life of the Chinese people. . . . It is also our intention, in the present given context, to truthfully engage in the construction of a theory and a practice of audio-visual documentation that is genuine, open, penetrating and expansive."[17] In August 1988, they started shooting an eight-episode series titled *Tiananmen Square* (completed in 1991) that was supposed to reflect the daily life and the historical significance of Beijing's monumental central square. Lying across the Forbidden City, it witnessed important moments of contemporary Chinese history: the first gathering of the May Fourth intellectuals, "parades" of the Red Army or the Communist Party, meetings of the Red Guards, and so on. Each of the episodes starts with the following statement: "We respect life just as we respect history." For Shi and Chen, modernity is outlined on a historical background; it is a dialectic between a present in the making and history—not only as it was experienced, but as it is recounted and handed over as part of various forms of ideological discourses, mythologies, and propaganda. Everyday life in Beijing takes place among streets and monuments in which the past is, somehow, engraved, and it is the shadow of the past that "marks" the present. In "The Old City" (episode 1), we are treated with extraordinary interviews with living relics of the past, such as immediate members of Pu Yi's family, and a former court eunuch who still remembers the beatings ordered by Empress Dowager Ci Xi. His words articulate complex feelings concerning history, for at some point, through a subtle conceptual "slip," having alluded to the succession of dynasties his fellow eunuchs had to serve, he seems to project into the present: "The emperor of today is like old wine in a new bottle." Is he still talking about imperial power, or insinuating something rather subversive about China's current rulers? Anyhow, a few minutes later, he breaks down in tears of gratitude to assert that "without the Communist Party, my life wouldn't be what it is today."

In "Habitats" (episode 2), the tape adopts a leisurely pace to enter the maze of small streets and inner courtyards that make up a working-class neighborhood just off the square and follows a Sunday afternoon spent by an extended family invited to taste "Granny Li's" cooking. "On The Way" (episode 7) explores various figures of modernity: a young man who has started his own advertising production company; an international fashion model; a former model running a school to train young women in modeling (as in the United Kingdom of the sixties—remember *Polly Magoo, Darling*—to be a fashion model has become a much coveted profession for young girls in Beijing). It also includes an exhibition of Chinese expressionist paintings; interviews with researchers at the Chinese Social and Cultural Research Development, whose task is to translate foreign academic and encyclopedic books into Mandarin; and a visit at the "Three-Flavors Bookstore," a sort of alternative cultural club for students and intellectuals.

The works of Shi Jian, Chen Jue, Zhang Yuan, and Wu Wenguang (who all know each other and eventually work together) demonstrate the emergence of a new artistic movement in Beijing. After *Tiananmen Square*, the Structure, Wave, Youth, Cinema Experimental Group produced several other videos, including *I Graduated!* (1992, 64 minutes), which was shown at the 1993 Hong Kong Film Festival. The tape is composed of interviews with students who had just graduated from more than ten universities and colleges in Beijing—precisely the class that experienced the Tiananmen Square events. Concealed between the spoken words of these interviews is the incredible upset and confusion represented by the events of the spring of 1989. Some became party members, some dropped out of school, some tried to commit suicide. The main contradiction is between people who have opted for a mindless rush for money and those whose life is more difficult or do not even have this option.

Zhang Yuan became involved in another aspect of youth culture through his friendship with rock singer Cui Jian. Popularized by a famous portrait in which he sings with a red blindfold over his eyes, Cui has become the symbol of the resistance of young Chinese to the repression following June 4, 1989. His songs can be heard everywhere, and his international reputation protects him, but he is nevertheless the victim of all sorts of repressive measures: his concerts are canceled, his exit visas denied, and so on. Zhang directed several music videos for Cui before embarking on his second feature-length project, *Beijing Bastards* (1993). The film, following Cui and his band in a series of loose narratives—playing, drinking, quarreling—throughout Beijing, had to be shot illegally, which almost prevented its premiere at the 1993 Locarno Film Festival.

Wu Wenguang directed a second video work, 165 minutes long, titled *1966, My Time in the Red Guards* (1993), which can be read as the clash between two forms of modernity. In 1966, the Red Guards represented the avant-garde political consciousness of the Chinese people. The teenagers who joined the movement did so out of a feeling that, since they didn't fight with Mao Zedong for the Communist revolution and didn't participate with him in the Great Walk, they had somehow been bypassed by history. Being a Red Guard was a way to become a hero of the revolution, contribute to the death of the old world, and make history. Wu interviews several cadres—engineers, academics, and "Fifth generation" filmmaker Tian Zhuangzhuang[18]—who talk about their involvement in the Red Guards *from the point of view of the teenagers they were at the time*. He then pits such interviews against images of the women of the all-girl band Cobra (a splinter from Cui Jian's rock group) rehearsing a song titled "1966, Red Train": the "modernity" of the post-Tiananmen Square youth is deliberately weary of political illusions and feeds itself on Western pop culture and various forms of "cool" and cynicism. Wu has obviously seen *Tiananmen Square* (and also, probably, *River Elegy*) when designing the structure of *1966*.

THE PLACE OF HISTORY

Through this constant dialectic between the representation of the present and the interpretation of the past, Chinese history remains a deeply polemical object, as demonstrated by the ten-episode television series (still to be completed) *Understanding China into the Maze of History*.[19] The series was initiated by Wang Shau-di, one of the few female filmmakers working in the Taiwanese industry. In particular, she wrote the screenplays of two major films—both directed by Wang Tung—that explored different aspects of Taiwanese history seen in the eyes of common and/or marginalized people: small peasants under the Japanese occupation in *Strawman* (1987) and illiterate soldiers of the Nationalist army trying to make a new life after 1949 in *Banana Paradise* (1989). In the latter film, written from many interviews conducted with veterans, she capitalizes on the 1987 lifting of martial law in Taiwan, which made it possible for filmmakers and artists to touch upon previously forbidden subjects—Taiwanese history being one such taboo. Yet Wang considers her exploration of history a means to delve deeper into the crisis of Chinese identity, which she views in terms that are not so different from Chen Kaige's: "Chinese have been morally sick for a very long time. Because the old beliefs have disappeared. They are frustrated in their political lives and economically have experienced all sorts of turmoil."[20] A turning point in her political consciousness as a Chinese was her meeting with Su Xiaokang, one of the two writers of *River Elegy*, then in exile in Paris. By then, Wang, disappointed with the state of the Taiwanese film industry, had decided to form her own television production company, ViewVision (although a literal translation of its Chinese title means "People's March"), to offer programs to the public television started in the mid eighties as part of the ongoing democratization of Taiwan. When I interviewed Wang in December 1989, the Taiwanese Public Television was not an independent company and did not have its own channel (it was run by the government and broadcast its programs at specific times on the three other television channels), but it had the advantage of being nonprofit and running better quality programs.[21] Wang produced and/or directed an extraordinary number of television series and programs through ViewVision, in which, with her partner Huang Li-ming (a former commercial television producer), she also has a training program for young filmmakers. *Six Martyrs* (1989), exploring various forms of resistance to abusive power at different moments of Chinese history, was a reformulation of the costume drama, an ever popular genre in Chinese cinema and television. *One Hundred Walks of Life* was an eighty-six-episode series documenting Taiwanese people at work; it included controversial issues such as the labor-management relationship. *Understanding China into the Maze of History* (1992, 54 minutes), whose production was unfortunately stopped after the second episode because of a conflict with the television station, can be read as the other side of *River Elegy*. It is an attempt to think of Chinese history as a whole, to read the past in order to understand the present, to use the most recent archaeological or historical discoveries to explore the genesis of power in the former Middle Empire—how, for example, what Marx and Engels called "the Asian mode of production" was the product of specific geoclimatic conditions, such as the necessity to organize the distribution of water to large populations in semidesert areas—and the traces it has left in Chinese psyche. In addition, it is impossible not to feel a certain poignancy in Wang's quest. Her parents left Mainland China in 1949 to follow the Kuomintang, so the inscription of her own history on the ancestral soil is, somehow, constructed as a lost object. In Taiwan, where the official doctrine is that the withdrawal on the island is a "provisional" strategy before recapturing the Mainland from the Communists (until recently one was put in jail simply for advocating "Taiwanese independence"), a painful fetishization of Chinese history takes place. Wang Shau-di and Huang Li-ming's series masterfully avoid this trap by presenting Chinese history as a succession of partially unanswered questions, rather than as a closed text.[22]

The work of Shu Lea Cheang represents another questioning of Taiwanese history, this time from the point of view of the diaspora. While Wang had studied at the University of Texas and felt compelled to go back home after Taiwan's expulsion from the United Nations, Cheang studied filmmaking at NYU and stayed in New York, becoming involved with alternative media groups and media activists such as Paper Tiger Television and Deep Dish Public Access Network. In 1990, she produced and distributed a television series (broadcast on Deep Dish and shown in galleries and museums) entitled . . . . *Will Be Televised: Video Documents from Asia*, whose statement of purpose reads as follows: "As video camcorders become more widely distributed in Asia, video makers have become active protagonists in the current social and political changes that are taking place in the region. The series is an archive of that movement." . . . . *Will Be Televised* is made of five one-hour episodes, one from South Korea (*Until Daybreak*), one from the Philippines (*A Legacy of Violence*), and three from China. The Chinese episodes include *Presenting River Elegy* (a fifty-seven-minute compilation of the original six-hour program) and also a program from Taiwan, *The Generation after the Martial Law* (1986–90, 60 minutes), curated by Ching Jan Lee and made up of agit-prop videos shot illegally by groups such as the United Houseless Association and the Green Team Video Collective. The martial law imposed in 1949 was lifted in 1987, allowing the establishment of an opposition party, the Democratic Progressive Party (DPP), but democracy is slow to settle in Taiwan. For example, two-thirds of the seats at the National Assembly are occupied by representatives elected *before 1948* who are supposed to represent the various provinces of mainland China. And the "Taiwanese economic miracle" has depended on an extreme modernization whose cost was paid for by the peasants, the aboriginals, and the environment. Yet, even though the activities of the Green Team are illegal, their videos can be found everywhere, in the markets or by mail order, and this is not one of the least contradictions of Taiwanese censorship.[23] The compilation prepared by Ching Jan Lee starts with extremely potent images (which became the visual trademark of the entire series): young demonstrators throw and destroy dozens of TV monitors against the gate of the state television building. It continues with a series of segments documenting the fight of the students, the farmers, the workers, the homeless, and the ecologists, as well as their violent repression by the police. At some point groups of students cover the TV crew vans with graffiti while screaming slogans through loudspeakers: "Journalists, reporters, where is your conscience? Why is the news distorted?"

It is this very distortion of the news that is the subject of Cheang's *How*

BÉRÉNICE REYNAUD

Was History Wounded (1990, 28 minutes, 30 seconds), which takes as a departure point what can probably be termed the founding moment of the new Chinese modernity: the June 4 massacre in Tiananmen Square. On the way to Beijing to document the Democracy Movement with her video camera, Cheang, like all foreign nationals, was evacuated at the beginning of June, first to Hong Kong and then to Taipei, where her family lives.[24] Then, in collaboration with Taiwanese intellectuals, she realized *How Was History Wounded* (currently distributed in Taiwan by the Green Team), in which she analyzes the process of propaganda used in both Taiwan and the People's Republic. Significantly, the Kuomintang *and* the Chinese Communist Party eliminate the content and meaning of the student movement. For Beijing it is the work of "hoodlums," while Taipei reads it, according to its own ideological interests, as anticommunist, easily forgetting that movements of popular protest are violently repressed in Taiwan (as exemplified by the Green Team tape). Cheang interviews Taiwanese militants and media activists, while keeping their faces in shadow so they can't be recognized (tactics similar to those used by the leaders of the Chinese Democracy Movement after the repression). One of the speakers sarcastically notices that repression is more complete and hypocritical in Taiwan than in the People's Republic of China. When the anchorwoman of CCTV (Central Chinese Television in Beijing) had to read the government's communiqué about the June 4 massacre, her face betrayed her emotion and silent reprobation. On the contrary, the anchors of the three Taiwanese networks (CTS, TTV, and CTV) looked quite happy when reading their propaganda texts. Capitalism seems a smoother, more efficient mode of ideological control than socialism. For all its repressive aspects, the current Communist regime makes possible these tears in the social fabric, these breaches in the political discourse that allow, even for a fleeting moment, a spark of individual revolt—while in Taiwan, television personalities are paid well enough to be "convinced" that the government's politics are in their best interests. "They are political prostitutes," comments the faceless young militant. Cheang masterfully quotes examples of TV news, but also inserts an excerpt of a prime-time soap opera sentimentalizing and distorting the meaning of the student movement: between a few tears for his sweet girlfriend killed by the Red Army, the student leader addresses his comrades, thanking the "help and support" they have received from the Taiwanese government! Another witness adds, "As in all third world countries, the TV is the most conservative of all the press organs." Cheang's video seeks to look beyond the glossy surface and the "spectacle society" provided by the "Taiwanese economic miracle": mechanisms of exploitation typical of a third world society still exist, albeit drowned in ideology and the neons of Taipei.

POSTMODERN PALIMPSESTS

Distant echoes of the Tiananmen Square massacre can also be found in the fifth video of the . . . . *Will Be Televised* series, *Only Something That Is About to Disappear Becomes an Image* (1990, 60 minutes), a compilation by Hong Kong artist Danny Yung of short pieces by members of the Zuni Icosahedron (also known as Zuni) group he founded in March 1982. Zuni, a loose collective of artists, is mostly known for the abstract, sculptural language of its group performance work, but its artists are also credited for being "pioneers of video art in Hong Kong." In 1983, they organized the first video art workshop ever held locally, from which works were created for the Hong Kong section of the First Hong Kong International Video Arts Festival. Since then, Zuni members have been actively involved in directing and producing video works (often in Hi-8 format) and organizing exhibitions and shows. Complex and "postmodern," Zuni's work assumes a critical position about Hong Kong's colonial situation, with its retinue of political repression, identity crisis, and alienation. There is practically no funding for the arts in Hong Kong, so Zuni members have full-time professional jobs (in academia, the government, or even as health technicians).[25] In addition, censorship specific to Hong Kong forbids cinema and the arts to be critical of the colonial government or even to shed an unfavorable light on a "neighboring country"—a euphemism for either Taiwan or Mainland China. This explains in part the indirect style through which Zuni members formulate their political statements. The ominous shadow of the People's Republic of China that keeps spreading further and further over Hong Kong, combined with the horror caused among the residents by June 4, exacerbates the problems of representation specific to a city that experiences itself as part of a perpetual game of difference and transition between the East and the West. With a triumphant capitalism governing its daily life and economic exchange and communism at its door supposedly marking its future, the stakes are very high in the megalopolis.

Only Something That Is About to Disappear Becomes an Image starts with a collaborative piece by Danny Yung and May Fung that "deconstructs" images, postcards, and stories about Hong Kong, while attempting to define its "hybrid identity" and sense of displacement through short fragments. "Stories about HK always turn into stories about somewhere else," a title says. Another states that the city's cultural identity is defined "only by difference." This piece is followed by a number of segments, often no longer than ten minutes each, realized by other members of the group: Victor Chan, Kuan Punleong, Ellen Pau, and Comyn Mo. One of these segments starts with a black-and-white home movie of some British settlers arriving in Hong Kong in the twenties. Then one hears a song that has become an ironical "trademark" of many a Zuni performance, a little nursery rhyme designed to teach English to Chinese children: "China is a big garden. / Flowers here are so beautiful . . . / Everybody's happy again."

In another segment entitled "She Said Why Me," May Fung shows a young woman walking blindfolded through the present, past, and probably future of Hong Kong. In "Private Collection," Comyn Mo (also an experimental filmmaker in his own right) examines the relationship between the postcolonial situation in Hong Kong and his most private obsessions. Ellen Pau is represented by two pieces, the secretive, highly metaphorical "Diversion," structured around images of a body climbing stairs or throwing itself against a wall, and the clearly political "Game of the Year," using pantomime to ridicule the television propaganda of the Chinese government.

Chinese American video artist Victor Huey noted that, if it is now relatively easy for Asian artists or activists to get hold of camcorders and video cameras, access to sophisticated systems of editing is more difficult. Chinese living in the United States or Canada don't have this problem, and they have asserted a strong presence in the media to explore their own divided identity. The original "immigrant stories," if they are tempted to indulge in nostalgia or "family romance," often lead to a political consciousness-raising about racism or postindustrial alienation—and eventually, as masterfully expressed by Trinh T. Minh-ha, to new ways of positing "identity" or "Asianness":

> Here, the becoming Asian-American affirms itself at once as a transient and constant state: one is born over again as hyphen rather than as fixed entity, thereby refusing to settle down in one (tubicolous) world or another. The hyphenated condition certainly does not limit itself to a duality between two cultural heritages. It leads, on the one hand, to an active "search of our mothers' garden" (Alice Walker)—the consciousness of "root values" or of a certain Asianness—; and on the other hand, to a heightened awareness of other "minority" sensitivities, hence a Third World sensitivity, and, by extension, of the necessity for new alliances.[26]

The works of Shu Lea Cheang and Valerie Soe reflect such concerns. In *Color Schemes* (1990, 28 minutes, 30 seconds) Cheang uses the image of the hand laundry (a traditional activity for Chinese immigrants) and juxtaposes it with a slightly irreverent reconstruction of the Last Supper to comment humorously on the mixing of races and colors characteristic of contemporary America, in particular the Lower East Side of New York, where Cheang lives. Is the melting pot a washout? Do good table manners define a "model minority"? Can one be "too ethnic" for one's own good? Is American democracy, as Malcolm X said, a table offering nothing but empty plates to some of the diners? The tape clearly defines the alliance outlined by Trinh between Chinese people and other "people of color."[27] In *All Orientals Look the Same* (1986, 1 minute), Valerie Soe mocks the stereotypes used against Asian people: she repeats in a loop the sentence that gives its title to the piece, while showing in rapid succession head shots demonstrating the great ethnic and physical diversity of "Oriental" people. In *Black Sheep* (1990, 6 minutes), she tells the strange story of her "Uncle Joe," born with six toes on each foot. He seems at first to have benefited from these stereotypes, since he was able, as a baby, to fool U.S. immigration authorities. His parents thought it was easier to give him the identity of an older brother who had died than to start all the paperwork from scratch. Yet this double status as an outsider and imposter marked Uncle Joe for life. His increasing marginalization, strange habits, and loneliness seem to ask the question of the "unspoken" status of homosexuality—or even of homophobia—in Chinese societies.

To be Chinese and gay while living in a Western society means to be subjected to a double displacement, but why, asks Richard Fung (whose family emigrated from South China to Trinidad and then to Canada) is Chinese homosexuality more often criticized than Caucasian homosexuality?[28] His landmark tape, *Orientations* (1984, 56 minutes), probably the first to address such issues in North American media, confronts the cliché according to which "all homosexuals are white." Fung interviews a number of Asian men and women who find themselves, because of their homosexuality, in the position of being "a minority within a minority." Their stories, told from a militant point of view and ending up in the defense of gay rights, are sometimes painful, sometimes funny: coming out, homophobia, racism, cultural identity, sexual and emotional problems. What the tape ultimately tries to define is how the speakers' most intimate being has been fashioned by their homosexuality *as well as* by their Asianness. More playful, *Chinese Characters* (1986, 21 minutes) explores the *jouissance* and the intercultural vertigo resulting from being both Chinese and gay. The piece, which starts with a quote by Confucius, "Food and sex are human nature"—evolves as a series of four variations on four erotic figures ("East," "West," "South," and "Down There") that describe the attraction among gay men of different racial backgrounds, the relationship to gay pornography, the dialectic between the subject and the object of desire, the erotic and alienating components of the gaze.

The current repression of homosexuality in Mainland China—where homosexuals are sometimes forced to undergo shock treatment—and the silence surrounding homosexuality in most Chinese communities seem to reinforce the cliché that homosexuality is perceived as "un-Chinese" and imported by the "foreign devils." It is quite probable that, on the contrary, the current homophobia recorded in the various Chinese communities is the result of contact with the West, where homosexuality exists as a specific, often marginalized or even militant lifestyle usually precluding heterosexual intercourse. For homosexuality was rather well tolerated in the imperial courts until the Qing dynasty (1644-1911) and peacefully coexisted with heterosexual practices, with wealthy, powerful men having both wives, concubines, and young male lovers or "favorites." Granted, with a few exceptions, the only remaining texts describe the sexual practices of the upper classes. The emperor's favorites could attain positions of incredible power and wealth, to the chagrin of more puritanical historians who saw in this practice a cause of the decay of the empire. The most ancient favorite recorded by history was Mizi Xia, who remained famous for an act of loving thoughtfulness: seeing the emperor arrive in the garden, he gave him half of the peach he was in the process of eating. Later, when Mizi Xia fell out of favor, the Emperor used the same event as a pretext to dismiss him as being selfish for giving his master only half of his peach. The incident was recorded as an example of the fickleness of imperial favor. "Men who eat half-peaches" became a poetic metaphor for homosexuality.[29] The following dynasties record love stories among men of equal standing—among scholars, for example, who, while being married and having children, had significant affairs with each other, the older man taking on the responsibility of finding a suitable wife for his younger lover. Yet, there is virtually no mention of female homosexuality, although it appeared that it existed and was, in some cases, well tolerated.

In his multilayered, fragmented explorations of Asian homosexuality, Ming-Yuen S. Ma posits himself at the receiving end of contradictory traditions: the sophisticated tales of "boy-love" in the Chinese imperial court and the contemporary "queer politics" currently expounded in the United States. Like Hong Kong itself, Ma's persona as an artist is constructed as a locus of exchange between the East and the West: born in the United States (and therefore a U.S. citizen), he grew up in Hong Kong, then came back to the United States to study and get involved in AIDS prevention work in New York's Chinatown, and eventually to act as a curator of Asian and Asian American film and video programs about gender issues. His short tape *Aura* (1991, 7 minutes) overlays allusions to the mythical peach-eating Mizi Xia with excerpts of the classic text of Japanese erotic literature, Ihara Saikaku's *The Great Mirror of Male Love,* over sensuous, colorful images of Asian drag queens. Ma describes *Aura* as "a deconstructive music video . . . , effect-ridden and totally overdone, a somewhat frivolous exploration of gender, identity, tradition and glamour." Ma's *Toc Storee* (1992, 21 minutes) is a palimpsest including translated and untranslated Cantonese, English, and phonetic renderings of English as spoken by native Cantonese speakers, to the point of being undecipherable. The tape expands the concerns of *Aura*—it uses the same sources, such as Bret Hirsch's and Ihara Saikaku's books—to posit Asian and Asian American gay men as desiring subjects marked by the intersection of several narrative traditions: classical Asian homosexuality and contemporary Western discourse that views Asian bodies as objects rather than subjects of desire. The gay love stories of the imperial courts often had violent, tragic endings, with the favorites executed or forced to suicide. Contemporary stories avoid the word "love," but AIDS has also contributed to put death in the pictures. Mixing interviews of Hong Kong–born gay men with images of an Asian male couple in bed, and again with footage of the 1991 Gay Pride March, Ma skillfully evokes a multilayered ideological landscape in which the subjects, their sexuality, their culture, and their memories are resounding with stories that are both "older and younger" than themselves, that repeat and contradict, that, quoting Trinh T. Minh-ha, are "at once a fragment and a whole; a whole within a whole."[30]

CANTONESE OPERA AND FEMALE MASQUERADE

Ellen Pau explores the homosexual connotations of another source of Chinese tradition, the Cantonese opera, in which all the parts were held by female performers, some of them in male drag. As with its counterpart, Peking opera, in which all the parts were held by male performers, this implies a rather intriguing reformulation of sexual roles and identities, thus opening up a space for dissension. Pau's *Song of the Goddess* (1993, 6 minutes) starts with the image of two famous Cantonese opera performers, Yum Kim-

Fai and Pak Sui-Tsin, who were not only "stage sisters"—one played the hero, the other his female lover—but shared a house together. "They were together in many stories," a written title explains. Yet the camera focuses on the *gaze*, erotically charged, that the two women exchange even in their most official photographs: is it meant to convey the fictional love portrayed on stage, or does it reveal the nature of their relationship? Pau interweaves images of this gaze with more personal allusions: shots of the New York City subway, a young woman in her bath washed with tenderness by the hand of another woman. Whose "stories" are being recounted here? Maybe those of all the Chinese women who secretly live their homosexuality.

In addition to splendid visual poems (*She Moves*, 1988, 3 minutes; *Drained II*, 1989, 6 minutes), Pau also directed a promo tape in collaboration with Edward Lam, another Zuni member, to publicize the latter's performance piece, *How to Love a Man Who Doesn't Love Me* (1990, 5 minutes 45 seconds). While homosexuality was still illegal in Hong Kong until the last few years,[31] Lam had been overtly gay in his work as a performance artist and curator (he organized the first Gay and Lesbian Film Festival at the Hong Kong Art Center).

Another female video artist from Hong Kong, Ansom Mak, also uses Cantonese opera (in her case, black-and-white footage of old Cantonese opera films) as a starting point for her most recent tape, *Two or Three Things I Know about Them* (1991, 39 minutes), a subjective inquiry about female homosexuality in Hong Kong. Ansom interviews a few women she knows and discusses with them issues of identity, role-playing ("femme" or "butch"), and perception by others. Each of the vignettes is staged in an unconventional way; one of the women, for example, refuses to show her face and is seen from the back walking through heavy traffic, in negative, her hair white and skin tone dark. The whole sequence can be perceived as a metaphor for the elusive reality of female homosexuality in Chinese culture. Finally, the artist puts herself in question, in an exchange with a female friend who critically, yet sympathically, comments on the making and the format of the tape.

THE INTERTEXTUALITY OF EXILE

The work of Zuni members or of artists who are close to them (Anson Mak, Wong Chi Fai), of a number of young Taiwanese video artists working experimentally (Ju Jieh Wang, Andrew T. L. Jon, and so forth), of Ming-Yuen S. Ma, and of Shu Lea Cheang define a specific form of intertextuality: in the case of the postcolonial subject, new meanings are created from the intersection, the conflict, the juxtaposition of different texts. Born in Hong Kong but currently working in the United States, Yau Ching has also chosen a plurality of voices to tell a story of exile, that of the artist Wen Yi Hou, a female papermaker and painter from Shanghai now living—like the videomaker herself—in downtown Manhattan. Her complex, visually compelling video portrait, *Flow* (1993, 38 minutes) is aptly punctuated by slowed-down shots of a dragon dance in

BÉRÉNICE REYNAUD

New York's Chinatown, overlaid by stanzas of a 1066 B.C. poem expressing the poignancy of regrets generated by exile:

Where the grounds are wet and low
There the trees of goat-peach grow
With their branches small and smooth
Glossy in their tender youth
Joy it were to me O tree
You know not consciousness . . .
. . . You know not home . . .
. . . You know not family . . .

Over images of Chinese tourists visiting Tiananmen Square, footage of army repression in China, or shots detailing her own papermaking activity, Wen Yi Hou evokes her teenage years during the Cultural Revolution, her hunger for reading, permanently frustrated by the rarity of available books. Gradually, though, a space different from the one produced by history is created in the piece, the more intimate space of the relationship between two women. This is done through a gentle settling in what constitutes now the urban territory of the displaced artist (who, as it turns out, lives in the same office building as the videomaker), through conversations while cooking, through the mention of difficult choices made in the young woman's life—having a child or an abortion, getting married to satisfy society's expectations, and then deciding to leave. The real work of the piece, though, is to translate not so much the femininity of the experience of exile as lived by this particular individual, but the *points of erasure* it involves, the junctures in which nothing can be expressed. For if intertextuality creates new meanings, it also involves, more tragically, a real *loss of meaning*, which Yau Ching evokes though the multilingual situation in which her subject has been forced. Wen Yi Hou compares her current situation in New York with the history of her family, who emigrated from a Cantonese-speaking province to Shanghai and therefore were considered "guests" for generations: "Sometimes I feel that I am just repeating their stories, and not in ways as good as theirs." Then she adds: "Even when I am speaking in Mandarin, I don't have enough confidence. Shanghaiese I have forgotten part of. English I never learned. . . . Cantonese I don't know. I'm Cantonese though. There's not one language I master completely. It seems it wasn't like that in China. Although I always had a feeling of loneliness, probably because I couldn't speak eloquently." This leads Wen Yi Hou to criticize the notion of identity that she discovered as central to her fellow artists in the United States. "I don't know where I come from. . . . My identity is no identity." But, instead of sinking in a facile form of existentialist despair, Hou's discourse shifts and becomes political in her refusal of the burden—so often imposed on minority artists—to *represent* an idealized community of Chinese artists, who turn out to be nothing else but a projection of Western fantasies about China.[32]

It is another aspect of Chinese modernity that Chinese American director Victor Huey explores in his forever-in-progress video work, *Rocking the Great Wall* (1993, 27 minutes in the version shown in Paris). In this highly personal collage of grainy black-and-white footage, archival documents, MTV, excerpts of concerts, and interviews, Huey recounts his own fascination with rock singer Cui Jian, whom he had met at an "underground" party in Beijing in 1986. Starting as a playful documentary about the lives of the members of Cui's band (with the obligatory footage about their childhood during the Cultural Revolution), the tape ends up asking pointed questions about what it means to be Chinese. The first of these questions involves the role of women. Huey alternates images of female bodybuilders, disco dancing, and displays of cover girls with the discreet walk of a grandmother whose tiny slippers are a reminder of once bound feet, and montages them with interviews with the members of the all-girl band Cobra. As a man—and probably as a Chinese man—he can't help being curious about their sexuality: "How do you choose between husband and music?" he asks them. The women laugh at him, refusing this Confucian dilemma and reversing the poetic cliché comparing a woman's youth and desirability to the fragility of a rose petal: "Men, you can always find. But music you can't! Once youth is gone, that's it!" Later, while interviewing Liu Yaun, a member of Cui Jian's group who has decided to live in exile in Oregon, Huey confronts his own displacement as an overseas Chinese: "As you live longer in America," he tells Liu, "you'll understand what it is to live in two worlds. You are now Chinese American." Then he shows Liu a tape of Cui Jian and some of his musicians he has recorded in Beijing for Liu, in which they address him, in a poignant attempt to bridge his absence. This section ends on the famous image of the young man trying to stop the tanks on Tiananmen Square, while Cui Jian sings. The tape concludes (provisionally) on a musician's cynical remark: "You'll tell your grandchildren: Oh yeah! Remember one day in August 1991. We had a very good gig! And we had to wait three years to have another one!"

VIDEO, TELEVISION, CINEMA

Like Wang Shau-di's television series, a number of the current video experiments attempted by Chinese artists are evidence of the crisis of commercial film production in their respective countries. In the early 1980s Taiwanese cinema seemed to have been redeemed for a while by the emergence of New Wave directors (Hou Hsiao-hsien, Edward Yang, Wan Jen, and Chang Yi) and screenwriters (Wu Nien-jen, Xiao Ye, and Chu Tien-Wen) who endeavored to tackle the problems of contemporary Taiwan in a realistic, albeit poetic manner. In spite of the international success of such films as Hou's *A City of Sadness* (Golden Lion in Venice in 1989) and Yang's *A Brighter Summer Day* (1991), New Wave directors continue to be marginalized in their own country. Between productions, Edward Yang wrote a play, *Likely Consequence,* which he directed with the members of an experimental theater group, later recording the production on video. Significantly, it is on video that Yang started his career, with the 1981 production of "Floating Leaf," a 145-minute episode of the television series *Eleven Women* produced

BÉRÉNICE REYNAUD

by the Taiwanese actress Sylvia Chang (who was to star later in Yang's breakthrough feature film, *That Day on the Beach*, 1983, 166 minutes—his masterful first foray into middle-class angst). While "Floating Leaf"—recounting the subtle disillusionment and loss of innocence of a small-town girl coming to the Taipei of her dreams—was subtle and realistic, *Likely Consequence* (1992, 45 minutes) boldly espouses the formal parameters of the play it mockingly "documents" and pushes to the limits the conventions of "canned theater." The spectators are seated on the four sides of a central stage, which is completely devoid of either prop or decor: actors play around the presence of invisible objects (a telephone, a door, a window). As in Yang's filmic work, the crisis of Taiwanese society is acutely seen through its effects on a middle-class marriage, and mostly through the eyes of the woman, perceived as the *sign*, the embodiment of this crisis. Coming home, a man finds the body of a dead man in his kitchen, while his wife feeds him a yarn about a traveling salesman trying to abuse her. The husband worries about the negative effect this incident may have on his career; the wife remembers the stages that have transformed her "love match" into a domestic nightmare. Then the husband finds a solution: "Why don't you undress this guy, put him on the bed, and tell people he was your lover and had a heart attack while making love to you!" The "fiction" here functions as a return of the repressed: isn't this exactly what happened, the truth the husband refuses to see? Isn't it a metaphor for Taiwan manufacturing its own alienation?

Still in Taiwan, a new generation of post–New Wave filmmakers have asserted themselves (Chen Kuo-fu, Huang Mingchuang, Ho P'ing, Ang Lee, Tsai Ming-Liang). Not surprisingly, Tsai—revealed at the 1993 Berlin Film Festival with *Rebels of the Neon God*—started his career directing flicks for local television. The best one may be *All the Corners of the World* (1989, 50 minutes), showing the disintegration of a lower-class family. The parents work as cleaners in a "love hotel," and the children help out by buying tickets to popular shows and reselling them to patrons waiting in line. The little boy's dream of becoming a writer is misunderstood by a boorish high school teacher, and the teenage daughter has a brief, yet violent and catastrophic brush with prostitution. Tsai's fascination with the youth culture, its rituals and sorrows, in an ever-tentacular Taipei, and his tenderness and talent at directing young, unprofessional performers work very well on the video format, even if they lack the visual splendor of *Rebels*.

While Hong Kong commercial cinema seems to be striving, auteurs more interested in aesthetics than in box office are also marginalized, and some are turning (or returning) to television and video production. In spite of the critical acclaim given his filmic work (including *Rouge*, 1988, and *Center Stage*, 1991), Stanley Kwan often finds it difficult to raise money for some of his projects. In 1992, he directed a fifteen-minute short film, *Too Happy for Words*, based on the screenplay and the clearly camp aesthetics of Zuni's Edward Lam. He has also accepted a commission from the German television ZDF to produce a half-hour episode provisionally entitled *My Lecherous Youth*, describing the genesis of homosexual desire. In between, he directed a documentary about Siqin Gaowa, a Mainland actress who appeared in his 1989 film, *Full*

Moon in New York. The *Siqin Gaowa Special* (1993, 45 minutes) draws the portrait of a first-rate actress and a complex woman through straightforward interviews, excerpts of films, and cinema verité sequences. Gradually the issue that emerges is that of cultural displacement. Born in Inner Mongolia, known for her work with some of the most respected Chinese directors (Ling Zifeng in *Rickshaw Boy* in 1982, Xie Fei in *The Women of the Lake of Scented Souls* in 1992), and appearing in films of some of the best Hong Kong directors (Yim Ho, Stanley Kwan), Siqin Gaowa left behind her in Mainland China the children of a previous marriage and now lives in golden seclusion in Switzerland, where she fights day after day against language and cultural barriers.

THE RETURN

Ann Hui, another major film director in Hong Kong, considered one of the luminaries of the New Wave that emerged in the early 1980s, decided, after the commercial failure of her latest feature film, *The Zodiac Killers* (1991), to dissolve her production company and to temporarily return to television.[33] Before directing such internationally acclaimed films as *Boat People* (1982) and *Song of the Exile* (1990), Hui had worked extensively for several television stations in Hong Kong (TVB and Radio Television Hong Kong) and was responsible for some of their best programs, including three episodes for the popular series *Below the Lion Rock*. In his article "The Television Work of Ann Hui," Shu Kei asserts that "when [Hui] was first employed by TVB, the station had largely taken over the functions of Cantonese cinema in the fifties and sixties: i.e. to provide mass entertainment."[34] He also reminds the reader that "many young filmmakers who worked in television between 1976-78—the 'Golden Age' of Hong Kong television—used the industry as a stepping stone to enter the big screen. Collectively they became a force to be reckoned with . . . to herald the 'Hong Kong New Wave,' a phenomenon which many people then considered pregnant with possibilities."[35] While Hong Kong film lovers mourn the drowning in commercialism of the hopes generated by the New Wave, it is again to television that Hui turned back to make innovative work. *The Prodigal's Return* (1992, 47 minutes) was produced by her "alma mater," Radio Television Hong Kong. A striking example of fictional documentary whose complex take on reality and masterfully evocative mise-en-scène could be appreciated even by a non-Chinese speaker who saw it without subtitles, the piece is thus the story of a "return" in more ways than one. For Hui, it is the return not only to television but also to a place of obsessive mourning, the memory of June 4, 1989. For her real/fictional protagonist, Taiwanese pop singer Hou De Jian—described by Hui as a "political dissident, writer, dandy of the two shores . . . , at once controversial and colorful"[36]—who had moved to Beijing and embraced the Democracy Movement, it is the story of his deportation back to Taiwan after his arrest on Tiananmen Square. Yet for him, no real "homecoming" is possible: Hou now lives in New Zealand, another displaced wanderer of the ever growing diaspora, suggesting that, since June 4, there is no place that a Chinese can rightly call "home."[37] Since the original events were not documented—they are "lost" and function as a historical void—Hui reconstructs Hou's detention, his relationship to his guards, the football matches watched together in the cold gray administrative buildings of mainland China, the transfer of the prisoner between Chinese and Taiwanese coast guards, the defiant gaze of the young man who stares back at his former captors and tells them—and the camera, and History, for at that moment he speaks in English—"I'll be back."

I'll be back. . . . Where? When? Who is getting back at whom? Which immense "repressed" is returning in this English phrase? It is no accident that one of Hui's chosen forms of expression when she directs feature films is melodrama, in which political impasses and historical upheavals are presented under the guise of emotional separation (between lovers or family members) and heartbreaks. Many of her films (the most successful in that respect being *Song of the Exile*) tell the story of an impossible return. Even the work of Zuni, Yau Ching, or Victor Huey contains moments in which erotic or emotional longing is used as a metaphor to evoke postmodern dislocation. Yet, if I may, I want to read in this "I'll be back" the possibility of another metaphor, which I would call "the return of the represented." It is no accident that, at this moment, Hui chooses to make her protagonist-subject speak *in English.* Indeed *The Prodigal's Return* was aimed at a local Hong Kong, and not an international, audience. Yet, *who* is Hou De Jian addressing, beyond the anonymous faces of his Chinese guards, beyond the receding shore of the mainland, beyond the Taiwanese authorities he defied by joining the movement of the Beijing youth, if not the West that had been complacently fabricating images of the inscrutable Orient, digesting reports of massacre and repression, consuming exotic tableaux of Chinese life? *I'll be back. . . .* From Beijing, Hong Kong, Taipei, or all the corners of the diaspora, I'll reclaim my own image. And, while cinema seems more appropriate to (re)establish a myth, video, through its versatility, appears the ideal tool for this reclaiming. In their diversity of format and strategies, the pieces discussed in this essay bypass the traditional dichotomy—is it art, is it television? For what they do is *systematically occupy a site* formerly occupied by (post)colonial discourse or agencies of repression. Hence a multifarious strategy—documentary, editing of archival footage, deconstruction of mainstream television, miniseries for mainstream television, fictional documentary, poetic essay, diary film, documentation of performance, avant-garde text, postmodern collage, agitprop pamphlets, historical reflection, visual poem—to insert, at every moment of the flow of images that surround us, at every articulation of the giant portrait of "China" manufactured by the Western media, an "insert," no matter how small, that says "I am watching *back.*"

One may object that this is an ethnocentrist point of view, that it is only through my not-so-innocent "curiosity" that I came in contact with these tapes, which were primarily destined for Chinese, and not Western, audiences. First, this is not entirely true. If one takes, for example, the series *Tiananmen Square*, one is struck by the care with which, in a situation of financial hardship, the members of the Structure, Wave, Youth, Cinema Experimental Group have designed and composed the subtitles (indeed the video format makes the subtitling operation cheaper, easier, and more accessible than on film). In their already quoted program notes the artists define their goal as

251

two-fold: "to truly communicate with the people who, like us, live in Beijing and on this land. For people in the outside world (*including Chinese people living permanently or temporarily overseas*), we hope to provide some information, *so they will understand our lives*" (italics mine). Furthermore, the reality of the contemporary audiovisual landscape, as well as the effects of domination of American and European media, shouldn't be dismissed. The images of "China" manufactured in the West are fed to Chinese (whether they are living in China or "in exile" in the West) as they are to Westerners. As discussed in several panels of the Network for the Propagation of Asian Cinema (NETPAC) conference, organized in November 1993 in Honolulu by the New Delhi film quarterly *Cinemaya*, Asians complain of not seeing enough films and videos by Asians. The mystifying representations of "Chineseness" produced in Western media are displacing Chinese spectators *in their own land* or in their own diasporic communities while contributing to maintaining the Orientalist gaze of Western audiences. From this point of view, one can say that, since all Asians undergo a contradictory process of (forced or not) Westernization in which media play a major part in producing Western culture, values, and lifestyle as universal objects of desire, they all are more or less "hyphenated," and that even the position of Chinese living in China is comparable to that of the Chinese American. The image of Fu Manchu, the Dragon Lady,[38] the asexual Asian man, the inscrutable and treacherous Oriental, as well as many more subtle misrepresentations of "Chineseness," are still dominant, producing in the Asian spectator what, in a 1990 article, I had pointed out as "very close to what Freud described as the *uncanny:* the image of someone who strangely resembles you, looks back at you, and . . . *it could be you, but it's not*; it's a caricature, producing a painful sense of displacement (since this uncanny image circulates more easily, has more currency than yours, doesn't it become more *real*? And where does that leave you?)."[39]

In an essay that discusses the complex reasons for which a film as blatantly Orientalist as Bertolucci's *The Last Emperor* is generally loved by Chinese audiences, Rey Chow concludes the necessity of "understanding Chinese modernity from the point of view of the Westernized Chinese subject/reader who is caught between the sinologist's 'gaze' and the 'images' of China that are sewn on the screen of international culture. Between the gaze and the image the Chinese experience of being spectators to *representations* of 'their' history by various apparatuses is being erased."[40] It is precisely against this erasure that these various video strategies assert themselves, and nowhere as acutely, maybe, as in Hong Kong. *Here's Looking at You, Kid* (1990, 8 minutes 45 seconds), created in collaboration by Ellen Pau, Yau Ching, and another Hong Kong artist Chi Fai Wong, articulates this process. Through montage of various examples of media representation of Chinese people, it displays the acute awareness that residents of Hong Kong have of being "trapped" between the Western gaze that turns them into exotic objects, their own alienated production of images, and the watchful eye of the Big Brother in Beijing—while being, paradoxically, one of the world's centers of film production. The sound track is a *karaoke* love song that celebrates the erotic and ambiguous elements at work in the gaze. Yet an image keeps coming back, obsessionally, again and again: that of a young street urchin followed by a British tourist shooting a travelogue in Hong Kong in the thirties. Until the kid turns around and *looks back at him.*

I had, while writing this text, a sense of *urgency* about the necessity of communicating information about artists that are making work *now*, often under difficult circumstances. In spite of the soothing words of the Chinese government, June 4 has accelerated history for all those interested in Chinese media.

This piece is the result of years of travel and research, which I was able to conduct with the help of many, both in the United States, France, and the three Chinas. In addition to the artists who lent their works and had extended conversations with me, and my "mentors" mentioned earlier, special thanks should be addressed to the following individuals: Claire Aguilar, Po-Chu AuYeung, Jane Balfour, Chris Berry, Elisabeth Cazer, Evans Chan, Terence Chang, Chen Kaige, Scarlet Cheng, Daryl Chin, Chiu Fu-sheng, Chu Tien-Wen, Peter Chow, David Chute, Abe Ferrar, Alan Franey, the late Renee Furst, Bill J. Gee, Sophie Gluck, Marlina Gonzales, Danièle Hibon, Minnie Hong, Hsu Feng, Vivian Huang, Marina Heung, Bono Lau, Li Cheuk-to, Wendy Lidell, Cheng-Sim Lim, Jill Lin, Professor H. K. Ma, Ian and Mira Macbeth, Gina Marchetti, Paul Mayeda Berges, Marco Müller, David Overbey, Jeannette Paulson, Peng Xiaolian, Jacques Picoux, Barbara Robinson, Catherine Sentis, Shan Dongbing, Shu Kei, Tan Dun, Stephen Teo, Trinh T. Minh-ha, Aruna Vasudev, Councillor Jeff Yao, John Woo, Wu Tian-ming, and my Asian students, Jo-Fei Chen, Ada Chu, Soo Kim, Angie Lee, Tamiko Murai, Meena Nanji, Tati Nguyen, Catherine Tse, and Liza Wong.

NOTES

[1] Chinese names traditionally start with the family name (usually one syllable, Xia or Su, for example), followed by the given name, which is often composed of two or several syllables (Xiaokang). Mainland China and Taiwan have different policies for the Western transcription of Chinese names (Mao Zedong versus Mao Tse-tung, for example), so given names in Mainland China are usually transcribed in one word (Xiaokang), while two words—which may or may not be hyphenated—will be used for Taiwanese names (Shau-di, Shu Lea). In Hong Kong people tend to have a Western version of their Chinese names (Ellen, Edward) and follow the Western order (given name first, surname second: Ellen Pau, Edward Lam). When they keep their Chinese name, they also keep the Chinese order (Yau Ching). An interesting case is that of Taiwanese artist Shu Lea Cheang. She kept her Chinese given name (Shu Lea) but, having lived in New York for more than fifteen years, has adopted the

Western order. Ming-Yuen S. Ma falls in the same category, and so does the Mainland artist Wen Yi Hou. Without exception, however, when the name of one of the artists mentioned is repeated, I have used their family name (Su, Wang, Pau, Lam, Cheang), no matter in which position it appeared in the initial mention of their full names.

[2] See Su Kaiming, *1840–1983: La Chine moderne— Histoire thématique* (Beijing, People's Republic of China: Editions du Nouveau Monde, 1987), 22.

[3] The following were episodes of the Opium War:

1781: The British East India Company sends its first big cargo of opium into China.
1800: Emperor Jia Qing forbids the sale of opium in China.
1838: Opium represents 57 percent of Chinese imports, totaling 40,000 chests of 60 to 72 kilo-

grams a year. The same year, the emperor orders the destruction of 20,000 chests of opium in Guangzhou.

June 1840 to August 1842: First Opium War with the United Kingdom.

1840: The British government decides to send gunboats to "open up" China's door by force.

1842: Treaty of Nanking (first of the "unequal treaties") with the United Kingdom. Cession of Hong Kong, opening of five trading ports (Shanghai, Guangzhou, Xiamen, Fuzhou, and Ningbo). A clause also imposes a unilateral most-favored-nation treatment. Su Kaiming writes: "The provisions of this treaty . . . marked the beginning of the transformation of China, until then an independent country, into a semicolonial state" (*La Chine moderne*, 28).

1844: More "unequal treaties": Treaty of Wang-hea with the United States, of Whampoa with France.

1856–60: Second Opium War. New "unequal treaties" (treaties of Tianjin) with the United Kingdom, France, Russia, the United States.

October 1860: Destruction of the Summer Palace by the French and British troops.

13 October 1860: The French and British armies enter Beijing.

Note: There is no such a thing as a "comprehensive" and "objective" history of China. To write this chapter, I used two books published by the Foreign Language Press/Editions du Nouveau Monde in Beijing: in addition to Su Kaiming's already mentioned book, I also consulted Bai Shouyi, ed., *An Outline History of China* (Beijing: Foreign Language Press, 1982).

4 Rey Chow, *Women and Chinese Modernity* (Minneapolis: University of Minnesota Press, 1991), 87.

5 "This was during the Russo-Japanese war . . . and . . . one day I saw a newsreel slide of a number of Chinese, one of them bound and the others standing around him. They were all sturdy fellows but appeared completely apathetic. According to the commentary, the one with his hands bound was a spy working for the Russians who was to be beheaded by the Japanese military as a warning to others, while the Chinese beside him had come to enjoy the spectacle.

"Before the term was over I had left for Tokyo, because this slide convinced me that medical science was not so important after all. The people of a weak and backward country, however strong and healthy they might be, could only serve to be made examples of or as witnesses of such futile spectacles; and it was not necessarily deplorable if many of them died

of illness. The most important thing, therefore, was to change their spirit; and since at that time I felt that literature was the best means to this end, I decided to promote a literary movement" (Lu Xun, preface to *Call to Arms,* trans. Yang Xianyi and Gladys Yang [Beijing: Foreign Language Press, 1981], ii-iii).

6 The "Fifth Generation" denotes the class that entered the Beijing Film Academy in 1978 and graduated in 1982. The best known are Chen Kaige (*The Yellow Earth, King of the Children, Farewell My Concubine*), Peng Xiaolin (*Three Women*), Tian Zhuangzhuang (*The Horse Thief, Li Lianying, the Imperial Eunuch, The Blue Kite*), and Zhang Yimou (*Red Sorghum, Ju Dou, Raise the Red Lantern*). Most of these directors had spent their teenage years in the countryside during the Cultural Revolution, so they were in their thirties when they graduated. "Fifth Generation" films, although often banned in China, have attracted major attention in the international arena.

7 Chen Kaige, interview with the author, Beijing, December 1990.

8 However, many Hong Kong residents, subjected to a forced bilingualism, are alienated in their use of language; many of them are now unable to read Chinese characters and use a form of pidgin English to understand Mandarin-speaking Chinese, for example. This is why Hong Kong films, shot in Cantonese, are always subtitled both in Chinese (Chinese characters are the same for all the Chinese dialects; only the pronunciation turns them into different languages) and English. Characteristically, most of the language used in Hong Kong video art (which, to survive, has to aim at some international art milieu) is English.

9 The first film Zhang Shichuan wanted to direct for Asia Motion Pictures was the adaptation of a stage play showing the ill effects of opium on a Chinese family, but he had to renounce this project because of the opposition of foreign importers of opium. See He Xiujun, "Histoire de la compagnie shanghaienne Mingxing et de son fondateur Zhang Shichuan," in *Le Cinéma chinois*, ed. Marie-Claire Quiquemelle and Jean-Loup Passek (Paris: Centre Pompidou, 1985), 45.

10 In the last few years, though, significant changes have taken place in the United States, thanks to the efforts of organizations such as Asian Cine Vision in New York and Visual Communications in Los Angeles, which promote Asian American media and organize festivals, retrospectives, and special events. The nature of Chinese American media has also changed, passing from a necessary "search for identity" and

BÉRÉNICE REYNAUD

recounting of "forgotten stories" to the articulation of an alternative cultural discourse somewhat ready to compete with the mainstream. That Hollywood itself is interested is a major sign of this change, and Wayne Wang's career is a good example of the complex dialectic of self-representation within or without the mainstream media. Wang's first feature, *Chan Is Missing,* became a cult film in both independent and Asian American circles—as Gus Van Sant's *Mala Noche* was a cult film in the independent and gay media network. This success interested the studios so much that Van Sant was given the opportunity to direct *Drugstore Cowboy.* Wang had to wait a bit longer before making a distribution deal with a major studio (Buena Vista) for *The Joy Luck Club.*

11 "Throughout his work, Derrida asks us to notice that *all* human beings are irreducibly displaced although, in a discourse that privileges the center, women alone have been diagnosed as such." So "the deconstructive discourse of man (like the phallocentric one) can declare its own displacement (as the phallocentric its placing) by taking the woman as object or figure" (Gayatri Chakravorty Spivak, "Displacement and the Discourse of Woman," in *Displacement: Derrida and After,* ed. M. Krupnick [Bloomington: Indiana University Press, 1983], 170, 173).

12 One usually keeps the "list of special thanks" at the end or the beginning of the text. Due to the collaborative, intercultural nature of my research, I thought it truly belonged to the body of the text itself.

13 Because of the unconventional relationship between image and sound in the first few minutes of *The Last Dreamers* (the interviewees are seen talking in their immediate surroundings while a title introduces them, but what they say is *not* heard), a Western venue sent back the tape to the distributor as "defective." One of the technicians of the Jeu de Paume thought that "there was something wrong with the sound" at the moment when one of the artists is shown painting, when the only noise heard is that of his brush on the canvas. A shorter version of the tape, deemed to conform to Western standards, exists, but without subtitles. However, we decided not to show it at the Jeu de Paume, for the real drama of *The Last Dreamers*—a struggle to find a voice within a new form of representation—needs time to unfold.

14 Sophie Laurent, Musée du Jeu de Paume, Paris, February 1993.

15 Zhang Xiz Ping's delirium is not subtitled in English in the tape. My student Catherine Tse helped me to come up with a partial translation: "Motherfucker! . . . Is it a man or a woman? God, can you hear me? . . . Hi, fucker, who am I? You listen to me. I'm telling all of you in this world: my last name is wrong. Motherfucker, where do I get my last name from? I'm telling all of you, I'm speaking. This is really painful. But what is it, I don't know. You motherfucker, I don't even know my last name." As I emphasized in a version of this essay given at the Sixteenth Asian University Film Conference (November 3–5, 1994), Zhang does not seem to be struggling with issues of sexual identity only, but with the more practical question of whether or not she should marry a foreigner (change her last name) to leave China.

16 Interview with Zhang Yuan, in the catalog of the Seventeenth Hong Kong International Film Festival, (Hong Kong: Urban Council, 1993), 115. (I am quoting the exact words of the English version of the interview printed in the catalog).

17 Production notes for *Tiananmen Square,* in the catalog of the Sixteenth Hong Kong International Film Festival (Hong Kong: Urban Council, 1992), 98. (I am quoting the exact words of the English version printed in the catalog.) *Tiananmen Square* was scheduled as part of the festival, but was withdrawn at the request of the Chinese authorities, after the catalog was printed. Through means that cannot be discussed here, I managed to screen four of the eight fifty-minute-tapes of the series.

18 Tian Zhuangzhuang's latest feature, *The Blue Kite* (1993), tells the story of a little boy who loses his father to the antirightist campaign of the late fifties, whose stepfather is killed by Red Guards, and whose mother is sent to reeducation camp during the Cultural Revolution.

19 The translation of the Chinese title is the one provided by the producers themselves.

20 Wang Shau-di, interview with the author, Taipei, December 1989.

21 The enactment of the Cable Television Law in July 1993 might have significantly changed the situation. See Philip Liu, "Cable TV Goes Legit," *Free China Review* (Kwang Hwa Publishing, Los Angeles and Taipei), November 1993, 32-37.

22 The four questions posed in the first two episodes of the series are "When did cities emerge in China?"; "What was recorded in the early writing systems?"; "Why were Mongols perceived as a race of speed?" (I am quoting the English translation provided by the

producers); and "What was the 'T'sung' [an engraved stone] used for?"

23 Another contradiction can be found in the existence of MTV clubs, mostly patronized by teenagers. Pirated, uncensored, and uncut videos (including foreign movies with or without nudity) can be rented and screened in small rooms by groups of people or couples.

24 Cheang used the footage she shot in Tiananmen Square in a five-channel video installation entitled *Making News/Making History—Live from Tiananmen Square*, originally commissioned by the 1989 American Film Institute Video Festival, and not discussed in this essay.

25 "No professional/amateur distinction operates to mystify Zuni's endeavor or to hinder involvement in its projects of collective creativity—even members of the executive board (like many Hong Kong artists) have daytime jobs. There is no assumption in Zuni that non-professional means uncommitted—one's life/work experience is something of value that one brings to the task of performance" (David Clarke, "Zuni Icosahedron in Context," unpublished paper).

26 Trinh T. Minh-ha, "Bold Omissions and Minute Depictions," in *When the Moon Waxes Red: Representation, Gender, and Cultural Politics* (New York and London: Routledge, 1991), 159; originally published in *Moving the Image: Independent Asian Pacific American Media Arts 1970–1990,* ed. Russel Leong (Los Angeles: Visual Communications, Southern California Asian American Studies Central, and UCLA Asian American Studies Center, 1991).

27 *Color Schemes* was initially presented as a multimedia installation including three monitors visible through the glass windows of three huge coin-operated washing machines, a long dining table, a neon sign flashing "Service and Self-Service," and a slide show of images of "Chinese laundries" throughout America. In some communities, religious organizations objected to the installation because of its use of images of the Last Supper. On the other hand, when the exhibition was on display at the Whitney Museum, the administration of the museum expressed concern about the requirement that the viewers insert quarters in the washing machines, because patrons would have already paid an admission to the gallery and shouldn't expect to be charged more. Cheang retained the idea of a "coin-operated installation" in her collaborative piece, *Those Fluttering Objects of Desire* (which, having only a tenuous link with Chinese identity, is not

discussed here): as in a peep show, the monitors would start only after a quarter was inserted in a slot, and then stop after a few minutes. The images offered to the viewers were eighteen different vignettes written and directed by women of various ethnicities and sexual preferences about female eroticism, interracial sex, lesbian love, and so on. When the images stopped, they were "blocked" not by a black screen, but by the images of male buttocks going up and down, as during missionary-type intercourse.

28 "The notion of the 'traditionalness' of the Asian communities has also been used as a reason for gay and lesbian Asians not to come out. However, from my decade of working with gay and lesbian Asians, the proportion of rejection and acceptance for those who do choose to come out to their families is not significantly different to those for white people. Yet whereas white homophobia is not interpreted to say anything about whiteness, there is a way in which Asian homophobia is assigned meaning. . . . I do feel . . . that the idea that the homophobia of an Asian is somehow 'worse' than that of a white person, or that it says something about Asianness, feeds into a racist discourse" (Richard Fung, "Center the Margins," in *Moving the Image,* ed. Leong, 66).

29 See Bret Hirsch, *Passion of the Cut Sleeve* (Berkeley: University of California Press, 1990).

30 Trinh T. Minh-ha, *Woman, Native, Other* (Bloomington: Indiana University Press, 1989), 123. This quote appears in the text of *Toc Storee*.

31 Repressive laws against homosexuality, directly inspired by British legislation, were actually not enforced. Homosexuality was eventually decriminalized out of a concern that, after 1997, Mainland authorities could use them to prosecute "dissidents."

32 Not surprisingly, Wen Yi Hou turns up as a "subject" in Trinh T. Minh-ha's already mentioned text, "Bold Omissions and Minute Depictions": "Perhaps vindicating and interrogating identity takes on a peculiarly active significance with displacement and migration. . . A familiar story of 'learning in America' is, for example, the one lived by artist Wen Yi Hou when she left Mainland China to further her education in the States: 'I was surprised that shortly after I started the program [at the University of California at San Diego], I was asked why my paintings were not traditional Chinese paintings. I was depressed. I did not have any value as a Chinese artist in their minds. . . . I am not a painter who has come to America to paint China. I am a painter from China who has come to

America to continue painting'" (Trinh T. Minh-ha, "Bold Omissions," 157, 160).

33 Since then Ann Hui has directed another feature film, *Summer Snow,* produced by Golden Harvest (one of Hong Kong's major studios) and shown at the Berlin Film Festival in February 1995.

34 Shu Kei, "The Television Work of Ann Hui," in *Changes in Hong Kong Society through Cinema,* catalog of the Twelfth Hong Kong International Film Festival (Hong Kong: Urban Council, 1988), 49.

35 Ibid., 52.

36 Ann Hui, quoted in the catalog of the Seventeenth Hong Kong International Film Festival (Hong Kong: Urban Council, 1993), 109.

37 Shu Kei—who, in addition to being a well-known critic, distributor and publicist, is also a filmmaker— deals with this issue in *Sunless Days* (an homage to Chris Marker's *Sans Soleil*), a piece commissioned by a Japanese television network to document the reactions to June 4 in Hong Kong. The film ends up as a melancholy reflection on the various aspects of the diaspora, from London to Australia to Canada and even Venice.

38 On "the Dragon Lady," see the tape by Deborah Gee, *Slaying the Dragon* (1988, 60 minutes). About other mystifying images of "the Oriental woman" in Western media, see Valerie Soe's *Picturing Oriental Girls: A [Re]Educational Videotape* (1992, 12 minutes).

39 Bérénice Reynaud, "Three Asian Films for New Cinematic Language," *Cinematograph* 4 (1990–91): 130–44.

40 Chow, *Woman and Chinese Modernity,* 29.

CHAPTER 18

TAKING AIM:
THE VIDEO TECHNOLOGY OF CULTURAL RESISTANCE

Monica Frota

TUNING THE INSTRUMENTS

A rifle is a practical idea
and an idea is a theoretical rifle.
A film is a theoretical rifle
and a rifle is a practical film.
~ JEAN-LUC GODARD

We are learning Brazilian culture to help ourselves hold on to our land, to protect ourselves. In the past, Kayapo have killed Brazilians and Brazilians have killed us in return. In that way, Kayapo almost disappeared. We almost lost our population. But now we no longer kill Brazilians with bullets or clubs. Instead we have learned Brazilian technologies or cultural ways. Look, this thing there [pointing toward the camera] is like a gun. This camera is like a weapon that we can use to protect ourselves.

~ MEGARON TXUCARRAMÃE, Kayapo leader

In envisioning films and videos and the technological apparatuses involved in the film-making experience as weapons,[1] both Jean-Luc Godard and the Kayapo leader Megaron Txucarramãe draw upon distinct and divergent experiences of media production. Despite the differences between their individual film- or video-making practices, they share at least one common feature that allows me to unite them across the borders of culture and language differences on the same page; namely, their understanding of filmmaking experience as political action.

Looking at the political efficacy of documentaries, five elements that define documentary practice in its complete form, from conception to screening—filmmakers, subjects, medium, products, and audiences—seem relevant. Studies have focused on the analysis of the binary relationships of filmmakers/subjects and products/

258

audiences. However, while these binaries have been analyzed extensively, not enough attention has been given to the element of the medium. Adherence to a generalized model based on the arbitrary isolation and binary association of these elements restricts our analysis of documentary practice, particularly the binary products/audience, because it presupposes the political efficacy of a documentary piece to be based solely on the existence of a final product and the product's relation with the audience. This emphasis does not do justice to documentary videomaking as political practice. An analysis of the complex set of interactive relations among all five elements of documentary practice promises to further our understanding of how documentary films and videos achieve or fail to achieve political efficacy. The medium necessarily contributes to determining the form and content of all stages of production, postproduction, and exhibition. I do not dismiss the notion that an image produced through any one medium is subject to being reproduced through another. Rather, I intend to call attention to the economic and practical aspects that define the politics of visual representation and its relationship with the medium involved.

FIGURE 1
Photograph by Monica Frota

FIGURE 2
Photograph by Monica Frota

I embarked on my own struggle toward a practical understanding of how films and videos operate politically in Brazil in 1985, when I entered into a collaboration with two friends, Renato Pereira and Luis Rios. The three of us formed a crew of anthropologists and independent filmmakers interested in making possible the use of videotape technology for, and by, segments of society that usually would not have access to the technological apparatus of audiovisual representation. Together we developed the Mekaron Opoi D'joi project,[2] through which we taught the Kayapo Indians of Brazil how to operate videotape technology.[3] Both Renato and Luis were anthropologists who became involved with video productions through their interests in the uses of videotape associated with anthropological practice. I, as an independent film- and

videomaker, was committed to exploring the uses of videotape technology as a means of transforming the existing power relations of visual representation and, in particular, of subverting the dominant and centralized control of the Brazilian broadcast system.[4]

The medium of videotape appeared to me as particularly well suited to these goals. Unlike film, videotape records not only images but also synchronous sound, and requires only one primary apparatus—a videotape camera with built-in microphone—to do so. The recorded videotape is then instantly ready for viewing. Conveniently, the primary apparatus of the video medium can be used not only to record, but also to play back videotapes on a monitor. These factors give videotape a comparative economic accessibility and immediacy, which allow those who are traditionally restricted to the status of subjects and audience members of films and videos to become active producers for and by themselves, thereby making video a mode of production practically and economically far more difficult to regulate than either television or film. In the 1980s in Brazil, videotape technology became a popular tool that generated many low-budget, community-centered media projects throughout the country. Such expressions of local populations and cultures facilitated popular resistance against the cultural homogenization that the broadcast system imposed. Some of these forays, particularly those developed by suburban neighborhood populations, proved their political efficacy by leading to the creation and establishment of local organizations to represent the community's interests to the Brazilian state and society as a whole.[5]

The Kayapo appropriation of videotape technology is the subject of the following pages, in which I intend to demonstrate how, by redefining who controls the means of production, indigenous media projects transform the existing power relations of image production and representation.[6] The Kayapo indigenous media experience indicates that the political efficacy of image production and representation is the result of a combination of forces that transform the traditional power relations involving filmmaker, subject, medium, product, and audience. I shall begin by addressing the concept of indigenous media in the light of the Navajo film project, the first project designed to teach an indigenous group the techniques of film production. I will then introduce the Kayapo indigenous media project. I argue that the Kayapo appropriation of video technology is not detached from the Kayapo's history of interaction with the larger society nor from their own cultural values. In discussing the Kayapo uses of videotape technology, I will describe an experience that involves behavior, conflict, determination, and struggle. I shall therefore define indigenous media production as a political project through which indigenous people effectively address their concerns and further their resistance against external domination.

THE NAVAJO FILM PROJECT

The first experiment relating to an indigenous people's use of film or video dates back to 1966, when Sol Worth and John Adair arrived at the Navajo reservation of Pine Springs, Arizona. Worth and Adair were interested in exploring the visual grammar that a "Navajo eye" would produce in the medium of film. When Worth and Adair first met with Navajo leader Sam Yazzie to negotiate their research project, Sam asked them, "Will making movies do the sheep any harm? Will making movies do the sheep good?" After Worth and Adair explained that making films would not affect the sheep, Sam asked them what would have been an obvious question to the Navajo, "Then why make movies?"

The sheep that were of such concern to Sam can be understood symbolically, for while Sam may not have been interested in the relevance of film for ethnographic research, he may have been wondering about the relevance of film for the Navajo themselves. Although Mekaron Opoi D'joi and the Navajo films resulting from the work of Adair and Worth are both projects that have enabled indigenous people to produce their own videos and films, they were distinct in their results. Before their contact with Worth and Adair, the Navajo never expressed any particular interest in producing their own films. Only when working with Worth and Adair on this "exploration in film communication and anthropology"[7] did the Navajo become involved in the production of films. The Mekaron Opoi D'joi project came about very differently.

The Navajo film project was the result of a sterile scientific experiment centering on the interests of its researchers. The project did not develop the potentialities of cultural and political resistance involved in forms of indigenous self-representation. Whether or not the project successfully served the interests of the researchers, it did not further the interests of the Navajos through film. Because the Navajo did not find film to be of any particular relevance to themselves, the project fell outside the most fundamental parameter that defines the existence of indigenous media experience.[8]

In comparison with the Navajo experiment, Mekaron Opoi D'joi was a collaborative experience between "us," the filmmaker-anthropologist outsiders to Kayapo culture, and "them," the members of the Kayapo, albeit with all the limitations that such an encounter presupposes. What made our project effective is that we did not try to adapt the Kayapo use of the camera to research needs. Rather, we attempted to adapt the camera to the Kayapo's cultural and political needs. The subjects of academic and theoretical discussions that arise from the Mekaron Opoi D'joi project are the result of our experience with the Kayapo rather than the motivation that had brought us to develop the project.

After conducting their research with the Navajo, Worth and Adair stated in their resulting book about the Navajo film project: "We can see that persons in different cultures approach the filming situation differently and make films that differ on several important parameters."[9] This leads me to ask whether a pattern or visual code can be discerned in the images shot by the Kayapo.

Significantly, although the Kayapo live in the middle of the forest and until recently lacked television contact with Brazilian society,[10] there are ways in which a "Kayapo visual aesthetic" would be largely influenced by a Western film-TV aesthetic. Like most Indians in Brazil, the Kayapo have become accustomed to the technical means of capturing images that modern society has developed. When members of the Kayapo villages go to larger cities they are exposed to television. Also, in the process of learning how to operate a video camera, the Kayapo were influenced by our own camera operation. This suggests the futility of trying to define a purely Kayapo visual grammar. On the other hand, it is useful to attempt to analyze the Kayapo's process of appropriating videotape technology and the resulting cultural and political implications; that attempt is the focus of this work's coda.

PRELUDE

The first direct experience of the Kayapo with the video camera was in 1985, through the Mekaron Opoi D'joi project. Nevertheless, the Kayapo, like many other Brazilian

Indian groups, especially those inhabiting the Xingu National Park,[11] had indirectly experienced both filmmaking and videomaking as documentary subjects for quite some time. Brazilian and international filmmakers and journalists had long filmed and video-taped the Kayapo.[12] As emblems of indigenous nationality, images of the Kayapo had become readily available merchandise in urban centers all over the world. Eighty per-cent or more of the images that Brazilian and international media have generated of Brazil's Indian populations have focused on the Xinguano Indian.[13]

In response to the commercial use of their images, the Metuktire began to restrict access of film and video crews to their villages, reducing the exploitation of their images substantially. Beginning in the late 1970s, any film or video production that intended to shoot the Metuktire had to negotiate charges for copyright with the reluc-tant and skeptical Indians. In contrast to their effective limitation of film and television crews' access to their villages, the Metuktire's ready acceptance of Brazilian television news crews during the episode of the Raft War indicates that in this instance the Metuktire intended to take advantage of the television broadcast system.[14]

Throughout the Raft War, the Metuktire mobilized Brazilian public opinion through their daily appearance on broadcast news. Scaring many through their portrayal of "bloodthirsty wild Indians" and appealing to far greater numbers supportive of the Indians and their cause, the Metuktire spurred the Brazilian public to action. Other factors contributed to creating widespread Brazilian sympathy for the Metuktire, among them the failure of the development projects implemented in the Amazon, which had not benefited society as a whole; an increase in public awareness of environmental issues and of the populations of the areas affected by developers; and the organization of political groups directly concerned with the Indians and supported by international envi-ronmental associations and human rights groups. Together, these pressures helped to prepare the way for Indian political movements of resistance. However, the Metuktire's canny manipulation of the Brazilian media was perhaps the key factor in their victory in the Raft War, and certainly the most germane to the Mekaron Opoi D'joi project.

Throughout the Raft War, Brazilian media focused its attention on the Metuktire, seizing on their bellicose ethos to portray them in images suggesting aggres-sion and horror.[15] As Metuktire leaders reported to us later, whenever news teams went to their village, the Metuktire demonstrated aggressive behavior and staged severe treat-ment of white "hostages." Performed for the television cameras, the Metuktire's ritual dramatization, complete with black war-painted bodies and war dances, demonstrated the Metuktire chiefs' awareness of the power and influence of the media, capturing the attention of Brazilian society much more powerfully than did their oral communications with government authorities.

Consequent to the Metuktire's manipulation of the news media, Brazilian newspapers printed many letters blaming the government for its role in bringing about the altercation. Associations of anthropologists, lawyers, students, and churches, as well as many private individuals, sent letters supporting the Metuktire. Politicians, architects, and members of organizations such as the Association for Environmental Protection and the National Association for Indian Support signed and sent to the president of Brazil a political manifesto supporting the Metuktire.

The impact of the Metuktire's performance on national and international audiences pushed the Brazilian government toward a solution that favored the Metuktire. The government agreed to accept Megaron, the young Metuktire leader who had represented the Metuktire in the mediations resolving the Raft War, as the first Indian to fill the position of director of the Xingu National Park. One year after these events, in June of 1985, my friends and I embarked on a trip to the Xingu National Park.

FIRST MOVEMENT

NEGOTIATING AN INDIGENOUS MEDIA EXPERIENCE

The idea of installing video equipment in Indian territory to enable a group of Indians to use the equipment was not new. In the mid-1970s, the administrator of the Xingu National Park, anthropologist Olimpio Serra, proposed to set up a video center and a mini–transmission station in the Upper Xingu. Contacts were made and some equipment was bought, but technical and bureaucratic obstacles impeded the project. The purchased equipment was never used, and after Serra's administration it became impossible to find out what FUNAI's office had done with it.[16]

When we made our first trip to the Xingu National Park we proposed to redevelop Serra's idea and to embark on a similar project. Following the suggestion of Megaron, the park's new administrator, we planned this trip as an experimental phase of the new project. We would circulate throughout the entire park in order to test the project's technical viability. We all agreed that this project would result from the joint efforts of the Indians and the three of us and that the costs would be divided. While we would provide equipment and sensitive material such as film stills and videotapes, they would provide transportation, gasoline supplies, and housing.

It soon became apparent that it would be impossible for us to divide our time evenly among the fifteen Indian groups who live scattered throughout the large park. It would be necessary to concentrate our work on one Indian group. We did not, however, exclude the possibility of later expanding the project to include other groups.

Simultaneously with our first trip to the Xingu park, the two Metuktire villages, which had been separated by the highway BR-080, were reuniting at long last. The Krumare and Ropni[17] groups chose a spot for their new village to the north of highway BR-080 in the Kapot area, which they had recovered through the Raft War. This place, which was still a makeshift camp when we first visited, became our headquarters when we returned to further develop the project in September 1985 and July-August 1987.

Our first problem was in making ourselves understood by the Metuktire. The obstacle was not so much the language itself as the history of past occurrences. To many Metuktire, film crews and reporters were trouble and not to be trusted. The Metuktire were skeptical of our assertion that we were not just one more crew seeking to commercialize their image. It was imperative that we position ourselves as different from the video crews with which they were familiar. Slowly, we won the trust of those individuals who had initially seen us as just another group of filmmakers in search of beautiful and exotic images.

We waited to record images until we had the approval of the chiefs of the group. In a meeting at the Men's House,[18] Megaron explained to the Metuktire chiefs why we were there. We initiated talks among ourselves, Megaron, and chiefs Raoni and Krumare only after the latter two had approved the project.

The Metuktire showed interest in recording the construction of the new village and suggested that this material be preserved for future generations. They began to look on the cameras as tools to help them in their intent to perpetuate *Mebênkokre kukràdzà*.[19] We were then able to place ourselves at their service. We recorded whatever they suggested: the construction of a new village, the clearing of land, hunts, and chants.

Not all the Metuktire had finished moving into the new village. A small group, including Kremoro, the oldest member of the entire Metuktire group, was still at the abandoned Jarina village. We went to this village and videotaped Kremoro sending a message to the new camp, explaining why he had not yet moved and when he planned to do so. Back at the camp, we decided to set up the first video viewing session that night, which we later recreated as a narrative, our own myth:

KAPOT'S NIGHT

It is night time in the Kapot. Our footsteps can be heard restlessly crossing the village square. We are living among the Metuktire, to the north of the Xingu National Park, overhearing scraps of conversation that leak out of the Men's House, and noises indicating that the final domestic chores of the day are still underway, the village oblivious to our presence. Camp fires spring up all around, lighting up one more night. We stop near the Men's House, the cameraman shifts the videocassette into position on an improvised stand, somebody turns on the generator, and in an instant there is one more light in the Kapot village. Women and children leave their huts, the children squeezing in ahead of the others, the men already approaching, dragging stools and mats. On the screen: the image and words that Kremoro, the oldest Metuktire chief, sent from the abandoned village.[20]

The viewing of Kremoro's message and of the scenes shot at the Jarina village caused a commotion, particularly for the Indians who had just moved from Jarina to the camp. After this night, the Metuktire took it on themselves to organize the video viewing sessions.[21]

Another crucial moment occurred when Megaron asked us to screen for the village the videotape of the news broadcasts that the Brazilian networks aired during the Raft War. The Metuktire, particularly males of the *mekrare* age-set,[22] enthusiastically watched the episodes in which they played "the wild Indian" for the television cam-

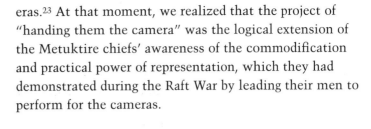

FIGURE 3
Photograph by Monica Frota

eras.[23] At that moment, we realized that the project of "handing them the camera" was the logical extension of the Metuktire chiefs' awareness of the commodification and practical power of representation, which they had demonstrated during the Raft War by leading their men to perform for the cameras.

FIRST INTERMEZZO

At the end of July 1985 we returned to Rio and spent ten weeks researching Kayapo history and ethnographic literature on the Kayapo. We found that the ethnographic works developed by researchers who lived among the Kayapo generally represent the Kayapo as "a revolving hierarchy in which dominance is exerted by age-grades of senior men and women over the younger age strata of Kayapo society."[24] In Kayapo society, dominance also depends on mastery of Kayapo culture. However, Kayapo interaction with Brazilian society and the knowledge appropriated

FIGURE 4
Photograph by Monica Frota

from this interaction escapes the traditional sphere of the elders' domain. Contemporary Kayapo social and political organization is largely influenced by the historical process of interaction with the Brazilian state.

We decided that before we could prepare a written description of our project we needed to return to the park. On this second trip we intended to deepen our relationship with the Metuktire and, as an aid in our search for financial support for the project's continuation, to make a short video in which the Metuktire themselves could address their interest in the development of the project.

SECOND MOVEMENT

In September of 1985 we returned to the Kapot village. Our relationship with the members of the village became more consistent. Small gestures marked our progress. We began lending our camera and videotape recorder to the village's inhabitants. Soon the chiefs designated a young man to learn how to use the equipment. Other young men came by themselves. One of them, Kiambiety, was so good at using the camera that in a short time he was moving around freely, followed by children, as he recorded the village's daily activities.

We began to find solutions to some of our initial concerns. As to the feasibility of installing videotape equipment at the Indian outpost, we now had no doubts. The equipment withstood the Xinguano wear and tear. The village's inhabitants learned to keep equipment in working order through simple operations like cleaning the videotape recorder's heads, while they were able to obtain more sophisticated maintenance services on their trips to Brasilia.[25]

Video viewing sessions became a social event. What we recorded was screened almost daily. The screening sessions were shifted from the central plaza to the Men's House. About three hundred Indians would gather to watch a program, including scenes depicting their own lives, as well as films about other Indian nations and scenes showing the lives of "white men" in the cities, a request made by the Metuktire during our first trip.[26]

During this second trip we felt that the Metuktire were already actively participating in the project. Daily, they operated the camera, decided what was to be shot, organized the video screenings, and, in an especially strong testimonial to the strength of their commitment, shared the ever increasing expenses involved in the project. The Metuktire regularly supplied gasoline for traveling within the park, recharged the video camera's batteries, and powered the electric generator for the video viewing sessions. Metuktire men brought to our house wild game and fish from their hunting and fishing expeditions. Women brought us potatoes and fruits. I was struck by their care for our well-being, particularly because an ongoing malaria crisis had sapped the strength of the village and made food scarce.

THE CAMERA AS A POTENTIAL GUN

It was during the malaria crisis that the Metuktire first recognized the political potential of the use of the video camera. Raoni was in radio communication with the authorities in Brasilia, seeking medical care for his people. Although the authorities had promised their support, they had not sent help. In the meantime, a child died of malaria and the people of the village became extremely upset.

Raoni decided that the video camera could be used as a weapon to defend them. He asked Renato and me to make sure that images relating to the malaria crisis were shot. He said:

> We must shoot everything that is happening now with the Metuktire. Before contact with the "whites" we did not have any disease. Now we have malaria, flu, everything, and the government does not send us the doctors and medicine that we need. They are responsible for what is happening here. If somebody else dies here, I will go to Brasilia and show them what they are doing to us. I will show it to everyone in the city. This camera is a weapon. (Raoni, Kayapo chief, personal conversation, 1985)

Raoni understood that the camera could generate a visual document that would demonstrate and denounce the negligence of the authorities. He intended to show the tapes in Brasilia, in order to engage sympathy and support from segments of the national and international communities. To make our camera instruction culturally relevant to the Metuktire, we decided to incorporate the analogy of the camera as a weapon into our pedagogical approach. We called the focus ring of the camera its "sight" and we taught the Metuktire to aim the camera before shooting as if they were aiming their guns. Good hunters they were, and great cameramen they became.

Expanding the Borders of the Project

On the same trip we proposed to the Metuktire that the Mekaron Opoi D'joi project should be expanded to include other Kayapo villages. The shared language, culture, and similar problems of the Kayapo and their dispersal over a wide but geographically continuous area led them to search for ways to unite in their resistance to the ever encroaching dominant society. Our observation of their use of radio to communicate with other Kayapo villages suggested to us that the video camera could complement the radio.

By radio, Megaron consulted the leaders of the Gorotire and A'ukre villages as to the possibility of our visiting these villages, and described the work we had been doing.[27] In the Kapot village, news of our forthcoming trip sparked a series of requests that we record messages for the villagers' far-off relatives. Kiambiety, the young man whose facility with the camera had led the chiefs to designate him as a cameraman, became responsible for the taping of all messages sent by the Metuktire group to Gorotire and A'ukre villages.

With Megaron we set out to Gorotire village. For this trip, Megaron cashed his paycheck from FUNAI to rent the airplane we used to travel between Kayapo villages. We spent two weeks with the Gorotire and the A'ukre villagers in Kayapo Indian Park. The scenario in Gorotire is very different from the one in Kapot. I noticed differences even before the airplane landed. The aerial view of Gorotire village immediately reminded me of a typical small Brazilian town in the middle of the jungle. Unlike a traditionally disposed Kayapo village, Gorotire's houses are not arranged in a circle.[28] At first it was difficult for me to make out the location of the Indian outpost, such were the similarities between the Indians' houses and FUNAI's office. Despite the noncircular geography of the village, the Gorotire had managed to rebuild a Men's House in a favorable position on the main "street," indicating Gorotire's resistance to the Brazilian "urban planning" imposed upon them by the Indian Protection Service (which was later replaced by FUNAI).

Immediately upon our arrival in Gorotire, we set up a video viewing session, the first of its kind in this village's history. The video screening session was busy. Literally all the Indians elbowed their way into the Men's House, which, obviously, was not built for such an occasion! We screened Raoni's message, which addressed problems common to all Kayapo groups, and discussed strategic matters. The emphasis on politics was the hallmark of messages recorded by the chiefs throughout the project. In his message to Gorotire village, Raoni first gave a report on the meetings in which he had participated in Brasilia. Unfolding a map of the Kayapo lands, Raoni articulated his plan to unify all Kayapo lands in one unique country:

> Long ago, before we were pacified, we would run in the forest by ourselves. But now, since we made peace with the whites, we came out to settle in this place from which I am speaking this to you. The Brazilians are always

encroaching on us and they hate us. You must know this. This is our new place in the Xingu. This (a map that he unfolds) is what a big chief of the whites gave to me. It is a picture of our old country. Our good land, I am going to tell you about it. Here is the Xingu River. This is where we are now. Here, the land is empty and these rivers here are also empty. Through this trail here, we can connect the park and Mekranoty's land, so that when our people visit each other, they do not have to see the whites. We need to keep the whites out of our way. We need to connect all our different lands and make just one big country again. So now that you can all see very well, very plainly, where we are, all you chiefs should support us. I am speaking to you at a distance by means of this videotape machine. Even though we are not together, we can communicate and support one another. (Raoni, Kayapo chief, message recorded on video to the Kayapo from Gorotire and A'ukre villages, 1985)

The attention Raoni's message aroused led us to examine the role that videotape could play as an information outlet in the future.[29]

The next day we discussed forming a video circuit between Kayapo villages with Payakan, a young man who was a leader of A'ukre and head of the Gorotire outpost.[30] Megaron and Payakan talked with Totoi and Kanho'm, two Gorotire chiefs, who gave their approval to the project and asked us to record their messages answering Raoni:

All of us here at Gorotire are very happy with this camera. We want to use it to record our dances, and our speeches. We are all happy with the idea that we can send messages to each other. We can send them also to the Brazilians. We can talk to the outside world about the bad Brazilians. We don't want to have raids or go to war, beat each other up with clubs or any of that stuff. The possibility of all the chiefs of our different communities talking to one another is good. Talking about the bad Brazilians or the evil Brazilians and what they are doing is good. (Kanho'm, Kayapo chief, message recorded on video to Raoni, 1985)

Accompanied by Payakan and Megaron, we flew on Gorotire's airplane to the A'ukre village. The showing of recorded scenes with the Metuktire and Gorotire led the men and women of A'ukre village to reschedule a celebration for an earlier date than had been planned originally, so that we could record the evolution of a dance and show it to the other villages.

When we returned to the Gorotire village, Payakan described the work and objectives we proposed to the warriors at a meeting in the Men's House. In our final discussions it was agreed that the Gorotire would acquire their own videotape recording unit and would collaborate with us on future trips to Kayapo villages at the Kayapo Indian Park and Mekranoty Reservation.[31] Depending on the financial support the project obtained, we would stay with the Gorotire for a set period to teach a group of Gorotire Indians how to use the equipment.

Unfortunately, the limit to our funds obliged us to return to Rio de Janeiro without having been able to take the material recorded at Gorotire and A'ukre villages to Kapot, which would only happen two years later, in 1987, on our third trip to the Kayapo's lands.

Since our departure in 1985, the Metuktire have tried to obtain their own equipment, which the Gorotire, in better economic standing, were able to do just a few months after we left. Meanwhile, we were often invited back to the village to carry on with the work. However, as we had not succeeded in raising the funds to provide video recording and screening equipment to the Kapot village, we felt that such a trip would not be productive. Although the project had become well known, no Brazilian foundation would support it. Because it was unique, the Mekaron Opoi D'joi project did not meet the guidelines of any of the few existing foundations in Brazil.

In fact, the Mekaron Opoi D'joi project still triggered predictable questions, such as: why give the Indians one more industrialized benefit? The tendentious reasoning behind this sort of question suggested—and suggests—that the relationship between whites and Indians is that of patron and the patronized, and that "we" (that is, "whites") are the guardians of "their" (Indians') future. The answer to this question is another question: Who are we to keep technology from them? In our society it is all too commonplace to see "primitive cultures" as a set of survival skills and traditional customs incapable of articulating with current history.

My next encounter with the Kayapo, on 11 March 1986, delighted me. Having breakfast at home in Rio de Janeiro I found the Kayapo on the first page of *Jornal do Brasil*.[32] Using the camera belonging to the Gorotire village, the Metuktire Indians had recorded the siege they had laid at the official residence of the Brazilian president, the Planalto Palace, in which they successfully demanded the removal of the FUNAI president, Apoena Meirelles. On this occasion Megaron said: "The Minister guaranteed he would dismiss FUNAI's president. We recorded this on the videotape, therefore, this time he cannot back down on his words."[33]

The apparent incongruity of a "high-tech exotic other" holding a video camera guaranteed the Kayapo space in Brazilian newspapers and direct access to the Brazilian public. Through contact with the national society the Kayapo had already traded their clubs for guns. Now they were appropriating the camera as a new weapon, while continuing to perpetuate their ethos as warriors.

After the Kayapo's successful political demonstration in Brasilia, it became clear to us that the Mekaron Opoi D'joi project was now fully in Kayapo hands and that the Kayapo had an understanding of the power relations that forms of representation necessarily involve. However, Metuktire's dependency on our and Gorotire's equipment was a problem. The Metuktire needed to have a camera of their own. In the beginning of 1987, as payment owed to them by a British television crew, the Metuktire asked for and received a complete videotape recording unit.[34] Immediately after the British crew had left their village, the Metuktire asked us to return to their village to continue our work. On this occasion Megaron enthusiastically said: "You must come back now, as this time we have our own camera. Now we are in business."

THIRD MOVEMENT

Our third trip to the Kayapo lands took place at the beginning of the dry season in the Xingu, a mild time, good for traveling by land and by river. The Metuktire had finished building their new village. Because they now had their own video equipment, we could train the young warriors more effectively than ever before.

This time I gave the Metuktire at the Kapot village some prints of photographs that I had taken on previous trips. We also brought copies of all the video footage that was produced throughout the project. The whole village enjoyed watching the material we brought from these previous trips. For the first time they saw their relatives on a video screen. The screening of the A'ukre village dances stimulated the Metuktire to perform old dances they had not done for a long time. As both Kremoro and Megaron had explained to us on our first trip,[35] there were now enough members of the large Metuktire group that they could perform rituals they had not been able to carry out when they had been split in two villages. The elders then decided to demonstrate the traditional dances they used to perform in preparation for raids against other Kayapo groups, in the days before they had ceased such attacks.

It was during this third trip that we visited the Kubenkokre village at Mekranoty Reservation. This time Kiambiety came with us. The Metuktire's enthusiasm during the recording of their messages was stronger than ever. At Kubenkokre village, we explained the project's nature and evolution to chief Bepkum and secured his support to set up the first video screening session. After watching their Metuktire relatives perform many old dances on video, the Mekranoty decided to perform a series of dances for the cameras to record.

Kiambiety took this opportunity to start teaching Nambre, another young man, what he had learned from us about operating the camera. Soon they were working together as a video crew. Knowing about the close kinship ties between the people of Kapot and Kubenkokre villages, Kiambiety passed the word that they might record messages for Kapot village. The villagers directly addressed their messages to relatives by name or reference to their kinship ties, sometimes presenting a long genealogy in the message. The tone of their messages was familiar, expressing the close relationship that exists among people of these two villages. They reaffirmed their alliances and asked for the exchange of gifts. They also recalled how they had fought in the past and stressed how happy they were to be able to talk to each other:

> Poin, Poinbá, I am sending you this message by the videotape recorder. We cannot see each other. Why have we split up? My dear, I behaved hatefully. I don't want to say harsh words to you. I am telling you that I am sorry for what

happened. This is what I want to tell you and that is all of my message. (Koko-ur, message recorded on video to her sister, 1987)

When we got back to Kapot I decided to spend more time with women. One question struck me: Why didn't women get more involved in the project and become camera operators? Women's participation in the project was restricted to two areas: they had been present in the audience during the video screening sessions, and they had messages to other Kayapo villages recorded by Kiambiety and other camera-men. Neither Kiambiety nor the others who had learned how to operate the equipment had taken the initiative to record women's activities. As young men they were expected to spend their time in the Men's House or in male activities such as hunting and fish-ing. As a result, women's matters were not being represented on video, and it concerned me that they were not able to record anything on their own. As a video-wielding female and the only woman on our team, I thought of myself as a potential model for Kayapo women. I took responsibility for trying to encourage the Kayapo women to participate in the project more directly.

Language was a problem. The Metuktire did not have a systematic prac-tice of learning Portuguese. Other than the young men who had training as health moni-tors, mechanics, shortwave radio operators, pilots, or other occupations involving manu-factured goods, few Metuktire, unless they had spent time in a city for medical treatment, knew Portuguese.

My first attempt to engage with the Kayapo women was through Vanessa Lea, a British anthropologist who had recently completed her doctoral disserta-tion on Kayapo society and the notion of wealth—*nekret*—and its transmission. Lea agreed to translate discussions between myself and Biri-Biri, an elder female chief. When I asked Biri what she thought about the young men's learning of videotape technology, Biri's first reaction was to ask Lea what she, Biri, should answer. A review of the inter-view reveals a kind of game between Lea and Biri. While Lea tried to obtain information without influencing Biri's answers, Biri evaded questions relating directly to the project. Lea's analysis of the complementary roles between men and women sheds light on Biri's apparent and uncommon "lack of cooperation." Unlike other anthropologists who had worked with the Kayapo, Lea describes the spatial organization of the village not as a peripheral ring regulated by male powers but as a "circular totality composed by 'hous-es,' as it were links of a chain":

> The "houses" which constitute the circle converge to the center, and simul-taneously, the role of women in Kayapo society is related to its internal dom-ination. The men's house faces the exterior, towards and beyond the circle, and they are the ones in charge of the external relations of the village. . . . Women guarantee the continuity of the "houses," delivering the new charac-ters that will enact the roles that identify the "house." Men take care of the

chain that links or separates the ones inside with the ones outside [Kayapo society].[36]

In keeping with this organization, our project, a link between the village and the outside world, belonged exclusively to the male sphere, and so fell outside Biri's province.

Disappointed with the results of my first attempt to get women involved in the project, I was happy to find a Kayapo woman, Panhô, who had learned some Portuguese when she had gone to São Paulo to seek medical care. She and I became good friends. Panhô gave me a bridge to the women's world. Through Panhô, I was invited to participate in some of the women's activities, such as gardening and body painting. But whenever I tried to hand the camera to the women, they treated it like a plaything. The women played with the camera as a child would with a toy. They liked looking at each other through the viewfinder, playing with the focus ring and joking about the way they looked out of focus. They paid no attention to my attempts to pass on to them the simple mechanics of shooting. They just were not interested in operating the equipment by themselves. They did, however, ask me to shoot them in the garden. They also made sure that I shot them painting themselves and their children. The women enjoyed seeing these images at the video screening sessions, but accepted that whatever came from the outside, which included modern commodities appropriated by the Kayapo (for example, the generator and the shortwave radio), was not their concern. Hence, the video equipment was for them part of the male sphere, which they incorporated into their activities only indirectly.

Because of my experiences with the Kayapo women, I more clearly understood why I was accepted into the men's society and activities readily, compared with Lea, who had told me how difficult it was for her to get invited to participate in men's activities such as hunts or fishing journeys. While I felt invited to participate whenever the men undertook such activities, the invitation was not so much for me as for the camera; I was simply allowed to accompany it. The camera's interface between the Kayapo men and myself positioned me as an androgynous character, a woman with a tool belonging to the male sphere. Following are my further thoughts on the politics involving the operation of the camera within Kayapo society.

CHIEFS (CLUBS), LEADERS (GUNS), AND OPERATORS (CAMERAS); OR, WHO HOLDS THE CAMERA, ANYWAY?

Times have changed, and the leaders have to change with them or they will no longer be leaders. ~ PROCONSUL, *Star Trek: The Next Generation*

Before we were pacified, we just knew our own knowledge, our own culture. Now that we have made peace with the whites, we are coming to know their culture, and many, many things of their culture. Let Kayapo learn white's culture. ~ MEGARON TXUCARRAMÃE, Kayapo leader, interview recorded on video, 1987

MONICA FROTA

Following their contact with the national society, the Kayapo needed leaders to act as intermediaries in their negotiations with Brazilians. Contact challenged the traditional power structures of the Kayapo. To increase their autonomy and to resist dependence on Brazilian government, the Kayapo had to create two new categories of men: leaders and operators.

Kayapo leaders have different roles from Kayapo chiefs, or *beniadjuòrò*.[37] In Kayapo society, a chief is a man who has the prerogative to lead the *ben* chant, which is performed during one of their most important rituals. Chiefs have followers and make decisions at the village level. Kayapo leaders do not lead the *ben* chant. Their circumference of power is external to the village. Leaders are spokesmen because they learned Portuguese and can serve as intermediaries between Kayapo and Brazilian society. A leader usually is of the *mekrare* age-set. In this way, a Kayapo leader, like every other Kayapo, is inscribed in the hierarchical age-set structure of Kayapo society, which defines his relations with elders. However, as he is the person who first has access to important information concerning the whole group, he is in a position to make decisions concerning the group in negotiations with Brazilians. Furthermore, leaders also have an income from the FUNAI and, in some cases, control over the income of the community.

The other category of men created by contact I call, for want of a better term, "operators." The operator is not as important as the leader, but both share some characteristics, such as an ability to speak and write Portuguese and a greater frequency of interactions with Brazilians. The operators are a group of men who were trained as health monitors, mechanics, shortwave radio operators, pilots, and workers in other jobs involving manufactured goods. These men are younger than the leaders. Usually they are part of the *menononure* or *mekrare* age-sets.

Operators occasionally go to the city to attend training classes, a constant source of excitement for those who travel and of jealousy for those who stay home. Sometimes operators have a personal income, as in the case of the Indian post's "chief," who is in charge of the daily radio communication with the other villages in the area and with FUNAI's office in Brasilia. The person who runs the Indian post is called *chefe*, which is the Portuguese word for chief. He is called this as a consequence of his power over the circulation of information and his responsibility in allocating the basic goods that come from the city, like gasoline and medicines.

The operators and leaders fulfill those needs of the community that exist as a result of interaction with the national society. Therefore, despite the limits on their power, operators have prestige within the community. The most important characteristic shared by operators and leaders is their political role as defenders of the Kayapo's autonomy.

I am always struck by how well the Kayapo, who have a profound sense of pride, have managed their relations with the external world. They recognize the importance of learning "things of the whites" as a way of maintaining their autonomy from the national society. At the same time, they see that modern goods could threaten

Mebênkokre kukràdzà. In fact, the Kayapo are deeply aware that maintaining their Indian identity is effective self-protection. At the Men's House, chiefs and elders gave many speeches criticizing young people not only for being too exposed to "the ways of the whites," but also for "not caring enough about *Mebênkokre kukràdzà.*" In keeping with this concern, the Kayapo are very selective as to which new "tools" they allow into their villages. Young leaders like Megaron have an important role in this process, as we found when we first negotiated our project with the Kayapo.

It is noteworthy that the decision as to who holds the camera varies among villages. In the village of the Metuktire, we made all initial negotiations relating to the project with Megaron and the group's chiefs. Megaron and the chiefs selected one young man, Katoptire, to learn about the camera. Katoptire is the youngest son of Kremoro, a former chief of the Metuktire. Kiambiety accompanied Katoptire. Kiambiety was much more interested in the camera classes than Katoptire. He listened closely to my explanations about how to clean the equipment and charge the batteries, details that are important but boring to learn and to practice. For a brief time Renato and I thought that the extreme interest of Kiambiety, in contrast to the lack of dedication of Katoptire, would somehow generate embarrassment. Kiambiety's father was not from the Metuktire group, but had moved into the Kapot village as a result of a dispute in his village of origin. This only increased my concern. Renato and I decided to talk with the chiefs to explain how important it was that the people involved enjoy what they were doing. Raoni simply said: "Fine. You teach whoever is interested in learning." Kiambiety, through his effort and dedication, became the best camera operator of Kapot village.

During our third trip to Kapot, after the village had obtained its own camera through Granada Television, we faced additional problems. A *mekrare,* the chief operator of the Indian post, clearly was trying to jeopardize the video screening sessions and the project by controlling our access to the generator. We had brought our own generator, but it frequently broke down. While this man told us that he also wanted to participate in the classes, he did not have time to dedicate to them. It was impossible for him to continue his activities as operator of the Indian post and participate in the project. As he became more and more jealous we tried to avoid him, which only increased his hostility toward us and the project. We responded to this situation by getting the chiefs on our side. Whenever he tried to jeopardize the project, we simply reminded him that the chiefs were counting on us. However, we were afraid Kiambiety would have problems after we left. This man suggested that the video camera should be kept at his house in the Indian post, an idea we opposed. Aware of the instability of Kiambiety's political position, we suggested to the chiefs that the equipment be kept in the schoolhouse, a politically neutral location. The chiefs accepted our suggestion.

During our visit, a group of six mineral prospectors looking for gold invaded Kapot, Kayapo territory to the north of the Kapot village. Megaron managed the situation with great diplomacy. He and several Metuktire warriors went to Kapot and captured the prospectors' airplane, preventing them from entering or leaving the area. He then called the Brazilian Federal Policy Force to take over the situation.

There was a lot of tension during these events. Some Metuktire men wanted to march to Kapot. Megaron's goal was to control the invasion while avoiding a direct confrontation, for which men in the village criticized him. While his strategy was clear and well planned, its success was not guaranteed. Megaron decided that the camera should document whatever happened, so that if anything went wrong, they would have a document that they could use in the future.[38] As Megaron said on this occasion:

> This camera is like a weapon that we can use to protect ourselves. Now we are communicating with Brazilians instead of fighting Brazilians. Through this camera we can send messages, our words to the cities. Our words in our defense. (Megaron Txuarramãe, Kayapo leader, interview recorded on video, 1987)

We decided to invite the older *mekrare* who was trying to jeopardize the video project to interview participants in the conflict with the prospectors. I felt this was an appropriate political decision for two reasons. First, an older man was needed to address the questions and, second, by bringing him a little closer to us and to Kiambiety, we might neutralize this man's intention to block the project. The strategy worked, temporarily.

Two years later, an anthropologist went to this village with a video camera he intended to donate. Knowing that Kiambiety had problems in gaining access to the equipment and knowing that Kiambiety was excellent at his work, the anthropologist mistakenly suggested, in a meeting at the Men's House, that the camera be kept in Kiambiety's house. The anthropologist's "solution," however, only aggravated what was already a tension-fraught situation for Kiambiety. The operator of the Indian post did not lose his chance to shame Kiambiety in public, leading Kiambiety to move out of the village without the camera.

An explanation for the conflict between the Indian outpost's operator and Kiambiety lies within the hierarchical organization of Kayapo society. The two men involved were both *mekrare*. But Kiambiety had become a *mekrare* much more recently than the other man. This put Kiambiety in a weak position in relation to him. Moreover, as one source of prestige is interaction with the outside world, the position of the camera operator brings prestige. The camera operator, when in the city, has been repeatedly photographed by the Brazilian and international press. Appearances in newspapers, magazines, and on television are not uncommon for Kayapo chiefs (*beniadjuòrós*) and leaders. Except for the chiefs and leaders, the Kayapo are presented to our society as a group, not as individuals, and rarely on the front covers of major magazines and newspapers. Because his responsibilities did not include speaking in the name of the community, Kiambiety's political power was not strong. That the press had extensively photographed him aggravated the jealousy existing within the village. The hierarchical structure of the age-sets was at odds with Kiambiety's excessive prestige.

Furthermore, in this case the camera can be understood as a foreign object appropriated *by* the community, *for* the community. At the end of the day, health operators leave their instruments in the pharmacy. The radio of the Indian post is located at another site, not in the operator's house. By placing a manufactured object in the house, it is understood that the object is a personal possession. Because the camera was given to the entire community, Kiambiety was not supposed to keep it in his house.

Payakan, from A'ukre village, was the chief operator of the Indian post in Gorotire village and an important leader in this village. Immediately after our trip to Gorotire village he bought his own camera and kept it with him in his house where he held private screenings of his footage. In Gorotire village, the camera was considered personal property rather than community property. Why is it that the video camera is taken as personal property in some villages and as community property in Kapot? To answer this question we need to examine the economy of these villages. Because of their contracts with mineral prospectors and lumber companies, Gorotire villages have substantial income. Conversely, Metuktire's only source of income is generated through the raft used to ferry cars across a river. This income is small, yet it is supposed to support the needs of all fifteen villages of a variety of Indian groups who live in the park. Therefore, Metuktire's economy can be characterized as an economy of subsistence, in contrast to Gorotire's surplus economy. In these villages characterized by a surplus economy, it is easy for some individuals with personal income to buy their own camera, which is virtually impossible for the people from Kapot.

Holding a camera always involves a power relation. Ethnographic and documentary filmmakers tend to acknowledge the power relations involved in filming other people. This raises both political and ethical issues relating to ethnographic filmmakers and subjects. Although in our project those who came to control the camera and those who were their subjects were from the same social group, the power of the camera is still an issue.

In a recent conversation with Megaron, he expressed his intention to allocate funds to buy an editing system that the Kayapo can use in Brasilia. This leads me to believe that the Kayapo are taking the final step in their appropriation of videotape technology. The proposed editing system in Brasilia would increase the Kayapo's access to editing facilities and, for this very reason, it would strategically remove the project from the editing installations in São Paulo. Moreover, I believe that the increase in access to editing facilities would lead to the Kayapo's circulation of edited tapes throughout their communities, a practice that was very effective during the Mekaron Opoi D'joi project and has been abandoned under the auspices of the Kayapo Video Project. Furthermore, the location of a Kayapo video center in Brasilia would strengthen the Kayapo's use of video to document their meetings and negotiations with the Brazilian government. Finally, the editing center Megaron proposes would give the Kayapo autonomy from any external force of control in their video production. Most recently Megaron informed me that the Kayapo videomakers had just created their own association, Ipre-re.[39] A threefold project, Ipre-re was created to guarantee Kayapo videomakers access to video cameras and editing facilities, to reestablish the exchange of videotapes among their villages, and to provide universities and other institutions outside their own community with a video databank of images produced by them. In support of the last objective, Megaron argues that many of the existing films and videos in which the Kayapo appear are not representative of how they see themselves and what they consider to be culturally relevant about their society.[40]

Despite the fact that the realization of the project still depends on financial allocations from foreign foundations, the Kayapo are displaying their will toward autonomy. The Kayapo are continuing to take control over the ways in which their society is represented, as well as technical and practical control of the apparatuses their use of the video medium requires. This tension between dependence and autonomy is typical of a struggle within Kayapo society that has been a constant since its first interactions with modern society. A preliminary stage of dependence is opposed by a usually effective push for autonomy, once again enabling the Kayapo to be the real agents in their appropriations of Western technologies.

REVIEWING THE PERFORMANCE

As a result of the project, Renato, Luis, and I were slowly able to learn from our experience with the Kayapo the far-reaching possibilities open to an Indian group able to record their lives on their own terms. Through the Mekaron Opoi D'joi project, the Kayapo themselves understood these possibilities in a number of ways. Their video productions undertake a fourfold project. At the internal level, within Kayapo society, the Kayapo use video to support the preservation of *Mebênkokre kukràdzà* and to strengthen communication among diverse Kayapo villages. Within Kayapo society, the video camera provides a motivation for the Kayapo to perform their rituals. Concomitant to the production of the images for their archive on Kayapo rituals, dances, and myths, Kayapo children and youth learn their *kukràdzà*. Another expression of *Mebênkokre kukràdzà* is afforded by the exchange among their villages of video messages in which Kayapo elders perform their traditional speeches. Furthermore, it is through these messages that chiefs and leaders express their internal political differences and their concerns regarding external domination, thereby furthering their strategies of resistance. At the external level, regarding national and international visibility, the Kayapo use video to document the agreements established with Brazilian government and to win sympathy from ever larger segments of Brazilian society.

Throughout the Mekaron Opoi D'joi project, the Kayapo, who metaphorically referred to the camera as a weapon, demonstrated the use of video as a tool for resistance against outside domination. That the Kayapo used video as an instrument of resistance is an interpretation based not on ahistorical idealism but rather on my observations of their experience of struggle and their understanding of the media's power, all of which I have set out to document in this chapter. The Kayapo's use of videotape technology cannot be detached from their interaction with Brazilian society and must be framed as a *political* project of self-representation and empowerment.

Furthermore, the Kayapo manipulation of our representation of them as "high-tech Indians" is also a culturally relevant affirmation of their identity, as they conceive their culture both from the points of view of change and of permanence. As Hall observes: "Cultural identity is not a fixed essence at all, lying unchanged outside history and culture. . . . It is always constructed through memory, fantasy, narrative and myth. Cultural identities are points of identification, the unstable points of identication or suture, which are made within the discourses of history and culture."[41] The Kayapo were determined that their appropriation of videotape technology should also reinforce their indigenous cultural values, demonstrating how, for groups of the so-called traditional societies who accept change, identity is a self-determinate and dynamic contemporary construction that hybridizes elements of their traditional values with appropriations of "modern society," through which they reaffirm their differences and create an alternative future for their existing present.

In short, instead of appearing as mere subjects of our films and projects, the Kayapo came to understand the use of video technology as a "praxis," that is, as a tool that they could use to transform their sociopolitical reality. The Kayapo appropriation of the medium of video reaffirms the notion that it is people who make their own history and that in the age of "the global village" one makes history by controlling the media of self-representation. The Kayapo, instead of having "us" paternalistically construct and manipulate their images, can now directly and thus effectively represent themselves to modern society as agents who speak and act for themselves. As Zavarzadeh has pointed out, "The binaries should not be allowed to be read as metaphysical fictions and thus as epistemological categories deconstructed by rhetorical strategies [because this would] blur the boundaries of exploiter-exploited and obscures social contradictions in the interests of the dominant."[42] Zavarzadeh's statement leads me to the basic question, Who, if not "us" rather than "them," are the ones who have access to the means of production? The Kayapo's appropriation of videotape technology points to a transformation and subversion of the power relations inscribed in the politics of visual representation. The ones who traditionally were subjects of our films are now autonomous beings of their own representation. Thus the oppositional concept of "us" and "them," what poet Abel Martín has termed "the essential heterogeneity of being," and the real differences that it involves are absolutely necessary for a transformative politics of representation.

MONICA FROTA

NOTES

This essay could not have been written without the insightful assistance of Emily Fisher. I would like to thank Nancy Lutkehaus for her encouragement of my thesis project while I was at the Center for Visual Anthropology–University of Southern California, from which this essay has resulted. I am also grateful to Terence Turner for his translation of the Kayapo video footage shot through the Mekaron Opoi D'joi project.

1 Throughout this chapter I will use the terms *filmmaking* and *filmmaker* without distinguishing between the experiences of producing films or videos. When such distinctions are relevant to the subject of discussion I will address them in the text.

2 *Mekaron Opoi D'joi* means "he who creates images" in the Kayapo (Gê) language. The male pronoun—he—is significant for our understanding of who, among the Kayapo, operates the camera. Later on in this chapter I will discuss this power dynamics between genders more extensively.

3 The Kayapo are an Indian nation inhabiting an extensive territory spread throughout the Brazilian Amazon rain forest. In the past, the Kayapo population lived in two or three villages. Today, their total population of three thousand is divided into fifteen villages, ranging from eighty to eight hundred individuals per village. Of the existing Kayapo subgroups, the Metuktire-Kayapo, to whom I will refer simply as Metuktire, formed the core of our project. Other Kayapo subgroups who participated in the project are the Gorotire-Kayapo of the A'ukre and Gorotire villages and the Mekranoty-Kayapo of Kubenkokre village. The Gorotire's villages are within the Kayapo Indian Park, and the Mekranoty's villages are within the Mekranoty Reservation. Metuktire's village, named Kapot, is located at the northern part of the Xingu National Park. The southern part of Xingu National Park is inhabited by representatives of other Brazilian Indian groups who are not part of our story. I use the term *Indian* rather than a term such as *Native American* or *indigenous group,* as the Kayapo, in relation to external Brazilian society, term themselves as Indians, a category that excludes all others as "white" persons.

4 Brazilian television institutions, like all existing Brazilian broadcast systems, are controlled by the state. However, unlike the U.S. transmission system that offers over three hundred venues of broadcasting and "more than 1200 public access facilities," the Brazilian broadcast system offers only six channels to the public, an oligarchical system of communication. Despite Brazil's development of advanced technology for transmission, such as optical fiber, for example, the country lacks a cable system, reinforcing control and restricting the access of independent productions to audiences. It is not by chance that Brazil's dominant network—Globo—was established under an authoritarian centralized state, the military dictatorship. The Globo network quickly developed an enormous television audience and in 1982 was the world's most watched commercial network, transmitting nationally and selling its own productions internationally.

5 Such initiatives culminated with the organization of the ABVP—Brazilian Popular Video Association—which, among other activities, facilitates the exchange among communities of local video productions. The ABVP is also engaged in a project that, through five regional centers spread throughout the country, will give diverse communities broadcast access via satellite.

6 The term *indigenous media* refers to a body of literature that discusses the relationship between indigenous people and their uses of videotape and film technologies. For further readings about indigenous media see Monica Frota Feitosa, ed., *Visual Anthropology Review: The Other's Visions,* vol. 7, no. 2 (Washington, D.C.: American Anthropological Association, 1991), and Faye Ginsburg, "Mediating Culture: Indigenous Media, Ethnographic Film, and the Production of Identity," in *Alternative Vision: Essays in Visual Anthropology, Cinema, and Photograph,* ed. Leslie Devereaux and Roger Hillman (Berkeley: University of California Press, 1995).

7 The expression refers to the title of a book in which Worth and Adair describe their film project with the Navajo: Sol Worth and John Adair, *Through Navajo Eyes: An Exploration in Film Communication and Anthropology* (Bloomington: Indiana University Press, 1972).

8 Members of international indigenous film- and video-makers' associations recently created the First Nations Film and Video World Alliance. They present-

ed a press release at the Yamagata International Documentary Film Festival in which they defined indigenous media as projects "to ensure absolute control over the portrayal of our images and stories." On the occasion members of the alliance also stated their certainty that "the effective use of film and video is crucial if native languages and culture are to survive."

9 Worth and Adair, *Through Navajo Eyes*.

10 Today some Kayapo villages have satellite dishes, which are used to watch news programs.

11 The Xingu National Park was created by the Brazilian government in 1961, under the leadership of two pioneers, the Villas-Boas brothers, who were brought to wide international attention when they were nominated for a Nobel Prize for their adoption of protectionist (and paternalistic) policies toward Indian groups. The fifteen Indian groups who live in the park, including the Metuktire-Kayapo, are represented as a metaphor for the Brazilian Indian that the Brazilian government has created and handily exploited through promotional tours of the park to influential visitors.

12 Besides films and videos, photographic collections, often in printed postcard form, focusing on the Kayapo circulate widely in Brazil and the European community.

13 Xinguano refers to the Indian populations inhabiting the Xingu National Park.

14 Separated for fourteen years and victimized by innumerable invasions of their land, the two Metuktire-Kayapo groups whose land had been split by highway BR-080, after years of unsuccessful negotiations with government representatives, in 1984 confiscated the raft that facilitates the crossing of the Xingu River by vehicles traveling along the BR-080 highway. This episode, known in Brazil as the Raft War, lasted for forty-one days and culminated in the Indians' reconquering of their lands, adding 3,520 hectares to the park, which represents approximately 10 percent of its entirety.

15 Among the Kayapo, women are considered eventempered (*uabore*) while bravery (*àkre*) defines the male ethos of the warrior. Warfare is a central component of Kayapo tradition. Warfare with other Indians was a system of conquest and proof of supremacy. Moreover, Kayapo males cultivate their sense of bravery from an early age. Kayapo male teenagers are expected to prove themselves by

successfully undergoing a series of rituals that involve pain.

16 FUNAI is an acronym for Fundação Nacional do Indio, the National Indian Service. FUNAI is the office of the Brazilian government that ideally should represent the Indians' interests and needs.

17 Raoni is the Brazilian adaptation for his original Kayapo name Ropni. As this Kayapo chief is internationally known as Raoni, and as *Raoni* is also the title of a documentary film by Jean Pierre Dutilleux and Carlos Saldanha (which in 1979 was nominated for an Academy Award as best documentary film), I choose to use Raoni instead of Ropni, with hopes that some readers will identify the person.

18 The geographic configuration of a traditional Kayapo village conforms to a circle—a sacred Kayapo form—which is also the guiding principle in all spatial organization of Kayapo villages. The female extended uxorilocal households encircle the plaza, which is the locus of ritual activity. In the center of the plaza stands the Men's House (*ngà*), which functions as a meeting place for the men's societies (*tchêt*) and as a dormitory for males prior to their becoming fathers, after which they move into their wives' houses.

19 The Kayapo's name for themselves is *Mebênkokre*, which literally means "people from the water's source." The expression *Mebênkokre kukràdzà* refers to Kayapo culture, in their own terms.

20 Monica Frota, Renato Pereira, and Luis Rios, "Kapot's Night," in *Antropologia Visual* (Rio de Janeiro: Museu do Indio, 1987), 12.

21 The following are the films and videos presented at the video viewing sessions on our first trip (July 1985):

Talks in Maranhão, Andrea Tonacci, Brazil, 1979, documentary on the Canela Indians.
The Arara, Andrea Tonacci, Brazil, 1982, documentary on the Arara and their contact with Brazilians.
Xingu, Intervideo and Manchete TV, Brazil, 1984, documentary on Indian groups inhabiting the Xingu National Park.
"National News," Globo TV, Brazil, 1984, news program about the political changes that occurred in FUNAI and Mekaron's assumption to office as administrator of the Xingu National Park.

22 Kayapo society is organized on the basis of gender and age-set categories. Men of the *mekrare,* the age-set immediately junior to the elders, constitute the majority of the group who, following the *ben-iadjuòrò*

(chief) participated intensively in the "wild" demonstrations staged during the Raft War.

23 Metuktire Indians, when asked about the Raft War, would simply joke by saying, "We were very wild." They made variations on this joke in a variety of situations, as a humorous cultivation of the male ethos of the brave warriors.

24 Terence Turner, "Os Mẽbẽngokre Kayapó: De communidades autónomas para sistema interétnica" (The Mebengokre Kayapo: History, social consciousness, and social change from autonomous communities to interethnic system), in *Historiados Indios no Brasil,* ed. Manuela Caneiro da Cunha (Sao Paolo, 1993).

25 Brasilia, the capital of Brazil, is the closest town in which this service is available. The "intense traffic" of airplanes between the park and Brasilia made this service readily accessible to Metuktire.

26 The following are the films presented at the video viewing sessions in Kayapo villages during our second trip (September 1985):

The Tribe Who Hides from Men, Adrian Cowell, England, 1972, self-defined as a documentary on a pacificatory expedition's attempt to contact the Krenakarore Indians, with the participation of the Metuktire.
Koyaanisqatsi, Godfrey Reggio, United States, 1984, fictional movie blending scenes of mechanized life with the minimalist music of Philip Glass.

27 Among the Gorotire, who number about eight hundred, there are representatives of almost every Kayapo group. Gorotire village draws refugees and immigrants from all Kayapo villages. Megaron chose to include Gorotire village in the expansion of the project because of its historical and political importance to the Kayapo nation. He chose the A'ukre village because of its proximity to the Gorotire village. The airplane the Gorotire village had recently acquired would make travel between the two villages quick and affordable.

28 The layout of Gorotire village points to its history as the first Kayapo group to be "pacified," in the late 1930s. The Kayapo who inhabit Gorotire participate in the region's larger economy. At the time of the first invasion of settlers, the Gorotire villagers collected Brazil nuts for sale to Brazilians. Later, the villagers also earned wages by working for crews who did mineral research in the area. Today Gorotire village fills all its needs, ranging from airplanes to medicine, with the substantial financial resources it has derived from gold prospecting and the exploitation of the mahogany hardwoods on its lands. In the strongest contrast to Metuktire's village, Gorotire's annual estimated income of around U.S. $ 2,000,000 gives it easy access to industrialized commodities.

29 This message was recorded four years before Raoni, Megaron, and the rock singer Sting made a tour through Europe, collecting sympathy, francs, dollars, pesos, marks, and pounds for the Mata Virgem Foundation (Rain Forest Foundation). The funds that the tour raised allowed the Mata Virgem Foundation to pay for the demarcation of what is today one of the largest Indian reservations in the world.

30 Payakan's intervillage leadership came about as a result of the A'ukre and Gorotire villages' geographical proximity and their participation in Maria Bonita's mining project, in which Payakan became a key mediator.

31 The Metuktire often insisted that we should visit the Kubenkokre village at the Mekranoty Reservation, of which the Metuktire are a subgroup and with whom they maintain strong connections.

32 Jornal do Brasil had the second largest circulation of any paper in Brazil at the time.

33 Jornal do Brasil (Rio de Janeiro), 14 March 1986.

34 Granada Television was producing The Kayapo, a film that was part of the Disappearing World series. During his involvement with this production, anthropologist Terence Turner learned about the Kayapo use of videotape and three years later began to work with several Kayapo groups in strengthening their technical knowledge of videotape postproduction. Supported by the Spencer Foundation, this undertaking, dubbed the Kayapo Video Project, has provided several Kayapo groups with cameras and facilitated their access to an editing system in São Paulo, hundreds of miles away from Kayapo villages.

35 Kremoro is a former chief and the oldest living Metuktire Indian.

36 Vanessa Lea, "Nomes e Nekrets Kayapó: Uma Concepção de Riqueza" (Ph.D. diss., Universidade do Rio de Janeiro, 1986).

37 Ben-iadjuòrò means "chief," or in Kayapo terms, "he who gives the ceremonial chants."

38 This usage is consistent with the origins of video technology, as an apparatus to support military and commercial surveillance.

39 *Ipre-re* means "god" in the Kayapo (Gê) language.

40 Discussing many of the existing documentary films on the Kayapo at the 1993 Yamagata International Documentary Film Festival, Megaron critized their use of a non-Kayapo voice-over narration. After screening his assembled forty-five-minute video about the Bemp naming ceremony at the First Nations Theatre in Yamagata, Megaron suggested that each Kayapo video should have two edited versions, both narrated by Kayapo voice-over—the longest one specifically for Kayapo audiences, and a second shorter version to be distributed to outsiders. For a second presenta-tion in Los Angeles, Megaron asked to reassemble his video, which he shortened to one-third of its original length.

41 Stuart Hall, "Culture, Identity and Cinematic Representation," *Framework,* no. 36 (1989): 71-72.

42 Mas'ud Zavarzadeh, *Seeing Films Politically* (New York: State University of New York Press, 1991).

CHAPTER 19

Video:
The Politics of Culture
and Community

Ron Burnett

THEORY AND PRACTICE

Portable video use has exploded worldwide. Since its appearance in the late 1960s video has become the medium of choice for larger and larger numbers of people. Community, gay, and feminist organizations; environmental and social advocacy groups; and mainstream and alternative political and cultural formations in North America, Europe, and the third world have made active use of video for information gathering, political agitation, and artistic experimentation. This has resulted in the distribution and dissemination of local and transnational debates and ideas across a wide spectrum of different contexts. There are a large number of assumptions governing this use of video, but perhaps the most important is that the electronic image can be an effective tool to *teach* and *inform* both practitioners and viewers. This is, in a sense, the philosophical and ideological basis upon which the video movement has built its credibility and which has encouraged the extraordinary growth in the production and distribution of a large variety of videotapes. Many of the best examples of political and artistic video production have developed out of the desire to transform images into useful arbiters of change and education. Underlying this process is the notion that electronic images will stop having a rarified and distant relationship to viewers, and instead, images will become the "site" of transformative activities. As a consequence, information changes into knowledge and knowledge transforms those who learn into activists in the communities of which they are a part.

Often, the impulse to use video for teaching and learning, for experimentation, and for the dissemination of political ideas relies on the electronic image in an untheorized fashion. In part, this is because of a profound antipathy to theory itself, but the underlying premise here is a devotion to, and a dependence upon, idealized notions of practice. The separation between theory and practice, the very idea of their separation, has hindered if not retarded the historical importance and effect of video within

283

both Western and non-Western cultures. Video production is seen as a craft. The creation of electronic images is as a result enframed by a variety of mystifications with respect to production, and one of the most important is that the camera as an instrument must be understood and learned about in much the same manner as one might learn how to draw or paint or use a still camera. In addition, there are a number of aesthetic assumptions with respect to images that are derived from the cinema, not the least of which is that electronic media generate moving pictures. There are professional standards derived from the history of cinema production (because both media make use of cameras) that have been imported in a wholesale fashion into video. The question is, How can all of these assumptions be examined *without* at least some theory? And why would one want to avoid enriching the critical and intellectual discourse that surrounds the use of video as a medium? As a practitioner myself, as an academic and a writer, I have found that the resistance to theory has in a general sense hobbled the growth and development of the video movement. But this resistance has a positive side as well, since what is often being looked for is a new way of conceptualizing practice, a dramatically different approach to audience and to viewing. So much of the political video movement depends on the creation of public contexts for discussion that there is a strong need to develop a more profound understanding of the grass roots, of the communities being addressed. It is also important to generate pedagogical models that will encourage open and honest exchange among participants in the production of videotapes as well as among the viewers who see them. But all of this will not shift the parameters of many present-day practices (and I will comment on them in this chapter) unless the artificial barriers that have been erected against theory are torn down. Many of the premises that have been used to justify the activities of various video groups and individuals are as "abstract" as any ivory tower theorizing. The paradox is that theory and practice inevitably inform each other, and it is only the narrowest of polemics that keeps them apart.

THE RIGHT TO COMMUNICATE

In southern or third world countries, video has been embraced in much the same manner as radio was for a previous generation, as a technology for training, education, organizing, information gathering, political agitation, and cultural preservation. Even more important, the appropriation of video has been seen as a key way for economically deprived communities to gain some measure of democratic control over information and communication sources now controlled either by the state or by multinational corporations. This grassroots activity has had a profound influence on the way in which very different communities in many parts of the world have thought about communications. At the same time, these activities are taking place within the context of societies that are undergoing profound change. The diasporic character and history of southern countries, the shifting terrain within which their communities now operate, and the politically and economically explosive situation they now find themselves in have provided fertile ground for the growth and development of new communications technologies.

These links between the old and the new, between societies in transition and communities undergoing a variety of complex changes, alter the landscape of meanings within which communications technologies operate. However one puts it (the shift from the modern to the postmodern, the movement from the colonial to the postcolonial), this hybridization has overwhelmed the more conventional critical, theoretical, and practical approaches that have been developed with respect to technologies such as video, television, and radio.

Access to communications technologies has been advocated as a constitutional right, to be written into the legal framework of all countries.[1] The MacBride Commission in 1980 called for "structural changes to equalize and balance the communication structure. Such balance is necessary, according to the proponents of the new order, if development—economically, politically, socially and culturally—is to be effectively promoted. This approach sees communication as the infrastructure of and precondition for economic growth, and thus, development."[2] I will argue that most of the *categories* in place for analyzing the efforts that have grown out of this suggestion, ranging from notions of participatory democracy to the horizontal nature of collective work with video to the various paradigms for understanding the role of mainstream media, have been very weak. There has been a lack of critical and evaluative work, although there are many descriptive efforts that end up justifying development work with communications technologies.[3] Even given this, the MacBride Commission Report was an important initiative and continues to exert tremendous influence because it suggested a paradigm shift in the political economy of communications in developing countries. The report also linked communications as a concept and as a practice to concrete notions of cultural development. It recognized and then enshrined the relationship between cultural and economic growth. It broadened the way communications was thought about, from the exchange of information to notions of the public sphere and democratic rights and freedoms.

The linkage between democracy and communications, however, incorporated ideas of citizenry, responsibility, and community from Western societies. This is an area that must be investigated with great care. Cultural specificity often precludes the simple transference of new technologies and ideas. More important, the evaluative, critical, and interpretive strategies that Western analysts use in relation to community and democracy have to be foregrounded. This is the only way to *prevent* assumptions of shared values from overwhelming local concerns and giving a strength to transnational ideas that end up duplicating neocolonial imperatives. As D. Barnlund suggests in an influential piece:

> The intercultural dialogue we seek concerning ethical standards is compounded, finally, by our diverse concepts of the nature and potential of communication in mediating these ethical values. The rhetorical premises of the west—our belief in the value of rational discourse, our faith in the emergence of truth from competing arguments, our confidence in the values of collabo-

THE POLITICS OF CULTURE AND COMMUNITY

ration—do not enjoy universal respect. Setting aside for the moment those cultures which refuse to contribute to such a dialogue, there remain many others which claim an intuitive truth that is higher than reason, who reject collaboration (especially among equals), who are unimpressed with arguments and mistrustful of words.[4]

I consider Barnlund's comments to be crucial. In most cases the question of an ethical framework for new communications technologies must be located within this intercultural debate. I would extend his and my own comments concerning specificity to most work with video in community contexts, irrespective of location in the north or south.

EMPOWERMENT

Artists, particularly in the West but also in developing countries, have gravitated to video in part because of its low cost and also because the medium encourages experimentation with images. There are now hundreds of video centers, some independent, others run by universities and museums, all engaged in activities that have legitimated video as a preferred medium for a variety of creative and political endeavors. The advent of multimedia in the middle of the 1980s has increased the hybridization of video and computer technology and has brought a variety of information systems together, with even greater potential for experimentation and research. One of the central presuppositions of this activity in multimedia is that it enlarges the base of participants who use and watch video. This encourages the spread and democratization of media technologies. At another level, the advent of cheaper and cheaper camcorders with near professional results (especially with Hi-8) has encouraged the proliferation of informal networks of communication and exchange. An example of this is *Video News Service* in South Africa, which operates through the exchange and placement of videocassettes in small communities throughout South Africa. These cassettes have become a precious commodity as they are often proposed as the only source of alternative news for groups of people who have limited access to broadcast technology. Another example is Video SEWA, which operates in India and is a unique example of the grassroots applications of lowcast technologies in local communities: "Video SEWA is the video cooperative of the Self-Employed Women's Association, trade union of some 30,000 poor, self-employed women in Ahmedabad, India."[5] A further example at an institutional level is Vidéazimut, or the International Coalition for Audiovisuals for Development and Democracy (located in Montreal, Canada). This organization has grown dramatically over the last four years. It works on the premise that alternative sources of information will encourage dramatic cultural, personal, and political transformations in the societies and people who make use of new technologies (they are now actively pursuing satellite and broadcast media to enlarge the distribution base for their work). Vidéazimut is made up of well over twenty organizations worldwide, from Peru and Mozambique to India and Hong Kong. Each of these often represent regions rather than countries and have a large number of smaller groups with whom they are associated. Vidéazimut has become a clearinghouse for the distribution of hundreds of videotapes shot by these groups.

There is a need to more fully explore why this type of investment is being made in video and whether it reflects an idealism for which the criteria of evaluation are often self-serving. The active implication of nongovernmental organizations (NGOs) in these efforts to spread the use of video must be analyzed as a Western phenomenon, very much related to notions of development, aid, and economic growth. Most of the NGOs in the field are supported by Western governments and aid organizations. They are managing video in much the same manner as they might approach a project on educating peasant farmers in the better use of their land. In other words, the medium is being treated as if it can serve the function of a formal and informal educational tool. In addition, video, like radio, is often described by NGOs as one of the most important vehicles for "giving a voice" to the disenfranchised.[6] The educational and pedagogical model in place here is derived from Paulo Freire and his work on the problems of literacy with South American peasants.[7]

The philosophy of "giving a voice" was recently critiqued in an editorial in the newsletter *Interadio,* which is produced by the World Association of Community Radio Broadcasters (also an NGO):

> More than any other mass communication medium, radio is accessible, affordable and easily appropriated by groups of people whose demands have traditionally been ignored by the mainstream media. Many marginalized groups are turning to community radio as a forum for expression, by-passing the corporate and state media rather than fighting to access them. Community radio often speaks of the need "to have a voice" and of the necessity of establishing community stations as independent voices. Community radio has also become known as the "voice of the voiceless" in many parts of the world. However, while the term voiceless may well refer to those who have traditionally been denied access to the media, labelling community radio as the voice of the voiceless demeans the very essence of community radio. The phrase voiceless overlooks centuries of oral tradition which preceded radio technology (traditions which are especially strong in Asia, Africa and among indigenous populations). It can also be interpreted as implying that people do not have a voice in their communities and in their everyday lives unless they have some kind of access to the media.[8]

This is an important caution but the issues it raises are generally overlooked, if not overwhelmed by the ongoing need to keep producing videotapes and radio shows. In order to more fully understand how traditional cultures interact with new technologies, the communities affected would have to "educate" the outsiders who bring the technology with them. The general claim made by video activists is that this in fact happens. It is to Lisa Vinebohm's credit that she questions those claims. But how does the history

THE POLITICS OF CULTURE AND COMMUNITY

of a culture foreign to those who visit it with the intent of introducing video become both culturally and discursively visible? At one level the distinctions in operation here between the inside and the outside, between the local and international, seem to have been undermined, if not overcome, by the rapid spread of communications technologies themselves. The result is that few societies are now without some experience of video, television, and radio. The various distinctions of "otherness" that have guided the introduction of video have changed almost entirely. What results are social contexts in which communities have developed sophisticated media strategies at an aesthetic and political level, often far removed from the concerns of the NGO groups who bring the media with them. This suggests that the kind of work that has to be done will take the politically astute video practitioner and activist into the realm of the interdisciplinary, as he or she engages with cultural, sociological, ethnographic, and political analyses of the community. But will these analyses and overviews be able to respond to the transformations that are taking place?

There is even more to the notion of voice than what Vinebohm suggests. One of the main assumptions of community video is that of empowerment. Voice stands in for all of the processes that supposedly lead to enhanced notions of community control of information and knowledge: "Dialogue is at the very heart of community access television. For this is a medium that is (or is supposed to be) interactive, user-defined and operating horizontally. A sharp contrast indeed to the centralized, one-way, top-down flow pattern of conventional media. This alternative communications system . . . has enormous potential to liberate the public from the controlled flow of information, experience and thought."[9] This quote summarizes many of the concerns of the alternative video movement in both the south and the north. Aside from the conventional bow to the hegemonic influences of mass media (which foregrounds the notion of dominance, control, and the efforts to generate a democratic response), there is the key thought of liberation from control, the opening up of hitherto closed spaces of experience, and the unveiling of different ways of thinking. Goldberg is referring to the entire process of community control, although she rarely defines the meaning of "community," and to the resulting sense she has that people, once empowered in the use of the medium, will gain a new understanding of their own viewpoints on the world, if not of their politics. How does the experience of images create the open-endedness that Kim Goldberg proposes? This is such an important issue and it is so profoundly bound up with notions of education and change that the models in use for the process she supports would need far more explanation than she provides: "Like the medical treatments of the barefoot doctors, community television was a shared tool belonging to a community of equals. However, in the community TV model, the distinction between 'doctor' and 'patient' breaks down. The medium becomes a tool of community self-healing."[10] How does the medium become a tool of self-healing? Empowerment begins with the presumption that something is missing either in the community or in people's lives. The intervention of the videomakers, accompanied by the use of the medium on the part of "ordinary" people, supposedly leads to shifts in identity and claims of self-determination.

Do all of the contingent factors that govern the production of meaning in a video contribute to the sense that meaningful exchanges can take place? What blockages are there to learning? Is the concept of horizontal participation an idealized projection on the part of the community workers who use video?

In asking these questions from a negative rather than a positive standpoint, I in no way want to belittle or even underestimate the importance of community efforts to use video. Rather, more time needs to be spent on the issues of empowerment, participation, democratic control, and communication. Although these terms are used in an almost continuous fashion to construct the discourse surrounding video politics, they remain a bit too flexible and are loosely adapted to fit into the constraints of each situation. I believe, given the fundamentally intercultural nature of many of the productions now circulating, that these issues must be dealt with in much more detail if there is to be a more profound understanding of the political implications of the work. Yet, I also believe that after nearly twenty-five years of effort, the utopian presumptions underlying the use of video in a variety of different communities have not been evaluated in great depth. To what degree are communities likely to evaluate a technology that, from the outset, potentially reconfigures their own modes of communication? To what degree have the proponents of this technology brought a critique of the medium with them? How well have we understood video from within our own cultures? This, it seems to me, is a crucial question. There are many possible and different interpretive and analytical approaches that could be taken with respect to video, but these would involve the type of theorization that practitioners often avoid. The critical literature on video is at best slim. If our own culture has been so hesitant in the development of video theory and criticism, then what impact does this have on the movement of the technology into other social and cultural contexts?

Part of the problem I have faced in researching the organizations involved in using and promoting video is that so much of what is being made is treated as information in the most ephemeral sense of that word. Although there is some discussion of aesthetics and form, the discourse is generally quite limited, in part because there seems to be no critical vocabulary with which to examine and analyze the material produced. Videotapes circulate and are shown to audiences, but the evaluations that follow are short-lived and rarely followed up. In addition, the arguments that have been developed to describe and analyze the production of community or political videotapes don't often concern themselves with questions of *how* or whether images communicate meaning, or to what degree analytical tools are in place for explaining the various relationships between different forms of cultural production and their reception and use by viewers. This resistance to theory and to critical practices suffuses, perhaps even dominates, the video movement. Can a video stand on its own? Can the "message" be transparently clear, even if the audience the video is addressing supposedly shares the premises of the communication? The videotapes depend upon the electronic image to do the work of revealing, if not creating, discursive spaces within which questions of identity and self can be addressed and as a result of which action can be undertaken. But can the image play that role without a creative pedagogical strategy that extends far beyond the boundaries of the image? How can that strategy be enacted without a careful reflection on the history of the medium, on its aesthetic characteristics and formal properties, and on the previous uses that have been made of images in all media?

ALTERNATIVITY

Some of these problems were addressed in a recent article by Kelly Anderson and Annie Goldson, "Alternating Currents: Alternative Television inside and outside of the Academy."[11] The authors bemoan the lack of contact between academics and video practitioners. They make the claim that there is very little interest on the part of theorists to examine the history and development of alternative media in the United States as well as elsewhere.[12] Although they clearly underestimate the work that has been done, they pinpoint a serious gap in the thinking about community and alternative media. There is an underlying moral imperative to the notion of alternativity that locates critique and analysis within a framework of oppositions to nearly all aspects of mainstream culture. (Examples of this approach can be found in the work of Paper Tiger Television and Deep Dish, both in New York.) This becomes the centerpiece of an evaluative strategy that is then applied to the videotapes produced in a community context. There is an ambiguous conservatism to this strategy and an underlying conformity to the statements about culture and ideology.

To what extent, then, is there some clarity with respect to the idea of alternativity? Anderson and Goldson suggest a number of different approaches. Their first assumption is that alternative television that is community based has a "precarious though binding relationship to the dominant economy of media production."[13] This refers to the various strategies that alternative producers and practitioners, as well as community workers, engage in with respect to funding and the acquisition of resources and equipment. The subject is a fascinating one because it is at the root of an economic activity rarely, if ever, measured. A number of objections could be raised here to the suggestion that we are dealing with alternative production processes. The first is that lowcasting now makes use of increasingly sophisticated equipment. Although not as costly as conventional broadcast technology, the investment can be considerable. Second, any effort to go beyond the immediate availability of basic resources involves grant requests to government or local agencies, corporations, or foundations. This issue has been debated before, and the argument is always that public or private aid pollutes, if not skews, the political track of advocacy that governs so much of the production at the community level. Yet, what seems to be at stake here is precisely the idealizations of the "alternative," which sees itself as outside the very institutions to which it is beholden. This is a circuitous route, full of potholes, but the most important point to keep in mind is that the terrain of practice opened up by relying on an alternativity trying to operate outside the conventional economic constraints that any technology imposes may be extremely limited.

Yet this could become a more dialogic process, and it could be more sensitive and aware of the institutional nexus within which it must operate, if there weren't such a strong dependence on the central idea of a dominant culture and on ideological control. There is no question that monopolies from Time Warner to News Corporation control the marketplace, and recent moves toward consolidation on the part of telephone and cable companies in the United States presage even more complex, although not necessarily uniformly similar, worldwide corporations. This is indisputable. But the terrain of communication, the place within which meanings as such are exchanged, interpreted, worked upon, is within the very communities that video activists want to politicize. If the model of dominance were to operate at the level, and with the intensity, suggested by the oppositional relationship between mainstream and alternative, then the very people who inhabit those communities would themselves not be accessible (nor, perhaps, would they even be interested in seeing anything different).

In part, this is because there are so many aspects to a community's activities that traverse the boundaries between what is acceptable and what is not, so much heterogeneity to the relationship between institutions and people, that questions of power and how to address the powerful cannot be answered from within the hazy traditions promulgated and supported by the easy dichotomy of alternative and mainstream. In some respects this opposition carries the same weight as the superstructure/base opposition, which did so much to undermine creative, theoretical, and critical work on culture from within the Marxist tradition. There is a simplicity to the opposition that cannot be sustained any longer. It is perhaps more necessary than ever to unmask the weaknesses of an approach that cannot account for desire, pleasure, and the contradictory politics of incorporation, which, it must be remembered, can be simultaneously experimental and co-opted. A large number of distinctions should be introduced which will reinvigorate the meaning of all kinds of media practices, without locking them into an intellectually convenient oppositional structure. This can only be done by recognizing how heterogeneous the work of the media is, how it is possible for a film like *Wayne's World* to present an analysis and critique of community cable television and be, at one and the same time, irreverent and part of the mainstream, a moneymaker and a joke on American cultural values.

THE PUBLIC SPHERE

Lili Berko has suggested that the advent of the portapak in the late 1960s broke the hold of broadcast television on the technology of electronic images:

> The coupling of the portable videotape recorder (porta-pak) with the advent of the videocassette offered artists and social activists alike an opportunity to participate in the production of images that were to shape their culture. The most revolutionary aspect of the porta-pak was its mobility. Through the

porta-pak, television production was not locked into a studio and the confines of the codes of such mediated experience. Through video, the mystique of production was shattered and the streets became equally important sites of textual inscription. Video soon became the vehicle through which the social world could be easily documented, the vehicle which would record the voices and the images of the Newark riots, or a Mardi Gras celebration; as such it proclaimed the public sphere to be its own.[14]

The trajectory of influences and changes launched by portable video certainly foregrounded the need for a reevaluation of the way in which mainstream broadcasters operated. For the first time, a radically different model of televisual practices was suggested by the lowcast process. A dialectic was created between two differing conceptions of the public sphere. On the one side were the networks and on the other was a new breed of videomaker devoted to local forms of expression and rooted in a specific community. It took many years for the networks to recognize the widespread effects of lowcast technologies not only on viewers and practitioners but on the ways in which our culture thinks about the circulation of knowledge and images.

Berko's analysis of the shift to the public sphere, of the reclaiming of a territory lost to mainstream media, stands at the juncture of an analytic space that has defined an entire generation of writers and practitioners. There are few texts or articles on video that have not made the claim for this break (which resonates with the symbolism of the sixties and is represented by the work of Nam June Paik and Michael Shamberg),[15] and most have made it with reference to the history of mainstream media. Much remains unexamined in this choice of approach. The most important point is that the analytical framework for the study of television at that time was in its infancy. In fact, there were very few departments of film studies in universities, let alone departments of media or cultural studies. There were, however, a number of crucial "sites" where media were analyzed, and for the most part they were dependent on communications theory as it had evolved from the 1930s.[16] I make this point because the attitude toward mainstream television and the public sphere that underlies Berko's approach is based on a hegemonic view of the role of the media, with the result that portapak activity is analyzed as if the practice of image creation was itself a sufficient, if not utopian, reclamation of lost territory. This occupation of a new space was seen as a political act with an immediate impact upon the environments and people in which video was used and shown. Yet the absence of contexts for the analysis of mainstream media in the late 1960s (which was in part a result of the "newness" of television itself) suggests that the initial shift to a populist view of portable television technology was based on a fragmentary and often reductive presumption about mass forms of entertainment and learning. This oppositional framework continues to be the premise for much of present-day video practice and theory, which still does not grapple clearly with the problems of audience, performance, and learning with regard to media production at the local, national, and international level. There is, therefore, a measure of continuity to the debate, a his-

292

RON BURNETT

torical underpinning to the contrasting attitudes that have been taken toward media technologies that address both large and small audiences. How have the various definitions of impact and change that underpin notions of grassroots activity and democratic access been used to give credibility to the use of video both in the community and as an artistic tool?

It is estimated that there are about four hundred groups working in popular video in South America, with a predominant number, two hundred, working in Brazil. Luiz Fernando Santoro, who is a professor at the University of São Paulo, has commented upon this phenomenon with the statement that for the most part these groups make use of video in three ways: "Historically, there have been three distinct moments in video work: the first was the use of video to share information within the movement (video as a self-organizational tool); the second, video used as counter-information (video as a tool for constructing discourse within the movement); and the third, present moment, where video is used to present an alternative view of the world to the collectivity at large."[17]

With respect to the first category Santoro uses, how is information shared? What are the public and private "locations" within which richly endowed discursive formations can and do develop? This is of course a question of pedagogy, of learning, a question of how important political issues can be raised and then discussed, if not acted upon. Within the utopian ideals of the video movement, the notion of sharing information reflects a desire to jump-start the learning process and also a desire to create open contexts for communication and exchange. As well, the presumption is that by making video in local contexts, the images will reflect the genuine needs of the people who participate and, as a consequence, formerly closed channels of communication will be opened.

Video is promoted by Santoro as perhaps the best way of democratizing processes of communication and providing access to the media, particularly for those presently excluded from power or conventional networks for the production and exchange of information. Underlying Santoro's third point about presenting local interests to the broader world community is the notion that video has become a tool to reach larger and larger numbers of people. Yet this will mean that video has changed from a lowcast medium to a broadcast medium. If this is true (and I am not convinced it is), then the underlying impulses I have been describing will have shifted. This means that the perceived need to reach more and more people will change both the aesthetic approach and fundamental assumptions about the technology. It will further professionalize what up till now has been informal, and, as Santoro puts it, "the accent is on making more complete programmes in order to get them broadcast."[18] The premature movement into broadcasting may not happen with the rapidity suggested by Santoro. Even if it does, all the questions of communication, learning, and social change will remain. Clearly, the desire here is to broaden the base within which important political and cutural statements can be made. Yet the problem is that the "public" Santoro wants to reach remains an imaginary construction that may to some degree refer to real indi-

THE POLITICS OF CULTURE AND COMMUNITY

viduals, but that for the most part suggests a context of experience that cannot be validated. The tension between public and private forms of knowledge and experience is played out at a contradictory level within the framework of video production. As notions of the public sphere broaden to include more and more communities, the heterogeneity of the videotapes being made could decrease. In many southern countries videotapes are used to make education more accessible to large numbers of people. Examples abound from the most basic (images that show people how to make use of clean water supplies) to more complex forms of education (how to develop communal structures for economic growth and diversification). The videotapes are meant to fit into the formal and informal networks of learning already in place. But who makes these videotapes? Where do the assumptions of learning and education come from? How are cultural differences dealt with? In fact, how are the issues of intercultural communication integrated into the videotapes, since they presumably would be used by a wide variety of people with different interests?

These are questions that are usually answered with the assertion that local people know and control the relevance of the videotapes. If they are adequately informed and involved, then the results will be seen as relevant and will perhaps have an even more profound influence on the community as a whole. But this remains a supposition, because the history of educational video in the north would suggest that learning from video is a complex task. Without delving into this issue at the moment, it is not very clear how people learn from images or even whether they do. That is not to suggest that viewers don't learn, but that the critera of evaluation remain vague and more attached to an imputed content than anything else.

The approaches here range from the formal to the informal. For example, Vidéazimut has run workshops in video production in a variety of different countries. These workshops are community based and are intended to provide local people with the tools they need to both understand and make videotapes. Most of the workshops are run on questions of technique (how to make videotapes, how to use the equipment, and so on), invoking a pedagogy that is rarely examined, and when it is, the evaluation is usually based on vague notions of empowerment through the use of video. In a sense Vidéazimut faces a conundrum well known to ethnographers and anthropologists. Outside observers and participants with the best of intentions and the most rigourous notions of the local, or the indigenous, are nevertheless *not* part of the communities with which they get involved. This obviously has an impact on the pedagogical methods that are chosen for training purposes, but an examination of the literature produced to date shows little awareness of those problems, which are fundamentally intercultural in character. How can critical methods of training be developed with respect to video? Is the terminology wrong to begin with here? What are the historical origins underlying the assumption that to learn a technology, you have to be trained in it? Are we dealing with craft-oriented approaches here, and what are the implications of that for critical analysis?

Yet although those contradictions seem to be a major characteristic of the use of video, I must also stress the positive side. Some of the preliminary research I have done on video-oriented projects, such as the Integrated Rural Project in Education, Health, and Family Planning (in the Honduras), suggests that with limited tools and cheap technology, video has been useful in opening up hitherto untapped energies for learning and debate. In this instance video and sound cassettes were used to provoke discussion on issues of central concern for the health and welfare of Hondurans living in small impoverished villages. This encouraged an open exchange of ideas, and the participants began to make tapes of their own and exchange them with other villages. Similar projects in Kenya, Senegal, and Bolivia point toward the potential strengths of this movement. Another major effort is the Village Video Network, cosponsored by the United Nations University and Martha Stuart Communications (now called Communication for Change). The network is nonprofit and has many participants from a number of African and Asian countries. "Women are a primary target and beneficiary of Village Video Network activities and women's groups (such as the Self-Employed Women's Association of Ahmedabad, India) are active participants in the workshops and exchanges made possible by the network."[19]

The German Foundation for International Development has been involved in a large number of projects in the south. They held a series of seminars on community communications between 1986 and 1990. A report on the seminars was written up in *Group Media Journal,* published in Munich. Manfred Oepen invokes three categories to describe a new paradigm for the use of media in the community: "They have gone from information diffusion *for* people to information seeking *by* and *with* people. Here, problem and practice-related information is generated through local or regional community processes and fed into existing media networks horizontally and vertically, to inform both central decision makers and community groups respectively." Oepen goes on to describe three key concepts of community communication: "access, participation and self-management."[20]

Those three aims were also the foundation upon which the Challenge for Change program was developed at the National Film Board of Canada (NFB).[21] In the late 1960s and early 1970s Challenge for Change was created to engage with processes of social change through the use of video and film. Broadly speaking, the desire to use the medium as an instrument for an activist relationship to Canadian society grew out of the recognition that the NFB, as well as politically committed cultural workers, needed to be involved in more than the production of films or videotapes. They needed to connect with, and better understand, the audiences and communities they were addressing. The aim was to extend the process of creation and production from an institutional nexus into a decentralized model, based on an idealized version of community involvement:

Films can teach, they can explain and they can move people to great depths of emotion. Having done all of these things, is it possible for films to move people to action? There is no question for most social scientists that carefully constructed communications, films for instance, can produce changes in attitudes, in those who adequately receive the communication. The use of adequately is of course a conscious one in that we know that people tend to misperceive that which they hear and see, and go through fairly complicated strategies of selective attention and selective perception.[22]

In fact, the audience became an obsession at the NFB, with specific people at the institution assigned to develop polling methods and questionnaires for distribution to the populace at large. After certain films or videotapes were shown on television, for example, the Film Board phoned people at random to see if they had watched and to pose questions if viewers said they were prepared to participate. The premise of this community-oriented work was pedagogical, political, and cultural, and it influenced an entire generation of activists devoted to the use of visual media for political purposes. The issue of connectivity to the viewer, to the community—the issue of the relationship between production and distributions—is what distinguished the efforts of the NFB from many similar organizations elsewhere. The traditions developed during the heyday of the Challenge for Change period were improved upon in the late seventies when the board decentralized and opened up a series of regional centers across Canada in an effort to build closer ties to the communities it was serving.

The idealism of Challenge for Change was based on notions of democratic access, the rallying call for anyone seriously interested in promoting the use of video in the community. The history of that period has not yet been written in great detail; suffice it to say that one of the most interesting aspects yet to be explored will be the relationship between the social work movement in Quebec in the early 1960s and the accelerated movement toward media use for educational purposes. The level of advocacy in both education and social work was very sophisticated, with tie-ins to provincial government departments and local municipalities. The use of video for the purposes of empowerment was embedded in a particular political context and surrounded by debates within Quebecois culture about the role of the media in culture and education. The specificity of the situation affected not only the videotapes being made but also the institutions that promoted them. The claims of that period and the video activism that followed were not as easily transferable to other contexts as was presumed at the time. In fact, it is startling to read the anecdotal comments about Challenge for Change by modern-day proponents of community video,[23] the decontextualized analyses of the films that were made, and the lack of understanding about the history of the National Film Board—in particular that many of the films were the site of conflicts between the English and French sections of the NFB (which had a definitive impact on what the film board meant by community).

Rick Moore, who wrote *Canada's Challenge for Change: Documentary*

Film and Video as an Exercise of Power through the Production of Cultural Reality,[24] quotes one of the members of Challenge for Change: "All across Canada (often with the help of Challenge for Change), citizens are picking up half-inch VTR cameras and learning to speak through them."[25] Moore then goes on to say:

> The assessment was not an exaggeration, geographically speaking. Challenge for Change had begun numerous projects across the country in which the primary emphasis was citizen access. Over twenty-three major projects were eventually completed, some in urban areas such as Vancouver, Halifax and Toronto. Some were done in rural areas such as Drumheller, Alberta. In many of these communities, Challenge for Change staff took on new titles. For example, "directors" were no longer directors, but "media counsellors" in charge of helping the local citizens use the media most effectively.[26]

Guided by a vague concept of change, firmly believing in the potential of video as a technology to empower people to "talk to each other," engaged in the legitimation of a public sphere with a hierarchy of discourses that workers at Challenge for Change rarely examined, the program nevertheless produced many important experiments in the field of community video. But the operative word here is experiment, and in some senses people and their communities became the site within which many different ideas of democratic involvement were tested. The problem is that the targets for these experiments were as much the members of the community as the image itself—the creation and construction of meaning within the confines of an electronic medium. And the often-expressed analysis of workers at Challenge for Change was that no other form of communication adequately responded to the needs of the people, as they understood them. But this is a confusion of levels. Experimenting on the image, testing its effectiveness with regard to change, is already fraught with contradiction. Applying these ideas to the relationship between the image and the spectator, the image and the community, just confuses the issues even more.

If it appears that I am referring to a historical situation that may not be relevant anymore, here is what Deirdre Boyle has to say: "Nearly 30 years since the video portapak launched an independent television movement in the United States, a new generation of video activists has taken up the video camcorder as a tool, a weapon, and a witness. Although the rhetoric of guerrilla television may seem dated today, its utopian goal of using video to challenge the information infrastructure in America is more timely than ever and at last practicable. Today's video activism is the fulfillment of a radical 1960's dream of making 'people's television.'" Boyle goes on to talk about the three components of video activism as they have coalesced in the nineties: "To be a tool, a weapon and a witness."[27] These three categories are as constitutive now as they were in the late 1960s and early 1970s. Their longevity is framed by the concept of empowerment. Yet an examination of the literature and research that has been produced in relation to video reveals very little evolution or depth with regard to empowerment as a *process*. Terms like *democratization* and *control by the community* appear over and over again, but these are assumed from within the activities of portable video *use*. There is not enough research about audience, about the ways in which video images work as devices of communication, if at all, or about questions that relate issues of representation to empowerment.[28]

Care must be taken in discussing the *effects* of portable technologies upon users and viewers. The evaluative tools we have for examining how these technologies have been appropriated, and then understood, cannot simply be reduced to an instance of the technology itself. While it is true that hundreds of groups started to use video in the late 1960s and early 1970s, that by *itself* does not suggest much about the aesthetic or political uses that were made of the medium. It will be important to account more fully for the difficulties that are posed in analyzing the subjective relationship that practitioners and viewers develop with video images. Is it true that advocacy video changes the ways in which people both analyze and act upon the social contexts of which they are a part? There is little but anecdotal evidence to suggest what these changes are actually about, to what degree and with what depth viewers and/or communities work upon the images they watch or create. This is as much a methodological problem as it is a theoretical and practical one. All the various problems of conflating class, ethnicity, color, and gender come to the fore here, in a notion of community that seems to rise above the contradictions and conflicts that are a part of any community's history.

HISTORY/TECHNOLOGY/COMMUNITY

By now it should be evident that I am concerned with the relationship between the history of video and popular and academic assumptions about how that technology can be used and responded to. I am also concerned with presumptions of impact and various hypotheses about change as they are refracted through the shifting parameters of technological growth and innovation. To what degree, for example, does the appearance of video coincide with the desire to link home photography with television? Does this explain the rapid acceptance of the medium by many different sectors of our society? Do the camcorder and the palmcorder presage a historical shift in the way in which electronic images will be watched, understood, and created? If we go back to Sony's invention of the half-inch black-and-white portapak, will we be able to delineate the social, cultural, and economic factors that contextualized the appearance of this new technology and its rapid acceptance by artists, news organizations, and community activists?

In retrospect it now seems clear that Sony was setting the stage for the VCR, having made the judgment that spectators would eventually want to control their own viewing patterns and also place their faith in the electronic image, in much the same way they had with photographs.[29] What led Sony to this hypothesis and is it valid? Why was the Sony Corporation able to anticipate this? Why did an American firm, the Ampex Corporation, which had invented video recorders in 1955 ten years before Sony introduced the portapak, not grab the opportunity in the same way? Why did the JVC Company in Japan choose the VHS format over Betamax (a superior technology) and thus quickly marginalize Sony's role in the first years of VCR development, even though Sony had been in the forefront some years earlier? Those are questions that this essay will not be able to answer, but they are part of a history that needs to be developed in any discussion of video if we are to broaden our understanding of technological change and the role of video in cultural development.

There is a "history" that can perhaps account for the new circuits of communication put in place by the advent of video. In particular one would have to develop an analysis of the implications of more and more people of vastly different backgrounds becoming comfortable with video as a device in the home. We would have to explore the link between the technology as a structure of possibilities in the political arena and its location within a postmodern context in which new kinds of histories (public and private) are being created in rather nonlinear ways. At first blush, it appears as if video permits a massive set of variables to be introduced into a world of endless disjunctures, where there is no clear or level playing field for the construction and maintenance of specific meanings. Yet it may be the case that as more and more electronic images are created for very specific contexts, the fragmentation will allow for an interchangeable flux of meanings to be sustained by hitherto undescribed modes of linkage.

The often-expressed desire of video activists to bring the people in the communities they work with together for the purposes of change and social cohesion is situated in a concept of community that is both naive and untheorized. Aside from the difficulties of gaining access to the rather complex and multilayered aspects of community life, the very notion of community is based on a denial of difference and on a vague conception of conflict resolution. As Iris Marion Young has put it: "The ideal of community, finally, totalizes and detemporalizes its conception of social life by setting up an opposition between authentic and inauthentic social relations. It also detemporalizes its understanding of social change by positing the desired society as the complete negation of existing society."[30]

Young goes on to talk about the efforts of political activists to radicalize and politicize the communities they work in. She claims that the notion of face-to-face relations "seeks a model of social relations that are not mediated by space and time distancing. In radically opposing the inauthentic social relations of alienated society with the authentic social relations of community, moreover, it detemporalizes the process of social change into a static before and after structure."[31] The implications of these claims for political work in the community with video are quite dramatic. They suggest that the assumptions of involvement and participation that video activists so vigorously pursued may have contributed to a static model of human relations, from which it was difficult, if not impossible, to build new paradigms of political and cultural activity.

The desire to bring people together around the practice of making videotapes has an initial ring of authenticity to it. In the literature of community video, there seems to be an almost apocalyptic result that is generated when the technology is introduced and then used. The effect is doubled when the images are shown back to the community, with the explicit presumption being that images provide a mirror that would otherwise not be available. Within this environment, the topography of ideas one uses to clarify or support political media activities needs to be carefully thought out. Although often discredited both from within and outside academic circles, the high culture/low culture dichotomy remains at the center of presumptions about what works as political communication and what doesn't. It seems clear that the arguments presently in place for the activity of viewing are strung out along a thin border between conflicting conceptions of passivity and nonpassivity. This dichotomy cannot account for televisual viewing, so we need an entirely different model. I bring this up because in the context of the arguments that have been developed around the legitimacy of video as a political tool, it is television, and by extension all of popular culture, that is the site of a lack, an absence that the community use of video or video advocacy will somehow fill. It is in the context of this notion of a loss of power to the mainstream media and to the consequences of technological innovation that the notion of empowerment draws its strength. Yet the question of empowerment cannot be answered from within the negative parameters of an opposition that promotes such a mechanical model of communication and exchange. So perhaps the very idea of empowerment as it has been theorized up until now needs to draw upon different sources that incorporate many *more* forms of cultural activity and that accept the diversity of needs, desires, and political priorities that communities, groups, or individuals encourage, create, and respond to.

Underlying the approach taken by the community video movement is a rationalist ideology of communication, centered on ideas of citizenship, identity, and empowerment through participatory, media-based activities. In fact, there is a need to move beyond generalized metaphors of the media to perhaps address the following question as it is posed by Nicholas Garnham: "Can we identify cultural forms or types of media practice that favor the formation of democratic identities and others which undermine such identities?"[32]

In one respect this seems like a naive question. In another respect it is at the core of the political assumptions that both guide and frame the use of video as a pedagogical tool. Although these points are not articulated by the institutions that have become the most important purveyors of video (and I should add other new technologies, in particular the computer), there is an assumed link between media practice and the public sphere. The premise is that images will contribute to the growth of social movements—viewers will also fit what they see into what they think about both with respect to their own identities and their sense of themselves as public and private personae (the contribution they can make to the social context in which they live). This notion of a "public subjectivity," a term articulated by Benjamin Lee, is essentially proposed as a holistic practice that moves citizenship beyond the narrow parameters of the community or nation-state.[33] In this respect public subjectivity comes to stand for a public sphere and a public culture that stretches far beyond the physical and psychologi-

RON BURNETT

cal boundaries of the community as we presently define it. It also stands for strategies of spectatorship that are dependent on intercultural and therefore more hybridized conceptions of what works as communication and what doesn't. The appropriation of video leads to forms of cultural expression that mix many different aspects of historically *differentiated* types of information. The problem is, to what degree can these histories be accessed when their specificity is both overwhelmed and diluted by the movement of ideas across many, often distinctive, cultures in one country or many countries? What are the attractions of different publics for the videotapes presented to them? To what degree and with what depth can public spaces be constructed where the videotapes can be evaluated? Can viewers gain access to their own and their neighbors' experiences of media images? Even more important, since so much of the viewing of electronic images is bound up with desire (the desire to know, sometimes combined with, and other times offset, by the desire to be entertained) and since the discursive articulation of desire is neither easy nor, generally speaking, public (and may even be antithetical to the culture involved), what kind of access can we gain to the way viewers learn from, and experience, video images?

It may be that Garnham's question merely reinforces the idea that instrumental forms of communication can be constructed to promote political involvement and change. Surely the time has come to alter, if not recreate, this kind of argument. I have found that some gay and feminist writers and videomakers have moved beyond the restrictive boundaries of instrumentality. (In particular, I would like to cite the extraordinary work of Sadie Benning.) Video advocacy, particularly in southern countries, is in deep trouble. Community video has rarely moved beyond the initial parameters of debate that established the movement. The time has come to examine these closed systems of thought and discourse and reflect on why they have played such a dominant role in grassroots work with video and why they have been used as the foundation upon which so-called alternative media institutions have been built. If the heterogeneity of "community" and the richness of the "local" can engage with the genuinely important shifts of emphasis represented by video and other emerging technologies of communication, then it may just be possible to redefine the meaning and breadth of alternativity at the creative, political, theoretical, and discursive levels. It may also be possible to rethink the history of visual technologies and their role in the development of idealistic notions of change. Technology has changed the role of the image in most societies. This may be the time to take a step back and examine the implications of such a major shift for cultures in the north and south.

I would like to thank the editors of this volume for their input and Haidee Wasson of McGill University for her suggestions and insightful comments on this article.

[1] See the International Commission for the Study of Communication Problems (the MacBride Commission), *Many Voices, One World* (London: Kogan Page, 1980), and *World Communication Report* (Paris: UNESCO, 1989). The latter lists a long series of reports that have come out of various countries and constituencies.

[2] Hamid Mowlana and Laurie J. Wilson, *The Passing of Modernity: Communication and the Transformation of Society* (New York: Longman, 1990), 58.

[3] See in particular Sara Stuart, "Access to Media: Placing Video in the Hands of the People," *Media Development* 36, no. 4 (1989): 42–45, and Chinyere Stella Okunna, "Communication for Self-reliance among Rural Women in Nigeria," *Media Development* 39, no. 1 (1992): 46–49.

[4] D. Barnlund, "The Cross-Cultural Arena: An Ethical Void," in *Ethical Perspectives and Critical Issues in Intercultural Communication,* ed. N.C. Asuncion-Landé (Annandale, Va.: Speech Communication Association, 1979), 8–13, cited in Jeffrey C. Ady, "Cultural Relativism and Global Equity in Media Access: A Challenge to Idealism through the 1990s," paper presented at the Sixth MacBride Roundtable, Honolulu, 20–23 January 1994, 10-11.

[5] Stuart, "Access to Media," 45.

[6] See Ad Boeren, "Getting Involved: Communication for Participatory Development," and Manfred Oepen, "Traditional and Group Media Utilization in Indonesia," both in *The Empowerment of Culture: Development Communication and Popular Media,* ed. Ad Boeren and Kes Epskamp (The Hague: Centre for the Study of Education in Developing Countries, 1992), 47–60, 61–78.

[7] Paulo Freire, *Education for Critical Consciousness* (New York: Seabury Press, 1973).

[8] Lisa Vinebohm, "The Power of Voice," *Interadio* 5, no. 2 (1993): 2.

[9] Kim Goldberg, *The Barefoot Channel: Community Television as a Tool for Social Change* (Vancouver: New Star Books, 1990), 6.

[10] Ibid., 10.

[11] Kelly Anderson and Annie Goldson, "Alternative Television inside and outside of the Academy," *Social Text* 35 (Summer 1993): 56-71.

[12] The authors seem not to be aware of the work of John Downing, whose *Radical Media: The Political Experience of Alternative Communication* (Cambridge, Mass.: South End Press, 1984) attempts precisely to link historical and theoretical concerns with practical experience. Various monographs such as Francis J. Berrigan, *Community Communications: The Role of Community Media in Development* (Paris: UNESCO, 1979), and Francis J. Berrigan, ed., *Access: Some Western Models of Community Media* (Paris: UNESCO, 1977); short articles such as, Terence Turner, "Visual Media: Cultural Politics, and Anthropological Practice: Some Implications of Recent Uses of Film and Video among the Kayapo of Brazil," *Commission on Visual Anthropology Review*, Spring 1990; and the work coming out of the *Group Media Journal* in Germany reflect an ongoing concern to grapple with the various issues that arise out of alternative use of the media. Also see Roy Armes, *On Video* (New York: Routledge, 1988).

[13] Anderson and Goldson, "Alternative Television," 59.

[14] Lili Berko, "Video: In Search of a Discourse," *Quarterly Review of Film Studies* 10, no. 4 (1989): 289–307.

[15] Michael Shamberg, *Guerrilla Television* (New York: Holt, Rinehart and Winston, 1971); Doug Hall and Sally Jo Fifer, eds., *Illuminating Video* (New York: Aperture Foundation, 1990).

[16] Two of the most important were the Annenberg School of Communications at the University of Pennsylvania and the School of Public Policy at the University of Chicago.

[17] Sylvia Roy and Nancy Thede, "An Interview with Luiz Fernando Santoro," *Clips* (a publication of *Vidéazimut,* Montreal, Quebec), May 1992, 3.

[18] Ibid., 14.

[19] Hamid Mowlana and Laurie J. Wilson, *The Passing of Modernity: Communication and the Transformation of Society* (New York: Longman, 1990), 142.

[20] Manfred Oepen, "Communicating with the Grassroots: A Practice-oriented Seminar Series," in *Group Media Journal* 9, no. 3 (1990): 4.

21 For additional information on Challenge for Change, see Ron Burnett, "Video/Film: From Communication to Community," in *Video in the Changing World,* ed. Nancy Thede and Alain Ambrosi (New York and Montreal: Black Rose Books, 1991), 54-60.

22 Dorothy Todd Hénaut, "Editorial," *Challenge for Change Newsletter* 1, no. 2 (1970): 3.

23 See a number of the essays in Thede and Ambrosi, eds., *Video in the Changing World* (Montreal: Black Rose Books, 1991).

24 Rick Moore, "Canada's Challenge for Change: Documentary Film and Video as an Exercise of Power through the Production of Cultural Reality" (Ph.D. diss., University of Oregon, 1987). This is one of the few sustained efforts at an analysis of the relationship of the National Film Board to Challenge for Change.

25 Elisabeth Prinn, "Vive le Videographe," *Challenge for Change Newsletter*, no. 8 (Spring 1972): 18.

26 Moore, *Canada's Challenge,* 119.

27 Deirdre Boyle, "From Portapack to Camcorder: A Brief History of Guerrilla Television," *Journal of Film and Video* 44, nos. 1–2 (1992): 67, 78.

28 These questions are addressed, albeit all too briefly, by Lili Berko in "Video: In Search of a Discourse," *Quarterly Review of Film Studies* 10, no. 4 (1989): 289–307.

29 Akio Morita, the founder and head of Sony, said of the VCR: "[It] will revolutionize television. It will change the concept of prime time so that *any* time can be prime time. Before the development of video recording, television was too fleeting. While it has been outstanding for conveying information, providing entertainment, and improving our culture, the sad fact exists that once a program is off the air it is gone forever for the T.V. viewer. Newspapers, magazines, and books can be read and kept for future reference. But this had not been so with T.V. programs seen in the home" (quoted in Nick Lyons, "The Age of Betamax," in *The Sony Vision* [New York: Crown, 1976], 211).

30 Iris Marion Young, "The Ideal of Community and the Politics of Difference," in *Feminism/Postmodernism,* ed. Linda J. Nicholson (New York: Routledge, 1990), 302.

31 Ibid., 305.

32 Nicholas Garnham, "The Mass Media, Cultural Identity, and the Public Sphere in the Modern World," *Public Culture* 5, no. 2 (1993): 264.

33 Benjamin Lee, "Going Public," *Public Culture* 5, no. 2 (1993): 165–78.

CHAPTER 20

FETAL TISSUE:
REPRODUCTIVE RIGHTS AND
ACTIVIST AMATEUR VIDEO

Patricia R. Zimmermann

As women, we now live under wartime conditions. Anita Hill, Murphy Brown, the Republican Party's attempt to deify family values, Zoe Baird, and the shooting of Dr. David Gunn at a Florida abortion clinic in March 1993 are all sites of newly fashioned feminist battlegrounds.[1] The Supreme Court's *Bray* decision upholding the right of Operation Rescue to block entrances to clinics in January 1993 signals a sharp retreat for women's reproductive rights. *Bray* legitimates the antiabortion movement's strategy of direct assault and annihilates women's bodies and right to choose.[2] These battlegrounds are constructed differently than geopolitical wars—the Gulf War, Bosnia, Somalia—where combatants fight with guns, missiles, and media propaganda for geographically demarcated places defined by borders. These wars against the female body occupy different locations.

Although these female body wars differ significantly from World War II or Vietnam with their postmodern inflection of new media technologies like satellites and CNN, which alter war representation through privileging instantaneous imaging, feminist battlegrounds are not defined exclusively or explicitly by geography.[3] Their borders are amorphous in the material sense, smudging the lines between media representations, political agendas, the female body, technology, and place. They cannot be mapped—analytically, physically, philosophically, critically—in quite the same way as geopolitical wars; gender and sexuality operate within a much more fluid and infinitely contestable expanse.

Gender, sexuality, and reproductive rights in the 1990s are difficult to "see" and to "situate," although they penetrate nearly every political discussion and media representation like a computer virus. Their polyvocal and fluid forms shatter borders between humans and machines and challenge the stasis of phallocentric systems of politics and representation. Donna Haraway identifies these shifting practices and mergers as the cyborg: "People are nowhere near so fluid, being both material and opaque. Cyborgs are ether, quintessence. The ubiquity and invisibility of cyborgs is precisely why these sunshine-belt machines are so deadly. They are as hard to see politically as materially. They are about consciousness—or its simulation."[4] In the case of the war over representation and reproductive rights, the cyborg provides access to these new places.

This argument about heterogeneity and cyborg identity must be hewn carefully, however, so as not to totally launch feminist media political strategy into the potentially unproductive realm of cyberspace unhinged from concrete social relations. The realpolitik dimensions of gender, sexuality, and reproductive rights located in the courts, the law, public policy, health care, and the real material lives of women remain vital to any feminist media agenda. The difference that I am trying to argue for here is that while realpolitik is necessary, it is no longer sufficient. We must also see representation as a material practice. The web of social relations within which women live is *also* an assemblage of technology and representation. Haraway's imagining of the cyborg, then, proposes not to jettison the "real," but to actually expand it, complicate it, demonstrate its multivocal construction that breaks down distinctions and domination.[5]

These feminist battles over reproductive rights track the disturbances provoked by women in a differently ordered and constructed public sphere that has transformed politics in the 1990s. The most recent and horrific concrete example of this collapse of the borders between representation and the "real" is the assassination of Dr. David Gunn, an abortion provider in Florida, by Michael Griffin, a prolife supporter. Although the shooting of Dr. Gunn marks the first death of an abortion provider and therefore signifies the escalation of the civil war against women to deadly heights, it also occurred within the context of increasing clinic violence during the last several years (bombings, arson, toxic chemicals injected into Planned Parenthood clinics, assaults against clinic personnel, vandalism, trespass, and physical confrontation of abortion providers). Prolife political strategy has shifted from ideological to physical warfare diffused to multiple clinics across the country. This explicit assault on the pregnant female body has unfolded for the last ten years, unimpeded by any intervention from the Justice Department to protect the civil rights of women or their access to health care.[6]

However, the prolife political strategy has itself not been confined only to the realm of the "real" or the domain of the "law." It too has obscured the boundaries between female bodies, representation, politics, and reproductive rights. Operation Rescue chapters have instituted a campaign called "No Place to Hide." The campaign features "Wanted" posters with pictures of doctors who perform abortions and their telephone numbers. Dr. Gunn was the subject of one of these posters. There is no simple cause-and-effect relation between these posters and abortion violence; that kind of analysis suggests an antiquated, hypodermic model in which media directly impels politics. Rather, these posters, the killing of Dr. Gunn, and the subsequent Planned Parenthood media campaign demonstrate quite forcibly that a new formation smearing the lines between media, technology, and politics has emerged that requires careful deconstruction if a new feminist media politics is to be forged.

The prolife movement is not defined on only one monologic level anymore; rather, it is *both* national and local, *both* ideological and physical, *both* for "babies" and against women, *both* invoking 1960s civil rights strategies and engaging more postmodern technologies like telephones, faxes, and amateur low-end video documentaries. In the case of Dr. Gunn, the attack against pregnant female bodies inscribed by choice was rendered physical by the killing of a male abortion provider, who himself traveled between clinics in Alabama and Florida. Thus, the pregnant female body was both absent and present simultaneously. Therefore, a feminist media strategy must not only reinsert the female body, but also include a reinvention of representation, media technology, and politics as multivocal constructions that travel between different discourses and terrains.

All of these feminist battlegrounds suggest the emergence of a new political territory, a region marked off not so much by material space or location as by a constantly shifting set of interconnecting relationships between the female body, new technologies, mass communications, political rights, and visual representation. The false borders between media and politics, discourse and representation, the body and technology have disintegrated. This new territory requires a rethreading of feminist media theory and practice. We must reimagine its possibilities for political intervention into the discursive and material conditions of women's lives.

In this chapter, I want to zero in on reproductive rights as a specific battleground of great importance to women in order to investigate the multiple dimensions of these realignments between media and politics, gender and representation, sexuality and visual imaginaries, the maternal and the pregnant body, the female body and the state. I argue that this collapsing of media and politics into a new configuration of power needs to be considered dialectically. On the one hand, this merging reveals a strategy for containing feminist articulations of reproductive rights within mass forms of communications dependent on capitulating to the discursive dominance of textuality. On the other hand, the blurring between media and politics offers a strategy for feminist intervention that arms the oppositional female body with new technologies like low-end video camcorders to build a new social and representational space that imagines new contexts and different material conditions. Along these same lines, Constance Penley and Andrew Ross have argued for the emancipatory potential of new technologies and for a revision of the definition of radical politics: "Activism today is no longer a case of putting bodies on the line; increasingly, it requires and involves bodies-with-cameras."[7]

Rather than pitting alternative media against dominant network or print media in a David-and-Goliath scenario of scarcity and heart versus abundance and manipulation—a common strategy of radical media politics in the 1970s and 1980s—in this chapter I want to play with the notion that all of these multiple registers—from the dominant media of commercials and news stories, to right-to-life videos, to activist video, to experimental art video—trace the contours of the multiple battlegrounds in the fight for reproductive rights. This variety of media charts the multiple formations of the female body: maternal, pregnant, militant, aborted, oppositional, cyborg. These typographies are not distinct, and often overlap. On a theoretical level, the political urgency of

PATRICIA R. ZIMMERMANN

media on reproductive rights hinges not on representation alone, but on its organization of the female body within these multiple zones.

If we junk these oppositions between dominant media and alternative media and concentrate instead on how the social, representational, and discursive dimensions of feminist reproductive rights merge, then the definition of political documentary must be revised, if not altogether abandoned as a false construct dependent upon separating media practice from politics in order to argue that each operates in a seesaw dependency with the other: politics creating the necessity of media intervention, media intervention changing politics and consciousness. If we begin with the supposition that these distinctions are no longer viable because new technologies, gender, and sexuality have problematized them, then we need to revamp our notion of political media entirely.

I start with an incendiary yet necessary assertion: political documentary theory and criticism (with a few exceptions like Julia Lesage, Julianne Burton, and E. Ann Kaplan)[8] has not sufficiently foregrounded the problematics posed by gender, sexuality, and new technologies. A large bulk of writing on documentary has been codependent on textual analysis or argumentation, locked into a Griersonian or neo-Marxist or religious conception of documentary redeeming the nation and the spectator through good works and good intentions, like a missionary to the masses of the uninformed. That a large body of documentary film and video has also depended on realist conventions of expository documentary or more deconstructive, interrogative, and self-reflexive forms is inconsequential. As redemptive works, these films and videos have attempted to rescue the spectator from ignorance or passivity.

As interconnected modalities rather than parallel tracks, gender, sexuality, and new technologies have the potential to revamp our theorization of political documentary. False theoretical oppositions between media texts and historicopolitical contexts must be destroyed if women are to survive. If both Donna Haraway as a feminist and Ross Perot as a renegade multimillionaire capitalist can redefine politics as the convergence of the body with the technological—where distinct borders between the aesthetic and the social, the private and the public, media and political identities fuse—then documentary theory also needs rehabilitation from its 1960s rhetoric of agitation and its fetishization of texts themselves as central to activating politics. Documentary needs to become a feminist cyborg guerrilla, going to the streets with amateur video cameras, just like the Buffalo Media Coalition for Reproductive Rights or Reprovision in New York City. But it needs to reimagine these streets in a less linear and more fluid way, with multiple voices and multiple political nodal points. While the fight for reproductive rights is increasingly bifurcated between the legal system as interpreter of the law and the clinics as enactments of it, a feminist documentary strategy for reproductive rights must interweave and travel between these two poles.

In this chapter, I fantasize how the use of amateur camcorders by reproductive rights activists to document demonstrations at clinics reconfigures the public sphere around abortion politics in the 1990s. I propose to investigate how the new social relations of production offered by amateur video technologies shift discussion about what constitutes political oppositional media practice away from a more monologic, formal analysis of textuality into a more dialogic politics of community and active spectatorship. I argue on two interwoven levels here: the mass-mediated version and the oppositional video revisioning of reproductive rights. I theorize the significance and possibilities of amateur media to generate a feminist oppositional public sphere in light of a repressed and repressive political and media context that represses the female body—in all its multiple forms—from representation. Second, I analyze how specific tapes negotiate reproductive rights activism within specific, multiple social formations of age, class, and race—terms not associated with reproductive rights in its earlier historical formations. These tapes insist on the presence of the female body. These tapes reimagine the relations between text and context, art and politics, spectator and participant with new technologies. This work functions as feminist guerrilla cyborgs, to rephrase Donna Haraway's ideas within a media discourse. These tapes invent a new social space for women.

But how do we justify disposing of residual modes of political documentary as though they were old tie-dyed T-shirts? Why is a feminist public sphere where art and politics, the private and public sphere amalgamate via video an urgent necessity during war on the female body? I would like to graph out two different trajectories on abortion, one textual and symbolic, the other discursive and legal, to show how both, although different, share reactionary structural similarities.

During the 1980s, feminists not only lost ground on the legal front for reproductive rights, but also experienced a retrenchment on the visual front as the antiabortion movement marshaled the visual representation of the fetus as its veritable smart bomb. As Margaret Cooper noted in a 1986 *Cineaste* article called "The Abortion Film Wars," since the dissemination of the antiabortion film *The Silent Scream* in 1986, the abortion debate has engaged both right-to-lifers and feminist media producers in combat over representation.[9] In her decoding of the complicated relationship between media spectacle and clinical experience in *The Silent Scream* and imaging technologies like ultrasound, Rosalind Petchesky has argued that not only has the pregnant body been effaced, peripheralized, and absented, but the fetus itself has been represented as "primary and autonomous." Petcheskey claims, "The strategy of anti-abortionists to make foetal personhood a self-fulfilling prophecy by making the foetus a *public presence* addresses a visually oriented culture. Meanwhile, finding 'positive' images and symbols of abortion hard to imagine, feminists and other pro-choice advocates have all too readily ceded the visual terrain."[10]

Discussing a wide range of reproductive discourse in the 1980s from newspapers, magazines, and television shows, Valerie Hartouni shows that the last decade can be characterized by the mass media's obsession with women and fetuses. She notes that an entire range of political debates about the family, the military, gays, careerism, hedonism, affirmative action, civil rights, and welfare, for example, have reproduction as their subtext. The imaging of the fetus deploys science to institute visual identification and bonding, to reintegrate women with an essentialist maternalism.

PATRICIA R. ZIMMERMANN

Hartouni observes that although the decade of the 1980s left feminists in a defensive and somewhat narrow position of defending reproductive rights, the context of these technologies, techniques, and representations are unstable and vulnerable. She states, "Contained in the disruption of conventional meanings and identities and their particular vulnerability to contestation are numerous possible political openings—multiple points of resistance as well as projects of reconstruction. Naming and seizing these possibilities, however, require imagination, a new political idiom, as well as a certain courage—to eschew a lingering attachment to things 'natural' and 'foundational,' and to jettison the essentialism clung to by all extant participants and opponents of the repro-tech drama."[11] All these writers acknowledge that the battle for reproductive rights has shifted to representation. Although Cooper sees hope in alternative documentaries that tell different stories about abortion, she does not theorize how these films could work to restructure the relationship between politics, media, and the female body. While Petchesky and Hartouni concur that the antiabortion movement has virtually seized the visual front, they do not propose concrete counterstrategies for feminists to regain visual culture and to imagine a concrete counterattack that places the female body within social relations.

Ultimately, representation alone is insufficient, vulnerable to endless recodings and recontextualizations. Signification without social relations poses no threat to the phallocratic patriarchal order. An activist, feminist oppositional media practice around abortion that includes the female body is vitally urgent. As both longtime reproductive rights activists and feminist cultural theorists know, our opponents in the culture wars and the female body wars can conjure up the easily digestible, romanticized codes and maternalized conventions of visual imagery of fetuses and children. They can marshal discursive homologies equating abortion to the Holocaust and slavery to invoke civil rights within a rhetoric dependent upon metaphor and emotion unhinged from historical specificities.

Conversely, the prochoice side has traditionally banked on cognitive and political arguments about a woman's right to choose and analysis of the problematic of women's differences from men within the U.S. health care system.[12] While valid, necessary, and compelling, these positions do not easily lend themselves to visual representation where the object itself could be reproduced, because the object—abortion rights—is a discursive construct with multiple dimensions and forms. Therefore, there is no simple, unmediated correspondence between object and image. A radical intervention into representation, then, must by necessity assemble different layers of images, discourses, bodies, and politics together to combat the way the image of the fetus appears to be consummate. These arguments are abstract and not easy to represent within Hollywood cinematic narrative conventions invoking desire or affect. In the 1990s, textual, contextual, representational, political, and argumentative modes have congealed into a new kind of social formation that is neither distinctly media nor distinctly political. Therefore, a feminist radical media practice requires decomposition of these arbitrary borders. I deliberately deploy the term *practice* here, following Foucault in *The Archaeology of*

Knowledge, as a way to suggest the disintegration of boundaries between the political and the representational, yet to avoid postmodernism's blurring of everything into a pluralist simulacrum in which power is disavowed.[13]

During the last year, the De Moss Foundation has aired commercials on the networks in selected markets and on CNN depicting a multiculturally correct group of about thirty smiling six-year-olds exiting a clean, suburban school. The Arthur S. De Moss Foundation, located in Philadelphia, is a rather curious organization, established nearly forty years ago by Nancy De Moss, wife of Arthur S. De Moss, president of the National Liberty Corporation, an insurance company located in Valley Forge, Pennsylvania. Upon Arthur's death in 1979, Nancy committed herself to celebrating what she terms "Life." Nonprofit and committed to producing educational publications and media presentations on what their foundation statement terms "major concerns within our society," the De Moss Foundation accepts no contributions. Instead, it asks that potential contributors donate money to one of the prolife organizations whose addresses are reprinted in a thirty-two-page glossy brochure that is mailed to anyone inquiring about the organization.[14] The television ads are part of an elaborate media campaign by the De Moss Foundation. In their own statement, they proclaim: "This campaign celebrates life. It deals with family values and treats a delicate subject in a kind and gentle way. It seeks to change minds, not laws, by getting people to think about a difficult subject in a new light. These spots simply ask the question: What could be more important than the right of someone to be born?"[15] The foundation refuses to disclose the names of the producers and will not circulate the tapes.[16]

In the current ad running on cable television, the voice-over proclaims that their mothers chose life for them, and that is why we can "see" them now. The De Moss Foundation has run this series of prolife, profamily spots for over a year during prime time. Other notorious spots feature happy white parents doting over a child in a playground, with a syrupy, concerned male voice-over explaining that the couple had considered terminating the pregnancy because they weren't sure they could afford a child.

With their classical, harmonious composition, soft lighting, pastel costuming, and bourgeois mise-en-scène, these slick commercials merge the commodity fetishism of advertising with the psychoanalytic overlays and conventions of Hollywood melodrama. These ads elaborate an emotional tapestry of the family romance. Here, both the production and representation of children collapse into each other: the 35mm image of the happy yet voiceless child is reproducible on the level of representation precisely because biological reproduction on the level of the woman's body was not tampered with by "unnatural" forces such as abortion. These De Moss ads invert the melodramatic modes of classical Hollywood style: rather than contradiction between sexuality and convention, between woman's independence and her place within the confines of the home, between repression and expression (tropes that form the resistant, oppositional potential of all melodrama), these De Moss ads present us with upscale versions of happy home movies where all contention is erased.[17]

This evening out of contradictions facilitates an affective response on

310

only one register—emotion. The subtext of this ad is that no other analysis—feminist, analytical, legal, social, political—is legitimate, because no available single image could overpower that of the beatific child. As in Holocaust and civil rights imagery, the child is figured as a survivor and the reason for continued vigilance. This strategy does not differ significantly from most television commercials, in which the fetishization of commodities—in this case, children—depends on addressing affective desire through the excessive opulence of the image design.

Most important, this ad pictures the child without the mother as parent, as an independent, autonomous being virtually outside of familial relations. Woman's body and mothering are invisible, not simply erased, which would suggest an active deletion. Carole Stabile has noted a similar move in mass media representations of fetuses: "The maternal space has, in effect, disappeared and what has emerged in its place is an environment that the fetus alone occupies."[18] Numerous close-ups amplify the child's identity, subjectivity, and presence while the mother is reduced to a verbal construct with no visual valence or power. In other words, the maternal space is jettisoned to the outside of the image as a sort of distant satellite, still transmitting but on the "outside," secondary to the needs or the image of the child.

Ann Kaplan, in her book *Motherhood and Representation,* describes this fusion of the mother and child to submit to the rule of the father as the maternal sacrifice paradigm. This paradigm establishes women's relationship to their children as one typified by loss of self, identity, and differentiation between women and their children.[19] Extending this paradigm to the elision of abortion in this ad, women sacrifice choice and autonomy from the nuclear family to live in a world where the rule of the father is inscribed on three different registers. First, a disembodied male voice-over asserts patriarchal authority. Second, 35mm commercial film production affirms technological authority. Third, access to prime-time markets on cable in the realm of distribution and diffusion confirms economic authority. Following most prolife imagery, the child (and in other media representations, such as magazine photographs, the fetus) is positioned as the glorified subject of the family romance, its subjectivity overpowering, engulfing, and annihilating the mother. The De Moss commercials merge the fetus and the child; each invokes and winds back on the other, inseparable in practice and discourse.

My second example of the complex discursive topography of abortion is none other than President Bill Clinton's reversal of five rulings on abortion on the twentieth anniversary of *Roe v. Wade* on 22 January 1993, only two days after he took office. Women's groups pressured the Clinton administration to initiate some significant interventions on abortion on this historic day to show the symbolic end to twelve years of Republican and Supreme Court chiseling away at *Roe v. Wade.* To summarize, the rulings reverse the prohibition on counseling women about abortion in federally funded clinics (the gag rule), permits military hospitals to perform abortions if the woman pays, reassesses the ban on RU 486, opens the way to provide money to international groups that provide abortions, and allows research on fetal tissue to proceed.[20]

On the discursive and political level, Clinton's actions on abortion signaled his debt to the women's vote that helped him to win the presidential election in the first place, despite the fact that during the campaign he equivocated that abortion should be safe and legal but rare. While his position on abortion is hardly a feminist stance on reproductive freedom, this statement serves to speak of abortion yet silence the feminist agenda. It should also be noted that during the transition, Clinton railed against women as "bean counters" for demanding more women appointees to cabinet positions in his administration. What has emerged in the Clinton administration's discursive construction of women is a splitting of the female subject into multiple parts, each of which can be handled in specific ways to curb the potential destabilization of neoliberal pluralism by a radical multiplicity. For example, abortion is severed from the discourse of equality and access, women appointees to cabinet positions are positioned as women and *not* as women interested in women's issues, and Hillary Rodham Clinton is remade as a pastiche of the perfect mother, supportive mate, glamorous fashion plate, and health care policy wonk. This disarticulation of the political complexity of women and feminism in the Clinton administration toward a more singular and controllable media image serves to modify and restrain the political power of women as a voting bloc and women's issues as politically volatile.

The Clinton reversals on abortion should not be so easily read and acclaimed as remedies to the legal setbacks of the 1980s and 1990s. These reversals are both similar to and different from the Supreme Court decisions of the 1980s (*H. L. v. Matheson* in 1983, *Webster v. Reproductive Health Services* in 1989, *Hodgson v. Minnesota* and *Ohio v. Akron Center for Reproductive Health* in 1990, *Planned Parenthood v. Casey* in 1992, and *Bray v. Alexandria Women's Health Clinic* in 1993). All of these Court decisions limit access to abortion yet keep the right to abortion intact. Clinton's reversals actually only invert what the Court has advocated: the right to abortion remains but access to abortion is not bolstered at all in terms of protecting equality, with the rulings covering only very specific areas like the military, scientific research, and disbursement of funds internationally. However, the rulings also differ from the Supreme Court decisions in that they open up the discourse on abortion, typified in the lifting of the gag rule. Thus, the Clinton reversals sever practice from discourse: the practice of abortion remains locked within the regressive Supreme Court rulings while the discourse on abortion is released from legal bondage.

However, despite what is on the level of policy a breath of liberal—but be apprised, certainly not radical—fresh air after the virulently antiwoman regimes of the past decade, on the level of visual representation and narrative structure, the *New York Times* coverage of the Clinton reversals structurally duplicates the De Moss Foundation's ads.[21] The news coverage of this event deleted women, feminism, and reproductive rights visually and discursively. Out of twenty-four paragraphs in the *New York Times* story, only one featured a response from a prochoice leader, Kate Michelman of the National Abortion Rights Action League. That sole sentence was located on the jump page, a visual and ideological displacement of women.

PATRICIA R. ZIMMERMANN

The bulk of the article covered various prolifers, from Cardinal Mahoney of Los Angeles to Senator Jesse Helms to the seventy-five thousand prolife protesters outside the White House. This discursive erasure of "women" and silencing of "feminism" is doubled in the two news photographs illustrating the story: on the front page, a group shot of about seven prolife men with picket signs, and on the jump page, a large crowd shot of the prolife demonstrators with the phallic Washington Monument centering the composition. This double move of silencing feminism and representing women has emerged as a strategy of the Clinton administration, in the example of Hillary Clinton's carefully orchestrated, yet mostly mute, press image. When Clinton announced that Hillary would head the task force on Health Care Reform, she did not speak. Yet the press coverage of Hillary, in biographies and anecdote, constantly affirms her strong voice in policy.[22] So her visual representation is split from her practice.

One could argue that these images of antiabortion protest are merely ideological capitulations to the inherent use of binary opposition in news coverage to establish a narrative conflict between large, overpowering forces such as the government and an angry mass movement. Yet on a more visual and visceral level, they underscore the repression of women as a class *and* the maternal as a complex multiplicity by the "law." Within the news coverage of the reversals, the "law" is figured in multiple forms that are *not* split apart discursively. The "law" is government, yet it symbolizes Clinton's authority to intervene and change government policy. The "law" in this media representation is caught between social debates yet also operates psychoanalytically as the rule of the father and language. If the entire context of the news during Clinton's first one hundred days is read as a Hollywood melodrama script with various roles and subplots, repression and contradiction erupt, signifying narrative excess and radical ruptures with patriarchy. During the same period that Clinton signed these abortion reversals, "nannygate" erupted on Capital Hill: Zoe Baird's nomination for attorney general was embattled by her employment of illegal aliens to provide child care.[23] Here, the contradictions that emanated from the Baird nomination emulated the classic ingredients of 1950s melodrama: woman as mother challenges woman as worker, the private and the public realms that constitute "woman" crash into one another. In the case of the attorney general nomination, Baird's position as a rich, elite professional superseded the gender issues of mothering in the discourse surrounding her employment of illegal aliens, yet the confirmation hearings vacillated between her qualifications as a legal professional and her disqualification as a mother who performed an illegal act. Further, the private realm of Baird's mothering and child care detoured the public realm of her ability to serve as attorney general. In this case, gender issues around mothering underscored class privilege as a "problem" for government service.

I would like to detour from unraveling the gender, class, ethnicity, colonial relations, and corporate collaborations trajectories of the Baird case and focus instead on the narrative structure of the maternal in news coverage from the period of January 21 to January 24, 1993. Within this time period, three breaking news stories opened up maternal space: the Clinton reversals on abortion, the Zoe Baird case, and the installation of Hillary Clinton into the West Wing of the White House. If we can reimagine this period not as news, but as a 1957 Douglas Sirk melodrama called, perhaps, *All That the Law Allows*, then we might envision parallel editing between the *benevolent* rule of the father in Clinton's discursive legal reversals, his *malevolence* toward women in leaving Zoe Baird hanging in the wind as the female replacement of the very same "Law" in the position of attorney general, and his *admission* of women to some truncated, silent form of power in Hillary's unpaid assumption as czarina of health care reform. Following the narrative patterns of classic melodrama, the phallic mother—the nonnurturing, sadistic, controlling mother—is in evidence in the Baird story. The mother who chooses to live in *both* the maternal realm of the private sphere and the social/economic world of the public sphere is punished, silenced, and exiled from the narrative, or, in this case, the Department of Justice. Despite the Clinton abortion reversals, the social annihilation of the phallic mother on the symbolic level and the political destruction of the "materiality" of mothering on the level of the real continued at a ferocious, almost pathological pitch.

How do these media trajectories—neoliberal, conservative and radical—relate to amateur video and the formation of a feminist oppositional public sphere around reproductive rights? Both examples are inflected with similar articulations of a subplot on sacrificial mothering as proper behavior for women, eradication of women's bodies and voice, and suppression of any discourse on abortion rights and access. In this way, the De Moss ads and the news coverage of the Clinton legal reversals demonstrate some of the very complicated congruencies between conservative and neoliberal politics, especially when understood in relation to various strategies for representing the female body. Both positions depend on disentangling women from mothering, mothering from social relations, social relations from representation, and representation from the female body. Both positions demonstrate an inability, or perhaps refusal, to situate women within a more complex, multiple formation.

It could be argued that President Clinton is actually the first truly postmodern president, not Ronald Reagan. I define *postmodernism* here as the separation of the signifier from the signified through the simulacrum available from new technology and as the refiguring of history and agency as representation. Clinton's particular inflection of postmodernism is not so simply a play of media surfaces: it is much more insidious. It revitalizes traditional liberal rhetoric of participation and social welfare but eviscerates subjects, social space, and history. Linda Hutcheon has argued that much postmodern art disposes of conventional history, interrogating instead the construction and ideological underpinnings of historical explanation: "In a very real sense, postmodernism reveals a desire to understand present culture as the product of previous representations. The representation of history becomes the history of representations."[24]

In the case of Clinton, it is important to make a distinction between postmodernism as a descriptive, covering term charting major alterations in the social order and postmodernism as an artistic strategy that revamps the relationship between representation and referents to create new meanings. Although both clearly overlap and

PATRICIA R. ZIMMERMANN

inform each other, Clinton's media construction of himself borrows its strategy from radical postmodern art, pastiching representations and history, yet denuding the reassemblage of radical critique. Barry Smart has identified postmodernism with a fundamental transformation in politics, technology, and capitalism, a shift from a public sphere based on justice to one based on performativity.[25] In the political sense, Clinton *performs* liberalism rather than *engages* it. For example, Clinton's penchant for the talk show format as a way to get in touch with "the people" to push his programs relies on his performing the role of open host, when in fact, the participants are carefully screened ahead of time. In an aesthetic sense, Clinton's particular inflection of the postmodern presents a *representation* of democracy as it diminishes the material, social relations that would provide *access* to participation in democracy, a political strategy typified by the Clinton abortion reversals. Clinton understands the power of new media technologies like cable, satellite, and e-mail, which glibly perform and evoke nineteenth-century formulations of small-town, rural democracy (the electronic town hall), yet completely guts them of any emancipatory possibilities to form a public sphere in the Habermasian sense of establishing truth through critical dialogue entered into equally. Cultural studies theory has shown how mediated relations are social and material. Clinton suggests access but does not ensure it for everyone, thus severing mediated relations from material ones.

A feminist oppositional political and media practice must dismantle all of these intertwined levels of representation, politics, media, technology, and the female body and be multistrategic. The De Moss ads and the Clinton reversals are both locked within conventions of home movies, commercials, state mandates, and melodrama that smooth over sexual and racial difference, struggle across common political interests, the historical position of women's bodies, and collective efforts on multiple sites. These two media representations systematically eradicate women's struggle and bodies by means of both the law and high-end, commercial media production. The law and high-end media blur together like a stereoscope.

Because media blackouts and restrictions have obliterated access to the public sphere for reproductive rights activists, the availability of small-format video provides a means to create multiple oppositional public spheres where art and politics converge like a Moebius strip. I would like to outline some of the contours of this media blackout on abortion to establish the urgency of these activist videos. As Nina Leibman has shown in a recent issue of the *Velvet Light Trap*, it was not until 1956 when the Production code was altered that Hollywood features could mention abortion. And even afterward, the few films that dealt with abortion constructed both sex and abortion as sordid.[26]

Steve Dubin, in his book *Arresting Images*, has outlined how the networks and the Right have effectively eliminated abortion discourse and representation from the public sphere: characters in mainstream television series rarely mention the word *abortion*. Network television has vehemently shied away from abortion since a character on a 1972 episode of *Maude* had an abortion and sent advertisers fleeing. An episode of *China Beach* that featured an abortion was not rebroadcast. Right-wing and antiabortion groups have also censured more avant-garde art that deals with abortion. The Heritage Foundation, a right-wing think tank recently notorious for its attacks on public television, attacked feminist artist Shawn Eichman's installation piece *Alchemy Cabinet*, a piece incorporating the remains of her own aborted fetus.[27]

The NBC production of *Roe v. Wade* epitomizes the instability that abortion poses and the way in which radical discourse on women's reproductive rights is contained. This 1989 docudrama was subject to extensive rewriting and network scrutiny to avoid bias, and is now widely available at video stores as a rental movie. The network made every attempt to present an unbiased, balanced show that would favor neither side in order to avoid charges of political advocacy. Although Holly Hunter, an actress identified with reproductive rights politics, performed the role of Norma McCorvey, the network inhibited her from granting interviews. Amy Madigan, an actress whose star image is one of a tough, uncompromising woman, played Sarah Weddington, the attorney for "Jane Roe." The script went through many rewrites in an attempt to maintain balance, and during shooting, the producers used a different title to stave off protesters during production. The program is structured in an almost ping-pong style, with scenes alternating between Norma McCorvey's life and Sarah Weddington's legal struggles juxtaposed against the district attorney's team fashioning opposing arguments. However, despite this "balance" between scenes, the emotional valence and spectator identification of the show resides with the two women: the melodrama of women's difficult negotiation between home, work, and the medical and legal establishments overpowers the more sterile legal arguments of the opposing side.

The casting of Madigan and Hunter, stars associated with commercial film rather than television, further situates *Roe v. Wade* within the history and conventions of the woman's picture and legitimizes abortion as a woman's right to control her life, a fundamental tension of classical melodrama. Although "Jane Roe" wins the case, the entire plot of *Roe v. Wade* revolves around the difficulties of Norma McCorvey's working-class life, and even includes the birth of the child she sought to abort. This narrative structure focuses the program on the victimization of McCorvey by social and legal systems, a trope identified with the position of women in classical film melodramas. The show aired the week after the Supreme Court heard arguments in *Webster v. Reproductive Health Services*, which further increased its political volatility. Some advertising executives argued *Roe v. Wade* was simply good television; its controversial and topical slant would secure good ratings and generate ad revenue. However, Reverend Donald Wildmon and the American Family Association endlessly harassed network sponsors to withdraw advertising. Many advertisers did back off, claiming that the show was too provocative. However, the advertisers who bought airtime at a significantly reduced rate were clearly focused on attracting the women's market, the typical audience for made-for-TV movies: Murphy's Oil Soap and General Foods.[28]

Both CBS's *Murphy Brown* and ABC's *Sisters* have featured main characters mulling over abortion but then choosing to have a baby, in a capitulation to the

PATRICIA R. ZIMMERMANN

prolife bias of the networks, according to a recent study by Fairness and Accuracy in Reporting (FAIR). Another study conducted by Fairness and Accuracy in Media shows that most abortion reporting relies on compromise and common ground in the abortion debate, presenting extremists and angry rhetoric.[29] Dan Quayle's condemnation of *Murphy Brown*, then, was flawed: she represents not the single *mother* rejecting the family, but the single *woman* locked into patriarchal and statist agendas on abortion. His conflation of mother and woman was off target. He should have applauded Murphy Brown for following the script and having the baby, instead of blaming the Los Angeles riots on her decision to become a single parent without a man.

The minimal coverage of the April 1992 Reproductive Rights March on Washington—considered the largest political demonstration in U.S history—by the *New York Times* and other major news outlets underscores the thoroughness of this media blackout. With the *Casey* decision gutting *Roe v. Wade* in June 1992, more commercial and "public" media have effectively detoured from any discussion of reproductive rights, evidenced most recently by the presidential election. Family values and the economy diverted discussion about reproductive rights and "real" family politics out of what emerged during the election as a newly defined, circumscribed, noncritical public sphere of CNN and talk shows by falsely separating them from the economy.

But what about independent film and video in these struggles over representation and reproductive rights, two terms that could be used interchangeably in the context of this argument? Of course, there have been some significant independent films produced about abortion in the 1970s and 1980s, such as *Holy Terror, Abortion: Stories from North and South, With a Vengeance,* and some others. However, compared with the amount of work produced on AIDS, there is a relative dearth of independent work on reproductive rights. The gendered context of production was highlighted for me in 1990 when I served as a film panelist for the New York State Council on the Arts, one of the largest funders of film and video in the country. Out of over three hundred proposals, not one was for a project on abortion, and over 75 percent, in my estimation, were for narrative films about personal issues by a diverse array of producers. B. Ruby Rich has railed against the gendered confines of independent film and video, noting that independents in the 1980s unconsciously internalized the Right's agenda to disembowel controversy in government-funded media by moving into narrative feature film. Because women have traditionally been positioned as outsiders in media production, she claims that the independent media scene has witnessed a gendered division of labor in the 1980s in the face of severe budget cutbacks (totaling a 50 percent reduction of funds over a twelve-year period): men produce narrative film, while women, she argues, have moved into video, a cheaper and more accessible format that is not so reliant on huge production budgets and can be produced more quickly.[30] In the case of reproductive rights media, the amount of work produced on video far exceeds the amount produced on film, a fact confirmed by a survey of current film and video rental catalogs.

What possibilities does video, especially low-end video, offer in this age of defunding and privatization of Corporation for Public Broadcasting (CPB), the Public

Broadcasting Service (PBS), and federal and state grants?[31] What sort of intervention do new technologies like amateur video provoke in an era of increasing concentration and centralization of all media industries? First, it is important to recognize here that the 1992 attacks against public television by Laurence Jarvik, the Heritage Foundation, the Family Research Council, and various conservative senators like Bob Dole and Jesse Helms were not new salvos against the so-called perverse, postmodern, antifigurative, artistic Left, but merely the pinnacle of twelve years of complaints by conservatives that arts agencies and public television evidenced a liberal bias that axed out conservative viewpoints.[32] Conservatives invoked the fairness doctrine, modernist social science notions of objectivity, and a return to traditional art forms to save media production from the terrors of postmodernist decentering of white male hegemony and linearity. Their arguments hinged on a three-pronged attack: first, invocation of a reinterpretation of the law that narrowed its scope; second, a philosophical rejection of postmodernism by reconstructing a romanticized and scientific truth claim; and third, a reinstitution of the boundary line between the high culture of form and the low culture of emotion and rage.

The Right's terror of this threat of instability—both political and aesthetic—was epitomized in the outcry against Marlon Riggs's black gay anthem, *Tongues Untied*, by Pat Buchanan and some conservative groups attacking local public television stations. It is not just sexuality that threatens the status quo here, as some radical cultural critics have claimed, but a proliferation of multiple sexualities and the situating of these differences within historical specificities. Some conservative congressmen cited Nina Totenberg's exposure of the Anita Hill sexual harassment as a misuse of public funds and a violation of senators' privileged access to testimony. Ironically following the plotline of the recent Hollywood film *Basic Instinct*, women with linguistic power—a journalist and a lawyer—were the root cause of social and aesthetic decline and the enervation of powerful white men.[33]

The defunding of PBS has been systematic and steady during the culture wars of the last decade. For example, in 1980, 27 percent of its funds came from federal sources, and in 1990, only 16 percent did, while corporate funding increased from 10 percent to 16 percent.[34] These figures illustrate what has amounted to, on the theoretical and political levels, the gradual erosion of a publicly funded, publicly protected, mediated public sphere. Thus, this napalm attack against the arts and public television occurred on two fronts: the economic base, which, according to conservatives, needed to be liberated from the state and privatized with free enterprise market relations, an argument that has been used to reinvent mass communications along capitalist lines in the former Eastern bloc; and the superstructure, which had exploded with a kind of uncontrolled postmodernist ecstasy of racial, sexual, gender, and regional difference whose deconstructive and historical strategies decentered traditional art forms and white male patriarchy. While the postmodernist theories of Lyotard or Baudrillard describe the destabilization of unified claims within language and difference, the decentering of white women and people of color as producers functions as a material attack. These new makers not only produce different media images but also occupy multiply marked differ-

PATRICIA R. ZIMMERMANN

ences of social and economic location, which alter the political relations of production and representation.

However, the underpinnings of this debate about the funding and programming priorities of Public Television and the National Endowment for the Arts are even more complicated when we focus on women, feminism, and reproductive rights. The 1980s witnessed two potentially contradictory movements: on the one side, the conglomeratization of media and drastic reductions in network public affairs programming, and on the other side, the dissemination of new technologies, like amateur camcorders and satellite communication, that decentralize and democratize media production and distribution.[35] This democratization and dissemination of access facilitated what I would like to call the explosion of "difference through diffusion," a term I utilize to denote the convergence of representation, politics, and technology. In this context, media groups like Paper Tiger Television and Deep Dish TV Satellite, AIDS activists such as ACT-UP, and reproductive rights media groups such as the Buffalo Media Coalition for Reproductive Rights have linked low-end, low-tech technologies with deconstructive argumentative and visual strategies. The amateur camcorder could be retrieved from the privatized confines of the bourgeois nuclear family—the gulag where all amateur media technologies have been deposited to stunt their democratic potential. This retrieval process pivots on two political moves: (1) access to media production to alter the social relations of production, and (2) discursive and textual realignments in the analysis of reproductive rights. Both moves could arrest the erosion of feminist public spheres.

The parallels between democratic access to media as potentially subversive of dominant media and unrestricted access to abortion as a woman's civil right are almost uncanny in both discourse and practice: both protect *differences of voices and bodies,* in particular female ones whose specificity poses unique interventions. A true democratization of both media and abortion rights depends on the practice and protection of access and not just on a commitment to equality and plurality. The issue of access, then, emerges as the fulcrum upon which "rights" can be imagined as articulations of multiple differences of voices on the level of discourse and multiple bodies on the level of practice.

As film and video are gradually defunded and privatized as a way to stem this explosion of access made possible by state-supported funding initiatives of the 1970s and technological advances of the 1980s, the Supreme Court in the last decade has maintained the construct of *Roe v. Wade,* but progressively limited access by a range of women in a series of repressive court rulings. The cumulative effect has been to privatize both media production and abortion, protecting them almost exclusively for the white middle class. Racial politics, most particularly the rollback of affirmative action law, underpins both of these discursive and legal moves.

Most significant, the conservative attack on public television and the arts has cited as precedent the abortion ruling on the gag rule in *Rust v. Sullivan* (1991) to argue for limitations of free speech and access to information when government funding is provided for the arts. Richard O. Curry has argued that the issues of abortion and freedom of expression are joined in *Webster v. Reproductive Health Services* (1989) and *Rust v. Sullivan*. The Webster decision upheld a Missouri law that prohibited spending public funds to counsel a woman to have an abortion. The American Library Association filed an amicus brief with the Court, asking the Court to consider the effect of the ruling on intellectual freedom and dissemination of material about sexuality in libraries. In *Rust,* the Court ruled that guidelines for federally funded family planning clinics that prohibited personnel from providing information on abortion were constitutional.[36] According to the American Civil Liberties Union (ACLU), conservative arts watchdog groups, especially the American Family Research Council and the Heritage Foundation, have initiated a series of court injunctions against certain forms of art by citing *Rust v. Sullivan* as precedent for limitations on free speech.

The ACLU has argued that "the *Rust* decision fueled arguments that the government may likewise prohibit 'indecency' in NEA-funded projects, or may deny arts grants for idcological rcasons. *Rust* was undoubtcdly a blow to frccdom of spccch, but it is far from clear that the Supreme Court will extend its reasoning to the arts funding context."[37] The ACLU advances three arguments against the importation of *Rust* as a precedent for arts censorship: first, *Rust* focused exclusively on medical services and delineated that content restrictions in areas expressly dedicated to speech activity were not included; second, private patient-doctor communication, the focus of the *Rust* decision, differs in scope from arts contexts and funding, which have "impact beyond the actual dollars spent"; and third, arts funding permeates an entire institution or work project, and is not as containable as abortion counseling.[38] These debates on freedom of speech and recent Supreme Court abortion rulings demonstrate quite forcibly how distinctions between arts production, the law, women's rights, abortion, and access have congealed.

Sean Cubitt, in his book *Timeshift,* argues that the proliferation of video technologies multiplies the number of sites for cultural struggle. They fragment a coherent market of consensus broadcasting with diffused and intensely localized practices. He writes: "We have to think of the term 'technology' as a centrifugal net of interacting discourses, and as a function of them: educational, legal, aesthetic, socio-cultural, scientific. . . . The first break is to rid ourselves of the prescriptive power of definition, and to think instead in terms of process and relations."[39] Cubitt's notion of inscribing technology within process and relations and removing it from static definitions evokes Donna Haraway's cyborg; the video maker, then, emerges as a sort of traveler between discourses and practices, a weaver of fractured social and aesthetic spaces and creator of new frontiers. Along this same line of excavating the radical potential of new technologies, particularly consumer technologies like camcorders, Dee Dee Halleck has observed, "The challenge is to develop Mumford's insights into emancipated uses of technology in a decentralized and genuinely democratic way. . . . In fact, it is evident that pockets of resistance have arisen that have the potential to evolve into more highly organized and autonomous centers of democratic communications."[40]

These discussions of the radical potential of consumer technology con-

PATRICIA R. ZIMMERMANN

centrate not on their dissemination and control by major corporations, but on their ability to increase access to production and to diffuse the sites where media intervention can occur.[41] Systematic exclusion of independent political voices can be challenged by inclusions of multiple voices via access to technology and a commitment to rephrasing the normative modes of production offered by commercial media. Rather than a technological nihilism that views all technology as reactionary and co-optive, Cubitt and Halleck argue that video technology presents possibilities to alter social relations that did not exist within previous media forms. Both of their arguments stress the context and usage of the technologies rather than their inherent properties. As the antiabortion crusade relocates to clinics, video has become increasingly important as part of the artillery that feminist groups can use to destroy ideology with visual evidence.[42]

The case of the Buffalo Media Coalition for Reproductive Rights (MCRR) exemplifies this move. They use low-end amateur camcorders to combat Operation Rescue clinic blockades. Their most recent tape, *Spring of Lies* (1992), chronicles the recent attacks in May 1992 against several abortion clinics in Buffalo, New York. The tape places the videomakers in the middle of the action through hand-held camera work. We hear their voices emerging from behind the camera. The videographers themselves frequently speak to the right-to-life protesters. The tapes are distributed to anyone for fifteen dollars, roughly the cost of a hardcover book. They are often used as courtroom evidence to document illegal barrier of entry to clinics by Operation Rescue. The MCRR tapes circulate in a different sphere from that of more traditional oppositional films of the 1970s, exploiting the proliferation of VCRs to form underground feminist networks. Although the videography of the tapes is often shaky and out of focus, their confrontational style overrides formal coherence with the feverish pitch of war photography.

While the tapes are shot in the 1960s style of aggressive cinema verité, with the camera provoking action from either antiabortion or reproductive rights activists, they document the extent of Operation Rescue's interference by placing the spectator in the subject position of a *pregnant woman* going to the clinic. These tapes put the pregnant female body—excised and exiled by the Supreme Court and mass media representations—back into abortion confrontations. They compare media representations of the attacks that even out the conflict with the immediate and visceral ambience of their own cinematography, in which the camera, and by extension representation, is often physically in the center of the struggle and debate. These tapes do not simply serve as alternatives to the networks, in the sense that research on anti–Vietnam War media has hypothesized the dialectic and binary opposition between alternative and dominant media formations. They provoke a new social usage of technology and a new social configuration of spectatorship as resistant, active, and social. The tapes function as a sort of feminist cyborg, the video technology provoking slippage between feminist intervention and representation, between technology and woman's body.

US Bans Abortion (1990), produced by Paper Tiger Television in New York City, also inserts the female body into the health care system surrounding abortion via low-end video technology. This thirty-minute tape discusses the Bush administration's restrictions on Title X, which provides funding for health care clinics for poor women. The restrictions would limit health care providers in clinics from providing information on abortion as an option to deal with pregnancy in federally funded clinics. The tape alternates between four feminist health care activists analyzing the impact of Title X restrictions on poor women's health and footage of a Women's Health Action Mobilization (WHAM) demonstration at the New York City Department of Health shot from the point of view of the participants.

The interview sequences with the four activists demonstrate how media representation, public policy on health care, and the specificity of the female body coalesce in both discourse and practice. These interviews are threaded in between the demonstration footage, providing analysis of the media blackout on Title X and analysis of its impact on poor women and women of color. These activists speak directly to the camera and argue that Title X restrictions could be potentially more devastating than the *Webster* decision, affecting over five million women and four thousand clinics.

Marianne Staniszewski, a cultural critic from the Rhode Island School of Design and a member of WHAM, explains that the media create our social landscape and collective memory; she claims that the lack of coverage on the restrictions can be directly related to the fact that they would affect marginalized groups of women: teenagers, people of color, poor women. Later in the tape, Staniszewski shows how the language of Title X redefines life as beginning at conception; she quotes from Title X: "The health care worker must promote the interests of the unborn child."

Tracy Morgan, a health educator who works in a clinic, narrates an example of how her work life would change under Title X restrictions. To a pregnant teenager coming to her clinic now, she would explain three options: prenatal care if she decided to carry the baby to term, adoption, and abortion if she chose to terminate the pregnancy. Morgan explains that under Title X, abortion would remain legal but she would be prohibited from mentioning it as an option. A young man in the group explains that although *Roe v. Wade* in 1973 made abortion legal, the strategy of the federal government has been to attempt to cut off women's access to abortion through measures like the Hyde Amendment, which revoked Medicare funding for abortion. He then describes his failed attempts to garner media coverage of the WHAM demonstration; he reasons that funding issues are not perceived by the mass media as a matter of rights. A WHAM activist concludes the tape by arguing that all the attempts to curtail abortion constitute "retaliation against the massive gains" made by women. She asserts: "We never achieved reproductive freedom. We have to incorporate all women from all classes, races, and ethnic backgrounds."

These interviews provide two lines of analysis. First, they establish the necessity for direct action demonstrations because of a virtual media blackout. Second, they provide a historical and analytical context for the more heated footage of the demonstration. The interviews, then, anchor our reading of the demonstration footage within the larger issue of health care as a right for all women. By delivering a political analysis of the regressive impact of Title X on women's health care, these inter-

PATRICIA R. ZIMMERMANN

views, although by white activists, discursively position the spectator in the subject position of a pregnant teenager of color by mapping how that specific body would be denied its rights.

Mirroring the camcorder strategy of *Spring of Lies*, the demonstration footage in *US Bans Abortion* is shot with low-end, hand-held video. The camera does not maintain an objectified, ethnographic distance from the demonstrators; rather, the camera itself emerges as a participant in the direct action. The camera records the march down a New York City street by WHAM activists from inside the demonstration, not outside on the sidewalks. Marchers speak directly to the camera in extreme close-up, explaining the reasoning behind their chant, "Abortion is health care, health care is a right." When the women enter the Department of Health to plaster the office with red tape to symbolize the effects of Title X restrictions, a young woman discusses why she is performing this kind of civil disobedience directly to the camera. WHAM activists wear surgical masks marked with X's to connote the consequences of Title X.

While coverage of demonstrations from the point of view of demonstrators has a long tradition in political documentary film, extending as far back as the Workers' Film and Photo League's coverage of demonstrations during the depression and continuing through oppositional film of the antiwar period, this camcorder footage offers a slightly different intervention. Rather than simply documenting the demonstration, the camera is at the eye level of the demonstrators, walking with them, stringing red tape on office walls, talking with them. The arbitrary border between videographer as omniscient and omnipresent and the subject as distant and passive is abandoned. This strategy is not merely a participatory form of media production to stimulate active spectatorship; rather, it situates the video camera and its operator within the sexualized and gendered subject position of a cyborg-like woman opposing governmental policy and fighting back for reproductive rights. Instead, the video technology of the camcorder and the body of the videographer are transposed into a gendered, moving, resistant force-field—a sort of counter-panopticon—whose project is equally the making of representation and the execution of political action.

In a move similar to that of *Spring of Lies*, *US Bans Abortion* uses camcorder video to both reinsert and reassert the pregnant female body. While the camera work in *Spring of Lies* positions the pregnant female body under virtual physical and psychical attack, the camera in *US Bans Abortion* imagines a pregnant, racialized, and classed female body of the future that bureaucracy and politics try to mute and restrain but that, in the end, refuses to be silenced or immobilized. While many film theorists have interrogated the multiple subject positions constituting female spectatorship, this cyborg-like confederation of the camcorder, reproductive rights politics, and the sexualized female body proposes a different twist on psychoanalytic identification and more ethnographic reception theory. Not only is the female body made visible and vocal, it is empowered and powerful through video technology that facilitates a militant subjectivity and a collective participation.

Another example of feminist oppositional public sphere video is a tape by the activist group Reprovision, part of the Women's Health Action Mobilization, called *Access Denied* (1991). In comparison to *Spring of Lies*, this tape works on a more explanatory than visceral level, yet also obscures the line between spectator and participant, the law and the body. While showing street demonstrations, the tape elaborates the multiple contexts of restrictions on abortion across race, age, and sexual preference lines, effectively deconstructing the complaint that abortion rights politics evidenced white middle-class, single-issue feminism of the 1960s and 1970s. Constructed in segments outlining reproductive rights issues within a larger context of race, health care, and teenagers, the tape interweaves demonstration footage with interviews, marking each segment historically with a short montage of archival footage deifying babies or mothers.

        Access Denied begins with clinic defense against Operation Rescue and interviews with WHAM volunteers and escorts. It then moves from the streets to the legal plane, where it discusses the Supreme Court *Webster* decision restrictions on abortion. An African American woman activist relates how *Webster* affects women of color, citing evidence that prior to 1973, 80 percent of illegal abortions were performed on women of color. Another black woman describes her friend's hemorrhaging from an illegal botched abortion. Moving to a discussion of the gag rule, a black male proclaims, "You can't cut information." Other segments refuse to position abortion as a single issue of privacy, focusing instead on the relationship between AIDS research and fetal tissue research and between prohibitions on sexual preference and the issue of women's right to health care, on a description of a menstrual extraction, and on teenagers protesting parental consent restrictions. On the argumentative and visual levels, *Access Denied* explicates the multiple geographies of abortion politics. The tape ends with the direct address to viewers: "Come join us." *Access Denied* depends on constantly circulating between the private and the public, between the law and the clinics, between health care and sexuality, itself forming a new location somewhere between these polarities. It constructs a discursive multiplicity that implicitly argues for reimagining the larger political context of abortion, one beyond a unified, white, middle-class discourse.

        Although it does not utilize hand-held, camcorder videography, Kathy High's remarkable new tape, *Underexposed: Temple of the Fetus* (1992), also centers on women's clinics as the space where the female body, technology, and politics converge. The clinical space outlined in this tape is not abortion providers, but rather clinics of the future that retrieve embryos and implant them in women desperate for children. Kathy High deciphers the clinical space within which women's bodies have been and will be suspended and the way new reproductive technologies continue the discursive move of separating women from their wombs, turning the womb into what one character in the tape calls "a fetal environment." The tape later visualizes this discursive amputation with images of wombs like spaceships. This clinical space entails a kind of feminist nightmare of male doctors controlling women's bodies through technology. One doctor asserts, for example, that in vitro fertilization "is therapeutic for these women, the best way for some women to resume useful lives." The clinic of the future, as imagined by *Underexposed: Temple of the Fetus,* is one where women are reduced to wombs.

Like *Access Denied, Underexposed: Temple of the Fetus* weaves together multiple discursive and explanatory modes to define the space within which reproductive politics operates.[43] It layers together several different genres to investigate the politics of new reproductive technologies, specifically in vitro fertilization: historical archival footage of pregnancy and birth; a fictional, docudrama-like story about a newscaster covering her friend's in vitro fertilization; straight documentary interviews with international feminists who study reproductive politics; and a science fiction narrative about the future control of in vitro fertilization by male doctors and corporations.

Deploying these multiple textual strategies to unpack the position of new reproductive technologies within a feminist health politics, *Underexposed: Temple of the Fetus* locates the pregnant and desiring-to-be-pregnant female body within a network of politics, practices, discourses, science, and imaginings about the future. The historical site of the female body is discovered through archival shots of C-sections, deliveries, and newborns. Because these old medical training films are juxtaposed with the fictionalized story of the news reporter covering the story of her friend's in vitro fertilization, their evidentiary and scientific claims are defused and their historical discourse, one that positions the female body as a passive receptacle of technology, is underscored.

Underexposed: Temple of the Fetus insists that scientific exploration of new reproductive technologies is inextricably linked to the state. In a faked interview in the future, the head of the newly formed Department of New Reproductive Technologies proclaims, "This is not just a baby, it is a national issue." By utilizing the conventions of network news interviews, the narrative sequences with doctors practicing in vitro fertilization and with the woman patient expose how scientific intervention into reproduction and pronatalist ideologies can be reframed as commonsense solutions and miracle cures for the complicated biological and social issue of infertility. The utopian possibilities of in vitro fertilization are undercut by the narrative of the tape, however: the woman who was implanted lost her baby at twenty-two weeks. In one faked interview, a woman proclaims that the doctor at the clinic "was looking at my stomach and seeing dollar signs."

The narrative of one woman's quest for a child now that her career is under way is located within two registers: the family melodrama of the impregnation and its subsequent failure told from the point of view of the woman patient, and rational, instrumental muckraking of the in vitro business by her best friend, an aggressive news reporter. Thus, the "story" of in vitro fertilization in this tape is multitiered, simultaneously narrated from the emotional and personal point of view of the female patient and logically, publicly exposed by a female news reporter. Both routes arrive at the same conclusion, a condemnation of the trivialization of women's reproductive autonomy. Both routes are positioned in this tape as equally important, equally urgent politically, functioning in a pas de deux with each other. Most important, the constant interplay between these two positions suggests that only a political strategy that can account for multiple and complex explanations at different levels simultaneously is viable.

Underexposed: Temple of the Fetus also suggests the sexual preference, class, and race dimensions of reproductive technologies. The female reporter interviews a pregnant lesbian couple who contend that the Department of Reproductive Ethics and Procedures, a government agency, restricts sperm to protect the unborn from AIDS. The couple explains they procured sperm from "two Harvard guys," and argues that they, too, constitute a nuclear family. In a later fictionalized interview, a black woman doctor exposes that in vitro fertilization is reserved only for middle-class white women. Consequently, *Underexposed: Temple of the Fetus* offers a critique of male-controlled reproductive utopias by rerouting its narrative trajectory into a failed pregnancy that then produces consciousness about how these technologies serve science, the state, and capitalism rather than women.

Underexposed: Temple of the Fetus establishes that historical images of birth and reproduction, scientific training films, and narratives about the utopian future prospects for reproductive technologies all concoct fantasies about the female body that rob it of autonomy, activity, and specificity. This fictionalizing of disparate materials and sources demonstrates the pacification of the maternal and pregnant body in discourse, practice, and image making. Actual documentary interviews with feminists from around the world who study the social consequences of new reproductive technologies are counterposed against these fantasy constructions of the female body that neutralize and confine the body within science.

Not only do these interviews provide a larger context and more analysis of the social and political ramifications of new reproductive technologies, they critique the truth claims of a scientific practice positioned as gender neutral. Gena Corea, author of *The Mother Machine*, describes scientists who work with new reproductive technologies "exploring something like galaxy 38" and use "woman-obliterating sentences." Joyanta Gupta, a sociologist, explains that these technologies operate within an ideology that sees women useful only as mothers, marginalizing women and giving them less and less say over their own bodies. Christine Ewing, a biologist, argues that the success rate for in vitro fertilization is actually less than 10 percent and advances that these technologies are actually a form of imperialism. Malina Karkal points out medical researchers in India focus on infertility, despite high infant mortality rates. A surrogate mother describes how wealthy couples will use the court system to their advantage to counteract the birth mother's claims on the child.

Through social and political analysis, these interviews mark off "truth" from a feminist perspective, demonstrating the multiple ways in which the real, material position of women and their bodies are excised from discussion and practices of new reproductive technologies. In some ways, these interviews function as guides through the fictional and archival material, locating the spectator within feminist deconstruction rather than melodramatic identification or passive awe of the spectacle of strange medical training films. Although these interviews are shot in exactly the same style as

PATRICIA R. ZIMMERMANN

the fictionalized interviews of the science fiction part of the tape, their veracity is discernible because they work in opposition to the utopianism of the other imaginary narrative. These interviews interrupt the futuristic narrative and historical imagery by continually reinserting women's needs into the discourse. They focus on women, not science.

As *Underexposed: Temple of the Fetus* alerts us, reproductive politics travels like a cyborg, reconstructing temporality along less linear, phallocratic lines: between historical formations that remove woman from the womb; new technologies that reconfigure the race, class, and imperial relations of reproduction; and male fantasies of a technological utopia where women's lack of individual control over her body aids patriarchal agendas for reproduction.

S'Aline's Solution (1991), a short experimental video by Aline Mare, utilizes technological and representational strategies similar to the more activist tapes discussed above, but formally manipulates the images to further specify that the tape speaks from the point of view of the female body, a voiced body that chose abortion over pregnancy. The very title of the tape suggests the cyborg merging of the medical-technological and the specified female subject: as saline solution is a method of abortion, S'Aline's solution is one particular, historical woman's solution to an unwanted pregnancy. Thus, the title of the tape does not only function as a pun on abortion, but demonstrates that the convergence of medicine and subjectivity constitutes the material site of abortion.

This compelling and evocative tape in many ways performs an ideological exorcism on abortion, wresting it from the limiting discursive domain of the law and public policy and sheathing it within not only the female body, but the speaking female subject and medicalized, imaged female organs. The tape specifies not only the female body, but the site of abortion through medical imaging technology that allows for close-up views inside the body and its organs. *S'Aline's Solution* traverses three different political registers: the social-medical organization of the female body; the imaginary, emancipated female body of a specific woman who chooses; and the aborted speaking subject. The female body, then, is split into three parts in the tape, each of which correspond to these intersecting registers: medical images of the interior female body; close-ups of a woman's mouth and images of a woman swimming; and lyrical voice-over that fuses assertion of personal choice, loss, science, and autonomy. Subjectivity here is redefined along multiple trajectories rather than linear unities.

The social-medical organization of the female body engaged in reproduction is presented through the use of slow-motion scientific imaging of female reproductive organs, sperm, ovum, and embryos. The tape opens with a traveling shot through the vagina into the womb through some sort of high-tech, miniaturized video camera accompanied by slow, eerie electronic music suggesting science fiction movies. This particular image presents a gendered intervention into the semiotics of the "traveling shot" of classical Hollywood cinema. Rather than moving through public space, this traveling shot literally invades the private and invisible space of the interior of the female. Access to the interior and interiority of the female is literally visualized as entry through the vagina. Various slow-motion, medicalized, high-tech images of sperm, ovum, and embryos floating in space unanchored to the female body emerge throughout the tape, evoking science, medicine, and the activity of the womb as mysterious melo-dramas and spectacles. The torpid and tedious speed of these images reduces them to abstractions and highlights how this medical imaging technology generalizes, ethereal-izes, and isolates reproduction from any social-political context. On the level of repre-sentation and politics, the lethargy of these images removes these sperm, ovum, and embryos from the antiabortion ideological construct that they *are* "life" by showing that they are actually only representations.

This visual strategy employs a pun on reproduction: while the images are severed from the referent of biological reproduction, they operate as an interrogation of visual reproduction and a deconstruction of antiabortion ideological constructs argu-ing that life begins at conception. In *S'Aline's Solution*, a woman's life begins when she chooses. Indeed, to underscore the physical and scientific difference between fertilized eggs and babies, the tape concludes with a birth scene, where a baby's head emerges from a woman's vagina. Although on first viewing this birth scene may appear to be out of place, the construction of the tape actually changes the signification of the birth. It simultaneously confirms on the level of representation the biological difference between fertilized eggs and babies and affirms on the level of feminist politics that, in choosing, a woman gives birth to herself.

The tape also employs live-action footage of a specific woman to coun-terpose a *specific woman's* body and identity to medicalized representations of an ideal-ized and sanitized construction of *Woman's* organs. The extreme close-ups of a woman's mouth and of a woman swimming compose another part of this splitting of the female body. These images also evoke a dreamlike quality through slow motion and some distor-tion from wide-angle lens videography, suggesting that subjectivity is tied to physicality. While the medical imagery dislocates female body parts with a scientific, fragmenting gaze, these image-manipulated close-ups and long shots of a specific woman relocate the right to choose abortion within the female body. The repeated use of close-ups of a woman's mouth link identity with speech.

S'Aline's Solution also crafts the aborted, female body as a speaking sub-ject and as an active participant in the abortion. The speaking, pregnant body counters medicalized images of female body parts as planets in some outer galaxy waiting to be explored. The sound track is composed of a somber, incantatory woman's voice-over intoning the words "I choose, I chose, I have chosen," then progressing into the formula for saline solution, a poetic description outlining the feeling of abortion ("Flesh of my Flesh, you will never be flesh. Bye-bye, Baby, Bye-bye. Animal, Vegetable, Mineral. Dissolve, Disintegrate. Dismember.) The voice-over concludes with an affirmation that abortion is located not within the abstract and ideological, but within the material, social relations of the gendered and sexualized female body.

In all of these tapes, video technology reinvents the political project of abortion rights through an emancipatory merging of technology and women's bodies.[44] If

PATRICIA R. ZIMMERMANN

the Supreme Court decisions have detached women from abortion, these tapes produce and reproduce women's bodies, restoring specificity to this war on the female body. The resistant, biological woman suspended between multiple discourses and identities is reinvigorated via the video camera, physically inserted into the action, her voice, body, and spectatorship central rather than erased as in the De Moss Foundation ads or Clinton's press conference or mass media narratives or the Supreme Court *Bray* decision. Rather than melodrama, these tapes function as combat videography mapping the location of the gendered body and voice in politics. Rather than texts or discourses, these tapes function as physical intersections between the body, abortion politics, and technology. To discuss them solely on the level of formal innovation as avant-garde texts or on the level of argumentative structure to elaborate political context is to miss their political agenda entirely.

A day after Clinton signed the reversals, prolife activists exclaimed they would now take their struggle to the streets, suggesting that the war on the female body is not simply discursive but physical, located within a specific time and location at clinics. However, the right-to-life invocation of sixties-style yippie politics is hopelessly outdated, because the street as a material place, although clearly important for activism in the 1990s, is insufficient for the struggle over reproductive rights and the gendered body.

The days when political activity solely focused on the streets could change the world and make it a better place are gone, looking more and more like a painted Volkswagen bus without an engine. The inability of the so-called Left to deal with the mass-mediated phantasmagoria of the Gulf War verifies that activist politics needs a different kind of vehicle, one with more power and an ability to maneuver over multiple terrains—real, discursive, and representational. We must recapture pleasure and desire in our consumption of media images just as we must see we need new technologies like camcorders. Picket signs alone are not enough, as they will be cast within residual modes and rendered ineffective and impotent, quaint signposts from another era demanding a different kind of intervention. One unified linear line of defense is inadequate, whether on the level of explanation or representation or political struggle. These low-end videos assert that the current war on women's bodies can only be fought by reimagining the woman's body within the construct of a feminist cyborg public sphere. Low-end video not only documents that women's bodies are the battlegrounds, to paraphrase a famous Barbara Kruger poster, but it also physically manifests that this new guerrilla construct of women's bodies as powerful video cyborgs is the fetal tissue of an emerging feminist public sphere.

1 I would like to thank Zillah Eisenstein for her helpful criticism of the original draft of this essay. I would also like to thank my research assistant, Lenore DiPaoli, for her diligent excavation of documents.

2 For a fuller explanation of the consequences of *Bray v. Alexandria Women's Health Clinic,* see "Clinic Access," pamphlet, National Abortion Rights Action League, n.d.

3 For discussions of how new media technologies like satellite, cable, and laptop computers altered the public sphere of reporting the Gulf War, see Craig LaMay, Martha FitzSimon, and Jeanne Sahadi, eds., *The Media at War: The Press and the Persian Gulf Conflict* (New York: Gannet Foundation Media Center, 1991); Douglas Kellner, *The Persian Gulf TV War* (Boulder, Colo.: Westview Press, 1992); Hamid Mowlana, George Gerbner, and Herbert I. Schiller, eds., *Triumph of the Image: The Media's War in the Persian Gulf—A Global Perspective* (Boulder, Colo.: Westview Press, 1992); Bruce Cumings, *War and Television* (London: Verso Books, 1992).

4 Donna J. Haraway, "A Cyborg Manifesto: Science, Technology, and Socialist Feminism in the Late Twentieth Century," in *Simians, Cyborgs, and Women: The Reinvention of Nature* (New York: Routledge, 1991), 153.

5 Haraway, "Cyborg Manifesto," 174.

6 Larry Rohter, "Doctor Is Slain during Protest over Abortions," *New York Times,* 11 March 1993, 1 and B10; Anthony Lewis, "Right to Life," *New York Times,* 12 March 1993, 29; David A. Grimes, M.D., Jacqueline D. Forrest, Ph.D., Alice L. Kirkman, J.D., and Barbara Radford, M.A., "An Epidemic of Antiabortion Violence in the United States," *American Journal of Obstetrics and Gynecology* 165, no. 5 (November 1991): 1263–68; "Highlights of Recent Violence against Planned Parenthood Clinics," Planned Parenthood flyer, 11 March 1993; see also a series of Planned Parenthood news releases issued on the heels of the Dr. Gunn shooting: "Statement by Pamela J. Maraldo, Ph.D., President of Planned Parenthood Federation of America Planned Parenthood Action Fund," 11 March 1993; "Statement by Pamela J. Maraldo, Ph.D., President of Planned Parenthood Federation of America Planned Parenthood Action Fund," 12 March 1993; "Planned Parenthood Establishes Clinic Defense Fund in Aftermath of Florida Physician's Murder," 12 March 1993; "Statement by Alexander C. Sanger, President and CEO, Planned Parenthood of New York City," 12 March 1993; "Statement by Dr. Pamela J. Maraldo, President, Planned Parenthood Federation of America Planned Parenthood Action Fund," 10 March 1993; "Unwanted in Any Florida City, David LaMond Gunn," Planned Parenthood flyer of clip from *Washington Times,* 12 March 1993.

7 Constance Penley and Andrew Ross, eds., *Technoculture* (Minneapolis: University of Minnesota Press, 1991), xv.

8 See, for example, E. Ann Kaplan, "Theories and Strategies of the Feminist Documentary," in *New Challenges for Documentary,* ed. Alan Rosenthal (Berkeley: University of California Press, 1988), 78–102; Vivian C. Sobchack, "*No Lies:* Direct Cinema as Rape," in *New Challenges,* ed. Rosenthal, 332–41; Patricia Erens, "Women's Documentary Filmmaking: The Personal Is Political," in *New Challenges,* ed. Rosenthal, 554–65; Linda Williams, "*What You Take for Granted,*" in *New Challenges,* ed. Rosenthal, 566–70; Julia Lesage, "Feminist Documentary: Aesthetics and Politics," in *Show Us Life: Towards a History and Aesthetics of the Committed Documentary,* ed. Thomas Waugh (Metuchen, N.J.: Scarecrow Press, 1984), 223–51; Julianne Burton, "Transitional States: Creative Complicities with the Real in *Man Marked to Die: Twenty Years Later* and *Patriamada,*" in *The Social Documentary in Latin America,* ed. Julianne Burton (Pittsburgh: University of Pittsburgh Press, 1990), 373–401.

9 Margaret Cooper, "The Abortion Film Wars: Media in the Combat Zone," *Cineaste* 15, no.2 (1986): 8–12.

10 Rosalind Pollack Petchesky, "Foetal Images: The Power of Visual Culture in the Politics of Reproduction," in *Reproductive Technologies: Gender, Motherhood and Medicine,* ed. Michelle Stanworth (Minneapolis: University of Minnesota Press, 1987), 58.

11 Valeri Hartouni, "Containing Women: Reproductive Discourse in the 1980s," in *Technoculture,* ed. Penley and Ross, 51.

12 See, for example, Laurence H. Tribe, *Abortion: The Clash of Absolutes* (New York: Norton, 1990); Shirley L. Radl, *Over Our Live Bodies: Preserving Choice in*

America (Dallas: Davis, 1989); and Susan E. Davis, ed., *Women under Attack: Victories, Backlash and the Fight for Reproductive Freedom* (Boston: South End Press, 1988). The most thorough study of abortion history and politics is Rosalind Pollack Petchesky, *Abortion and Woman's Choice: The State, Sexuality, and Reproductive Freedom* (Boston: Northeastern University Press, 1985).

13 Michel Foucault, *The Archaeology of Knowledge and the Discourse on Language* (New York: Harper Colophon Books, 1972), 125–28, 186–88, 190–95.

14 Statement by the Arthur S. De Moss Foundation, "Life. What a Beautiful Choice," brochure published by the Arthur S. De Moss Foundation, n.d.

15 Ibid., 1.

16 Letter to author from Rebecca S. McKay, for the Arthur S. De Moss Foundation, 3 March 1993.

17 These tropes of melodrama have been elaborated in Laura Mulvey, "Notes on Sirk and Melodrama," in her *Visual and Other Pleasures* (Bloomington: Indiana University Press, 1989), 39–44, and "Melodrama inside and outside the Home," ibid., 63–77.

18 Carole A. Stabile, "Shooting the Mother: Fetal Photography and the Politics of Disappearance," *Camera Obscura* 28 (1992): 180.

19 E. Ann Kaplan, *Motherhood and Representation: The Mother in Popular Culture and Melodrama* (London: Routledge, 1992), 76–106.

20 Gwen Ifill, "Clinton Ready to Act on Two Abortion Regulations," *New York Times,* 17 January 1993, 21; Robin Toner, "Anti-Abortion Movement Prepares to Battle Clinton," *New York Times,* 22 January 1993, 1, 16; "Since Roe v. Wade: The Evolution of Abortion Law," *New York Times,* 22 January 1993, 11; Robin Toner, "Clinton Orders Reversal of Abortion Restrictions Left by Reagan and Bush," *New York Times,* 23 January 1993, 1, 10.

21 My argument here analyzes one article and two photographs from Toner, "Clinton Orders Reversal."

22 See, for example, Robert Pear, "Hillary Clinton Gets Policy Job and New Office," *New York Times,* 22 January 1993, 1, 23.

23 Deborah Sontag, "Increasingly, Two-Career Family Means Illegal Immigrant Help," *New York Times,* 24 January 1993, 1, 32; Gwen Ifill, "Clinton's Blunt Reminder of the Mood That Elected Him," *New York Times,* 24 January 1993, E3.

24 Linda Hutcheon, *The Politics of Postmodernism* (London: Routledge, 1989), 58.

25 Barry Smart, *Modern Conditions, Postmodern Controversies* (London: Routledge, 1992), 171.

26 Nina C. Leibman, "The Way We Weren't: Abortion 1950s Style in *Blue Denim* and *Our Time*," *Velvet Light Trap,* no. 29 (Spring 1992): 31–43.

27 Steven C. Dubin, *Arresting Images: Impolitic Art and Uncivil Actions* (New York: Routledge, 1992), 131–37.

28 "The Advertiser That Didn't Balk," *Ms.* 18, no. 2 (July 1989): 75; Judith Graham, "NBC's 'Roe' May Turn Off Advertisers," *Advertising Age,* 1 May 1989, 1, 85; John Leonard, "Their Bodies, Their Selves," *New York Magazine,* 15 May 1989, 117; Mark Lasswell, "Movie of the Week," *Rolling Stone Magazine,* 1 June 1989, 40; Judith Graham, "'Roe' Advertisers Risk Boycotts," *Advertising Age,* 15 May 1989, 2; "Roe vs. Wade," *People Weekly,* 15 May 1989, 9-10; Verne Gay, "'Roe vs. Wade' Sells Out, but Did the Advertisers Sell Out to Boycott Threat?" *Variety,* 17 May 1989, 1.

29 Neil DeMause, "The Great Abortion 'Compromise,'" *Extra,* September 1992, 25, 26, and "Can Men Spot Sexist Premises in Abortion Debate?" *Extra,* September 1992, 26.

30 B. Ruby Rich, "The Current State of Independent Film and Video," keynote address, University Film and Video Conference, Ithaca College, Ithaca, N.Y., 16 June 1990.

31 For a very thorough discussion of the attack against public broadcasting and a clear scorecard of the major players in the debate, see Josh Daniel, "Uncivil Wars: The Conservative Assault on Public Broadcasting," *Independent,* August/September 1992, 20–25. See also Walter Goodman, " Pull the Plug on PBS?" *New York Times,* 22 March 1992, H33; Martin Tolchin, "Public Broadcasting Bill Is Sidelined," *New York Times,* 5 March 1992, A14; Mark Schapiro, "Public TV Takes Its Nose out of the Air," *New York Times,* 3 November 1992, H31; "Attacks on CPB and ITVS Threaten Funding for TV Documentaries," *Documentary,* May 1992, 1, 8-9.

32 Kim Masters, "Big Bird Meets the Right Wing," *Washington Post,* 4 March 1992, 21; William J. Eaton and Sharon Bernstein, "GOP Senators Blast Public Broadcasting," *Los Angeles Times*, 4 March 1992, 11; Kim Masters, "Hill Clash Set over Public TV," *Washington Post,* 3 March 1992, 14; Robert Knight, "Free Big Bird," *Miami Herald,* 6 March 1992, 8C;

FETAL TISSUE

Laurence Jarvik, "Monopoly, Corruption, and Greed: The Problem of Public Television," reprint of a speech delivered as part of the Heritage Foundation Lecture Series, 25 February 1992; Richard Zoglin,"Public TV under Assault," *Time*, 30 March 1992, 58; S. Robert Lichter, Daniel Amundson, and Linda S. Lichter, "Balance and Diversity in PBS Documentaries," unpublished research study (Center for Media and Public Affairs, Washington, D.C., March 1992).

33 Martin Tolchin, "Public Broadcasting Bill Is Sidelined," *New York Times,* 5 March 1992, 7; Patti Hartigan, "Targeting PBS," *Boston Globe,* 4 March 1992, 18; Howard Rosenberg, "On the Urge to Purge Public TV," *Los Angeles Times,* 6 March 1992, 34; Mike Mills, "Charges of Liberal Bias Stall PBS Funding Bill," *Washington Times*, 7 March 1992, 16; John Wilner, "Stealth Senators Sought; One Admits He Placed Hold," *Current*, 2 March 1992, 3; "Statement by Donald Ledwig, President, Corporation for Public Broadcasting (CPB) on the Reauthorization of CPB, Which Is Being Debated on the Senate Floor," Corporation for Public Broadcasting Press Release, 3 March 1992; "Making Public Television Public," *Heritage Foundation Backgrounder*, pamphlet, 18 January 1992.

34 Mills, "Charges of Liberal Bias," 17.

35 Ben Bagdikian, *The Media Monopoly* (Boston: Beacon Press, 1992); Ken Auletta, *Three Blind Mice: How the TV Networks Lost Their Way* (New York: Random House, 1991); Douglas Kellner,"Public Access Television and the Struggle for Democracy," in *Democratic Communications in the Information Age,* ed. Janet Wasko and Vincent Mosco (Norwood, N.J.: Ablex, 1992), pp. 100-13; Gladys D. Ganley, *The Exploding Political Power of Personal Media* (Norwood, N.J.: Ablex, 1992).

36 Richard O. Curry, *An Uncertain Future: Thought Control and Repression during the Reagan-Bush Era* (Los Angeles: First Amendment Foundation, 1992), 59-61.

37 Marjorie Heins, director, American Civil Liberties Union Arts Censorship Project, "The First Amendment, Censorship, and Government Funding of the Arts," American Civil Liberties Union position paper (New York, n.d.), 3.

38 Ibid., 4.

39 Sean Cubitt, *Timeshift: On Video Culture* (London: Routledge, 1991), 13–14.

40 Dee Dee Halleck, "Watch Out, Dick Tracy: Popular Video in the Wake of the Exxon Valdez," in *Technoculture*, ed. Penley and Ross, 217. For a discussion of the use of camcorders for AIDS education and empowerment, see Alexandra Juhasz, "WAVE in the Media Environment: Camcorder Activism and the Making of HIV TV," *Camera Obscura* 28 (1992): 135–50.

41 This argument on increasing access to media production as a democratic right has also been argued by media producers working in public access in less urban and smaller communities. See, for example, Chris Hill and Barbara Lattanzi, "Media Dialects and Stages of Access," *Felix* 1, no. 2 (Spring 1992): 98–106.

42 See Steven Greenhouse, "Praise and Protest on Clinton's Decisions," *New York Times,* 24 January 1993, 6; Adam Clymer, "Abortion Rights Supports are Split on U.S. Measure," *New York Times,* 2 April 1993, A16; Felicia R. Lee, "On Battle Lines of Abortion Issue: Debate Rages On outside of Clinics," *New York Times,* 17 May 1993, B1, B4; Felicity Barringer, "Slaying Is a Call to Arms for Abortion Clinics," *New York Times,* 12 March 1993, A1, A17; Alisa Solomon, "Harassing House Calls," *Village Voice,* 23 March 1993, 20.

43 Many feminist theoreticians have advanced similar arguments that reproductive technologies are controlled by men, thereby circumscribing and limiting choice. See, for example, Michelle Stanworth, "Reproductive Technologies and the Deconstruction of Motherhood," in *Reproductive Technologies,* ed. Stanworth, 10–35, and Hilary Rose, "Victorian Values in the Test-Tube: The Politics of Reproductive Science and Technology," ibid., 151–73.

44 I would particularly like to thank Scott MacDonald, Sally Berger, and Kathy High for alerting me to these tapes on reproductive rights. I would also like to thank the distributors of these tapes for their generosity in loaning me preview copies for this article. *Spring of Lies* is available from the Media Coalition for Reproductive Rights, P.O. Box 33, Buffalo, NY 14201. *US Bans Abortion* is available from Paper Tiger Television, 339 Lafayette Street, New York, NY 10012, 212/420-9045. *Access Denied* is available from Women Make Movies, 462 Broadway, Suite 501, New York, NY 10013, 212/947-9277. *Underexposed: Temple of the Fetus* is available from Video Data Bank, 37 S. Wabash Avenue, Chicago, IL 60603, 312/899-5172. *S'Aline's Solution* is available from The Kitchen, 512 W. 19th Street, New York, NY 10011, 212/255-5793.

PATRICIA R. ZIMMERMANN

CHAPTER 21

FEMALE TRANSGRESSION

Laura Kipnis

Toward the end of Oliver Stone's *The Doors*, Jim Morrison— that militantly self-destructive rock-and-roll god and sixties emblem of desire—now reduced by drugs, booze, and fame to impotence and death games, finds the only way he can sing in tune during a recording session is if his girlfriend, on her knees, gives him head in the recording booth during his solos. On one's knees is, of course, fairly typical of the position of women in Stone's films. From movie to movie, as Stone stakes out his increasingly epic project of defining, for the world, the American experience of the sixties—its foreign policy, domestic politics, and here, its culture—that experience is, it goes without saying, described as centrally phallic. "Rock is cock, baby," one of his entourage tells Morrison, just as he seems to be detumescing on both fronts. The close identity between the preeminent cultural form of a generation and triumphantly phallic sexuality is made evident by both the screenplay and the mise-en-scène, as numerous plot points in the film turn, quite literally, around Morrison's cock—its rise, its fall, its travels and travails—transformed by Stone into the icon of a decade. When Morrison finally whips it out and waves it around onstage (although discreetly out of frame in Stone's veiled direction of the scene), it's a protorevolutionary act, a confrontation with state power that stands in for the countercultural politics of the decade, and is, in the same way, doomed: the act precipitates Morrison's final downfall in a lengthy prosecution by southern criminal justice, precipitating as well, for this film, the effective end of the sixties. (And for the benefit of leftists with nostalgia, Stone summons William Kunstler himself—that last surviving icon of sixties counterculture justice—to defend the phallic exposure.)

      If rock is cock, what *The Doors* also tells us, recreating documentary footage of omnipresent screaming girl fans at every limo stop, hotel, and stage door, is that women wanted some of it—although their access was as sycophants, groupies, and muses. As Morrison struts and waxes poetic, Stone shows us endless scenarios of frenzied women beside themselves with desire, whipped up into a lustful hysteria. I'm not arguing with either the historical veracity or the message of these images—that the position offered (and accepted by) women in sixties rock and roll was organized by male sexuality. Rather, I'm impelled to ask, So what would the sixties have been like if Jim Morrison had no cock? This is the vulgar, surprising, and subversive question posed by Suzie Silver's video, *A Spy (Hester Reeve Does the Doors)* (1991). What would culture be like if culture recognized the degree to which both representation and its various culture industries revolve around questions of sexual difference and phallic power, yet didn't, as opposed to earlier feminist dictates, eschew pleasure? And what would the role of women be—what would the sexuality of women be, what would desire be about for those screaming girl fans—if not predominantly organized around the phallus?

However, Silver's tape, like the recent work of a number of younger women (often lesbian) videomakers who tackle issues of sex and representation, bypasses traditional feminist analysis, bypasses feminist film theory dicta about visual pleasure and the male gaze, and simply (although not so simply) performs cultural upheaval. It turns a blind eye on (or perhaps just winks at) recognizable feminist figurations like oppressor/victim, subject-who-looks/object-who-is-looked-at, male pornography/female erotica and instead invents new political forms and gropes toward new forms of knowledge and new political subjects.

A Spy, appropriating the music video form, portrays performance artist Hester Reeve as a female drag Jesus Christ, lip-synching the Doors' erotomaniacal tune "The Spy" against a changing faux-psychedelic background of sixties porn films—where naked women frolic in hippy free-love orgies for male spectators—and other ironically bizarre imagery. Bearded, wearing only a loose loincloth, sporting a crown of thorns and a pious expression, with each naked breast painted as a mocking angel's face, Reeve transforms Jim Morrison's lyrics into a female transgression of the male-center-stage cults of both Christianity and rock and roll, claiming for her own the mantles of cultdom, tragedy, and omniscience. As Hester's Christ intones, in Morrison's voice: "I'm a spy in the house of love / I know the dream you're dreaming of," the religious, sexual, patriarchial, and psychopaternal resonances of the lyrics come unraveled one by one, through the transgressive insertion of a female into the cults of Christ and of rock sex-god Morrison. It's an appropriation that transforms the possibilities of the female position, from supplicant to subject—off our knees in more ways than one: a politics that starts with the body, the female body. For a woman to impersonate Christ, flaunting her breasts in a floozy mockery of the divine, is a more sophisticated and more transgressive deployment of bodily politics than, say, immersing a cross in urine (artist Andres Serrano's contribution to the NEA culture wars), because it insists on the centrality of gender in the complex of church–state–social body, which the controversy about Serrano's work symptomatically elided.

If Silver's tape is representative of a certain rethinking going on in women's video, one of the primary issues being rethought is the question of pleasure. As Laura Mulvey's 1975 essay "Visual Pleasure and Narrative Cinema" set an agenda for a generation of feminist film theorists in its analysis of how women are positioned in Hollywood cinema through the regime of scopophilia, it simultaneously issued a call for

LAURA KIPNIS

practitioners to create alternate media that smashed the pleasure of dominant forms. One of the main problems with Mulvey's prescriptive was that it demanded, and produced, a modernist and elitist countercinema as an antidote to the power of the male gaze, one whose sole audience was the traditional audience of high culture. Its attack on the pleasures of popular culture was an implicit attack on the audience of popular culture as well, on the masses who would find sitting through a screening of *Riddles of the Sphinx* a form of torture. As a politics, it suggests leadership by a vanguard (or avant-garde) elite who will lead the populace to true consciousness, reforming their imaginations and sexualities along the way.

Mulvey's attack on the pleasures of the cinema and on pleasurable looking was shared by (and reflected in) the first generation of feminist video. This was work—appearing around the same time as Mulvey's essay—that also set itself the task of critiquing and reforming the manner in which women are subjugated in dominant culture and representation, and its tactics, too, generally entailed renouncing dominant form and subverting, denying, or attacking pleasure in looking. A paradigmatic example is Martha Rosler's 1977 *Vital Statistics of a Citizen, Simply Obtained*, in which a passive Rosler is stripped, her body systematically and exhaustively measured, and the measurements recorded by two male technocrats in lab coats. Throughout this ordeal Rosler's voice-over expatiates on measurement as a form of social control, particularly on the sanctioned terrorism of anthropometry—that is, the measurement of the human body.

Although not directly sharing Mulvey's concerns with either cinema or the unconscious, Rosler's tape too takes up the question of how women are positioned by the gaze (although the particulars of this gaze differ from Mulvey's) and further shares, as its political aesthetic, a tactics of negation and of smashing pleasure. For Rosler, the gaze is not described as specifically gendered, but is part of an abstract complex of power that includes the state, science, and all forms of measurement, bureaucratization, and technical rationality, and that is deployed primarily against women's bodies (and is, through its internalization, a primary component of female subjectivity). All measuring—and women's bodies are, more than anything else, subject to normative measurement—is connected to the bureaucratic engineering of everyday life, which is in turn connected to female masochism and disempowerment, as well as to what seems like all other forms of dehumanization and evil, in a speculative, somewhat Frankfurt School–inspired commentary. Rosler's analysis of this all-powerful scientific scrutiny is even more sweeping than Mulvey's description of the scopophilic gaze: for Rosler, scrutiny and its handmaiden, measurement, are central not only in what she calls femicide, but in racism, colonization, and the Holocaust.

This is a tape that was a cornerstone of feminist video, enormously important both at the time and since: it's a tape that also encapsulates the position that later women's video, in works like *A Spy*, reacts against. Looking at it again after fifteen years, *Vital Statistics* is, in both its polemic and its formal strategy, an experiment in radical unpleasure. Using her own naked body as a gambit, Rosler's unrelenting voice-over endeavors not only to strip the experience of looking of any interest, pleasure, or curiosity, but to stigmatize any traces of such experience in the viewer. But pleasure and curiosity are the invariable expectations of looking at a screen, whether film or video, and a naked body is always enough of a frisson to arouse at least some minor interest on its own: that's precisely why performance and video artists take off their clothes. Here, though, one's initial engagement with the visual experience of the tape indicts the hapless viewer, snapping the cage door shut in a perfect double bind: one is implicated, through a chain of associations made by the lecturing voice-over, in a vast array of evils, from racist IQ testing to crimes against native peoples to mass extermination of human beings.

Although the sort of evaluative vision being implicated is, I assume, primarily that of the male viewer, as a female spectator one doesn't look at a woman's naked body neutrally or unevaluatively or without curiosity, either, whatever one's sexuality. (Although sexuality is, along with pleasure, completely evacuated from this tape.) Do I like this body, what does it do to me, am I turned on, what are her breasts like, what is her body like compared with mine? But any response to this naked body—evaluative, curious, sexual—is elided into yet another form of domination, along with any propensity the female viewer might have for bodily self-measurement or self-evaluation, or even for wearing makeup. Although the voice-over allows that, for women, such things as self-measurement are imposed on us as on victims, we're implicated in our own victimization, guilty to the extent that we're knowing, or even unknowing, participants.

The viewing positions offered by Rosler's tape seem to be, on the one hand, self-excoriation or, on the other, denial (that is, being politically correct—another form of maintaining appearances). Me? I don't do/like/think that. The trouble is, I do, and I assume most other women do as well, at one level or another. Although I imagine that what Rosler had in mind as a viewing response was something more like a radical refusal, it always was a fallacy of both the Left and seventies feminism that you can browbeat a populace into enlightenment, indicting them for their pleasures, berating them for their moral failures, offering little or nothing in the way of vision or utopia, and expect them to obediently fall into line. What Rosler offers, besides the feel-bad viewing experience, is the authority of her own analysis—that is, more authority. This analysis is sweepingly undialectical, however, and to a large degree ahistorical. (It's obvious that there's always been a progressive side to social science, in both its inception and its practice, and even that statistics and statisticians, who get a particularly bad rap here, are crucial tools for the Left—in fact, the only feminist issue that most women can still unite around is pay equity, which would be nowhere without statistics on the wage differential.)[1] What seems unthought in Rosler's work is how the browbeating voice-overs partake of kinds of domination formally similar to that which she's critiquing, or that this attack on power simply substitutes a different version of power. As the voice-over tells us repeatedly, "This is a work about coercion." And although it may have been Rosler's plan to make the point coercively, there's no imagining of a space outside coercion; while the tape criticizes the heartlessness of scientists and intellectuals, it is itself heartless. It's an aesthetic strategy that does everything possible to reinforce the oft-expressed folk wisdom/fear/ suspicion that the Left has a particular talent for authoritarianism.

LAURA KIPNIS

There *is* pain here, buried beneath the analysis, pain that women share at the degradations inflicted on female bodies and psyches, but no language to access that pain outside of its overreaching language of intellectual mastery.[2] Its refusal of pain seems bound up in its repudiation of pleasure: what's left is intellect and correctness. Neither, however (from the current vantage point), seems sufficient (or perhaps even necessary) to an aesthetics of political transformation that aims to be both radical and democratic.

What Rosler does unequivocally bring to her work is an articulated politics, a clear understanding that, politically speaking, there are oppressors, there are crimes, there are enemies, and it's the task of a political video art to name them. Later video concerned with trying to reformulate the politics of pleasure and gender, of looking and sexuality—work that often implicitly responds to Mulvey and earlier feminist video—is often less politically explicit, working at engagement rather than distantiation. The tactics here usually entail reappropriating narrative, humor, and visual pleasure. Vanalyne Green's 1989 *A Spy in the House That Ruth Built* is often cited as a tape that aims to reverse the regime of the male gaze, an example of a woman turning the tables on male objectification of women. It's a work that's savvy in its incorporation of feminist theory while rarely deploying theoretical language; one of its great strengths is that it has both accessibility and sophistication. (It's usually one or the other.) It's also extremely pleasurable. The tape is presumably autobiographical, that is, it's narrated in the first person with Green as the protagonist—although all assumptions of autobiographical verisimilitude should be held skeptically, I tend to think, since autobiography always relies on fictional techniques (and demands selective amnesia). The subject is, at the manifest level, Green's relation to the male world of baseball, which for a three-year period in her life had all the earmarks of obsession.

Baseball functioned, for her, as parable, metaphor, and an arena for the experience of an array of desires—sexual, familial, and cultural. It also provided a medium for a host of transgressive fantasies, most of which center around wanting to fuck baseball players. (Her fear of seeming like someone who wants to fuck a baseball player is matched only by her fearful desire to do exactly that.) The brilliance of the tape is the way baseball, our national sport, is transformed, in a kind of feminist guerrilla-semiotic trench war, into a hostage terrain, through whose captive dramatis personae, playing fields, and lingo Green explores the complexity of female sexuality: the way that female desire is often wrapped up in ambivalence and disappointment, and the contradictions (for those doomed to heterosexuality) between resenting and wanting men. Treading on this very male domain and daring to make its metaphors her own is, like Suzie Silver's *A Spy*, in itself a transgressive act—and Green, too, is a self-proclaimed spy. And in the process she introduces a new (or little-heard-from) subject position: the female voyeur.

Her sexual fantasies are on the road to realization when she receives press passes that allow her to take her video camera onto the playing field and aim it at the ballplayers. "Could they tell where I was angling the lens of my camera?" she asks as a bulging crotch comes into view, or a well-rounded male posterior, or as the camera roves up and down a player's muscular thighs. She uses the camera in a way women rarely have, which is to force her desire on us—desire that, however, she's more unabashed about pronouncing than doing anything about.

Her flatfooted technique, as she laments, needs work, although her playing-field interviews with some of the players and managers are hysterically funny clashes of gendered cultures. "Do the players have to wash their own uniforms?" she wants to know. "What sort of food do you like to cook?" she asks one. And when she earnestly explains to a baffled-looking minor leaguer that she's interested in baseball because the origins of the game are thought to have been in some kind of prehistoric fertility ritual, his stunned incomprehension makes her realize that if she wants to get anywhere with these players she's going to have to find a different approach.

FIGURE 1
Vanalyne Green, *A Spy in the House That Ruth Built* (1989)

But the tragicomedy of the tape is that Green (or to be more precise, Green's character) has too many inhibitions and her desire is too wrapped up in intellectualization to either get what she thinks she wants from these male bodies she so volubly lusts for, or to respond in the affirmative when one finally (somewhat crudely) approaches her (a response she later rues); and she lacks the talent for objectification, too. She envies these guys their unselfconscious exhibitionism, but try as she might to objectify them, she can't help but feel sorry for them as she pins them with her viewfinder. Try as she might to turn the tables, the ballplayers emerge as too human, too poignant, too afflicted with career anxieties, disappointments, and injuries to be simple objects of lust. I don't know if there's a lesson here about gender differences when it comes to sexual looking (other female testimony says otherwise) or whether her inability to carry through relates to the other, buried, narrative level of the tape.

Green's often comic explicitness about her lust for ballplayers (a player stands over her at perfect blow job distance, she tells us, as she goes off into a wistful reverie about his massive thighs) is in contrast to a veiled reticence about the tape's subnarrative, one of familial, perhaps incestuous sexuality, which is repeatedly alluded to but remains mysterious and inexplicit. Baseball, which grabs our attention so engagingly, ends up functioning as not so much a metaphor as a displacement. The transgressiveness of speaking female desire in one arena distracts from desires less able to

338

be spoken or named: childhood sexuality, and the daughter's desire for the father—which may or may not have been reciprocated. Green makes reference throughout the tape to her own father and to a triangulated familial sexuality, delivering insights like "Daughters have sexual feelings for their fathers, and I am a daughter." At one point she lets her camera linger for an uncomfortably long time on a little girl, maybe four or five years old, sitting in her father's lap in the stands at a minor league game. As this little blond subnymphet writhes adoringly in her daddy's lap in an unconscious reenactment of those old *Playboy* Vargas cartoons of the bombshell temptress-secretary in the boss's lap, all our cultural discomfort and denial around issues of childhood sexuality well up. The tape seems to struggle to associate its transgression of naming a woman's desire (that is, desire to fuck ballplayers) with an even greater transgression, but one that, in the end, remains too threatening or painful to completely unveil.

The tape finally resolves on an unexpected note of playing-it-safe: it transforms itself into a reform plot. Having been transgressive in speaking her desire, Green is quick to reassure us, at the end, that those desires have been renounced in a triumph of self-realization and new insights about male desire for women and home. And now, she no longer wants to fuck ballplayers. The journey of the tape has been one of victory over transgressive desire and the narrative return of the good girl. Perhaps if that more subterranean, more "infantile" narrative was worked through more fully, the tape wouldn't have to end so resoundingly, and I think depressingly, under the insistent banner of "maturity." For a girl, oedipal desire and incestuous sexuality—whether acted on or not—mean being caught up in the alternation between two positions: bad girl flaunting (I really wanted it) and good girl denial (I never wanted it), and the tape itself seems stuck alternating between these two roles. The intelligence of Green's tape is in the way she manages to tie female Oedipal desire to masculine culture itself—that is, to our national culture. What this tape reveals is that, for a woman, the connection to dominant culture *is* always Oedipal—a lust for the father. To experience that desire invariably means being caught in the terror and danger of abjection, humiliation, rejection, and betrayal.

That having been said, there's something a little boring about good girls, about maturity and renounced desire. Perhaps these are desirable qualities in life where there are bills to pay, jobs to get to, and all the other mundane things that maturity lends itself to, but can't art still be the place where transgression reigns? If Green's autobiographical persona were more of a punk rocker, a skydiver, if perhaps Green, the author, allowed her narrative to resolve itself with more abandon and less sobriety, there might still be a realm of transgression that remained in place as a challenge to "the house that Ruth built." One of the built-in problems of the autobiographical first person is the all-too-understandable desire to elicit admiration and respect for one's person, to protect one's self. Risking not being liked or being disapproved of, being a bad girl on a national scale—the position of performers like Karen Finley or Holly Hughes—is, of course, dangerous in any number of ways. The way the tape gets to its narrative resolution doesn't diminish its achievements, though, particularly in its form of address, which manages to be popular and to perform critical analysis, to put dominant conventions and culture on the line without indicting pleasure, desire, or the audience.

It's also the case that for female desire to be both transgressive and heterosexual is, particularly in the current political scene, a tough balancing act. It's interesting that the work of a number of younger lesbian video artists has lately embraced romance (Cheryl Dunye's 1991 *She Don't Fade* and Sadie Benning's 1992 *It Wasn't Love,* among others): one question this raises is whether speaking desire from a nonheterosexual identity is a politics in and of itself. In today's political climate—after the recent NEA wars and the 1992 Republican convention—I'd want to answer, on the one hand, yes. But while work like Jane Cottis and Kaucyila Brooke's 1990 *Dry Kisses Only* and Cottis's 1992 *War on Lesbians* turn outward, to interrogate the conscious and unconscious constructions of the identity "lesbian" and the nervous circulations of "lesbian" desire in the media and the polis, counterpart works that turn inward, toward the self, romance, and interiority, don't necessarily indicate the same willingness to interrogate the categories that construct identity, for example, the ideologies that surround romance or sexual identity itself. The brilliant exception is, of course, Julie Zando's ongoing exploration of the sadomashochistic underpinnings of all sexuality and desire, brought home in a series of tapes that intrepidly expose the imbrication of childhood sexuality, shame, and adult desires. Her latest tape, *Uh-Oh!,* a rereading of *The Story of O*—now reenacted with a country western motif and an all-woman cast—isn't just a fashionable rehashing of S-M as a kinky possibility for the sexually blasé, but instead powerfully appropriates the classic text as a narrative of the inequities of power that underlie all coupledom. Sadomasochism, it tells us, is the dirty little secret at the heart of all love.

To the extent that it resists proclaiming itself as a new norm, one of the techniques that works to subvert fixed identities and overcertainty is inversion—a term that was, not so ironically, at one point the psychiatric establishment's term for homosexuality. Interestingly, two aspects of recent women's work feature inversion as a favored aesthetic and political tactic. There's a growing body of video inflected by queer politics, aggressively inverting heterosexuality and precariously maintaining difference. (Precariously because difference always risks—or perhaps, within liberal pluralism, demands—incorporation, often as style innovation.) Of work by artists who proclaim queerness as a sexual-political identity, I'm struck by the exuberance of nineteen-year-old Sadie Benning's *It Wasn't Love.* Benning has been making tapes since she was sixteen—in her room—and this is by far her best work to date. Mostly about a crush on an older woman and a crazy plan to drive from Milwaukee to Hollywood that never happens (they make out in a fast food parking lot instead), it's simultaneously rebellious and wistful. Embracing queerness as a banner allows Benning a lot of outlaw tropes, and it's the bad-girl stance that's the source of all this energy and ebullience rather than a traditionally feminist agenda promoting incorporation and equity. (Although clearly, the existence, exhibition, and distribution of this work is indebted to feminism and the inroads of feminist video.) Gender becomes a kind of play rather than a form of oppression (she vamps for the camera in drag, both female and male), and queerness is a

LAURA KIPNIS

license. It's a tape that refuses victimhood, sees desire as having its own integrity, and uses sex to carve out a sphere of freedom. Benning's irony about gender and her final thank you to "bad girls everywhere" signal an exit from some of the more constricting aspects of an earlier feminist video politics, when the charge of "not feminist enough" rained down frequently. (Although I've heard that the counterpart charge of "not queer enough" now also gets made.) This is work that issues a plaintive "fuck you" to straights, parents, authorities, and other downers, including any dictates on either correctness or pleasure, whether social or sexual, and Benning's repertoire of formal techniques and stylistic devices—notably her camera work with the cheesy Fisher-Price Pixelvision camera—succeeds in creating a unique low-end visual pleasure, even reviving a sixties-style sex-rebel utopianism along with it. There's an expansiveness to this work, and a generosity to the audience that reads like a renewed call for a politics of inclusion rather than incorporation, and Benning's invitation to join her in her room and party on the margins makes so much political video seem, by contrast, pinched and joyless.

Inversion also crops up as a favored technique in what might be called an aesthetics of the grotesque, which celebrates the marginal and the excessive, parody and exaggeration, and regularly features flagrant bodily exposure, gender masquerade, and a focus on anything polite society deems inappropriate for public comment or display. The grotesque is in opposition to the norms of bourgeois society and the bourgeois body, or what Mikhail Bakhtin calls the "classical body," a refined, orificeless, unsmellable, laminated, proper body. Largely through the influence of Bakhtin's work on Rabelais, the grotesque has sparked renewed interest as a political aesthetic in academic literary theory, and this, in combination with the historiographical movement toward everyday life, popular culture, and the marginalized and popular classes as subjects, has given rise to a growing canon of historical and theoretical investigations of carnival, low culture, transgression, and the margins.[3] The interest of feminist theorists has now been piqued by the possibilities of the grotesque as a feminist aesthetic strategy and by the power of the female grotesque as an emergent political figure.[4] Not surprisingly, the same sorts of stirrings can be felt in the aesthetic realm—which is, after all, of the same historical and political moment. And obviously the grotesque has been a recurring aesthetic motif that gets revived and reformulated at different historical and political pressure points for varying purposes.

Female transgression as spectacle and strategy has been powerfully deployed in performance art, notably by Karen Finley and Annie Sprinkle, and the female grotesque is a terrain whose possibilities are just beginning to be explored. Finley, who at times smears herself with chocolate, egg yolks, and glitter; spits and growls; and, most famously, crams tubers up bodily orifices, makes defying the proper a central technique of her work, transgressing all boundaries, proprieties, and bodily norms. In transforming herself into a female grotesque, her long poetic excoriations of society's violence toward women's bodies seem spoken almost directly from the body—a body unveiled, and unbound by the social. It's a voice that lays claim, through the power of the grotesque, to a peculiar form of authority to speak the unheard and the unspeakable, and that is, surprisingly, being heard (all too clearly, it seems, given the government's response via the NEA).

In video, there is Erika Beckman and Mike Kelly's *Blind Country* (1989), a completely idiosyncratic work, which seizes on the grotesque to chart the embarrassments of the male body. The subjection of this male body to the logic of an infantile dream language produces a new bodily form and a previously unseen form of male bodily spectacle—a male body not only unbound by rationality but stripped of phallic authority through its forced reversion to an infantile state. Suzie Silver's *A Spy*, discussed earlier, also invokes the grotesque, deploying a strategy of excess and vulgarity, inviting all looking as opposed to critiquing or subverting visual pleasure: its gender parody, its religious defiance, its rock-and-roll female grotesque embodied by Hester Reeve set loose an unruly parodic body—an unruly transgressive female body in drag—onto the unsuspecting culture.

But the most serious practitioner of the grotesque in video art must be Cecilia Condit. Her earlier tapes, *Beneath the Skin* (1981) and *Possibly in Michigan* (1983), are fantasy narratives of the morbid, the macabre, of violence and death, which plumb both the body's materiality and what the unconscious makes of it. In *Not a Jealous Bone* (1987), Condit invents a gothic fairy tale of aging, bodily decrepitude, and death: our eighty-something heroine, Sophie, comes upon a magic bone that contains the secret of youth, which, as in any proper fairy tale, she loses, fights for, and finally regains. "Old people want to live and young people just don't want to grow old," the tape tells us, probably the most benign insight it delivers as Condit masterfully manipulates the response of the young to the process of aging and bodily decay: denial. "It doesn't matter what you're told, it's never you who will grow old," she mocks us, and then prods us to remember just what it is our denial signifies; it's the resistance to admitting into consciousness the inescapable fact that being alive is really an inexorable march toward death. Condit uses the camera to inventory Sophie's aging, sagging body—wielding shots of withered flesh, of corn plasters, and teeth grinning from a glass, when they're not chomping right at the camera lens. At the same time her sound track delivers a mocking singsong nursery rhyme of the indignities of aging flesh, whose childlike cadences only serve to magnify the cruelty of the lyrics:

> Maybe when I'm eight-five, I will have a stroke and die
> Maybe when I'm eight-six, I will fall and break my hips
> Maybe when I'm a hundred-two, I'll have a lift and look like new
> Maybe when I'm ninety-three, I'll do well to hold my pee.

It's a shocking, impolitic, and impolite vantage on the aging process, shocking because it refuses the politely veiled speech and the sentimentality that public discussions of aging are generally conducted through, which function to mask the revulsion and dread that—at least in our culture—the subject of aging invokes. Having confronted us with the inescapable materiality of the body, of our bodies, Condit then

LAURA KIPNIS

inverts the horror of aging onto the human tragedy of lost childhood. Sophie's search is not only for the secret of youth but also for her mother, who even as death nears, Sophie yearns for still. Even at eighty-five, even on your deathbed, Condit tells us, you'll still be longing for, and will never find, maternal plenitude. Life is cold and cruel, death comes sooner than you want to think, and still we're driven by the inescapable will to live.

Condit's frankness about the indignities of aging is in sharp contrast to another art video on old women, Suzanne Lacy's *Whisper, the Waves, the Wind* (1986).

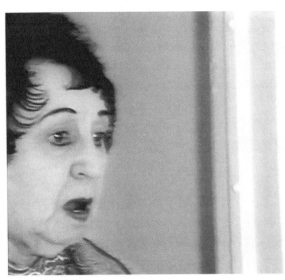

FIGURE 2
Cecelia Condit, *Not a Jealous Bone* (1987)

Lacy, a California feminist first-generation performance and video artist, made this tape to document a large-scale performance piece she created in which 154 women aged sixty to ninety-nine were instructed to dress entirely in white and were bused to the ocean, where they strolled along the beach, gathered in groups, and discussed their lives (while watched by an audience from the cliffs above). The narration track celebrates aging women, "elevating them to goddesses, oracles, voices of experience," insisting on their physical beauty, valiantly asserting that "elderly" is not a negative term. Lacy places the onus on a discriminatory society for its failure to appreciate the wisdom and beauty of older women, taking the position, in the tradition of the positive images approach, that negative stereotypes can be reformed through countering with positive ones, through education, raised awareness, and sensitivity.

What the tape doesn't account for is the unconscious, for the irrationality and fear that is part of the response to aging and the prospect of dying, or for ambivalence—particularly about the maternal body. It seems to presume that the horror of aging is superficial enough that it can be rationalized away. But clearly, while public policy should concern itself with the rights of the aging, with fighting discrimination and providing benefits, Lacy's address is to private policy, which is less available to reform. "Shoulds" have no effect on the unconscious. And what the positive images approach, in general, has always had a problem with is the kernel of truth—often in a false guise, but powerful nevertheless—in stereotypes. Stereotypes take grip and keep gripping us precisely because so often they manage to condense some elements of truth, some real, often unvoiced fear, some buried panic—dehistoricized and stripped of context—but deeply meaningful nevertheless. This insistence on the beauty of aging women, on uplifting messages and positivity, completely neglects the kernel of truth in the stereotype, which is what Condit forces in our faces through a symbolic, nonliteral language: that young people's contempt for the old is inextricable from denial of death and the aging process, and all the reform movements in the world will have little effect on this denial because the visceral horror of the aged, of withered flesh and decrepit bodies, is a matter of life and death. Literally.

Not a Jealous Bone refuses polite speech and positive images. In this tape, death pulls at you from everywhere, from television images, from under manhole covers, from sudden bursts of violence that disrupt the everyday, from haunting memories of dead parents, from the betrayal of one's own aging body. And while we so politely mourn the dead, we can't help but gloat that it's them and not us. When Condit dares voice the oh-so-impolitic, triumphant cackle of the living—which manners and internal censors would never give voice to—she forces us to dive straight into our own denial:

> Tough luck mom,
> Poor mom.
> You are dead but I am still alive
> I may be old but—
> You're dead.
> Don't let being dead go—
> To your head.
> Shame you had to die so young.
> You are dead but I am still alive.

Condit's anti-reformism, her refusal to tiptoe politely around the most difficult subject of all, strikes me as having, in the end, more potential reformist effect by forcing us to confront the dread that Sophie's aging body inspires instead of denying it, like polite citizens, like good girls. She uses the grotesque as a conduit to the unsaid and the unsayable—to a new form of knowledge that all the lecturing and good intentions in the world can never access. This tape acknowledges the unspeakable cruelties of living, and taps into something of the beauty as well, a beauty all the more moving because it's not based in sanctimony, piety, or interdictions.

The transgressions of the current crop of women video artists aren't only a product of individual inspirations. They're also the effects of a specific series of reformulations around questions of pleasure and audiences, both inside the video world as well as within wider cultural and aesthetic discourses and practices, and within feminist theory, as well. But I'd like to suggest that this reconsideration of the pleasure issue isn't simply relevant to debates over representation, or to debates over sexuality and representation, where it's mostly been carried out. It's not even most productively thought about in narrowly cultural terms. How audiences are constituted and addressed is a pressing political issue, not only for feminism but for any possibility of political transformation. And if feminism (at least by name) has largely lost its audience—as countless polls of college-aged women tell us—the reason, I'd suggest, has largely to do with issues of address, or what in political language is sometimes called interpellation: it isn't "speaking to" the audience it needs to reach. Instead, it's received as a series of interdictions: against (hetero)sexuality, humor, popular culture, pleasure. And censoriousness is boring. The languages of radical unpleasure or moral instruction are not, at least currently, succeeding in speaking to the audiences we need to address. The good news is that the work of artists like Silver, Benning, Green, and Condit are suggesting new possibilities and new forms of address—pleasurable address—not to mention new possibilities of female resistance, refusal, and transformation (maybe even transformation for everyone) as they stomp over all the proprieties, all the interdictions, one by one.

NOTES

The tapes discussed in the essay are distributed by Video Data Bank (37 South Wabash, Chicago, IL 60603, 312/899-5172). Thanks to Mindy Faber, Kate Horsfield, and Ayanna Udongo for their help.

[1] See, for example, Lucy Horwitz and Lou Ferleger, *Statistics for Social Change* (Boston: South End Press, 1980). Thanks to Rick Maxwell for suggesting this point.

[2] I have to say, before anyone else does, that I think my own work has often shared this trait with Rosler's.

[3] Mikhail Bakhtin, *Rabelais and His World* (Bloomington: University of Indiana Press, 1984). See also Peter Stallybrass and Allon White, *The Politics and Poetics of Transgression* (Ithaca, N.Y.: Cornell University Press, 1986).

[4] See Mary Russo, *Female Grotesques: Carnival and Theory* (Milwaukee, Wis.: Center for Twentieth Century Studies Working Papers, 1985).

CHAPTER 22

JULIE ZANDO'S PRIMAL SCENES AND LESBIAN REPRESENTATION

Judith Mayne

A number of contemporary lesbian film and video artists are challenging, in a variety of ways and from multiple perspectives, assumptions about lesbian representation.[1] Such assumptions include, of course, the pathologizing perspective, whether deliberately homophobic (such as right-wing pronouncements) or unconsciously so (such as theoretical formulations that take heterosexuality as unquestioned paradigm). But the assumptions challenged in recent lesbian work also include the celebratory ones that have characterized much lesbian representation from "within," as it were. Indeed, I would argue that some of the most exciting film and video being produced by lesbians today takes on the complex and difficult project of challenging, simultaneously, both heterosexual presumption and the myths of lesbian representation that exist within lesbian communities.

For instance, Su Friedrich's film *First Comes Love* (1991) is a condemnation of the virtually universal prohibition against homosexual marriage. Yet that condemnation is presented in a decidedly ambivalent way. After a series of candid images of the various preparations for different church weddings, a rolling title interrupts those images to list the countries where homosexual marriage is illegal—practically every country in the world. After another series of images of newlyweds, the final title image of the film reveals the one exception: "In 1990 Denmark became the first country in the world to legalize homosexual marriage." Two modes of documentary observation are juxtaposed—the cinema verité style of capturing weddings either about to begin or just concluded, and the more detached, dry style of authoritative recitation. In the process, different assumptions that lesbians bring to the institution of marriage are juxtaposed, as well—simultaneous envy and detachment, desire and repugnance. As a result, the very notion of a single, monolithic lesbian view on marriage is questioned.

Lucretia Knapp's videos perform this challenge in yet another way. In a manner reminiscent of Todd Haynes in *Superstar*, Knapp uses Barbie dolls in *Erotica* (1989) and *Sally Cheesey Raffelyell* (1992) in a parodic way. In both tapes, the dolls are lesbianized. Their short haircuts and butch clothing make evident how *un*representable lesbian style is in popular cultural forms like Barbie dolls. And yet, at the same time, the tapes play on the opposite impulse as well, the visibility of lesbianism, whether in porn or in talk shows. Like Kaucyla Brooke and Jane Cottis in *Dry Kisses Only* (1990), a hilarious lesbian rereading of supposedly heterosexual films like *All about Eve* and *The Great Lie*, Knapp reads the conventions of porn (in *Erotica*) and talk shows (in *Sally Cheesey Raffelyell*) ironically.

A question often raised among lesbians, as among members of virtually any marginalized and politically disenfranchised group, is whether it is possible to use mass cultural forms toward, if not "positive," then at the very least "productive" ends— that is, whether lesbians should even attempt to use the talk show format (or pornography, or marriage rites), if they function therein as freaks on display. Friedrich and Knapp turn the traditional formulation of this question on its head by using such institutions and making fun of them simultaneously. The very question of "using" already established forms of popular institutions and mass culture is thus playfully—and forcefully— set aside in favor of a more complex notion of lesbian use value where lesbians are understood as always both inside and outside dominant forms.

In this chapter I want to examine how, in the video work of Julie Zando, such challenges to both prevailing lesbophobic and ingrained lesbian assumptions are addressed. Zando's videos are stunning representations of the complexities of lesbian desire. Stylistically, her work traces an erotics of video form. Zando's video camera moves almost constantly, and one of the most typical devices of her work is a constant framing and reframing of her subjects. As Amy Taubin puts its, "Zando's primary expressive and organizational tool is her hand-held, herky-jerky, intrusive camera, which effectively turns every factual statement into a question, marked moreover, with subjectivity."[2] Zando uses the qualities of video to great advantage, particularly insofar as grain and resolution are concerned. When shot in extreme close-up, for instance, her subjects appear both near to and far from the viewer, distorted by the extreme angle and grain, yet caught as well in a moment of vulnerability. Indeed, Zando plays constantly with the implications of exposure to the video camera, whether it be of her or her subjects.

Like Friedrich and Knapp, Zando challenges prevailing orthodoxies, both those of dominant institutions and those of lesbian culture. In her case, the challenge proceeds across two registers—that of psychoanalysis and that of narrative. The failures of psychoanalysis vis-à-vis lesbians and gay men have been detailed enough that there is no need to rehearse them here, although just as important have been the efforts of theorists like Teresa de Lauretis and Judith Roof to read those failures as the limitations, not of psychoanalysis itself, but of particular practitioners of psychoanalysis.[3] Similarly, Zando's videos are less concerned to critique psychoanalysis for its shortcomings than to reframe the very question of what it means to talk about psychoanalysis in lesbian terms. Zando undoes and reframes the question of lesbianism and psychoanalysis by situating psychoanalysis as a theory less of psychic truth or verifiable experience than of narrative. Now, in and of itself, this use of psychoanalysis as a theory of narrative is nothing new; rather, what is specific to the inquiries undertaken in Zando's work is the definition of psychoanalysis and narrative in relation to lesbian representation.[4]

Narrative is not defined exclusively in the psychoanalytic terms of, say, transference and countertransference, or imaginary and symbolic, in Zando's work, for her video narratives have a very specific resonance vis-à-vis lesbian representation. One of the most persistent myths of lesbian identities is the notion that one "becomes" a lesbian as a result of a very specific intersection of experiences; that is, one of the narratives most common in lesbian culture is the fixing of lesbian identity to a particular moment, a particular experience, a particular time. Coming-out stories are the most popular version of this lesbian narrative, whereby one identifies a particular experience as the turning point of one's sexual life. To be sure, there are some lesbians who are convinced that one is "born" a lesbian, but this too is a version of the lesbian narrative of identity; in this case identity is decided well ahead of any lived experience. Popular versions of the lesbian narrative of identity invariably include scenarios of childhood (as a child I always preferred the company of girls, or I was a tomboy) and adolescence (I got crushes on my female teachers; I was more attracted to female than male characters on television; I was obsessed with Doris Day/Natalie Wood/Greta Garbo . . . or James Dean). The very notion of lesbian identity is produced, in other words, across a narrative structured by a series of revelatory, self-sufficient moments of recognition.[5]

Let me take that lesbian narrative of identity back to psychoanalysis: it is as if, within lesbian representation, there is a preoccupation with the primal scene, with a founding moment of sexual identity. I am admittedly using the term "primal scene" in a metaphoric way, although there is a connection to be made, I think, between how fantasies of the primal scene have been theorized in psychoanalytic writing and how fantasies of lesbian identity have been narrativized in lesbian writing. In contemporary film theory, fantasy has provided the basis for an important revision of theories of the cinematic subject that have reproduced the very traits of dominant culture—that is, a subject that is white, male, and heterosexual. An essay by Jean Laplanche and Jean-Bertrand Pontalis, "Fantasy and the Origins of Sexuality," has been extremely influential in this rethinking of the cinematic subject. Elaborating on their claim that "fantasy is the fundamental object of psychoanalysis,"[6] Laplanche and Pontalis distinguish three "original" fantasies: "Like myths, they claim to provide a representation of, and a solution to, the major enigmas which confront the child. Whatever appears to the subject as something needing an explanation or theory, is dramatized as a moment of emergence, the beginning of a history." They then define three such fantasies of origins: "the primal scene pictures the origins of the individual; fantasies of seduction, the origin and upsurge of sexuality; fantasies of castration, the origin of the difference between the sexes."[7]

Of the three primal fantasies described by Laplanche and Pontalis, the primal scene has particular relevance for sound-image forms like film and video, which rely precisely on the relationship between participant and observer and on the spectator's knowledge as a function of sound and image. Additionally, an understanding of film in relationship to fantasy challenges any monolithic definition of the cinematic

JUDITH MAYNE

subject, for Laplanche and Pontalis emphasize that fantasy scenarios offer "multiple entries."[8] It is not coincidental, then, that fantasy has been the point of departure for challenges to film theory's own compulsory heterosexuality. In a study of Sheila McLaughlin's film *She Must Be Seeing Things,* for instance, Teresa de Lauretis argues that the film articulates a *lesbian* version of the primal scene, where the positions of onlooker and participant are occupied by women.[9]

Throughout Julie Zando's work, lesbian desire inflects fantasy and rubs against the grain of dominant psychoanalytic thinking, just as fantasy inflects lesbian desire and rubs against the grain of some cherished myths of lesbian identity. In suggesting that Zando's tapes interrogate the space where these fantasies intersect, I do not want to reduce her work to an intellectual or theoretical exercise. For what is so exciting and stunning about that work is its visual density, its sonoric field, its narrative richness. Bill Horrigan says of Zando's work that it "evidences the application of a sympathetic intelligence, *une raison ardente,* onto lived values, in the passionate interest of restoring to the subject (themselves/us: we're both of us I) the possibility of an imagined wholeness always partly lost."[10] Zando's tapes are theoretically challenging, to be sure, but this is not theory that seeks easy hierarchies or master narratives. Rather, in Zando's work, theory is an engagement in complexity, contradiction, and most of all, in lesbian pleasure, visual and otherwise. As Zando herself puts it: "I like theory as an intellectual game but I prefer it when I can apply it to my own experiences. I don't want my tapes to act as a light where my role is to flip the switch and illuminate some theoretical concept. I'm more interested in putting the viewer's finger into the socket allowing the shock waves to carry the message in a sudden jolt of understanding."[11]

My discussion of Zando's work is based on five tapes: *The Bus Stops Here* (with Jo Anstey, 1990), *The A Ha! Experience* (1988), *Let's Play Prisoners* (1988), *Hey, Bud* (1987), and *I Like Girls for Friends* (1987). All of these tapes share a concern with the implications of the primal scene for psychoanalytic and lesbian storytelling, and they share stylistic features, as well—the persistent framing and reframing of the subjects, complex and sometimes dissonant relationships between sound and image track, competing and often opposing narratives. Zando herself is present in her tapes, whether as a literal performer (in *The A Ha! Experience, I Like Girls for Friends,* and *Hey, Bud*) or as an offscreen but audible narrator (*Let's Play Prisoners*). Zando's visible authorship is very much a collaborative endeavor, for she appears in her tapes with Jo Anstey, whose writings are the basis of—and in many cases are recited by Anstey herself in—*Let's Play Prisoners, The Bus Stops Here,* and *The A Ha! Experience.*

The Bus Stops Here and *The A Ha! Experience* are the most "obviously" psychoanalytic of Zando's tapes. In *The Bus Stops Here,* a complicated family triangle becomes the scene for the juxtaposition of heterosexual and lesbian desire, maternal and paternal objects, and differing views of psychoanalysis as, alternately, talk therapy and drug therapy; Jacques Lacan also makes an appearance as "Jack," the father. *The A Ha! Experience* contains perhaps the most explicit representation of the primal scene, for here a daughter, returning home from an evening out with a man, imagines her mother in her bed. That Zando herself appears in the role of a young woman in a heterosexual relationship gives a sense of how complicated the representation of lesbianism is in her work!

Yet despite the apparent heterosexual intrigue of *The A Ha! Experience*, I would argue that Zando situates lesbian desire fully center stage. In *The A Ha! Experience,* the young woman returns to an apartment after saying good night to the man. In the bathroom, she removes her jewelry and her clothing, and it is not always clear when we are seeing her or her image reflected back to her (and us) from the mirror. As she proceeds to her room, she describes her shock at seeing her mother in her bed. Zando juxtaposes two classical psychoanalytic scenes of recognition—the mirror stage and the primal scene. In both cases the identification of woman as object of desire is at stake. During the bathroom scene, Tony Conrad, from behind the camera, speaks of his own need to be logical and instructs Zando to repeat an action. Hence the moment of (illusory) self-recognition in the mirror is complicated by the control of that image by a very literal masculine presence. So too is the primal scene segment complicated by Conrad's voice once again, as well as the reappearance of the male lover.

Yet those elements of domination are countered by the woman's fantasy of her mother speaking to her from her own bed. If there is a single absent presence in the tape, it is the mother. Masculine control is exercised on Zando's body in a virtual catalog of the techniques that have been ascribed by feminist film theorists to the (male) cinematic control of the female body: close-ups of her, framing of her within the frame, and sexual display for the camera; in addition, her hands are bound by her male lover, and Tony Conrad not only directs her but yells at her at one point. Yet, the last freeze frame of Zando's face in the tape is accompanied by Zando's voice-over: "Mother, you are my camera."

The A Ha! Experience opens up an encounter, in other words, between lesbian and heterosexual desire, and in other of her works Zando pursues that encounter with more and more attention to the implications of the phrase, "Mother, you are my camera." *The A Ha! Experience* also gives some sense of how much Zando stretches the very definition of "lesbian representation." Forget about so-called positive images of lesbianism; if you are even looking for *literal* images of lesbians, you will be disappointed in Zando's work. Some of her tapes represent (more explicitly so than *The A Ha! Experience*) lesbian scenarios—*Hey, Bud* and *I Like Girls for Friends*, for instance, are inquiries into televisual images and take lesbian relationships as their point of departure and conclusion, and *The Bus Stops Here* has a lesbian character. In *Let's Play Prisoners*, which seems to me Zando's most sustained and complex inquiry into the relationships between lesbianism, desire, and narrative, there is little that can be described as a precise, specific, lesbian image, but there very definitely *is* a lesbian narrative. That seeming paradox—a lesbian narrative without the specific lesbian image—constitutes one of the most challenging aspects of Zando's work.

In *The Bus Stops Here,* lesbian desire is by and large spoken by others. Judith, the clinically depressed lesbian sister of Ana, the novelist who is having an affair with Judith's therapist, rarely speaks, and more frequently her desire and her story are

FIGURES 1 AND 2
Julie Zando and Jo Anstey, *The Bus Stops Here* (1990). (Photo: Fred Ciminelli.)

spoken by others—the therapist, the psychiatrist who prescribes different drugs for her, or the male voice-over (who Zando describes as the metanarrator) who gives her history. In another way, lesbian desire itself is appropriated by her sister, whose novel in progress, read aloud in the tape, is about lesbian attraction and seduction. If Judith's story (and by extension her lesbianism) is largely told, narrated, and appropriated by others, this is part of a larger pattern in the tape whereby women rarely narrate their own stories but are "told," rather, by male figures of authority—psychoanalytic and psychiatric authority, specifically.

Yet throughout the tape, lesbian narration threatens to upset the fit between male domination of women and heterosexual control of lesbian desire. Each of the three principals in the tape—Ana, the therapist, and Judith—tells of a disturbing encounter in a public place. In Ana's case a man exposed himself and masturbated on a bus, and the therapist, also while on a bus, saw a well-dressed woman sucking her thumb. For both Ana and the therapist, the scenes provoke masturbatory fantasies, and the recounting of the tales is strongly evocative of primal scene fantasies, with their emphasis on staging and on the unacknowledged presence of the observer. In addition, the sexual fantasies that result from the encounters in public places occasion the multiple identifications typical of fantasies. Ana, attending a class (during which feminist film theorist Kaja Silverman's voice is heard describing the components of fantasy), imagines a man describing masturbating on the bus, and shots of her on the bus are intercut, thus identifying her as occupying, simultaneously, the position of male masturbator and female onlooker. When the therapist fantasizes about the woman he has seen on the bus, his voice is heard reading aloud the fantasy of lesbian seduction from Ana's novel.

Finally, Judith too has an encounter in a public place that she describes, but once again the psychiatrist introduces the story, so that when Judith faces the camera and speaks, she is speaking through the psychiatrist. Judith describes seeing a woman eating a bagel while her eyes are bulging out, and she describes her discomfort. "You know eating like that is such a very private time, you never expect to see anyone watching you," she says. "I had turned away, embarrassed that I had seen her so vulnerable." As Judith tells of the encounter, we see images of Ana and the therapist drawn from their "bus" encounters. But unlike their scenarios, Judith's story leads to no masturbatory fantasy, no movement across different positions in the fantasy. Rather, the tape concludes with a dream of hers, but told by the psychiatrist, and from which she is virtually absent. Hence the problem of lesbian narration is that it exists only to be appropriated by others.

Let's Play Prisoners is divided into two sections entitled "Remembrance" and "Recognition," suggesting a process of discovery not unlike that of the therapeutic

FIGURES 3 AND 4
Julie Zando, *Let's Play Prisoners* (1988). (Photo: Ellen Spiro.)

situation. The psychoanalytic analogy situates childhood experiences as always the product and projection of a privileged, adult hindsight. The talking cure, with its accompanying dynamics of transference and countertransference, is the model undertaken here; virtually every

aspect of the tape is concerned with conversation and with the dynamics of power therein.[12]

Stories of games played by little girls are read and reread in the tape. The first words heard in the tape belong to Jo Anstey, who reads aloud from her own short story. Anstey's reading of her story is directed by Zando off camera, with an occasional hand entering the frame to adjust Anstey's dress or even, at one point, to slap her to elicit an appropriate response. Zando instructs Anstey to repeat certain lines or to adjust her tone. The relationship between the two women changes in the course of the tape, as does Anstey's appearance, particularly insofar as makeup is concerned. While at the beginning of the tape Anstey and Zando appear to be comfortable in their relationship, tension between them (whether real or performed) emerges as the tape continues. In the first section of the tape, Anstey does pretty much what Zando asks her to do, but in the second section, there is more visible resistance on Anstey's part.

Anstey's reading of the story alternates with a young girl's (Zando's niece) recitation of identical passages from the story. Just as Zando directs Anstey's reading, the girl's mother (also offscreen) reads passages aloud, which the girl then repeats. During the first part of the tape, the story concerns games between two young girls in which one is the prison guard and the other the prisoner, and as the story progresses to tell of other games (particularly in part two), the relationships of power become more and more clearly identified as modeled on the mother-child relationship. It is not only the story, as recited by Anstey and the girl, that makes the imprint of the mother-child relationship more and more foregrounded, but also the editing of the tape. Home movie–type images of mothers with their children, or babies "posing"—however unconsciously, however awkwardly—for the camera, are gradually intercut into the alternation between the two storytellers, Anstey and the young girl. For instance, Anstey says of her friend: "She gave me piggybacks, but I wanted to show her I could pick her up, too." At that moment, we are confronted with a visual match, as it were, but now of a mother picking up her child. When the girl storyteller is shown lying on the ground and speaking the words "'You tie me up,' she said," an image of a baby lying in a similar position is intercut, suggesting, of course, their common status as "tied up" by the mother and the camera.

To my mind the most striking and haunting images of *Let's Play Prisoners* are those that begin the tape and are repeated at key moments throughout: extremely fluid and fragmented close-up shots of two female bodies accompanied by the eerie musical score of the film (written by Paul Dickinson), over which we hear the first words of the film, recited by Anstey: "She said, 'Let's play prisoners. Pretend you've just tried to escape.'" Even though Zando uses the grain of video to great advantage, an effect heightened by the use of black and white, these particular images have the additional texture produced by the video camera used, a Fisher-Price camera marketed for children. Like Sadie Benning, who also uses the distorted effects of this toy camera to great advantage, Zando uses a "toy" to ironic effect in a tape so concerned with putting into question the sanctity of childhood memories.[13]

Jo Anstey appears on camera after this prologue, along with the title "1) Remembrance." While the alternation between Jo, directed by Julie, and the girl, directed by her mother, would suggest a parallel between Jo and the girl (both directed by the women off camera), an additional factor complicates somewhat this parallel. For during the first few alternations from Jo's story to the girl's story, Zando's camera centers not on the little girl but on one of her girlfriends, who walks back and forth in the background during the entire tape. The friend functions as a witness in the video, a bystander seemingly both engaged and perplexed by the spectacle she is witnessing. The friend has no specified position or place within the proceedings; she never speaks, has no narrational role comparable to speaker (Jo, the girl) or director (Zando, the girl's mother). Despite— or rather because of—this lack of specified position in connection with the narrative, Zando's camera tracks this little girl's movements frequently. Indeed, during the girl's recitation of the story, the camera moves in more sweeping, distracted movements, as if the witness pulls the story off balance somewhat, disturbs any possible equilibrium in the movement back and forth from Jo to the girl.

If I am tempted to see the girlfriend as the tape's spectator, it is (I hope) not because of some compulsive need to assign her a fixed position, but rather to describe her as something more than a purely disruptive, marginal presence. For her relationship to the entire proceeding, as both participant (she "enacts" one of the games described by Jo) and observer, as within and without, seems to me to embody the way Zando's video challenges the spectator to read through her own memories of childhood without becoming immersed in nostalgia or sentiment.

The "remembrance" section of the tape concludes with a series of disruptions. Voice-over narrators speak of the mother's power over the child, unconditional love, the power implicit in the other's affirmation of her love, and the loss of power. None of these voices is synchronized with the image track. The naked female bodies appear again to mark the transition to the second part of the tape, entitled "Recognition." The "recognition" here is the increasingly clear link between the girls' games as narrated in Jo's story and the relationship between mother and child; thus, what was presented as something of an interruption, or rather an eruption, in the first part of the video here becomes an integral part of the narration itself. Put another way, the way the home movie–like images of mothers and children appear during "Remembrance" suggests symptoms not yet understood, and the style of "Recognition" suggests, rather, a more complex interweaving of the different levels of "Remembrance."

The primary game recounted in "Remembrance" is the prisoner game of the tape's title, and it culminates in a fusion of past and present when Julie hits Jo on the head to get the desired reading of the story. The two games recounted in "Recognition" are more clearly defined as to how girls' games are modeled on the mother-child relationship. The first, "floppy doll," has the one girl becoming totally passive as the other grabs hold of her and lets her hang, and then drops her. In "Remembrance," a vivid match between the game and the tape's present tense occurs when Julie, acting like the dominant girl in the story, slaps Jo; a somewhat different match occurs in the second part, when the girlfriend in the background holds the girl in the way described in the "floppy doll" game.

The second story in "Recognition" tells of how the two girls refused to go to the bathroom all day, and made signs at each other during school, the combination of pleasure and pain (or at least discomfort) creating a secret bond between them. The game changes when the more controlling of the two girls insists that they wet their pants "like little kids." In both games, then, the common denominator is the passivity of the one and the power of the other, and the passivity mimics the dependence of the child's basic needs—whether moving around or getting its diapers changed—on its mother.

As in part one of the tape, the second section is interrupted by a series of voice-over narrators: "Your source of power is an illness. . . . I want to sever the ties between us, between mothers and children." The tape concludes with the voice-over narration now taken up by Jo and the mother, so that techniques that previously marked difference and separation are collapsed. The toy-video-camera images of the female bodies return, while Jo tells the story (in voice-over) of the two girls not going to the bathroom all day. Something changes in the images of the bodies, for the toy camera continues— seemingly seamlessly—to record a bathroom (but, as with the bodies, the images are fragmented) as Jo continues the story of how Jill, the dominant friend, insisted that she wet her pants. Jo's story concludes with her inability to go to the bathroom, and her attempt to make amends to her friend. Her last line is: "I couldn't do anything without her."

The mother's voice tells more or less the same story (with some variations), and the image track consists of the by-now-familiar images of the girl (and her girlfriend in the background). However, the images are distorted, not enough to be unreadable but enough to suggest a parallel with the toy camera images of the female bodies (and the attendant imprint, as it were, of the little girls on the grown women, and vice versa). In addition, there is, in this conclusion, rapid cutting within the scene, whereas before the only cutting that took place was to introduce the home movie–like images of mothers and children. Hence, the various aesthetic devices that had previously signified different material and different registers are here combined, so that it is no longer possible to easily separate one from the other—just, one might add, as it is impossible to separate adult fantasies of childhood from the supposedly "real" experiences of childhood. "Recognition" is a more complex narrational and visual process of association.

Whereas Jo's version of the bathroom story ends with the girl begging her friend to forgive her for not being able to go through with wetting her pants, the mother's version stops at an earlier point, when the girl is inside the toilet stall. "I couldn't go, and I couldn't go out without going," she says. And on those words—a loop back from the previously uttered end to the story—the tape concludes. The paradox at the heart of *Let's Play Prisoners* is precisely there, the paralysis of refusing to submit to the power of the other and refusing simultaneously *not* to submit.

While *Let's Play Prisoners* is obviously preoccupied with power as it is manifested both in the mother-child relationship and in all subsequent relations between women, I think it is a mistake to read the tape too literally in terms of a particular parallel between mother-child and woman-woman. To be sure, Zando's tape challenges a tendency in feminist theorizing to idealize the mother-child bond as pure fusion, and she challenges as well the idealized notion of lesbianism as the recreation of that fusion. In this sense, Zando's tape is evocative of the critical difference that Judith Roof has elaborated between heterosexual and lesbian narratives of the mother. Taking the writings of Nancy Chodorow and Julia Kristeva as symptomatic of a heterosexual tendency to idealize the mother-child bond, Roof says: "If we see the relationship to the mother as one of lack instead of a nostalgia for plenitude suggested by Kristeva and Chodorow, if these lesbian stories privilege the moment of separation from the mother rather than the time of unity with her, we can see the genesis of an ironically heterogeneous desire as opposed to the nostalgic desire that characterizes heterosexual accounts of mothering."[14] In Zando's tape, a lesbian remembrance allows the recognition of the complexity of the power relationship in both childhood games and mother-child relations. Put another way, then, *Let's Play Prisoners* is less an indictment of the power struggles that characterize relationships between women (although it may well be that on a secondary level) and more an exploration of the ways "remembrance" and "recognition" are always a function of one another.

While the mother-child relationship is certainly important in its own right in Zando's work, it also functions as a paradigmatic dualistic framework, that is, a model for the either/or of autonomy and dependence.[15] As I've suggested, *Let's Play Prisoners* works through, in narrational and visual terms, the implications of binary frameworks. The relatively strict two-termed oppositions and parallelisms of the first half of the video (Jo's reading/the child's recitation; the relatively straightforward imagery of Jo's and the girl's narration/the more fragmented and distorted imagery of the female bodies) are transformed in the second half, so that the division between "recognition" and "remembrance" is, paradoxically, a putting into question of any such easy division.

Hey, Bud also relies for its initial structure on a much bolder two-termed opposition. The tape opens with images of women—their faces for the most part invisible—in colorful vintage gowns. The use of a wind machine and the sound of camera shutters clicking suggest a photo shoot and, by extension, the conventional definition of woman as object of the look.[16] During the opening minutes of the tape, these images alternate with a close-up of a woman cutting her toenails and a female voice-over reflecting on the significance of Bud Dwyer—the Pennsylvania official who committed suicide in front of television cameras during a news conference. The woman's voice describes Dwyer as a pornographer; "*Hey, Bud,*" she says, "you dramatized a private act in a public forum."

In *Hey, Bud,* Zando's own video style works through and against that of televised news, and one of the characteristics of her work is an engagement on many levels with the institutions of television. Indeed, *Hey, Bud* "cites" television advertising, journalism, and MTV and reworks their apparent differences in a meditation on the video form as one that flattens the distinction between voyeurism and exhibitionism. Similarly, in *I Like Girls for Friends,* a woman leans on her elbow and faces the camera in a style reminscent of the Calvin Klein jeans advertisements of some years back, where female models (like Brooke Shields) spoke in a confessional mode to the camera. In Zando's tape, the young woman's image and voice do not match—the female voice-over is unsynchronized for the most part to the image. Accompanied by generic pop music, the woman's voice begins talking about lesbianism in some of the cliché terms that have characterized the mythology of lesbianism—I like girls for friends better than boys, I'd rather be with girls, and so on. But the story the woman tells is one that moves far beyond both the "confessional" mode of advertising and the mythology of lesbianism as female bonding intensified. For she tells a tale of abuse by her female lover.[17]

Hey, Bud takes further this principle of juxtaposition. From its initial visual and sonoric opposition between what also might be called public and private views of the female body, the tape alternates between repeated images of two of the women (Zando and Anstey), still dressed in their vintage gowns, as they enter a room, primp, and eventually kiss and embrace; and the televised footage of Dwyer committing the act of suicide. As in *Let's Play Prisoners,* although in a more exaggerated way given how disparate the two tracks seem initially to be, binary oppositions are broken down. The tape combines in different ways the supposedly "public" act of Dwyer's suicide and the supposedly "private" seduction of two women in a room, all the while undoing any such easy opposition between private and public, subject and object of the look, or voyeurism and exhibitionism.

The conclusion of the tape plays on the notion of "climax." To the accompaniment of a woman's heavy breathing on the sound track, rapid alternation occurs between the black-and-white, grainy footage of Dwyer preparing to kill himself and lush, color images of one of the women (Anstey) combing her hair as the other (Zando) watches and moves to embrace her. During the most rapid montage of these image tracks, Anstey's hands, combing her hair, seem to be superimposed upon those of Dwyer preparing to kill himself. If Dwyer's suicide was, as the female narrator claims early on, an act of pornography, it has no money shot, so to speak. The first time I saw the tape, I cringed in expectation of the man's head being blown to bits before the camera. Zando (like most newscasters) stops short of showing the actual moment of suicide. Zando's climax is, rather, the juxtaposition between the seemingly disparate images of man and woman and the positioning of a lesbian narrative as inescapably connected to public theater.

I noted previously that in *Let's Play Prisoners,* there is a lesbian narrative with no specific lesbian image. If *Hey, Bud* seems initially to contradict that separation of image and narrative, it is only to challenge from another direction the relationship between image and narrative. For the image of the two women embracing remains difficult to "see," obscured and overpowered by the spectacular display on television. It is just that difficulty that constitutes the power and the beauty of Zando's work.

In conclusion, I would like to return to the question of how Zando's work may be seen in the context of contemporary lesbian representation. I have characterized Julie Zando's work as engaging critically with myths of lesbianism that exist both in dominant culture and lesbian culture. Zando's engagement with lesbian culture from within means that her work exists against the backdrop of a number of assumptions. For instance, Zando's work is never identifiable as "lesbian" in the sense of celebratory, positive representations of lesbian life, from *Desert Hearts* to *Claire of the Moon,* from uplifting documentaries to Naiad romances. Throughout this essay I have been arguing that Zando's work, in relationship to more popular (among lesbians, at least) forms of lesbian representation, offers a more intense theorization of the very stakes of lesbianism and representation. But in some ways this argument for the particular quality of Zando's work could be seen as an easy way out, and one that affirms a problematic dualism between "popular" and "avant-garde" work.

Laura Mulvey, in her classic 1975 article "Visual Pleasure and Narrative Cinema," speaks of the "passionate detachment" that will allow audiences to view the conventions of mainstream cinema critically.[18] If Mulvey herself has seemed more inclined toward the "detachment" side of the formulation, its "passionate" quality is always there, too, a love of the very forms that rely so extensively on woman as object. While Mulvey's work has been subjected to extensive commentary, revision, and argument, the concept of "passionate detachment" remains nonetheless as one of the most provocative and most undertheorized aspects of her approach to cinema.[19] Zando's work, it seems to me, is characterized by passionate detachment, directed both at dominant representational forms and at lesbian mythologies.

Now by situating Zando's work in this way, in relationship, that is, to the founding text of feminist film theory, one might think that I am appropriating Zando to the feminist cinematic canon, but what I want to suggest instead is that Zando's work exemplifies a process that I see in other works of lesbian representation, as well—an embodiment of passionate detachment that challenges feminist theories of representation, not just for their homophobia, but for their simplistic either/ors, their easy moralizing about dualisms, their insistence on making clear and absolute distinctions between what is patriarchal and what is not. Hence Zando's work—like that of Su

Friedrich, Lucretia Knapp, Sadie Benning, Midi Onodera, and Cheryl Dunye (to name but a few)—suggests that the complexities and contradictions of lesbian representation may well define a new, more theoretically challenging "scene" of feminist alternative representation.

Perhaps the stakes of "passionate detachment" in Zando's work are best exemplified in the way one of the most divisive and controversial of lesbian issues is addressed—lesbian sadomasochism. There is much in Zando's work to suggest the shadow of sadomasochism, from her investigation of power to her explorations of how violence intersects with sexuality. But these are not tapes that take up any identifiable position—that is, nowhere does Zando's work proselytize either "for" or "against" lesbian sadomasochism. Rather, Zando's work opens up a space within contemporary debates about lesbian sexuality. And in this sense Zando's work shares an important preoccupation with other contemporary lesbian works similarly concerned with exploring and redefining our very definition of lesbian representation. Lynne Fernie, codirector (with Aerlyn Weissman) of the remarkable feature *Forbidden Love*, an exploration of lesbian culture of the 1950s and 1960s, from oral histories of lesbians to a reenactment of the appeal of lesbian pulp novels, has said, "It's really the s&m controversy that made this film possible."[20] I take Fernie's comment to mean that whatever else one might say about debates concerning lesbian sexuality, the controversy has introduced the kind of active, engaged debate necessary for any representation to thrive. Now in many ways Zando's work would seem to be quite different from *Forbidden Love*, but what they share is that sense of passionate detachment that encourages viewers to rethink their own assumptions about what it means to talk about lesbianism and representation in the first place. In the process, some of the problematic dualisms that have characterized debates and discussions about lesbian representation may well become obsolete.

NOTES

An earlier version of this essay appeared in *Quarterly Review of Film and Video* 15, no. 1 (1993): 15-26.

1 For assistance in the preparation of this essay, thanks to Melodie Calvert, Bill Horrigan, and Julie Zando.

2 Amy Taubin, "The Deep: Lures and No Exits," *Village Voice,* 13 November 1990, 51.

3 Judith Roof, *A Lure of Knowledge: Lesbian Sexuality and Theory* (New York: Columbia University Press, 1991); Teresa de Lauretis, "Perverse Desire: The Lure of the Mannish Lesbian," *Australian Feminist Studies,* no. 13 (Autumn 1991): 15–26.

4 On psychoanalysis and narrative, see Donald P. Spence, *Narrative Truth and Historical Truth:* *Meaning and Interpretation in Psychoanalysis* (New York: Norton, 1982), and Peter Brooks, *Reading for the Plot: Design and Intention in Narrative* (New York: Random House, 1984).

5 Bonnie Zimmerman's description of the lesbian coming-out novel is relevant here: "Whether it conforms to the *bildungsroman,* the religious tale of exile, the novel of awakening, or the picaresque, the lesbian coming out novel takes its pilgrim on a progress toward wholeness" (see *The Safe Sea of Women: Lesbian Fiction, 1969–1989* [Boston: Beacon Press, 1990], 38).

6 Jean Laplanche and Jean-Bertrand Pontalis, *The Language of Psychoanalysis,* trans. D. Nicholson-Smith (London: Hogarth Press, 1973), 317.

JUDITH MAYNE

7 Jean Laplanche and Jean-Bertrand Pontalis, "Fantasy and the Origins of Sexuality," in *Formations of Fantasy,* ed. Victor Burgin, James Donald, and Cora Kaplan (London and New York: Methuen, 1986), 19.

8 Ibid., 22-23. For a more extended discussion of fantasy in relationship to contemporary film theory, see my book *Cinema and Spectatorship* (London and New York: Routledge, 1993), esp. chap. 4.

9 Teresa de Lauretis, "Film and the Visible," in *How Do I Look? Queer Film and Video,* ed. Bad Object-Choices (Seattle: Bay Press, 1991), 223–76.

10 Bill Horrigan, "Essay: Question," *Frame/work: A Journal of Images and Culture* 2, no. 3 (1988): 38.

11 Helen Molesworth, unpublished interview with Jo Anstey and Julie Zando, 1992, 6.

12 As Zando herself puts it: "Just as an analyst directs the therapeutic session, the camera directs perception and experience. In psychoanalytic terms the camera 'normalizes' experiences in a deliberate, self-conscious way; my tapes often remind the audience of the camera's analytic privilege (its power to interpret and mediate experience). Like Bertolt Brecht, I am interested in self-conscious direction, except that I interpret the process as a kind of 'counter-transference'" (see Julie Zando, "Symptoms and Stories: The Narrative Cure," in *Breakthroughs: Avant-Garde Artists in Europe and America, 1950–1990,* ed. Wexner Center for the Arts [Columbus, Ohio: Wexner Center for the Arts, 1991], 7).

13 These images suggest, at once, the relationship of infant to the mother's body and the relationship of lover to lover. As Cynthia Chris puts it: "As the desired object of either infant or lover, Zando portrays the body as a contested arena on which the other will experience victory or defeat, as a stage on which something will be made to happen, as the setting for a story about to be told" (see Chris, "Girlfriends," *Afterimage,* April 1989, 21).

14 Roof, *A Lure of Knowledge,* 114.

15 As Christine Tamblyn puts it: "Female dyads enacting dominance/submission rituals are obsessively constructed and reconstructed in *Let's Play Prisoners*" (see Tamblyn, "The River of Swill: Feminist Art, Sexual Codes, and Censorship," *Afterimage,* October 1990, 12).

16 Sandra Haar suggests that *Hey, Bud* is edited "to suggest, at once, ritual and fashion photography" (see Haar, "Self-lessness," *Fuse,* June-July 1990, 45–46).

17 In so doing, parenthetically, she alludes to many of the figures that appear throughout Zando's work; she refers to herself as treated like a "floppy doll" by her girlfriend, and footage of Zando and Anstey from *Hey, Bud* appears here briefly.

18 Laura Mulvey, "Visual Pleasure and Narrative Cinema," *Screen* 16, no. 3 (Autumn 1975): 15.

19 The introduction to Annette Kuhn's *Women's Pictures: Feminism and Cinema* (London: Routledge and Kegan Paul, 1982) is titled "Passionate Detachment."

20 Lynne Fernie, quoted in B. Ruby Rich, "Making *Love,*" *Village Voice,* 17 August 1993, 58.

CHAPTER 23

WEDDING VIDEO AND ITS GENERATION

James M. Moran

Although home movies have been popular since the introduction of cheap cameras and projectors in the 1920s, the advent of video technologies in the 1980s has compromised the "home mode" of family representation, one whose localized practices have been allied with folk art, compared to avant-garde cinema, and appraised as noncommercial popular culture. Undoubtedly, the codes of the home mode have themselves been shaped by domestic ideology and consumer imperatives; nevertheless, in certain critical quarters, the home mode has been championed for its imagined radical potential: that is, the broad access of the masses to the means not only of production, but to distribution and exhibition, as well. Ironically, the only real material advances of the home video revolution so far have been primarily technological rather than sociopolitical. The economic advantages of the video system have not only rendered the film apparatus obsolete, thus requiring a new cycle of leisure spending, but have also renewed the hegemony of a profitable industry specializing in family videography. This network of entrepreneurs is a new manifestation of late capitalism: a second-order constellation of professionals whose product simulates the home mode while diffusing it with instrumental values.

As objects of cultural analysis, commercial event videos fall outside the typical lines of theoretical inquiry. As media, they are neither broadcast nor publicly exhibited. As commodities, they are neither mass produced nor advertised. Their producers cannot be located within specific, centralized institutions. And their audiences are always local at the most microdemographic levels, yet cross all categories of ethnicity, gender, sexuality, and age. Formal approaches are equally puzzling. Wedding videos, for instance, although nonfictional, lack the critical perspective of documentary. And while, in general, they tell a story, indeed largely the same story, does it makes sense to categorize them as narratives, or as genre for that matter? Less than cinema, more than a home movie, but aspiring to television: commercial event videos complicate conceptual models of "mass media."

In the sense that they are both everywhere and nowhere (a research dilemma), event videos illustrate postmodern dispersal and implosions of classic binaries: private/public, amateur/professional, artisanal/industrial, to name a few. As simulations of the home mode, they hybridize production and reception, conflate autobiography and ethnography, confuse original and copy, and thus suggest unexplored configurations of image representation, self-identity, and memory. At the same time, as they increasingly infiltrate the home mode, commercial event videos demonstrate the continuing need for critical theory to situate their influence within the broader political economy and to examine the ways in which the capitalist values of professional videographers invest in, appropriate, and alter home mode conventions as they delimit and perhaps reinvent the genealogical traditions of family and domestic culture that, ironically, they have been hired to preserve.

The traditional wedding video is emblematic of these nascent video practices.[1] Although still in its infancy, the wedding video industry is finally coming of age. In 1992, American couples paid professionals over a billion dollars to record their marriage ceremonies. Revenues are predicted to grow dramatically over the next decade, suggesting that what had been formerly smiled upon as a passing fad now commands serious attention as an important business trend. The local cottage trade of the 1980s has matured into a national network of video associations led by pioneering figures, whose high expectations for increasing financial profit and cultural esteem extend well into the next century.[2] Not surprising for an industry so committed to preserving domestic values, these entrepreneurs are self-consciously forming their own professional families.

Inevitably, the wedding video has fast become a staple of the "family gallery" worthy of theoretical consideration.[3] A former wedding videographer myself, I first formulated intuitive hypotheses in the mid-eighties when working to understand how, why, and for whom clients wanted their ceremonies preserved. Since then, rapid innovations and advancing technologies have required that I substantiate these early speculations with primary research and interviews with current practitioners. For this reason, rather than speak in the first person from experience alone, I have fused the voices of various videographers with my own—one that, in effect, reflects a third-person masculine point of view. As an advocate of nonsexist writing, I adopt this voice, not in deference to phallocentric conventions of English prose, but in reference to a predominantly patriarchal industry. In short, although the wedding video is arguably a "woman's genre," its producers are primarily men.[4] The consequences and complications of this gender issue are central to my investigation.

Of equal importance are the subjective notions of heritage, memory, and autobiography that play crucial roles in the reception of this peculiar documentary form. Adopting conventions from home movies, television broadcast, still photography, cinema verité, and narrative filmmaking, the wedding video intersects several protocols of spectatorship and constructs new audience communities. In an effort to construct a coherent argument tracing the historical, structural, and technological import of this hybrid development in family photography, I explore the wedding video in terms of its "generation" in several senses of the word: as genealogy, as copy, and as production.

FIRST GENERATION: GENEALOGY

In *The Family Album* (1986), a montage of silent home movies recorded from the twenties through the sixties, director Allan Berliner illustrates and confirms the genealogical traditions of American family photography. Dramatizing the human cycle, he structures his documentary in groups of images spanning the average lifetime. From infants at their mothers' breasts and children on a grandma's knees, to young adults at their first proms and older couples' anniversaries, iconic moments are synchronized with independent audio tracks compiled from private tape recordings of various family gatherings, such as birthday parties, holidays, and vacations. Berliner's inspired unity of autonomous visual and audio tracks, whose corresponding effects seem so natural, illustrates our culture's timeless performance of familialism across boundaries of ethnicity, geography, and technology. At the same time, Berliner's ability to recognize the universal similarities between the various sounds and images reveals a generic protocol whose shared expectations maximize domestic ideology: the family album records an individual's rites of passage in such a conventionalized way that all family albums are alike. A series of cycles whose arrangement shapes memory, secures identity, and generates tradition, these forms of family exhibition are at once historical and ubiquitous, a syntactic progression of paradigmatic moments. As Berliner's film amply depicts, the wedding governs this sequence as its pivotal event. A generation of generations, it climaxes the narrative of the child in its exposition of the adult. Both a personal rite of passage and a communal experience, it marks and erases individual difference. Pointing toward the couple's future together but observing the heritage of their past, it heightens a sentimental awareness of the passage of time and affords a diachronic continuity.[5]

As a medium that accommodates material from virtually every visual and audio source—still photographs, film, television broadcasts, electromagnetic tape, and computer graphics—video is well suited for recording the wedding celebration. Incorporating the couple's childhood photos, old home movies, favorite songs, poems, and prayers into the footage of the ceremony itself, many wedding videos synthesize a nostalgic past with an expectant future into a summary chronicle of life in a liminal present. As an animated family album, the wedding video is at once *something borrowed*—an accumulation of visual media whose essential differences are homogenized—and *something new*—an electronic rendering that completes and replaces its predecessors with a new edition. A supplement to the couple's personal history and its telos, the wedding video makes an adult declaration of independence in both its form and its content.

THE TECHNOLOGY GAP

Thus, at the same time that they manifest their technology as something new, wedding videos contrast their media antecedents as *something old*. Like the grainy, black-and-white film stock that dates *The Family Album*, the photographic technologies that precede and are surpassed by video mark the couple's passage from "where we were then" to "where we are now." As children growing up with photographic artifacts antedating

JAMES M. MORAN

their birth, many couples eagerly turn to video as a more contemporary expression of their era: "Every generation must reach a *modus vivendi* that simultaneously embraces and abandons precedent."[6]

Despite the intended harmony of the marriage celebration, its planning frequently creates friction between generations. The surrender of authority from parents to their children regarding issues of invitations, seating arrangements, and menus often comes at the expense of bitter argument, whose urging proceeds as much from a crisis of identity as from matters of taste and decorum. Prompted by the wedding's liminality to evaluate their new positions in life, parents may unwittingly resist or reject the wishes of their children as threatening portents of change. As personal anecdotes and popular wedding literature reveal, the presence of video at the ceremony and reception stirs equally lively debates, whose lines are drawn roughly between junior and senior parties. Often described as cheap and corrupt by older generations, video is condemned as a poor rival to still photography, the "proper" medium for recording the event. Perhaps this denial of the camcorder in favor of the camera expresses a nostalgic desire, a parental longing for a return to the past. While the older technologies of flash and shutter signify a period unspoiled by sophistication, video's cutting edge drives a wedge between the good old days and the years to come, between new life and life declining. The relative simplicity of erstwhile processes renders a more inviting, comprehensible past: "Yesteryear's forms and functions were integral to life when we learned how things worked, whereas those of today often seem baffling because they stem from later, unfamiliar innovations."[7]

Juxtaposing the old and the new, pointing to the past and the future, celebrating the child and revering the parent, the wedding video simultaneously widens and bridges the generation gap. Where the wedding reception invites all age groups to participate in communal festivity, the reception of the technology that records it marks the breach between them. If the content of the wedding video narrates a story of timeless unity, its form nevertheless betrays the contingencies of its historical determination. The current generation, whose wedding videos mark the present as a site of change, also run the risk that their artifacts, too, will someday be out of date, supplanted by upstart technologies.[8] Like all generations before them, their resolution will inevitably fade over time.

YOU ARE CORDIALLY INVITED TO A CONCEPTION

Because of its ability both to transport older photographic images into the more contemporary video format and to invite future generations to look back upon those of the past, in many respects the wedding video is a medium of time travel. Children, in particular, are fascinated by the time just before their entrance into the world, the period before their birth when their parents existed before them. As Roland Barthes declares, "That is what the time when my mother was alive *before me* is—History."[9] A curiosity about roots, a desire to understand parentage, and a need for an explanation of personal existence promote fantasies of returning to key figures in the past to generate an event that has already made an impact on one's identity.[10]

Popular movies like *Back to the Future* dramatize perhaps the most satisfying and taboo of time travel narratives: the primal scene fantasy of being on or before the scene of one's conception. Observing parental intercourse or acting as one of the participants—in effect becoming one's father or mother—has stirred the western imagination in modulated forms from *Oedipus Rex* to *La Jetée*.[11] Like literature and cinema, the wedding video and family album tap into these desires. In Berliner's film, for example, several audio tracks record parents recounting stories of their first meeting, first date, and wedding proposal for their children. In one subtle but revealing shot, a man's hand appears from behind a bedroom door, places his pair of shoes carefully beside a woman's pair outside in the hallway, and closes the door behind him.

Although scenes of consummation are nearly unthinkable in conventional wedding videos, this amusing detail demonstrates how the moving image is better able than the still photograph to record the wedding ritual as a process of sexual investigation rather than merely its pose.[12] Those infamous moments at the reception—the garter and glass-breaking customs, both of which symbolically enact the groom's rupture of the bride's hymen—add just that *something blue* that anticipates the night of passion to come, perhaps even a scene of conception. If it is gratuitous to suggest that children enjoy watching their parents' wedding videos for reasons of sexual curiosity and voyeuristic pleasure, it seems indisputable today that the incest taboo takes on sublimated forms, camouflaged even within the wedding video itself. The most obvious display revolves around the "first dance" of the bride and groom, virtually an excuse for the bride's father to cut in for final "dibs" on his daughter and for the groom to reciprocate with his mother. The audience gazes on in admiration, applauding with enthusiasm. From the dance floor to the TV monitor, parents generate desire in their posterity, relooped and recycled in the wedding video.

SECOND GENERATION: COPY

TAKE ONE: "THE BRIDE SWORE BACK"

Rosie's wedding was a dream come true, but her video was a nightmare. At the end of the day's celebration, Jim, her videographer, a novice to the profession, confessed to Rosie's family a cardinal sin, his head hanging low in shame: somehow he hadn't gotten *it* on tape. Any of *it*. Inexplicably, he had pressed record when he meant pause and pause when he meant record. Sure, he had gotten footage: beautiful shots of the church floor's marble mottling, plenty of dancing feet at the reception, even the photographer's sneer and the janitor's smile. For all intents and purposes, Jim argued, these things *were* part of Rosie's wedding. Yet after viewing the remains, Rosie let out a silent scream. "This is *not* my wedding!" she finally cried. "This is a sick joke! This is avant-garde!"

Why was Rosie so upset? Why did she demand her money back? What was so scandalous about Jim's video? The answer lies in the question: quite simply, Rosie didn't want *Jim's video*—she wanted *her wedding*. Not its representation, but its replication. Not its reproduction, but its simulation. "Everybody knows" what a wedding is, after all. And it is the videographer's contractual duty to show exactly what everybody knows. A subjective labor indeed. Which of course begs for theoretical elaboration. Thus, in this section, the wedding video will be discussed as a procession of simulacra, and, as a generation of copies, its relationship to the actual event will be explored regarding memory, originary status, imaginary presence, critical transparency, defamiliarization, festive viewing, and community audience.

THE WAY WE WEREN'T

A phenomenon of the wedding day is that the bride and groom remember less about it than anyone else. Trembling with nerves, obsessed with details, bouncing from guest to guest, they have little time for reflection. The couple desire, therefore, to fix this seminal event permanently in recorded images.[13] They crave the past in a recoverable form, which, unwittingly, may supplant their personal memories altogether. In its effort to recover a consciousness of the ceremony, the wedding video serves as a form of electronic recollection, a recorded reverie that highlights the event with conventional images. Moments are selected that have pertinence not only to the idiosyncratic personal memories of the married couple, but to the community audience of friends and family at large: the wedding march, the exchange of rings and kisses, the honeymoon bon voyage. These moments frame the wedding video's selection of "appropriate" material that renders the marriage ceremony and its reception not exactly as it is, but as most would like it to be remembered. Elective and partial, in essence, the wedding video reflects the functions of human memory even as it replaces them: "Memory transforms the experienced past into what we later think it should have been, eliminating undesired scenes and making favoured ones suitable."[14]

The wedding suffers a technological repression. Both camcorder viewfinder and editing deck simplify and purify the ceremonies in a joint process of selective attention and retention. Focusing on images, actions, and figures with a predetermined value and revising aspects of the perceptual experience without "proper" ideological motivation, the video valorizes certain incidents over others: bowing in respect at the minister's benediction, over paying him for his services; toasting the couple's success, over bitching about the in-laws; drinking champagne, over smoking cigarettes; dancing, over sitting; smiles, over frowns. Overlooking incompatible religious faiths, family politics, personality conflicts, boredom, and unhappiness, the wedding video makes life seem more pleasurable than it really is.

A TWICE-IN-A-LIFETIME OPPORTUNITY

A wedding video signifies that memory is simply not good enough. Duplicated, the original ceremony diminishes recollection in favor of the potential for its replication. The reality of the event is, therefore, not what happened, but what is retold, what is recorded rather than remembered. Rendered a visible past, the marriage and its reception reify a captured spontaneity more animated than the actual encounter: "The event as represented is the one that is experienced and remembered. The status of the original—and indeed the individual destination between original and copy—is further demoted. The reproduction is now *more* important than the original."[15]

Or rather, going one step further, the reproduction *becomes* the original (stored in a safe place), from which all other copies are generated. The status of the original itself is in jeopardy: a *mise-en-abyme* proceeding from video copy to video master to wedding ceremony to ceremony rehearsal to ceremony model, itself a catachresis derived from its historical series. In the logic of Baudrillard, the wedding video reproduces a ceremony that itself simulates its imaginary paradigm: "Here are the models from which proceed all forms according to the modulation of their differences."[16]

By standing in for its historical referent, the wedding video sustains the marriage vows as an evidentiary alibi. Recalling the dreaded prospect of losing one's wedding ring—for some a superstition portending bad luck between spouses—many couples fear erasing or taping over their wedding videos. For most, of course, this upsetting loss of images represents an irretrievable loss of memories. For others, like those who consider a wedding ring replacement a poor substitute for the "real thing," their deprivation represents an irredeemable loss of authenticity, the source of whose replacement could only be, impossibly, another "original" ceremony. These superstitions underline our culture's ideological pressure against serial marriage, one that compels the videographer, like the betrothed, to "get it right" the first time: "Everyone hopes to be married only *once,* and during your wedding you have only *one* chance to be sure that your photos capture those magic moments!"[17]

UNTIL DEATH DO YOU PART

Wedding photography wants to capture life. Yet unlike the wedding album whose conventions it borrows, the wedding video suffers neither spatial paralysis nor the temporal delay of processing. Protensive, in motion, its photographic referent shifts between what has been and what is. Here is a telling difference: a common convention of the wedding video is to tape the photographer posing the bride and groom for group shots. The contrast is deconstructive, as video reanimates and disorders the embalming artifice of the still photograph.[18] An electronic mode of message transfer that causes all of its images to appear live, videotape transmission and live broadcast are indistinguishable from each other; only editing and postproduction effects offer clues that the ceremony has been recorded. Wedding videos readily exploit this association during playback on the television monitor, evoking the ceremony's origin as both living testimony and public event. Like Chuck and Di, every couple can watch their wedding on TV.

This sense of the wedding video's imaginary presence is rooted in a domestic ideology shared by its form and content: "Video is not life, of course, any more than any art is. Unlike the other arts, though, it approaches the pace and predictability of life, and is seen in a perceptual system grounded in the home and the self."[19] This perceptual system is also grounded in phonocentrism, an ideological faith in the unity of signifier and signified in speech, reflected in the general belief that the wedding video's synchronized sound more purely and naturally communicates the event. Its audience imagines themselves to be in the unmediated presence of the wedding's participants: the minister's blessing, the best man's toast, the drummer's beat, conversation, clinking glasses—even the whisper of the bride and groom. The advantage of sound, in fact, is the primary reason many couples opt for video in the first place. It imbues the ritual images with an aura of authenticity.

CAN I GET A WITNESS?

A surefire way to damage that aura is to tape an "aberration" that violates the integrity of the event. For example, editing conventions out of sequence—the bride throwing her bouquet before cutting the cake or the groom's mother being seated after the processional—may invite cries of protest. Another infraction, particularly unforgivable if he is neither friend nor family, is the unauthorized appearance in the video of the videographer himself, whose presence proclaims his identity, exceeding the self-defining performance of the ceremony.[20]

Neither a single-minded journalist looking for a good story nor a detached ethnographer receptive to all meanings, the wedding videographer is expected to perform both in theory and in practice as an implied but anonymous witness to the event he is transmitting. He must think of the wedding video as a medium of presentation more expositive than interpretive. He must adhere to rather than question the values and symbols being celebrated.[21] As David Craig pointedly advises his professional colleagues, the videographer must therefore deny his authorship: "A human testimony of commitment recorded on videotape can be watched and heard 100 years from now. Think of it! Who's going to care who the videomaker was 50 or 100 years from now?"[22]

In this effacement of the videographer and his camcorder, in its critical transparency, and in its photographic naturalism, the wedding video shares to a limited degree in the tradition of cinema verité, whose style guides the viewer without commentary.[23] The desired effect of both genres is a direct, immediate, untampered "reality" achieved with a small crew rigged with lightweight synch-sound equipment maneuvered with minimal contrivance. Realizing that the presence of video at the wedding is an intrusion, most videographers subscribe to an ideal whose aims are an invisible technology and a remote operator.[24]

This striving for "authenticity" that conceals the manipulations of the videographer's hand harks back to the earliest distinction between formalism and realism that marked primitive cinema at the turn of the century. A hundred years later, videography has spawned its own versions of Méliès and Lumière; that is, videographers who hotly debate the primacy of studio editing over live mixing, of digital over analog recording. Those who prefer to concentrate on the artistry of the wedding video celebrate new technologies that manipulate the video image, adopting a variety of special effects from wipes and flips to digital paint and 3-D animation. For this growing minority, the wedding video provides an outlet primarily for the videographer's creativity. For the vast majority, however, such special effects should be used sparingly and tastefully. They argue that the bride wants a wedding video, not an f/x demo. They condone only the simplest, the most straightforward, the most "natural" effects and transitions that present the wedding "as is."

ROLE REHEARSALS

The marriage ceremony "as is," of course, remains a purposefully staged, somewhat inauthentic event, teetering between naturalized conventions and their acute self-consciousness. Set to music, with its costumed principals choreographed on an elaborate proscenium before a gathered audience, the wedding prevails as the longest-running

FIGURE 1
Videomaker magazine cover, August 1987

perennial theatrical production in history. Commercial and popular literature evoke histrionic metaphors more frequently than any others to describe the event: a "Broadway play" with an "organized script" and "cast of characters," whose "dress rehearsal" offers them the opportunity to practice for the ceremony. Enter the videographer, who conceives of the rehearsal as a chance to practice for the video. Soon his enthusiasm spreads among the performers, their parents, and the minister, who join in as his cast and crew. Before they can yell cut, the church's theatrical background has become a movie set.[25]

The videographer's intervention has a defamiliarizing effect. Exposed by the roving camera eye turned inward, the members of the wedding may begin to feel as uncomfortable in their roles as in their floor-length gowns and tight cummerbunds. Soon, the ceremony appears doubly artificial, as the participants realize that they are neither being themselves nor acting at being themselves, but acting at being themselves performing mythic roles for the event's duration. See how flustered the "maid of honor" suddenly feels when the camera catches her on hands and knees smoothing out the wrinkles of her best friend's enormous train. Watch how often the "best man" swallows when he realizes that the toast he wrote on a cocktail napkin the night of the bachelor party will be recorded for posterity. Where the flash of still photography fuses these "hieratic personae" into unified identities, video pans around to reveal the person behind the persona.[26]

A LITTLE BIT SOFTER NOW, A LITTLE BIT LOUDER NOW

The tension between these symbolic roles and the plight of their performers perfectly juxtaposes the wedding video's paradoxical nature: literal and contrived, natural yet syn-

JAMES M. MORAN

thesized, immediate but distanced. Like its electronic representation, the wedding day is itself two-faced, being divided between the marriage ceremony and the reception, between the sacred and the profane. While the ceremony's spectacle enforces strict boundaries between its performers and respondents, the reception's festivity blurs distinctions, allowing respondents the chance to perform, to dance, to drink, to make "fools" of themselves in general. By juxtaposing the day's events within a single frame of reference, the wedding video transforms both celebrations into a single occasion for reception, and carries the festive atmosphere into the living room, blurring yet another distinction between the events, the performers, and the home viewer.

Decontextualized from its religious moorings, the church ceremony as observed from the couch no doubt loses its sanctified aura. The minister's lisp, demurely ignored on the wedding day, becomes ripe for speculation. Great-aunt Flo's sincere but quavering "Ave Maria" now brings down the house. Cousin Bob's *GQ* good looks yield oohs and aahs of delight. The suppressed giggle, the held tongue, and conversations hushed in the hallowed confines of the tabernacle can be freely expressed in louder tones,[27] a difference similarly marked between theatrical film presentation and home video viewing.

Home respondents exert greater control over the proceedings. They can fast-forward through the boring parts, analyze their dancing skills in slow motion, admire their outfits with freeze-frame, or replay that momentous kiss over and over again. Recontextualized, the wedding on video offers unexpected ways of participating in an altogether different experience.[28] The home audience can say and see more: their view is not blocked, so to speak. No participant at the ceremony can attend to every important moment, except, of course, the videographer, who records and sequences each subevent into a singular affair equalizing access to the occasion as a whole.[29]

WE ARE GATHERED HERE TODAY

Everyone can attend a wedding video. Its reception is open to all.[30] The small scale of the images on the TV monitor lend it a domestic aesthetic, gathering friends around the hearth of a Sony or Magnavox to watch, eat, drink, and be merry. The community audience is infinitely diverse, but for heuristic purposes can be divided among three geometrically disproportionate groups, each sustaining a distinct yet overlapping experience of the wedding video: the performers of the actual procession, the respondents and spectators actually in attendance, and all others not in attendance.

The first community—consisting of the bride, groom, maid of honor, best man, attendants, parents, and minister—is indeed the most privileged group. Their points of view, many of which are denied the videographer, forever remain on the "inside" as personal memories incapable of being shared directly on screen. Thus, the wedding can rarely be relived as it was performed, but only as observed. This handicap for the majority is an advantage for this handful who, standing outside the ceremony for the first time, can step out of their responsible roles and enjoy the spectacle as festive viewers.

The second community—comprising the invited guests—is the most efficacious group. These are the video's main enunciators, its implied spectators. Their perspectives sustain identification, inviting the viewer to inhabit the event through their mediation as the primary audience. Unquestionably, the key to a good wedding video's emotional subtext is its well-timed reaction shots. Placed to follow the audience observing the event from within, they provide a syntagmatic coherence.[31] Thus, as they unfold over time and are situated in an implied point of view, the wedding video's images can be read as a narrative text.

The third community—an amorphous assemblage of indefinite magnitude—is both the most and the least invested group. Clearly, friends and family unable to make the event may appreciate and enjoy the video as their only opportunity to review the celebration, to witness the marriage, and to "meet" the guests in a sort of receiving line in reverse. For strangers and mere acquaintants, however, the video can run on endlessly as a tiresome record of attendance.[32] Because memory is so personal, a purely "amateur" wedding video, whose focus is less concerned with telling a story and more with documenting familiar faces, is generally considered less pleasurable. These average viewers are then subject to the video's "average effect."

On the other hand, the "professional" video underlines the wedding's basic outline, provides the implied narrative text, and frames its reception according to the spectator's familiarity with wedding conventions learned by attending real ceremonies and from watching their depiction at the cinema, on television, and, of course, in other wedding videos.[33] Tied to the history of wedding representation, the video promotes universal audience comprehension through shared cultural codes. Like home movies, whose ideology of production assumes that audiences can best enjoy private films if they follow a logic of continuity grounded in ubiquitous performances of familialism,[34] the wedding video tells a timeless tale of matrimony.

THIRD GENERATION: PRODUCTION

Although individual differences of occasion (and opinion) may prove the exception, the protagonist of this tale is usually the bride herself. A man and a woman may be joined in marriage, but, as Barbara Tober succinctly puts it, "we look at a couple, but we see a bride."[35] Brightly arrayed in rarefied apparel, she draws all eyes, while the groom, in dark attire, fades into the background. A victorious symbol in the lives of many women, the wedding in American culture has historically been a woman's day. In *The Eternal Bliss Machine*, Marcia Seligson explains: "While little boys are dreaming heroic dreams of conquering worlds, little girls are yearning for transformation. . . . As marriage is the single event which will presumably guarantee that metamorphosis, it is, naturally, the day for which her entire life has been in preparation."[36] Although changing times have certainly tempered this dated notion of the wedding's definitive import on contemporary women's social choices, the ceremony today nevertheless remains a bride-centered affair.

FIGURE 2
Elaine Holliman, *Chicks in White Satin* (1992)

QUEEN FOR A DAY

What, exactly, is a bride? Like beauty itself, with which she is closely identified, the "bride" is a catachrestic figure,[37] an icon whose referent can be constituted only by the accumulation of a series of brides, a simulacrum whose model is imaginary: the magazine photograph, the store window mannequin, the soap opera star. In this respect, the "bride" has no significance beyond herself and is temporarily liberated, even in heterosexual ceremonies, from her referent as "woman" defined by a phallocentric order. No longer her father's daughter and not yet her husband's wife, she is a figure on the threshold between symbolic identities. Although the actual marriage ceremony performs her transition and reinstates her into patriarchy, in the wedding video the bride's liminal power is preserved, femininity reigns, and masculinity is subordinate, adjunct, other.

Like Barbie, who, despite her ongoing relationship with Ken, is always a bride but never his wife, her living model dons a costume fashioned strictly for the occasion. Its spectacular grandeur and sheer visual hyperbole lend it a "magical" power sustaining the bridal image for as long as the bride wears it, even well into the reception after the exchange of vows and rings.[38] Only at day's end, when they return to the party in their street clothes, do "bride and groom" bid the company farewell as "husband and wife," returning to the established order. By the magic of rewind, however, this inevitable moment can be endlessly delayed in the wedding video, whose spectators never speak of a "good wife," but only admire "such a beautiful bride."

As the star of her own show, then, the bride achieves a celebrity status,[39] flaunting her role, whose ritualistic significance tends to hold itself at a distance from the woman who plays it. Her costume, a "hyperbolisation of the accouterments of femininity," masquerades a divergence between her self and her mode of self-presentation.[40] This asymmetry between bride and woman suggests an allegory of image and identity: of "femininity" constructed as a performance that resists patriarchal positioning. Certainly, the "bride" is a signifier of "to-be-looked-at-ness." It is questionable, however, whether her image must necessarily be completed by the gaze of male desire in order to have meaning.[41] Lesbian weddings are a case in point. As documented by Elaine Holliman in *Chicks in White Satin* (1992), Heidi and Debra Stern-Ellis celebrate a marriage ceremony in every way traditional but one: they forgo the groom. Initially, this violation of so totemic a ceremony produces spectatorial shock, whose uncomfortable anticipation is aptly dramatized by Heidi's mother. Yet as the film (and the wedding) gradually proceed, the image of two women at the altar fully dressed in white gown and veil suggests less an absence than a doubling: one notices an extra bride rather than a lack of groom.[42] Even under such unconventional circumstances, the wedding is reconfirmed as a bride-centered occasion. Without her appearance, the wedding would lose its primary spectacle.[43]

At first questioning the political correctness of wearing veils, whose connotations suggest patriarchal submission, Heidi and Debra eventually don them, resolving that "not everything has to be a major political decision." Choosing veils because they are dramatic, sexy, and look good with the dress, these brides ignore their negative association with the symbolic order in favor of predominantly feminine notions of beauty. Thus, these garments are transformed into symbols of feminine, homoerotic empowerment that transcend their signification of consent to compulsory heterosexuality. Redefining sexual commitment without rejecting the traditional form of its celebration, these women are able to participate in a common fantasy structure of conventional romance *without* ensuring "their continued psychic investment in their oppression."[44]

GENDER AND GENRE

As *Chicks in White Satin* demonstrates, there are certain advantages to categorizing wedding video as a woman's genre. Because the wedding is part of women's subculture that exists alongside the dominant, patriarchal culture of marriage, and to the extent that women participate in the ceremony as a mode of empowerment, its recording functions, like soap opera, melodrama, and romance, as a genre catering specifically to "feminine" pleasures and viewing practices. The "feminine," as I conceive it, is not an ontological category. Rather, it signifies a marginalized, discursive subject position as the site of accommodation or resistance to patriarchal symbolic structures. While this position is subject to changes in both the cultural dominant and interpretive communities, historically it has been associated with women's relation to cultural production, which is not identical to women's social and material existence. Therefore, while I would be mistaken to conflate the female with the feminine, it would be ingenuous to reject their linkage, in the process denying centuries of patriarchal ideology that has conjoined both (oppressing one and denigrating the other), as well as dismissing the culturally defined differences between the ways real men and real women may experience cultural texts.

To the degree that we wish not to replicate the female-feminine conflation by equating gender with genre, we should therefore conceive of the wedding video as a woman's genre only with caution. Obviously, it is usually consumed and enjoyed by a married couple, a bride *and* a groom. Yet, in that it is designed within the domain of bridal culture, which insistently caters to women, the video functions as a double text, participating in the dominant discourse of marriage and the subcultural fantasy of romance: "a gendered categorization supported by the central place these genres accord socially mandated feminine concerns: family, domestic life, personal relationships, and 'feelings' which frequently run to tears."[45] Like the traditional romance, the wedding video's hero acknowledges openly the preeminence of love and the attractions of domesticity; its heroine breaks with her mother to fulfill a new identity with him; both commit to marriage and look forward to a life blessed with happiness.

Although often the literary wedding represents the epitome of classical narrative closure, coming as it does at the end of comedy and romance, the wedding video shares more with the structure of serials, as its place within the home mode of family representation falls closer to the beginning of the "life script" between the bride's birth and death. As Ien Ang notes, like the genealogy of family albums, soap opera narratives are centered on significant family rituals, such as births, deaths, and marriage.[46] So too, they are centered on divorce, marking the primary distinction at which the narratives of soap opera and wedding video diverge. For if it is true that the wedding ceremony in the soap opera is as much concerned with foreshadowing future conflict as it is with celebrating harmony, thus preserving the serial form's "endless middle," then the wedding video's open text signifies not a happy ending, but a utopian beginning.[47] Nonfictional, and therefore more invested in preserving only blissful memories, the wedding video safeguards the "endless prelude" of autobiography: "a beginning without middle (the realm of fiction) or without end (the realm of history)."[48]

MY VIDEOGRAPHER, MYSELF

The complex relationship of autobiography to the wedding video is wonderfully illustrated by *Videomaker* magazine, an industry trade journal whose cover story in one issue offers professional videographers "pointers" for recording successful wedding videos, accompanied by a photograph of a bride in full regalia peering through the viewfinder behind a camcorder (see figure 1). Are the editors here suggesting that the bride videotape her own wedding? She'd have to be ambidextrous, double-jointed, or extremely ambitious to pull off such a feat. No, what the photo suggests is simply another allegory of production: a wedding video should be construed as the bride's own story.[49] While technically a *biography in production*, it should seem like an *autobiography in reception*.

As a social and technological arrangement, the wedding video production is a hybrid collaborative form that both facilitates and conflates autobiographical and ethnographical expression. This partnership of bride and videographer sustains the common ideology of the home mode that the wedding video tries to simulate: an attitude that the person behind the camera has little to do with the photographic process, that "the presentation of oneself and manipulation of oneself are *more* important than controlling and manipulating the symbolic content from behind the camera."[50] Rather than merely posing his subject, the wedding videographer speaks with, not for the bride, and thus complicates the division of self and other in traditional ethnographies and the autobiographical notion that only one person can have authentic knowledge of her self, particularly an iconic "self" artificially constructed and nonidentical to the woman performing it.[51] As the subject of vision and object of representation, the bride constitutes the classic autobiographical divided self who regards herself in the mirror of her own prose. Video lends itself even more to this doubling, because the bride may see herself in a monitor while her recording is being generated. Here enters the videographer, hired to do the "writing" for her. Sharing rather than usurping the site of representation, subject meets subject in a self-conscious awareness of self *with* the other rather than *against* her.

This intersubjective mode of co-creation is playful. As John Fiske notes, "In so far as play is a representation of certain aspects of the social world, the power of play involves the power to play with the boundary between the representation and the real, to insert oneself into the process of representation so that one is not subjected by it, but, conversely, is empowered by it."[52] In planning and coordinating the wedding herself; providing the videographer a shot list; contributing photographs, music, and creative ideas for the video; and often reviewing the rough cut for criticism prior to final copy, the bride exerts a considerable degree of control over the rules of her representation. Her image as "bride" is neither hers nor the videographer's, but a shared projection of both, a manufactured subjectivity with no single site or body where it is naturally confined. The bride's "femininity" is, therefore, the product and the process of both re-presentation and self-presentation, a cultural palette from which both woman and videographer draw to paint the bridal portrait. Such a process is coproductive, not in its questionable potential to feminize or desexualize the male and thus increase his sensitivity, but more radically in its potential to provoke a recognition of himself as gendered and a realization of the likelihood that his "masculinity," like the bride's femininity, is nonidentical and, thus, nonessential to the sexes producing them.

One might suggest that the wedding video bypasses Foucault's Panopticon, whose structure obliges the woman to monitor herself with a patriarchal gaze. Subjected not by prescriptions of the symbolic order but by conventions of feminine fantasy, the bride-as-subject is visible to herself and others through imaginary categories. Moving from the law of the father to the desire of the mother, the wedding video reflects the typical bride's matriarchal identification. In her book *My Mother, Myself*, Nancy Friday explains how her marriage made her feel particularly close to her mother: "As I planned the details . . . I think I had her pleasure in mind. . . . [F]or the first time in my life when a judgment of taste had to be made, I did it her way."[53] Friday's sense of herself as her mother's desire speaks directly to a central tenet in Lacanian subject construction: "One always locates *the other in one's own image*."[54]

Commercial literature abounds with examples of the wedding as a production choreographed by a mother-and-daughter team: "Many women find an ally in their mothers, no matter what their ages. With a unified voice, brides and their mothers can often conspire to create a wedding satisfying to both their dreams."[55] Because the bride's mother normally oversees the videographer during the reception, she acts as her daughter's agent, channeling her influence through the apparatus with her own instructions and suggestions (often reinforced by her checkbook). The intersubjective mode is,

374

JAMES M. MORAN

therefore, complicated by the introduction of a third subject actively producing the bridal image, adding a twist to David Lowenthal's description of autobiography as "a record by oneself of what its *preceding* selves have chosen to remember of their predecessor."[56] By imagining the bride as both she and her mother imagine herself through each other, the videographer acts as one of the bride's several *competing* selves in constructing her self-image.

STUCK IN THE MIDDLE WITH YOU

As an actor relates to a role through her director or a student to a novel through her teacher, so a bride, her mother, and the videographer identify through each other to each other. As Bakhtin notes, "Man does not possess a sovereign internal territory, he is entirely and always on a frontier; looking inside himself, he looks *into the eyes of an other* or *through the eyes of another*."[57] We might call this model of subjectivity a periscope. Both/neither mirror and/nor screen, the periscopic gaze deflects lines of identification along indirect paths between subject and image. This shift in the subject is partially a result of an electronic space both inside and outside of which the bride (person) simultaneously becomes in the camera viewfinder a bride (image) to be seen as a bride (recording) on a television monitor. Thus, Metz's phenomenological "double movement" of projection and introjection can be seen in terms of the projection of the videographer's consciousness and the introjection of two "feminine" subjectivities into a unified visual space.

As a conduit between the camera and the monitor, the wedding videographer undergoes a symbiosis with the apparatus, extending his psyche into the electronic medium whose images become part of his consciousness. Part human, part machine, he functions something like a cybernetic organism, yet another liminal construct well suited to record the liminal image of the bride. Masculine and feminine identities blur in the simultaneous fusion of production and reception possible only with video. The rapid exchange of self and image has a powerful decentering effect. Rather than merely split, the videographer's cybernetic, nomadic subjectivity is splintered by ever changing positions. On the other side of the viewfinder, the posing subject experiences a similar refraction, as Barthes describes: "In front of the lens, I am at the same time: the one I think I am, the one I want others to think I am, the one the photographer thinks I am."[58] Between the two subjects, the videotape both records and erases their differences as it multiplies their possibilities.

For example, as a privileged member of the wedding, the videographer scopes out distinct vantage points during the ceremony's production that, upon its reception, can be shared by all: expository views from the balcony, peeks over the best man's shoulder, intimate close-ups of the couple's newly beringed fingers.[59] Fading from one subjective position to another, the spectator experiences the wedding as many in one, like the individual ushers and bridesmaids who don uniform fashions to express their unity. The wedding video thus offers subjective variation as it reconfirms the ceremony's consensus ideology.

TAKE TWO: "THE BRIDE LOOKED BACK"

Jim finally got used to his camcorder. In fact, as we've seen, it became a part of him. And so at Josie's wedding he was trying his hand again. This time it was steady. In control of the medium. Cool. Bridesmaids, flower girl, ring bearer: all proceeding on schedule. Ah, here comes the bride. He's ready: focus set, thumb posed on telephoto, record light ON. All smiles, Josie passes Jim at center pew, her veil and flowing train a sight to behold. He follows, panning, zooming in for a close-up. Not close enough, he moves into the aisle. Josie pulls ahead, Jim pursues, retracing her steps, tracking her from behind: what great pov! She's gonna love it! But wait—what's this? Abruptly, Josie has interrupted her approach to the altar, turned about face, and is staring Jim down through his viewfinder. What's going on here? She's got yards to go! Could it be that she's had a change of heart? Laughter begins rolling through the congregation, as an incredulous Josie points to the floor. Jim pans down to follow her cue, and *his* heart stops cold: My God! He's been *standing* on her dress! Talk about your show stoppers.

Later, Jim apologized. He was getting used to that, too. But to his wide-eyed surprise, Josie had found the whole episode most amusing. In fact, against Jim's strongest protestations, she insisted that his faux pas be included in her video. Jim couldn't imagine why. Just watching her through the viewfinder, he knew how she must have felt. He himself had never been so self-conscious in his life.

"I know," Josie slyly replied. "Your face was beet red."

"Then why won't you let me tape over the damned thing?"

"What, and miss out on seeing *my* expression?"

Here, in a small Catholic church in upstate New York, did the magic of video turn Josie into the videographer, and Jim into a blushing bride.

CONCLUSION: EXCHANGING THE BRIDE

To conclude with such an upbeat anecdote would have been appropriate only for a purely redemptive reading of the wedding video's capacity to deconstruct gendered oppositions. Unfortunately, such a utopian presumption would seem a bit too disingenous on my part, and unsound in terms of critical theory. For, despite the capacity of the wedding videographer to underwrite equitable subjectivities and to share the process of representation with his client, transcendent moments such as that shared by Jim and Josie cannot efface the gendered structural inequalities of the political economy in which the wedding video circulates as a commodity. As the home mode becomes increasingly commercialized, the intersubjective process is reduced to a means for consumption that sells feminine identity as product and that diffuses the bride's subjectivity, memory, and pleasure with instrumental values. By investing in the conventions of her self-display, the wedding videographer's bottom-line investment in the bride will be her cash, of course, not her consciousness.[60] The exchange of self and other is reconfigured in the consumer realm as an exchange of image and capital, of memories for a fee. Depending upon the bride's economic status, therefore, the quality of her video will be determined far less by the investment of her creative agency than by her capacity to afford designer options within her financial means. The difference, we might say, between a one- and two-camera setup, between cabled and wireless microphones, between in-camera and postproduction effects, is also a class difference, whose economic exigencies prescribe the technological resources employed and mark the limits of the video's formal possibilities and its capacity as self-portrait. The clear exchange of vows on audio, for instance, or of rings in close-up, valued for their religious and private sentiments, become subject more to the dollar sign than the sign of the cross, to commercial rather than interpersonal exchange.

Although temporarily liberated *in* the video from her patriarchal signification, the bride *on* video reenters a paternalist economy in which her image functions as a commercial fetish symbolically linking women in a relationship to the goods and services of the wedding industry naturalized by the institutionalized matrimonial system. As a display window for the consumer imperatives of bourgeois marriage, the wedding video preserves a memory of abundance provided by capitalism. The cornucopia of its mise-en-scène—bouquets of flowers, shimmering gowns, five-course meals, ten-layered cakes, stretch limousines—perpetuates the capitalist relations of production as it advertises the services of florists, dressmakers, caterers, chefs, and chauffeurs to future brides-to-be.[61]

The catachrestic liminality of the bride here becomes Taylorized: she functions in the series as a model endorsement of commercial wedding enterprises, divested even from the power of her gown, whose reification as a commodity displaces the significance of the woman wearing it to a status not unlike the store-window mannequin who had modeled it before her. The particular and idiosyncratic arrangements of her wedding, which during the video production process had inflected her participation in the co-construction of her identity, are homogenized in the marketplace. Displayed to prospective clients in his studio and at bridal shows as a demonstration of the videographer's skill, the bride's personal wedding video becomes an alibi for male professionalism exploiting the bride's image and autobiography in the service of public enterprise: *her* self-portrait becomes *his:* a mirror of the videographer's creativity and a vehicle for his self-promotion. In the realm of commodities, the intersubjective mode breaks down, confining the bride's empowerment to the "feminine" realm of subjectivity and representation, while the videographer advances in the "masculine" world of agency and production.

In short, the wedding video empowers women only to a degree that cannot escape containment in a patriarchal economy that writes her power and denies her agency. The industry's ideology of male professionalism continues to engender myths of female-related technical incompetence,[62] to regulate access to the means of production, and to position women as consumers in the sphere of business relations. Stamping a price tag on the value of her wedding day, it is the male videographer, in the final determination, who regulates the bride's memories and her display, for better or for worse.

1 With one exception, the scope of this paper focuses primarily upon the heterosexual, Judeo-Christian, church-based weddings and receptions popularized by the media. Although grounded in concrete examples, much of the following theoretical speculation assumes the existence of a "model" or "ideal" wedding from which real weddings and their videos are derived. Increasingly, more couples—whether homosexual, previously divorced, highly creative, or simply independent—are forgoing certain customs and redefining the ceremony to their own specifications. Yet, in assenting to a marriage ceremony in the first place, they are always already working from or against a traditional paradigm. It is this paradigm that concerns us here. Consider this essay, then, the expository chapter of a much larger work whose body would account for more specific cultural practices, including differences in religious, ethnic, and sexual orientation.

2 This optimism prevailed at the Wedding Video Expo '93, held July 26–29 in Las Vegas, Nevada, and organized by Roy Chapman, founder and editor of *Wedding Videography Today,* the leading industry trade journal. As an invaluable source of primary research, the convention offered seminars, panel discussions, trade shows, and competitions for those in attendance. Many of this essay's theoretical speculations regarding production have been grounded in the statements and practices of the industry's leading figures, who have either led the exposition's series of presentations, demonstrated examples of their work, or written articles in various trade publications.

3 If currently the most popular, wedding videos are only a branch of what many event videographers are calling the "living family tree" rooted in recordings of seminal events: birth, bar or bat mitzvah, holy communion, graduation, wedding, birthday, anniversary, retirement, and death (video's final frontier). This essay represents only a chapter of life's video narrative.

4 The ratio of men to women in local video associations nationwide is approximately 9:1.

5 A common musical selection at many weddings, "Sunrise, Sunset," clearly expresses this sentiment: "Is this the little girl I carried? Is this the little boy at play? I don't remember growing older, when did they?" Sung from a parent's point of view, the emo-

tional ambiguity of the lyrics underscores the event's liminality for both the rising and setting generations.

6 David Lowenthal, *The Past Is a Foreign Country* (New York: Cambridge University Press, 1985), 72. Fredric W. Rosen makes the connection more explicit: "The generation of people being married today is the first to be raised on the televised image. The TV has been baby-sitter to kids when their parents were not home, their companion as single adults, and now the medium for recording the most important of life's events, among them, their weddings" In (Rosen, *Shooting Video* [Boston: Focal Press, 1984], 164).

7 Lowenthal, *The Past,* 62.

8 Videographer David Craig admits that "video is a cute gimmick they will enjoy laughing at 50 years from now with their grandchildren" (Craig, "Wedding Video Movies: Pointers for 'Once in a Lifetime' Productions," *Videomaker,* June-July 1987, 34).

9 Roland Barthes, *Camera Lucida: Reflections on Photography*, trans. Richard Howard (New York: Noonday Press, 1981), 65.

10 See Constance Penley, "Time Travel, Primal Scene, and the Critical Dystopia," in *Close Encounters: Film, Feminism, and Science Fiction,* ed. Constance Penley, Elisabeth Lyon, Lynn Spigel, and Janet Bergstrom (Minneapolis: University of Minnesota Press, 1991), 68–71. The music recording industry recently inspired one fulfillment of this desire in Natalie Cole's duet with her dead father, Nat, on "Unforgettable."

11 Children's play frequently manifests this curiosity. Playing "house" is one example. Another is the popular nursery rhyme observing, "First comes love, then comes marriage, then comes baby in a baby carriage."

12 For an alternative "wedding video" that does indeed record the couple's very public scene of consummation, see *The Continuing Story of Carel and Ferd* (Ginsberg, 1970–75).

13 A brochure advertising Key Video Productions in Rochester, New York, reads: "You've dreamed about your wedding all your life, planned for months to make the dream come true, and then—poof—it's all over so quickly. Well, maybe the day will be over, but the memory will be alive forever because of the magic of video."

14 Lowenthal, *The Past,* 206.

15 Daniel Dayan and Elihu Katz, *Media Events: The Live Broadcasting of History* (Cambridge: Harvard University Press, 1992), 210.

16 Jean Baudrillard, *Simulations* (New York: Semiotext(e), 1983), 101.

17 Abigail Van Buren, *Dear Abby on Planning Your Wedding* (New York: Andrews and McMeel, 1988), 75. Videographer David Craig confirms, "The thing to remember about a wedding is that we are to assume there will be only one for the couple—which means you must do your utmost to get it right the first time" (Craig, "Wedding Video Movies," 33).

18 The rivalry between still photographer and videographer is legend in the industry, but their distinct responsibilities have narrowed considerably. During a panel discussion addressing questions about the future of wedding videography at Expo '93, the majority of industry leaders predicted that, arguably, the videographer would supplant the photographer in the advent of "still video," the proclaimed successor to silver halide. Using a floppy disk, high density resolution, and color printers, this new electronic technology provides crisp, clear, and lifelike images that rival chemical prints. One disk, which holds up to fifty images, can be erased and used over to better advantage than celluloid. The technology offers instant playback, minimal processing, importation to computers for storage and further manipulation, and digital transference by modem. The debate, nevertheless, continues.

19 Douglas Davis, "Filmgoing/Videogoing: Making Distinctions," *Video Culture: A Critical Investigation,* ed. John G. Hanhardt (Rochester, N.Y.: Visual Studies Workshop Press, 1986), 273.

20 During his seminar at Expo '93, Jim Myers of Video Tape It! handed out a list of twenty "Commandments" to his audience. Number seven reads, "Thou shalt not be part of the movie, being careful to avoid reflections, shadows, and multi-camera angles that reveal thyself."

21 See Dayan and Katz, *Media Events,* 80–83.

22 Craig, "Wedding Video Movies," 33. Roy Chapman of Classic Events Video may agree with Craig that his signature will seem irrelevant in a century, but for the present he exploits it, not in defense of auteurism, but as a marketing tool. Cognizant of his rising reputation for excellence in the Washington, D.C., area, Chapman has come to realize that his surname more frequently than his company name is cited in the client referrals that drum up business. Comparing a spectator who pays to see *Jurassic Park* because it is a film by Steven Spielberg rather than a product of Universal to a bride who chooses a videographer for his name rather than his organization, Chapman underlines the personal rather than corporate affiliation that defines the service/patron relationship in the wedding video business.

23 Sean Cubitt regards the wedding video's obliteration of the processes of production, its transparency, and its construction of an ideally coherent subject position as structured by the logic of classical realism: an oscillation between invisibility and formalism, universality and particularity, capitalism and individualism. See *Videography: Video Media as Art and Culture* (New York: St. Martin's Press, 1993), 4–7.

24 For example, Acclaim Video Production has recently invented "The Observer," a remote camera conversion developed as an alternative to the distraction that the operator creates. The product's advertising brochure reads: "Brides love it because there is no operator stealing her show. . . . The last thing the bride wants is a videographer getting all the attention."

25 David Craig insists on calling his works "wedding video movie productions," considering them as feature-length films. In Craig, "Wedding Video Movies," 35. Despite her mild aversion to video, Barbara Tober, editor of *Bride* magazine, betrays its influence upon her description of the wedding ceremony: "The bride and her bridegroom are stars at their own show . . . with the footage, if not the ratings, to prove it" (Tober, *The Bride: A Celebration* [New York: Abrams, 1984], 116).

26 Dayan and Katz, *Media Events,* 116.

27 Can it be a coincidence that "Shout!" is frequently the last song played at the reception?

28 See Dayan and Katz, *Media Events,* 134–41, on festive viewing roles and readings.

29 The sequence usually "reads" as follows: morning preparations, arrivals at the church, the ceremony, the receiving line, picture taking by the photographer, ride in the limo to the reception, the reception, farewell to the couple. Some videos include footage of private parties held afterward, or video clips from the proposal, the rehearsal dinner, and honeymoon if available. One memorable video included signing the marriage license and shopping for rings.

30 Many wedding videos insert "stills" of the invitation as a prologue.

31 Dayan and Katz, *Media Events,* 115.

32 Wedding consultant Marjabelle Young Stewart complains: "Many of the videotapes I have seen are not skillfully done, consisting as they do of long, boring scenes of people going through the receiving line or dancing and eating" (Stewart, *Your Complete Wedding Planner* [New York: St. Martin's Press, 1989], 99).

33 The distinction between "amateur" and "professional" can only be touched upon briefly here, but is an important one that defines the event videography industry. The amateur video, equated with a hand-held, shaky, entirely subjective camera, is denigrated by the professional as the work of "Uncle Charlie," a relative or friend of the bride. The professional video, on the other hand, is equated with a stable, steady, more objective camera, as Jim Myers so forcefully suggests with his twelfth commandment: "Thou shalt realize and utilize thy tripod, which has been created for thee, setting thee apart from amateurs." If, as Patricia Zimmermann has demonstrated, amateur home movie guides have gauged quality by the aesthetic standards of Hollywood cinema, the professional home video industry now aspires to the broadcast standard of network television. One should hesitate, however, to group professional videographers with TV journalists and documentarians, who broach their subjects with a critical intervention. More like "professional amateurs," wedding videographers still admire Uncle Charlie's naive but sincere perspective, if not his inept technique. For detailed analysis of mid-century American home movie ideology and its relationship to classical Hollywood narrative style, see Patricia R. Zimmerman, "Hollywood, Home Movies, and Common Sense: Amateur Film as Aesthetic Dissemination and Social Control, 1950–1962," *Cinema Journal,* Summer 1988, 23–44.

34 In 1955, Roy Pinney counseled home movie makers that "a mediocre movie is one that only your family can enjoy. A good movie can entertain an audience that doesn't know the actors" (Pinney, "Better Home Movies," *Parents Magazine,* June 1956, 26).

35 Tober, *Bride,* 11.

36 Cited in Jacqueline McCord Leo, *The New Woman's Guide to Getting Married* (New York: Bantam Books, 1982), 11.

37 See Roland Barthes, *S/Z: An Essay,* trans. Richard Miller (New York: Noonday Press, 1974), 33–34.

38 "Brides who . . . buy their wedding dresses are usually torn between choosing something which is so perfect for the event it will never look right for anything else, or compromising with a dress which will look good, though not marvelous, at the altar, yet can be turned into an evening gown afterwards. The compromise is rarely successful; there is nearly always something about the dress, and the girl inside it, which shrieks bride for ever more, no matter what the alterations or how many trips it has made to the dyers" Ann Monsarrat, *And the Bride Wore . . . : The Story of the White Wedding* (New York: Dodd, Mead, 1973), 200.

39 The connections between brides, celebrity, and role-playing are wonderfully illustrated in the "Special Celebrity Weddings Issue" of *People Weekly,* 26 July 1993. Here the act of "performing the wedding" takes on an almost literal meaning.

40 Mary Ann Doane, "Film and the Masquerade: Theorising the Female Spectator," *Film Theory and Criticism: Introductory Readings,* ed. Gerald Mast, Marshall Cohen, and Leo Braudy, 4th ed. (New York: Oxford University Press, 1992), 766.

41 As an ego ideal, the bride may be a signifier of her own narcissistic gaze.

42 Although the appearance of two brides might seem doubly "excessive," it would be difficult to argue Mulvey's position that Heidi and Debra are figures for each other of Freud's voyeuristic fetishism that defuses male Oedipal guilt and the threat of castration.

43 It should be noted that Holliman's work was nominated in 1994 for an Academy Award in the category of Best Documentary (Short Subject). On the one hand, therefore, her piece must be distinguished from professional wedding videography per se, particularly in its implicit criticism of homophobia and its interview techniques. On the other hand, the actual commitment ceremony itself is filmed precisely according to the current conventions of wedding videography, which only further emphasizes the lesbian twist. In short, my point is that, regardless of the medium, the photographed traditional wedding apparently begs for the spectacle of a bride.

44 In *Feminism without Women: Culture and Criticism in a "Postfeminist" Age* (New York: Routledge, 1991), 43, Tania Modleski suggests that the conventional romance does ensure the psychic investment of women in their oppression.

45 Christine Gledhill, "Speculations on the Relationship between Soap Opera and Melodrama," *Quarterly Review of Film and Video* 14, nos. 1–2 (1992): 105.

JAMES M. MORAN

46 Ien Ang, "Melodramatic Identifications: Television Fiction and Women's Fantasy," in *Television and Women's Culture: The Politics of the Popular,* ed. Mary Ellen Brown (London: Sage, 1990), 79.

47 For example, "We've Only Just Begun" is a popular song often performed at the wedding reception. Although the soap opera wedding provides crisis and complication rather than resolution, ABC Video has recently packaged three anthologies of wedding highlights from its most popular soap opera series. Reedited from the context of their narratives, these representations of marriage look much like wedding videos, illustrating that the utopian pleasures of these ambivalent events seem to resonate with fans on the same par as their potential for subversion.

48 Louis A. Renza, "The Veto of the Imagination: A Theory of Autobiography," *Autobiography: Essays Theoretical and Critical,* ed. James Olney (Princeton, N.J.: Princeton University Press, 1980), 295.

49 Industry professionals unflaggingly refer to the wedding video patron as "the bride" rather than as "the client," "the bride and groom," or even "the couple." Although most will highlight the groom in a portion of the video, videographers in general conceive of brides and their mothers as the primary market.

50 Richard Chalfen, *Snapshot Versions of Life* (Bowling Green: Bowling Green State University Press, 1987), 60.

51 The professional male videographer rarely, it would seem, presumes an ability to "read like a woman," or to "take over" her position. Often not trusting his native instincts, he will rely upon his wife, lover, or sister to review his rough cut before submitting a final copy to the bride. As Jim Myers's sixteenth commandment proclaims, "Thou shalt always solicit a female perspective of thy work, as they are the main audience and are much more sophisticated human beings."

52 John Fiske, *Television Culture* (New York: Routledge, 1987), 236.

53 Cited in Leo, *New Woman's Guide,* 5.

54 Joan Copjec, "The Orthopsychic Subject: Film Theory and the Reception of Lacan," *October* 49 (1989): 58.

55 Diane C. Elvenstar, *First Comes Love: Deciding Whether or Not to Get Married* (New York: Bobbs-Merrill, 1983), 248. David Craig concurs: "It's important to find out not only who has 'written the script,' but who's 'directing the play.' This may be the same person—usually the bride or the mother of the bride" (Craig, "Wedding Video Movies," 36).

56 Lowenthal, *The Past,* 207.

57 Quoted in Sean Cubitt, *Timeshift: On Video Culture* (New York: Routledge, 1991), 177.

58 Barthes, *S/Z,* 13.

59 There are, of course, eccentric points of view that extend this argument, but for simplicity's sake, I will put off their analysis for another occasion and briefly mention a few (just to think about). Particularly interesting are instances of direct address to the camcorder: the old college roommate from Australia who yells "Hi Mom!" to a woman halfway around the world who will surely never receive the greeting; the best man's farewell to the couple to "Have fun on your honeymoon" from which they will return before hearing it; or the beaming young mother encouraging her baby to "wave at the camera, honey." Who exactly is that wave for? These odd moments deflect lines of identification that may never reach a destination, or if they do, are belated, negated, or endlessly reflexive. A final favorite occurs when, stopping to notice the camcorder alone on a tripod in the record mode, guests draw near to photograph it. How do spectators identify with such moments? Ex-centric pov offers little chance for unity with an image. Biography, autobiography, interview, documentary, home movie, blind recording: all of these forms collapse as soon as these wonderful moments come into view, eliding even a periscopic gaze in their kaleidoscopic implosion.

60 The majority of seminars at the Wedding Video Expo focused upon marketing strategies—for example, "How to Create a Demand for Your Services," "Increase Bookings with Your Own Bridal Information Video," "Sensational Selling," "Direct Marketing," and "Maximizing Your Profits."

61 Many wedding videographers earn referrals from caterers, tailors, florists, limousine services, and bands by editing detailed footage of the cake, wedding gown, flowers, limo, and musical numbers into individual demo displays each business can play for prospective clients. Interestingly enough, when videographers describe their work in its relation to the couple's personal investment, they use metaphors of cinema (narrative), but in relation to financial investment, metaphors of television (advertising).

62 The discourse of professionalism distinguishes the ama-teur from the au-teur, an engendered distinction between lover and author, ingenuity and skill, feminine and masculine, women and men.

CHAPTER 24

VISION AFTER TELEVISION:

TECHNOCULTURAL CONVERGENCE, HYPERMEDIA, AND THE NEW MEDIA ARTS FIELD

Michael Nash

THE END OF VIDEO ART (AND TELEVISION)

The least that can be said is that we have witnessed the death of video art in the United States. By "video art" I mean the formal category defined by discipline-specific Great Society arts funding, theoretical resistance to electronic mass culture, and the self-serving historiography of curators seeking job security. There are almost no "video" festivals in the United States anymore. The "blue-chip" video artists—Gary Hill, Nam June Paik, Bill Viola—have been absorbed by the traditional arts establishment and now concentrate on creating collectible video installations. Decisions to produce film or video are dictated almost entirely by distribution issues and practical considerations; emerging and established video artists like Sadie Benning, Tom Kalin, Marlon Riggs, and Bruce and Norman Yonemoto have sought salvation in feature film projects, planned or recently completed. It was said a decade ago that video art may have been the only art form to have a history before it had a history,[1] and now its history is *history* before we had a chance to mourn its passing.

Disestablishment of television, the ultimate cause that united video artists and independent documentarians for years, no longer galvanizes the field for a variety of reasons. Distinct philosophical and stylistic shifts have muted the dichotomy between video art and television, as artists and activists seek to participate in TV culture in order to revitalize the medium's modalities and pursue the illusive goal of cultural democracy. Media artists are making works for television,[2] television is making occasional opportunities available to artists,[3] and most work that practices media critique has not only abandoned repudiation of the medium, it now engages television's methodology as an efficacious vernacular, "playing both ends against the middle" to make a kind of television that presents and critiques itself.[4] It is this success of video art, and the cultural shifts it enunciated and evinced, that is partially responsible for its "failure" as a fine arts form in the current decade: the media revolution is to some extent being televised or looks like television, and the battle lines are completely blurred.[5]

Once the great punching bag for new theory, TV is presenting deconstruction with a moving target. In fact, television's critique of itself is more pervasive, and in some ways is more persuasive, than its critique by media art. Ranging from Gary Shandling's deft faux talk show hit *The Larry Sanders Show*, to John Kricfalusi's and Bob Camp's genre-mutating toons *Ren and Stimpy*, to *Mystery Science Theater 3000*'s sophomoric running commentary on bad films, to *Beavis and Butt-head*'s sneering adolescent interrogation of adolescent music videos, to the Eveready Battery commercial's ubiquitous ad parodies broken up by the cymbal-crashing pink bunny, the current wave of "antitelevision" programs keeps television one self-critiquing step ahead of video art's best efforts to serve as the loyal opposition.[6] After a decade of subjecting the talk show format to withering denigration, David Letterman has raised self-parody to the industry standard, as witnessed by his fourteen-million-dollar-per-year contract to host CBS's new flagship talk show. Now, news anchors, sportscasters, MTV's VJs, and Nickelodeon's network promotions all make it a point to acknowledge the lameness and absurdity of the medium's formats, conventions, and protocols.

More than anything else, the friendly fire to which television has subjected itself has made guerrilla raids against the evil empire largely irrelevant, and, like the United States, now deprived of an archrival's bracing threat, "alternative" video has lost its moral imperative. Add to this advertising's—especially music video's—annexation of the entire history of twentieth century avant-garde film and video techniques for its flavor-of-the-week posturing of new consumer goods: the collapse of media art's secondary role as purveyor of experimental visualizations has deprived it of even the formal ground on which it once stood.

Convergences within the media arts field has also fueled its diffusion. In the last decade we have witnessed the merging of theory, documentary, and art-making into new kinds of critical television,[7] metacritical media,[8] and activist advocacy[9] that make distinctions between criticism and art as irrelevant as distinctions between news and entertainment on television. Distinct formal categories are breaking down, and strict adherence to genre—the self-enforced codes of "documentary," "experimental," and "narrative"—is less and less the norm, as choices about approach and strategy are increasingly driven by the exigencies of personal content. Video art seems to have forecast its diaspora in the past several years through a wide range of hybrids and mixed modalities: artists are embracing documentary techniques, documentarians are manifesting experimental sensibilities, narrative works fluently mix modes, and activists advocate their views with any persuasive means available.[10]

So, video art is dead. So what? These changes in postmodernist media arts practices have hardly been noticed because they are dwarfed by their sociocultural and technological surroundings. This merging of art and criticism and documentary and television and alternative video into a vestigial media arts field is a minor manifestation of a millennial vortex that is almost incomprehensibly large and powerful, a crush of convergences of the largest information systems in the world. Yes, video art has become a historical footnote, but television is in its twilight, too. At the on-ramp of the information superhighway, the movie studios, TV networks, cable companies, telephone companies, computer companies, consumer electronics companies, and publishers are poised to converge into massive new systems of cultural distribution based on digital technologies emerging in this generation.[11] When fully implemented, this will complete the century-long relocation of the dominant site of cultural experience from the "proscenium arch" to the "home."

In order to envision artistic life after television, it is necessary to understand how this convergence will come to critical mass and to reconsider all the essential questions about the realization of vision, the dialog between artist and audience, the underlying structure of the artistic experience, and the politics of media representation.

EVERYTHING THAT RISES MUST CONVERGE: THE PATH TO CHANNEL 1

The most crucial fact of life in the posttelevision generation we are about to enter is the eventual collapse of the networks into a single bitstream of information that will enter the home as user-determined programming and services. The technological circumstances privileging the place of a few monolithic networks who provide transmitter-to-receiver programming to millions of people simultaneously—already irrevocably ruptured by cable systems offering over fifty channels of somewhat differentiated programming—will change completely in the next twenty years or so, as fully digital delivery and playback of all entertainment and communications media will provide an exhaustive library of choices available at the viewer's discretion.

Even before fiber-optic rewiring gets all the way to the homes of America and makes this possible, digital compression and new switching technology will allow a massive expansion of cable services that will come through existing copper coaxial cables for the last quarter mile. During the next few years, cable (and Direct Broadcast Satellite) will expand analog television's spectrum in many communities to somewhere between 250 and 500 channels. When this happens, we are promised that new cable decoder boxes[12] and digital-to-analog conversion will let us select any program we want from a library of thousands of choices, or make a phone call (video or audio), or do catalog shopping, or play computer games against a friend in another home or city, or experience a live, interactive sex fantasy.[13]

Home video platforms will also be radically transformed by this convergence of analog and digital technologies.[14] Coming from the computer side, digital video formats such as QuickTime for the Macintosh and Digital Video Interactive for IBM's PC platform now make crude-motion video presentation available as a feature of CD-ROM technology—the Voyager Company just succeeded in putting a complete feature film on a CD-ROM disc designed for consumer use for the first time, and a flood of such products will follow from a host of companies.[15] Focusing on analog end use for the near future, Time Warner, AT&T, Sony, Matsushita, Sega, Pioneer, and many others are spending millions in the anticipation of spending billions on a format with CD-ROM or better capabilities that will have a digital-to-analog converter to feed the one hundred-million-home existing installed base of TV sets that are already used six to eight hours a day for electronic media entertainment.

Some technology will emerge by the mid-1990s—probably not Laser-Active, possibly 3DO, perhaps something not yet announced, like Apple's not-so-secret development of an operating system with either Sony or Matsushita—that will combine home entertainment technology with computer technology and establish a standard for software developers.[16] The first platform to combine analog laserdisc-quality replication of image and audio, CD-ROM interactive capability, and digital-to-analog conversion at a price point below five hundred dollars, even without recording capability, will almost certainly capture the market during the transitional window of opportunity.

That window will close sometime in the next century when most of the United States converts to a fully digital communications, culture, and "intertainment" environment. Universal installation of a fully digital installed base will let us download from massive file servers almost any cultural material ever produced and engage in any interaction with it we desire. Blockbuster live events (particularly sports), premieres of special programming of the kind Home Box Office now produces, and major news coverage are likely to remain in the province of networks for some time, but over the next generation or so, "network programming" will come to denote the writing of computer code for systems of information exchange rather than the presentation of a schedule of TV shows. The concept of a predefined channel will probably enjoy a nostalgic afterlife—something akin to seeing Shakespeare performed in replicas of the Globe Theater—but the even more dominant media culture of the future will be configured as patterns of ones and zeros available to each spectator on almost completely user-driven schedules: one channel, your channel. At this crucial point in the history of civilization, Channel 1 will emerge as the conduit between almost infinite data and individual perception, limited only by the on-line user's time and money. This is how electronic media will complete its metamorphosis from one form of information about the world to *the* world of information about form. Maybe.

HYPERTEXT, HYPERMEDIA, AND INTERTEXTUALITY (IN-FORMATION AND RE-VISIONS)

Will the computer "kill" television within the next generation? Will PowerBook-wielding intellectuals win American culture back from the couch potatoes hypnotized by infomercials? To many, the computer revolution is seen as one that will establish the primacy of reading over viewing. Forget about the death of the author—we are talking about the complete inversion of transmitter-to-receiver configurations that have defined the distribution of cultural production since the dawn of civilization.

Various theorists and academics foresee a new world in which the computer's present role as a Promethean manipulator of text will be combined with powerful organizational programs and other forms of digitized media into a new kind of book that will revitalize the role of literacy in culture. The first products to utilize CD-ROM capability were text products that offered storage of huge reference works on five-inch platters, and the book model predominates among nongame products.[17] Freed from the page and the linearity of the book's spatial configuration, able to roam anywhere within an information environment instantly, the written word is being hailed as a "hot new medium,"[18] and hypertext—meaning the presentation of written words within a dynamic network of literary and diagrammatic interconnections—is seen as the salvation and fulfillment of the intellectual practice of writing.[19]

When a poststructural theoretician trained in literary analysis sees a small window of QuickTime video surrounded by a screen full of words that are linked for instantaneous intervention, she must think that hypermedia on CD-ROM is the ultimate platform for the application of deconstruction to media culture. What could be better than a flickering little rectangle of demystified motion pictures engulfed in a sea of text given the power to instantly determine the context for meaning and the flow and sequence of presentation?

This relationship between the proportions of text and video on the screen is not inherent in the technology, of course, as full-screen, full-motion digital video on home computers of at least VHS quality is probably only a few years away. But the really significant flaws in this thinking have to do with a failure to look beyond established notions of what reading and hypertext mean.

Reading is the activity of pursuing and apprehending meaning. It is an engagement between subject and object that yields a perception specific to a time, a place, a unit of information, and a human being. Converting symbols presented on a surface into semantic constructs is one very sophisticated kind of reading, but to think that this is the essence of reading is to think that receiving patterns of light and forming images is the essence of vision. Since seeing is the physiological process underlying what we tend to think of as reading and vision, and redefining reading is central to the efficacy of hypermedia, this point is worth a departure.

Vision is clearly more than receiving light through an optical mechanism. A range of complexities asks the conventional viewpoint questions it can't effectively answer: how to explain routine phenomena like mental imagery and dreams; famous experiments where subjects fitted with image-inverting lenses righted their visual field; instances of war wounded with visual cortex damage who still see a complete visual field; cases of the fully sighted who don't recognize their families or even their own reflections (the famous case lending the title to Oliver Sacks's *The Man Who Mistook His Wife for a Hat*).

On an intuitive level, we know vision is more than optics and neurology. The mechanistic paradigm is haunted by "the ghost in the machine"; the imaginal psychology of self—the unitary physical identity we infer from the perception of our selves situated behind our eyes looking out at the world—is inexplicable in neuroscien-

MICHAEL NASH

tific terms, but it underlies our most fundamental assumptions about reality and identity. This phenomenon reaches far beyond the simplistic notion of a mind-body split and
can't be explained away as an enactment of received ideas about dualism. Scientifically
speaking, there is no "I" behind these eyes squinting in an effort to compose this sentence, and no "you" behind yours reading these words, but every exchange we will ever
have in our lives will be predicated on this overwhelming sense of orientation to each
other and to the world.

Research in visual perception concludes that we see objects and events
as culturally given conceptual representations of the world and our existence in it.
There are patterns of essential characteristics, structural parameters of meaning, that we
project outward, determining what we see or can see. Bill Viola calls this "Life as
Rorschach Test," and it isn't just a figurative notion. In literal terms, projection by the
spectator and reception of the spectacle are perhaps equally important in the activity of
seeing. One theory even proposes that high-level neural trigger units, "cognons," integrate and store mental representations, and later fire images at targeted sense stimula-
tion to give unitary perceptions their exterior quality. Two thousand years later, we are
remarkably close to ancient Greek theories of visual fire streaming out from observer's
eyes to engage opposing efflux and image the world.[20]

Another way to understand this is to think of seeing as reading (that is,
the pursuit and apprehension of meaning). In reading, the symbol system is just as important as the physical laws of sight. The activity of seeing is similarly governed by a cultural ecology: seeing is a construction of meanings governed by a shared visual language.

If seeing and reading are dialogues between inner and outer domains,
then intertextuality in a hypertext environment takes on far greater complexity and
significance than cross-indexing or nonlinear, nonconclusive writing. New theories
about the brain suggest that language manifests "cross-modal matching."[21] A word can
represent the thing itself—its sight, touch, sound, or even its imagining—so that the
modes of perception and their representations become interchangeable and any given
configuration of form can ultimately be understood in more than one way. The word
lemon simultaneously and interchangeably refers to a fruit, a yellow color, an acidic
smell, a sour taste, and the concept of lemon-ness. Subject-object and reading-writing
relationships are traditionally understood in mechanistic terms, but they are, more
accurately, the negotiations between the self in the world. They can be seen, heard, or
tasted, or they can be thought. If we try to understand the computer as though it were a
mind, rather than trying to understand the brain as though it were a computer, it is possible that a whole new kind of "hyperliteracy" will emerge from "hypermedia" and
"hypertext," a new intertextuality that will allow any given mode of representation to
be the spine of organization and will enable associative leaps of discovery of which poets
and mystics dream. In this context, an interface design might use words, with their millions of nuances of meaning, as the engine of intertextuality—modeled after the way the
mind uses words to link associations—rather than pursuing the linkage of repurposed or
newly composed words to other words and media as the goal of hypermedia.

Rather than turning to technology for templates to guide us into this brave new world,[22] let us turn to ourselves and our artists and try to understand what is essential to artistic dialogue, and what cultural experiences we need to deepen our humanity and enrich our lives. Poetry's broad influence on art and culture attests to its significance as inspiration, metaphor, model and strategy. Understood as the triumph of content over form,[23] poetry can offer an essential guide to the incarnation of a meaningful new media arts field and suggest some illuminating models and perspectives that might provide hypermedia with some points of departure.

What more is poetry than a literary composition in a historically established conventional form? Well, quite a bit more, although its reduction to the somnolent study of rhyme, meter, and reference is the standard didactic introduction from which many of us never recover. The "Open Form" movement that led to the renaissance in American poetry earlier in this century broke the bondage of academic convention with liberating ideas that reversed long-standing assumptions about acceptable formal strategies and the contents that could be made to fit them. Running throughout the thinking and writing of these New American poets is the recurring expression of an emptiness or desire or vision that will become the poem finding the form it needs. W. S. Merwin argues: "Obviously, it is the poem that is or is not the only possible justification for any form, however theory runs. . . . The consideration of the evolution of forms . . . belongs largely to history and to method. The visitation that is going to be a poem finds the form it needs in spite of both."[24]

Ron Silliman, one of the leaders of the Language Poets that followed, supports this idea in more analytic terms: "The focus of the work to be written is felt as a blind spot in the subjective matrix, a primal lack toward which the writer is driven. This is the essential truth of the cliché that poets write only those poems which they *need*. Each successful poem abolishes (but only for a time) the lack and subtly reorganizes the structure of the subjective matrix."[25]

It is in this sense that poetry is the triumph of content over form. How does such a process manifest itself? Poems occur in time, proceed by intervals between elements, and unfold inside-out. These three most important aspects of poetic form—temporality, association, and inscape—provide a useful starting point in exploring how the new media's intertextuality can aspire to the condition of poetry.

By temporality, I mean the qualities of the poem that reflect and require time. W. S. Merwin explains how the formal patterns we think of as poems fundamentally revolve around this way of perceiving and organizing experience: "What is called its form may simply be that part of the poem that had directly to do with time: the time of the poem, the time in which it was written, and the sense of recurrence in which the unique moment of vision is set."[26] Merwin's conception of the poem's three qualities of time provides one blueprint for a multitemporal approach to hypermedia: it is possible to present the work of art in its experiential time, to define the work in terms of the time it took to create it, and to present the interval of its echo, and it is possible to cross-reference all three into a new kind of temporal aesthetic.

Believing that "duration is to consciousness as light is to the eye," Bill Viola brings these different qualities of time into expressive configurations in his video-tapes, "musical thoughts" (Carlyle) orchestrated to echo the tangled rhythms of consciousness. Understood as psychically interactive video, the work opens up individual perception to a series of linked and parallel engagements. One of Viola's characteristic devices is to hold an image long past the point of surface recognition, right up to and then past the threshold of boredom, until a perspective shift occurs, revealing new contents within the image in a dynamic interplay with the viewer's imagination. Duration becomes a process of revelation, as the time it takes to make something, watch something, and think about something produces a new time signature for consciousness and intervals of discovery. Viola frames extended duration so as to turn mirages into apparitions (*Chott El-Djerid*, 1979) or a mountain into a pile of rocks (*Hatsu Yume*, 1981). The sustained close-ups of animals' eyes in *I Do Not Know What It Is I Am Like* (1987) similarly set up exchanges where zoological anonymities become creatural identities.

FIGURE 1
Bill Viola, *I Do Not Know What It Is I Am Like* (1986). (Photo: Kira Perov.)

Such engagements of subjective duration might be one form of research into creating hypermedia maps of temporal poetics. What do we think about when there is only one unit of meaning to think about for an extended period of time? The undulation of interconnections that evolves through time might be traced by tracking the intrapsychic events that occur in subjective consciousness placed in suspended engagement.

These ideas about temporality help us understand a poetic experience of form emerging through time, but what is it that is experienced? Another important aspect of poetic form is the concept of association. While prosody and narrative continue to concern many contemporary poets, under the influence of surrealists, particularly the great Spanish poets of the early twentieth century like Federico García Lorca and Juan Ramón Jiménez and their Peruvian compatriot Cesar Vallejo, dynamic association has become a prominent strategy. Poet and translator Robert Bly refers to it as "leaping poetry," and such work is characterized by dramatic shifts in levels of experience and qualities of perception expressed within the poem. The Russian poet Voznesensky is quoted as saying, "Rhyme has become boring. In poetry the future lies with the ability to associate."[27]

Poems proceed by mapping new relationships between feelings, images, behaviors, ideas, perceptions, and expressions. The associative space creates a range of characteristics with its various qualities of integration, resonance, irony, incongruence, simultaneity, and parallelism. Imagine the possibilities when associating between the written word, or another unit of meaning, and any other unit of meaning in words, images, or sounds. These possibilities are introduced in very compelling fashion by Bill Seaman's interactive hypercard-stack-driven laserdisc installation, *The Exquisite Mechanism of Shivers* (1992). Seaman's poetry machine allows the spectator to reflect upon and recast evocative terms and expressions in interchangeable constructions with literally millions of selectable or random possibilities, with each expression linked to brief moments of imagery and music that provide a vast range of interpretive framings. To experience the work is to rediscover poetry's revelatory power, as a virtually endless stream of hermeneutic challenges revitalizes our ability to create meaning.

Such engagements of associative construction are perfectly suited to the postcritical strategies of the "new" theory and its repurposing of the texts and media of the past. Gregory L. Ulmer writes of saprophytes (organisms like mushrooms that live off dead matter) and argues, "If normal critics adhere to the model of the poem as living plant . . . it might be useful to emblematize post-criticism as the saprophyte, growing among the roots of literature, feeding off the decay of tradition." Advocating a strategy of "montage-allegory" to create a "symbiotic ecology" between present and past, he believes this "provides the very technique for popularization, for communicating the knowledge of the cultural disciplines to a general public."[28] Given the fact that media deconstruction is now seen everywhere from rap videos to soft drink commercials a decade later, Ulmer's assessment of this strategy's potential reach seems unquestionable. Inventing new saprophytic relationships between "writing" and the texts of the past, as an extension of our model of poetic association, suggests some key elements in envisioning the possibilities of hypermedia as criticism and art and both in simultaneity.

Gary Hill is one of the most important contemporary artists inventing new relationships between poetry and imagery and theoretical discourse. Absorbing and enlarging this discussion, his work in video is, and is about, a new form of writing. Extending a dialogue between semantics and consciousness that Hill has advanced since the late 1970s, *Incidence of Catastrophe* (1987-88) depicts the synesthesia of reading and the dreamwork of the text. Inspired by Maurice Blanchot's novel *Thomas the Obscure* and the experience of observing his child acquiring speech, Hill's heuristic tour de force grounds the viewer in the activity of becoming the text through a succession of evocative scenarios and motifs that detail a gradual descent into language and its labyrinth of representational configurations. Literacy is seen as soul-sickness, the videotape's final image of the drowned man before a wall of words expressing the abjection of the body in Western society's semantic culture. Hill's writing *on* Blanchot, with its layers of amplification so remarkably well positioned, should be studied by anyone who wants to under-

FIGURE 2
Gary Hill, *Incidence of Catastrophe* (1987–88)

stand the potential of fusing poetic association with critical practice in hypermedia. Hill himself will undoubtedly fulfill his vision in the hypermedia domain: a proposed interactive installation, *Which Tree*, will present viewers with a maze of interconnected branch points, allowing them to wander through a forest of images and words to discover the "texts" of their own thinking patterns. He created the single-channel videotape *Site Recite* (1989) as a prologue: this stunning preview moves across and around a tabletop graveyard—bones, butterfly wings, eggshells, seed pods, crumpled notes, skulls—in a series of seamless edits that present a continuous flow of focused detail close-ups. The taxonomy of dispossession, "little deaths [that] pile up," is juxtaposed to a narration on the linkage between semantic self-consciousness and visual experience. Through the window of this text, the objects on the table come to model how consciousness affixes itself to material manifestations and how memory is constituted by the collection of empty vessels.

While these ideas and models of poetic association are promising, it isn't necessary to pair words with images in order to achieve the condition of poetry in traditional media or hypermedia. Poems rely upon vision to reveal themselves and their worldviews, and this inside-out transformation is central to the experience of poetic form. The Romantic poet Gerard Manley Hopkins invented the word "inscape" to denote intrinsic form, the pattern of essential characteristics in objects and perceptions. Denise Levertov expands upon Hopkins's idea, asserting, "There is a form in all things (and in our experience) which the poet can discover and reveal."[29] In this sense, as Robert Kugelmann put it, "Seeing is a way of dreaming the soul of things."[30]

As I stare into the open space in front of me searching for the words that will help explain how this process of probing the inscape of perceptions matters to hypermedia, I am engaging—in a very rudimentary way—in the activity that is the soul of poetic vision. As John Rajchman writes of Foucault's "art of seeing," "Through one's work one tries to say something as yet unsayable, or to see something as yet invisible, and so opens out a space of a sort of rhythmic 'disappearance' of oneself in and through one's work."[31]

It is in this sense that poetry becomes *poiesis*: probing into emptiness, into lack, we project our minds into the world and create new correspondences between inner and outer spaces. The space on an empty canvas can take days to fill, the space inside a journal can be immense, and the space inside an intertextual domain like a personal computer can extract years of intellectual life. Hypermedia offers a potential quantum leap in the dialogue between mind and inscape, a virtual Plato's cave for the visionary experience—that is, if it's not immediately filled with all the detritus of the past.

In one elaboration of this possibility—utilizing an interface concept without words—The Residents produced a CD-ROM for the Voyager Company called *Freak Show* (1993) that offers an exploration of a computer-animated twilight zone. The premise of the piece is that while the show under the big top is intriguing (we see a brief display of the talents of each freak), the real stories are contained in the trailers where the freaks live, behind the tent. The spectator can maneuver within these environments and "click" on elements to collect clues about various freaks' identities, including The Residents. Fetishes, fantasies, bizarre rituals, and tragic secrets are revealed (one can also peruse the history of freaks) in a theme park for the imagination where we find many aspects of ourselves and come to better understand alienation by exploring alienage and our fascination with it. While various "virtual museums" miniaturize the art history of the past, projects like this one point toward the poetic possibilities of projecting into and envisioning hypermedia's inscapes.

STORY TIME

This concept of intertextuality based on the poetic model is not intended to exclude the role of narrative—in fact, the death of narrative is a hugely misunderstood notion in the new media discourse. Jumping from one place in a text, film, or song to any other place in any other text, film, or song doesn't constitute a "nonnarrative experience." The tyranny of the single narrative line through a data space authored by one person has already been overthrown, but it is supplanted by the new narratives "written" by the course consciousness takes through information fields.

The impulse to "narratize" experience is endemic to the structure of consciousness[32] and takes root from our mortality. Every heart has a fixed number of beats, and that absolute rhythm propels the story of our lives from one perception to another, linking units of meaning in a finitude so that all roads lead to where we are. We need greater understanding of narrative possibilities, not less: as a nation of remote-control freaks channel hops television viewing into oblivion, one can only imagine where we will be when the options increase by the thousands. Great stories teach us how to link elements into our own narrative explorations.

An example of how we can learn intertextual narratization from the traditional story form is provided by Robert Altman's *Short Cuts* (1993). Extending an approach that had previously reached its zenith in film with *Nashville* (1975) and in video with *Tanner '88* (1988), Altman adapted nine short stories by Raymond Carver and added two of his own to provide the human events for a three-hour film. A sweeping panoramic portrait of a social environment that maps the intersections between desire, disappointment, frailty, and evil, it is perhaps the first millennial film of Altman's generation, a decidedly unmoralistic work about America at the moral crossroads. He locates dozens of characters in geographic proximity and then follows the trails of coincidence, tangent, and narrative association to relate all eleven stories in "sequential parallel." The spectator is reminded of the methodology when Altman wishes to underscore an element of linkage, either thematic, visceral, or compositional.

In *The Player* (1992), Altman made a movie about the illusion of Hollywood, and here he explores the reality of that other Los Angeles that pays the spiritual dues for its alter ego; these are Robert Altman's "instructions to the double," our double, the dark recesses of American experience that define our national impasse-time. Altman's gift to us in this film is a profound lesson about narratizing observations of behavior into a vision of community that takes us beyond the exile of the self. *Short Cuts* is a model of how a technologically interactive narrative might work to take us beyond technofetishistic games with computers into a spiritual journey.

THE TRANSITION

The transitional window of twenty years into a digital system for the exchange of culture will be a crucial time for the new media arts. More than the limits of technology and economics, the limits of end-use demand will dictate the opportunities for the new media. When the United States converted from radio to TV in the late 1940s and early 1950s, almost all programs were versions of radio shows with the same stars—one of the early terms for the technology was "radiovision"—and this relationship dictated TV's formats for the generation that followed and beyond. What are they planning to do with hundreds of slots soon to be available via DBS or fiber-optic cable? They are going to have pay-per-view movies starting every fifteen minutes taking up eight channels at once, to better compete with home video renters and retailers. Cable conglomerates know that people will pay to see movies and they aren't sure what else they'll want to experience.

Even if installation of the digital playback base speeds ahead of the delivery system installation, the market for products to "read" is not going to approach the market for products to "watch" for quite some time because of ingrained behavior patterns. The vast majority of people still see the computer as a workstation in the office or the study and the TV as the fun station in the living room.

Eventually all-digital delivery and playback will replace analog TVs, which will then share many similarities to computers. But it took twenty years to wire up for cable TV—and a sizable minority of the United States still isn't wired. It will cost hundreds of billions of dollars to rewire the country and fully convert the installed base of playback systems, so there is no way that the existing base of TV sets is going away for quite some time. For at least the next generation, the analog TV will enjoy a transitional window, and a whole revolution will unfold in increments, a year at a time, a platform at a time, driven by what TV spectators learn to demand.

TCI Cable is doing something that is either entirely brilliant or massively stupid. To a test market near their base in Denver, they are offering around two thousand viewing choices on demand through remote control selection. What happens once a selection is made is laughably low-tech: an attendant has five minutes to scramble to a vault of tapes, grab the selection, and put it in a VCR. Why would one of the largest cable companies in America do this? Because they know that they have to seed demand for interactive programming before they invest in the hardware that will make it a large-scale reality.

The parallel for new media artists is to accept the limits of the authoring systems and capacity of the transitional technologies—all technologies are, after all, transitional—and envision hypermedia's future now. While a number of artists have experimented with emerging interactive technologies, these have been almost exclusively in the realm of institution-based installations. Artists must go to the new venues as they emerge and make products and programming for the venues themselves. Key opportunities may open up in the next few years for a number of reasons.

There is a paucity of programming to fill a five-hundred-channel environment (even with half the capacity given over to pay-per-view) and a lack of capital to produce for "narrowcasting" because TV production has been skewed toward mass advertising budgets. Artists must exploit their ability to create low-budget programming before infomercials, home shopping, and every TV show made before the present moment gluts the paths into America's homes. While a lot of work has been created for television by artists up to this point in relationship to existing media arts venues, the total wouldn't fill one channel for a year, and much of it has consisted only of attempts to use television to distribute production created for entirely different distribution contexts. A generation ago, the emergence of cable technology was rhetorically embraced as an important new artists' venue, but public funding and community access, extensions of the Great Society models, were the almost exclusive basis of "guerrilla television." What is required is a completely different approach to funding and programming and a takeover at the level of programming enterprises and production companies to recast entire venues via media-arts-informed perspectives, but in a fashion that accepts who television audiences are, how television distribution works, and how it will be radically altered in the next two decades.

Simple multichannel interactive programs—the use of several channels with viewer options to make content decisions, such as the multicamera live sports program experiments in this country and Canada—may be one method whereby artists' intertextual strategies start to find their audience. Recent work by Van Gogh TV, such as their Documenta-based interactive television project of 1993, suggests how steps might be taken in bringing existing technologies such as phones, modems, video phones, and satellite links together into a dynamic telecommunity bulletin board for the exchange of information and public art.

Those interested in combining critical and aesthetic strategies have an excellent opportunity to create demand for truly oppositional deconstruction by taking advantage of the limits of crude digital video over the next few years. With QuickTime and DVI able to fill only a small window on most personal computers, the screen must be occupied by companion content, so there may never be a better time to combine radical applications of literary criticism with film and television, although as we have discussed, this is not in and of itself sufficient to redefine the possibilities of the new media. Interactive products that support repeated use really demand a depth of construction that may help create a receptive audience for the density, ambiguity, and complex engagement afforded by artist-produced hypermedia. If people do learn to truly read media, they will become an empowered audience, ready for new experiences with a new kind of media art and criticism.

But if artists primarily respond to the emergence of the new platforms by repurposing existing artworks as hypermedia in the hopes of finally getting neglected work distributed, the opportunity will be squandered. New technology and distribution systems require new creative engagement; artists must make computer software products for the base of users who are supporting this production or the formulation will fail. We must learn to approach marketing as audience development and not some egregious compromise of artistic principles.

None of these new production and distribution opportunities will dramatically change the role of art in culture—such shifts are always incremental—but they may ensure that the media arts legacy extends into the next century. This is not at all certain in the climate of recent setbacks.

FREEDOM OF INFORMATION ACTS

If any single circumstance defined the transformation of art in the United States over the past decade, it was President George Bush's firing of National Endowment for the Arts chairman John Frohnmayer in 1992, in anticipation of a radical-right-wing political ad. Pat Buchanan's campaign spot featured a tantalizing glimpse of *Tongues Untied*, a publicly funded and broadcast experimental video celebrating black gay identity.[33] Here, the war on culture waged by the evangelical Right and the war through culture waged by artists came into ecliptical alignment.

Distancing itself from largely apolitical formalism over the last decade or so, art has increasingly come to be defined by the politics of its content, distribution, and cultural and sexual representation. Utilization of mass media modes of address has come to be seen as a crucial strategy for social change. Heightened visibility has brought these confrontational agendas to the attention of the Right—not otherwise entirely aware of alternative culture—and its unequivocally provocative content has threatened just about every cherished belief in the Bible Belt. Arts funding has thus become a political football and a great issue with which the Right can raise funds. Attacks on the arts endowment in the early 1990s became as much a part of any conservative's routine as attacks on abortion rights, equal opportunity measures, or school prayer prohibitions. This is a dramatic series of developments: that an assault on a president's arts funding position would be a key part of a challenger's campaign strategy and that the firing of the NEA chairman would be that president's most crucial defense of his right flank were completely unthinkable five years earlier.

While the political tide in the United States has momentarily turned, the Right is powerful enough to keep the Clinton administration in check: at this juncture Attorney General Janet Reno is moving forward with an appeal of a federal court ruling that a clause requiring publicly funded art to be "decent" was unconstitutional, an appeal initiated by Bush appointees.

The end of public funding is in sight, and most of the field's publicly funded centers are mortally wounded. Clearly, the new media arts must blaze their own trails and create self-sufficient private support through commercial distribution. In the private sector, controversy about provocative content can "sell,"[34] but in the public sector, previous controversies have irreparably eroded the political base for arts funding and are hampering adventurous programming.[35] Beyond turning the tables on recent content controversies, this process is an important step in developing new relationships between artists and their constituencies.

The fight for the future of American culture hasn't seen anything like the all-out war that will be fought by the radical Right to keep provocative art and oppositional advocacy off the public utility master file servers of the nation in the fully digital future. Pornography will always have an audience on any platform, but truly transgressive work by artists openly challenging the boundaries of identity is under growing threat of suppression. As technology compresses the culture into increasingly more centralized storage, it is frighteningly clear that concentration of media power is the most important problem faced by whatever is left of the counterculture. It is imperative that artists, critics, curators, activists, and other cultural workers seize opportunities early in the technological transition to create a community of readers in search of new ideas.

Forget about the death of video art: failing to understand what's at stake during what may be only a brief window of opportunity at the inception of a new media arts field could irreparably harm the vitality of American culture for generations to come.

NOTES

1 Bill Viola, "History, Ten Years, and the Dreamtime," *Video: A Retrospective* (Long Beach, Calif.: Long Beach Museum of Art, 1984), 19.

2 For example, videotapes by Mark Rappaport, Shelly Silver, and Bruce and Norman Yonemoto, all carefully configured as broadcast video art works, position themselves within television's stylistic terms and genre expectations. Their success hinges, in part, on being recognized as some form of television, however far-out. Helping mass media to become its own worst enemy, the Yonemotos have refined in *Made in Hollywood* (1990) a perpetually self-critical and self-mutating form of soap opera expertly grafting simulated media culture to conversational art theory. A travelogue poised perfectly within kitsch Americana, Rappaport's *Postcards* (1990) is an inspired marriage of postcard worldview and television melodrama. Silver's *The Houses That Are Left (Part One)* (1990) is an ambitious film/video dramatic comedy pilot that also mixes in documentary and deconstructive modes with exceptional fluency.

3 Video art has occasionally found its way into the most adventurous programming of cable enterprises like MTV, USA, HBO, and Bravo and public-television-produced media art series like *Alive Television* (formerly *Alive from Off Center*) and *New Television*. These programs not only recycle existing art, but also help fund and, in the case of *Alive,* commission new work. There have been a few recent forays into the realm of commercial television by independent feature filmmakers such as David Lynch (*Twin Peaks,* 1989–90) and Nicolas Roeg (a made-for-TV *Heart of Darkness* in progress for TNT), following up on projects from the 1980s by Robert Altman (*Tanner '88* series, 1988) and Peter Greenaway (*TV Dante* series, 1983–). Various new forms of public television funding, such as the National Asian-American Television Association and the Independent Television Service, promise even more hybridization, for example, Janice Tanaka's moving one-hour personal documentary about the effect of the Japanese American internment on her father and family, *Who's Going to Pay for These Donuts, Anyway?* (1992).

4 Steve Fagin's *The Machine That Killed Bad People* (1990) is a particularly cogent example: one of the leading exponents and practitioners of theory-inclined video art has created a self-described two-hour experimental TV miniseries, unabashedly engaging the television context as a working paradigm for the production of intellectual culture.

5 In 1985, the leading video art curator during the field's inception, David Ross, wrote of "the success of the failure of video art": while video art had not liberated television from monopolistic corporate oppression, some great work had been created on its own terms (Ross, "The Success of the Failure of Video Art," *Videography,* May 1985). As video art's ascendant star—he is currently director of the Whitney Museum of American Art—Ross is another example of video art's absorption by the traditional art world.

6 A medium with a history of going its critics one better—this legacy extends back to the talk shows and specials of Ernie Kovacs in the 1950s and early 1960s, Mel Brooks and Buck Henry's *Get Smart* in the 1960s, *Saturday Night Live* in the 1970s, and Andy Kaufman in the 1970s and 1980s—television is now effectively parody-proof. See my "Parodying Parody: The San Francisco International Video Festival '84," "Andy Kaufman: Performance Provocateur," and "In the Beginning: Ernie Kovacs," *High Performance,* Winter 1984, for a historical context of this phenomenon. See also my "Andy Kaufman's Last Laugh," *Art Issues,*

March/April 1990, and *Kovacs and Kaufman* (Long Beach: Long Beach Museum of Art, 1989).

7 Works by Robert Beck (*The Feeling of Power: #6769,* 1990); Connie Coleman and Alan Powell (*Stat-ic,* 1989); John Goss (*"Out" Takes,* 1989); Alan Henderson, Richard Metzger, and Ann Magnuson (*The Power of Pussy,* 1991); Bob Paris (*Behold, I Come Quickly: The Strange Revelations of Reverend Swaggart,* 1990); and Elia Suleiman and Jayce Salloum (*Introduction to the End of an Argument (Intifada): Speaking for Oneself . . . Speaking for Others,* 1990) all demonstrate illuminating refinements in the application of critical theory to the textual analysis of television by engaging the medium's modalities.

8 Spoken and written texts are being used to inject critical dialogue into the body of the work in a didactic fashion. This is partly an extension of the social and political commentary provided by contemporary art, and this tendency also indicates the growing need for cultural criticism of and via electronic media. But what particularly distinguishes this new wrinkle is the extent to which video artists are now articulating cultural criticism, aesthetic theory, and even self-critique as interventions into the work—often establishing a separate "voice" for this commentary—assuming the role traditionally reserved for the art critic. Examples of works employing self-criticism include Vanalyne Greene's *A Spy in the House That Ruth Built* (1989), filled with expository asides that present a running play-by-play of her motives in making a tape about her sexual and sociological obsession with baseball, concluding with an ex post facto assessment of what the tape "means"; Jeanne C. Finley's *At the Museum: A Pilgrimage of Vanquished Objects* (1989), a devastating critique of the museum as context for culture articulated by written texts that constantly counterpoint and undermine the narrator's tour of the Oakland Museum; and Erika Suderburg's *Diderot and the Last Luminare: Waiting for the Enlightenment (A Revised Encyclopedia)* (1992), a presentation of reinvented meanings that simultaneously questions and supplants the role of order in knowledge.

9 Artists' advocacy works are so numerous that whole categories of video festival competitions must be reconfigured: as a judge at the Fifteenth Atlanta Film and Video Festival, my colleague and I had to create a category separate from documentary, narrative, and experimental—"Advocacy"—to reflect the dozens of videotapes that used experimental techniques to comment on contemporary issues, works that made

their own point of view so primary that they violated the cinema-verité-dictated parameters of documentary practice.

10 This is what most impressed me about the survey of hundreds of independent film and video works submitted for review to the NEA Media Arts Production Grant review process in which I participated in 1991, and provided by the entries of the Fifteenth Atlanta Film and Video Festival. These comments are revised from my statement in the festival catalog, *Fifteenth Atlanta Film and Video Festival* (Atlanta: Image Film and Video Center, 1991).

11 To get a sense of how visible this convergence is, see the cover story by Philip Elmer-Dewitt, "The Info Highway: Bringing a Revolution in Entertainment, News and Communication," *Time,* 12 April 1993, and Ken Auletta, "Barry Diller's Search for the Future," *New Yorker,* 22 February 1993.

12 For a discussion of the various players emerging in the competition to supply this technology, see Jonathan Weber and Carla Lazzareschi, "Box Wars: Whose Gizmo Will Be atop Your TV Set?" *Los Angeles Times,* 7 June 1993.

13 Undoubtedly, sex will play a key role in establishing the installed base for interactive media, just as it did for the VCR in the 1970s. *Virtual Valerie* is reportedly one of the best-selling computer software products to date. See Tony Reveaux, *New Media*, May 1993, 38. See also Gerard Van Der Leun, "This is a Naked Lady: Sex Is a Virus That Infects New Technology First," *Wired,* Premiere Issue, 1993.

14 For a rosy view, see Bob Young, "The Shape of Things to Come: Interactive Technology, Computer Animation Are Bringing New Dimensions to Home Video," *Los Angeles Times* TV Times, 21 March 1993.

15 The product is a QuickTime 1.5 CD-ROM version of Richard Lester's *A Hard Day's Night* (1964). It runs at a rate of approximately twelve frames per second in a small window on the computer screen. For two assessments of this release, see Peter Lewis, "At Last, a Movie Fits on a CD-ROM Disk," *New York Times*, 13 April 1993, and Ty Burr, "Hard to Handle: Beatles on CD-ROM," *Entertainment Weekly*, 14 May 1993.

16 A good overview is provided by George Mannes, "The Incredible Shrinking Videodisc," *Video,* July 1993. For a reality check on 3DO, see Joe Flower, "3DO: Hip or Hype?" *Wired,* May-June 1993. Prognostications about Apple's future plans come from Frederic E. Davis (contributing editor for *Windows Sources* and

Wired and former editor-in-chief of *MacUser*), interview with author, 30 March 1993.

17 Even with the recent surge in multimedia, text-only products are the largest category of titles, approximately 45 percent of the market, and the best-selling multimedia titles are reference works. See Reveaux, *New Media,* May 1993, 38-39, 42.

18 See Paul Saffo, "Hot New Medium: Text," *Wired*, May-June 1993.

19 See Jay David Bolter, *Writing Space: The Computer, Hypertext and the History of Writing* (Hillsdale, N.J.: Erlbaum, 1991), 21–25, 107–19.

20 For citations supporting all these assessments and an application of this perspective to the understanding of visual art, see my "Eye and I: Bill Viola's Double Visions," *Parkett,* June 1989.

21 Alberta Steinman Gilinsky, *Mind and Brain* (New York: Praeger, 1984), 457–63.

22 Artificial intelligence (AI) is a profoundly inverted project, and the mechanistic paradigm on which it is based is fundamentally flawed. See Rupert Sheldrake's brilliant rebuke of mechanistic biology and articulation of his theory about morphogenesis in *A New Science of Life: The Hypothesis of Formative Causation* (London: Blond and Briggs, 1985) and his comments on AI in *The Presence of the Past* (New York: Random House, 1988), 184, 214–15.

23 Admittedly, form and content gain meaning in relationship to each other, so placing them in strict opposition is problematic. This conception of poetry as a triumph of content over form is not only meant to mirror the pejorative obverse—"a triumph of form over content"—but is a shift in emphasis intended to challenge conventional ideas about form and therefore the form-content dichotomy itself.

24 W. S. Merwin, "On Open Form," *The New Naked Poetry* (Indianapolis: Bobbs-Merrill, 1976), 279.

25 Ron Silliman, "Disappearance of the Word, Appearance of the World," *The New Sentence* (New York: Roof Books, 1987), 13.

26 Merwin, "On Open Form," 277.

27 Bly has become particularly unfashionable, but his short and sweet postulation of these ideas is worth acknowledging. See Robert Bly, *Leaping Poetry* (Boston: Beacon Press, 1975).

28 Gregory L. Ulmer, "The Object of Post-Criticism," *The*

MICHAEL NASH

Anti-Aesthetic: Essays on Postmodern Culture, ed. Hal Foster (Port Townsend, Washington: Bay Press, 1983), 105–6.

29 Denise Levertov, "Some Notes on Organic Form," *Naked Poetry* (Indianapolis: Bobbs-Merrill, 1969), 141–45.

30 Robert Kugelmann, *The Windows of the Soul* (Lewisburg, Pa.: Bucknell University Press, 1983), 34.

31 John Rajchman, "Foucault's Art of Seeing," *October,* Spring 1988, 115.

32 See Julian Jaynes, *The Origin of Consciousness in the Breakdown of the Bicameral Mind* (Boston: Houghton Mifflin, 1976), 29, 63-64, 216–19.

33 Over a "suggestive" but relatively tame thirty-second excerpt from *Tongues Untied*, Buchanan's spot declared: "In the last three years, the Bush administration has invested our tax dollars in pornographic and blasphemous art too shocking to show. This so-called art has glorified homosexuality, exploited children, and perverted the image of Jesus Christ. Even after good people protested, Bush continued to fund this kind of art. Send Bush a message! We need a leader who'll fight for what we believe in. Vote Pat Buchanan for president." *Tongues Untied* (1989) is a widely acclaimed tour de force by Marlon Riggs, a Bay Area artist who makes experimental works and more conventional documentaries. It provides a remarkably rich assessment of the black gay experience through an arts variety show format that combines poetry and musical performance, personal narrative and ethnographic documentary.

34 Examples are numerous, ranging from banalities like Madonna's hyped-out book to artistic triumphs like Todd Haynes's homoerotic tour de force *Poison,* which was attacked by the radical Right and did well theatrically and in home video.

35 Obviously, the public funding of art is now in perpetual jeopardy, but the more insidious effect may be in the self-censorship many art institutions implement to limit their individual liability. For example, Dennis Barry was perceived as a major hero after the Contemporary Arts Center in Cincinnati beat a pornography charge precipitated by an exhibition of the works of Robert Mapplethorpe. Within a year, Barry and one of his curators pulled a work by Andrew Krasnow containing an American flag made of human skin from their "Mechanica" exhibition for fear that they would be subject to further attacks and loss of community support (Krasnow, in several interviews with the author, January-March 1991).

ROSANNA ALBERTINI is a researcher specializing in eighteenth-century philosophy at the University of Pisa. As a writer, she has merged her theoretical work within philosophy and history with a focus on contemporary art. She edited, with Sandra Lischi, the first Italian anthology of writings on video art, *Metamorfosi della visione* (1985). She has written essays for anthologies and catalogs in Italy, France, and Belgium, and organizes screenings for the Museo d'Arte Moderna in Bolzano, Italy. She currently writes for *Art Press* (Paris), *Flash Art* (Milan), and *L'Unita* (Rome).

RAYMOND BELLOUR is director of Research at the Centre National de la Recherche Scientifique (CNRS) in Paris. He is the author of numerous books, including *Henri Michaux ou un mesure d l'être* (1965) and *L'analyse du Film* (1979). He edited, with Jean-Jacques Brochier, *Dictionnaire du cinéma* (1966).

JOHN BELTON teaches film in the Department of English at Rutgers University. He is the author of *Widescreen Cinema* (1992) and *American Cinema/American Culture* (1994).

GREGG BORDOWITZ is an activist, videomaker, and writer living in New York. For six years he worked at the Gay Men's Health Crisis coproducing the *Living with AIDS* cable show. He has recently completed a one-hour-long experimental autobiographical film, entitled *Fast Trip, Long Drop*.

RON BURNETT is the director of the Graduate Program in Communications and an associate professor of Cultural Studies in the Department of English at McGill University. He founded and edited *Ciné-Tracts Magazine* and has published a book entitled *Explorations in Film Theory* (1991) and *Speaking of Parts* (1993), an essay on the work of filmmaker Atom Egoyan. His essays have appeared in numerous journals and books worldwide, covering the areas of photography, television, video, multimedia, and film. His latest book is *These Images Which*

Rain Down into the Imaginary (1995), and two further books are in preparation, *Countries of the Mind* and *Postmodern Media Communities.* The former is a study of the political and cultural dimensions of Quebec nationalism.

JACQUES DERRIDA is *directeur d'etudes* at the Ecole des Hautes Etudes en Sciences Sociales, Paris, and professor at University of California, Irvine. Almost all of his more than thirty books have appeared in English translation, most recently *Specters of Marx* and *Points . . . Interviews, 1974–1994,* both of which were translated by Peggy Kamuf. He has recently contributed an interview to the volume *Deconstruction and the Visual Arts: Art, Media, Architecture,* edited by Peter Brunette and David Wills.

SARA DIAMOND is the executive producer of television and artistic director of media and visual art at the Banff Centre for the Arts. She is a television producer and director, video artist, curator, critic, and teacher who has represented Canada at home and internationally. She recently received the Bell Canada Award in Video Arts, the most prestigious Canadian prize for video art.

MONICA FROTA is a Brazilian independent film- and videomaker who lives in Rio de Janeiro. She holds a master of visual anthropology degree from the Center for Visual Anthropology at the University of Southern California. Her most recent work, *Taking Aim,* a video on the Kayapo's appropriation of videotape technology, was awarded the Grand Prix at the 1995 Hiroshima International Film Festival.

BILL HORRIGAN is Curator, Media Arts, at the Wexner Center for the Arts at The Ohio State University, and coproducer of the public television series *New Television.* Recent projects he has organized include *Chris Marker: Silent Movie, Bruce and Norman Yonemoto: Three Installations,* and, for the American Center in Paris, *This Body, This Soul, This Brick, These Tears: Disorder Today.*

DAVID E. JAMES is the author of *Allegories of Cinema: American Film in the Sixties* (1989) and the editor of *To Free the Cinema: Jonas Mekas and the New York Underground* (1992). He is professor of Critical Studies in the School of Cinema-Television at the University of Southern California in Los Angeles.

LAURA KIPNIS teaches at Northwestern University. She is the author of a collection of essays and videoscripts, *Ecstasy Unlimited: On Sex, Capital, Gender, and Aesthetics* (University of Minnesota Press, 1993). She received a 1993 Guggenheim Fellowship for video art and a 1995 Rockefeller Fellowship for Media Criticism.

TETSUO KOGAWA is professor of media studies at Tokyo Keizai University's Department of Communications. He has written thirty books, including *Critique of Information Capitalism* (1985), *Future of Electronic Man* (1986), and *Cinema Politica* (1993).

JUDITH MAYNE is professor of French and women's studies at Ohio State University (since 1976). Her most recent books include *Directed by Dorothy Arzner* (1994), *Cinema and Spectatorship* (1993), and *The Woman at the Keyhole: Feminism and Women's Cinema* (1990).

JAMES M. MORAN is currently a doctoral student in the School of Cinema-Television at the University of Southern California. Formerly a professional wedding videographer, he is writing his dissertation on commercial appropriations of home video.

MICHAEL NASH is president and creative director of Inscape, a partnership he formed with Home Box Office and Warner Music Group to produce, publish, and market interactive CD-ROM titles. Prior to forming Inscape, Nash oversaw the Voyager Company's award-winning Criterion Collection laser-disc label and was executive producer of The Residents' *Freak Show* CD-ROM. Formerly media arts curator of the Long Beach Museum of Art, Nash is a contributing editor of *Art Issues* and has authored more than one hundred articles and essays on media and art.

CHON A. NORIEGA is an assistant professor in the Department of Film and Television at the University of California, Los Angeles. He is the editor of *Chicanos and Film: Representation and Resistance* (University of Minnesota Press, 1992). He is guest editor of special issues of *Jump Cut* and *Spectator* (both fall 1992) and coeditor of *The Mexican Cinema Project* (1994) and *The Ethnic Eye: Latino Media Arts* (forthcoming). He has curated film and art exhibitions for the Whitney Museum of American Art, the American Museum of the Moving Image, and the Robert Flaherty Seminar, among others.

MICHAEL RENOV, professor of Critical Studies in the School of Cinema-Television at the University of Southern California, is the author of *Hollywood's Wartime Woman: Representation and Ideology* (1988), editor of *Theorizing Documentary* (1993), and coeditor with Jane Gaines and Faye Ginsburg of the Return of the Real book series for the University of Minnesota Press.

BÉRÉNICE REYNAUD is a U.S. correspondent for the French film monthly *Cahiers du Cinéma* and for the daily paper *Libération*. In English, her work has been published in *Screen, Sight and Sound*, the *New York Times*, the *Village Voice*, the *Independent, Afterimage, Tikkun, Cinematograph, Black American Literature Forum, Transitions, Cinemaya*, and *Fuse*. A correspondent for the Créteil International Women's Film Festival (Paris) and for the San Sebastian International Film Festival (Spain), she has curated film and video exhibitions specializing on work by women, independent filmmakers, people of color, and third world directors. She was awarded a Rockefeller Foundation Scholar-in-Residence Fellowship at the Whitney Museum in 1990 and is currently teaching at the California Institute of the Arts.

MARLON RIGGS was a videomaker, writer, and educator who produced a rich body of video works that have been extensively exhibited and broadcast internationally. His tapes included *Ethnic Notions* (1986), for which he won an Emmy, *Tongues Untied* (1989), *Affirmations* (1990), *Anthem* (1991), and *Color Adjustment* (1991). His most controversial work, *Tongues United*, engendered a powerful public debate on censorship, African American gay male representation, and the politics of public funding for the arts. In addition to his artmaking, Riggs taught in the Graduate School of Journalism at the University of California, Berkeley. He died of AIDS in 1994 at the age of thirty-seven.

MARITA STURKEN has written extensively about independent video for more than fifteen years and is working on a book about the politics of cultural memory. She is assistant professor in the Annenberg School for Communication at the University of Southern California.

ERIKA SUDERBURG is a curator, multimedia artist, teacher, and writer who works in photography, film, video, bookworks, and installation. Her work has been exhibited internationally at various institutions, including Capp Street Projects, the American Film Institute, the Museum of Modern Art, Los Angeles Contemporary Exhibitions, Millenium Film Workshop, The Kitchen, Kunstlerhaus, and Grazer Kunstverein. She is currently an associate professor of art at the University of California, Riverside.

CHRISTINE TAMBLYN is an assistant professor in the Department of Visual Arts at Florida International University in Miami. She has published more than one hundred articles and reviews in art magazines, catalogs, textbooks, and anthologies. Her performative lectures, videotapes, and computer art have been shown widely.

MAUREEN TURIM is professor of film studies in the Department of English at the University of Florida. Author of *Flashbacks in Film: Memory and History* (1989) and *Abstraction in Avant-Garde Films* (1985), she has also published articles on a wide range of theoretical, historical, and aesthetic issues in cinema and video. She is currently completing a book, *The Films of Oshima: Images of a Japanese Iconoclast*.

PATRICIA R. ZIMMERMANN teaches in the Department of Cinema and Photography at Ithaca College, Ithaca, New York. She is the author of *Reel Families: A History of Amateur Film* (1995) and *Endangered Species: Documentaries and Democracies* (University of Minnesota Press, forthcoming).

INDEX

compiled by Eileen Quam and Theresa Wolner

A

A Ha! Experience, The (Zando), 349-50
Abbott, Jennifer: *Skinned*, 204
Abortion, 317
Abortion rights. *See* Reproductive rights
Abramovic, Marina, 144
Access Denied, 324
Accessory Transit Company (Lozano), 196
Acconci, Vito, 155, 180; *Recording Studio from Air Time*, 125
ACLU. *See* American Civil Liberties Union
Activist video, 17, 174, 177
ACT-UP, 319
Adair, John, 260-61
Adams, Ansel, 36
ADS Epidemic, The (Greyson), 203
Advocate, The, 189
Agony and the Ecstasy, The (Mitchell), 190
Agueda Maritínez, 213
AI. *See* Artificial intelligence
AIDS: activism, 175, 181, 319; cable program, 173, 182; and censorship, 203; documentary work, 181; Memorial Quilt, 2; PSAs, 204; in soap operas, 167-69, 171n3, 172n4; and television, 165-70, 175; and unborn, 326; in videos, 173, 175, 177, 181, 182, 203-4
Alchemy Cabinet (Eichman), 316
Alice in Wonderland, 202
All about Eve, 347
All Orientals Look the Same (Soe), 243
All the Corners of the World, 249
Alternative history. *See* History
Alternative media, 3, 99n30, 174, 290-91
Altman, Robert, 392-93; *Player*, 393; *Short Cuts*, 392

A.M. Radio Was His Only Friend (Werden), 191
Amateur: vs. professional, 380n33
Amelia Productions, 194
American Civil Liberties Union (ACLU), 320
American Family, An, 86
American Family Association, 185
American Film Institute, 15
American Library Association, 320
America's Funniest Home Videos, 13, 15
Ampex videotape recorder, 61, 63, 298-99
Ancona, Victor: *Videography*, 41
Anderson, Kelly, 290
Anger (Cohen), 85, 90
Anima (España), 220
Animal Kingdom, 201
AnOther Love Story (Douglas and Micallef), 204
Anstey, Jo, 352-55; *Bus Stops Here*, 349, 350-51, 351
Anticensorship. *See* Censorship
Arbus, Diane, 191
Archaeology of Knowledge, The (Foucault), 309
Arresting Images (Dubin), 315
Art: image of, in video, 29-50. *See also* Video art
ART COM: address, 224
Art museums: and video medium, 208
Art of Memory (Vasulka), 4-5, 11, 136, 149-64, 160-64
Art video. *See* Video art
Artificial intelligence (AI), 55, 398n32
As a Wife Has a Cow (Wyngaarden), 202
Asco art collective, 207, 214, 215
Asia Motion Pictures, 233
Asian Cine Vision, 234
Assumptions, 173-84

Astruc, Alexandre, 83
Asyndeton, 24
Audience: as activist of access, 59
Audio technology, 61, 62-64, 69
Augustine of Hippo, Saint, 98nn13, 15; and autobiography, 125; *Confessions*, 79, 80
Aumont, Jacques, 47
Aura (Ma), 245
Autobiography, 124-33; in avant-garde film, 125; vs. biography, 133n4; and confession, 79, 98n5. *See also* Confession; Video diary
Avant-garde, 16, 47, 180; autobiography in, 125; and Chicano video, 207
Aztlán, 216

B

Baby Dolls (Werden), 191
Back to the Future, 364
Bad Day at Black Rock, 7
Baillie, Bruce, 84
Baird, Zoe, 304, 313
Bakhtin, Mikhail: on classical body, 341; on semiotics, 59n6; on subjectivity, 375
Baldessari, John, 138
Baldwin, James, 187, 188
Balser, Michael, 204; *Survival of the Delirious*, 203
Banerjee, Himani, 204
Banff Centre for the Arts, 204
Barnlund, D., 285-86
Barthes, Roland, 35; on mana-word, 100n43; on the personal and history, 363; on photographs, 67; on realism, 135; on subjectivity, 375
Bätschmann, Oskar, 37, 39
Batsry, Irit: *Leaving the Old Ruin* and *Simple Case of Vision*, 141
Battle of San Romano, The (Uccello), 32
Bazin, André, 61, 71n2
Beavis and Butt-Head (TV show), 383
Beckett, Samuel, 139, 145
Beckman, Erika: *Blind Country*, 342
Beijing Bastards (Yuan), 238
Beneath the Skin (Condit), 342
Benglis, Lynda: *Now*, 125
Benjamin, Walter: on angel of history, 5; on art and reproduction technology, 30, 57, 60n23, 68, 69, 71n2
Benning, Sadie, 382; *If Every Girl Had a Diary*, 87; *It Wasn't Love*, 17, 21-22, *22*, 87, 340-41; *Jollies*, 87; *Me and Rubyfruit*, 87
Berko, Lili, 291-92
Berlin, Symphony of a Great City (Ruttman), 118
Berliner, Allan: *Family Album*, 362
Bertolucci, Bernardo: *Last Emperor*, 252

Betamax, 64, 299
Bettelheim, Bruno, 194
Beverley, John, 209-10
Beyond the Helms of the Sensors, 204
Biggs, Simon: *New Life*, 32-33, 34; *Temptation of Saint Anthony*, 32, 33, 34
Binge (Hershman), 17, 20-21, *21*, 87, 88, 127, *127*, 128; and self-transformation, 22
Birnbaum, Dara: *Wonder Woman*, 173
Birri, Fernando: *Tire Dié*, 211
Birthday Suit—with Scars and Defects (Steele), 191, *191*, 197
Bisexual Kingdom, The (Schroder), 201
Black Sheep (Soe), 243
Blanchot, Maurice: *Thomas the Obscure*, 390
Blind Country (Beckman and Kelly), 342
Blood Risk, 204
Blue Moon (Werden), 192
Blush Productions, 200
Boat People (Hui), 250
Bociukiw, Marusia: *Bodies in Trouble, Night Visions*, and *Playing with Fire*, 201
Bodies in Trouble (Bociukiw), 201
Body: as discursive site, 190
Body Art magazine, 189
Bolo, Bolo (Rashid and Saxena), 204
Border Brujo (Gómez-Peña), 213
Boschman, Lorna: *Butch/Femme in Paradise, Drawing the Line, Our Normal Childhood, Scars*, and *True Inversions*, 201
Boswell, James, 124
Boudreau, Charlene, 201
Boutet, Richard: *Suzanne et Lucie*, 193
Bowery in Two Inadequate Descriptive Systems, The (Rosler), 174
Boxer Rebellion, 231
Boyd, Blanche McCrary: *Mourning the Death of Magic*, 102
Boyle, Dierdre, 297
Brakhage, Stan, 47, 84, 125, 207
Brazil: popular video in, 293
Brazilian Indians. *See* Kayapo Indians
Breathing through Opposing Nostrils (Greyson), 200
Brecht, Bertolt, 90, 94, 100n44
Bride Stripped Bare by Her Bachelors, Even, The (Duchamp), 33
Bright, Suzie: *Sexual Reality*, 189
Brighter Summer Day, A (Yang), 248
Broadcast television: vs. film, 65; live vs. video-tape, 66; and nationalist history, 3; technology, 65-66, 72n20, 123; as transmission, 65; vs. video art, 16, 51-52, 72n20, 174

Brooke, Kaucyila: *Dry Kisses Only*, 340, 347
Broughton, James, 207
Brown, Peter, 80
Browne, Nick, 82
Buchanan, Pat, 318
Buffalo Media Coalition for Reproductive Rights (MCRR), 307, 319, 321
Bumming in Beijing (Wenguang), 234, 235-36
Burden, Chris, 130
Burden of Representation, The (Tagg), 95
Bus Stops Here, The (Zando and Anstey), 349, 350-51, *351*
Butch/Femme in Paradise (Boschman), 201
Butler decision, 189
Bye Bye Kipling (Paik), 58

C

Cage, John, 139, 144, 145
Cage, La (Paradis), 203
Camcorders, 13-14, 25
Camera: as instrument of confession, 82-84; and memory, 1. *See also* Photography
Camino, Luis F.: *Velazquez Digital*, 32, 34
Camp, Bob, 383
Campbell, Colin: *Conundrum Clinique*, 192; *I'm a Voyeur*, 192; *Love Life*, 192; *No Voice Over*, 192-93; retrospective of, 206n21; *Skin*, 193; *Snip, Snip*, 199; *True/False*, 192
Campbell, Peg: *Common Assault*, 194; *Rule of Thumb*, 194; *Sign of Affection*, 194; *We Will Not Be Beaten*, 194
Canada: censorship in, 189-90, 197-200; video environment in 1970s, 196; video sex in, 189-206
Canada's Challenge for Change (Moore), 296-97
Canadian Broadcasting Company (CBC), 193
Cane, Candie, 197
Cantonese opera: and female masquerade, 245-46
Carel and Ferd, 87, 90, 100n38
Carlomusto, Jean, 173; *L Is for the Way You Look*, 180
Carnalitos, 213
Carver, Raymond, 392
Casa de Las Américas, 209
Cavell, Stanley, 2
CBC. *See* Canadian Broadcasting Company
CBS logo, 31
CCTV. *See* Central Chinese Television
CD-ROM, 384-85, 386
Censorship, 185-88; of AIDS material, 203; in Canada, 189-90, 197-200; and community standards, 187; of homosexuality, 185-88
Center for Public Broadcasting (CPB), 209, 317

Central Chinese Television (CCTV), 241; *River Elegy*, 229-30, 239
Cezanne's Composition (Loran), 47
Cha, Theresa Hak Kyung, 113
Challenge for Change (Canada), 295-97
Chaperons rouges, 194
Cheang, Shu Lea, 230, 234, 240; *Color Schemes*, 243; *How Was History Wounded*, 240-41; *Will Be Televised*, 240
Chen Jue, 236-37
Chen Kaige, 232
Chiao, Peggy, 234
Chicano Art Movement, 207, 214, 218
Chicano Cinema Coalition, 214
Chicano experimental video, 207-28; *testimonio* in, 209-11
Chicano Movement, 216
Chicano Ur-nation, 216
Chicks in White Satin (Holliman), 371-72, *371*
China: and colonialism, 232; film/video in, 229-57; identity in, 234; and modernity, 229-32; portrayal of history, 238-41; and postmodernism, 241-45; Western influence, 232-38
China Beach (TV show), 316
Chinese Characters (Fung), 202-3, *202*, 244
Ching Jan Lee, 240
Chion, Michel, 143-44
Chitty, Elizabeth, 196-97; *Desire Control*, 197
Chocolate Grinder, No. 2, The (Duchamp), 33
Chow, Rey, 229; *Woman and Chinese Modernity*, 231
Chronique d'un été (Rouch and Morin), 83, 86, 89, 90
Cine testimonio, 211
Cinema: alternative, 99n30; aura in, 71; genealogy of, 62; impure, 18; language of, 66; movement in, 66-67; and photography, 67; technology of, 62-63, 66-67, 71; and television, 106; vs. video, 62-63. *See also* Film; Motion picture industry
Cinema 1 (Deleuze), 53
Claire of the Moon, 357
Clark, T. J.: *Painting of Modern Life*, 49n29
Clarke, Wendy: *Ken and Louise*, 91, 92-94, *93*; *Love Tapes*, 87, 89-91, *90*, 97, 100n42; "One on One," 87, 91-97, 100n45, 101n53; *Ricky and Cecilia*, 94-95
Clinton, Bill: on abortion, 311-15, 329
Clinton, Hillary Rodham, 313, 314
Close, Chuck, 45
Close Encounters of the Third Kind (Spielberg), 151
Coalition for the Right to View (CRTV), 198
Cohen, Maxie, 145; *Anger*, 85, 90; *Intimate Interviews*, 85, 88

Collective memory: camera image as, 1; maintenance of, 3; and video, 4
Color Schemes (Cheang), 243
Come See the Paradise, 7
Commission, The (Vasulka), 149-50, 151
Common Assault, A (Campbell), 194
Communication for change, 295
Communication technologies: access to, 284-86
Community: and video, 283-303
Compulsion to Confess, The (Reik), 78
Computers: development of, 59; as electronic brain, 58-59; as interactive, 58; as interface to social life, 59; for processing and storage, 58-59; technology, 58-59; and television, 385
Condit, Ceclia: *Beneath the Skin*, 342; *Not a Jealous Bone*, 342-44, *343*; *Possibly in Michigan*, 342
Condy-Berggold, Craig: *Fresh Talk*, 204
Confession: and autobiography, 79, 98n5; and criminology, 95; defined, 79; developmental perspective, 88-89; electronic, 84-86, 99n32; first person, 85, 100n35; in literature, 81; and Protestantism, 88; and psychoanalysis, 79-80; on television, 82, 95, 96; as therapeutic, 80-82, 84, 98n11; on video, 78-101. *See also* Autobiography; Video diary
Confessions (Augustine), 79, 80
Confessions of a Chameleon (Hershman), 87, 126, 128, 129
Confused, 204
Conspiracy of Silence (Hershman), 124, 132
Consumer video, 27; and video art, 14, 17
Continuing Story of Carel and Ferd, The (Ginsberg), 86-87
Contrast ratio, 71
Conundrum Clinique (Campbell), 192
Cooper, Margaret, 308, 309
Cores, Gena: *Mother Machine*, 326
Cottis, Jane: *Dry Kisses Only*, 340, 347; *War on Lesbians*, 340
CPB. *See* Center for Public Broadcasting (CPB)
Craig, Kate: *Delicate Issue*, 197
Criminology: and confession, 95
Cronenberg, David: *Videodrome*, 54
CRTV. *See* Coalition for the Right to View (CRTV)
Cubitt, Sean, 104; *Timeshift*, 320
Cult of the Cubicles (Kuchar), 78, 87
Cultural history, 1-2; and television, 3; video as, 2, 12
Cultural resistance: and video technology, 277-78
Cultural Revolution (1966-76), 232, 247
Culture: dominant, defined, 175, 176; politics of, and video, 283-303
Curry, Richard O., 319-20

D
Damn Interfering Video Activists (DIVA), 175, 209
Day of the Dead. *See* Dia de los Muertos
Days of Heaven (Malick), 43
de Beauvoir, Simone: *Very Easy Death*, 219
De Certeau, Michel: *Practice of Everyday Life*, 13, 15-16, 21, 24, 26
de Lauretis, Teresa, 196, 347, 349
de Man, Paul, 219
De Moss, Nancy, 310
De Moss (Arthur S.) Foundation, 310, 329
Dead Man Was a Woman, The (Wyngaarden), 202
Deep Dish Satellite Network, 209, 240, 290, 319
Delerium (Videographe), 193
Deleuze, Gilles, 149, 153; *Cinema 1*, 53; on virtuality, 60n16
Delicate Issue (Craig), 197
Delivre-nous du mal (Paradis), 203
Demonstration of the Fear and Pain, A (Tomczak), 196
Deren, Maya, 84, 207
Derrida, Jacques: *Truth in Painting*, 39-40; on video as new art, 73-77
Descartes, René, 74, 77n1, 136, 142
Desert Hearts, 357
Desire Control (Chitty), 197
Desire Incorporated (Hershman), 124, 130, *130*
Di Meglio, Clara, 81
Dia de los Muertos, 217, 218, 220
Diary video. *See* Video diary
Digital theater sound, 69
Dinesen, Isak: *Out of Africa*, 167
Disturbance (Hill), 74
DIVA. *See* Damn Interfering Video Activists
Doane, Mary Anne, 20
Documentary: elements of, 258-59; function of, 84, 99n33; and the poetic, 105; as preservation, 84
Dolby, Ray, 63-64
Dolby Laboratories, 63-64
Dole, Bob, 318
Doors (rock group), 333-34
Doors, The (Stone), 333
Doroshenko, Peter, 43
Douglas, Debbie: *AnOther Love Story*, 204
Downey, Juan: *Looking Glass*, 29, 34-35
Drawing the Line (Boschman), 201
Dry Kisses Only (Cottis and Brooke), 340, 347
Dubin, Steve: *Arresting Images*, 315
Dubuffet, Jean, 138, 139, 140
Duchamp, Marcel, 33-34, 35; *Bride Stripped Bare by Her Bachelors, Even*, 33; *Chocolate Grinder, No. 2*, 33

Dufour, Lorraine: *Ma vie c'est pour le restant des mes jours*, 193
Dunye, Cheryl: *She Don't Fade*, 340
Duras, Marguerite, 38
Dworkin, Andrea, 189, 194; *Pornography*, 189; *Women Hating*, 189
Dwyer, Nancy, 135

E

Edison, Thomas, 62
Egoyan, Atom: *Speaking Parts*, 27
Eichman, Shawn: *Alchemy Cabinet*, 316
Electronic Confessional, The (Lewis and Lewis), 99n32
Electronic Diary (Hershman), 20-21, 88, 124-32, *127*; monologues in, 88
Eleven Women (Yang), 248-49
Elizabeth I, 202
Empowerment: and media access, 286-90
Emshwiller, Ed, 139
Entelequía (España), 222
Enzensberger, Hans Magnus, 119
Erotica (Knapp), 346-47
España, Frances Salomé, 220-23; *Anima*, 220; *Entelequía*, 222; *Espejo*, 213, 221-22
Espejo, El/The Mirror, (España), 213, 221-22
Estes, Richard, 46
Eté—double vue (Kuntzel), 35-40, 47
Eternal Bliss Machine, The (Seligson), 370
Eulogy, 112-15
Eveready Battery commercial, 383
Everyday Echo Street (Mogul), 87
Ewing, Christine, 326
Examination. *See* Self-examination
Exile: and intertextuality, 246-48
Experimental video: Chicano, 207-28; "I" in, 209; vs. television, 208
Exquisite Mechanism of Shivers, The (Seaman), 390

F

Fabo, Andy: *Survival of the Delirious*, 203
Fairness and Accuracy in Reporting (FAIR), 317
Falcon Cable Television, 215
Family Album, The (Berliner), 362
Family Research Council, 318
Family values, 304
Fanni, Cosey: *Music for Stocking-Top, Staircase and Swing*, 193
Fargier, Jean-Paul, 74, 149
Fascist in Love (McP), 204
Fashion as a Social Control (Women in Focus), 194
Female masquerade: and Cantonese opera, 245-46

Feminism: documentary films, 193; feminist video, 124, 133n6, 341, 344; on pornography, 189, 195-96; and reproductive rights, 304-9, 326. *See also* Women artists
Femme et le Film, La: *Chaperons rouges*, 194
Fight Back (Speak Out Productions), 194
Fighting Chance (Fung), 202
Film: vs. broadcast television, 65; colorization, 70; as medium, 71; and self-evaluation, 115; technology, 61-72; and video, 51-52, 61-72. *See also* Cinema
Film Portrait (Hill), 133n3
Findlay, David: *Gender, Lace and Glass*, 204, *205*
Finley, Jeanne: *Nomads at the 25 Door*, 4, 10-11
Finley, Karen, 339, 341
First Comes Love (Friedrich), 346
First Person Plural (Hershman), 127-28, *127*, 132
First-person video confessions. *See* Confession
Flow: defined, 2; in television, 108; video image as, 103, 104
Flow (Yau Ching), 246-47
For Memory (Karlin), 102, 115-18, *116*, 120-21, 122n22, 122n23
Forbidden Love (Zando), 358
Foucault, Michel: *Archaeology of Knowledge*, 309; on confession, 79-81, 85, 88, 96, 97; *History of Sexuality*, 79-80; *Madness and Civilization*, 79; on seeing, 391
Four Shadows (Gottheim), 47
Frank, Robert, 45
Frankly Shirley (Moores), 200
Freak Show (Residents), 392
Freedom of Information Acts, 395-96
Fresh Talk (Condy-Berggold and Marshall), 204
Freud, Sigmund, 1, 82, 86, 92, 98n8, 112
Friedrich, Caspar David, 43, 44
Friedrich, Su: *First Comes Love*, 346
Frohnmayer, John, 395
From Another Time Comes One (Longboy), 204
From Caligari to Hitler (Kracauer), 52
Full Moon in New York (Lam), 249-50
Fung, Richard: *Chinese Characters*, 202-3, *202*, 244; *Fighting Chance*, 202; *Orientations*, 202, 244; *Out of the Blue*, 202; *Steam Clean*, 203, *203*

G

Galerie Nationale du Jeu de Paume (Paris), 234
Galleries. *See* Art museums
Gamboa, Harry, 207, 214-17; *Chicano Male*, 215; documentaries of, 215; *El mundo L.A.*, 213, 215-17
Gaowa, Siqin, 249-50
Garcia, Roger, 234

Gay Men's Health Crisis (GMHC), 173, 175, 177, 184n2

Gender, Lace and Glass (Findlay), 204, *205*

Generation after the Martial Law, The, 240

Genet, Jean: *Querelle*, 189

German Expressionist cinema, 150

German Foundation for International Development, 295

Gerz, Jochen, 145

Giacometti, Alberto, 139

Giant (Stevens), 43

Gibbons, Joe: *Onourown*, 17, 22-23

Ginsberg, Arthur: *Continuing Story of Carel and Ferd*, 86-87

Giroux, Suzanne, 41

Global Taste (Rosler), 174

Gloria tapes (Steele), 197

Glueck, Grace, 41

GMHC. *See* Gay Men's Health Crisis (GMHC)

Godard, Jean-Luc, 180; on film and metaphor, 258; on history and identity, 109-12, 120; *Passion*, 47, 109; *Soft and Hard*, 109, 110-12; Sonimage, 109

Goldberg, Michael: *Orgasm*, 190

Golden Voyage (Vasulka and Vasulka), 29-32

Goldson, Annie, 290

Gómez-Peña, Guillermo: *Border Brujo*, 213

Good Boy, A (McP), 204

Gorewitz, Shalom: *Ten Thousand Things*, 145

Gorotire village, 267-69, 281n27-28

Gottheim, Larry: *Four Shadows*, 47

Graham, Dan, 174, 180; *Rock My Religion*, 174

Great Expectations (Hawley), 194

Great Lie, The, 347

Great Mirror of Male Love, The (Saikaku), 245

Green, Vanalyne: *Spy in the House That Ruth Built*, 87, 337-40, *338*; *Trick or Drink*, 87

Green Team Video Collective, 240

Greenaway, Peter, 143

Greyson, John: *ADS Epidemic*, 203; *Breathing through Opposing Nostrils*, 200; *Jungle Boy*, 200; *Making of Monsters*, 200; *Moscow Does Not Believe in Queers*, 200; *Urinal*, 200; *Visual Evidence* workshop, 200-201, *201*

Griffin, Susan: *Pornography and Silence*, 196

Gronk, 214

Groot, Paul, 41

Grossberg, Lawrence, 207-8

Grotesque, female, 341-42

Group Media Journal, 295

Groupe Intervention de Video: *Chaperons rouges*, 194

Guattari, Félix, 53

Guevara, Ché: *Reminiscences of the Cuban Revolutionary War*, 210

Gunn, David: shooting of, 304, 305-6

Gupta, Joyanta, 326

Gutenberg Galaxy, The (McLuhan), 55

H

Hahn, Sandra P., 217-20; *Replies of the Night*, 217-19; *Slipping Between*, 213, 219, 224

Hall, Doug: *People in Buildings*, 45-46, *46*, *47*; *Storm and Stress*, 40, 44-45, *45*

Halleck, Dee, 174, 320

Hanson, Miriam, 108

Haraway, Donna, 308

Harems (Paradis), 203

Harman, Susan, 201

Harouni, Valerie, 308-9

Hawley, Gay: *Great Expectations*, 194

Haynes, Todd, 185

Health Care Reform, 313

"Heat Is On, The" (conference), *199*

Hegel, G. W. F.: on "Absolute Geist," 55; and metaphysics, 60n17

Hegemony: cultural, 81; defined, 175

Heidegger, Martin: on history of technology, 55; on memory, 55-56; on metaphysics, 60n17

Heimatfilme (homeland films), 106, 121n11

Helms, Jesse, 318

Hemphill, Essex, *188*

Henry Kissinger Won the Nobel Peace Prize (Kibbins), 200

Here's Looking at You, Kid, 252

Heritage Foundation, 316, 318

Hermandad National Media Center, 209

Herron, Willie, 214

Hershman, Lynn: *Binge*, 17, 20-21, *21*, 22, 87, 88, 127, *127*, 128; *Confessions of a Chameleon*, 87, 126, 128, 129; *Conspiracy of Silence*, 124, 132; *Desire Incorporated*, 124, 130, *130*; *Electronic Diary*, 20, 88, 124-32, *127*; *First Person Plural*, 127-28, *127*, 132; *Longshot*, 124, 131-32, *131*; private and public discourse of, 89, 100n40; *Seeing Is Believing*, 124, 128-29, *129*; and self-obsession, 124; *Shadow's Song*, 124, 132

Hey, Bud (Zando), 349, 350-51, *351*

Hill, Anita, 122n27, 304, 318

Hill, Gary, 47, 74-77, 382, 390-91; *Disturbance*, 74; *Incidence of Catastrophe*, 390, *391*; *Site Recite*, 391; *Which Tree*, 391

Hill, Jerome: *Film Portrait*, 133n3

History: alternative, 3, 102-23; as circular, 102; construction of, 1-2, 5-7; cultural, 1-2, 3, 12; and home, 11; and identity, 109-12, 120;

nationalist, 3; and popular culture, 7; and postmodernism, 3, 12; as process of displacement, 10; and stability, 11. *See also* Memory

History and Memory (Tajiri), 4, 5-8, 9, 10, 12

History of Art (Janson), 37

History of Sexuality, The (Foucault), 79-80

Holliman, Elaine: *Chicks in White Satin*, 371-72, *371*

Holocaust (television documentary), 116

Holy Joe (Sarahan), 202

Holy Terror, 317

Home movies, 109-12

Home video, 15; and pornography, 15; and family ritual, 84

Homeless (Logue), 145

Homosexuality: censorship of, 185-88; in China, 244-45; erotica, 199, 201; and pornography, 189, 200-201. *See also* Lesbian representation

Hong King Film Festival, 234

Hopkins, Gerard Manley, 391

Hopper, Dennis: *Last Movie*, 131

Horn, Rebecca, 138; *To Sleep as Little Spoons*, 143

Hou, Wen Yi, 246-47

Hour of the Filmmakers (Kluge), 106

How to Love a Man Who Doesn't Love Me (Lam), 246

How Was History Wounded (Cheang), 240-41

Howard, Earl, 41

Huang Li-ming, 239

Huey, Victor: *Rocking the Great Wall*, 248

Hughes, Holly, 339

Hui, Ann, 250-51; *Boat People*, 250; *Prodigal's Return*, 250; *Song of the Exile*, 250; *Zodiac Killers*, 250

Hunter, Holly, 316

Hypertext, 387

I

I Can't Believe What I Saw (Schroder), 201

I Do Not Know What It Is I Am Like (Viola), 389, *389*

I Like Girls for Friends (Zando), 349, 350, 356

If Every Girl Had a Diary (Benning), 87

Ihara Saikaku: *Great Mirror of Male Love, The*, 245

"I'll Bet You Ain't Never Seen Noth'n Like This Before" (Werden), 191

I'm a Voyeur (Campbell), 192

In the Dark (Steele and Tomczak), 199

In the Realm of the Senses (Oshima), 190

In Those Days (Mellinger), 17, 25-26; oral history structure, 25

Incidence of Catastrophe (Hill), 390, *391*

Incident Jones, L' (Paradis), 203

Independent Television Service, 209

Informational reproduction: and mechanical reproduction, 57

Instant replay, 65

Integrated Rural Project in Education, Health, and Family Planning (Honduras), 295

Interactive mode: defined, 100n36

International Coalition for Audiovisuals for Development and Democracy, 286

International Public Television Festival, 185

Interrogation. *See* Self-examination

Intertextuality: of exile, 246-48; and narrative, 392; poetic model for, 388-92

Intimate Interviews (Cohen), 85, 88

It Wasn't Love (Benning), 17, 21-22, *22*, 87, 340-41

It's Not My Head, It's My Body (Riseau Video des Femmes), 194

J

Jabès, Edmond, 140

Jacobson, David, 158

James, William, 81

Jameson, Fredric: on ennui, 118, 120; *Political Unconscious*, 27, 28n19; on television, 3; on text, 208; on video, 103-4, 208

Janson, H. W.: *History of Art*, 37

Jarvik, Laurence, 318

Jenkins, Bruce, 41

John, Jasper, 144

Jollies (Benning), 87

Joyce, James: on modern man, 231; *Ulysses*, 190

Judith Williamson Consumes Passionately in Southern California, 18

Jungle Boy (Greyson), 200

Jurassic Park, 69

JVC Company, 299

K

Kafka, Franz, 57; *Penal Colony*, 154

Kalin, Tom, 382

Kaplan, Ann: *Motherhood and Representation*, 311

Kapot village, 264-65, 274-75

Karkal, Malina, 326

Karlin, Marc: *For Memory*, 102, 115-18, *116*, 120-21, 122nn22, 23

Kayapo Indians, 258-60, *259*, 261-78, *265*, 279n3, 280n15, 280n18, 280n22. *See also* Metuktire-Kayapo Indians

KCET-TV, 214

Kelly, Elsworth, 139

Kelly, Mike: *Blind Country*, 342

Ken and Louise (Clarke), 91, 92-94, *93*
Kibbins, Gary: *Henry Kissinger Won the Nobel Peace Prize*, 200
Kitchel, Nancy Wilson, 49n23
Klier, Michael: *Riese*, 118-21; and silent cinema, 118
Kluge, Alexander: and history, 120; *Hour of the Filmmakers*, 106; on interventionist media, 106-9; and silent cinema, 108, 118; *Why Are You Crying, Antonio?*, 106
Knapp, Lucretia: *Erotica*, 346-47; *Sally Cheesey Raffelyell*, 346-47
Knights, Karen, 195
Kracauer, Siegfried: *From Caligari to Hitler*, 52
Kraus, Rosalind, 124
Kricfalusi, John, 383
Kuchar, George, 78; *Cult of the Cubicles*, 78, 87; *Weather Diary #3*, 17, 19-20; *Weather Diary* series, 19-20, 87
Kugelmann, Robert, 391
Kuntzel, Thierry, 155; *Eté—double vue*, 35-40, 47; interview with, 48n12
Kwan, Stanley, 249

L

L Is for the Way You Look (Carlomusto), 180
Lacan, Jacques, 38, 98n9
Lady Killer, The (Schroder), 201
Lam, Edward: *Full Moon in New York*, 249-50; *How to Love a Man Who Doesn't Love Me*, 246; *My Lecherous Youth*, 249; *Siqin Gaowa Special*, 250; *Too Happy for Words*, 249
Language Poets, 388
Laplanche, Jean, 348-49
Larry Sanders Show, The (TV show), 383
Larsen, Ernest, 18
Last Emperor, The (Bertolucci), 252
Last Movie, The (Hopper), 131
Laurent, Sophie, 234, 235
Lea, Vanessa, 271
LEAF. *See* Legal Education and Action Fund (LEAF)
Leaving the Old Ruin (Batsry), 141
Lee, Benjamin, 300
Lefebvre, Henri, 14
Legal Education and Action Fund (LEAF), 189
Lesbian representation, 346-59. *See also* Homosexuality
Leslie, Alfred, 45
Lesskow, Nikolai, 57
Let's Play Prisoners (Zando), 349, 352-55, 357
Letterman, David, 383
Lettre à un amant (Paradis), 203
Levertov, Denise, 391

Levine, Paula: *Mirror, Mirror*, 204-5
Levine, Sherri, 30
Lewis, Howard R. and Martha E.: *Electronic Confessional*, 99n32
Lexiconning, 70
Liebman, Nina, 315
Life Goes On (television program), 171-72n4
Likely Consequence (Yang), 248, 249
Lipton, Eunice, 35
Lister, Ardele: *Sugardaddy*, 197
Little Red Riding Hood tale, 194
Logue, Joan, 130; *Homeless*, 145
Longboy, Zackery: *From Another Time Comes One*, 204
Longshot (Hershman), 124, 131-32, *131*
Looking Glass, The (Downey), 29, 34-35
Loran, Erie: *Cezanne's Composition*, 47
Lord, Chip: *Motorist*, 17, *24*, 24-25
Los Angeles riots, 218
Lost, Lost, Lost (Mekas), 83-84
Louise's Breasts. See Seins de Louise, Les
Love Life (Campbell), 192
Love Tapes, The (Clarke), 87, 89-91, 97, 100n42; set-up, *90*
Lozano, Jorge: *Accessory Transit Company*, 196
Lucier, Mary: *Ohio at Giverny*, 29, 40-44, *41*, *42*, 49n30; *Wilderness*, 43-44, *44*
Ludlam, Charles, 173

M

Ma, Ming-Yuen S.: *Aura*, 245; *Toc Storee*, 245
Ma vie c'est pour le restant des mes jours (Morin and Dufour), 193
MacBride Commission Report, 285
MacCabe, Colin, 110
McCorvey, Norma, 316
MacKinnon, Catherine, 189, 194
McLaughlin, Sheila: *She Must Be Seeing Things*, 349
MacLean, David: "Marilyn," 204, *204*
McLuhan, Marshall, 138; *Gutenberg Galaxy*, 55; as pop star, 102
McP, Art: *Fascist in Love, Good Boy, Seize in Love*, and *Statues in Love*, 204
Madigan, Amy, 316
Madness and Civilization (Foucault), 79
Magnetic recording technology, 63
Magnetophons, 63
Magritte, René, 29-32
Mahoney, Cardinal, 313
Mak, Ansom: *Two or Three Things I Know about Them*, 246
Making of Monsters, The (Greyson), 200

Malick, Terrence: *Days of Heaven*, 43
Mama (Zhang), 236
Man with a Movie Camera (Vertov), 118
Manufactured Romance (Ramsden), 197
Mapplethorpe, Robert: banning images of, 185; use of male models, 36
Mare, Aline: *S'Aline's Solution*, 327-28
"Marilyn" (MacLean), 204, *204*
Marin, Louis, 39, 40
Marker, Chris: *Sans Soleil*, 1
Marlowe, Kellie: *Out on Video*, 199
Mars, Tanya: *Pure Nonsense*, 202; *Pure Sin*, 202; *Pure Virtue*, 202
Marshall, Teresa: *Fresh Talk*, 204
Marshalore: *You Must Remember This*, 197
Martha Stuart Communications, 295
Martín, Abel, 278
Matshushita, 64
Maturana, Humberto, 56
Maude (TV show), 315
May Fourth Movement, 231
MCRR. *See* Buffalo Media Coalition for Reproductive Rights (MCRR)
Me and Rubyfruit (Benning), 87
Media arts: and television, 382-99. *See also* Alternative media
Mekaron Opoi D'joi project, 259-78
Mekas, Jonas: *Lost, Lost, Lost*, 83-84
Mellinger, Jeanine: *In Those Days*, 17, 25-26
Memories from the Department of Amnesia (Tanaka), 4, 8-10, *9*, 12, 17, 25, 26, 112, 114-15, *114*, 117, 120
Memory, 102; collective, 1, 3, 4; construction of, 1-2; cultural, 1-2, 3, 12; and electronic amnesia, 54-56; as fragments, 115; and history, 115-18; and identity, 4; and media, 55; oral, 55; personal, 4, 7, 8, 11, 12; and postmodernism, 3, 12; and video, 1-12. *See also* History; Screen memories; Video memory
Mendieta, Ana, 132
Merleau-Ponty, Maurice: on perception, 54; *The Visible and the Invisible*, 54
Merwin, W. S., 165, 388
Metaphysics: defined, 60n17; and immediacy of video, 84
Metuktire-Kayapo Indians, 262-65, *265*, 266-69, 270-71, 279n3, 280nn12, 14
Metz, Christian: on cinema, 67-68; on semiotics, 52, 59n2
Micallef, Gabrielle: *AnOther Love Story*, 204
Michelman, Kate, 312
Mieville, Anne-Marie: on history and identity, 110, 120; *Soft and Hard*, 109, 110-12

Miller, Henry, 142
Miller, Nancy, 219
Mirror, The (España). *See Espejo, El/The Mirror*, 213
Mirror, Mirror (Levine), 204-5
Mitchell, John: *The Agony and the Ecstasy*, 190
Modernity: and China, 229-32
Mogul, Susan: *Everyday Echo Street*, 87; *Prosaic Portraits, Ironies and Other Intimacies*, 17, 23-24
Mom Tapes, The (Segalove), 87
Monet, Claude, 40-44, 49n29
Money Talks, Bullshit Walks (Werden), 191-92
Montage: and art history, 35
Moody, Ken, 36, 37-38
Moore, Rick: *Canada's Challenge for Change*, 296-97
Moores, Margaret: *Frankly Shirley*, 200, 201; *Surely to God*, 201
Mooto, Shani: *Wild Women of the Woods*, 204
Morgan, Tracy, 322
Morin, Edgar: *Chronique d'un été*, 83, 86, 89, 90
Morin, Robert: *Ma vie c'est pour le restant des mes jours*, 193
Morrison, Jim, 333-34
Morse, Margaret, 25, 107
Moscow Does Not Believe in Queers (Greyson), 200
Mother Machine (Corea), 326
Motion picture industry, 69. *See also* Cinema; Film
Motorist (Lord), 17, 24-25, *24*; production values in, 25
Mourning the Death of Magic (Boyd), 102
Mulvey, Laura: "Visual Pleasure and Narrative Cinema," 334-35, 357
Mundo L.A., El (Gamboa), 213, 215-17, *216*
Munsterberg, Hugo, 67
Murphy Brown (TV show), 316-17
Museum of Modern Art, 31, 48n5
Music for Stocking-Top, Staircase and Swing (Fanni), 193
Music videos, 383
My Father Sold Studebakers (Sweeney), 87
My Lecherous Youth (Lam), 249
Mystery Science Theater 3000 (TV show), 383

N

Narcissism, 124, 137
Narrative. *See* Intertextuality; *Testimonio* narration
NASA, 68
Nashville, 392

National Abortion Rights Action League, 312
National Endowment for the Arts, 319, 395
National Film Board (Canada), 193, 295-96
National Gallery: Micro Gallery, 32
National Liberty Corporation, 310
Nauman, Bruce, 137, 180
Nausea art collective. *See* Asco art collective
Navajo film project, 260-61
Networks: collapse of, 384
New American Cinema, 84, 207
New German Cinema, 121
New Life, A (Biggs), 32-33, 34
New Wave cinema, Taiwanese, 248-49
NFB. *See* National Film Board (Canada)
NGOs. *See* Nongovernmental organizations
Nichols, Bill: on interactive mode, 100n36;
    Representing Reality, 100n36
Night Visions (Bociukiw), 201
No Voice Over (Campbell), 192-93
Nomads at the 25 Door (Finley), 4, 10-11
No-movies, 215
Nongovernmental orgnizations (NGOs), 287
Not a Jealous Bone (Condit), 342-44, *343*
Now (Benglis), 125
NYPD Blue (TV show): confession in, 95, 96
Nyst, Jacques-Louis, 140; *Object*, 137

O

Object, The (Nyst), 137
Odenbach, Marcel, 158
Odhaimbo, David: *Priapic Black Stud, The*, 199;
    Skinned, 204
OFAVAS. *See* Ontario Film and Video
    Appreciation Society (OFAVAS)
Ohio at Giverny (Lucier), 29, 40-44, *41, 42*,
    49n30; critical reception, 41
111 (Sarahan), 202
One Hundred Walks of Life, 239
"One on One" (Clarke), 87, 91-97, 100-101n45,
    101n53
Ong, Walter J.: *Orality and Literacy*, 55
*Only Something That Is About to Disappear
    Becomes an Image*, 241-42
Onourown (Gibbons and Oursler), 17, 22-23
Ontario Board of Censors, 198
Ontario Film and Video Appreciation Society
    (OFAVAS), 198
Ontology: of photographic image, 61; relativity,
    57; of television, 179
Open forum movement, 388
Operation Rescue, 321
Opium War (1860), 232
Oral culture, 55, 210

Orality and Literacy (Ong), 55
Orgasm (Goldberg), 190
Orientations (Fung), 202, 244
Oshima, Nasia: *In the Realm of the Senses*, 190
Other Love Story, An. See AnOther Love Story
    (Douglas and Micallef)
Our Normal Childhood (Boschman), 201
Oursler, Tony: *Onourown*, 17, 22-23
Out of Africa (Dinesen), 167
Out of the Blue (Fung), 202
Out on Video (Marlowe et al.), 199

P

Paik, Nam June, 47, 51, 64, 99n31, 109, 122n14,
    144-45, 180, 208, 382; *Bye Bye Kipling*, 58
Painting of Modern Life (Clark), 49n29
Paley, William, 48n5
Paper Tiger Television, 17-18, 174, 180, 209,
    240, 290, 319; *US Bans Abortion*, 321
Paradis, Marc: *Cage*, 203; *Délivre-nous du mal*,
    203; *Harems*, 203; *Incident Jones*, 203; *Lettre
    à un amant*, 203; *Reminiscences Carnivores*,
    203; *Voyage de l'ogre*, 203
Paradise Lost (Tomczak), 196
Passage de l'image (exhibition), 50n38, 77n
Passion (Godard), 47, 109
Patton, Gregory, 165
Pau, Ellen, 234; *Song of the Goddess*, 245-46
Pauli Schell (Werden), 191
PBS. *See* Public Broadcasting Service (PBS)
Peacock, Jan: and the elegiac, 120; *Wallace +
    Theresa*, 112-14, *113*, 117
Penal Colony, The (Kafka), 154
Penley, Constance, 306
People in Buildings (Hall), 45-46, *46, 47*
People in Buildings II (exhibit), 46
Pereira, Renato, 259
Petchesky, Rosalind, 308, 309
Phi phenomenon, 67
Photography, 61, 67; and memories, 117; and
    representation, 95; wedding, 366, 379n18. *See
    also* Camera
Pierce, Charles S., 53
Place with No Name, A (Schroder), 201
Planned Parenthood, 305
Plateau, Joseph, 67
Player, The (Altman), 393
Playing with Fire (Bociukiw), 201
Poetry: and intertextuality, 388-92
Poison, 185
Political Unconscious, The (Jameson), 27, 28n19
Pontalis, Jean-Bertrand, 348-49
Pornography: feminine, 196-97; and home

videos, 15; porn wars, 194-95; and social dysfunction, 189. *See also* Video sex
Pornography (Dworkin), 189
Pornography and Silence (Griffin), 196
Portapak: effects of, 298; electronic news gathering (ENG), 64; and public sphere, 291-92; Sony, 84; and video art, 64, 84, 122n14
Possibly in Michigan (Condit), 342
Postmodernism: and history and memory, 3, 12; postinteriority of, 27, 28n19; of video, 105
Poussin, Nicholas, 35-40
Practice of Everyday Life, The (De Certeau), 13, 15-16, 21, 24, 26
Preservation: of video and television tapes, 2-4
Priapic Black Stud, The (Odhiambo), 199
Prime Cuts (Wong), 193
Prodigal's Return, The (Hui), 250
Professional: vs. amateur, 380n33
Prolife movement. *See* Reproductive rights
Prosaic Portraits, Ironies and Other Intimacies (Mogul), 17, 23-24
PSAs. *See* Public service announcements
Psychoanalysis: and confession, 79-80
Psychology: of video and film, 61-72
Public Broadcasting Service (PBS), 209, 317-18
Public service announcements: on AIDS, 204
Public sphere: shift to, 291-94, 300; and social space, 106, 108
Public television, 185; and community standards, 187; majority vs. minority perspective in, 187-88; programming priorities, 318
Pure Nonsense (Mars), 202
Pure Sin (Mars), 202
Pure Virtue (Mars), 202

Q

Quayle, Dan: on *Murphy Brown*, 317
Querelle (Genet), 189

R

Radio: critique of, 94, 100n44; as transmission, 64; and video 62, 284
Radio Television Hong Kong, 250
Raft War, 262-63
Raindance (video collective), 3
Rajchman, John, 391
Ramsden, Anne: *Manufactured Romance*, 197
Rape Is a Social Disease (Women in Focus), 194
Rashid, Ian: *Bolo, Bolo*, 204
Rayns, Tony, 234
Realism, 46; in video art, 134-46
Rebels of the Neon God, 249
Reclaiming Ourselves (Women in Focus), 194

Recording Studio from Air Time (Acconci), 125
Reeve, Hester, 334
Reik, Theodor: on confession, 78, 80, 82-83, 86, 89, 97-98n2, 99n23, 100n41
Reminiscences Carnivores (Paradis), 203
Reminiscences of the Cuban Revolutionary War (Guevara), 210
Ren and Stimpy (TV show), 383
Renan, Sheldon, 215
Replies of the Night (Hahn), 217-19
Representing Reality (Nichols), 100n36
Reproductive rights: and activist video, 304-32; and advertising industry, 315-17; and feminism, 304-9; independent work on, 317; prolife movement, 305-6
Reproductive Rights March (*1994*), 317
Reprovision, 307
Residents (rock group), 392
Respectable Lie, A (Women in Focus), 194
Richards, Nelly, 190
Ricky and Cecilia (Clarke), 94-95
Riese, Der (Klier), 118-21
Riggs, Marlon, 382; *Tongues Untied*, 180, 185-88, *186, 188*, 318, 395
Rios, Luis, 259
Riot Tapes, The (Segalove), 87
Riseau Video des Femmes, 194
Rising Sun, 61
River Elegy (CCTV), 229-30, 239
Robert, Simon: *Incident Jones*, 203
Rock music: as phallic, 333-34
Rock My Religion (Graham), 174
Rocking the Great Wall (Huey), 248
Roe v. Wade, 311, 319
Roe v. Wade (docudrama), 316
Roof, Judith, 347
Rosler, Martha, 16, 174, 180; *Bowery in Two Inadequate Descriptive Systems*, 174; *Global Taste*, 174; *Vital Statistics of a Citizen, Simply Obtained*, 335-37
Ross, Andrew, 306
Rouch, Jean: *Chronique d'un été*, 83, 86, 89, 90
Rousseau, Jean-Jacques, 125, 126
Royalle, Candida, 206n21
Rule of Thumb, A (Campbell), 194
Rust v. Sullivan, 319-20
Ruttman, Walter: *Berlin, Symphony of a Great City*, 118

S

Saint Augustine of Hippo. *See* Augustine of Hippo, Saint
S'Aline's Solution (Mare), 327-28

Sally Cheesey Raffelyell (Knapp), 346-47
Sandoval, Humberto, 216, *216*
Sanjinés, Jorge, 211
Sans Soleil (Marker), 1
Santeros, 213
Santoro, Luiz Fernando, 293
Sarahan, Joe: *Holy Joe*, 202; *111*, 202
Saussure, Ferdinand de, 52-53
Saxena, Gita: *Bolo, Bolo*, 204
Scapes (Vasulka and Vasulka), 31
Scars (Boschman), 201
Schnitzler, Arthur, 134
Schroder, Elizabeth: *Bisexual Kingdom, I Can't Believe What I Saw, Lady Killer, Place with No Name*, and *Where Does the Mess Come From?*, 201
Seaman, Bill: *Exquisite Mechanism of Shivers*, 390
Second Decade, 204, *204*
Seduction, 197
See Evil (Steele and Tomczak), 199-200
Seeing Is Believing (Hershman), 124, 128-29, *129*
Segalove, Ilene: *Mom Tapes*, 87; *Riot Tapes*, 87
Seins de Louise, Les, 193
Seinsvergessenheit, 55
Seize in Love (McP), 204
Self-Employed Women's Association (SEWA) (India), 285, 295
Self-examination, 80-82, 97, 115. *See also* Confession
Seligson, Marcia: *Eternal Bliss Machine*, 370
Semiotics: and literature, 59n6; and phenomenology, 59n2; and video art, 52-53
Serra, Oliumpio, 263
Serra, Richard, 154
SEWA. *See* Self-Employed Women's Association; Video SEWA
Sex, Lies and Videotape (Soderbergh), 27
Sex on video. *See* Video sex
Sexual abuse, 194
Sexual Reality (Bright), 189
Shadow's Song (Hershman), 124, 132
Shandling, Gary: *Larry Sanders Show*, 383
Sharp, Willoughby, 138
She Don't Fade (Dunye), 340
She Must Be Seeing Things (McLaughlin), 349
She Works Hard for the Money (Women against Pornography), 194
Shi Jian, 236-37
Short Cuts (Altman), 392
Sign of Affection, A (Campbell), 194
Silent film, 108, 118
Silent Scream, The, 308
Silliman, Ron, 388

Silver, Suzie: *Spy*, 334
Simple Case of Vision, A (Batsry), 141
Siqin Gaowa Special, The (Lam), 250
Sisters (TV show), 316
Site Recite (Hill), 391
Sitney, P. Adams, 125
Six Martyrs, 239
Skin (Campbell), 193
Slipping Between (Hahn), 213, 219
Smithson, Robert, 43
Snip, Snip (Campbell and Werden), 199
Soap operas, 167-69, 171n3, 172n4
Social space: production of, 13-28; public sphere, 106, 108
Soderbergh, Steven: *Sex, Lies and Videotape*, 27
Soe, Valerie: *All Orientals Look the Same*, 243; *Black Sheep*, 243
Soft and Hard (Godard and Mieville), 109, 110-12
Sommer, Doris, 210
Song of the Exile (Hui), 250
Song of the Goddess (Pau), 245-46
Sony, 109; contest sponsorship, 15; portapak, 84; VCR, 64, 298-99
Sound recording. *See* Audio technology
Spaces I (Vasulka and Vasulka), 32
Speak Out Productions, 194
Speaking Parts (Egoyan), 27
Spielberg, Steven: *Close Encounters of the Third Kind*, 151
Spring of Lies, 321, 323
Sprinkle, Karen, 341
Spy, A (Silver), 334
Spy in the House That Ruth Built, A (Green), 87, 337-40, *338*
Staniszewski, Marianne, 322
Star Trek, 112, 130
Starling Man (Wyngaarden), 202
Statues in Love (McP), 204
Steam Clean (Fung), 203, *203*
Steele, Lisa, *199*; *Birthday Suit*, 191, *191*, 197; *Gloria* tapes, 197; *In the Dark*, 199; *See Evil*, 199-200
Stein, Gertrude, 134
Sternberg, Leo, 35
Stevens, George: *Giant*, 43
Stevens, Wallace, 113
Stockhausen, Karl Heinz, 109
Stone, Oliver: *Doors*, 333
Storm and Stress (Hall), 40, 44-45, *45*
Story of O, The, 340
Story of Red, The (Werden), 192
Storytelling, 57
Strand, Paul, 36

Strawman, 239
Structural coupling, 56
Structure, Wave, Youth, Cinema Experimental
    Group, 237
Subjects: disenfranchised, 176-77
Sugardaddy (Lister), 197
Surely to God (Moores), 201
Surveillance. *See* Video surveillance
Survival of the Delirious (Balser and Fabo), 203
Suzanne et Lucie (Boutet), 193
Sweeney, Skip: *My Father Sold Studebakers*, 87
Synecdoche, 24

T

Tagg, John: *Burden of Representation*, 95
Tajiri, Rea: *History and Memory*, 4, 5-8, 9, 10, 12
Talking heads: in China, 236; vs. talking group,
    211
Tanaka, Janice: *Memories from the Department
    of Amnesia*, 4, 8-10, *9*, 12, 17, 25, 26, 112,
    114-15, *114*, 117, 120; *Who's Going to Pay for
    These Donuts, Anyway?*, 4, 8-10, 12
Tanner, 392
Taubin, Amy, 347
Techno-analysis, 83
Techno-therapy, 84
Tele-Advising (White), 82, 99nn23, 24
Television: catastrophe coverage, 20; and cinema,
    106; commercial, 174-75, 176; community-
    based production, 175-80; and computers,
    385; and confession on, 82, 95, 96; consumers,
    13; and defensive action, 178; defined, 68;
    development of, 59; and distraction, 25; vs.
    experimental video, 208; flow of, 2, 108;
    high-definition, 70-71; and history and mem-
    ory, 2-3; as interactive, 166; and media arts,
    382-99; and national identity, 12; as proac-
    tive, 178; as representation, 13; as reproduc-
    tion, 66; and scanning technology, 72n8; and
    self-evaluation, 115; as sending and receiving
    device, 58-59; serial format of, 2; as situation,
    177; technology, 58-59, 64-65, 66, 68, 70-71,
    72n8, 384-85; as transmission, 64-65; vs.
    video, 64, 177, 208; and video arts, 382-85;
    viewpoint dependency of, 170. *See also*
    Broadcast television
Temptation of Saint Anthony, The (Biggs), 32,
    33, 34
Ten Thousand Things (Gorewitz), 145
Ten To Eleven, 106
*Terrible Uncertainty of the Thing Described,
    The* (exhibit), 45
Testimonio narration: of España, 221, 222-23; of

Gamboa, 215-16, 222-23; of Hahn, 219-20,
    222-23; vs. oral history, 210; and plural self,
    209-11
That Day on the Beach (Yang), 249
That's Not Me They're Talking About (Women
    in Focus), 194
Third World Newsreel, 174
Thomas, Clarence, 119
Thomas the Obscure (Blanchot), 390
Tian Zhuangzhuang, 238
Tiananmen Square, 237-38, 251
Time compression, 70
Timeshift (Cubitt), 320
Tire Dié (Birri), 211
Title X restrictions, 322-23
To Sleep as Little Spoons (Horn), 143
Tober, Barbara, 370
Tomczak, Kim, *199*; *Demonstration of the Fear
    and Pain*, 196; *In the Dark*, 199; *Paradise
    Lost*, 196; *See Evil*, 199-200
Tongues Untied (Riggs), 180, *186*, *188*; artistic
    and social merit, 186; awards and honors,
    185; censorship of, 185-88, 318; homoerotic
    imagery, 187; identity in, 188; obscenity
    in, 187
Too Happy for Words (Lam), 249
Totenberg, Nina, 318
Tradition: defined, 175-76
Transmission technology, 56-58, 64-66
Transsexual Lifestyle, 193
Travessos, Almerinda, 201
Treaty of Nanking (*1842*), 231
Treichler, Paula, 165-66, 167
Trick or Drink (Green), 87
True Inversions (Boschman), 201
True/False (Campbell), 192
Truth in Painting, The (Derrida), 39-40
Tube metaphor, 56, 58
TV. *See* Television
2 Live Crew (rap group), 185
Two or Three Things I Know about Them (Mak),
    246
Txucarramãe, Megaron, 258, 272, 276

U

Uccello, Paolo: *Battle of San Romano*, 32
Ulmer, Gregory L., 390
Ulysses (Joyce), 190
Umaku Group, 211
Underexposed, 324-26, 327
Understanding China into the Maze of History,
    239
United Houseless Association, 240

United Nations University, 295
Urinal (Greyson), 200
US Bans Abortion (Paper Tiger Television), 321, 323

V

Valdez, Patssi, 214
Valentini, Norberto, 81
Vancouver Art Gallery, 199
Varela, Francisco, 56
Varela, Guillermo "Willie," 207
Vasulka, Steina, 136; *Golden Voyage*, 29-32; *Scapes*, 31; *Spaces I*, 32; *Vocabulary*, 31
Vasulka, Woody: *Art of Memory*, 4-5, 11, 136, 149-64, *160-64*; *Commission*, 149-50, 151; *Golden Voyage*, 29-32; *Scapes*, 31; *Spaces I*, 32; *Vocabulary*, 31
VCR. *See* Videocassette recorder (VCR)
Velazquez Digital (Camino), 32, 34
Velvet Light Trap, 315
Venturi, Lionelli, 41-42
Versailles Treaty, 231
Vertov, Dziga, 65; *Man with a Movie Camera*, 118
Very Easy Death, A (de Beauvoir), 219
VHS. *See* Video home system (VHS)
Vidéazimut, 286-87, 294
Video: as access medium, 51-60; collectives, 3; definitions and usage of term, 62, 63, 64, 71n1, 73, 103, 105; experimental, 180; in the field, 295-98; future of, 181-82; history of, 298-301; immediacy of, 84; as medium, 177; memory, politics of, 1-12; movement in, 67; panning and scanning, 70; and self-transformation, 22; small format, 14; systematic solipsism of, 84; technology, 61-72, 209, 258-82, 393-95; time, 134; as transmitter, 56-58. *See also* Experimental video
Video art, 122n14; as alternative, 16, 383; and artisanal potential, 99n31; vs. broadcast television, 16, 51-52, 72n20, 174, 382; on cable television, 397; and consumer video, 14, 17; defined, 64, 73-74; end of, 382-84 interpreters of, 75; limits of, 30; as medium, 66; in 1960s, 16; on public airwaves, 130; realism in, 134-46; and semiotics, 52-53; technology, 64, 103; and television, 382-85; as transformative, 65-66. *See also* Media arts
Video confessions. *See* Confession
Video culture. *See* Visual culture
Video diary, 18-19, 105. *See also* Autobiography; Confession
Video Free America exhibition. *See* Videofreex
Video home system (VHS), 64, 299

Video News Service (South Africa), 286
Video SEWA, 286
Video sex: in Canada, 189-206; and censorship, 189-90; and interactive media, 398n13; and voyeurism, 205
Video surveillance: and censorship, 200
Videocassette recorder (VCR), 64, 68, 298-99, 303n29
Videodrome (Cronenberg), 54
Videofreex, 3, 86, 100n38, 174
Videographe collective, Le, 193
Videography (Ancona), 41
Videomaker (magazine), *368*, *373*
Videor, 73-77
Videotape recorder (VTR), *61*, *63*
Videotape technology, 66
Vietnam Veterans Memorial, 2
Village Video Network, 295
Vinebohm, Lisa, 287-88
Viola, Bill, 138, 142, 208, 382, 387, 389; *I Do Not Know What It Is I Am Like*, 389, *389*
Virilio, Paul, 74, 77n3
Virtual reality (VR): defined, 60n16; as interactive, 53; and perception, 53; and video, 53, 59
Visible and the Invisible, The (Merleau-Ponty), 54
Visions of the U.S. (contest), 15
Visual Evidence (series), 200-201, *201*
Visual perception, 386-87
"Visual Pleasure and Narrative Cinema" (Mulvey), 334-35, 357
Vital Statistics of a Citizen, Simply Obtained (Rosler), 335-37
Vocabulary (Vasulka and Vasulka), 31
von Foerster, Heinz, 142
Vostell, Wolf, 99n31, 109, 122n14, 140
Voyage de l'ogre (Paradis), 203
Voyeurism: and video sex, 205
VR. *See* Virtual reality (VR)
V/TAPE (Toronto): address, 206 n. 24
VTR. *See* Videotape recorder (VTR)

W

Wallace + Theresa (Peacock), 112-14, *113*, 117
Wang, Norman, 234
Wang Shau-di, 248
Wang Tung, 239
War on Lesbians (Cottis), 340
Wasserlein, Frances, 194
Waugh, Tom, 211
Wayne's World, 291
We Will Not Be Beaten (Campbell), 194
Weather Diary #3 (Kuchar), 17, 19-20
Weather Diary series (Kuchar), 19-20, 87

Webster v. Reproductive Health Services, 316, 320, 324

Wedding videos, 99n34, 360-81; as preservation of family ritual, 84, 369-70; as representation of past, 362; vs. wedding photography, 366, 379n18; as women's genre, 372-73

Weddington, Sarah, 316

Wegman, William, 137-38

Werden, Rodney, 200; *A.M. Radio Was His Only Friend*, 191; *Baby Dolls*, 191; *Blue Moon*, 192; "*I'll Bet You Ain't Never Seen Noth'n Like This Before*," 191; *Money Talks, Bullshit Walks*, 191-92; *Pauli Schell*, 191; *Snip, Snip*, 199; *Story of Red*, 192

Wertheimer, Max, 67

West, Mae, 202

Weston, Edward, 139

WHAM. *See* Women's Health Action Mobilization (WHAM)

Where Does the Mess Come From? (Schroder), 201

Which Tree (Hill), 391

White, Mimi: *Tele-Advising*, 82, 99nn23, 24

Who's Going to Pay for These Donuts, Anyway? (Tanaka), 4, 8-10, 12

Why Are You Crying, Antonio? (Kluge), 106

Wiegand, Ingrid, 141

Wild Women of the Woods (Mooto), 204

Wilderness (Lucier), 43-44, *44*

Wildmon, Don, 185, 187

Will Be Televised (Cheang), 240, 241

Williams, Raymond: on cultural hegemony, 81; on flow, 2; on flux, 126; on hegemony, 175; on tradition, 175; on transmission, 64-65

Williamson, Judith, 18

With a Vengeance, 317

Wittgenstein, Ludwig, 75

Woman and Chinese Modernity (Chow), 231

Women against Censorship, 198

Women against Pornography (Victoria, B.C.), 194

Women artists, 333-45. *See also* Feminism

Women Hating (Dworkin), 189

Women in Focus, 194

Women's Breast Self-Examination, 193

Women's Health Action Mobilization (WHAM), 322-24

Wonder Woman (Birnbaum), 173

Wong, Ain-ling, 234

Wong, Paul, 200, 206n21; *Confused*, 199; *Prime Cuts*, 193

Wooster, Ann-Sargent, 41

World Association of Community Radio Broadcasters, 287

World images, 149-64

Worth, Sol, 260-61

Wu Wenguang: *Bumming in Beijing*, 234, 235-36; *My Time in the Red Guards*, 238

Wyngaarden, Cornelia: *As a Wife Has a Cow*, *Dead Man Was a Woman*, and *Starling Man*, 202

X

Xia Jun, 229

Xingu National Park, 262, 263, 264, 280n11

Xun, Lu, 231

Y

Yalter, Nil, 137

Yamate, Yuriko, 26, 114

Yang, Edward: *Brighter Summer Day*, 248; *Eleven Women*, 248-49; *Likely Consequence*, 248, 249; *That Day on the Beach*, 249

Yankee Doodle Dandee, 7

Yates, Frances A., 54

Yat-sen, Sun, 231-32

Yau Ching: *Flow*, 246-47

Ybarra-Frausto, Tomás, 217

Yellow River (China): as metaphor, 229-30

Yonomoto, Bruce, 382

Yonomoto, Norman, 382

You Must Remember This (Marshalore), 197

Young, Iris, Marion, 299

Youngblood, Gene, 215

Yung, Danny, 241-42

Z

Zando, Julie, 346-59: *A Ha! Experience*, 349-50; *Bus Stops Here*, 349, 350-51, *351*; *Forbidden Love*, 358; *Hey, Bud*, 349, 350-51, *351*; *I Like Girls for Friends*, 349, 350, 356; *Let's Play Prisoners*, 349, 352-55, 357; *Uh-Oh!*, 340

Zhang Shichuan, 233

Zhang Yuan: *Beijing Bastards*, 238; *Mama*, 236

Zodiac Killers, The (Hui), 250

Zuni Icosahedron, 242, 246, 249